P9-APJ-237

"David Broder portrays vividly the inheritors of power, sketches their actual and potential linkages, points toward the frontiers they are exploring, and winds up hopeful for a future which—warts and all—may yet surpass the recent past." —James David Barber, *Transaction*

"An engrossing study, an important book. Keep it around for a few years, and check off the names as his subjects climb higher."

—*Louisville Times*

"The most influential political writer of the current age, Broder has written a book that can best be defined as 'necessary.' . . . Its importance lies in the fact that it is the first to come along that offers any specific clue to the identity of this country's future leaders."

—*Dallas Times Herald*

"A work that will be read carefully by scholars and politicians, as well as by the general public . . . catches American politics at one of history's sharp turns, and like a sharp photograph, brings the action into clear focus" —*Detroit News*

"A significant work on the changing American political scene and the future of the nation as it heads into the next century"

—*Atlanta Journal-Constitution*

"David Broder is in a class by himself . . . a compelling book that is as much about the past as it is about the future." —*Trenton Times*

"A fascinating study of 'younger America' . . . Broder shows a keen ability to dissect and explain new alliances whose power to varying degrees has been either underestimated or misunderstood."

—*Houston Chronicle*

"Simply indispensable . . . the service Broder has performed in introducing us to the new generation of public servants is, in itself, a public service." —*Washington Star*

"David Broder's book gives new meaning to America's changing political society. He writes with clarity, and his keen sense of political history, past and present, has provided a meaningful statement of what's in store in the decade ahead." —*Lewiston Daily Sun*

PENGUIN BOOKS

CHANGING OF THE GUARD

David S. Broder is the national political correspondent and an associate editor of the *Washington Post.* His twice-weekly syndicated column appears in more than 260 newspapers across the United States and abroad, and in 1973 he won the Pulitzer Prize for Distinguished Commentary. Mr. Broder was born in 1929 in Chicago Heights, Illinois, and received his B.A. and M.A. from the University of Chicago. He began his newspaper career on the Bloomington (Illinois) *Daily Pantagraph,* went to Washington in 1955 to work for *Congressional Quarterly,* and later worked for the *Washington Star* and *The New York Times* before joining the *Post*'s reporting staff in 1966. He is the author of *The Party's Over: The Failure of Politics in America* and coauthor, with Stephen Hess, of *The Republican Establishment: The Present and Future of the G.O.P.* In addition, he contributes articles to many magazines, appears frequently on such television shows as *Today, Meet the Press,* and *Washington Week in Review,* and regularly gives talks to various college and civic groups around the country. Mr. Broder and his wife, Ann, have four sons and make their home in northern Virginia.

David S. Broder

CHANGING OF THE GUARD

POWER AND LEADERSHIP IN AMERICA

With a New Introduction to the Penguin Edition

PENGUIN BOOKS

Penguin Books Ltd, Harmondsworth,
Middlesex, England
Penguin Books, 40 West 23rd Street,
New York, New York 10010, U.S.A.
Penguin Books Australia Ltd, Ringwood,
Victoria, Australia
Penguin Books Canada Limited, 2801 John Street,
Markham, Ontario, Canada L3R 1B4
Penguin Books (N.Z.) Ltd, 182–190 Wairau Road,
Auckland 10, New Zealand

First published in the United States of America by
Simon and Schuster 1980
Published in Penguin Books with a new Introduction 1981
Reprinted 1984

Copyright © David S. Broder, 1980, 1981
All rights reserved

LIBRARY OF CONGRESS CATALOGING IN PUBLICATION DATA
Broder, David S.
Changing of the guard.
Bibliography: p.
Includes index.
1. United States—Politics and government—1945–
2. Pressure groups—United States. 3. Elite (Social sciences)—United States. 4. Power (Social sciences).
I. Title.
JK271.B658 1981 306'.2'0973 81-5897
ISBN 0 14 00.5940 7 AACR2

Printed in the United States of America by
Offset Paperback Mfrs., Inc., Dallas, Pennsylvania
Set in Times Roman

The job titles and descriptions of individuals profiled in this book were correct as of April 1, 1980.

The author gratefully acknowledges permission to quote from the following: "Alienation and the Decline of Utopia," by Kenneth Keniston; copyright © 1960; reprinted from *The American Scholar,* Volume 29, Number 2 (Spring 1960). *Dynamics of the Party System: Alignment and Realignment of Political Parties in the United States,* by James L. Sundquist (Brookings Institution, 1973), pages 41 and 42; copyright © Brookings Institution, 1973. *The Promise of American Life,* by Herbert Croly; copyright 1909 and renewed 1937 by Macmillan Publishing Company, Inc. *The Rise of the Unmeltable Ethnics,* by Michael Novak; copyright © Michael Novak, 1971, 1972.

Except in the United States of America,
this book is sold subject to the condition
that it shall not, by way of trade or otherwise,
be lent, re-sold, hired out, or otherwise circulated
without the publisher's prior consent in any form of
binding or cover other than that in which it is
published and without a similar condition
including this condition being imposed
on the subsequent purchaser

In memory of Bruce Biossat, who would have liked these young people, even if he did not entirely approve of them.

And for Ira Kapenstein and William A. Steiger, who would have been in this book, had they lived.

Contents

Introduction to the Penguin Edition

A funny thing happened to this book on its way to becoming a paperback. Interviewing and research on *Changing of the Guard* began in the spring of 1978. The final manuscript changes were made early in 1980, and the book was published in September of that year. Two months after I proudly proclaimed the thesis that the decade of the 1980s would see the coming to power of a new generation of young leaders sharply different from their predecessors of the Great Depression–World War II generation, the American people elected the oldest President in our history. Ronald Reagan, 69 years old, not only extended the hold on the White House by men who were in uniform during World War II, he seemingly knocked my thesis of imminent generational change into a cocked hat.

How then do I have the temerity to send this poor battered notion out into the world again, in the Reagan era, in this paperback format? Because, frankly, the basic thesis of this book still holds: The 1980s will be a decade of generational change, as momentous as we have ever seen in our country—and full of implications for an altered direction in our politics and government. That change may be made all the more dramatic by the fact that the latest of the World War II vets to occupy the Oval Office is also the oldest of the lot.

There is a generational fault that cuts across Ronald Reagan's Washington, and it produces as much tension as the San Andreas fault in his home state of California. As with geology, so with politics: Eventually the pressure will reach the point where the landscape will be altered.

The simplest way to convey the situation is this: Ronald Reagan was born during the presidency of William Howard Taft. His first political hero was Franklin Delano Roosevelt. He began to serve in public office during the time of Lyndon Baines Johnson. And he came to Washington with a Congress barely more than half of whose members had begun their service before Jimmy Carter was elected President.

Reagan's view of the world was formed in the Dixon, Illinois, of the

1920s. As he describes it, it was a simple, secure life in a seemingly stable small-town atmosphere. But that security was disrupted by the Depression, which cost Reagan's father his job and made young Reagan a devoted New Dealer. Like most other Americans, he saw in FDR the architect of economic salvation, and later, the leader of the worldwide alliance that saved democracy from the dictators. But Reagan's own life was hardly that of the typical American. He went to Hollywood, became a star of some magnitude, moved smoothly into the new medium of television, and emerged in the 1960s as the possessor of perhaps the best political voice, style, and presence since Roosevelt's—but a voice that was raised on behalf of conservative ideas and causes far removed from the philosophy of the New Deal.

There are two views of the source and significance of Reagan's victory. One holds that it was simply the by-product of the public's frustration with inflation, the Iranian hostage situation, and the political inadequacies of Jimmy Carter—shortcomings that were well reflected even in the interviews with Carter's own young lieutenants in Chapter 4.

The other viewpoint regards Reagan's victory as a much more important milestone, a reaffirmation of the conservative and Republican trend that was visible in the Nixon victories of 1968 and 1972, but was interrupted (temporarily) by Watergate. Because of Reagan's electoral landslide over Carter, and the even more surprising election of the first Republican Senate in twenty-six years and the halving of the Democratic margin in the House of Representatives, there were some who felt that Reagan's inauguration might mark the start of a new political era.

That may prove to be the case, but among those who were very cautious in embracing that judgment were the two Republican pollsters quoted in Chapter 15. Richard Wirthlin, who in 1980 served not just as Reagan's pollster but as his chief political strategist, said in an interview at inauguration time, "There was no party realignment in 1980. The number of people expressing an affiliation with the Republican Party did not change from 1978. . . . What we're dealing with now is an electorate that, as an act of faith, has cast its votes for Republican candidates without affiliating with the Republican Party. Our success—especially on inflation—will determine whether they take the next step."

Robert Teeter, who did the polling for Vice President George Bush in the primaries and assisted Wirthlin in polling for the Reagan-Bush ticket, took a similar view. "Almost by definition," he said, "a realignment has to cover two or three elections. . . . We will have to wait until 1982 and 1984 to see if this is a long-term change."

Both Wirthlin and Teeter pointed out that while Reagan had improved on the normal Republican share of the votes of younger people, he had not increased the low turnout of those under-40 citizens. "I'm still waiting for that baby-boom generation to make its commitment," Teeter said.

Most Democratic analysts agreed with Teeter and Wirthlin that the first test of the "realignment theory" would come in the 1982 congressional election. The only instance in the twentieth century when the party in control of the White House gained seats in the midterm election was in 1934, two years after FDR's first victory. That feat, as much as his 1936 landslide, gave shape to the Roosevelt coalition and confirmed the long-term Democratic dominance of our politics. A similar victory by the Republicans in 1982 would do much to clarify the significance of what happened in 1980.

All this suggests that the men and women who will determine whether Reagan's victory is an isolated event or the start of a new era will almost certainly be men and women of the new generation. Of the seventy-four freshmen elected to the House in 1980, seven were in their twenties, twenty-five in their thirties, twenty-three in their forties, and only nineteen were past fifty—the somewhat arbitrary cutoff for inclusion in this book. Even in the Senate, once a most patriarchal society, ten of the new members were in their thirties or forties, while eight were in their fifties.

Reagan's election in 1980 also served to elevate to prominence and power a number of the exceptionally promising younger Republicans who were profiled in this book. The most spectacular rise may have been that of David Stockman (Chapters 1 and 6), who moved at age 34 from being a junior member of the minority party in the House of Representatives to the Cabinet-level position of director of the Office of Management and Budget, arguably one of the half-dozen most influential posts in the entire government. Stockman, as Chapter 6 notes, was part of a group of young conservatives whose ideas and approaches were very much at odds with those of the older generation of right-wing Republicans. They were open both to intellectual mentors and to mass-media communicators. They saw themselves as brokers of ideas, in much the same way that members of FDR's "brain trust" had seen themselves.

Stockman's rise was no accident, for his intellectual force had been felt by everyone in the House and in the Washington community who had met him in his four years in Congress. He was picked in the summer of 1980 as the chairman of the energy subcommittee of the Republican Platform Committee, and then—because he had once worked as a staff man for John B. Anderson—was asked to help Reagan rehearse for his September 1980 debate with the independent presidential candidate. Reagan was so taken with Stockman that he again asked for his help in preparing for the climactic debate with Carter in the final week of the campaign, and he finally rewarded Stockman with the budget directorship.

While Stockman was probably the intellectual heavyweight of this young conservative group, the best-known and most popular figure was Representative Jack Kemp of New York (Chapter 6), the former professional football quarterback who became the ardent exponent of "supply-side" economics, with its emphasis on deep, continuing cuts in the tax rates. He was the coauthor of the Kemp-Roth bill, calling for a 30 percent across-the-board reduction of tax rates over three years. After some initial hesitation, Reagan accepted the gospel of supply-side economics and made the Kemp-Roth bill the cornerstone of both his campaign and the economic policy of his administration.

A longtime Reagan protégé, Kemp chaired the defense subcommittee of the Platform Committee, gave a rousing and well-received maiden address to the GOP convention in Detroit, and was the subject of a flattering vice-presidential boom. After the election, his House Republican colleagues chose him as chairman of the House Republican Conference, the caucus leadership spot from which Gerald Ford rose to the presidency.

Kemp was not the only young Republican featured in this book to gain a leadership position in the House. Trent Lott, the Mississippian who appears in Chapter 13 as a young Southerner switching parties to make his first bid for elective office, moved into the position of Minority Whip. Richard Cheney (Chapter 3), Jerry Ford's former White House chief of staff, became chairman of the House Republican Policy Committee after just one term in Congress. Mickey Edwards of Oklahoma (Chapter 6) became an assistant Republican House Whip and chairman of the American Conservative Union, succeeding Robert Bauman of Maryland, who had the misfortune of being defeated for re-election to the House after acknowledging his participation in homosexual activities.

The gains were even more dramatic for the young Republican senators, as their party claimed its first majority in that body in a generation. Bob Packwood of Oregon (Chapter 3), Alan Simpson of Wyoming and Orrin Hatch of Utah (both in Chapter 12) became chairmen of full committees, while Senators John Danforth of Missouri (Chapter 3) and Richard Lugar of Indiana (Chapter 16) took over major subcommittees. To round out the 1980 election picture for the Republicans, Governor Pete du Pont of Delaware (Chapter 3) won a smashing re-election victory and E. Clay Shaw, Jr., the Mayor of Fort Lauderdale, Florida (Chapter 13), was elected to the House of Representatives.

Reagan's election, and the Republican victories in the House and Senate, also focused fresh attention on the other wing of the New Right, more concerned with such social issues as abortion, gun control and prayer in schools than with economics. The network of fundraising, research, and political-action groups they developed outside the formal framework of the Republican Party impressed the mass media and alarmed the previously complacent Democrats.

Richard Viguerie, the master of computer mailings and relentless promoter of anti-union, anti-abortion, anti–gun-control causes, and Paul Weyrich, a founder of the Heritage Foundation and a variety of other think tanks and political-action groups (both men are profiled in Chapter 6) became familiar television figures immediately after the 1980 voting. They claimed credit for mobilizing a good portion of the Reagan vote and for defeating a long string of liberal Democratic senators. Weyrich and Viguerie are both Catholics, but they formed an alliance with a group of fundamentalist Protestant clergymen, the most publicized of whom was the Reverend Jerry Falwell of Lynchburg, Virginia, 47, founder of the Moral Majority. (His absence from this book is an omission I now regret.) Together they helped mobilize the support of conservative candidates by many previously politically inactive adherents of the white evangelical churches. After the election, they asserted their goals, in often strident terms, to the officials they had helped elect.

Viguerie, Weyrich and such allies as John T. (Terry) Dolan (Chapter 6) of the National Conservative Political Action Committee (NCPAC) were quick to jump on the Reagan Administration for the lack of appointments from their own circle. The point I made in the conclusion of the book appears to have been borne out by the staffing decisions of the Reagan Administration: Those who were "outsiders" to the structure of the Republican Party remained largely outsiders in this Republican administration. Margo Carlisle (Chapter 6) did move from being staff director of the unofficial Senate GOP Steering Committee (an informal conservative caucus) to the same position in the formal Senate Republican Conference (the caucus of all GOP senators). But Viguerie, Weyrich, Dolan, David Keene, former chairman of Young Americans for Freedom, and such conservative public-interest leaders as James D. Davidson (Chapter 5), Raymond Momboisse and Ronald Zumbrun (both in Chapter 8) were overlooked, at least in the first round of staffing of the Reagan Administration.

In contrast, Stockman and the other New Right economic conservatives, most of whom had operated strictly within the context of the Republican Party, were given positions of real influence by Reagan. In the concluding chapter of the book, I noted the intellectual vigor of this element of the GOP as one of the signal developments of the 1970s, and said, "It will be surprising to me if there is not a significant political reward for the party that leapfrogs the opposition in the realm of policy ideas. At some point in this decade, the Republicans will probably have a chance to test their policies from the White House."

That chance came sooner than many had expected. Some observers feared it came before the ideas themselves had been well developed and well tested. But as these words are written, the test is under way. If supply-side economics turns out to be a powerful enough weapon to slow the growth of federal spending and reduce the burden of federal taxes, and if that in turn proves to be the promised key to reviving the economy and curbing inflation, then Stockman, Kemp and Co. will be hailed as heroes and be able to set their own timetable for the political future. But if it fails—and that conceivably could happen even before this paperback is in the bookstores—then those promising young men may spend the rest of their lives making alibis for the opportunity that they squandered.

For the Democrats, the 1980 election decimated a whole generation of leadership. Jimmy Carter, Walter Mondale, George McGovern, Birch Bayh, Frank Church, Edmund Muskie—all presidential contenders in the 1970s—were turned out of office by the 1980 election. Of the five Democrats who were listed on the 1976 New Hampshire presidential primary ballot, only one—Representative Morris K. Udall of Arizona—remained in public office after the 1980 election.

For the first time in a generation, the dominant congressional party had to acknowledge its repudiation by the voters. Not only did the Democrats lose their Senate majority for the first time in twenty-six years, but they were outpolled by the Republicans in the popular vote for the House of Representatives—a clear threat to their control of that body after the post-Census reapportionment.

Even before the grim returns were in, one of the brightest of the young Democrats profiled in this book, Senator Paul Tsongas of Massachusetts (Chapter 2), made a speech signaling the impending change. Speaking to the national convention of Americans for Democratic Action, founded more than thirty years earlier by Hubert H. Humphrey and dedicated to perpetuating the flame of New Deal–Fair Deal liberalism, Tsongas said in June 1980, "The Reagan candidacy is the result of the bankruptcy of liberalism. Either we're going to leave the future to conservatives, with all their Cold War baggage, or we're going to begin to find a new rationale or definition of liberalism.

"Liberalism must extricate itself from the 1960s," he went on, "and we must have the answers that seem relevant and appropriate to the generation of potential liberals. If the basis of liberalism is just 1960s rhetoric, then the last meeting of liberals will inevitably be held in an old people's home."

While some of the old-generation liberals grumbled at his heresy, Tsongas continued, "If we are to mobilize a new generation to move forward with liberal leadership, we must understand that the average young American is just that—part of a new generation." For Tsongas, the key to that new liberalism was an understanding of the implications of energy and resource scarcity and the changed nature of America's relationship to the resource-rich nations of the Third World. He later said plainly that he thought his own colleague, Senator Edward M. Kennedy of Massachusetts, had lost his bid for the 1980 Democratic presidential nomination when he defended a cheap-energy policy in a time of growing shortage.

After the election, Tsongas plunged into writing a book on his own views. It was part of a process of intellectual self-renewal that took place inside the Democratic Party—and that was long over-due. Plainly uncomfortable with the policies and programs they had inherited from their predecessors, the Democratic survivors quickly created a variety of forums for the long-postponed debate on the future direction of their party.

That debate promised to be wide-ranging, for the Democrats were deeply and evenly divided. After the 1980 election, for example, it took the surviving House Democrats three ballots to decide between two of the able young legislators profiled in this book, Representative David Obey of Wisconsin (Chapter 16) and Representatives James Jones of Oklahoma (Chapter 2), for the key position of House Budget Committee chairman. Jones, the Lyndon Johnson-trained skeptic of Great Society programs, finally prevailed over his more traditionally liberal rival.

Their contest was symbolic of the thrust to power of the young Democrats described in many chapters of this book. Representative Christopher Dodd of Connecticut (Chapters 2 and 12), a Peace Corps alumnus, was elected to the Senate and joined Tsongas on the Foreign Relations Committee. Senator Gary Hart of Colorado (Chapter 2), who had proclaimed, "We are not a bunch of little Hubert Humphreys," was one of the few liberal senators to achieve re-election in 1980. And John D. (Jay) Rockefeller IV (Chapter 2) won a handsome and lavishly financed second-term victory for Governor of West Virginia.

A host of younger House Democrats moved into the power structure as subcommittee chairmen. Among them were Representatives Norman Mineta of California (Chapter 1), Michael Barnes of Maryland, Thomas Harkin of Iowa, Timothy Wirth of Colorado and Albert Gore, Jr., of Tennessee (all in Chapter 2), Robert García of New York (Chapter 10), Julian Dixon of California (Chapter 11) and James Blanchard of Michigan (Chapter 12). And as they moved higher on the pyramid themselves, their interest in rebuilding the shattered structure of their party grew.

There were of course some casualties and some dropouts among the Democrats in 1980, but fewer among those interviewed for this book than one would have guessed, given the carnage. Bill Clinton (Chapter 13) was an upset victim in his bid for a second term as Governor of Arkansas. John Cavanaugh (Chapter 2), the Representative from Omaha, Nebraska, retired from the House, saying he needed a sabbatical from politics.

But there were also some advances. Barney Frank (Chapter 16), the outspoken state Representative from Boston, Massachusetts, moved up to the House of Representatives. In the spring of 1981, San Antonio elected Henry Cisneros as the first Hispanic mayor of a major American city (Chapter 10). And in defeat, a number of the Carter appointees profiled in Chapters 2, 4 and 5 moved into position for races of their own in 1982. Sam Brown went back to Colorado, Richard Celeste to Ohio, Jack Watson to Georgia, Neil Goldschmidt to Oregon—all with an eye on governorships or other political prizes. As expected, the two young men closest to Carter, Jody Powell and Hamilton Jordan, turned to writing and television, Jordan from a base at Emory University in Atlanta and Powell from Washington. Lawyers like Stuart Eizenstat, David Rubenstein and Matthew Nimetz joined law firms that will keep them close to the center of Democratic Party developments. The Mondale circle—Jim Johnson, Richard Moe and the rest—took jobs that allowed them time to work on preparations for his undeclared 1984 presidential campaign. Anne Wexler (Chapter 16) and Sarah Weddington (Chapter 9) left the Carter White House for consulting and publishing jobs—again staying close to the political arena.

Farther from the White House, the networks regrouped and readjusted to the new political configuration. Activist women, blacks and Hispanics prepared to battle the Reagan Administration on behalf of social programs that had lost their political support with the change of party control. Public-interest groups—particularly those involved with environmental issues and civil liberties—reported a surge in contributions and memberships from people concerned about Reagan's intentions in those areas. Charles Halpern, one of the public-interest lawyers interviewed in Chapter 8, commented after Reagan's victory that "Public-interest advocacy will be more urgently needed. There may be less reasoning with the government and more litigation, but the goals will remain the same." Some of the advocates who had moved into government under Carter, like Jim Moorman and Joe Onek, moved back into law firms, where they could pursue their causes from the outside once again. As Eleanor Holmes Norton (Chapter 11) put it, "We know we have gained our strength in the past in times of adversity and I think we will see that again."

For some of the "makers and takers" of opinion described in Chapter 15, Reagan's election also brought altered circumstances. Patrick Caddell and Peter Hart saw their presidential candidates—Carter and Kennedy, respectively—defeated, while Wirthlin and Teeter, as noted, played major roles in the Republican victory. Columnist George Will played host at Reagan's first postelection Washington dinner party—and was satirized for doing so by Garry Trudeau in a two-week *Doonesbury* sequence.

At the end of 1980, the Census Bureau reported its official population figures, showing that the shift of people and political power from the older cities, the Northeast and the Midwest to the suburbs, and the Sunbelt of the South and the West had been even greater than the estimates used in this book. At the same time, the bureau confirmed that the decline in voter participation, which is discussed in Chapter 1, had continued apace in 1980, with only 53.9 percent of the voting-age population embracing the candidacies of Reagan, Carter or Anderson.

For all the change that the Reagan-Republican victory brought in 1980, the greater change—the change of generational control—is still to come. The men and women who will lead America up to the beginning of the new century are not those who were born near the start of the present century. All around Washington, and all around America, those young people are dreaming their dreams and making their plans. The competition among them is the one that will, I am convinced, shape our future.

It is that strong sense of the struggle still to come that gives me the nerve to send this book out to the public again.

David S. Broder

Washington, D.C.
May 1, 1981

To conceive the better American future as a consummation which will take care of itself—as the necessary result of our customary conditions, institutions and ideas—is admirably designed to deprive American life of any promise at all. The better future which Americans propose to build is nothing if not an idea which must in certain respects emancipate them from their past.

—*Herbert Croly*, The Promise of American Life

1 · The Next Ones

AMERICA IS CHANGING HANDS.

In the 1980s the custody of the nation's leadership will be transferred from the World War II veterans, who have held sway for a generation, to a new set of men and women.

These newcomers—the next ones in a leadership succession that goes back to the youthful men we call the Founding Fathers—are the products of a set of experiences different from those which shaped the dominant American personalities of the past quarter-century.

They do not carry the memories or the scars of the Great Depression. They were not part of the victory over totalitarianism in Italy, Germany and Japan.

The next ones who will take power—the babies born between 1930 and 1955—were shaped in a very different time. Theirs has been a time of affluence and inflation, of extraordinary educational advance, and of wrenching social change and domestic discord.

They were immunized against the childhood diseases and exposed to endless hours of television. Their wars were fought in Korea and Vietnam, and if fewer of them returned as casualties, none returned as victors.

They saw America open the space age—sending men to the moon, cameras and measuring instruments to distant planets. But they also saw the premature close of what their parents had called "the American century," as industrial obsolescence and resource dependency curtailed everything from the strength of the dollar to the use of the family car.

In their brief time, such familiar institutions as the two-party system and the nuclear family, with its male breadwinner, a housewife and two children, have become endangered species.

Millions of the older members of this generation have seen their daughters "liberated," and thousands of the younger members have spent nights in jail after some civil-rights or antiwar protest.

They have argued and sometimes fought with each other over civil rights, equal rights, the right to life and a dozen other causes. They have been through lunchroom sit-ins, Vietnam teach-ins and Watergate break-ins. At one time or another, some of them have been "clean for Gene" and others have been keen for Proposition 13. They have embraced a good many heroes, and discarded most of them. Having come of age in the traumatic decade bracketed by the murder of one President and the forced resignation of another, they have lost whatever romantic idealism they may have held about politics and government. Lamenting the lack of leadership, many of them have turned off and tuned out.

The men and women of this next generation have one other characteristic in common. Every President for whom they have been eligible to vote so far has been a man who was in uniform during World War II.

When that war ended, Dwight D. Eisenhower was the commanding general of the armies that liberated Europe and Jimmy Carter was just a midshipman at Annapolis. But they and all the presidents in between—John F. Kennedy, Lyndon B. Johnson, Richard M. Nixon and Gerald R. Ford—are part of a common pattern. The greatest mobilization of economic and military and human power in this nation's history caught them in its grip and pushed them ahead to a position far beyond their early imaginings. They rode that fast express to the Oval Office by different routes and with different timetables, but for all of them the war was a vital element in their careers.

Eisenhower, the professional soldier with twenty-six years of service behind him, was ready to quit in frustration at the slowness of promotions when suddenly he was advanced from colonel to five-star general in the space of four years. A succession of sensitive political-military commands made Eisenhower a presidential favorite of both parties, and his victories in 1952 and 1956 were as much a celebration of America's historic achievement in liberating and rebuilding Europe as they were a tribute to his own personality and good sense.

Kennedy's was a triumph of a different sort: the saga of a junior officer who survived a brush with death in battle only to face new risks and hazards in his political career. The wartime tale made the PT-109 tie clip, worn by his aides and supporters, the most important political symbol of a whole generation of politics. The Kennedy legend came to embrace not only military heroism but the symbolism of the Harvard-educated grandson of Irish immigrants struggling to overcome the prejudice that had barred the presidency to Roman Catholics.

By comparison, Lyndon Johnson's was, on the surface, a more prosaic story—but *only* on the surface. The precocious Texas politician had come to Capitol Hill as an aide as early as 1931, was elected to Congress in 1937 and lent his support to the one-vote majority that kept the draft act alive in 1941 before Pearl Harbor. A member of the Naval Reserve, he took a five-month leave of absence from Congress to serve on active duty early in the war, then returned to his political chores. But the war remade politics for Johnson, as it remade his native state into a forerunner of the "New South" of industry and commerce and urbanization. Johnson changed with Texas, broadening his political and financial base beyond his original Hill Country populism to embrace the interests of the expanding oil, aircraft, banking and communications industries. Before the war, Johnson had tried and failed in a bid for the Senate. In 1948, three years after V-J Day, he was elected to the Senate and was on his way to power.

Richard Nixon and Gerald Ford were also naval officers, for whom wartime service meant their first extended look at a world much larger than the towns where they had grown up and gone to college. When these young lawyers came home—Nixon to Orange County, California, and Ford to Grand Rapids, Michigan—they were determined to play their part in shaping the world they had seen. Plunging into politics, they became advocates for the twin World War II ideals of military strength and international cooperation. When the Soviet Union challenged both those principles, Nixon and Ford, like Kennedy and Johnson and almost all their contemporaries, easily adopted the anti-Communist ideology of the Cold War. Where the Democrats actively promoted the growth of the welfare state that had been born in the 1930s and '40s, the Republicans simply acquiesced in its inevitability. But all four Navy veterans were men of their times, in everything from their use of the Central Intelligence Agency to their expansion of federal grants-in-aid.

Finally, in the last election of the 1970s, came Jimmy Carter, who sounded like none of these predecessor presidents. His chief claim as a candidate was that he was an "outsider," one who had no part in what Eisenhower had called, at the beginning of this cycle, "the mess in Washington."

Carter was provably innocent of Washington connections. When Kennedy, Johnson, Nixon and Ford were all members of the House, hearing General Eisenhower argue for the Marshall Plan and NATO, Jimmy Carter was far away, moving from port to port as a Navy submarine officer. Intent on following an uncle's Navy career, Carter took an extra year of schooling to prepare for his entrance exams to Annapolis—and thereby missed active duty in World War II. Even though his class was accelerated to graduate in three years, he was still a year away from being commissioned when Japan surrendered. The nuclear submarine then became the focus of his career, and it was not until 1953, when Nixon was Vice President, Kennedy and Johnson senators, and Ford a rising member of the House, that Jimmy Carter got back to Georgia to begin his civilian business and political career. To emphasize his role as a newcomer, he repeatedly said he had "never met a Democratic President."

But on the evidence so far in hand, it appears unlikely that Jimmy Carter will be seen by history as heralding the start of a new generation of political leadership. Far more likely, he will be viewed as the tail of the passing parade, or at most, as a transitional figure in our politics. He was a bit slower than his predecessors in getting where he was going, but he bore the stamp of some of the same experiences that had shaped them.

Like them, he carried sharp, clear memories of the Depression, of the time that unemployed migrants were given handouts from the kitchen of his father, "Mr. Earl." And like them, he followed the battle maps of World War II with the intensity of personal involvement.

Carter's roots, like those of all the other postwar presidents except Kennedy, were in small-town America, not in the great metropolitan areas where the demographic transformation of modern American society has been taking place. Except for the civil-rights struggle (in which he was more a spectator than a leader), he felt the great social conflicts of the 1950s and '60s but dimly. He remained aloof from the fervor of the controversy over the Vietnam war and the earlier urban and campus riots. He also seemed personally insulated from the more fundamental, if less violent, changes in the life-styles and attitudes of millions, the alterations in the sexual and social relations of men and women, and the changes in the structure of the family, the church and the community.

In the presidential campaign of the nation's bicentennial year, much of Carter's appeal lay in his ability to evoke and symbolize the traditional values of a disappearing America. He was welcomed by many as a hard-working, churchgoing, independent businessman, with a devoted help-meet wife, linked by history and the networks of an extended family to his land, his community, his nation and his God. But it was significant that throughout his campaign and in his presidency, Carter has shown a conspicuous weakness in his appeal to the group that, as we will see, may hold the key to the next generation's politics. They are that "bubble" of the baby boom—now 25 to 35 years old. And they are not Carter's voters any more than he is, in any real sense, their kind of President.

In their own time and in their own way, each of the past presidents has been a challenger of the *status quo,* an energizing force in the politics of his own community, state or nation. As befits a five-star general, Eisenhower entered politics at the top. But he still had to prove himself against the established favorite for the 1952 Republican nomination, Senator Robert A. Taft of Ohio. He prevailed by mobilizing thousands of previously inactive voters to come out to Republican conventions and primaries, where they challenged and defeated Taft and the Old Guard.

That pattern has persisted. Kennedy won the nomination for his House seat in a ten-man primary field, of which he was the youngest. He defeated an incumbent Senator (Henry Cabot Lodge) six years later, and eight years after that beat the Senate Majority Leader (Lyndon Johnson) for the Democratic presidential nomination and outpolled the incumbent Vice President in the general election.

Although Johnson is thought of, in retrospect, as an "establishment Democrat," he was a 29-year-old maverick and the only New Dealer in a seven-man race for special election to the House of Representatives. He got to be Senator only by beating out the Governor of Texas, Coke Stevenson.

Nixon, as has often been told, answered an advertisement placed by Republican fund raisers looking for a candidate bold enough to challenge a supposedly entrenched incumbent, Representative Jerry Voorhis, in 1946, and he did the job for which he had hired on, against the odds. In his first Senate race, he had to beat the person who had beaten the incumbent in the primary. To become President, he had to beat the incumbent Vice President, Hubert H. Humphrey.

Ford was the "Young Turk" Republican in Grand Rapids who took on the four-term isolationist Republican incumbent, Bartel J. Jonkman, and beat him in the primary. Later, he challenged and defeated two other Republican elders in his climb to the leadership of his party in the House, the post from which he was elevated to the vice presidency and then the presidency.

Carter was the challenger and the underdog in every campaign he ever ran, from his first try for the Georgia state Senate in 1962 to his battle with former Governor Carl Sanders in the 1970 gubernatorial race. In 1976, it was "Jimmy Who?" challenging almost a dozen better-known and more heavily credentialed Democrats in the primaries and then tackling the incumbent President of the United States.

In compiling this record of challenges and upsets, the World War II veterans have shown themselves tough and aggressive politicians. But their generation is also showing its age; its pace is slowing visibly. Eisenhower barely caught his breath between the time he left the service and the time he entered the presidency. For Kennedy, it took fifteen years; for Johnson, twenty-one years; for Nixon, twenty-three years; for Ford, twenty-nine years. Even with his delayed exit from uniform, Carter was twenty-three years a civilian before reaching the White House.

What was a fresh wave in our politics has become a stagnant pool of leadership, from which the voters pick their presidents with obvious and increasing reluctance. Voter turnouts—which jumped significantly with Eisenhower and Kennedy—have been declining in each successive presidential election since 1960. The voters of today, in increasing numbers, question the relevance of yesterday's heroes.

It may be that the World War II veterans can extend their grip into the 1980s. In the winter and spring of 1980, the Democratic primaries saw Carter easily defeating the challenges of two younger men, Senator Edward M. Kennedy of Massachusetts, 48, and California Governor Edmund G. (Jerry) Brown, Jr., 42. (Brown gave up his presidential ambitions, at least for 1980, in April of that year after defeats in Maine, New Hampshire and Wisconsin.)

The probable Republican challenger to Carter appeared likely to be the 69-year-old Ronald Reagan, who spent World War II as one of the "Culver City commandos," grinding out training and propaganda films while serving in the Army Air Corps. (Ages are given throughout this book as of 1980 birthdays.)

If one looks more broadly at the positions of power in Washington, the pervasive grip of that generation is even more impressive. A majority of the leaders of the House and Senate, a majority of the Supreme Court and several of the members of the Cabinet are also World War II veterans, with many of the exceptions being even older.

And yet it is almost an actuarial certainty that at some point in the 1980s, the grip of the World War II veterans on the positions of power in American public life will be broken by the inexorable passage of time. By the end of the Eighties, a youth who was 17 when the Japanese surrendered will be into his seventh decade—not too old to be a President or a Speaker of the House or a Chief Justice, but old enough to be thinking of retirement.

Meanwhile, a new generation is pushing forward, nudging toward the time when its members will take command. And they are, in many respects, both the echoes and the opposites of their parents.

The complexities of that generational relationship are explored in some detail in the pages of this book, but perhaps the best opening clues are provided by a look at the differences one finds within specific families. From the Adamses of Massachusetts to the Tafts of Ohio to the Lees of Virginia, bloodlines have been important in our politics. In the course of interviewing people for this book, I found myself talking to several sets of fathers, sons and daughters, whose careers in politics I had covered as a journalist. Two sets of interviews were particularly intriguing. The first was with the Browns of California: former Governor Edmund G. (Pat) Brown, who served in that office from 1959 to 1967, and two of his children, Kathleen Brown Rice, an elected member of the Los Angeles Board of Education since 1975, and Jerry Brown, who has been Governor of California since the same year. The second was with the Scrantons of Pennsylvania: William W. Scranton, the former U.S. Representative, Governor of Pennsylvania (1963–67) and Ambassador to the United Nations, and his eldest son, William W. Scranton III, who has been Lieutenant Governor of Pennsylvania since 1979.

The Browns are Democrats and the Scrantons Republicans, but the most significant differences in their views were generational, not partisan. The family members were interviewed separately, but because they were viewing similar issues, from opposite sides of what was once called "the generation gap," and because communication between parents and children in these families has remained close, what ensued was a kind of dialogue within each family on the aspects of political leadership which are some of the concerns of this book.

In late 1978, when we talked in his prosperous Beverly Hills law office, Pat Brown, now 75, was a very contented fellow—as high-spirited as he had been twenty years earlier when he had defeated William F. Knowland by a million votes to become Governor, or in 1962, when he gave Richard Nixon the beating that people thought (mistakenly) had ended Nixon's career. Jerry Brown had just been re-elected Governor by a margin exceeding Pat Brown's 1958 record. And daughter Kathleen, 35, was compiling the record that would enable her to lead the ticket in her own race for re-election to the school board in 1979.

Pat Brown said there were two big differences in politics now and when he was running—one in technique and one in substance.

"Television," he said, "has changed campaigns entirely. When I first ran for Attorney General [in 1950], I spent most of my time in newspaper editors' offices trying to persuade them to give me support, because the editorial endorsement was so important. Now, it's all television. Jerry beat Evelle Younger on television, because he was much better-looking, younger, more alert. Reagan beat me the same way. He was an actor, six or seven years younger than I, and I'd begun to get a little bit shopworn. They just wanted a change of face.

"But the real change," he said, "is that after the New Deal, the Fair Deal, the War on Poverty and the Great Society, the whole Democratic Party has retreated into conservatism."

Brown's comment on television was a truism, though it was also a self-serving rationalization of his own loss to Reagan, which had other causes than simply the difference in their TV appearance. But his comment on the "retreat to conservatism" was doubly interesting. Brown himself had created, as his daughter Kathleen had put it earlier that day, a California version of "the Humphrey-Johnson-Kennedy Great Society type of program" in his eight years as Governor. And Jerry Brown had, since the passage of Proposition 13 the previous June, become the leading apostle of what many called "the new conservatism."

Pat Brown said he agreed with the characterization of his own record. "I was known as a profligate spender," he said, "because I passed bond issues and borrowed with the veterans' loans and raised taxes. And we built the universities and the medical schools, and the freeways and the water system, because, of course, California was growing at a tremendous rate at that time. . . . But since Watergate and the other exposures, people have become disillusioned with government, and the whole focus of attention is on the incompetency of government." In part, he said, that blame is unfair, because "government takes all the jobs that private industry can't make money on, like mass transit . . . and then they blame government for not balancing its books." But also, he said, the public has added new expectations that were not part of the equation he had to solve.

"The whole issue of the environment has gotten much more sensitive," Brown said. "When I was building the freeways, everyone was for them. Now they say freeways create smog and noise and they cause a separation in our urban centers.

"Now, people are convinced that government is spending too much money, and they're demanding all these programs be cut back. But I don't think this conservatism is going to last more than a few years. This is a temporary situation. It was caused by high property taxes, which became exorbitant because of the increased value of land. I don't think it was caused by too much government spending. And at the end of this period, I think the accumulated problems and difficulties are going to bring back the need for government to invest in things that only government can do—in colleges and universities, in water supplies, mass transit, parks and all the rest."

Part of the conservative backlash, the former Governor said, could be blamed on the fact that "people have not done the job of selling the importance of the public sector." That sounded like an implied criticism of his son, who had opposed Proposition 13 until its passage, but then had moved adroitly to become the leading proponent of the budget cutting it required, and, in 1979, even recommended a mandatory balancing of the federal budget by constitutional amendment or, if necessary, constitutional convention.

Pat Brown was quick to assure me he was not criticizing Jerry. "I am absolutely convinced that if Jerry had not done what he did . . . he would have been defeated for Governor." Brown said that as early as January 1978, his son had known from private polling that Proposition 13 was likely to pass, "but Jerry, with a lot of guts, went out and fought it with all his heart." Afterward, "they said that he flip-flopped. Well, I flip-flopped too, on capital punishment," Brown said, recalling one of the great controversies of his own governorship, when he balked at permitting the death sentence to be carried out and finally, under great pressure and over his son, Jerry's, public protests, assented. "I let people die, after the people passed the law. I mean, you raise your right hand to enforce all the laws of the state. And I think the thing to do is to try to enforce it [Proposition 13], give it everything you have. If it fails, which it's going to do, because there won't be enough money to keep the services going that people want, then they can't blame Jerry for it."

When I talked with Kathleen Brown Rice, that same day in late November 1978, she was preoccupied with an issue that seemed enduringly controversial—school busing. She was, in many ways, more of a "natural" politician than her brother, Jerry—"a throwback to the old man," some Democrats would say, admiringly, although, like Jerry, she had inherited her mother's handsome features.

"I just feel I am rocketing through the generations at supersonic speed," she said, when I had told her why I wanted to interview her. "Growing up, I was raised on a sort of political idealism, and whether it's integration or affirmative action, or special education or bilingualism—all those are areas I'm involved with as a board member—I just find the ideals of yesterday are not as easy to put into reality as I might have hoped.

"I have the feeling," she said, running her fingers through her hair, "that when my father was in office, everything was growth. The university system was built up, public education was improved, and vast sums of money were invested. . . . He set so many of these things in motion, and now we're having to pick up the bills, and pay the price that inflation has added. . . . And I'm finding that people are not as willing to pay the price, not just in dollars, but in personal terms, when it comes to something like integration with which I'm involved."

Two months earlier, Los Angeles had begun a large-scale busing program under court order. "It was peaceful," Rice said. "It was, in many ways, successful, and in a great many ways, it was a real failure. I mean, thirty-one thousand white kids just didn't show up. And I've said—and it seems to incite some groups to react violently—we should slow down just a bit, consolidate our efforts and gains and keep moving forward. Specifically, I think we should expand the programs that are working and that have parental and community support. By and large, those are voluntary programs of the magnet-school type. I don't think you should turn up your nose at them. And don't try to make integration into a penance to be paid by the white society, because I think that they've shown that they're not going to pay the price—or at least, a large number of them aren't."

She said she worried about the pressures and tensions being generated not only in the schools but in the society. "When I was growing up," she said, "I had a library card that was worn thin. And now people have television sets. Every house and apartment building in Watts has an aerial on the roof, and the same in the *barrios* of East L.A. And what they're watching portrays the middle-class American dream. And every middle-class family wants these great little pleasure domes—the Winnebago summer home, the Genie push-button garage-door opener, the hot tub. So they use their credit cards and ready-reserve accounts, and then they turn around and tell the government to tighten up its spending and operate on a fixed budget. . . . When we're talking to parents in the San Fernando Valley and telling them we're going to send their children back, not to the Fairfax-Wilshire area where they grew up as children, but to the East L.A. areas where their grandparents had come from, they feel threatened. They don't want to go backward. They want to keep moving forward and have their children's opportunities broader than their own.

"I don't think that public education is going to solve the human-relations crisis of civilization," said the daughter and sister of the two governors. "We've tried it and we haven't been too successful at it. . . . We should be making efforts, because we're all a part of the community in which we live, and we have responsibilities and obligations in that regard. But don't put that whole trip on us. We're having a hard enough job teaching kids to read, to write and to do arithmetic. In fact, we're having one hell of a time getting a teacher to go to a classroom in the inner-city areas. We have a steady stream of day-to-day substitutes. . . . So I would like to focus my efforts on making sure that we get good, qualified teachers into every classroom in the school district, that we teach basic skills, and that we continue to move in the direction of accepting our social responsibility."

She was talking with haste and emotion now, and she paused before going on. "It seems like we've perhaps bitten off more than we can chew," she said. "We have to scale back our expectations; not abandon them, but do them in a more credible manner so that the public will invest more trust and more energy and more money in our operation. For public education, at any rate, I think if we continue to pretend that we can solve the world's problems, I think we'll see the end of public education."

When I saw Jerry Brown a few months later, I asked him if he agreed with his sister Kathleen that it had been easier to be a liberal in their father's time than it was in theirs. Jerry Brown is one of the quickest-thinking dialecticians in public life—a reflection of both his years in the seminary and his Yale Law School training—and he immediately began to pick the question apart.

"If that means liberalism as a historic phenomenon, associated with an era in the Fifties and Sixties," he said, "I think that would be true. But even then people were beginning to hedge their bets. When my father was inaugurated, he entitled his program 'responsible liberalism.' And the addition of the word 'responsible' I interpret as an attempt to balance some of the fiscal realities with the spending initiatives that are associated with liberalism."

Brown ticked off the changes that have occurred since then—in population, technology and world power relationships—to buttress his familiar contention that we live in "an era of limits." "When productivity was growing three and a half percent a year, generating a fiscal dividend, that allowed for a different kind of government initiative than when it's growing at less than one percent a year. So we have to analyze carefully what initiatives we're going to undertake.

"But," he said, in proper dialectical fashion, "if we mean by liberalism the willingness to use government institutions and authority to promote the general interest, to invest in the human beings that make up society, to respect people on their own individual merits, to be open to the future, to seek a more equitable society, then it is as vibrant today as it's ever been. But if we're trying to prop up the images and the concepts of twenty-five years ago and trying to apply them to a very changed world, well, obviously it will seem a little bit out of date."

In his rapid rise in politics, no one has ever accused Jerry Brown of being "out of date," though some have worried about his skill in riding every big wave that came ashore on the California beaches, from ethics-in-government to ecology to exploration to budget balancing.

I asked the Governor if he agreed with his father's guess that the latest phenomenon—Proposition 13–style budget cutting—would be one of the briefer fads.

"Well, obviously," he said, "people can't have an anti-government mood for a prolonged period of time. That doesn't make any sense. The government is the servant of the people, and there should be some measure of goodwill between the constituents and their representatives. . . . The paradox is that I represent a very progressive state, with a progressive tax policy and very compassionate social programs. But we're in a period now where there is fiscal excess. Inflation reflects that, and so does the decline of the dollar, the inability of the Dow-Jones average to move above what it was in 1966, the lack of investment. So we have to retool and reanalyze. . . . It just so happens that capitalism goes through recurring challenges, and we happen to be in one right now. And the people are hungry for leadership."

I asked him what kind of leadership such a period required, and his answer, I am afraid, came unintentionally close to parodying *Doonesbury*'s parody of Governor Brown.

"I think it takes very bold leadership," he said. "Bold leadership. Big thinking. Thinking for the year 2000. Where does America fit in? Where does the planet, where do we as a species, fit into the whole flow of things? I emphasize space, energy, job training and technological leadership. And I do that because we can't get blinded to the fundamental by cyclical dislocations. And the fundamental fact is that the planet is filling up with people and technology, and we have to respect the limits. We have to be cognizant of the 'greenhouse effect' and the long-term mutations in human genes.

"I think people want leaders to discuss the big picture, not the little pictures," he said, the words tumbling out at an accelerating pace. "How do we maximize the quality of life for the people in this country, consistent with the legitimate aspirations of other people living in other lands?" Brown asked himself. And then he answered: "I believe that proper technological leadership, proper respect for the environment, and a willingness to continue the exploratory destiny of this country in space will lead toward a more positive political future. I expect space to have the same role in the next century as the oceans held in the 19th century. There is nothing larger or more mysterious than the universe, and exploring is really the hallmark of a great nation and a great people."

We were now far removed from Pat Brown's worries about the budget-cutting impact on social programs and Kathleen Brown Rice's struggle to get regular teachers into Los Angeles' classrooms.

Jerry Brown came partway back to earth, saying, "In the shorter term, our challenge lies in the energy area, to find renewable resources and more benign sources, a decentralized energy source." He had emerged as a proponent of small-scale, household solar power and a leading critic of nuclear power plants. Speaking of the nuclear scientists, he said, "I don't think we want a priesthood of experts who control the few power plants on which we all depend." Development of solar and other unconventional power sources will "provide employment and the good feeling that comes from achievement," Brown said, "but it will also take investment, and that means shifting from excess consumption to greater savings. It means less indulgence today and therefore more discipline and a leaner life-style than people perhaps are prepared to accept.

"But they will accept it," he affirmed. "Our institutions are durable. All that is lacking is leaders who can articulate that vision to the people of the country. . . . If people get a vision of where this species is evolving, they will wish to participate in it. Their interest will be rekindled. You might even have them starting to vote again."

The problem, said this most contemporary of leaders, is that "the moment is always more powerful than the future, and today's indulgence will carry a greater weight than tomorrow's greatness." And then, almost as if he were ruminating philosophically and not speaking personally about the presidential campaign he was about to undertake, Brown concluded: "Originally, the one who can stand up and say, 'This is what must be done' will not be understood or listened to. But ultimately, if the person is right for the historical period ahead, the people will listen."

The overall challenge facing the leaders of California during the period when the Browns were in the governorship was that of helping a society adjust to rapid growth. Difficult as that task may be, it is probably an easier—and more enjoyable—assignment than that facing those who take responsibility in an area of economic decline. That was the challenge facing the Scrantons of Scranton, Pennsylvania. The family had prospered and become a part of a political and economic aristocracy during the time that the hard-coal mines of northeastern Pennsylvania were pouring forth their riches. The wealth permitted Marion Margery Warren Scranton to be the grand dowager of the Republican National Committee from 1928 to 1951. Her son, William W. Scranton, had a less enviable introduction to politics, as head of a local committee trying to attract new business to a city—and a state—that were suffering from an obsolescent transportation, industrial and resource base. When Bill Scranton ran for Congress in 1960, it was in hopes of bringing outside help from Washington to his beleaguered district. I first heard his name while riding the press bus behind John F. Kennedy's campaign motorcade to Scranton—an incredible, slow progress through masses of people along the highway—when a local reporter passed along the judgment that the Republican who was likely to come to Congress that year was a man who might make his mark in a larger scene. I covered Scranton through his two years in the House, where he was one of the handful of liberal Republicans who occasionally helped give Kennedy a victory on an economic or social-policy issue; in his election as Governor in 1962; in his reluctant and foredoomed opposition to the nomination of Barry Goldwater in 1964; and still later, in his service as Ambassador to the United Nations for his friend and Yale Law School classmate President Ford. When I found myself in 1978 covering the campaign of William W. Scranton III for Lieutenant Governor of Pennsylvania, it was like opening the first page of the sequel to a favorite novel.

The sequel, so far, has proved to be at least an equal to the earlier volume. That does not surprise the father. For he is not only a partisan of his son as a politician but an admirer of the generation of which he is a part.

"I happen to have a very strong feeling," Scranton, now 63, said when we talked in 1979, "that young America is very good, and that, generally speaking, it's driving in the right direction. Their educational standard and therefore their intelligence of approach to things is higher than we've ever had . . . but I don't think they've gotten fused yet into exactly where this is going to lead them. Although I think the motivation generally is very good and the determination is there to make this a better world, I think they are finding it harder, not easier, to give leadership to the causes they feel. . . . I think it is more difficult now to gain a majority consensus as to what ought to be done and, even more importantly, to come up with a program you can dynamically put across."

Scranton himself, at least in my judgment, was an underrated public official, in large part because he was one of the most understated public officials. The economic power he had inherited perhaps made him consider it bad form to throw his weight around. Many mistook his relative lack of ambition for a lack of conviction, and that was an error, for in both Congress and the state capitol, Scranton showed himself a man quite ready to take risks and make enemies in order to make his influence count.

But his view of the current scene, he said, was that "the institutions are not as strong as they were, and even if you get control of one and use power in the right sense of using power, it isn't as effective as it used to be. . . . What people in the country felt as a reaction to Watergate and other problems . . . has proliferated power tremendously and made it more difficult to bring the elements together to put a program across." Scranton cited the shift of authority from the President to Congress, and the dispersal of power inside Congress to the hundreds of subcommittees. But it was not limited to Washington, he said. "When you get into state government, where I had more practice, I do think it was easier, even ten or twelve years ago, to have an executive program that you could get through the legislature than it is today." His own state, he noted, had suffered through repeated crises—payless paydays and the rest—because of the inability of governors and legislators to work out their differences on the budget. All this, he said, was evidence that "the new thinking in America—in my judgment, at least—has not yet really jelled."

But Scranton said he was optimistic the process would have a positive outcome. "In the first place," he said, "I think the diffusion is partly, at least, an offset to what was too great a concentration of power [in the presidency], whose evil results we all saw. Now the pendulum has swung to the opposite extreme. But eventually it will come back to what I hope will be a very reasonable middle where it would be near impossible to have an imperial presidency again but at the same time power would not be so diffused that you couldn't act at all."

And then Scranton returned to his point about the impact of education on the political institutions. "The high level of education and the high standard of knowledge will help on this, eventually," he said. "It has been a diffusive factor in the immediate past and present, I think, but it will help in the long run, because it creates a constituency which is more reasonable and presumably more intelligent about keeping things on an even course and making progress.

"The British," he said, "have stultified themselves because they didn't go in for mass higher education." America, after World War II, took the opposite course, taking both the risks and rewards of a more widespread diffusion of education and knowledge. In the Sixties and early Seventies, many of those on the campuses were alienated by their own government's policies, and some of them, Scranton said, developed "a tendency to love diffusion. The idea was that if I'm different from anybody else, therefore I'm good. . . . They got terribly turned off, a lot of them, for a while. But now I think they're digging back in and attempting to make it better from the inside, rather than being revolutionary from the outside."

William W. Scranton III, 32, was never a revolutionary. With his name, no one would have believed it. But he was certainly "turned off" by what he saw happening in his country, his government and his party, and for many years was preoccupied with an inward-looking search for his own true character. His may, in fact, be the only recorded case of a person's following the course of Transcendental Meditation (TM) to a job on the Pennsylvania Republican State Committee.

The junior Scranton remarked that when his father was in public office, "I was probably the least interested in politics of any of the children." He went off to Yale while his father was Governor, graduated in 1969, and ran several small weekly newspapers in his native northeastern Pennsylvania region. But his overriding interest in this period of his life was TM, a technique for release of psychic tensions, and he proselytized for its adoption by others. "I can be accused of being part of the 'me generation' or the 'me decade' or whatever Tom Wolfe called the Seventies," he said. "I spent a great deal of time involved with TM, and it's still very much a part of my life. But it enabled me to turn outward. Because I was able to fulfill that demand in myself for privacy and for introspection, I gained the confidence that allowed me to go into politics. I would not have been able to go into politics without it, I'm convinced.

"You know," he said, "a lot of it is family influence. That's a subtle force. It's one you don't really realize until you get outside of the family and are able to see the family from outside. It's as if you grew up in a smokehouse: you wouldn't know it was smoke; you'd just think it was the atmosphere. In my father's generation and my grandmother's generation—both strong influences on me—your duty was always outward. You never indulged yourself. Any kind of personal concern they were always uncomfortable with. I think this generation saw that the world couldn't be fixed that way, and so we inevitably turned back inward. And there was a lot of indulgence in that attitude. I think there are excesses on either side, and I think the world is looking for a balance at the moment. It occurred to me in 1976 that politics was something that I might enjoy doing." He became a field worker for the Republican state committee, "enjoyed it tremendously," and in 1978 (aided greatly by his family name and connections) won a three-way fight for the GOP nomination for Lieutenant Governor and was elected that November.

"What got me started," he said, "was just a personal revelation that if I was made to do something, this was probably what I was made to do." It was a return not just to a family tradition but to his inherited party allegiance that Scranton marked in 1976. "I was a bit of a controversial figure, actually, when I first ran for this office," he said, "because, as a newspaper editor in 1972, I endorsed George McGovern. I did that for two reasons. First of all, I was very much a product of that generation and that time, and I think my generation was full of moral judgments: The war in Vietnam was bad. North Vietnamese were noble. Mao Tse-tung was a fine guy. We tended to be absolute in our judgments. I probably tended to be less absolute than most. But I was extremely indignant about what I perceived to be a lack of candor in public leadership. I was very strong in my endorsement of McGovern, because I thought what was going on in the Nixon Administration was absolutely wrong. I was very indignant about having that kind of situation, and I said what I said when it counted. . . ."

The broader reason behind his revolt, Scranton said, was that "in the turmoil of the Sixties, when my political awareness began to form, there was a time when the political iceberg of America began to break up. It was more than just Vietnam. It was an emergence of a different way of looking at the world—naive in some aspects, helpful in some, and in some . . . even corrupt. But it was an emergence of a new world-view. . . .

"We've come out of the New Deal time, and even though Richard Nixon, Gerald Ford and maybe even Jimmy Carter, to some degree, still live in the shadow of the New Deal, that method of political leadership is beginning to crack. It's beginning to crack under the pressures that broke loose in the Sixties and continued in the Seventies . . . and I don't know when or in what form it will recombine. It may be decades. You see the Kennedys and the Browns and the Carters arguing over which direction to push the Democratic Party, and you see the Republican Party feeling hopeful about the demise of the Democrats and yet, at the same time, unsure of where it is going."

In their first months in office, Scranton and Republican Governor Richard Thornburgh were caught up in the problems created by the accident at the Three Mile Island nuclear power plant. They drew widespread praise for their calm good judgment in that chaotic situation. As the Governor's deputy for both civil defense and energy, Scranton had reinforced for him —with regard to the behavior of the utility company—the tendency of leaders to "get defensive as soon as something threatening has happened" and learned again, as with Watergate, that "it's the wrong thing to do. You have to be open to ideas, wherever they may originate.

"Look at Jerry Brown," he said. "He had credibility when he was doing incredible things. When he is trying to be credible, he loses credibility—which is the sort of Zen paradox that he would enjoy. His first term, he flew in the face of traditional political thinking and forced a kind of new-age outlook. Very impractical, not an administrator, but at the same time, extremely attractive. He ran well against Carter [in 1976] because I think people saw the boundary being expanded somewhat, and they ran to that. Not because Jerry Brown had the answer, but because they saw an opening. And I think there is going to be more of that. The boundaries are going to expand and be broken.

"I think," said this self-disciplined, well-educated product of shrewd business people, "a lot of politics is intuitive. It's not the square in-boxes and square out-boxes. A lot of it is off the wall. And that's the charm of politics. The times are putting a premium on that, putting a premium on boldness and experiment, and that will continue while these old forces of politics are breaking up and until the new patterns recombine.

"How they will recombine I don't know. I think for a time, there's going to be very much of that flow that Jerry Brown likes to go with. A rigidity, a resistance to change is going to bowl over a lot of people, I think. And the question I have to ask myself late at night is, 'What are you going to be in that process?' "

The question that young Bill Scranton asked himself is one that hundreds of his contemporaries in politics have had to address. But few of them could draw on their parents for the kind of advice and experience that a Bill Scranton, Jerry Brown or Kathleen Brown Rice could. In many instances, they were traveling paths that their parents could not have imagined.

Consider some of the biographies of people we will meet in later chapters:

• When World War II broke out, thousands of Nisei—Americans of Japanese ancestry—living on the West Coast were interned in detention camps as potential security threats. A 10-year-old boy who came out of the camps amazingly unembittered, who fought for the United States in

Korea, later became the Mayor of California's fourth-largest city and is today a prospect to be a future Speaker of the House of Representatives.

• At the end of World War II, a Mexican-American enlisted man was returned from the Philippines to a hospital in San Antonio to recover from malaria. His roommate's sister, the child of a revolutionary printer who had been forced to flee Mexico years earlier, took a liking to him. Today, their 33-year-old son, one of the youngest people ever chosen as a White House Fellow, is the leader of the San Antonio City Council and a good bet to become San Antonio's first Chicano Mayor.

• In the early 1960s, the Peace Corps sent two volunteers to northern Guatemala to see what help they could give the natives of that most rugged and primitive section of the country. Today, one of them is the first woman president of the New York City Council and the other is one of the President's top political aides.

• In 1963, two young Southerners made their first visits to Washington. One of them, a black man from rural Alabama, was the speaker whose inflammatory rhetoric had to be cooled because of the potential for disturbances among the thousands gathered before the Lincoln Memorial at the massive civil-rights march on Washington. The other, a white youth from Houston, took a nondescript fund-raising job with a struggling conservative organization on Capitol Hill. Today, the black man has completed three years of running a $100-million government program sending organizers into communities across America, and the white man has become the impresario of a right-wing computerized mail propaganda and fund-raising network that is altering the face of American politics.

• In 1968, a young man who had gone into politics and government largely to escape having to compete with his father's formidable reputation in science once stayed up all night drafting the introduction to a federal-commission report. A sentence he wrote became one of the most memorable, and controversial, statements of the decade: "Our nation is moving toward two societies—one black, one white—separate and unequal." Today, that same young man sits in an office high in New York's World Trade Center, running one of the largest public agencies in the world, the Port Authority of New York and New Jersey.

• In 1969, a precociously bright 17-year-old high-school student from South Orange, New Jersey, was suspended for distributing anti–Vietnam war literature in the halls. His appeal eventually wound its way into the state Supreme Court, but the case was mooted, because by then he was on the verge, at 26, of breaking one of America's last surviving political machines and becoming the first elected Executive of Essex County, New Jersey.

• In 1973, the 28-year-old, red-haired daughter of an itinerant Texas Methodist minister, making her second courtroom appearance anywhere since receiving her law degree, persuaded a majority of the U.S. Supreme

Court that women had a constitutional right to abortion. Six years later, that same young woman, now an assistant to the President, was walking a narrow line between radical feminists and conservative women as she tried to find her way in the escalating battle over equal rights.

• In 1960, a young man from upstate New York helped John F. Kennedy win the "mock convention" at Notre Dame. Twenty years later, he was masterminding Ronald Reagan's bid for the presidency, working with a pollster who had upset his Republican family in 1964 by signing his name to a "Professors for Johnson" ad.

• In 1962, when John and Robert Kennedy sent 320 federal marshals to the University of Mississippi campus to protect James Meredith, its first enrolled black student, a young Navy veteran and law student sat watching, bemused and embarrassed, as state officials lined up police dogs to face the overwhelming federal force. Today, the same young man sits in the U.S. Senate, the first Republican elected from Mississippi since Reconstruction.

• In 1962, eager to "become a guerrilla and go to Vietnam and fight Communism," this young conservative came to Washington and joined the CIA. Ten years later, by then an avowed Marxist, he was sitting on the Detroit Recorders Court bench, presiding over part of what he insisted was "the criminal injustice system" of the United States.

As these examples, drawn from the more than three hundred interviews that make up the heart of this book, suggest, the next generation of American leaders is almost certain to bring different perspectives to government, politics and the forging of the American future, just because its members were shaped by experiences so dissimilar to those which molded their parents in the Depression–World War II era.

What one quickly discovers in talking to the emerging leaders is an acute self-awareness of those differences. They know who they are and what has made them that way, and they think of themselves not just as individuals, but as parts of groups or networks that were formed in some shared experience of their youth or early adulthood.

That experience can be as broad as having grown up in one of the new frontiers of American society: the Sun Belt of the South and West or in the kaleidoscope called Suburbia. Or it can be as elusive as a "feel" for that new avenue of political communication, the television tube.

But, more often than not, what one finds is that the thinking and the vision of this next generation were formed in one specific circumstance or experience of their lives. For some, their destiny was in their race or in their gender or in their condition. Coming of age as a black, or as a Hispanic, or as a woman, meant something different in the period of rights-and-pride assertiveness of the 1960s and '70s from what it had in the 1930s or '40s. But it has also turned out to be very important, for the future alignments of American politics, whether you happened to spend a certain fall weekend in 1960 at the Buckley estate in Connecticut or the summer of 1964 in Mississippi. Those who went through certain National Student Association conventions; those who graduated from the University of Texas or Ole Miss, or Notre Dame or Yale Law School, in certain years; and those who were in San Francisco in 1964 or Chicago in 1968 —all are acutely aware of who else was there, and what that experience meant.

The interviews were a reminder that even in this nation of 220 million people, we function as parts of identifiable clusters or networks of peers, those to whom we are bonded by geography, history or common loyalty.

In ways that we can now, perhaps, begin to explore and define, those networks of young people, forged in the 1960s and '70s, will shape our politics, government and society increasingly from now until the end of the century—when they, in turn, will give way to those who are barely teen-agers today.

The cycle of generational change—and of generational conflict—is an old and familiar one in history, philosophy, literature and drama. The debate at the time of the American Revolution concerned the justification for the "child," America, revolting against the "mother country," Britain. In his tract *Common Sense,* Thomas Paine wrote that if Britain is, as some say, "the parent country . . . then the more shame upon her conduct. Even brutes do not devour their young, nor savages make war upon their families, wherefore, the assertion, if true, turns to her reproach. But it happens not to be true." In another treatise defending the Revolution, Paine argued, "Every age and generation must be free to act for itself in all cases as the ages and generations which preceded it. . . . Man has no property in man; neither has any generation a property in the generations which are to follow."

While the generational analogy was central to the external debate between the colonists and the home country, there is little evidence that the Revolution pitted a younger generation against an older one on this side of the Atlantic. Thomas Jefferson was only 33 when he wrote the Declaration of Independence. But among the fifty-five delegates to the 1787 Constitutional Convention, there was a considerable disparity in ages, reflecting the fact that men of two generations—not one—had fought in the Revolution. George Washington was 55 at the time of the Philadelphia convention. Alexander Hamilton, who had been his aide-de-camp during the Revolution, was 32. But neither the philosophical nor the political divisions of the time coincided with generational lines. The young did not consistently side against the old. There was no need for youth to band together defensively in a society in which they were respected and influential at an early age.

Generational differences in American politics have only rarely been so sharply drawn as to attract explicit attention from the historians. Where they have been noted, they are mainly in third-party or "reform" movements.

Probably the first instance in American history of a "youth politics" was the burgeoning of third parties spurred by the emergence of the slavery issue, in the 1840s, and the revolt of some people against the "machine" tactics of Tammany Hall. In 1835, the ranks of New York City's Democrats were divided by charges of monopoly control and special-interest influence. Younger members formed an Equal Rights Party, quickly dubbed the Loco-Focos, with a "Young Men's General Committee" and an "Old Men's General Committee." It was a short-lived effort, but in 1848 a more substantial breakaway occurred, with the Free-Soilers and the Barnburners angered when the party refused to endorse the Wilmot Proviso, which would have prohibited the extension of slavery into the newly incorporated territories of the American West. John Van Buren, Martin Van Buren's son, was able to pull the former President into the Barnburner revolt, despite serious misgivings on his father's part. The spirit of that movement and of the Free-Soil rebellion was captured in the memoirs of L. E. Chittenden, a delegate to the Vermont Democratic convention and later a leader of the Vermont Free Soil Party. "On the day it [the Democratic convention] met," he wrote, "I should complete my 24th year." Chittenden spoke against squatter sovereignty, and "an ancient Democrat, whose mind was impervious to argument, then arose and observed that as 'the boy has spoken his piece, we might as well proceed to the business of this convention.' No one else spoke. There was a subdued affirmative vote and a sharp 'No!' from the six to the resolutions. . . . The opposition party of six walked out of the convention . . . and the first Free Soil Party formed in this Republic." Recalling the incident, Chittenden became nostalgic: "Even now, there is a sensation of fun about the whole affair, for we were all then enjoying life in the freshness and vigor of that youth which, alas! never returns."

The Whigs too were feeling the pull on their younger members from the Liberty Party and the Free-Soilers, and the result was a realignment that ultimately formed the Republican Party.

Although there were elements of generational struggle in the Populist revolt (William Jennings Bryan was 36 when he captured the Democratic nomination in 1896), they were subordinated to the regional and economic conflicts of the period. The next political upheaval in which generational forces were dominant came a bit later, during the Progressive era. James Sundquist, in his book *Dynamics of the Party System,* noted that

> The displacement of conservative by progressive party leadership was to a large extent a generational phenomenon. The typical conservative leader was of

the generation that had come to political maturity in a simpler age, before the Industrial Revolution and an exploding urbanization had transformed America . . . The typical progressive was of a newer generation, drawn into politics by concern about the problems arising from industrialization and urbanization. He was young and issue-oriented. Patronage might be a means to the end, for the progressive, but it was not itself the goal of politics. . . .

When [Robert M.] La Follette [Sr.] was nominated for governor [of Wisconsin] in 1900, a veteran Wisconsin politician wrote, "A new cult has arisen and forced its way to the front. Never before were so many new faces seen in a Republican state convention in Wisconsin. The majority are young men whose enthusiasm has taken the place of experience."

La Follette was almost 40 years younger than the Republican party boss, Senator Philetus Sawyer, whom he overthrew. "The average age of the important progressive leaders who upset the Southern Pacific Railroad machine in California," George Mowry found, "was a little over 38." The men who led the successful revolt against the "czar" of the House of Representatives, 71-year-old Speaker Joseph G. Cannon, were on the average 30 years his junior.

The Progressive movement faded as a political force with the onset of World War I. But it left behind an important heritage of ideas. Direct primaries, popular election of senators, sunshine laws, fair-labor-standards laws, consumer and occupational-safety legislation, conservation laws, regulation of campaign finances and a national health program were all foreshadowed in its platform.

Discontent in the agricultural Midwest took the Progressives' "trust-busting" zeal one step further. The Nonpartisan League, which was founded in North Dakota in 1915 and quickly spread to the other Plains states, not only unified farmers' sentiment against the Minneapolis-based grain monopoly, but demanded state intervention in agriculture: state-owned grain elevators, mills and packing plants and state-administered farm-insurance programs. Allying with urban labor forces, the Nonpartisan League put together a formidable bloc, and by 1919 North Dakota had enacted the entire league platform. After World War I, however, with popular fear of Bolshevism running high in the aftermath of the Russian Revolution, the Nonpartisan League fell into disrepute: It was accused of disloyalty and socialism, and disappeared as quickly as it had sprung up. Its remnants in Minnesota formed the basis for the Farmer-Labor Party, which later allied with the state's Democrats to dominate that state's politics.

Institutionally, the greatest victory for Progressivism may have been the revolt against Speaker Cannon. Representative George Norris of Nebraska put together a coalition of Democrats and insurgent Republicans in 1910 which not only defied and discredited Cannon but radically reduced the authority of the Speaker: The uprising cut back the Speaker's power to appoint members of committees and designate chairmen, restricted his discretion in recognizing members for floor debate and removed him from control of the powerful Rules Committee.

The description Sundquist gives of the age gap in the revolts that overthrew Czar Cannon (or the Old Guard Republican boss in Wisconsin) could apply equally well to the revolts that shook the House of Representatives in the decade between 1965 and 1975. The House is an important barometer of intergenerational tension, because it is the point of entry to national politics for ambitious young leaders. It is not accidental that four of the last five presidents began their political careers there. And it is of the greatest significance that the past decade has been one of continual generational upheaval in the House leadership.

It began on a modest scale, inside the minority party, and with a most unaggressive-looking leader, Gerald R. Ford. As noted earlier, Ford had come to Congress as a result of defeating an entrenched Republican incumbent, and, despite his quick entry into the heart of the congressional Republican establishment (as symbolized by his membership on the Appropriations Committee and in the informal Chowder and Marching Society), his willingness to lead a charge had not been forgotten. In 1963, some of the "Young Turks," led by 39-year-old Robert P. Griffin of Michigan and 37-year-old Charles E. Goodell of New York, ran the 49-year-old Ford against 67-year-old Charles B. Hoeven of Iowa and captured the No. 3 spot in the leadership, the chairmanship of the House Republican Conference. Two years later, in 1965, Ford challenged and defeated 64-year-old Charles A. Halleck of Indiana and became the House Republican leader.

In both contests, questions of ideology and personal competence were less important than the generational tensions. Hoeven and Halleck were carry-overs from the New Deal years, having entered Congress in 1943 and 1935, respectively. Ford drew his strength from the junior members of his party. His 73–67 victory over Halleck came in the wake of the 1964 election debacle, in which the GOP sustained a net loss of 38 seats. More than half the Republicans who had come to Congress before Ford's arrival were defeated or retired in 1964. "In the final analysis," said Robert L. Peabody in his book *Leadership in Congress,* "it was the bottom-heavy structure of the House Republican Party which made victory possible for Ford. The bulk of his support, and certainly the organizational nucleus of his campaign, came from members elected since 1956."

The era that began with Ford's elevation was one of extraordinary change in the House leadership of both parties, and of upheaval in the rules and power relationships of that body. Between 1965 and 1979, throughout which time the Democrats were in the majority, the House had three different speakers, four different majority leaders and four different majority whips. On the GOP side, there were two different minority leaders, two minority whips and four conference chairmen. The 19 standing committees of the House in existence since 1965 (with the exception of the now-defunct House Committee on Un-American Activities) had 57 different chairmen and 63 different ranking minority members in that fourteen-year period. By 1979, there were only 70 Democrats and 31 Republicans still serving who had been there when the period of upheaval began in 1965. By contrast, despite the wreckage of the Republicans in 1964, there were 148 House members—more than one-third of the total body—serving in 1965 who had been there fourteen years earlier.

This recent period has seen not only a reshuffling of the membership deck in the House but a recasting of some of its most basic rules and procedures. Once again, the ferment began on the Republican side under the prodding of such young Ford supporters as Donald Rumsfeld of Illinois and Thomas B. Curtis of Missouri, and then was taken up and brought to fruition by young Democrats.

In a short span of years, the House sharply reduced the secrecy surrounding its committee markup sessions, where bills are actually written; opened its payrolls, personal and campaign finances to public scrutiny; switched from unrecorded to recorded votes on most floor amendments; introduced electronic voting systems and computerized information retrieval; and allowed televising of its own floor sessions. Most important, it decentralized its entire structure of authority—by a series of rules changes—shifting effective control from a handful of leaders and senior committee members in each party and magnifying the influence of individual members.

The climax of this extraordinary transformation came in the period immediately following the 1974 election, when 75 freshman Democrats, the largest such class in years, arrived on the scene. This was not the familiar breed of congressional politicians, who had served a protracted apprenticeship in local office or the state legislatures while waiting their turn for a House seat to become available. Many of them—31—were in elective office for the first time. They were activists who had been mobilized by concerns over Vietnam, the environment, consumer affairs or some other cause, and the Watergate climate permitted them to win in districts that were normally safely Republican.

When they caucused in Washington after the election, they quickly discovered that many of them had made a similar promise to their constituents: to "change things" in a government that had lost the confidence of millions of voters. Having just witnessed the forced resignation of a

President, they were not disposed to believe that anyone in the congressional hierarchy had a "divine right" to his post. To the shock of many of their elders, they rejected the concept of seniority automatically guaranteeing committee chairmanships, and they requested—indeed, almost demanded—that the incumbent chairmen come before them to justify their continuation in office. In the party caucus, they forced a change in the chairmanships of three powerful committees—Banking and Currency, Agriculture and Armed Services—and came close to unseating the chairmen of other committees as well.

The two classes that succeeded them—in 1976 and 1978—were neither as large nor as iconoclastic. But neither were they cut from the same cloth as House members traditionally had been. The House has not settled back into its old ways at all, for the gap between its older-generation leaders and the younger people who make up the mass of its membership—in attitude and experience—is almost unbridgeable.

The man who must make the effort to bridge the gap, however, is the Speaker of the House, Thomas P. (Tip) O'Neill, Jr. O'Neill, 68, is a product of the old-school ward politics of Cambridge, Massachusetts, where, as he said, "leadership came from party loyalty, and party loyalty emanated from the grass roots—the precinct worker and the doorbell ringer and the fellow who had the car out front to get Mrs. Murphy to the polls, and his partner who had Mrs. Sweeney, at the next house, ready when the car came back. I remember fifty years ago, when I was just a kid starting out in politics—and I'm talking about the '28 campaign of Al Smith—only four people in the precinct didn't vote. We got them all out."

The Speaker's father, the first Thomas P. O'Neill, was a leader in that system—Grand Knight of the Knights of Columbus, head of the Temperance Society, city councillor and, perhaps most important in terms of the jobs it means for the neighborhood, Superintendent of Sanitation and Sewers. Tip O'Neill went to Boston College, then into the Massachusetts Legislature, became its Speaker, took John Kennedy's seat in the U.S. House of Representatives and moved up to become Speaker of the House.

But history, that fickle mistress, did not make Tip O'Neill Speaker until there were hardly any congressmen left who had any idea of the kind of disciplined, structured party politics in which he was raised.

"Everything has changed about the Hill," O'Neill said in 1979, mentally comparing the House of today with the one he had entered as a freshman in 1953. "A good many of the members coming into Congress now never came through the organization, never rang a doorbell in their life, never were a precinct worker, never stayed late at the polls, never brought people to an election, weren't brought up in the realm of party discipline. They never served on the city council or a state legislature, or as a mayor or a county officer. They come right in at the top. They're totally independent. A lot of them, like my own son Tommy, were on the threshold or had achieved success in business or a profession, but wanted to come into politics. They're not just off-the-street people. We have more Rhodes scholars and more Sorbonnes and more doctorates and more masters of every description. They're young, qualified, highly educated people. . . . And they're all so media-oriented. In years past, fellows around here would be frightened to go on a program like *Meet the Press* or *Face the Nation*. But these guys say, 'I know more about what they're going to ask me than they know, so why should I have any fear?'

"It all turned around in the Seventies," he said. "The youth of America were turned off by the war and Watergate and recession. But the ones who weren't turned off, they wanted to come down to Washington and change the establishment. They wanted to open it up. They wanted to take the power out of the hands of the committee chairmen. And they wanted all the votes in committee and on the floor to be record votes."

I remarked to the Speaker that "to most people, those changes would sound very good."

"In the overall," he said, "I think it's done good. I was always opposed to the seniority system, but not for the same reason that these young fellows around here are. I believe in rewarding party loyalty. I believe that the chairmen of the committees should be the ones whose philosophy is most in accord with the majority of the body . . . and who are able and competent to carry it out. They [the young members] don't think about party loyalty. They were interested in spreading the power. But in spreading the power, we now have 152 subcommittees, each one with its own staff, each one trying to make its own chairman look good. And it's just hard as hell to put the pieces together and put the legislation through."

In attempting to lead this independent, highly decentralized House, Tip O'Neill could hardly look to the example of the speakers under whom he had served. "Sam Rayburn," he said, "wouldn't know but 20 members of the House. That was all the people he needed to deal with. I know every Democratic member of Congress. I go to all their caucuses. The freshman caucus. The sophomore caucus. The junior caucus. The black caucus. The Jewish caucus. The Mexican caucus. The Northeast caucus. The Middle American caucus. The steel caucus. The women's caucus." In addition to the formal party structure of the steering committee and the whip organization, O'Neill said, he had begun setting up task forces on major bills, headed by "these young fellows like Norm Mineta [Mineta is the third-term Nisei Representative from California who spent his boyhood in the internment camps] who are as frustrated as I am in trying to get things passed, and they involve their friends and they become part of the action. But the party discipline just isn't there."

O'Neill was not alone in that view. One morning in 1978, nine senior members of the House, drawn from both parties, gathered with me in the "Board of Education" room, where Rayburn had held his private caucuses, to talk about the newcomers to Congress. Their comments were then relayed, anonymously, to a similar round table of junior members.

The newcomers were told that their seniors had this to say about them, as a group: "You have no ideology, or you are not as 'ideologically pure' as your predecessors; you expect to be immediate participants in the legislative process; you want immediate solutions, and this sometimes makes Congress less effective in its policy making; you are argumentative, making it harder to reach consensus; you play the outside game; you're more independent; you're disrespectful of traditional leadership. You're responsive to your constituencies, but you're also highly responsive to single-interest groups. You are very good politicians, but some of you are opportunistic and self-serving. You are darlings of the media, you exploit the media; you're not loyal to political parties; you're not legislative craftsmen; you're anti-government; you're brighter; and yet, for the most part you are, as one of your elders said, 'lacking in personal accomplishment in the political or business world.' "

There were a few stunned looks around the table as the nine junior members—again drawn from both parties—listened. The first to react was Norm Mineta. "First of all," he said, "that's such *bullshit!* We have a much brighter group who are willing to take on very seriously the discussion of national legislative policies. I think we take on that task much more seriously than our predecessors. That's why a lot of them are bailing out [of Congress]. There are maybe three or four times as many recorded votes a year, so they have to be accountable for more; they've got to do more reading, more studying, be better briefed, and I don't think they're up to the task. Our younger members here are much more prepared on legislation—whether it's in their own committee or not. It used to be that if it was outside your committee jurisdiction, you didn't even think about it, you just automatically accepted it. But now we've got people who are all over the place, and I just think that's a much healthier situation."

His colleagues went on in a similar vein, challenging the criticisms their elders had made. The arguments echoed the earlier intergenerational conflicts in American political history, as when *The New York Times* described the Loco-Focos as "pledge-spouters, resolution-mongers, small-fry of small politicians, small lights, fireflies of faction."

What is different now is that there are so many of these young people that even the heaviest epithets cannot halt their inexorable march to power. As Peter Drucker pointed out in his 1976 book *The Unseen Revolution,* the "unprecedented" fact is that "American society . . . now faces a period during which there will be two centers of demographic gravity," competing with each other for control.

One of those centers is the population of older people, those past retirement age or rapidly approaching it, like Tip O'Neill and his House contemporaries. "The number of people over 65 and of 'survivors,' especially widows, 55 to 65 years old . . . now amounting to some 30 millions . . . will reach 40 millions or so by the mid-Eighties," Drucker said.

The second group—of equal size—is the baby-boom generation, the bulge of population created during the decade following World War II.

In many respects, the course of American history since the early Sixties can be traced as the shock wave of that generation's impact on long-standing customs and institutions. Its members overturned social norms and then began applying the force of their numbers to political authority. The high-school principals were the first to encounter the rebelliousness of this generation, but they were soon joined by the college deans and the assembly-line foremen. And then it was presidents of the United States and congressional-committee chairmen who were being threatened by masses of anti-establishment youths.

They were first known as "the beat generation." Their parents, who had experienced privation during the Depression and rationing during World War II, indulged them—perhaps to excess. The parents, having known poverty, craved material things. Their children, not surprisingly, rejected what they perceived as acquisitiveness. Brought up on the child-rearing principles of Dr. Benjamin Spock, members of this generation were encouraged to speak freely and to assert their individuality. They did, creating the "youth culture" of the 1950s and '60s. A young actor named James Dean made a movie titled *Rebel Without a Cause* which became a cult favorite. Buddy Holly introduced rock-and-roll, and the older generation condemned the sexuality of its performance. Ed Sullivan's television cameras studiously avoided Elvis Presley's controversial lower torso—"lest," as *The New York Times* put it in a 1977 obituary, "his wiggling hips be shown." Restlessness and protest became the dominant themes of literature and music. Jack Kerouac wrote *On the Road.* Allen Ginsberg published his poem *Howl.* Bob Dylan began singing about racism and war. The arts moved into the coffeehouse, a place appropriately underground, foreshadowing the "subversive" culture of the late Sixties.

The Beatles came to America in 1964, and remained one step ahead of youthful taste, beginning in cute style with "I Wanna Hold Your Hand"

and moving toward social protest and heavier-metal sounds, sounds taken ever further by Mick Jagger and the Rolling Stones. By the end of the 1960s, the rock culture and the drug culture had become thoroughly enmeshed, and jointly labored to widen sensory perception and to transcend the limits of a narrow world. The Beatles sang of LSD under the name of "Lucy in the Sky with Diamonds." Janis Joplin, a singer who died of an overdose of heroin, was admired as a sort of anti-paragon. Her harsh, strained voice was ugly by the standards of a previous generation. The press quoted her mother as saying that Janis, with her naturally lovely voice, could have made opera her career. The point of Joplin's art was that she didn't. *Bel canto* held no charms for her, and no charms for her generation.

The psychedelic visions of hashish, mescaline and LSD influenced the optical illusions of "serious" art as well as the colors of fashion, the shocking pink and bright orange of a peyote dream. Skirts rose steadily during the 1960s, and then wildly fluctuated from the mini to the midi to the maxi, reviving a theory of the linkage between stock-market fortunes and cautious or uninhibited exposure. Dance was frenetic; a million forms gyrated, beginning with the twist and the frug and moving on to an even more complete free form. Luci Baines Johnson watusied across America for her father's 1964 campaign. It was a time for experimentation. Sexual relationships, with the advent of the birth-control pill, became casual. There were "happenings," "sensitivity-training" sessions, Woodstock, yoga and yogurt. It was a time to be beat, cool or hip, to dig, groove, turn on or trip—the words changed as fast as the styles.

The more political disputes of the era were tied to this impatience with repression. As more and more of their students wore blue jeans and long hair, the schools found they could no longer insist on standards of appearance. They were also challenged on their administration, as students demanded a hand in setting policy and determining the curriculum. "Relevance" became the criterion for course selection, and the issues of the external world invaded the quiet of the campus. The "free-speech movement" shook Berkeley. Vietnam stirred protests and strikes and frequent acts of violence.

And then almost as suddenly as it seemed to have begun, the turbulence began to subside. The generation began to age. The protests lost their force as the draft ended—and as the impact of the Kent State killings took hold. The consumer and environmental movements began. And, as Peter Drucker pointed out, "the members of this group [began] forming families and getting started on work and careers. They entered what in many ways is the most conservative age of man . . . the age in which concerns with salary and job, with the mortgage on the home, the pediatrician's bill and the schooling of one's children tend to predominate."

But the quiet that descended on the country in the mid-Seventies was different from that of the earlier generation, for the country itself had been changed by the passage of time. In 1960, at least 77 million Americans, or about 43 percent of the total population, had personal memories of the Depression and World War II. These were people who had been born before 1925. They were at least 15 years old when FDR stopped being "Dr. New Deal" and became "Dr. Win the War." They were at least 20 when Japan surrendered. But today the great majority of Americans were too young to have any—or more than the most fleeting—memories of the Depression and World War II. Nostalgia for them is hearing the Beatles—not Glenn Miller.

The members of this new generation of adults are substantially more affluent, educated and white-collar than their counterparts in 1960. For the first time in our history, the typical adult American has more than a high-school education, the median number of years of study rising from 10.8 in 1960 to between 12 and 13 years in 1980. In 1960, two of every five American adults had less than an eighth-grade education. Today that is true of only one in five. Two of every five adult Americans had a high-school diploma in 1960, compared with two of every three Americans today.

In terms of occupation, in 1960 the number of white-collar workers barely exceeded the number of blue-collar workers; today, the ratio is about 3 to 2. Income is up accordingly, in spite of inflation, and earning power has increased substantially. Median family income in constant 1978 dollars rose from $12,374 in 1960 to $17,640 in 1978—an increase of about 40 percent. And the percentage of families whose income was over $25,000 in constant 1978 dollars nearly quadrupled in those eighteen years from 7.4 percent to 27.9 percent. At the same time, the average numbers of hours of work declined, affording both more leisure time and more income. Recreational spending increased fivefold; the number of overseas travelers quadrupled, and the number of two-car families did the same.

By the end of the Seventies, nearly half of America's women were working or seeking jobs. Fertility rates dropped to a new low. Life expectancy increased three years and, for women, approached 80. One marriage in three ended in divorce.

Significant as all these changes are for the makeup of the country, there is another change of equal importance for American politics. Since 1960, millions of Americans have dropped out of the voting process—declining to participate in that most basic ritual of democracy. The percentage of eligible voters casting a presidential ballot reached a 20th century peak in 1960, when an estimated 58.5 percent of adults cast ballots. It has declined in each election since then, reaching at least a provisional low in 1976, when 54.4 percent of those eligible came to the polls.

The decline has been pervasive, but not even, across various segments of the population. There is a sharp age gradient to the falloff. Younger people, those under 35, have always voted in lesser numbers than those who were somewhat older, probably reflecting their greater mobility and lack of stable involvement in a community. But in this recent period, the younger citizens' voting has declined even more rapidly than that of middle-aged and older voters. Census Bureau studies show the difference between 1964 and 1976. (Earlier years are not available.) In those twelve years, the percentage of those over 55 who voted declined by 5 points; the drop-off among the middle-aged (35–54) was 8.8 points; and the decline among voters under 35 was 11 points.

The overall dimensions of the nonvoting population give a strong hint of the forces that are gathering—or waiting to be marshaled—in the 1980s. According to the nonvoter study of the Committee for the Study of the American Electorate (CSAE), nearly 70 million Americans failed to cast ballots in the 1976 presidential election, and 82 million did not take part in the 1978 voting.

Close to half those 1978 nonvoters (46 percent) were people under 35, while only 30 percent of those who did vote were equally young. The nonvoters are likely to be poorer, less educated and more urban than the voters. And yet 74 percent of the nonvoters are white, 20 percent are in the upper income brackets and 23 percent live in suburbs. At least 15 million of the nonvoters are real "dropouts," people who once voted with some regularity and have given up the habit.

As the CSAE nonvoter study pointed out, the falloff in voting has occurred in the same time period in which many of the mechanical and political barriers have been removed from the polls.

Curtis Gans, the executive director of the study, said in a 1977 speech: "Within the last decade and a half, the poll tax was outlawed, discrimination at polling places on the basis of race or language was legally eliminated, young Americans between the ages of 18 and 21 were enfranchised, residency requirements were eased, unreasonable and inequitable registration dates were discarded, and many states initiated various devices to increase the level of participation, including mobile registrars, postcard registration, expanded voter information and even election-day registration."

Why, in the face of all that, did voting decline so sharply? The main reasons mentioned in the CSAE study's survey sounded like a litany of complaints, not about the difficulty of getting into the polls, but of finding motivation to go:

"Candidates say one thing and then do another," said 68 percent of the nonvoters. "It doesn't make any difference who is elected because things never seem to work right," said 55 percent. "Watergate proved that elected officials are only out for themselves,'' said 52 percent. And ''All candidates seem pretty much the same,'' said 50 percent.

Perhaps most poignant, and most pertinent for our purposes, is the fact that when the nonvoters were asked about the political figures of their lifetimes they admired most, the most recent name on the list (and the most frequently mentioned) was John F. Kennedy. No one who has emerged since 1960 drew more than a scattering of mentions. And the one thing they said would most likely induce them to vote in the future would be ''having a candidate worth voting for.''

It is not just the habit of voting that has been broken; so has the pattern of voting behavior among those who do mark their ballots. The oncoming generation of political leaders is the product of a period of rising independence in our politics. Data from the University of Michigan's Center for Political Studies show an erosion of support from both parties and an increase in the number of people calling themselves independents. As with the phenomenon of nonvoting, the disaffiliation from the political parties is concentrated most heavily among the younger voters. In 1952, according to the CPS data, 25 percent of those who were first eligible to vote considered themselves independents. Twenty years later, 51 percent of the first-time voters were independents, and every age group up through 65 included more than 25 percent independents. The trend continued into the 1976 elections, with the highest percentage of independents —over 48 percent—found among the 18-to-24-year-olds.

The change in party identification has been matched by an actual change in voting behavior. The proportion of people reporting they voted for a President of one party and a Congressman of the other doubled between 1952 and 1976 (from 13 to 25 percent). There has been a parallel upsurge in the number of states choosing a Governor and Senator of opposite parties in the same election.

The causes of this fundamental change in the way this generation responds to politics and politicians will be discussed in many of the chapters of this book.

One of the causes, as Pat Brown pointed out, is the advent of television as the principal means of political communication. Today's voter prides himself on being able to make a more sophisticated evaluation of the strengths and weaknesses of individual candidates than did his straight-ticket-voting parent, because he has seen those candidates on his living-room television screen. The result has been to create a demand for telegenic candidates, and a large and lucrative industry has developed among specialists in presenting them on the flickering tube.

A second basic reason has been the mass movement from the cities to the suburbs, from the bailiwicks of the political bosses to the arenas of the political volunteers. The old-fashioned political machine was the product of the big city. It developed first in the period of mass immigration, as a device for delivering certain minimal social services—for jobs, food, coal—to recent arrivals, in return for their votes and political support.

Where it survived into the last half of the century, as in Chicago, it was the best available device for sustaining hierarchical control of competing and conflicting population elements, usually on behalf of the dominant economic interests of the city. That kind of machine is disappearing, even in Chicago. In moving from city to suburb a family is uprooting itself from its past and asserting a desire to throw off the constraints and disciplines of city life—including the political disciplines. It is also choosing a more homogeneous environment, where there are few clashes—racial, ethnic or economic—that require political mediation. Thus, just as hierarchical party organizations are the "natural" structure for the older cities, so horizontal, volunteer, nonhierarchical structures are at home in suburbia.

A third factor which has contributed to the basic change in our voting patterns is the "homogenization" of politics. The Solid South, which ever since the Civil War has been the backbone of the Democrats' strength, gave Republicans increasing proportions of its presidential vote from 1952 through 1972, and elected scores of Republicans to other offices. But with the enfranchisement of blacks, Democrats staged a comeback in the 1970s, and the region is now one of the most competitive political areas in the country.

While the South was going through its oscillation, many of the traditional Republican bastions of the North were seeing the same phenomenon in mirror image. Maine, New Hampshire and Vermont developed vigorous Democratic parties. Wisconsin, Michigan, Iowa, Kansas, Nebraska, Minnesota and Oregon—states that were the birthplace and bedrock of the Republican Party—became important sources of national leadership for the Democrats and vigorous two-party battlegrounds.

A fourth basic change is that as the country emerged from the Depression and World War II into a period of sustained postwar prosperity, the sharp economic and class lines that marked the New Deal period began to erode. While there was little income redistribution in that period, the living standards of millions of Americans improved so rapidly and significantly that their class identification weakened. Auto workers could no longer be easily motivated to come to Cadillac Square (later renamed Kennedy Square) in Detroit for their traditional Labor Day rally, because many of them were off at the lakes with their powerboats for the weekend.

Organized labor found itself falling out of comfortable collaboration with other elements in the New Deal coalition—such as ethnic groups and urban machines—over the Vietnam war and other foreign-policy issues and the social policies pushed by the "new constituencies" of women and minorities. Big business, recovering from the shock of the New Deal, became increasingly involved and sophisticated in its politics and, in the 1970s, mobilized campaign funds that dwarfed the war chests of the unions and the political parties.

Instead of the Depression worries about job security and unemployment, the pervasive economic and social problem for the younger generation of Americans has been inflation. Ever since the mid-1960s, when the rising costs of the Vietnam war and the Great Society began to have an impact on an inflation rate that had held at 3 percent or below for the previous fourteen years, families have been struggling with an escalating cost of living.

By the end of the 1970s, inflation had become an overriding political issue—a distorting and frightening factor in the lives of many families who found themselves working harder to gather dollars whose value eroded almost as rapidly as they could be accumulated.

Inflation was one, but only one, of the forces that Americans found unfathomable and upsetting as the 1980s began. As a people, they had gone through a protracted period of accelerated social change, and they were suffering the after-effects of what Alvin Toffler had called "future shock"—the too-sudden alteration of the social environment.

In the space of a few years, the "rules" had changed as to what was accepted and proper in the relationship between parents and children, between husbands and wives, and between the races. Barriers of space and time that had stood for generations were obliterated suddenly in the rush of technology. The jet airplane and the superhighway offered greater mobility than any society had known before. Airline pilots commuted 300 miles to their jobs in order to enjoy the beauties of the West, and millions of less-privileged contemporaries plied back and forth from their suburbs to their city jobs for the same reason. Television brought the events of the world into every living room in the land. And yet, along with this speed and freedom of transportation and communication, there was a growing sense of the shattering of old community ties—of the weakening of the infrastructure of the national society.

In a short time, the same America which had come within a single vote of eliminating the draft just months before Pearl Harbor was spending over $100 billion a year to maintain its position as the preeminent military and political power in the world. The destructive power of its weaponry defied the imagination, and yet, in the two wars following the victory over fascism, the United States was denied its initial objective and sent home in frustration. Nor could the incredible U.S. economic machine protect Americans from having their vital energy supplies threatened by a group of underdeveloped countries. They discovered how to exploit America's insatiable appetite for oil and, by classic cartel practices, extracted more and more bounty from the United States for their treasuries, thus fueling the inflation that mocked America's seeming prosperity.

Finally, the massive government that was built in a frantic burst of energy to meet the twin crises of the Depression and World War II appeared to many Americans to have acquired a destructive momentum of its own. Concern about the proliferation of programs and regulations grew as fast in the 1970s as the programs and regulations themselves had multiplied in the previous 30 years. At the apex of that government—the presidency—the concentration of decision-making authority grew so great that it spun spectacularly out of control. As the system malfunctioned from its overload, individual politicians and office seekers increasingly severed their ties with others in government, or even in their own party, and pursued a politics of personal ambition and self-aggrandizement. Their views reflected a strong sense that the formulas and philosophies of the past were outdated and irrelevant, but a great uncertainty about what would—or should—replace them.

In round-table discussions with members of Congress and executive-agency officials in their thirties—people chosen because of their promise for even more significant leadership roles in the future—what emerged was a pervasive sense that the political and governmental formulas and approaches of the past were finally receiving an overdue examination.

Over and over, these men and women spoke of the tensions and frustrations of living in a time when there were neither heroes nor models nor philosophies one could look to with confidence, and when the discipline previously imposed by party loyalty was not there to dictate policy choice, either.

"I'm not entirely sure what my political philosophy is," said Representative James Blanchard, a Michigan Democrat. "Nor do I have any major leader to look to as someone I want to follow, which I think is very typical of members of Congress today."

A Republican colleague from Michigan, Representative David Stockman, observed that the passage of the Great Society legislation in the mid-Sixties had ended thirty years of ideological debate. "If the government wasn't doing anything to rescue the cities, to save the housing industry, to transform education, to change the ghettos, you could have great debates. But that debate was broken with the Eighty-ninth Congress after 1964. We started doing all those things, and I can't run now *against* Medicare, or aid to education, any more than the Democrats can run *for* those things, because they're already on the books. All I can do—or they can do—is propose better ways of doing it, more effective, less costly ways. And that's why ideology has declined."

At the discussion with the agency officials—all appointees of a Democratic administration, it should be pointed out—the focus was almost entirely on the problem of fulfilling the promises that were implicit in the programs passed in the 1960. "People want far more from their government than government has been used to delivering," observed Frank Raines, then a deputy director of the Office of Management and Budget and the highest-ranking black official in the history of that "super-agency." "People like us are probably very much to blame for creating those expectations. Even the routine government agencies—Social Security, the Post Office, Internal Revenue—aren't run as well now, from the standpoint of the average citizen, as they were ten years ago. They just aren't."

As the 1980s began, public dissatisfaction with the performance and the cost of government had reached the point where it was politically possible to imagine an upheaval that might overturn the long Democratic predominance at all levels of government in this country.

But the people pressing for change were not only Republicans. Many of the younger Democrats were as impatient with the formulas of the New Deal–Great Society era as any GOP critics. One of them, Representative Timothy E. Wirth of Colorado, complained that his party leaders had "absolutely no strategy" for confronting either the question of inflation or the need for improved governmental efficiency and relief from the "overregulation" of society. Seeking such strategy from current leaders in Congress, he said, "is like pushing on a rope."

But neither Wirth nor Raines nor Stockman nor Blanchard, nor any of the others among the hundreds interviewed for this book, was pessimistic about the future. "I think," said Tim Wirth, "the younger people understand the complexities more thoroughly and are more willing to deal with the ambiguities, are more willing to cross party lines and explore new ideas, more willing to threaten or confront the old ways of going about our business."

That statement seems palpably true. What the changing of the guard promises America in the 1980s is not a pat solution to all its problems, but a long-overdue fresh look at those concerns. There is no one vision of the future that emerges from these young people but a set of partial alternatives, based on the experiences and insights they have gained in their widely varying political educations.

It is those experiences and visions to which we now turn.

SURVIVORS AND HEIRS

Let the word go forth from this time and place to friend and foe alike, that the torch has been passed to a new generation of Americans, born in this century, tempered by war, disciplined by a hard and bitter peace, proud of our ancient heritage, and unwilling to witness or permit the slow undoing of those human rights to which this nation has always been committed, and to which we are committed today at home and around the world.

—John F. Kennedy, 1961

You are coming to maturity at a time which history will remember as a great period of emancipation for young Americans. Your generation has the opportunity to participate more fully in the American adventure than young people have ever been able to do since Revolutionary times 200 years ago.

—Richard M. Nixon, 1971

We have been through too much in too short a time. Our national nightmare began with the assassination of John Kennedy, and went on to include the assassination of Robert Kennedy, and of Martin Luther King, Jr., and the wounding of George Wallace. We watched the widespread opposition to the war in Vietnam, and the division and bitterness that war caused, and the violence in Chicago in 1968, and the invasion of Cambodia, and the shootings at Kent State, and revelations of official lying and spying and bugging, the resignations in disgrace of both a President and a Vice President, and the disclosure that our security and law-enforcement agencies were deliberately and routinely violating the law. No other generation in American history has ever been subjected to such a battering as this.

—Jimmy Carter, 1976

The bold confidence of John Kennedy's and Richard Nixon's challenges to young America is mocked by the mournful history recited by Jimmy Carter. The last twenty years have seen dramatic—and often disconcerting—turns in the national mood, and they have been a period of unrivaled instability in the presidency, the symbol of the national government.

Not since Dwight D. Eisenhower left the White House at the start of the Sixties has America seen what it once thought of as a "normal" presidency—a two-term tenure by the same man. Rather, the presidents of the past two decades have been either the victims or the perpetrators of a sort of national shock treatment—or, in some cases, both.

Kennedy began with the Bay of Pigs fiasco, endured the Berlin Wall and Cuban missile crises, which brought the Cold War perilously close to open conflict, and then was gunned down in Dallas—a tragedy which, as much as any other, shattered the optimism of the nation. Lyndon Johnson used surprise as a weapon of governing, but the escalation of American involvement in Vietnam led to a surprise that not even he could have anticipated—his withdrawal from the 1968 presidential race and his forced retirement to Texas. Richard Nixon, his successor, was at least as secretive as Johnson. But he was driven from office—forced to resign early in his second term—because he could not keep two secrets: the fact that there had been White House involvement in a break-in at the Democrats' Watergate headquarters, and the fact that he had recorded incriminating evidence of his own involvement in the cover-up of that crime on secret tapes in his own office. Gerald Ford, his successor, was a much more open man, but only thirty days into his presidency he shocked the nation by issuing a full pardon of Nixon—an act from which he never recovered politically. Finally Jimmy Carter, seemingly the most stable and shockproof of them all, took the country with him on an incredible roller-coaster ride in the last half of 1979. Plagued by polls that gave him the lowest rating of any President since World War II, Carter went into a ten-day retreat at Camp David in July of that year, and came down from the mountain with the decision to reshuffle his Cabinet and bring outsiders into senior positions on his White House staff. He plunged into a round of cross-country appearances, almost as if the campaign for re-election had begun—but his standing in the polls still declined. In the autumn, when Ted Kennedy officially announced his challenge to Carter's renomination, the President's position seemed politically hopeless. But in the final two months of the year, attention shifted from Carter's shortcomings to the drama of the American hostages in Iran and the Soviet invasion of Afghanistan. Carter abandoned the campaign trail—and, at least temporarily, surged to a height of popularity he had not enjoyed since his first year in office.

Yet for all this turbulent history, the White House and its occupants have remained a magnet for young people drawn to political and public life. And so this book begins by looking at some of the young men and women whose presence in politics today can be traced to the personalities, programs and policies of the last five presidents. In many cases, the connection is direct: They were hired to work on the campaigns or the White House staffs. In other cases there was no personal link, but only an unforeseen connection. When John Kennedy started the Peace Corps, when Lyndon Johnson started the War on Poverty, and when both of them and Richard Nixon sent thousands of Americans to fight in Vietnam, they did not do so primarily to involve new people in politics. But each of those movements has produced a crop of younger politicians who would not have arrived—at least with their current views—were it not for the acts of those presidents.

Because of the turbulence of the times through which they have come, it is appropriate to label these "presidential recruits" as survivors. Many of their contemporaries who were brought into politics at the same time and in the same way came away disillusioned and defeated.

But if they are the survivors, they are also the heirs of these presidents. Different as they are in background, experience and outlook, they display, perhaps more clearly than any others in this book, the dilemmas and doubts that are so much the heritage of the past twenty years of

American leadership. They are, in one way or another, searching for a consensus—a set of goals and programs that somehow was lost during the past two decades.

Their quest sets the recurring theme of this book.

2 · Kennedy-Johnson

THEY ARE NO LONGER YOUNG, the youths of Camelot. Ken O'Donnell, the tight-lipped, totally dedicated political aide and appointments secretary, went to his own early grave, still mourning the murdered President. Larry O'Brien, the legislative wizard who ran congressional relations, now worries about franchises, attendance and television ratings as commissioner of the National Basketball Association. Ted Sorensen, who was 24 when he brought his brain and his typewriter to Kennedy's Senate office, is 52 now, and practicing law. Press Secretary Pierre Salinger is still plump and plucky, but an expatriate in France. Others, like Lee White, Myer Feldman and McGeorge Bundy, have gone back to the legal or academic careers they had begun before the summons came to the New Frontier. No one from the Kennedy White House staff was in elective public office as the 1970s ended.

If the heritage of a past President were carried forward only by his immediate staff, or if influence in this country were limited to the holders of elective office, the previous sentence would end the discussion of the impact of the Kennedy years on those who shape the future of American politics. But obviously neither of those assumptions is valid. Presidents influence successive generations in a great variety of ways, both direct and indirect. A presidency is like a stone dropped in a pond; the farther from the center, the wider the circle of its influence. This chapter is organized around those concentric circles of influence which center on the presidencies of John F. Kennedy and Lyndon B. Johnson: first, the members of their immediate staffs; second, those who were activated into politics by their campaigns; third, those who were brought into public service by the programs they created—the Peace Corps, the War on Poverty, the White House Fellows; and, finally, the veterans of the American involvement in Vietnam, which began in Kennedy's time and reached its peak under Johnson.

All these are, in a real sense, "children of the Sixties," and of the two presidents who dominated that decade. But the most powerful part of the Kennedy-Johnson legacy may be one of mood—the belief that America, under an optimistic, activist and charismatic president, can accomplish any goal it sets for itself, on earth or in outer space. As the 1980s began, the relevance of that early-Sixties spirit was being debated and tested by the presidential candidacy of Senator Edward M. Kennedy, seen by some as reincarnating the broken dreams of the earlier decade and by others as an anachronism, a relic of a time and a leadership style that cannot be recaptured.

In its time, that spirit was strong medicine. Although John Kennedy's victory in 1960 was narrow, the theme song of his campaign, "High Hopes," seemed to catch the mood of the country. In those years, everything seemed possible. America replaced its oldest President with the youngest it had ever elected. It rejected one of its historic prejudices: the barrier to a Roman Catholic's occupying the White House. It began a period of steady, dramatic economic growth. It stared down the only other superpower, the Soviet Union, in the Cuban missile crisis. And it began to tear down the walls of segregation that had endured for a century since slavery was ended.

Progress on some fronts, particularly in Congress, was slower than the young men in Kennedy's White House had expected. But by 1963, when Kennedy was struck down, they were beginning to learn the pathways to success. Many of them stayed on to help Lyndon Johnson carry through those Kennedy initiatives in the remaining year of Kennedy's term, and to launch the Great Society, which embodied the vision of a President even more activist, optimistic and unconstrained in his dreams for the nation and the world than Kennedy had been.

After the 1964 election, Johnson gradually replaced the Kennedy men with a staff of his own—one that was larger in numbers and at least equal in talent. And yet, eleven years after Johnson went into retirement, only one alumnus of *his* White House staff held elective office.

The lone Johnson alumnus is Democratic Representative James R. Jones, 41, of Tulsa, Oklahoma, who is, as it happens, one of the most influential members of the House of Representatives, even though he has less than eight years of seniority.

Jones is an Okie from Muskogee, the son of a rural mail carrier, reared, like Johnson himself, in an atmosphere of politics. Like Johnson, he came to Washington in his early twenties, right out of college, to work for a home-state Congressman. Volunteer work as an advance man on the 1964 campaign earned him a White House staff job, and at 27, Jim Jones found himself the President's appointments secretary—a post he held for the last two years Johnson was in office.

Two years after Johnson retired, Jones was back in Oklahoma running for Congress, and after a narrow defeat in 1970, he was elected on his second try in 1972. Jones has none of the obvious dominating personality traits that marked his mentor, but he nevertheless has displayed a Johnsonian knack of coalition building. Serving on the House Ways and Means Committee, he has fashioned *ad hoc* coalitions of Republicans and moderate-to-conservative Democrats that reshaped capital-gains taxes and trade, investment and energy policies.

Jones was a good advertisement for the Johnson recruiting system, which, over the long years of his service, brought dozens of talented young Texans (and a few out-of-state strays) to Washington for training in the art of politics and government.

"Johnson had an eye for young people," Jim Jones said. "And he really encouraged them to get into government. And he gave them responsibility. What I noticed when I went to the White House was that Johnson expected you to have the talent to be there; he gave you the assignment and expected you to run with it, and then chewed your ass out if you didn't do it right. At the end of the day, you were totally wrung out, but he got more than 100 percent out of what you thought you were capable of doing."

But Jim Jones stood out, not just for his quality but as the only Kennedy-Johnson White House aide to gain elective office. Others, like Sorensen, Salinger and O'Donnell, tried and failed in their campaigns. But most of the others, as Johnson's able counsel, Harry McPherson, said of himself and his colleagues, "didn't have the gumption to go chase it."

How much of their reluctance can be attributed to the unhappy last chapters of their presidents' careers can only be guessed. But it was certainly not lack of interest in politics that held them back. McPherson, Sorensen and most of the other lawyers who worked for Kennedy and Johnson have wielded significant political influence, advising candidates, polishing speeches, serving on presidential commissions.

Joseph A. Califano, Jr., the Brooklyn kid whom Johnson picked from the immense Pentagon bureaucracy to manage his Great Society domestic program, became one of the "superlawyers" of Washington and then was recycled as the controversial Secretary of Health, Education and Welfare in the first thirty months of the Carter Administration. Matthew Nimetz, one of Califano's White House assistants, came back in the Carter years as Undersecretary of State. Johnson's daughter Lynda Bird Robb heads Carter's advisory council on women's issues.

More broadly, many Kennedy and Johnson White House aides have continued to contribute significantly to the discussion and understanding of public affairs. Kennedy's National Security Adviser, McGeorge Bundy, ran the Ford Foundation for many years, while the counterpart in Johnson's term, Walt Whitman Rostow, teaches at the Lyndon B. Johnson School of Public Affairs at the University of Texas at Austin. S. Douglass Cater, Jr., Johnson's education specialist, directs the Aspen

Institute for Humanistic Studies; Roger L. Stevens, his assistant for the arts, now manages the Kennedy Center in Washington. Arthur M. Schlesinger, Jr., and John P. Roche, thinkers-in-residence for Kennedy and Johnson, respectively, have resumed active careers as teachers, authors, newspaper columnists and political polemicists.

The press secretaries who served the two presidents have all remained active in public roles. Pierre Salinger, who stayed on briefly after JFK's assassination as Johnson's first press secretary, is a novelist, television and magazine journalist and sometime political organizer—he helped direct the McGovern-for-president campaign. Bill D. Moyers, LBJ's second spokesman, became publisher of *Newsday*. George E. Reedy, the third, wrote a significant study of presidential power, *The Twilight of the Presidency,* and has served as dean and professor at the Marquette University School of Journalism. George Christian, the last of Johnson's press secretaries, has become one of the most influential lobbyists and political consultants in Austin.

But it would be a major mistake, in measuring the historical impact of these two presidents, to assume that their political heritage is measured only by the subsequent activities of those who were in their direct employ.

Of all the campaigns that have shaped the next generation of political leaders, none was more important than the Kennedy-Johnson campaign of 1960. From politicians nearing 50 to those barely more than 30, one hears, time and again, of the signal impact of that 1960 race. Here, briefly, are six examples.

At 49, Norman Mineta of California is perhaps the most widely admired Democrat to enter the House of Representatives in the 1970s. He was the leader of the huge freshman class elected in 1974, and while in his third term was chosen to head the task force on inflation and budget policy that was critical to the political well-being of his party. Many of his contemporaries regard him as a future prospect for Speaker of the House.

But until 1960, Norm Mineta expected to be a Republican. His background is remarkable. When he was a youth in San Jose, California, he and his family were among the thousands of Japanese-Americans rounded up after Pearl Harbor and sent to internment camps. The attitude among his friends, when they returned to San Jose, Mineta said, was "It was the damn Democrats that stuck us in those damn camps, and why the hell should I . . . register as a Democrat?"

Mineta expected to follow his father into the insurance business, and "during high-school days, through college and the time that I was in the service [during the Korean war], I used to be very pro-Republican."

But, he said, when he tried to become active in the local GOP organization, he was rebuffed by the question "How much money do you have to contribute?"

"About that time, my own feelings about civil rights, fair housing, fair employment, were beginning to jell. . . . And then the Kennedy-Nixon election campaign came along, and there was an undercurrent of very strong anti-Catholic feeling in that race, and that just sent me up the wall. So in 1960, I reregistered and became a Democrat and worked in the campaign."

Like so many of the others discussed in the course of this book, Mineta has experienced the kind of rapid escalator rise which the American political system can provide. Whatever else its failings, American politics does give access to power and growing influence for those with ability and ambition. In Mineta's case, he moved from campaign volunteer to member of the city human-relations commission and housing authority to the city council, and in 1971 he became the first Japanese-American Mayor of a major U.S. city.

Down in Texas, Bob Armstrong, now 48, was a young lawyer just out of the University of Texas when he was asked to handle three counties for the Kennedy-Johnson ticket in 1960. Three years later he won a seat in the Texas House of Representatives, and since 1970 he has been the state land commissioner, handling oil and gas leases on all the public lands in Texas, and the chairman of the last two Democratic presidential campaigns in the state.

Armstrong has walked a narrow line between the environmentalists, who have supported him in all his races, and the oil-industry forces, which play so important a role in Texas politics. While applying one of Johnson's favorite biblical maxims, "Come, let us reason together," to his own job, he has cultivated useful alliances with a succession of Democratic powers in Washington. His position in Texas politics is much like Mineta's in the House of Representatives; he has great expectations.

The 1960 campaign caught Gary Hart, now 43 and the senior Senator from Colorado, as a graduate student at the Yale Divinity School, aiming toward an academic career as a teacher of philosophy and religion. "I'd never really considered any alternative profession," Hart said, "but the 1960 campaign opened up the possibility of public service as a reasonably attractive avenue to pursue, and it ultimately led me to switch to law school."

Hart was only two-thirds of the way toward a law degree when Kennedy was assassinated, but he followed his new interest to Washington, working for Robert Kennedy in the Justice Department and for Stewart Udall (a Kennedy ally) in the Department of the Interior. Eventually he found himself campaign manager for George McGovern in 1972, and then, back home in Colorado, won an uphill battle for the Senate in 1974.

Carl Wagner was only 15 in 1960, a mailman's son in the Mississippi River town of Lansing, Iowa, but he found in John Kennedy "the first politician to spark my interest and imagination. . . . I would guess everyone my age remembers 'Ask not what your country can do for you; ask what you can do for your country.' "

As a graduate student in political science at the University of Iowa, Wagner worked in the 1968 anti-war campaigns of Eugene J. McCarthy and Robert F. Kennedy, and in the 1970s toured the liberal movements and causes—from hunger hearings in Washington to economic development in Wisconsin, from the McGovern campaign to political organizing for AFSCME (the American Federation of State, County and Municipal Employees). At the end of 1978, he came to rest at what seems to have been a predestined job: the top political assistant to Ted Kennedy.

Predestination may also be the word for the Senator's press secretary, 32-year-old Tom Southwick, a second-generation Kennedyite. His father, Paul Southwick, was a New Hampshire newspaperman who came to Washington with the Kennedy Administration, worked as a deputy to Salinger in the White House and eventually became an Assistant Secretary of Commerce in the Johnson Administration.

Tom Southwick boasts that he was "the first member of my family to endorse John Kennedy. My parents were for Adlai Stevenson early on. I was in the sixth grade at the time, and I was the only kid who was for him."

"The sense of purpose and the sense of hope" that Kennedy conveyed to Southwick shaped his own career. He was a Senate page while in high school, then, after Harvard, a reporter in Washington, and has been Kennedy's press secretary since 1977.

A similar journey has been made by Mark Siegel, the 33-year-old campaign consultant and Democratic Party insider. Siegel was a precociously bright and eager Brooklyn kid of 13 who got "very excited by Kennedy and worked very actively in his campaign. I was, at thirteen, the guy in charge of mailing all his political paraphernalia throughout New York State—all the bumper stickers and the posters and the buttons. And I met Senator John Kennedy several times during that campaign, and that's what turned me on to politics, and I've never turned off."

At Brooklyn College, Siegel became an activist in the anti–Vietnam war movement, and later, while doing graduate work at Northwestern, was a volunteer for Robert Kennedy in the 1968 Indiana primary.

Armed with a Ph.D. and a thesis on the Democratic Party delegate-selection reforms, Siegel came to Washington in 1972, and, after a year on the staff of Senator Hubert H. Humphrey, moved to the Democratic National Committee as the in-house rules-and-reform expert. He spent eighteen unhappy months in the Carter White House as a deputy to Hamilton Jordan, serving as the Administration's chief link to domestic Jewish groups. But the 1978 sale of warplanes to Egypt and Saudi Arabia as well as Israel spurred him to leave. A year later, he was a central figure in organizing the draft-Kennedy movement that laid the groundwork for another Kennedy candidacy.

In the course of interviewing people like these, I learned to expect a special note of excitement—a kind of nostalgic yearning—when they recalled the impact of that 1960 campaign on them. But I never heard the personal effect of John Kennedy on young people described better than it was by Daniel Whitehurst, now the 32-year-old Mayor of Fresno, California.

"We moved to Fresno when I was ten," he said, "and the first year we were there, 1958, my dad and mother met Kennedy. He spoke at the Elks Club, just starting his initial push for the presidency, and my dad was so impressed he changed registration. He'd been a lifelong Republican, but he became a Democrat. . . . We're Catholics, and that was a big part of it, I know that. . . . In this area, there was still discrimination against Catholics, and for him to see a Catholic guy doing that well, I think he identified with that.

"I was in the eighth grade when he came as President to the Central Valley," Whitehurst recalled, "and I was kind of swept up in the Kennedy mania, whatever it was." It was August 18, 1962, and the occasion was the start of construction of the San Luis Dam, part of the vast California water system. Kennedy arrived at the construction site by helicopter, "and as he came down the ramp, there was a Marine band that played 'Hail to the Chief,' and he stepped out. I mean I had goose bumps, and I don't think anybody there didn't have goose bumps. He was striking in his appearance to me. I was thirteen or fourteen at the time, probably, and I'd never seen a President before." After a slight delay, Kennedy appeared on the platform, where he was to make his speech and to push the plunger on the dynamite charge that would start the project. "When he came up on the platform," Whitehurst recalls, "there was another wave of applause and cheers, and the band was playing again, and his first line was: 'It's a pleasure to be here to blow up this valley.' And he had me. Whatever he wanted, I was going to do. . . . And the impact he had on me, in those very formative years, was that government was a noble profession, a high calling and a worthy thing to do. And I still feel that way."

For Daniel Whitehurst, the impulse that Kennedy planted has been the shaping force in his life. As president of the student body at St. Mary's College, advocating curriculum changes and the admission of women; as a labor-union intern; as a lawyer with a master's degree in urban studies; as a refugee from both law practice and the family funeral business; and as a city councilman, Whitehurst has been pursuing that ideal. In 1977, when he was 29, he defeated the 65-year-old incumbent mayor by a margin as thin as Kennedy's 1960 edge over Richard Nixon, and since then he has been struggling with what he calls "the very difficult transition of Fresno becoming a major American city." Moving away from "an era when politics was very personal, where the insurance broker for the city was an old chum of the city-council members," to what he called "a more professional and objective approach to management," Whitehurst has rattled as many old-timers in Fresno as Kennedy did during his thousand days as President in Washington.

In his first two years, there was a wholesale change of faces in Fresno's government. Retirements, resignations and firings led to the replacement of the city manager, the city attorney, the police chief and the entire civil-service board. New people were named to the planning commission and other citizen bodies. Whitehurst recruited a Fresno version of "the best and the brightest" to replace the appointees of the previous Mayor, a milkman who had become an official of the Teamsters Union. He even supported a Republican over a Democrat for the state Assembly.

But even as he followed the example of his boyhood hero, Daniel Whitehurst acknowledged that the times—and the mood—were depressingly different now from what they had been back then. "I'm in this," he said, "because of the image that I got of government when Kennedy was President. . . . But as I go and talk to high-school groups and college groups, I sense a very negative attitude about government, and I think that becomes a self-fulfilling prophecy. Good people are discouraged from getting into it, and then the people's fears and apprehensions about government become true. . . . There are days when I feel charged up and excited about what I think I'm accomplishing for the city and there are days when I think nobody gives a damn and I ask myself, 'What am I doing this for?' "

The doubts that Daniel Whitehurst expressed about himself and his profession of politics are hardly unique to him. As will be seen in this chapter, and often throughout the book, the core of confidence in government and politics has been badly eroded in the minds of many of those who were drawn toward them in the Sixties.

But before turning to their questions, I want to focus on some other people who were recruited through such Kennedy-Johnson programs as the Peace Corps, the White House Fellows program and the War on Poverty—and through one venture that escaped the controls of both those presidents, the war in Vietnam.

A remarkable number of those who call themselves "children of the Sixties" can look back to a common experience in one of the most famous and enduring of the innovations of the Kennedy years: the Peace Corps. In its first eighteen years, the Peace Corps sent more than 83,000 volunteers abroad. "The experience of having been a part of that is widely shared," said Richard F. Celeste, a 1963 Peace Corpsman who was named director of the organization in 1979 by President Carter. "And it's a very strong network. It's like Yale Skull and Bones used to be in the Foreign Service, but instead of there being fifteen people a year, this is a network that produces thousands."

Kennedy introduced the Peace Corps proposal during the 1960 campaign—three times, in fact. It was floated first in early October, in a press release which drew little attention. Nine days later, he offered the idea to an approving audience of 10,000 University of Michigan students at an impromptu rally at two o'clock in the morning—an hour that precluded national publicity. Finally, on November 2, he made the idea the centerpiece of a major televised speech at the San Francisco Cow Palace, calling for "a Peace Corps of talented young men and women, willing and able to serve their country . . . as ambassadors of peace."

The idea was anything but new. William James, in his celebrated 1904 essay "The Moral Equivalent of War," suggested that "draft-age young men be put to work building, not destroying." There were elements of the idea in the church-sponsored International Voluntary Services and Operation Crossroads Africa, both started in the 1950s; in the Quaker work camps; and in the Experiment in International Living, which dates back to 1932. In 1958, Democratic Representative Henry Reuss of Wisconsin, whose wife and daughter had both been involved in the Experiment, suggested formation of a "Point Four Youth Corps" to link foreign aid with volunteer workers. And in June of 1960, Senator Humphrey introduced a bill to establish a "Peace Corps of American young men to assist the people of the underdeveloped areas of the world to learn the basic skills necessary to combat poverty, disease, illiteracy and hunger."

Kennedy created the Peace Corps by executive order six weeks after he became President (it was later given statutory authority) and put the project in the hands of his brother-in-law, Sargent Shriver, who had led Experiment groups when he was in college.

To launch the fledgling organization, Shriver assembled a group of impressive young people. Among them were Bill Moyers, now an influential television journalist; Franklin Williams, now president of the Phelps-Stokes Fund, which supports education in Africa and in the United States; Harris Wofford, former president of Bryn Mawr College; Warren Wiggins, now president of the TransCentury Corporation, a management-consulting firm in Third World development; Jack Vaughn, now director of Pierce International, a consulting firm dealing in aid to developing countries; Douglas Kiker, now a political reporter for NBC News;

Richard Ottinger, a six-term member of the House of Representatives; and Charles Peters, founder and editor of *The Washington Monthly*.

Shriver came to the Peace Corps with a personal conviction that the affluent Fifties had weakened the moral fiber of American youth. A biographer wrote that he liked to quote Will Durant's observation that "nations are born stoic and die epicurean." So the Peace Corps was made tough. Most applicants had just received their college degrees, but in the first year, only 17 percent of them passed the written exam, only 7 percent entered the rigorous physical and language training, and only 3 percent made it into the field. Shriver believed from the start, he said in a 1979 interview, that "the most important value" of the Peace Corps would be found not in what it did for the host countries, but in what it did for the volunteers and, ultimately, for the United States. "I believed that, having spent an extended period of time living in a different culture, they would come back with a deeper appreciation of their own society. And I hoped that when they came back to this country, they would move into the area of political service and public service, and play a significant part in transforming, improving, modifying the way we do things ourselves."

Unlike many other hopes of the Sixties, that one has been substantially realized. Celeste said that a 1979 computer run found about 800 returned volunteers in Washington, D.C., including about 150 congressional staff members. Shriver said that in his travels around the world as an international lawyer, he continually found Peace Corps alumni in U.S. embassies.

Senator Paul Tsongas, 39, a Massachusetts Democrat who was one of the first-year recruits, found the Peace Corps "the formative experience of my life. If I have a meeting with someone and I find out he's a former Peace Corps volunteer, there's an instant sort of attachment. It's like having old war buddies." Tsongas came out of Lowell, Massachusetts, with the Republican inclinations of his Greek-immigrant father, who ran a dry-cleaning business. "When I graduated from Dartmouth, the farthest I'd been from New England was Annapolis, Maryland, when Dartmouth swam against Navy," Tsongas said. "So I had a very insulated existence. I was in the first group that went overseas, and I didn't know what the hell I was getting myself in for.

"I ended up in a village in Ethiopia with five other Peace Corps volunteers, and I didn't go anywhere on vacations, just stayed in the village. I broke away from the others and set up house by myself, with my students. I took the ten best kids in the school and I lived with them, just a total immersion in their culture. And, you know, nothing I've ever done before or since has ever given me the same feeling."

Tsongas is clearly not exaggerating. When he came home from Ethiopia to study at Yale Law School, he found the first year "catastrophic." So strongly out of place did he feel, working through torts and contracts, that he developed a speech impediment. As soon as he had his law degree, he headed back to the Peace Corps as a training coordinator in the West Indies, returning in 1968 only because he wanted to work in Robert Kennedy's short-lived presidential campaign.

By that time, Tsongas himself had the political bug, and he moved up the ladder from Lowell City Councillor to Middlesex County Commissioner to U.S. Representative before winning a Senate seat in 1978. Once there, he resumed his advocacy of Third World policies that had their origin in his Peace Corps experience.

Carol Bellamy, 39, the President of the New York City Council, was another of the early volunteers who had her life direction changed by the Peace Corps. She was from "a good Republican family" in Plainfield, New Jersey, and had gone to Gettysburg College. "I was sent to Guatemala," she said, "along with Tim Kraft [later to be President Carter's appointments secretary and the manager of his 1980 re-election campaign]. It just took me out of the track that I was on, and gave me time to think about what I wanted to do." When she returned, it was to law school at New York University, and then to a Wall Street firm, where she organized a volunteer group of attorneys, first in support of civil rights and then in opposition to the Vietnam war. Meetings with other returned Peace Corps volunteers also introduced her to the women's movement, and friends from all three of those causes—civil rights, the peace movement and the women's movement—helped her win her upset victories as an anti-organization insurgent, first for the state Senate and then, in 1977, for her position as the No. 2 official in the New York city administration.

A good friend of Bellamy's, Donna E. Shalala, 39, a former Assistant Secretary of Housing and Urban Development and now president of Hunter College, found the Peace Corps "a jarring experience." She had grown up in the security of a large Lebanese-American family in Cleveland (the family political hero was Robert A. Taft) and the equally protected environment of the Western College for Women in Oxford, Ohio. Politically, she was touched by Kennedy's inaugural address and the experience of joining in support of the early civil-rights sit-ins. But nothing had prepared her for the Peace Corps.

"It was very tough," she said. "I was in a mud village in southern Iran. There weren't a lot of people around who spoke English. I was twenty years old and had a very difficult assignment. I learned about discrimination against women for the first time. . . . The experience had more of an impact on me than my college and pre-college years."

When Shalala returned, she found "all the returned Peace Corps volunteers were either going into Middle East or other area studies or going into the urban business." She chose the latter course, and took her master's degree and doctorate at Syracuse University. Later, Shalala became director and treasurer of the Municipal Assistance Corporation for the

City of New York, the agency created to help the city through the fiscal crisis of the late 1970s, and then brought her urban expertise to Washington when Carter became President.

The fourth in this sampling of Peace Corps alumni is unlike the others. Christopher J. Dodd, a Democratic Representative from Connecticut, grew up in a political household: His father, Thomas J. Dodd, was a two-term Representative and two-term Senator from Connecticut. Chris Dodd, now 36, went into the Peace Corps after graduating from Providence College in 1966 and was assigned to the Dominican Republic. He arrived shortly after President Johnson had sent in the Marines to protect American lives and property and to quell suspected Communist-backed rioting. "Then," said Dodd, "Johnson literally dumped in millions and millions of dollars as a penance, and that left a bad taste in my mouth. I had long arguments—not arguments; I guess you don't argue with your father—maybe long discussions." The elder Dodd was a staunch anti-Communist and a close friend of Johnson's. But his son said, "I think I had an influence on his thinking in his last years, helping him see there were moderate elements in these countries, and we were allowing ourselves to be pushed around and bullied by people who constantly raised the fear of Communism taking over, when in fact that wasn't the case at all."

Dodd, like Tsongas and Bellamy, came back from the Peace Corps to law school and then went into politics, winning a seat in the House in 1974. A fellow member of that class was Representative Timothy E. Wirth, a Colorado Democrat. Wirth was an alumnus of the White House Fellows program, created by Lyndon Johnson in 1964 (at the suggestion of advisers John Gardner and Eric Goldman). Designed to bring outstanding young people, early in their careers, into government for one year's exposure to the White House and the Administration decision-making process, the highly selective program matches a Fellow one-on-one with a senior member of the Administration—a Cabinet secretary, an assistant to the President or the Vice President—whom the Fellow serves at the special-assistant level. Through 1979, 245 promising young people had been chosen for the program. Coming from diverse racial and ethnic backgrounds, they were impressive in their education and accomplishments. The alumni of the group have gone on to distinguish themselves in business, the law, teaching, the military and other professions—as well as in government.

Wirth is the first product of this program to reach Congress, but several others will appear at various points in the book.

The larger creation of the Johnson years that has contributed significantly to the new generation of American leadership was the War on

Poverty. Sargent Shriver, who moved from the Peace Corps to the War on Poverty, said the latter program had more diverse objectives than the former. "But the fundamental, overarching objective," he said, "was to release all different kinds of people to do for themselves what they had been unable to do in the past because they weren't given a chance. That's why we called the anti-poverty agency the Office of Economic Opportunity. And many of them have become rather distinguished people."

If the White House Fellows program was avowedly elitist in its standards, the ethic of the War on Poverty was one of "maximum feasible participation" by those receiving federal assistance. It was an institutionalization of the participatory democracy practiced in the civil-rights movement, and the forerunner of other such movements which have altered the face of American politics in the past fifteen years. But the War on Poverty did more than that. It provided (however inefficiently) crash-course training in middle-class management skills, with commensurate salaries, for thousands of poor people who had no other way to acquire such credentials.

The alumni and alumnae of the anti-poverty program are scattered all across the nation now, and they turn up in subsequent chapters on community organizers, public-interest lawyers, the women's movement and growth-area politicians from the West, the South and suburbia. They are probably most heavily concentrated in the chapters on blacks and Hispanics, who were special targets, for obvious reasons, of the War on Poverty. A 1978 survey of 210 black mayors, city councilmen and state representatives by Peter E. Eisinger of the University of Wisconsin found that one-third of them had had experience in at least one of the anti-poverty programs. As Rochelle Stanfield said in a retrospective fifteen years later in *The National Journal,* "The 1964 Economic Opportunity Act, in which Congress wrote Johnson's War on Poverty into law, has long since expired. But thousands of people who helped fight the war have not only survived but moved into positions of leadership today." She quoted Hyman Bookbinder, an early anti-poverty official, as saying, "It gave an opportunity for leadership to a lot of people who had only seen closed doors before."

It also changed career directions for some people who were themselves about as far from the poverty line as was imaginable.

John D. (Jay) Rockefeller IV, an heir to one of America's great fortunes, was pointed toward a career as a State Department Far East expert when he took an assignment from Sargent Shriver to work in an anti-poverty effort in the tiny town of Emmons, West Virginia. Attracted by the state, Rockefeller entered local politics by running for the West Virginia House of Delegates, and in 1976, on his second try, was elected Governor of West Virginia.

Neil Goldschmidt, the former Mayor of Portland, Oregon, who was named in 1979 as Secretary of Transportation in the Carter Cabinet, was far from Rockefeller's class in wealth. But he is a middle-class professional whose career was given a decisive turn by his involvement in the War on Poverty.

A native of Eugene, Oregon, a graduate of the University of Oregon and an early civil-rights activist, Goldschmidt came out of law school at the University of California at Berkeley and went into an OEO-sponsored legal-services office in a low-income Portland neighborhood.

"I was getting more and more angry all the time about the problems the people I was representing had with the police department and the city," he said. "And then the City Council voted to put curfews on all the parks to keep the hippies out; their response to a cultural problem was just to pretend it didn't exist. . . . And I had the reaction a lot of my friends did: 'This is ridiculous; we've got to get those turkeys out of there!' "

In 1970 Goldschmidt was elected a City Commissioner, and, after barely a year of being the loser in regular 4–1 votes, ran for Mayor, winning election in the spring of 1972, when he was not quite 32.

His political base was in the neighborhoods and his main issue was the freeways—or as he put it, "stopping the forces outside the community that are mangling it."

"There was one freeway—eight lanes, with two lanes of median bus strip—that would take out five thousand people, destroy one percent of the city's housing stock, schools and everything. And I took it away from them. I said, 'Look, if you want to move to the suburbs, you can't be five minutes from your job. You can't expect us to give up our neighborhoods and you can't expect to travel over the back of the city, because you're going to kill the city doing that kind of stuff.' "

His success in fighting freeways and developing a successful mass-transit system made Goldschmidt a logical candidate to take over the federal Department of Transportation in the Carter Administration. But before leaving Portland in his second term as Mayor, Goldschmidt launched another effort which showed that the concerns he had acquired in his anti-poverty days had not been forgotten. He began attacking the problem of hard-core unemployment through the mechanism of federal economic-development funds. In return for using the federal grants to acquire and clear low-cost factory sites, Goldschmidt required the new industries to sign long-term agreements with Portland's manpower agency to hire their new employees from training programs for the hard-core jobless. "What we're trying to demonstrate," he said, "is that it's possible to move these folks into private-sector employment without taking jobs away from somebody else."

That was an idea that Lyndon Johnson would have liked.

Dwarfing the Peace Corps, the White House Fellows program and even the War on Poverty as a learning experience for those who came of age in the Kennedy-Johnson years was another national effort for which neither president would willingly have taken credit. It was the war in Vietnam.

Between August 10, 1964, the date of the Gulf of Tonkin Resolution, and March 29, 1973, when the last American combat troops were withdrawn by President Nixon, 8,744,000 Americans served in the military and 2,594,200 were assigned to tours of duty in the Indochina theater. Official Pentagon casualty figures listed 57,145 killed, 153,303 wounded and, in mid-1979, 1,363 missing in action and unaccounted for. The high point of the war, in terms of both American forces in the theater and American casualties, came in 1968.

It was the longest war in American history and probably the most divisive since the Civil War. The domestic protest against American involvement led directly to Johnson's decision not to seek re-election in 1968, and forced his successor, however reluctant he may have been, to accelerate the American withdrawal and thereby ease the way for a Communist victory.

But despite the fact that it consumed a disproportionate share of the nation's wealth (an estimated $165 billion) and an even larger amount of its political will and energy, Vietnam was not the universal experience for this generation of politicians that World War II was for their fathers.

At its peak, World War II, according to the Department of Defense, saw 12,550,000 Americans in uniform. The Korean conflict mustered 3,718,000, but the Vietnam-era peak was only 3,548,000. The Selective Service System drafted 9.9 million men during World War II, but in the longer Vietnam war, the draftees numbered only 1.7 million. During World War II, military service was a patriotic bond uniting a generation. During the Vietnam period, on the other hand, draft "avoidance," to employ the most polite term, became almost a way of life for those who would normally constitute the nation's leadership elite.

As Lawrence Baskir and William Strauss said in their book on the Vietnam generation, *Chance and Circumstance,* "The draftees who fought and died in Vietnam were primarily society's 'losers,' the same men who got left behind in schools, jobs and other forms of social competition. . . . Few of the nation's elite had sons or close friends who did any fighting. . . . At the end of World War II, blacks comprised 12 percent of all combat troops; by the start of the Vietnam war, their share had grown to 31 percent. In 1965, blacks accounted for 24 percent of all Army combat deaths."

Baskir and Strauss noted that "35 men from the Harvard class of 1941 died in World War II, and hundreds more saw combat duty." By contrast, they noted, James Fallows, "a *Harvard Crimson* editor from the class of 1970, surveyed his 1200 classmates and counted only 56 who entered the military, just two of whom went to Vietnam." Fallows wrote a famous essay in *The Washington Monthly* in 1975, recounting his strategy in evading military service by starving himself to get below the minimum weight for draftees. A few years later, the same Jim Fallows was named chief speechwriter for the first President to take office following the fall of Vietnam.

As that example suggests, opposition to the Vietnam war and draft resistance are hardly the barriers to government service that they were after World War II. As late as the 1960 campaign, Hubert Humphrey was still answering charges about his lack of a World War II military record. By contrast, the ranks of public office today are filled with anti–Vietnam war protestors.

But there are also people who were turned to politics by their service in Vietnam. Dennis Koehler, 39, a Palm Beach, Florida, county commissioner, is one of them. A Lutheran minister's son, he received an ROTC commission after graduating from the University of Wisconsin – Milwaukee and volunteered for Vietnam in January 1965. "My assignment was with a civilian-clothes intelligence outfit," he recalled. "I was advising Vietnamese officers on running their agent nets.

"I did that for a year, and I must confess that . . . it never began to sink in on me what the Americans were doing over there, other than that the Vietnamese seemed to be pretty uncooperative. . . . When I got to Vietnam, the number of Americans that had been killed over there was about the same as the number who jumped off the Golden Gate Bridge. So the impact of the war on the country wasn't apparent to me."

It was not until he returned to Fort Holabird, outside Baltimore, for further intelligence training in 1966 that Koehler confronted the "war issue." In an evening graduate-school political-science class at Johns Hopkins University, he wrote a research paper on the rationale for the American intervention in Vietnam. "I used all the resources available at the Army Intelligence library," he said, "and I thought I put together a pretty nice little paper. And I can't forget how the professor and the students in that class began to dissect that paper. Of course, pride of authorship was my first reaction, but as they asked more and more questions, I realized I was agreeing with them, with the anti-war position, and not the position that the military and the State Department and the Administration had been taking."

Those doubts continued to grow until the winter of 1968, when Captain Koehler was ordered back to Vietnam for his second tour. "I took nine days in Hawaii on the way to Vietnam, and most of that time I spent on the beach, pondering whether or not I should refuse to go, and get myself arrested and trucked off to Fort Leavenworth, as some people were doing at that time. . . . I thought about it long and hard and finally decided that whatever I'd want to do in the future would be terribly hamstrung if I did that. . . . So I chose finally to go."

This time, Koehler was assigned to the 25th Infantry Division, manning the area between Saigon and the Cambodian border. "Two things happened to me over there," he said. "One, I became totally convinced that the war was absolutely wrong, and that if I was a Vietnamese, I would have been a Viet Cong myself. . . . The second thing was, I was sickened by the environmental destruction I saw. In our area we had B-52s, herbicides, chemical defoliants, and teams of tractors with big heavy blades and chains, all just mowing down everything in sight. . . . They took out whole forests and whole areas of the countryside. . . . And I came away from there thinking that I wanted to get into something that had to do with saving the environment."

Discharged in September of 1969, Koehler enrolled in the pioneering environmental-law course at George Washington University Law School, joined Vietnam Veterans Against the War and participated in the Washington protest marches. After graduation, he worked for the Environmental Protection Agency, then moved to Florida for further work in environmental law and eventually landed a job as environmental control officer for Palm Beach County.

In 1976, after less than two years in the county, he challenged a 63-year-old incumbent county commissioner and won, despite some adverse publicity about his having thrown his medals on the Capitol steps during one of the anti-war protests in 1971.

As commissioner, Koehler has adopted one policy that he also attributes to his Vietnam service: All his files are open to the press and public. "I had a reaction against intelligence files and overclassification," he said. "Hidden files and locked drawers are anathema to me."

If Vietnam made Dennis Koehler an environmentalist and the intelligence service made him loathe official secrecy, the war had equally unconventional effects on others who moved from the military ranks into politics.

In 1979, the Congressional Vietnam Veterans' Caucus (organized largely to seek special counseling and other assistance for those veterans experiencing serious readjustment problems) numbered seventeen members of the House and two senators. One morning, seven of those veterans met at the invitation of Representative David E. Bonior, a Michigan Democrat, to talk about the way the service had affected them, their careers, and their outlook on political life.

Neither the tone nor the substance of their "war stories" bore any resemblance to what one would have heard from their fathers.

Bonior, a bearded 35-year-old, led off: "Well, I was out of college . . .

and joined the Air Force, basically, to avoid the draft, I guess, and served four years, from 1968 to 1972. I was stationed in California. I served as a cook for two and a half years, washing pans and cooking eggs, and then was an education counselor."

Representative Don Bailey, a Pennsylvania Democrat, 35: "I probably would have been drafted, I imagine, but I joined after I was out of the University of Michigan. Joined the Army. I spent fifteen months in Vietnam with the 101st Airborne Division, and about twelve months of that was on-line combat in the field. Not reluctantly. I'm one of those who does not apologize for my involvement. I'd fight it again. . . . I haven't had any regrets."

Representative Leon E. Panetta, a California Democrat, 42: "Basically, I completed ROTC at Santa Clara in order to get a deferment to [go to] law school. . . . After law school, I had to go in with my ROTC requirement. I went to Fort Holabird in the intelligence service and then was assigned out to Fort Worth, where I spent most of the time—although assigned to intelligence—basically defending a lot of the AWOLs and war resisters."

Representative Thomas R. Harkin, an Iowa Democrat, 41: "I went to college [at Iowa State University] on a Navy ROTC scholarship, so they had a claim on me. I spent five years as a Navy pilot, starting in November of 1962. One year was in Vietnam. I was flying F4s and F8s on combat air patrols and photo-reconnaissance support missions. I did no bombing. I don't know what I would have done if I had been ordered on bombing missions. But I did no bombing."

Representative Albert Gore, Jr., a Tennessee Democrat, 32: "I volunteered for the Army in 1969 when I graduated from Harvard, and I served in Vietnam. I felt that was the right thing to do. I was opposed to the war —very strongly. My father [former Senator Albert Gore, Sr., of Tennessee] was a vigorous spokesman in opposition to the war policies in the Senate." Young Gore said that he "felt I had a duty to the country" to enlist, but there was a political consideration as well. Tennessee calls itself the Volunteer State. With the senior Gore facing a tough re-election battle (one he ultimately lost to Bill Brock, now the Republican National Chairman), young Gore said it might be "counterproductive for him [his father] if I did anything but volunteer. I felt I could best help end the war by strengthening his hand—and that meant volunteering."

Representative Michael Barnes, a Maryland Democrat, 37: "I graduated from college in 1965, got a one-year deferment from the draft to go to Europe to study international economics, and the last few days over there I got my draft notice. So I came back and made what all my friends thought was a much worse decision. I joined the Marines. I did not go to Vietnam, although it was the height of the Vietnam war. My major combat experience was defending the Capitol building as part of a squad of Marines assigned here during the riots in 1968."

Representative John Cavanaugh, a Nebraska Democrat, 35: "I was drafted into the Army after my first year of law school in 1968. I spent most of my two years in Germany, guarding the I.G. Farben building from antiwar demonstrators."

Don Bailey told me in a later conversation that he thought the others in the round table "didn't speak for the real Vietnam vets at all."

Bailey said he had gone to Vietnam with "mixed feelings, thinking it might be a more nationalistic struggle than an ideological one." But after nine months in combat, he was convinced that the South Vietnamese were fighting for their freedom and deserved America's help. "It did something to me to see the bones of two hundred South Vietnamese civilians who had been chopped to pieces by machete when their village was overrun. . . . There's a huge bitterness in me because of the myth and the lie of the leadership strata in this country and the mass media, who played up the anti-war demonstrations while a lot of good people were bleeding and dying over there. It turned my stomach, I'll be frank with you."

When he came to Congress in 1979, Bailey placed on his office desk, in a display case, a leaflet distributed by Vietnam Veterans Against the War, containing an anti-war statement from Republican Senator Mark O. Hatfield of Oregon. "It was taken from a North Vietnamese major we killed while he was trying to ambush us," Bailey said, his voice still quivering with suppressed anger.

"Vietnam made me excessively ideological, some people would say. It made me a crusader for human rights—everywhere—because I think democracy has to have an ideology to survive. But it also made me more conservative. It taught me to fear the police power of government, and to be more skeptical of the growth of judicial and administrative power, which operate without democratic restraints. It changed my thinking in a lot of ways, because I went there a typical JFK-LBJ liberal, and now a lot of people think I'm a conservative."

In acknowledging that the war had changed his outlook, Bailey is typical of his contemporaries—even if he is different in many other ways.

"You can't overstate the effect that serving in the military at the time of the Vietnam war had on people," said Mike Barnes. "The cynicism that was created, the jokes about your buddies' coming back in green bags . . . and then the fact that they *did* come back in plastic bags—you had to develop some way to deal with that."

Because most of them were both part of the Vietnam war effort—largely for reasons not of their own choosing—and critics of that effort, the veterans said they see themselves as a fragile bridge between the opponents of the war and those older Americans who were offended by the opponents' tactics. "It's been a real plus, politically," said Leon Panetta, "because it's given me the ability to relate to what the [older] veterans are saying but also to the people who opposed the war."

Tom Harkin said his status as a veteran "gave me a legitimacy that I otherwise would not have had" in Iowa, running against a strong Pentagon supporter in 1972 and 1974. Several of the others said they had used their status as veterans to soften the opposition of those who might otherwise feel no "empathy," to use John Cavanaugh's word, for their views.

And yet, most of them conceded, they are spiritually much closer to the anti-war protestors of their own generation than they are to the World War II veterans. "The only communality I see between us and the older veterans," said David Bonior, "is the fact that we shared an experience of being displaced from our regular lives. In terms of values, it's a very different ball game. We're very different in what we're about than what they were about."

On the other hand, said Albert Gore, "there's no rancor at all" among the Vietnam veterans he knows toward the anti-war activists. "I was opposed to the war, and most of the others felt it was pretty stupid, but they were going to go anyway."

Cavanaugh, the son and grandson of Omaha Democratic politicians, went straight from the Democratic Convention of 1968 into the Army. He had been caught up, like so many others, in the drama that summer in Czechoslovakia, where Soviet power crushed the incipient liberalism of Alexander Dubček's government. "It was really traumatic," he said. "Dubček had just been overthrown the week before, and there were tanks and troops rumbling through Prague. And I came to Chicago, and you had a feeling that a similar cataclysmic occurrence was about to transpire in this country. . . . The ferocity of the police, the blatant ignorance and insensitivity of [Chicago Mayor Richard J.] Daley. . . . It seemed as though everything you had been taught couldn't happen to this country was happening. The institutions of government were not serving the interests of the people, and the people in the streets didn't know what to do so they became equally vicious. . . . It presented me with a terrifying glimpse of what could happen if the leadership is not wise enough to take the country where it really should be going."

Where Cavanaugh went from protest to the military, Bonior moved from the military to protest. When Bonior, on his return from service in 1972, was elected to the Michigan Legislature, his first act as a public official was to join a group of anti-war autoworkers from his district in the "anti-inaugural protest" at the start of Nixon's second term.

"Being in the service, and particularly in the role I was in," said Leon Panetta, "defending a lot of kids who were coming in and questioning what was happening, gave me the ability to challenge the process, to challenge the system and ask questions about it.'' That habit, once formed, has proved a hard one to break. Panetta, then a Republican, came to Washington to work in the Office of Civil Rights in the Nixon Administration's Department of Health, Education and Welfare. He questioned its go-slow enforcement policies so vigorously that he found himself forced out of his job and, eventually, his party. When it came time for him to run for Congress, he did so as a Democrat.

As Albert Gore said during the round-table discussion, the ''pervasive effect'' of Vietnam has been to increase the skepticism about the accepted assumptions of the past. ''The best and brightest constructed the greatest tragedy this country has had in a century,'' Gore said. ''So how can we any longer take for granted the wisdom of policies, simply because they're in place and are vigorously defended? Don't we have to ask tougher questions and get more personally involved in the analysis of what we're doing? That's what Vietnam is all about, and it's had a pervasive effect along those lines.''

Mike Barnes said, ''Every generation goes through that period of questioning its elders. But what Vietnam did was to put all of us out in the streets, and made us go to a degree of questioning and challenging the institutions of society that previous generations in this country had simply never reached. And that's brought to Congress a good many people—a lot of whom never did serve in the military—who are even more vocally challenging the institutions of society.''

Gore drew another contrast—and a fundamental one. ''The generation that won World War II,'' he said, ''came back into the mainstream of this country on the heels of the greatest victory in the history of mankind. And the pervasive sense was one of optimism, of conquering new worlds, even harnessing the atom for peace. To some extent, it was the last step in the process of expansion across the American continent. And then we went into Southeast Asia and we stopped. And we started coming back the other way. And now we're focusing our attention not on the New Frontier, but rather on finding better solutions for our problems here at home.''

Gore also said that after Vietnam, and the shocks that have followed it —Watergate, the energy crisis and the rest—''the number of shared assumptions'' among America's political leaders is far reduced.

At the end of World War II, there was broad agreement on the outlines of the developing welfare state at home and a foreign policy aimed at containing Communism. That consensus embraced most Democrats and many Republicans as well. It was based on the reality of America's dominant military position and its seemingly limitless economic capacity.

By the end of the Seventies, events had shattered the euphoria about how much America and its government could accomplish at home or abroad. And with that loss of confidence came a cracking in the old consensus.

John Cavanaugh could argue—and did—that "I don't see any conflict between the ability of government to inspire aspirations . . . and a realistic perception of the limitations" on its own, or the country's, capacities. But most of the other "children of the Sixties" saw that the reversal of the optimism of the World War II veterans, the growth of skepticism or cynicism, and the recognition of the real limitations on American resources posed a challenge to the nation's leadership it has not yet begun to meet.

The first two post-Vietnam presidents—Gerald Ford and Jimmy Carter—were notably ineffectual at leading the government or rallying public support. The waves of young people who inundated Congress in the mid-to-late Seventies overthrew the older leadership structure, based on the authority of committee chairmen and a handful of party leaders, but quickly found themselves sinking in a legislative swamp, unable to make satisfactory policy choices in many areas of critical national importance.

Ironically, one of the few young legislators who appeared to be consistently effective in this time of political transition was Lyndon Johnson's protégé Jim Jones. His success in molding coalitions of conservative-to-moderate Democrats and Republicans from his junior position on the House Ways and Means Committee appeared to be a vindication of the enduring values of some old political maxims.

"The lessons I learned from Lyndon Johnson," Jones said, "were, first of all, to understand who the key players are in Congress and know the procedures. Then, bring in those key players in the formative stages of a policy, so it becomes not just your policy, but the policy of a broad range of people.

"The other thing that I gained from Johnson with regard to Congress was his sense of timing and the mood up here. I guess you can't inherit intuition, but you can certainly hone intuition by knowing the things to look for. . . . And another thing is boldness—to know what your ultimate goals are, how much time you're prepared to commit to achieving them, and then being willing to shove in the stack to achieve those goals. . . .

"Lyndon just worked and worked and worked, massaging every group that had anything to do with policy, from congressional groups to the press to private organizations. And I find, in the limited capacities that I have in Congress, that all of those lessons still work."

But the measures that Jones managed to pass were not the traditional Democratic programs. He was on the side of cutting social-program spending to help balance the budget. He sought to cut taxes on corporations and middle-income investors. He tried to free the oil companies from regulation and reduce the taxes on their profits. And more often than not, he won—even when both Jimmy Carter and Ted Kennedy were lined up against him.

It was a conservative package which seemed, to some, far from his mentor's Hill Country populism. But Jones insisted that "had Johnson been alive and in Congress, he wouldn't have been doing things much different from what I'm doing. . . . I think he would also trim back considerably some of these government programs, because government has become so large it's become the oppressor."

For those inheritors of the Kennedy-Johnson tradition who regarded that definition of government as heresy, however, the Seventies were a time of political confusion.

Tommy O'Neill (more formally, Thomas P. O'Neill III), the 36-year-old son of the Speaker of the House, saw his own political career blossom in the Seventies. The Boston College graduate was elected to the Massachusetts House of Representatives in 1972. Two years later, he parlayed the family name and his own alliances in the party's liberal wing to victory over four rivals for the Democratic nomination for Lieutenant Governor. He was elected that November and re-elected in 1978.

Despite his personal success, there was no one more anxious than Tommy O'Neill for the Seventies to be over. "I just hope now," he said, "we've seen the effect of the assassinations of the Sixties, of Vietnam and of Watergate. There's been a dismantlement of almost every single political institution in America. And what's left are people who have never grown up in an institution, who have no appreciation of it, and have turned to what they think to be a new brand of leadership. There's a narcissism in American politics right now that makes me hope the Seventies go out the window just as quickly as they came in."

Tommy O'Neill had his own reasons for concern. In his first four years as Lieutenant Governor, he served with Governor Michael S. Dukakis and carved out a useful role for himself as Massachusetts' "man in Washington." All of the state's and many of the localities' grant applications were channeled through O'Neill's office, and he and his staff used his good Washington contacts to push their requests through the bureaucracy and Congress. But the Dukakis administration was politically inept at home, and in 1978 the Governor was upset in the primary by Edward J. King, a maverick and very conservative Democrat. King had pulled together a number of single-issue constituencies, particularly the opponents of abortion and the advocates of the death penalty, and had promised tax-burdened voters a massive rollback in their property levies. King and O'Neill had no greater personal rapport than they did agreement on the issues. But after some wavering, O'Neill remained on the ticket and mobilized enough traditional Democratic support to stave off a Republican challenge.

When he complained about the turn that politics had taken, he was certainly thinking of his own state. But the application was broader than that. It focused on what he called "the egocentric, single-issue candidate" who, he said, was also "part of the fallout of the Vietnam-Watergate period. Our heads were spinning so much from 1963 right through 1974 that we hardly had an opportunity to sit back and objectively view what had taken place in this country. . . . And what we got coming into politics in the Seventies was the type of man or woman who offered this baffled, befuddled voter the quick solution, the single idea that was going to fix everything. And I really hope that the Eighties relieve us of that single-issue, emotionalized approach, the candidates with the simple solutions. They have just ripped at the very foundation of our two-party system, and I am now more convinced than I ever was that the two-party system was one of the greatest strengths of this country. I would like, in 1980, to be able to tell you that by 1990 we will still have a two-party system, but I'm not sure I can do that."

O'Neill, who had received his introduction to presidential campaigning while passing out literature for John Kennedy in 1960, found himself twenty years later working in the campaign of Ted Kennedy, the man he thought most likely to revive the Democratic Party as an instrument of progressive policies.

But others of his age, reared in the same tradition, were no longer even sure they knew what those policies would be. As Carol Bellamy said poignantly at a reunion of 1960s activists in 1978: "A decade ago, our key issues and goals were clear: social justice for the poor; equal rights for minorities; an end to America's bankrupt foreign policy. . . . There were scenes of horror, but a kind of special certainty. We knew our goals, we knew our friends and we knew our enemies. I wonder if we will ever be as certain again."

Her friend Donna Shalala said, for example, that "the biggest problem in developing an urban program is that we don't have consensus among the urbanists." There was even dispute, she noted, about what constitutes an urban area. Their predecessors in the Sixties had a "body of literature" from which to draw their programs. "Many of the programs don't appear to have worked," she said, "and we critiqued those programs, but all we had when we got here were the critiques. We didn't have a new agenda, the way they did in the 1960s."

What Shalala said about urban policy—reinforced by her own searing experiences in the near-bankruptcy of New York City, that laboratory of 1960s liberalism—was the central theme of Gary Hart's thinking.

As the manager of George McGovern's 1972 presidential campaign, Hart had ridiculed the efforts of such McGovern rivals as Senator Edmund S. Muskie of Maine and Hubert Humphrey to find a "center position" on the Vietnam war. "There is no center," he would say. "You either defend that mistake or you condemn it." Two years later, running his own Senate race in Colorado, Hart tried (with some success) to bury those differences by asserting they were an affliction of the older generation, not his own. His slogan suggested that a change of faces would break the deadlock. "They had their turn," his billboards said. "Now it's our turn."

Hart was cold-blooded in rejecting the New Deal policies of the past. "We are not a bunch of little Hubert Humphreys," he told me in 1974—in what turned out to be an accurate preview of the economic and social-policy revisionism of many of the young Democrats elected to Congress in that Watergate year. They have been far less sympathetic to organized labor, and far more concerned about middle-income taxpayers, than many had expected.

But five years after his "turn" in the Senate began, Hart had to concede that consensus was still elusive. Whether it is energy policy, economic policy or foreign policy, he said, "there is a failure of consensus in America on almost all matters of national policy." The shattering began, he said, with the assassinations of the Kennedy brothers and Martin Luther King, Jr. It was compounded by Vietnam and Watergate, and then further exacerbated by the discovery—through the oil embargo—of the new vulnerability to external limitations by energy, the environment and a no-longer-subservient physical and political world. In the McGovern campaign, in his own race and since, Hart said, he has been "out flailing the bushes," looking for someone with ideas and concepts to guide policy in this drastically altered environment, "and finding no one out there." The old Democratic policies are "beginning to run into a stone wall" of resistance to ever-larger government, leaving, as Shalala and so many others have said, "a huge conceptual vacuum."

In one interview, Hart suggested that the argument was essentially between two generations of Democrats, between "those who have espoused the traditional New Deal approaches to social problems and economic problems, as opposed to those who are coming into public office in Congress, in governorships, in state legislatures around the country, who are attempting to question some of the premises upon which the Democratic Party has operated."

His friend Carl Wagner, Ted Kennedy's political aide, noting the two opposing centers of demographic balance described in the last chapter, said, "it is arguable that consensus will be formed when my generation [he is 35] assumes leadership, which may be some time away but indisputably will happen."

"There is much less clarity, in terms of what the vision of the future should be, than I would like," Wagner conceded, "but to a very large extent, our activity has been focused on removing the unsatisfactory elements of the present—ending discrimination, ending the war, and sort of righting wrongs. To a very large extent, those efforts have been successful. But that does not automatically lead to setting out a vision of the future."

Wagner argued, perhaps with a bit of peer-group prejudice, that "the best candidates in the history of American politics come from our generation," at least in terms of "our understanding of media, campaigns, elections . . . the process of public communication."

But others in his own generation have a different view. Carol Bellamy said, "I see more and more people running for office on fewer and narrower issues. I've said to people that Westway [a controversial New York City highway project] is not the Vietnam-war issue of this decade, but they treat it that way."

In the House of Representatives, the part of the national government most altered by the impact of the arrival of large numbers of the next generation of politicians, there was growing concern as the 1970s ended that the leveling of the old leadership structure had gone so far as to render the House ineffectual as a legislative body.

Christopher Dodd, a "very peripheral" part of the leadership (by his own description of his role as a deputy whip), said "it's awfully hard" to mobilize Democrats on any legislative issue. "The last thing I would say to someone of my class is 'I want you to vote this way because Tip [Speaker of the House Thomas P. O'Neill, Jr.] wants us to vote that way.' I just would never think of saying that to a younger member. . . . They don't want to feel as though they have to be responsible to the leadership. They see *themselves* as being leaders. And that is why I question the ability of the institution to come to terms, in the long run, with the problem, unless we decide that some people have got to be the pawns or the foot soldiers and others are going to have to be the leaders. But in the framework in which we are operating politically, I see a hard road ahead of us to achieve that."

Dick Celeste, the Peace Corps director, offered an intriguing—but chilling—theory of why this style had developed in the new generation of politicians, and why it might be hard to alter. Celeste observed that "if we view leadership as a highly individualized phenomenon, it poses a real challenge to this country in the immediate future. It's going to be much harder in the days ahead, because our experience did not necessarily equip us to give that kind of leadership. Those of us who have had this experience of being involved in the movements of the Sixties—whether it be the Peace Corps or the march on Washington—were one of many people, all of whom are basically equal. So we have an enormous impulse to work by consensus, to involve people in the process, to be concerned about the process itself. Well, if you're oriented to that process, it's very different from the style of a person who stands up and articulates boldly a posture and tugs people along to that position."

Celeste's analysis certainly fits the young members of the House who overthrew the seniority system, opened up committee sessions to public scrutiny and made other basic changes in the operations of Congress. They were process-oriented, sought to broaden opportunities for participation—and have proved, so far, to be unable to generate effective leadership, across the board, from their own ranks.

Indeed, by the end of the 1970s, the quest for leadership—not just in Congress but in the White House as well—had become the overriding concern of politicians and voters alike. And it was this issue of leadership which Ted Kennedy cited as his reason for challenging Jimmy Carter for the nomination in 1980. But as soon as he entered that race, the "leadership" debate began to swing from Carter's supposed shortcomings to the relevance of the values and programs and myths of the early 1960s—all of which Kennedy seemed to embody.

The debate was first joined in a dramatic setting, when Carter came to Boston in October 1979 to dedicate the John F. Kennedy Library, housing the papers and memorabilia of the slain President.

With the library at his back, with the stage filled with Kennedy family members, and with an audience dominated by veterans of the Kennedy Administration and admirers of the former President, Carter found his text in one of John Kennedy's favorite maxims: "Change is the law of life."

While declaring that "the essence of President Kennedy's message—the appeal for unselfish dedication to the common good—is more urgent than it ever was," Carter argued that "the world of 1980 is as different from what it was in 1960 as the world of 1960 was from that of 1940. . . . The problems are different. The solutions, none of them easy, are also different."

Point by point, Carter reminded the Kennedy audience of the historic forces that made it unlikely that anyone, even another Kennedy, could follow John Kennedy's path without stumbling.

"After a decade of high inflation and growing oil imports," he said, "our economic cup no longer overflows. Because of inflation, fiscal restraint has become a matter of simple public duty. We can no longer rely on a rising economic tide to lift the boats of the poorest in our society.

We must focus our attention . . . directly on them. We have a keener appreciation of the limits now—the limits on government, the limits on the use of military power abroad. . . . We are struggling with a profound transition."

When Carter sat down, Ted Kennedy arose and, with all the power at his command, summoned the dream to live again. "As President," he declared, "Jack was a glory on the mountaintop. The New Frontier of which he dreamed touched deep and responsive chords in the American character. . . . In dedicating this library to Jack, we recall those years of grace, that time of hope. The spark still glows, the journey never ends, the dream shall never die."

Those present that day, including the Kennedy partisans, gave the honors for oratory to Carter, even though his was not the message of pure adulation. But that was only the beginning of the leadership debate—not its conclusion. Many Democrats saw Ted Kennedy as a figure whose essential appeal was a nostalgic wish to recapture a vanished past, rather than deal with the hard choices facing America in the future.

But Paul Tsongas, Kennedy's Senate colleague from Massachusetts, argued just the opposite proposition: that in a "time of wrenching readjustment, a psychic racheting down of our expectations, Ted Kennedy would be a good President. He is one of the few people who could take us through the dislocation process and prevent us from succumbing to the demagoguery of the Right."

Whichever view was accurate, what was striking about Kennedy was the fact that he was, at 48, so atypical of the politicians of his generation, both in his experiences and in his views. While many of them were in Vietnam or in the streets in the Sixties, he was in the Senate. The decade saw him not only struggling to master his new legislative and political responsibilities but trying to cope with the murders of two brothers, a near-fatal airplane crash, the drowning accident at Chappaquiddick and the strains on his marriage. Throughout the Seventies, when most of his contemporaries were trying to launch their political careers, he was constantly weighing the option of running for President of the United States, a step he finally decided to take as the decade ended.

With the death of Hubert Humphrey, he became, at a premature age, almost the last of the old-style liberals in the Senate, a living link to the optimism and programmatic ambition of the early Sixties. Some of his positions were innovative: He was a leader, for example, in the fights to ease government regulation of the airline and trucking industries. But most of his speeches and stands—whether calling for a comprehensive tax-supported national health-insurance plan or government controls on oil and gas prices—reflected more of an enduring faith in federal initiatives and federal regulations than most of his Democratic contemporaries could muster. While the dreams of the New Frontier and the Great Society were viewed with skepticism by most of the Democratic political recruits of the Sixties, Ted Kennedy was exerting his powerful influence in an effort to make them live again.

Not surprisingly, Kennedy attracted to himself young men who shared that vision and purpose. Tom Southwick, his press spokesman, said, "Kennedy . . . likes to have a lot of different opinions" from his inner-circle advisers, "and he likes you to make your argument strong."

But among the five top-ranking members of Kennedy's personal office staff (others served him in his committee and subcommittee chairmanships) at the time of his declaration of presidential candidacy, only one could be counted as a serious deviationist from traditional liberal Democratic views of foreign and domestic policy.

Richard E. (Rick) Burke, 27, who was Kennedy's administrative assistant, worked as a political volunteer for the first time in Hubert Humphrey's 1968 presidential bid. Burke was the sixth of eight children in a Connecticut family of divided political loyalties. His mother was a liberal Democrat; his father, the president of American-Electro Industries, a Republican. There was a similar ambivalence in Burke's own views.

He began working as a volunteer in Kennedy's mail room while he was studying accountancy at Georgetown University, and moved up in the Kennedy bureaucracy to office manager and administrative assistant, while completing work for a master's degree in business administration. His loyalty is unquestioned, but his views are iconoclastic in the Kennedy inner circle.

"My perception of it is that government is so bureaucratic at this point that it's become inefficient," Burke said. "And the inefficiency has caused business, the basic backbone of the American economy and society, to be very suspicious of government. They seem to be in conflict now because they don't understand each other. . . . Business is there basically to make money, but at the same time, in making money, it's helping the country and the economy"—and therefore, presumably, ought to be cherished, rather than harassed, by the government.

Carl Wagner, Kennedy's political aide, came to him from the anti-war and McGovern campaigns, lamenting the fact that "I don't think our generation has produced a vision of the future. I don't think there's consensus on it. I don't think it's been articulated." But Wagner was an organizer, not a philosopher, and the absence of that vision did not inhibit him from promoting a Kennedy candidacy during 1979 or plunging joyfully into the campaign once the Senator sanctioned it.

Tom Southwick, the press secretary, was a perfect pragmatist in his view of the future. "I think one has to deal with issues in the Eighties as they come up," he said. "I think the answer, for example, isn't always more government; it may often be less government," citing airline and trucking deregulation as an example.

But Southwick also said that the real choice for the Eighties was expressed in the speeches Carter and Kennedy gave at the Kennedy Library dedication, with Carter, as he put it, "talking about an era of limits in which our cup no longer overflows," while Kennedy "was saying we can deal with these problems; they're no more difficult than we've faced in the past.

"In certain areas," Southwick conceded, "it is an era of limits. There's no question that eventually we're going to run out of oil. But I don't think there's any reason we can't develop the resources to replace oil. I think it's just a matter of giving people confidence that when we get over the hump, things are going to be better on the other side."

That updating of John Kennedy's "High Hopes" approach to the 1960 campaign was seen even more clearly in the two men who were Kennedy's senior advisers on foreign and domestic policy, 32-year-old Jan H. Kalicki and 46-year-old Carey Parker.

Kalicki is a product of the same foreign-policy factory that took two foreign-born youths and turned them into America's last two national security advisers, Henry A. Kissinger and Zbigniew Brzezinski. His background is exotic. He was born in England of a Polish father, whose family had been in the World War II government-in-exile in Great Britain, and a Bolivian mother, whose father had been an envoy from his country to Spain, France and Great Britain. His parents, students in London when they married, moved to California to continue their academic careers when Jan was three. He graduated from Columbia; took a doctorate from the London School of Economics; taught at Oxford, Princeton and Harvard; had a fellowship with the Council on Foreign Relations; and from 1974 to 1977, when he joined Kennedy, worked for Kissinger's protégé Winston Lord as a member of the State Department's policy-planning staff.

A specialist in China and disarmament issues, Kalicki saw Vietnam as a lesson in the importance of "not getting overinvolved in what is essentially an internal-insurgency kind of situation," but denied any "trauma" for "the people of my generation who did not feel that they shared a direct responsibility for what went on in Vietnam."

Nonetheless, he was critical of Brzezinski and the Carter Administration for failing to rebuild what he regarded as a "shattered consensus" on the basic precepts of American foreign policy and for mishandling (in his view) U.S.–Soviet relations. In phrases echoing Kissinger's own criticism of his successor, Kalicki said it was an error at the outset of the

Carter Administration to confront Russia simultaneously with an ambitious new arms-control package and a highly publicized human-rights campaign.

"The first priority should have been to conclude the SALT II treaty right away, in my view," he said. "We had a structure there at Vladivostok [the Ford–Brezhnev agreement, negotiated by Kissinger in 1975] which was possible to elaborate. . . . And we could have done it, I believe, in the spring of 1977 with strong bipartisan support." As for human rights, he said, "It was very much a problem in coming out openly and taking a stand in which we could not hope to make progress, rather than pursuing this very firmly but quietly with the Soviets . . . confronting them openly and making it impossible for them to respond in a positive way."

The new Dr. K. shares his predecessor's disdain for the State Department bureaucracy. "I spent five years in the State Department and the Arms Control and Disarmament Agency," he said, "and it was quite extraordinary how difficult it is for bureaucracies to respond to the obvious and to do the necessary."

If Kalicki represents a kind of throwback to the positions of the National Security Adviser of recent Republican years, then Carey Parker, his domestic-policy counterpart on Kennedy's staff, is an embodiment of the basic beliefs of his predecessors, such as Ted Sorensen and Joe Califano, in earlier Democratic administrations. The same faith in a strong President, an energized bureaucracy and the wisdom of pragmatic intellectuals that sustained them sustains Parker, who is himself one of the most superbly educated men in public service.

The son of a Bryn Mawr, Pennsylvania, surgeon, Parker graduated from Princeton, won a Rhodes Scholarship to Oxford, next earned a Ph.D. in human biology and genetics from Rockefeller University and finally took a law degree from Harvard Law School. From 1965 through 1968, he was at the Justice Department, and he joined Kennedy's staff when the Republicans took over the Administration.

"Never really an activist" in the anti-war movement, Parker said he thinks Vietnam caused "a great change in perception" about the situations in which the United States should intervene in foreign fights, "but I don't see, as part of that fallout, a sense of limits on government power generally.

"I think myself the lesson of Vietnam is not so much that government across the board is less effective or has limits that are inherent in its ability to deal with more complicated problems, but that we no longer have the unlimited ability to intervene in situations regardless of their immediate effects on us," he said.

Consistent with that belief, Parker rejected the idea that the New

Frontier or Great Society programs were failures. The problem, he said, was the "diversion of resources" needed by those programs to the war in Vietnam and the neglect or abuse of those domestic efforts by the Nixon and Ford administrations. "I think had Hubert Humphrey been elected in 1968, the effectiveness and the reputation of the Great Society programs would be much different than they are today. I think there would have been a greater confidence in the ability of government to deal with questions like housing, transportation, health and education."

Parker said he also believes that the Vietnam and Watergate reactions have tipped power to Congress, which is "too easily influenced by well-funded groups" and special interests. "I think the leadership qualities that the President can bring to his office are more resistant to the local parochial pressures that can be brought to bear on individual members of Congress."

That kind of strong President, he said, can also provide leadership for a bureaucracy that is just waiting to have its potential tapped. "Over the past decade that I've been working here, I've certainly been impressed with the quality of the people who work in the executive branch. . . . I think the federal government is in good hands, and I'm not one who is either appalled at the size of the bureaucracy or alarmed at the problems in terms of the competence of the bureaucracy."

A similar sunny confidence surrounds his view of the intellectual challenges of managing the economy in a time of high inflation. "I think," Parker said, "the challenge is in implementation more than in the directions of policy. To the extent there are differences between Kennedy and the Administration over economic policy, for example, I think they revolve largely around the degree to which price-wage policy is restrained or implemented." He endorsed the Senator's view that what was missing from Carter's guidelines policy was the personal jawboning that John Kennedy and Lyndon Johnson had applied. "I don't think there's a new or novel solution there waiting to be discovered," he said. "I think it's going to take a coordinated fiscal policy and monetary policy and an incomes policy that will be very effectively implemented."

Consciously or not, Ted Kennedy seemed to have surrounded himself with a set of young people for whom the myths of the American past—ranging from the belief that what was good for business was good for America to the belief that there were few problems too tough for an energetic President to solve—had survived, almost untarnished by the experiences of intervening years.

As a rival to the politically battered Jimmy Carter, Ted Kennedy, at the outset of his campaign, seemed to be a formidable force. As a prospective opponent for the Republicans who were still searching for their own internal consensus after some shattering experiences of their own, he was a man to be feared.

But twenty years have gone by since young people like Norm Mineta and Mark Siegel and Gary Hart and Dan Whitehurst thrilled to John Kennedy's voice. Almost as much time has elapsed since Paul Tsongas, Carol Bellamy, Donna Shalala and Chris Dodd took their youthful idealism into the Peace Corps.

And in that time, many illusions—about America and its leadership—have been shattered. Reviving them might be a large challenge, even for a Kennedy.

3 · Nixon-Ford

DURING THE WATERGATE HEARINGS, Senator Joseph M. Montoya, a New Mexico Democrat, asked 30-year-old Gordon Strachan, a junior member of the White House staff caught up in the unraveling tale of official duplicity, what he would say to other young people concerned about the future of the country and weighing the risks and rewards of public service.

"My advice," said Strachan, "is to stay away."

It was easy to see why someone who had been working in Richard M. Nixon's White House would say that. Before Watergate ran its course, it took its toll not only on the President and such senior associates as John Mitchell, H. R. (Bob) Haldeman and John Ehrlichman, but on a score of younger people who had been imprudent enough to cast their lots with the Administration.

Watergate ruined or soured—even if, in some instances, it did not end—the political lives of many young men who were, like Gordon Strachan, still in their thirties in 1974, when it all came crashing down: John Dean, then 35; Dwight Chapin, 33; Kenneth Clawson, 37; Egil Krogh, 34; Jeb Stuart Magruder, 39; Herbert Porter, 36; Ken Rietz, 32; Donald Segretti, 32; Hugh W. Sloan, Jr., 33; Ronald Ziegler, 35.

In a certain sense, Strachan's advice was hardly necessary, for the great majority of young people found it very easy to stay away from the Republican Party and its presidents in the Sixties and Seventies. For those young people who were first eligible to vote in 1960, only 26.9 percent identified with the Republican Party, according to the University of Michigan's Center for Political Studies, compared with 30.7 percent who called themselves independents and 42.3 percent who identified themselves as Democrats. In every presidential election of the Sixties and Seventies, including Nixon's two victories, voters under 30 gave the Democratic nominee a larger share of their support than any other age group.

Ironically, in his long years at the center of the Republican Party and national politics, a span of almost three decades, Nixon drew hundreds, perhaps thousands, of young people into his campaign staffs, his personal entourage and his Administration. Like their counterparts from the Kennedy and Johnson years, some of the early recruits, like Nixon's first campaign manager, Murray Chotiner, are no longer living. Others, like former Secretary of State William P. Rogers and former Secretary of Health, Education and Welfare Robert H. Finch, are retired to lucrative law practices, more or less satisfied with the memories of their own careers.

In this chapter the focus is on those who joined Nixon late enough in his official life—and who were lucky enough to avoid the ruin of Watergate—so that they have most of their political futures still ahead of them. We will look at them and at some of the young people who were associated with Nixon's successor, Gerald R. Ford, and at some of the real newcomers to that Nixon-Ford mainstream Republicanism, on whom the future of the GOP also depends. In a later chapter in this book, we will return to the Republican scene to examine some of the "new conservatives" who are playing an increasing role in their party's affairs and most of whom had distant, if any, links to Nixon and Ford.

Those who concern us here, who come from the same mainstream Republican tradition as the last two GOP presidents, have all had to ask themselves what caused that tradition to fail—politically or morally.

J. Stanley Pottinger, now 40, was one of those late recruits to the Nixon Administration. He grew up in Ohio Republicanism, an admirer of the flinty integrity of Senator Robert A. Taft. After Harvard Law School, he moved to California, and it was from there that he was persuaded by Bob Finch in 1970 to take the powder-keg job of civil-rights enforcer at the Department of Health, Education and Welfare. Later, under Ford, he was Assistant Attorney General for Civil Rights.

"I came to Washington," he said, "with the notion that there was a level of wisdom reposing in these buildings that I discovered did not exist. You have the best and the worst of everything here. You have the best people I ever want to be associated with in government—people of the highest integrity and humor, people who work hard, selfless people. And then you have egomaniacs, people who have no respect for any sense of community or individual rights. That is a maelstrom that was all new to me, and the net effect of it was that I came to see that the major difference in the quality of government . . . came out of individuals' dedication to doing what is right under the Constitution.

"I think Richard Nixon was smart," Pottinger said. "I think he had a capacity to understand political forces that was unusual. But I also think he lacked character and was unable somehow to place a moral value on those political forces. And I think his downfall had nothing to do with the cover-up or Watergate, or any of the other technical points. I think it had to do with a widely held and growing perception that the person simply did not have a moral control of the power that he understood how to use . . . I think that anybody who was up there close in those years has got to see how important that is."

James A. S. Leach was up there close in those years, and he shared Pottinger's view about what was fundamental. Leach, who is 38 now, had likewise inherited his Republicanism from his Iowa businessman father, but was disillusioned by what he saw of his party in the Sixties. "The Republican Party seemed to be lacking in youth and vitality," he said. "It seemed to have little to say on the poverty issue or the civil-rights issue, which were the issues of the Sixties, or on the war in Vietnam, which should have been the issue of the Sixties for the minority party."

But from junior-high-school days on, Jim Leach had dreamed of being a Foreign Service officer, and that remained his goal as he studied at Princeton, Johns Hopkins and the London School of Economics. Hired by the State Department in 1968, he was assigned to the team drafting the first-round strategic-arms-limitation treaty with the Soviet Union—about as challenging an assignment as a junior officer could hope for.

But on the Monday after the "Saturday Night Massacre," in October 1973—when Nixon's effort to contain the Watergate investigation led to the firing of Special Prosecutor Archibald Cox, the resignation of Attorney General Elliot L. Richardson and the dismissal of Deputy Attorney General William D. Ruckelshaus—Jim Leach resigned from the Foreign Service.

His reasons were clear. "The person I most respected in the Administration [Richardson] had been fired," he recalled, "for reasons I could not support. A Foreign Service officer is directly a presidential appointee. I felt that if you cannot support the President you are working for, you cannot be in the Foreign Service."

Leaving the Foreign Service, however, did not mean leaving government for Jim Leach. He returned to the family business in Davenport and in 1974, that year of Republican misfortune, took the GOP nomination against the incumbent Democratic Congressman from his district. He ran a good losing race, considering the circumstances, and in 1976, on his second try, won a seat in the House of Representatives.

Those in the Nixon-Ford Republican mainstream who have survived the rigors of the 1970s have learned what Leach's career demonstrates: the importance of durability and persistence. Those qualities also characterize John P. Sears, who, despite being mauled in the Nixon White

House infighting, has emerged at age 40 as one of the most widely respected Republican political pros of his generation. His bold performance as the manager of Ronald Reagan's 1976 presidential bid won wide praise, and even when he was fired by Reagan on the day of the New Hampshire primary in 1980, Sears' reputation as a political strategist remained intact. He represented, perhaps as well as anyone can, the cast of mind of the Nixon survivors.

In a certain sense, his relationship to Nixon was accidental. A farmer's son from upstate New York, who took his Republicanism from his father and his Catholicism from his mother, Sears was, from the beginning, a political pragmatist. In his first campaign experience, he helped a friend win the presidency of the senior class at Notre Dame because "frankly, I was very tired of standing in lines at Notre Dame, and I gauged that if I had a friend in as president of the senior class, I could just call him up and get the tickets I wanted, or whatever. And it worked." Later, he helped his friend deliver the Notre Dame mock convention of 1960 to John F. Kennedy. On the basis of that success, Sargent Shriver offered him a job in the Kennedy campaign, but Sears turned him down. Thus, his Republican credentials were intact when in 1965, after graduation from Georgetown Law School and a clerkship with a New York City judge, he was interviewed by Nixon for a job with the firm of Nixon, Mudge, Rose, Guthrie and Alexander.

Sears had already pretty much decided to join another Wall Street firm, headed by former presidential nominee Thomas E. Dewey, but Nixon, Mudge offered him $500 more in starting salary. "And it was not until the following Christmas," he recalled, "that I found out I'd made a horrible mistake, because at Dewey's firm one such as myself normally got a $2,000 Christmas bonus."

On such matters do careers turn. But what stuck in Sears' mind, as he left the interview with Nixon, was something else. Rather than the awe he had expected to feel for Nixon—"I hadn't met people like that, ever" —"I remember walking out of there and getting on the elevator and thinking, Why is it that I feel sorry for that man?

"Here was this man who had run for President and done all these other things, and yet you could tell right away that he was the one that wasn't at ease—not you. And I thought, Here's this man who, as far as anybody knows, has all these qualities. And he really doesn't have them. It must be fierce for him."

Despite these doubts, Sears began doing some political chores for Nixon, as well as the legal work they shared, and by the time the 1966 midterm campaign came, those political tasks were time-consuming enough that Nixon asked him to take a leave from the firm. He became part of the Nixon campaign staff that fall, and, in 1967, was one of the first four people hired to organize Nixon's comeback presidential campaign.

As that campaign gathered momentum, more and more people were brought in by Nixon to take over its direction. Mitchell, Haldeman, Ehrlichman and the rest squeezed Sears further and further from the center of power. In the general election, he was sent off to campaign with Spiro Agnew. In the White House, he was given legal work and pushed away from political decisions. Haldeman and Mitchell were suspicious of the young lawyer who seemed to have as many friends among the press as he did in the White House Mess. Eventually, when their hostility grew too great, John Sears, not yet 30, having helped crucially in what Jules Witcover called "the resurrection of Richard Nixon," found himself out of the White House, once again practicing law.

"It was pretty embittering for me," he recalled much later, but it was not a surprise. Early on, he had learned that "there were no privileged people around Nixon. . . . There was nobody there who, because of past loyalties or anything, could call upon him any better than anybody who just happened to be there. . . . I remember Murray Chotiner telling me once that, by his estimation, he'd been disloyally treated twelve times. So it was no big deal to him."

It was a bigger deal than that to John Sears. In the terrible spring of 1970, shortly after he left the White House, circumstances threw us together at the Institute of Politics of the John F. Kennedy School of Government at Harvard. It was there, one night, that Sears heard the news of the U.S. invasion of Cambodia, and there that he saw the protesting students "trash" Harvard Square. The promise of the Nixon campaign, the hope that he would "bring us together," was crumbling before his eyes. And in his frustration, he kept repeating, "Damn it, it didn't have to be this way. It didn't have to be this way."

Sears, who instinctively seeks the middle ground in politics, has come to believe—like Leach and Pottinger—that the failure of Nixonian politics can be traced to the character of Richard Nixon.

"To this day," Sears said, "it's an intriguing thing about Nixon. You find a man who had tremendous strengths—well beyond human capacity, in some regards. And tremendous weaknesses, well beyond imagination. And very little, if any, discernible middle ground in between. There was always this big struggle over Richard Nixon inside Richard Nixon . . . but never the happy medium."

Sears has come to see Nixon not as an aberration, but as a symbol or symptom of the political schizophrenia of his time. The real wound of Watergate, he said, was that Nixon, who had concealed and suppressed his inner anxieties to the point that he was seen as "no extremist . . . but an eminently rational . . . competent man," portrayed himself on the tapes as one "preoccupied with . . . foolish things."

Nixon's failure, Sears believes, built on—and compounded—the earlier failures of Lyndon Johnson's version of "consensus politics." Johnson, in his expansive way, had tried to embrace in his Great Society every interest of every major constituency from big business to the women on welfare. It was a natural posture for a politician raised in Texas when it was essentially a one-party state. But in Sears' critical perspective, the Johnsonian consensus amounted to nothing more than "a bunch of very disparate separate interests, with Johnson with his arms around them, saying, 'Let us reason together.' The whole impression was that the middle of American politics was simple pie dividing. And the so-called consensus was just giving everybody . . . a piece."

By the time Johnson's and Nixon's presidencies had run their unhappy course, Sears said, public confidence in politicians of the middle had been badly eroded. And yet, in his role as a campaign manager, all his instincts tell him that that is where the voters are.

"The country has no ultimate interest in whose philosophy is right," Sears said, arguing that what was "right" at one time will almost certainly be "wrong" at another period. "It has a direct interest . . . in terms of future generations . . . in whether the structure of the country will continue to move. . . . We've made change a god here. We expect and want change. We believe in some strange way that there's truth in change. It's probably not true, but that's what we believe. That's us."

Like so many other good politicians, Sears has internalized his perceptions about the country's character so completely that his own philosophy is no more than a mirror image of what he sees "out there." "I don't have any deeply felt attitudes about there being any ultimately good or bad way to do anything," he said. The real task of leadership is simply to "sense what the society is capable of, and what's on its mind."

Sears' totally pragmatic approach brought him frequent criticism from the more ideologically inclined Republicans—particularly in the party's right wing—who are instinctively distrustful of that nondoctrinaire view of politics. Many of them never forgave him for persuading Reagan, on the eve of the 1976 convention, to announce that if he were nominated, he would choose as his running mate Senator Richard P. Schweiker of Pennsylvania, a pro-labor Republican with progressive credentials. Sears saw the Schweiker tactic simply as a way to pry loose a few Eastern votes for Reagan; others saw it as a betrayal of Reagan's conservative principles, and they rejoiced when Reagan purged Sears from his 1980 campaign.

There was a larger point behind that immediate dispute, and one affecting Republicans of all stripes. Just as the excesses of traditional liberalism embodied in Lyndon Johnson's Great Society and the bitter divisions engendered by the Vietnam war caused many younger Democrats to become skeptical of their inherited faith in an activist government, so the waverings and ultimate destruction of the Nixon Administration brought many Republicans to wonder about the intellectual and moral underpinnings of their own party's approach to government. Long before Nixon succumbed to the exposures of criminal wrongdoing in his Administration, he had tested the faith of his fellow partisans by rewriting traditional Republican doctrine to suit his immediate policy or political needs. Republicans (including Nixon) had always been advocates of a free market, but it was Richard Nixon in 1971 who slapped comprehensive wage and price controls on the economy. Republicans (including Nixon) had always been staunchly anti-Communist, but it was Nixon who pulled the last American troops out of the fighting in Vietnam, who declared "détente" with the Soviet Union and reopened relations with China. Republicans (including Nixon) had always preached the virtues of limited government and decentralized control, but it was Nixon who gave the nation its first $200 billion budget and who asserted, in 1973 and 1974, a doctrine of executive privilege so sweeping as to make FDR and LBJ seem like pikers.

In the Nixon years, Republicans learned ruefully to remember John Mitchell's admonition to "watch what we do, not what we say." And when the modest, well-meaning Jerry Ford succeeded Nixon, it was the pent-up frustration with the political vagaries of the previous six years that fueled the continuing intraparty challenges to his authority.

When Ford, after barely withstanding Reagan's insurgency, lost to Jimmy Carter, many mainstream Republicans felt the first priority for their battered party was to redefine what it stood for.

A year after Carter occupied the White House, Republican Senator Bob Packwood of Oregon, now 48, invited other Senate and House Republicans and elected statewide GOP officials to a weekend issues conference at Easton on Maryland's Eastern Shore. About 40 of them, mainly people Packwood's age or younger, showed up for the first session, and, encouraged by favorable press publicity, almost 100 of them and their spouses attended the second edition of the Tidewater Conference in 1979.

Aside from a weekend of informal relaxation, including beer, crabs and piano sing-alongs, what Packwood was offering was a chance for Republicans to hammer out—through a process of consensus-seeking round tables—party positions on basic economic- and foreign-policy questions.

"You have to show cohesion among your congressional and statewide Republican officials," Packwood said, "to have credibility as a party. So I try to skip the issues like abortion and gun registration and control of the Panama Canal. All they do is divide us. I'm trying to find those issues upon which we agree and the elected Democrats disagree. And then make those our Republican platform."

It seemed like a simplistic notion, but Packwood had seen the usefulness of a similar approach back home in Oregon. In 1965, when he was starting his second term in the Oregon Legislature, he invited about 300 Oregon Republicans to a weekend brainstorming conference at the Dorchester House, a resort hotel on the Oregon coast.

The Dorchester conference became an institution and, among other things, helped provide Packwood a statewide organization for his first successful Senate bid in 1968. More important—at least in Packwood's view—such meetings offer Republicans a chance to overcome the reputation for ingrained negativism which has kept them for so long a minority party.

"For years," he said, "the Republicans would not accept the legitimacy of the New Deal. For years, our attitude was, 'Let business do it.' From Lincoln's time to Roosevelt's, it worked pretty well. But then along came the Depression, and it wasn't working at all. And when all a guy wanted was the right to join a union, our answer was 'No.' Social Security? 'No.' Minimum wage? 'No.' Medicare? 'No.' We didn't have any other plan. Just 'No.' So what is the average voter inclined to think after a while? 'They said all this time business would take care of me, but they didn't, and they hit me over the head when I wanted to join a union, and all the Republicans said was No. No. No.' "

Packwood's ambivalence on the long Republican identity with business is perhaps more understandable if one knows his own personal history. His father was for almost thirty-five years the lobbyist in Salem for Associated Oregon Industries, a catchall employers' group. Packwood grew up in a home filled with the conversation of legislators, lobbyists and journalists. "Interestingly," he said, "although my dad lobbied for employers, he was never an apologist for them. He had a scrapbook that he kept, and when I got into my teens he showed it to me, of things that the employers, over the years, had said they could not afford. He had a whole history of things they said they couldn't afford, but then when they had come, business still managed to survive. He said to me, 'Son, businessmen will always say they can't afford it. And they're not lying. They simply cannot see beyond where they are. And what they will do when it comes is bundle it up and pass it along in the cost of their products.' "

That notion of "bundling it up and passing it along in the cost of their products" has become a keynote of Packwood's own approach to a Republican alternative to New Deal–Fair Deal–New Frontier–Great Society social programs. And he thinks the public is ready for an alternative.

"I think the tide is turning," he said, "because in the last ten years the federal government has begun to touch a lot of people that it never used to touch. The weight of regulations from new agencies like the Occupational Safety and Health Administration and the Environmental Protection Agency has been felt in the working place, causing disruptions and even layoffs. Many of the ambitious social programs of the 1960s have fallen woefully short of their objectives.

"But just as the Republicans, from 1930 to about 1970, could not grasp the fact that business had not produced correctly, now the Democrats, who have fathered most of these programs, cannot grasp the fact that they don't work right," Packwood said.

Packwood said he was convinced that "we're never going to have national health insurance in this country," because employer-subsidized health-insurance plans for the workers—which are not taxed as if they were wages—have so narrowed the constituency demanding that new federal initiative. "You talk to any business agent of a respectable union, aged thirty-five or under, and health insurance is off the bottom of his list of priorities. It's provided by employers."

Other social needs, like day care and advanced education, he argued, could equally well be met outside government through a combination of labor-management agreements and tax credits. Packwood lobbied for these ideas at the Tidewater Conferences, but mainly sought to orchestrate those meetings to produce an impression of intraparty unity on positive programs. By choosing the issues carefully and encouraging the employment of language that papered over policy differences, the first two Tidewater Conferences were able to produce two- or three-paragraph statements on subjects ranging from the balanced budget to strategic relations with the Soviet Union, which were portrayed in newspaper and television stories as evidence that Republicans were "getting their act together."

But there was less agreement at the third conference in 1980. It is one thing to write a brief statement durable enough to make the next day's papers, and it is something else to deal with the hard choices that await a party responsible for governing America in the last two decades of this century. The legacy of the Sixties and Seventies did little to help—and may actually have impeded—today's Republicans from defining what it is they really believe.

Josiah Lee Auspitz, a 39-year-old political philosopher, was one of the young men recruited from the Harvard campus into the Nixon White House. Like so many others, he was struck by the extent of the effort Nixon made to camouflage the absence of a philosophical or moral core to his own politics.

"Nixon's style . . . was always to portray himself as the only person who could accommodate both wings of the party and, in fact, create a center faction in the party," Auspitz said. "But his technique in doing this was not to find a common ground to draw people together, but to find a way to play them off against each other. To the Rockefeller people he'd say, 'Well, if it's not me, it's going to be Reagan, and you know how I hate those right wingers. They did me in in California [in his losing 1962 race for Governor], the John Birchers and all the rest.' To the Reagan people he'd say, 'If it's not me, it'll be Rockefeller, and you know how I hate those liberals. They've been against me ever since the Hiss case.' That was his style. And of course, that was the way he was able to keep center stage. So the factional warfare intensified during his Administration."

Auspitz was one of the early presidents of a small organization called the Ripon Society, which, for most of the past two decades, has been struggling to provide the Republicans with a set of identifiable programs of their own. Ripon has been a target of attack, almost from the beginning, from conservative elements in the GOP who sought to categorize it as a Rockefeller front group. But, as the presence of Auspitz and several other Riponers in the Nixon Administration suggests, it is very much in the mainstream tradition of the party.

Originally, Ripon was a Cambridge phenomenon, started by a group of graduate students at Harvard and the Massachusetts Institute of Technology. "Ripon was a reaction to Kennedy," Auspitz said. "He made politics a noble, daring, bold kind of thing to do. . . . I believe Ripon's first statement, a call to excellence in leadership, was really a kind of Kennedy-inspired thing." When it began, in 1962, as a kind of thinking Republicans' society, it was called the American Bow Group, a transplanting of the Oxford-Cambridge intellectual arm of the British Conservative Party. When Thomas E. (Tim) Petri, now 40, came home from a Peace Corps tour in Somalia and became the group's first full-time employee, he suggested it should have a more American name. It was renamed for the Wisconsin town—near his home—that claims to be the birthplace of the GOP.

The founders of Ripon were determined to keep it small and select, and they restricted its membership to graduate students and young professionals, even threatening lawsuits against prospective undergraduate chapters.

It first attracted notice by the quality of some of its policy papers—outlining the rationale for the all-volunteer armed services, for example, or the negative-income-tax approach to welfare reform. But it remained a tiny organization, with a meager budget augmented by occasional gifts from such liberal Republican financiers as Walter Thayer. What finally put Ripon on the political map was the critique of the Goldwater campaign called "From Disaster to Distinction." The report, analyzing both the strategic misconceptions and the political costs of the 1964 Goldwater fiasco, infuriated conservatives. At a press conference, Dean Burch, then Republican National Chairman, denounced it as a stab in the back by the allies of Nelson Rockefeller.

The idea of the group appeared again in a book titled *The Party That*

Lost Its Head, which declared the Republican Party to be in a state of "civil war, still cursed with the incubus of extremism," and desperately in need of being "regained by the majority from which it was seized during the last few years. The right wing represents a small minority of Republicans," coauthors George P. Gilder and Bruce Chapman said, "but the evident strength of this minority is greatly inflated by the impotence of the moderate and progressive Republican majority." Warning that Goldwater's place could easily be taken by "the pop-politician, ruggedly handsome, blond, alliterative Ronald Reagan—the party's hope to usurp reality with the fading world of the Class-B movie," they urged progressive Republicans to assert their own "distinct ideological identity." Unhappily, the two men they identified as leaders in that effort symbolized the futility of the cause: Senator Thomas H. Kuchel of California, the assistant minority leader, was only months away from defeat for renomination when the book appeared. Mayor John V. Lindsay of New York was destined to become first a Democrat and then a symbol of dated political trendiness. But Chapman, now the secretary of state of Washington, and Petri, elected to Congress in 1979, have both seen their own political careers blossom, and both believe that a Republican majority can be achieved.

"When you talk about the middle of America," Chapman said, "which does not have great hates, which does value traditions, which wants to see improvements within the system, and which has a very high degree of responsibility about community life, you are talking about a very powerful group of people. If you were to go to any small or middle-sized town and say, 'Who is it that goes out and works for the school levies? Who goes out and works for the United Way? Who runs the capital drive for the new swimming pool or for the addition to the library?' you'll find a lot of moderate Republicans."

If it is not for lack of numbers that the progressive Republicans have failed, neither is it for lack of ideas. Where they have criticized their party, they have, more often than not, been right. They said during the Goldwater years that Republicans were politically dumb as well as disloyal to their heritage to write off black votes, and after enough defeats, their party leaders—especially in the South—have come to agree with them. They were right in their criticism of the Vietnam war, and they were right when they said that mediocrity was not the criterion for selecting Supreme Court justices. More positively, the Riponers were among the first to point to decentralization of power from Washington as an important political imperative; before Jimmy Carter exploited it as an issue in winning the presidency, people like Petri and Auspitz were trying to move the Nixon Administration—as junior staff people—into serious efforts at governmental reorganization.

Despite this record, Ripon and its alumni have had relatively limited success in helping the Republican Party define a distinctive program for itself. They have never managed to build a permanent political network, with fund-raising, political-action and propaganda arms, such as their intraparty antagonists of the Right (who will be discussed in Chapter 6) have developed over the past twenty years. Rather, they have tied themselves to passing political stars, like Rockefeller and Lindsay, whose own success in national Republican politics has been very limited. In 1980, they flocked to the presidential banner of Representative John B. Anderson of Illinois.

While some of the Ripon alumni have had greater luck in their personal political ventures, the overall mission of the organization remains unfulfilled. "There is still a need for conceptualization," Auspitz said in 1978. "Ripon never had a program. Just a set of concepts, but each of them was an important and good Republican concept. After the experience of the Nixon years, the group really became quite politicized, and everybody wanted to do active politics. There's nothing wrong with doing that. It's just that once an organization is set up to do one thing, to try to convert it to something else is very difficult, and you usually end up doing neither very well."

The kind of organizational and financial resources that Ripon was never able to assemble have been brought into being by the American Enterprise Institute, a public-policy research center which, while not formally connected with the Republican Party, has become a major supplier of its ideas. AEI, as it is known, is to a major degree the creation of two generations of the Baroody family—Lebanese-American Catholics with a lively intellectual curiosity and an eclectic circle of friends. William J. Baroody, Sr., the former president and guiding spirit of AEI; his son William J. Baroody, Jr., who succeeded him as president in 1978; son Joseph, senior partner in a politically active Washington public-relations firm; and son Michael, director of research and communications at the Republican National Committee, together make up a kind of family holding company for conservative ideas.

When the senior Baroody joined AEI in 1954, it was a small organization preaching free-enterprise ideas in a capital dominated for twenty years by New Deal thinking. It has been only in the Seventies—and particularly since the downfall of Nixon and the defeat of Ford—that AEI has blossomed to its present size and begun to rival its more liberal neighbor, the Brookings Institution. AEI's 1979 budget was $9.5 million, and the number of full-time scholars and staff members totaled 160.

In part because their own background as Catholics and ethnics is out of the ordinary for Republicans, the Baroodys have brought into AEI the leavening influence of some Democratic intellectuals, who have been in dissent from some of the tendencies in their own party during the Seventies. Such writers and thinkers as Ben Wattenberg, Michael Novak and Irving Kristol have accepted the hospitality of AEI and, in turn, have helped stimulate the thinking of the many former Nixon and Ford Administration officials who have moved to AEI from the public payroll.

Bill Baroody, Jr., now 43, is one of those transfers. He came out of Holy Cross and the Navy and joined the staff of then Representative Melvin R. Laird of Wisconsin in time to serve as Laird's aide on the 1964 Republican platform committee (while his father, the senior Baroody, was a behind-the-scenes adviser to Barry Goldwater). He went to the Pentagon with Laird, and then to the Nixon White House in the final days of its agony. Baroody succeeded Charles Colson on the Nixon staff, and when Ford became President he was given responsibility for the White House Office of Public Liaison, which served as the contact point between the Administration and hundreds of private groups and associations with an interest in government policy.

It was in the course of those meetings, Baroody said, that he observed that "the leaders of just about every organized element of American society, if properly approached and engaged, want to be part of the solution and not part of the problem."

In his White House job and, more insistently, since taking over AEI, he has begun to articulate a view of the "missing middle ground" of American politics and government which both he and his father describe as a secular expression of several principles well known to Catholic theologians.

In a 1976 commencement address at Seattle University, young Baroody said, "We Catholics know the Church fell out of balance for a time by the assertion of the one principle, the hierarchical, over another equally valid principle, that of the community. Just as Vatican II sought to correct that imbalance," he said, "the new politics seeks the same restoration of balance in the sphere of politics."

As Baroody sees it, the New Deal philosophy had exalted the role of the federal government as the solver of national problems, and the Republican opposition, in response, had glorified the freedom of the individual it said was threatened by the growing authority of the state.

Now, he said at Seattle, that polarization is beginning to "merge into a new politics of the center," based on an expanding role for the "mediating institutions." "Mediating institutions" are no more than those familiar units, the family, the neighborhood, the racial or ethnic group and the voluntary association. But in Baroody's view, a major political change could be brought about simply by making it the goal of government policy to strengthen those institutions and then using them to perform social functions which otherwise would have to be done by the state.

As an example of this approach, he cited the Ford Administration's decision to handle the wave of Vietnam war refugees not primarily through a new federal bureaucracy, but by involving "families, churches, neighborhood groups and other volunteer organizations, whose function, at least in part, has always been the 'socialization' of individuals."

When the junior Baroody moved from the White House to AEI, he expanded an ambitious project designed to show how the "mediating structures" could be given enlarged roles in child care, education, law enforcement, social welfare, housing and health care. Books on all those areas were being written by AEI scholars in 1979, and from the books and conferences, Baroody promised, eventually would come specific policy proposals.

Baroody held out the hope that "this new politics of the center," once given specific content, might "restore the balance between the private and public sectors in America . . . and lead to a commonsense coalition" of majority dimensions.

It seems likely, however, that even if the intellectual product of this ambitious effort is as solid as Baroody hopes, it will have to contest for dominance—within the Republican Party—with the growing movement of economic conservatives whose emphasis is much more on the virtues of the free market than on the magic of "mediating structures."

In the meantime, Republicans must make do with what they have. The brief presidency of Gerald R. Ford did little or nothing to supply the party with programs and policies for the future. But it did remind Republicans—in a positive way—of the fundamental importance of an upright personal character, a welcome contrast to the lesson his predecessor left as his legacy.

I found that question of character very much on the minds of many of the younger Republicans interviewed. Stanley Pottinger told a story he said illustrated the importance of "moral leadership—a phrase I heard so much in the early Seventies that I gagged on it, but now find myself using."

It was shortly before the 1970 election, and a small group of HEW officials were giving Elliot Richardson, then Secretary of that department, their opinions on how to handle a Southern school-desegregation case they feared might have adverse political consequences.

"All these things went back and forth," Pottinger said, "and Elliot just sat there doodling. And finally it came time for him to say something. I was anticipating word from the mountaintop. And he said, 'I think the first thing we are going to do is start with the proposition that we will do what is right.'

"I was so angry at that moment," Pottinger recalled. "I thought, What kind of pap is this? But as time wore on, and I joined him again at the Justice Department for a time, and watched the agony of that department in the Agnew and Nixon investigations, I came to understand that 'piece of pap' as one of the most powerful things that a political leader can say. You can't say it too often. Just say, 'Let's do what's right. Let's don't get too cute.' "

Republican Senator John C. Danforth of Missouri, 44, who came to the Senate in the 1976 election after serving eight years as state attorney general, was another who put heavy stress on character and candor as the prime requisites for public officials. That was natural enough for Danforth, an heir to the Ralston-Purina fortune, who, like his classmate and fellow Senator Gary Hart, had earned degrees from both the law school and the divinity school at Yale and (in Danforth's case but not Hart's) was an ordained Episcopal minister as well.

Danforth made an impressive debut in the Senate, emerging quickly as a skillful spokesman for his party on tax and economic policy. But what struck colleagues about him was the remarkably detached attitude he had about the importance of his own role.

"Fortunately," he said, "the world is not waiting with bated breath for some new bill to be passed by Congress. You know, the ground honestly does not tremble when we do something. The world is changed very rarely by new laws that are passed. Much more important is the kind of attitudes that people have. When I was attorney general, I tried to make it clear that law enforcement really depended on the willingness of most people to obey the law. And in like manner, the future of the country depends less on what Washington-inspired initiatives there are than on the general attitude of the people. So I think the worst thing a politician could be, next to a racist, is a demagogue. And the best thing he could be is somebody who is able to evoke in the public a sense of trust and a sense of their own responsibility in making the world a little better."

In a similar vein, Richard Carver, the 43-year-old Mayor of Peoria, Illinois, who in 1979 broke the Democrats' traditional grip on the chairmanship of the U.S. Conference of Mayors, said that in his experience in city government he had learned that "you can only do those things that the voters trust you to do."

All the emphasis on the moral qualities of leadership could be viewed as an alibi for inaction. But as Carver's example made clear, that was not the case with these young Republicans.

Carver came out of the Air Force at 25 at a time when his home city of Peoria was showing clear signs of the same sort of decay that afflicts many middle-aged industrial centers. The voters had just rejected an annexation referendum, and to Carver "that didn't make sense." So with a few other friends, and no experience, he put together an organization that drummed up enough support for another vote which led to the city's doubling its size and increasing its tax base and population by about 40 percent.

After serving an apprenticeship on the city council under a Mayor who was opposed to accepting any federal aid and whose main accomplishment was the repeal of a utility tax that was supposed to finance urban renewal, Carver in 1973 was elected Mayor himself. Since then, the city has begun to address its problems—with a mixture of federal support and local initiative.

In 1980, Carver tried unsuccessfully for the Republican nomination for Senator from Illinois. But with the ambivalence that seems so characteristic of these younger Republicans, he insisted in an interview that fundamentally he was "committed to solving Peoria's problems at the Peoria level," rather than relying on Washington.

As I listened to them, it became clear that the young Republicans' aversion to federal policy making was more than just a rhetorical bow to the supposedly conservative temper of the times. Both the men who served as Jerry Ford's White House chief of staff, Donald Rumsfeld and Richard Cheney, said they had become more conservative in their outlook as a result of what they had seen in Washington.

Both had credentials from which to speak. Rumsfeld, 48, served for seven years as a U.S. Representative from Illinois before taking a series of domestic-agency and diplomatic assignments from Nixon and serving Ford first as White House staff chief and then as Secretary of Defense. Cheney, 39, was a congressional aide, an assistant to Rumsfeld and finally Rumsfeld's White House successor, before going home to Wyoming to start his own House career by being elected its Representative in 1978.

"Those years during the Nixon and Ford administrations," Cheney said, "made me more conservative than I was when I started. Having watched the final throes of the Vietnam war, having tried to fight poverty at OEO [the Office of Economic Opportunity], I saw how difficult it is to have government programs well designed to achieve any significant results. . . . There are all too often unanticipated consequences that flow from actions that were motivated by the best possible intentions but that nevertheless have negative effects on the society."

Rumsfeld echoed the same skepticism. The example he cited was Nixon's decision to create a White House "special-action office" for drug abuse. "We had a problem," he said, referring to drug abuse. "The country was worried about the problem. It was clear that the other bureaucracies were inept and unsuccessful, and the problem was becoming worse. It was politically appealing and dramatic to create an office in the White House that would clear away that problem. The only difficulty was that it didn't.

"I hope that people will be less ready to run to the federal government for solutions to problems, because so many times the federal government is really not capable of solving those problems. Action is an appealing thing, but action to no purpose breeds cynicism, and that's a big price to pay for a superficial sense of action—creating cynicism, turning people off, draining the reservoir of trust in the country."

I heard much the same thing when I went up to Wilmington, Delaware, to visit Pierre S. (Pete) du Pont IV, 45, a member of the state's first family, who had been elected Governor in 1976 after serving in the state legislature and in the House of Representatives.

Du Pont said that he was fresh from an argument with then Secretary of Energy James R. Schlesinger, who had demanded to know what had happened to the "moderate, thoughtful Congressman" he had known when du Pont was in Washington from 1970 to 1976.

"I said, 'I'll tell you what's happened to me,' " du Pont said. " 'I've had to go back to Delaware and live under this federal bureaucracy, and I think it has made me very much more hardheaded, considerably more conservative and very antagonistic to what the federal government is constantly forcing me to do. My schools are being run by a federal judge. My prisons are being run by a federal judge. Construction of a new hospital for New Castle County has been delayed a year and a half because of federal judges' fiddling around with various lawsuits. Every other week, I wake up and hear Joe Califano [then Secretary of Health, Education and Welfare] telling me that he is going to send a special team to these seven target states to investigate whether we are complying with something or other.' I mean the red tape and the morass and the harassment from Washington is endless, and I've really joined the ranks of those who want to be left alone."

That desire was widely shared as the Eighties began, but while the slogan "Don't Tread on Me" is as old as the country, it does not constitute an adequate policy by itself for a political party. Especially not when many of the federal interventions of which du Pont and others complained were the result of courts' attempting to secure compliance with what they interpreted as constitutional prohibitions against racial discrimination or cruel and unusual punishment.

The Republicans' eight-year brush with responsibility for the executive branch of the national government under Nixon and Ford ended so unsatisfactorily that there was a temptation for many of them just to condemn the central government—and let it go at that.

But people as serious as Carver, Cheney, Rumsfeld, Danforth and du Pont knew that there were dangers to both their party and their country in encouraging that kind of blind negativism. Lacking a clear concept of their own of what Washington should—or should not—be doing, they were often reduced to hand wringing—and storytelling.

"I'm concerned about the fact that there's a premium on oversimplification," Jack Danforth said. "I'm concerned about the too-easy-to-understand positions like Proposition 13 and let's-keep-the-Panama-Canal. All you hear are the extremes of the Left and the Right, and us moderates are such vanilla characters, we put you to sleep. I often tell people that the answer to their problems isn't in Washington, that it's in their own communities and their own homes. . . . I think that kind of realism about government and its role is very healthy. But it too often goes beyond that, to a kind of orneriness, a kind of us-against-them negative approach."

Not long after du Pont had vented his own frustration with his "get-off-my-back" speech in our interview, he reversed field to express his own fears that the constitutional convention some conservatives were promoting in 1979 to require a balanced federal budget could be the "scariest thing" ever to occur.

"Can you imagine what the abortion people and the anti-abortion people, the right-wing nuts and the left-wing nuts and the in-between nuts would try to put in the Constitution?" he asked.

"The special-interest groups, the pressure groups have destroyed the center," du Pont said. "I gave a graduation speech last June about the Gilbert and Sullivan operetta *Utopia Limited.* It's about a kingdom ruled by an absolute monarch who is followed everywhere by a person called the Public Exploder. And anytime the king strays and does anything wrong, it is the duty of the Public Exploder to blow him up with dynamite, right on the spot.

"And as they say in the play, it works terrifically. It is despotism tempered by dynamite. Well, that's what we have in America today—a Public Exploder mentality. We have a powerful chief executive, but the minute he steps out of line, some pressure group tries to blow him up—rhetorically, if not physically. And I think that's the problem for the future of America. When is there going to be a center?"

The spiritual heirs of Nixon and Ford were having as hard a time answering that question as the Eighties began as were the disciples of Kennedy and Johnson. And the young men and women brought to the center of power by Jimmy Carter and Walter F. Mondale were having no better luck with that question.

4 · Carter-Mondale

MAX CLELAND IS A SURVIVOR. The 37-year-old triple amputee who was named by President Jimmy Carter to head the Veterans Administration embodies, as much as any one person in public life can, both the agonies and the hopes of the past twenty years.

In 1965, Cleland was working as an intern for a Congressman from his native Georgia, but an impulse to keep "pushing my personal frontier further and further, testing myself to see just how good or how strong or how tough I was" took him into the Army paratroopers, to Vietnam and finally, to the siege of Khe Sanh.

"There's an element of insanity in all of this," he said, sitting in his bright blue-walled office, overlooking Lafayette Park and the White House. "But I always did want to be out front. . . . Well, I was a little bit too far ahead and ended up on the wrong end of a grenade explosion and that landed me in the hospital for eighteen months."

The grenade had rolled off a supply truck. Cleland dived for it, but it exploded before he could toss it away. As he told Myra MacPherson of *The Washington Post,* "The explosion blew me backwards. I opened my eyes and saw my right hand was gone. My right leg was gone, and my left foot. I saw my left boot lying off to one side. . . . I fought to stay conscious because I knew as long as I did, I was alive."

There were eighteen months of hospitalization, with many moments of despair—and of bitterness directed at the VA doctors and bureaucrats, against whom Cleland would later testify to a Senate committee.

But the man who came out of the hospital a triple amputee—the right arm severed at the shoulder, both legs above the knee—was undefeated in spirit. Pushing a wheelchair at breakneck pace, driving his own specially equipped car, Cleland picked up the broken pattern of his life—and politics.

When he left the hospital, Cleland selected a state Senate district in suburban Atlanta and in 1970 defeated the Republican incumbent. That was the same year Jimmy Carter was elected Governor of Georgia, and the two men quickly became friends and allies. When Carter became President, there was no doubt whom he wanted to run the Veterans Administration.

"I've got to tell you a story," Cleland said, spinning his wheelchair to face the White House. "I was a student here [at American University, on a semester leave from Stetson University] in the fall of 1963. A lot of people can't recall, but in the early Sixties being a student meant being involved in government and politics. We were part of the New Frontier. We were part of the new, emerging generation, and it was a noble, laudable enterprise. I was sitting in the gallery when the Senate approved the nuclear-test-ban treaty in the fall of 1963. They took our group on a tour of the White House that November. I was in the Oval Office seventy-two hours before the assassination. I was one of the last people to see the Oval Office as it was under Jack Kennedy. The next time I went in the Oval Office was on January 20, 1977, when Jimmy Carter invited me as his first official appointment. So I feel now we're kind of picking up where I left off back in 1963, when government stood for peace, not war, when it stood for human rights and ideals and not the reverse, and when people tried to make government more sensitive and humane."

Substantively, however, Cleland said, "We're in a totally different era. Then, government was the tool for reform. Now, government itself has to be reformed. . . . The basic liberal Democratic assumption that was present in this country for forty years from Roosevelt through Lyndon Johnson is no longer the presumption in American politics today."

There was an obvious irony in this comment coming from a man who headed one of Washington's larger and more expensive bureaucracies (the VA had, in 1979, about 235,000 employees and a budget of $19 billion). When Cleland was asked if he thought inefficiency was built into bureaucracy, he said, "It's built in, but I think it can be unbuilt, too. I've tried to spot the idiocies that keep our people from being effective, that keep our programs from working, the little daily nonsensities that you run across in any large organization."

His efforts included such major managerial changes as doubling the size of the VA's internal-auditing office and putting together what he called the agency's first long-term planning-and-evaluation program. But there was equal emphasis on "sensitizing" the bureaucrats to their face-to-face and telephone contacts with their clients.

"I've been on the other side of that desk," Cleland said. "I've been that veteran seeking to be hospitalized, and I've dealt with people who asked me my claim number before they asked me my name. It happened to rub me very much the wrong way, and I'll never forget it, and I guess that's one reason why I have such a passion to make the VA system better than that."

Making the whole government "better than that" was one of the main promises of Jimmy Carter's 1976 campaign for the presidency. Endlessly on the long trail from the Iowa caucuses to the November election, he intoned the hope that the government might become "as good and honest and decent and truthful and fair and competent and idealistic and compassionate, and as filled with love, as are the American people." It was a staggering goal, and in practice it has proved to be staggeringly difficult to achieve. The young Georgians who followed Carter north to the capital, their colleagues who entered the Administration through their connection with Vice President Walter F. Mondale, and the young people who landed on the White House staff more by luck or contrivance than through personal connections—all received a liberal education in the perils of political leadership in the first three years of the Carter-Mondale Administration.

In the course of interviewing a dozen of the young Administration officials for this book, I was acutely conscious, of course, that they were far less detached observers of politics and government than were the alumni of the previous administrations discussed in the preceding two chapters. When we talked, all of them were aware that 1980 was an election year in which Carter and Mondale expected to be on the ballot. I tried to circumvent that problem—and succeeded to some extent, I think—by stressing that this book was not an effort to evaluate Carter's presidency, but to look beyond it, through the eyes of some of those who had shared its experiences with him.

Specifically, it was my purpose to look at the kind of people who had been recruited for government by Carter and Mondale; to draw them out on the quality of their own experience near the center of power; to learn whether it had whetted their appetite for further political involvement or whether it had been disillusioning; and finally, to inquire what lessons they had drawn about what makes leadership possible in this difficult period.

Whatever the political futures of Carter and Mondale, most of these young people will survive and play a further role in politics and government. Max Cleland, who had been elected to the state Senate and defeated for Lieutenant Governor of Georgia before coming to the VA post, was typical. He said that when the Carter Administration ends, "I guess I'll revert to a business-as-usual mode and get back on the treadmill of elective politics."

Ironically, two of the people who could well close out their political careers when Carter's term in office ends are the two best-known young men in his circle: Hamilton Jordan, 36, the White House chief of staff, and Joseph L. (Jody) Powell, Jr., 37, the presidential press secretary. They have been with Carter almost every step of the way since he began his pursuit of the Georgia governorship back in 1966, and their very closeness may make it unlikely or unappealing for them to seek political careers independently of him.

Powell remarked in a 1979 interview that "I don't have this idea that Jimmy Carter is the only President that we've ever had or ever will have that's good enough for me to want to work for . . . but it's very unlikely I could serve someone else as effectively." Jordan said in mid-1979 that "When I get through here, I don't plan to continue in politics. . . . I don't plan to stay in Washington and be a lobbyist and I don't plan to go back home and run for anything. What I'd like to do is go back to school and then write. Probably fiction. I think I have a talent for writing, although I've never honed it, and I'd like to try that. And travel. But it's surely not going to be politics the rest of my life."

That is not surprising, considering how much politics has consumed Jordan's—and Powell's—adult life. Their biographies are well known. Jody Powell grew up on a farm outside Vienna, Georgia, about thirty-five miles from Plains. He graduated from high school with top grades and a reputation as an agile quarterback, and went on to the Air Force Academy. In his senior year, Powell was accused of cheating on a history exam and resigned from the academy, completing his undergraduate work at Georgia State University in Atlanta.

Jordan was raised in Albany, Georgia, "I loafed my way through" the University of Georgia and, after being rejected for military service, went to Vietnam with the International Voluntary Service. Jordan was a bank trainee and Powell a graduate student at Emory University when they signed on with Carter for the campaign that led to his election as Governor of Georgia in 1970 and as President six years later.

Jordan's maternal grandfather had been an active Georgia politician, president of the state senate for many years. Powell heard political talk from his schoolteacher mother and was majoring in political science himself. But both of them said it was unlikely they would have chosen to spend more than a dozen years in politics at the start of their professional careers had Jimmy Carter not happened to come along. "I decided early in my life," Jordan said, "that this was a talented and intelligent and very committed person," and made a commitment himself which has taken on dimensions he could not have imagined.

Aside from their loyalty to the one boss they have ever known well, Powell and Jordan have been spurred by one other force: a deep pride in —and a certain defensiveness about—their native South.

Jordan inherited something of an anti-establishment bias from his grandfather, who was always a factional foe of the Talmadges, Georgia's reigning political dynasty. He said he was attracted to Carter in 1966 (as he had been, four years earlier, to Carl Sanders, the man Carter was to defeat for Governor in 1970) "because here was a man that was going to move Georgia forward and represent the South in an honorable way."

"It's just impossible to exaggerate how important that was to a lot of young people in the South," he said, "a whole generation of Southerners who grew up with the country basically looking down their nose at them and their region, being told that they were bigoted and biased and bad. . . . A lot of it was media and television and the emotionalism of the civil-rights movement. But we were told we were not as good as everybody else, in a kind of media-imposed inferiority complex. The reaction a lot of us had was that 'We'll show you we can solve our problems down here as well as you can and we can produce progressive politicians just like you can.' There was a good dose of that in me."

As I listened to Jordan and Powell talk about those shaping experiences, what came through was not only their desire to vindicate their region, but their distaste for the Northern liberals and the mass media whose disdain they had known in their youth.

Powell's mother had been a quiet critic of segregation, "so when the *Brown* decision came along and later when the demonstrations and marches began, there was no question in my mind about what was the right thing to do," Powell said. "But there were conflicting emotions involved. I could not, frankly, help resenting to some extent the feeling that my region of the country and my people were being picked out. . . . There was an element of self-righteousness and a holier-than-thou sort of attitude, particularly on the part of whites from other parts of the country."

Jordan also had conflicting reactions to the civil-rights movement, because his own family was deeply split by the issue. His uncle Clarence Jordan (actually his father's first cousin, but, as he said, "they were raised more like brothers than cousins . . . very close") was a visionary of deep religious conviction who founded an interracial farm commune after World War II in President Carter's deeply conservative home county—Sumter County—and endured years of vigilante terror from outraged whites. "Clarence was much loved by my family," Jordan said. "They loved Clarence and they respected him, but they thought he was a little crazy, and they wondered how a guy who had grown up in the same town, the same environment, the same cultural experience had somewhere along the line got this crazy notion that blacks were as good as whites."

Albany, Georgia, where the Jordan family lived, was one of the toughest segregationist strongholds in the state. "It was one of the few places," Jordan said, "and I don't mean to sound bragging about this, that successfully thwarted Martin Luther King's integration drive. . . . I have a vivid memory—I must have been thirteen or fourteen or fifteen—of seeing Martin Luther King on trial in a federal court in Albany, and Andy Young and a lot of other blacks marching outside." During those times, Clarence Jordan would be on the streets in the demonstrations and addressing the meetings in the black churches. "He would always come to our home and see our family, and bring his own family," Jordan recalled, "but he would always come at night and he would never talk about, you know, why he was in town. He knew the way my mother and father felt."

I asked Jordan how he had felt at the time, and he said, "Kind of ambivalent. I had a feeling that whites had not been fair to blacks, but I felt the demonstrations and everything were a great threat to my way of life. So I had contradictory feelings." Later, as he grew older and times changed, Hamilton Jordan and his parents "came to see that Clarence had been right." The elder Jordan brought a black man onto the Albany draft board he headed, and Hamilton himself paid visits to his Uncle Clarence and came to know him as "the very special human being" he was.

Ironically, his connection with Clarence Jordan was the source of yet another ambivalent relationship—this time involving Vietnam. Jordan went off to witness the war "mostly out of curiosity," he said, and believing, vaguely, that "our country was doing the right thing." But the group of International Voluntary Service workers he joined were mainly pacifists or people "violently against the war, people from Berkeley and Harvard" and similar places. "Many of them had heard Clarence lecture at their colleges, and I was a little bit of a hero to them, but they found out that I wasn't as good as Clarence was" on the issues—and he was rebuffed.

Once Jordan reached Vietnam, "it was quickly obvious . . . our country was participating in the destruction of a society, for whatever reason," and when he was sent home ill, he came back with the conviction that "we were in a god-awful mess and had no business being there."

But always there was the ambivalence. And always the sense that those other people were, as he said, "looking down their nose" at him and others like him.

It is impossible to be certain how much the sense of being looked down on by others who considered themselves the leadership elite of their own generation contributed to the attitudes some of Carter's Georgia aides displayed when they came to Washington. But there was surely an element of that defensiveness in their almost-deliberate disdain for the protocol and conventions of official life. In a more fundamental way than perhaps even they knew, they felt themselves outsiders.

Jack Watson, 42, another of Carter's senior staff members (secretary of the Cabinet and assistant for intergovernmental relations), found himself an outsider earlier in his career, at Harvard Law School. Watson had gone through Vanderbilt on a Navy ROTC scholarship and spent three years in a Marine unit trained for reconnaissance behind enemy lines and for securing landing zones used in helicopter assaults. The experience, he said, "gave me a deep respect for many aspects of military life and discipline. We were parachute-qualified and scuba-qualified and demolition-qualified . . . a very military unit. In many respects, a military elitist unit. . . . I say that because I was not one of the early ones to be sensitive to the Vietnam war. I did not pay much attention to the antiwar demonstrations, nor was I sympathetic to them at all." While Watson was a bit of an outsider among the Carterites, with his Harvard Law School degree, he felt even more a stranger while in Cambridge. "I was treated like I was some strange, alien creature," he said of his Harvard classmates. "They really could not believe that I had actually been a Marine. To them, 'Marine' was a pejorative term, an epithet. To me, it was a label of the highest honor and distinction."

But Watson was different from Powell or Jordan, not only because he was somewhat older but because he plainly envisaged a political role for himself beyond his service to Carter. His ambitions had been kindled early. He grew up in Pine Bluff, Arkansas, where he was president of his class and its representative at the American Legion–sponsored Boys State in 1955. At that mock political convention, Watson opposed and defeated Fred Akers, now the University of Texas football coach, for election as "governor." He was taken to the state capitol to be sworn in. "The moment of supreme thrill," he recalled, "was to be escorted from the Governor's office, through the huge doors of the House of Representatives, to be announced as the governor of Arkansas Boys State, and to walk down that aisle with everyone standing in the House chamber, and to take the rostrum and give an address to a joint session of the Arkansas Legislature. That had to be one of the highest moments of my life!"

Watson came into Carter's orbit through two circumstances. After law school, he joined King and Spalding, the Atlanta firm whose senior partners included Griffin Bell and Charles Kirbo, who were later to be Carter's Attorney General and chief private adviser. And he took on extracurricular duties with the Atlanta Crime Commission, which gave him expertise in the problems of alcoholism and, later, mental health. He met Carter through Kirbo, traveled with him occasionally in his gubernatorial campaign, raised funds, wrote speeches—but never officially joined the staff. Later, during the governorship, he became the part-time chairman of the policy board of Carter's Department of Human Resources, and still later, while Powell and Jordan were engrossed in the presidential campaign, Watson organized a separate group in Atlanta to plan Carter's transition to the presidency. After the election, there were serious conflicts between the Watson group and the campaign group, particularly between Watson and Jordan. While the latter's supremacy on the White House staff was quickly established, Watson carved out a substantive role for himself that may prove a useful building block in his own career.

Stuart Eizenstat, 37, Carter's highly regarded domestic-policy assistant, is like Watson in the sense that his appetite for politics and government predates his relationship with Carter and is likely to survive it as well. The son of an Atlanta wholesale shoe distributor, he came out of the University of North Carolina with a reputation as a hardworking, skillful researcher. He was serving as a student intern in the office of a Georgia Congressman in the summer of 1963, and the great civil-rights march of that August "had a very major impact on me. I think I was hooked permanently on politics from that summer on," he said.

"Up to that point, I had not really been confronted with the civil-rights issue very directly. I had gone to a segregated high school, and I can't say that I thought too deeply about it at the time. . . . It was just a fact of life I accepted." Heading toward a Howard Johnson's in Raleigh one Sunday morning with a group of fraternity brothers, he found some black students staging a sit-in in the parking lot. "I remember saying to one of the kids I was with, 'Why are these students doing this?' And somebody said, 'They're not allowed to go in the restaurant, because they're black.' And I said, 'If that's the case, I'm not going to go in either,' and so some of the others went without me."

Both his political involvement and his sensitivity to civil-rights issues deepened as Eizenstat returned to Washington almost every summer after 1963. In the summer of 1966, while studying at Harvard Law School, he was working on civil-rights problems in the general counsel's office of the Office of Education—and doing two volunteer jobs at night. Three nights a week, he went to the Head Start office, working with "kids who were going out into rural Mississippi and Alabama checking on compliance with the civil-rights requirements. They were being tailed by the state police, and they were really, frankly, putting their life in danger. And this had real impact on me. . . . The other two evenings, I volunteered as a tutor for an Urban League remedial-reading program in Northeast Washington, which, really for the first time, brought me into personal contact with poor, underprivileged kids.

"The civil-rights thing came quite naturally to me, once the issue was focused, because I was also a member of a minority group," Eizenstat said. But the other great issue of the 1960s—the Vietnam war—"was one that, frankly, I was more ambivalent about. . . . I remember reading one of the early articles against the war by [Democratic Senator] Frank Church [of Idaho]. It had quite an effect on me . . . and from that time on, maybe 1963 or 1964, I thought it was a mistake. But when I was asked to work in the White House in 1967, I frankly didn't have any qualms of conscience about working for an administration that was involved in the war."

Eizenstat landed a job in the Johnson White House through some of the Young Democrats he had met during his previous Washington summers, and in 1968 he became research director of the Humphrey-for-President campaign.

When he moved back to Atlanta at age 25 to start practicing law, he was something of a seasoned political veteran. As such, he was very much in demand, and he worked as a volunteer issues director in Carter's 1970 campaign, very much as he worked for Sam Massell, Maynard Jackson and Andrew Young in their races for Mayor or Congressman in other years. While he did other part-time chores for Carter, it was not until the presidential campaign that Carter had a full-time job of sufficient interest to offer Eizenstat. His work as the issues director made him a natural choice to be the domestic-policy coordinator in the White House.

Watson and Eizenstat see themselves as insiders in a political system that extends well beyond Jimmy Carter's own career, and thus are more likely to be "survivors" of his presidency than are Jordan and Powell. "I think that the American political system is one that is very much an incremental system," Eizenstat said, "and it can be affected more by people inside the structure than it can by mass movements outside." While Eizenstat said that some in the Carter White House "have such a deep personal commitment to this President that they would feel uncomfortable working for another administration," he made it plain that that comment did not apply to himself. "I have been interested in government for a long time," he said, "and I don't expect my interest to diminish; if anything, it's been heightened."

There is little doubt that the memories of the heady day as Boys State governor fill Jack Watson's mind with dreams of being a real governor someday. And others in less-publicized positions on the Carter and Mondale staffs are—like Watson, Eizenstat and Cleland—people with a lifetime commitment to politics and government.

Jim Johnson, 37, Mondale's executive assistant, figured that his current service in Washington is actually his sixth tour of duty in the capital. He was reared in a deeply political home. His father, A. I. Johnson, was one of those who joined Hubert Humphrey in merging the separate liberal factions into the Democratic-Farmer-Labor (DFL) Party of Minnesota in 1944. When Jim Johnson was 12, he sat in the St. Paul hotel meetings where votes were solicited to make his father Speaker of the state House of Representatives. Jim Johnson got his first lesson in political tactics when a member who was believed too ill to vote was carried in on a stretcher to give A. I. Johnson a 66-to-65 victory. Young Johnson did his first door-to-door campaigning while a student at the University of Minnesota and took his first Washington job in 1965. Like so many others in later chapters, he came to the capital to work for the National Student Association. Over the next dozen years, while earning a Ph.D. at Princeton and serving as public-affairs director for the Dayton-Hudson Company in Minneapolis, he had five other campaign and governmental assignments in Washington.

Richard Moe, 44, Mondale's administrative assistant, is another one whose credentials seem almost too extensive for his age. The son of a Duluth physician, he has been hooked on politics since he volunteered in Humphrey's 1960 campaign and found himself a driver for the Senator. Later, he worked as administrative assistant to the DFL mayor of Minneapolis, then to the Lieutenant Governor of Minnesota, and for more than five years was finance director and chairman of the DFL Party. He became Mondale's administrative assistant in 1972 and has been in that position ever since.

Another Mondale man, Bertram W. Carp, has become one of Eizenstat's two deputies on the domestic-policy staff. Carp, 36, a graduate of Stanford and the anti-war movement (to his later chagrin, he declined to vote in the 1968 election between Humphrey and Nixon), came out of law school into a job in the general counsel's office of the Department of Health, Education and Welfare. When the Nixon Administration began purging "overzealous" civil-rights enforcers, he latched on to a job with Mondale's staff and worked for him until his present White House assignment began.

Several of the junior staffers in and around the White House were people who might have been there with any Democratic president elected in 1976. David Rubenstein, 31, another Eizenstat deputy, was a Baltimore junior-high-school student during the Kennedy Administration. While others were caught by the glamour of the young President, Rubenstein was more practical. "Either because of my more introverted nature or the recognition at an early age that I didn't think anybody Jewish could get elected to a very high office, I thought it would be much better if I aspired to be a staff person or adviser. . . . I thought that if you worked at the White House at an early age, you could look back for the rest of your life on something worthwhile."

Rubenstein took as his model Theodore C. Sorensen, Kennedy's assistant, and all the time he was at Duke University and the University of Chicago Law School, he was thinking about "finding the right opportunity, making a good enough reputation, making the right contacts and finding the right candidate I could work with."

As part of his plan, Rubenstein went to work for the New York law firm whose partners included not only Arthur Goldberg and Ramsey Clark, but also Ted Sorensen. "I spent about two years working reasonably closely with him, and he recommended me to [Democratic Senator] Birch Bayh [of Indiana], and I took that job [chief counsel of the Senate Subcommittee on Constitutional Amendments, which Bayh chaired] in part because Bayh had just started running for President."

Tragically, for Rubenstein, the Bayh candidacy did not survive the year's second primary in Massachusetts. But the Sorensen connection worked again. "I think it was Ted," Rubenstein said, "who suggested that I interview with Stu Eizenstat, who was putting together an issues staff of bright young Washington types [for the Carter campaign]." Eizenstat assigned him to run the "opposition research," tracking what Ford, Reagan and other Republicans were saying, and brought him along to the White House as his assistant.

W. Bowman (Bo) Cutter, 38, the executive associate director of the Office of Management and Budget (in effect, its third-ranking official), was just as careful as Rubenstein in his preparation for White House service—but luckier. A Virginian, Cutter was attracted early by Carter's qualities and threw in with him in 1975 before most people knew his name. A Rhodes Scholar from Harvard, with advanced degrees from both Princeton and Oxford, Cutter had worked in private industry and a Washington think tank, managed a successful Senate campaign in Illinois and run (unsuccessfully) for the legislature in Virginia himself before he signed on as a deputy to Watson on the transition team. "Carter was somebody I felt completely congenial with," he said. "I liked the idea of a Southern President. . . . And also, it seemed to me that I had spent ten years developing exactly the kind of skills that I was going to want to use in government."

By comparison with Rubenstein's and Cutter's carefully plotted assault on their White House jobs, Kitty Schirmer's ascent was almost artless. The specialist on energy issues on Eizenstat's staff, Schirmer, a blonde who seems younger than 31, disconcerted tough oil men who had trouble dealing with somebody who looked so much like their debutante daughters.

A product of New Canaan, Connecticut, a highly Republican suburb of New York City where, she said, "the teachers were all Democrats," Schirmer was recruited for the civil-rights movement by an activist minister in her family's Presbyterian church, and led into the anti-Vietnam teach-ins by her friends at Wellesley College.

She came to Washington after graduation and found a job, by chance, in the newly opened Environmental Protection Agency. Starting as a glorified secretary in the office of EPA Director William Ruckelshaus, Schirmer acquired increasing authority in the fledgling agency by the simple device of volunteering for any project that no one else on the Ruckelshaus staff wanted or had time to handle. "There were so few people available to do so much," she said, "that they were willing to give a very green twenty-one-year-old enough authority to go off to the OMB [Office of Management and Budget] meetings and represent the agency. It was real on-the-job training."

When EPA began to slow down and toxic substances lost their charm, Schirmer moved to Capitol Hill, working for the late Democratic Senator from Michigan Philip A. Hart. "And that was really my introduction to energy," she said. "The Energy Policy Conservation Act of 1975 was the hot ticket on the agenda. Hart was a conferee on that bill at the time that he was ill, and he was kind of critical, because there was a very even division on many issues among the Senate conferees. So we ran a system where I was his surrogate in those meetings, and would call him on what was going on, and I really became much more deeply involved in the process than a staff person ordinarily would have."

In that fashion, the international-law major from Wellesley became a sort of energy expert—at least enough of one that when Eizenstat began calling around looking for help on the Carter campaign's issues staff, several people suggested Schirmer for the energy spot. "I had not been a strong Carter partisan during the primaries," she confessed, "but it was Hart who gave me the push to go. He said these things come around only once every four years, and you ought to take the opportunity."

The step, from the campaign to the White House, was for her, too, a short one. And so it was for Timothy G. Smith, 32. Smith was not quite born in the White House, but the next thing to it. His father, the late Merriman Smith, was for many years the White House correspondent for United Press International, the gravel-voiced, mustachioed, much-loved man who traditionally closed the presidential press conference with the shout, "Thank you, Mr. President." "I was talking politics when I was nine or ten years old," Smith said. "I could easily have gone into journalism, but I always felt that a limitation of journalism was that you were never more than an observer."

Smith came back from Wesleyan University and a year at Oxford to join the Muskie and McGovern campaigns in 1971 and 1972 and then went to the University of Virginia for law school. Working in a Washington law firm, he went to Philadelphia in May 1976 to help the Carter people monitor the conduct of the primary-election voting. He took a leave from August to November to manage Carter's (losing) campaign in Virginia, and went to the White House as deputy appointments secretary, helping

Tim Kraft set up that office. "I wanted to get back to law, so I went over to the Justice Department as special assistant to the head of the antitrust division, and was there for about a year and a half," helping run a review of antitrust procedures. He returned to the law firm, but began spending considerable time in 1979 as legal counsel to the Carter re-election committee, continuing an in-and-out pattern that seems likely to persist throughout his professional life.

The Carter campaign also provided transportation to the White House for some less likely passengers. Greg Schneiders, 33, deputy to Jerry Rafshoon in the Office of Communications until they both resigned in 1979 to prepare for the 1980 campaign, was a Georgetown University student and operator of two Washington, D.C., bars before Carter came along. The agnostic son of a psychologist at Jesuit schools, with three sisters who are nuns, Schneiders met Carter at a 1975 Boston fund raiser for which his brother, Paul Schneiders, was desperately trying to recruit guests. Impressed by what he heard, he began volunteering and was hired to travel with the candidate. "I started January first," he recalled. "We went out to Iowa, and the candidate had a severe cold and a temperature of 103 and was in a bad mood, and I was the only person with him, and I lost my overcoat in the Atlanta airport before we ever got off the ground—you know, an auspicious beginning."

Schneiders proved to have the even temperament it takes to survive the recurrent crises of a campaign, and a detached, sensible view of political strategy that belied his years. His candor came to be valued both by Carter and by reporters covering the emerging contender. Unlike John Sears in the Nixon entourage, Schneiders was not penalized for his popularity with the press, and he wound up his White House tour in good standing with both the press and the President—a rare feat for anyone.

Kit and Evan Dobelle were also Carter coattailers. Now 35, the Dobelles did not meet Carter until January 1976, when he came campaigning in Pittsfield, Massachusetts, where Evan was in his third year as Mayor. They became enthusiasts and began traveling to other states to help Carter. Eventually, Evan joined the group planning the logistics of Carter's New York convention operation, and during convention week Kit assisted in moving the flow of visitors through the Carter suite. After the election, Carter summoned them to Washington and asked Evan to become his chief of protocol and Kit to work with him "as a team." Fifteen months later, Evan was shifted to the job of treasurer of the Democratic National Committee and Kit became the chief of protocol. In 1979, they moved on again—this time with Evan becoming temporary chairman of the Carter re-election committee and Kit becoming chief of staff for First Lady Rosalynn Carter.

What is remarkable about their saga is that through a busy pre-Carter political life, both Evan and Kit Dobelle had been active Republicans. She was the granddaughter and daughter of Republican officials in Hamden, Connecticut, and he had worked on GOP campaigns from San Francisco to Wilmington, Delaware. When they met in Boston in 1966, Evan's first reaction was to suggest to his friend Howard Phillips, the ultra-conservative then heading the Boston Republican Committee, that Kit would be an ideal person to fill a vacant spot on the GOP ticket for register of probate in Suffolk County. Despite their help, she received only 25 percent of the votes against the Democratic incumbent, Louis Musco. Of course, as the Dobelles pointed out, Musco had certain advantages. His campaign cards were in the shape of a football. On one side was the Boston College football schedule. On the other was a picture of Musco with Jackie and Ted Kennedy, probating the will of John F. Kennedy.

The Dobelles said their conversion to Carter and the Democratic Party had no ulterior motive, and certainly not the idea of winding up with a pair of jobs providing a $100,000 income in Washington. "He was just saying what I felt so strongly that I wanted to help," Kit said. "We never considered the consequences—pro or con," Evan added.

Nonetheless, they and many others like them whose most visible qualification was their willingness to work in Carter's long-shot political campaign made their way to power on his coattails. Although the pattern was hardly unique to the Carter White House, it bothered some people that this was the kind of staff Carter assembled. James Fallows, a young man from California and Harvard who joined Carter late in the campaign as chief speechwriter and stayed in that role for the first two years of the Administration, vexed his former colleagues when he wrote in a post-resignation memoir in the *Atlantic Monthly* of June 1979 that "Carter created an administration in which . . . people were more concerned with holding their jobs than with using them." In a devastating anecdote, Fallows quoted an unnamed Georgian as saying to several others on Air Force One, "You know, there really ought to be a place for people like us between the elections, someplace we could rest up and get ready for the next one."

The charge that they were merely passing the time between campaigns or lacked any governmental skills was bitterly resented by those Fallows left behind. David Rubenstein, the Sorensen protégé and Eizenstat deputy, said, "Our people are probably as good as, if not better than, most others, including the Kennedy staff, which I admired and still do." It was true, he conceded, "that many of the senior people here would not have been on another White House staff, if you did a computer survey of the most talented people in the country . . . because they just didn't have national reputations. But that doesn't disparage them. It just indicates that you really can't judge White House staffs by artificial standards that sometimes professors and others like to use."

As Fallows observed in his *Atlantic* article, the characteristic style of the Carter White House staff was captured in Annie Liebowitz's famous *Rolling Stone* photograph of its leading spirits, Powell and Jordan, dressed as Butch Cassidy and the Sundance Kid. It was "the laid-back, Mr. Cool" undergraduate style, not very subtly mocking the pretensions and protocol of official Washington. "Somebody like Hamilton or Jody," said Tim Smith, "is able to assess political situations and courses that the President ought to take in a way that, to me, is refreshingly free from emotion or cant. They believe in him personally, as an honest guy trying to deal in an unorthodox way with some difficult things that need attention. But it's more a problem-solver outlook than a crusade, which makes it more fun."

Halfway through 1979, with Carter staring at polls that showed him trailing Ted Kennedy badly in trial heats for renomination, the atmosphere in the White House changed. Jordan was given full power as chief of staff and swapped the open-necked sport shirts and slacks that had been his standard office wear for conservative pin-striped suits and patterned neckties. Powell gave up his bantering style at press briefings, and everyone down through the ranks was given to understand that discipline was the order of the day.

But even in the more disciplined atmosphere of 1979, few of the people in the nonideological Carter White House were pursuing specific policy goals of their own. Dick Moe, Mondale's man and a veteran of twenty years of Minnesota liberal politics, had a "war trophy" on a shelf in his office. It was a model of an American aircraft carrier with a torpedo in its side, a symbol of success for his White House task force in upholding Carter's veto of a 1978 defense authorization bill which included funds for a nuclear-powered carrier. (In 1979, Carter relented and signed the nuclear-carrier authorization bill, rather than risk another veto fight.)

Such trophies were missing in most other White House offices, because their occupants were not that emotionally involved—now or in their past—in particular causes. Most of them were not marchers in the civil-rights or anti-war protests of the Sixties, and they came to the White House for personal, not ideological, reasons. Rubenstein said he thought "I'd get educated and learn as much as I could about various types of domestic policy. . . . I wasn't ideological in the sense of saying, 'Here are five things that I personally want to get done. . . .' It wasn't that. In fact, there's nobody here who I've met who's like that. . . . Carter set out some goals in his campaign which attracted some of us, and you have a general sense you'd like to accomplish them. . . . But the White House staff tends to attract more pragmatic people—unfortunately, too pragmatic in some cases."

Like their predecessors, the Carter-Mondale people have found the White House a mixture of exhilaration and frustration, of fulfillment and fatigue. "You live by your wits in a job such as this," said Kitty Schirmer. "There is nothing like this environment that I've experienced anywhere in government. . . . Substantively, there's no amount of expertise you can bring to this job that's going to prepare you for more than half the specific issues that you're going to have to deal with in the course of a given week. . . . You can wander from understanding how many bowhead whales should live in the Beaufort Sea and how many could be killed by the natives . . . to a fifteen-minute education on whether the hockey-stick type of intermediate heat exchanger in the Clinch River breeder-reactor is the appropriate one or not. . . . It's as expansive an environment as I've ever encountered."

But it is also a job that requires fourteen-hour days, six days a week, under constant deadline pressure. When one sees David Rubenstein walking up 16th Street at 10:30 P.M., a clean suit in a plastic bag slung over his back, headed to his bachelor apartment after another day at the White House, the glamour of the job is barely visible.

"My own experience has been extremely positive," Greg Schneiders said, "and I suspect that's true for most of the others. But in a learning experience, things are more difficult in many ways than we had anticipated. . . . Pat Caddell [Carter's pollster] said shortly after the inauguration that the occupation is not nearly as much fun as the war. And it's not. It is more tedious, more difficult, and the virtues required tend to be much more of the perseverance variety than the sharp-insight dramatic-action variety. . . . A campaign is itself a very compressed experience, and with a very specific goal and a specific outcome. None of that is true of an administration . . . so that tends to make it less fun."

Nonetheless, it is clear that whatever Carter's political fate, many of the young people who have worked for him will be coming back for more. Evan Dobelle said he would stay with Carter as long as Carter wanted him, but "then I'll go out . . . and probably run for office." Bo Cutter, who also plans ahead, said, "I would love a chance to be the chief of staff of the White House someday."

"Personally," said Greg Schneiders, "I see this as preparation for whatever else I do, and since I'm interested in politics and in public policy, I expect there's a reasonable chance that I'll try to find something else to do in this area after this Administration."

"I may leave it for a while," said Kitty Schirmer, "or at least, I may leave Washington and do a different kind of government. . . . State government is of some interest to me. Local government. I can see at some point in my career deciding that it would be fun to be mayor of a town like Bridgeport, Connecticut, or, I don't know, Oshkosh, Wisconsin. . . . I can also see working in the private sector for a time, in corporate planning. . . . But I will have a continuing involvement in government."

"I'll probably stay in Washington," Tim Smith said, "and I'll be interested in who is President after Carter. "I really wouldn't be able to restrain myself." And not surprisingly, David Rubenstein, while saying he will need "a decompression chamber" after the marathon effort in his current job, also was sure he would be back for another tour. "When you get here and you see how much fun it can be working full time, dealing every day with things that are on the front page of the papers and on the evening news, that everybody's talking about around town, you begin to say, 'There's no way that I can ever go back to Shirkieville.' "

What is true of the Carterites is even more true of the Mondale-related staff members, both because of their longer-standing commitment to government and politics and because of their understandable hope that Mondale's role (and theirs) may increase in the years ahead.

Dick Moe said he thought Mondale's staff was "more traditional" than Carter's, "and while we've been with Mondale a long time, eight or ten years down the road, I can imagine that some of us, at least, will be back here in some other context, doing something."

"My interest in public affairs and in government and in politics is certainly going to dominate the rest of my life," Jim Johnson agreed. Bert Carp said the salaries offered by private business—especially to lawyers like himself—mean that "most people like me are going to be lost to government by the time we reach age forty." But in the next breath, he said that as for himself, "I'll probably stay in government as long as I can. I love it. And it's all I've ever done."

On the assumption that more than a few of the Carter-Mondale staff members will be recycled into politics and government later in this century, the interesting question is what ideas and impressions they will carry with them because of their current experience in and around the White House. Any answer must be provisional, because, at the time they were interviewed for this book, that experience was incomplete. But several themes emerge strongly from their comments.

One is the now-familiar view—expressed by White House alumni of both parties from Kennedy's time onward—of the fundamental importance of understanding the constraints on the capacity of the United States as a nation and on its government.

"We've grown up, all of us," Dick Moe said, "in an environment where we were taught that in America anything's possible, that with American technology and ingenuity and determination, any problem can be solved. There's still a desire to believe that, but it simply isn't being candid with ourselves."

It was particularly striking to hear these constraints emphasized by people like Moe who had absorbed the liberal promises of the New Frontier and the Great Society. In a series of speeches in 1979, Stuart Eizenstat, who was part of that same tradition, argued that "we live in a time of raw realities, because for the first time we are beginning to be cognizant that there are finite limits to our own natural and budgetary resources." Instead of the optimistic belief that the economic pie will grow sufficiently to afford generous social policies without serious self-sacrifice, he said, there is a "fear of the future to which social progress has difficulty accommodating.

"I first worked in the White House under President Johnson," Eizenstat said. "He launched the Great Society in 1965 with an inflation rate of 1.9 percent and a budget deficit of about $1.6 billion. I ask whether the Great Society would have been launched with a $50-billion deficit and inflation averaging 8 percent for the three years before we took office—which is what we inherited."

Jim Johnson stressed that in his view the policies of the past were not failures. "If you look at the sweep of what's happened from the time I went to college in 1961 to today, in terms of arms control, détente, civil rights, civil liberties, poverty, housing, education, a whole range of issues, I think there's cause for fairly substantial optimism. But," he said, "I don't think there is by any means the same confidence in government, or the same fascination with government, or the same assumption that all we need to do is create a program and a problem will be solved. . . . I don't have any illusion that the federal government is the answer, and I think most of the people I've grown up with see it as less of an answer today than it was in their earlier years."

"I continue to believe in programmatic approaches to a lot of domestic problems," said his colleague Bert Carp, "but I have come to appreciate the extent to which trying to do that runs afoul of the massive dead hand of bureaucracy. . . . I wish I believed that the same energy and talent would be brought to bear on the job-training program or day-care program as are brought to bear in making and marketing the Xerox machine. I just think the federal bureaucracy is a kind of lazy place. I think they are demoralized, and we may be partly responsible for that. . . . Liberals and the people who administer their programs have become terribly conservative. . . . We have a terrible time generating any excitement. Everybody just wants to keep doing what they've been doing."

Kitty Schirmer, who began her governmental career as an environmental regulator, said, "My belief in the government's ability to solve the problem via regulation has changed dramatically in the last couple of years. I understand the nobility of the motives . . . but the regulatory process assumes by its very nature that everything out there in the country is the same, and that the same set of standards ought to apply. And in fact, that's not the case. . . . I'm much more cautious about mandatory prohibitions or regulations than I once was. . . . Government has enormous impact on society . . . and I'm not sure we think it through all that well."

The second major theme that came through in their comments was the observation that leadership of any sort had been made far more difficult by both the institutional and intellectual fragmentation that occurred during the 1960s and '70s. Jody Powell suggested that it may be the transition from one generation to the next that is at the root of that problem.

"It seems to me, at least hypothetically," he said, "that the ending of the domination of American politics by the World War II–Great Depression people—those who were old enough to remember and be shaped by those two events—may be part of it. Those of us who are younger, while we will have certain shared experiences with some of our colleagues, will lack the degree of common experience that almost all our predecessors had in the Depression and the war."

Whether or not that theory is valid, Powell said, "the whole question of fragmentation, of the inability to reach consensus on important issues, the pushing and pulling of regional and economic interests, tends to make the making of any policy very difficult."

Individual staff members focused on separate pieces of the puzzle. David Rubenstein, on Congress: "I thought this [the White House] was a good place to get something done, but that was before I got here and realized all the power is in Congress. When I was [working] in Congress, it seemed like all the power was here, but it's clearly up there. . . . The most frustrating thing to us . . . is you propose stuff to Congress and they just change it all around; the interest groups get to work up there and they just wear it down. We are now at the point where we will do whatever we can to get something done without having to send legislation to Congress, and Congress tells us, 'Don't send legislation to us, because we aren't going to be able to solve the problem.' "

Kitty Schirmer, on division and cynicism in public opinion: "I'm not sure that our country responds all that well to problems that you can't see, and I'm not sure people like dealing with them. In the energy area, one can certainly think of specific instances where, had our performance been better, one or another preferable result might have come about. But

I'm not sure that would have made an enormous difference in the overall readiness of the United States as a social and political entity to deal with the energy problem. I don't think behavioral changes as fundamental as those which we're basically engaged with in the energy issue can be hurried . . . especially when there is this continued belief, which distresses me so, that the institutions and the problems are so big and so unpleasant that there's really nothing that I, as an individual, can do about it."

Jim Johnson, on the exhaustion of policy ideas: "I wouldn't shy away from calling it an intellectual failure . . . although part of it relates to what I think is, in fact, a much greater complexity of issues. . . . The fragmentation and the number of new complexities in dealing with energy in the last five years is staggering. But it's not just energy. . . . Program by program, if you look at hunger, if you look at housing, or transportation, or jobs, or whatever it is, it seems as though we are between generations of ideas. Where we had ideas, we tried them, and then we altered them, thinking that we had learned some things, and now in a lot of areas we have been through the second generation of failure and are trying to figure out what to do next. . . . The breaking of that analytical link in a lot of social and economic and energy areas is devastating politically. If you can't describe how to get from here to there, even if you can get everybody to agree where you want to go, it's awfully hard to get anybody to follow."

Bert Carp, on the breakdown of political structures: "I think that the increasing weakness of the political parties is a very damaging thing, because it weakens the whole process of coalition building and it removes a lot of political roots to reality. . . . We're losing the kind of grass-roots representativeness that I think the party gave. . . . And so you've got this kind of single-interest domination of the legislative process which I think is very harmful. I really believe in the back room, as long as it is a representative back room, because I think that's where you work out the compromises and accommodations that can make government work. And I think we're losing that back-room kind of accountability mechanism."

David Rubenstein, again, on the bureaucracy: "You have to be a very determined person really to get things done through the bureaucracy; it's almost as bad as dealing with Congress. I think presidents—this President as well—have had very little time to deal with their own branch of government. . . . The business of running the government is left to subordinates, and administering the laws doesn't take much of a President's time. It's very unusual. A corporate executive will spend a lot of his time running the corporation. A President spends very little of his time running the government."

As is his role and his custom, Stuart Eizenstat pulled these scattered observations about the fragmentation of intellectual and political authority into a coherent analysis, which emphasized six key points. In slight paraphrase, they were:

First, there is a basic conflict between the public's desire for greater services—especially in the areas of health, education and the quality of the physical and social environment—and its resistance to government spending and regulation.

Second, the task of reconciling these conflicts is impeded by the lack of tested doctrine to solve the policy riddles embodied in such problems as energy shortages and "stagflation."

Third, the struggle for scarce resources has increased the tensions between sections and regions in America, putting added strains on the political system.

Fourth, the increasingly well-organized economic interest groups have mobilized strong forces in Congress and the bureaucracy to defend or, if possible, expand their claims on the federal budget.

Fifth, Congress itself has seen a fragmentation of its institutional authority as power has been dispersed into hundreds of small subcommittees, each of which is susceptible to interest-group pressures from its own clientele.

And sixth, the influence of party loyalty has been so diminished that appeals by presidents or congressional leaders based on that allegiance are of negligible impact.

The result, Eizenstat said, and most of his colleagues agreed, is that the task of presidential leadership has become far more difficult than it was in the past.

Having wallowed in and struggled with this formless political morass, the Carter-Mondale staffers have obviously been forced to think about what would give it shape and coherence; what would enable a President to lead.

"Every day that I'm here," Stuart Eizenstat said, "makes me recognize that the most efficient type of democracy is a parliamentary system with a fairly stable set of parties, as in Great Britain. You can get your programs through, and if you can't, you get another government." But Eizenstat said he was not sure that a parliamentary democracy would "necessarily work in a country this diverse," and had put the idea aside as impractical. What he did hope, he said, was that "the post-Watergate antipathy toward the presidency" would dissipate to the point that presidents could regain some of the discretionary authority they lost in the late Seventies. "The discretionary authority of the President has just markedly diminished as a result of the Watergate experience," he said, "and I think the pendulum has swung way over in the wrong direction. Congress has added something like fifty legislative vetoes [over executive-agency regulations and decisions] in the last four or five years. They let the President's wage-and-price control authority expire. They threatened last year to take away his authority to impose import quotas. They are threatening this year to take away his authority to recommend a gas-rationing plan. Today, the President does not have sufficient authority to act. I think he ought to have authority to order wage and price controls. I think there ought to be a certain limited number of high-priority energy projects of critical national importance where the President would have authority delegated to supersede local and state requirements and even the regulations of his own federal establishment."

For the most part, Eizenstat's colleagues rejected basic structural changes and were more skeptical about the issue of discretionary authority. "I wouldn't touch the structure of government," Dick Moe said. "I think that there is a genius in the constitutional balance of powers that, for all of its frustrations, is the best safeguard we could possibly have against abuse of power. . . . it shouldn't be easy to do profound things quickly—and believe me, they don't come easily."

Where Moe and Eizenstat and several others agreed was that there might be less "parochialism" in Congress, less interest-group influence, if public financing of campaigns were available to its members. They also joined many members of Congress in the belief that the proliferation of subcommittees, while spreading power, had impeded action and increased the opportunities for special-interest influence.

Others suggested tinkering within the executive branch. Tim Smith argued, "There's probably got to be . . . more centralized control of the executive branch in the White House. . . . Obviously, the Haldeman stigma has hurt the prospects for that, and I'm aware of the President's wanting Cabinet government and decentralized decision making. . . . But there are so many interagency disputes, you need a referee, and I think the referee has to be a political person, not just a career person from OMB [Office of Management and Budget]." Evan Dobelle said he thought "the Vice President ought to run the Cabinet, keeping the programs together" on behalf of a President too busy to play that role.

But these were minor notes. The major, and oft-reiterated, theme was that presidential leadership in a time of political fragmentation must rest largely on the process of communication.

It was not lost on any of the Carter-Mondale staff members that this has been an area where Carter himself has been judged deficient by many outside critics. Jody Powell said, "I try not to be overly defensive about those who say, 'If the President just had a better speechwriter, or if he was just a better orator, or if he just screamed and shouted at people, like Lyndon, or if he fucked 'em in the ass, like Nixon, that it would make a difference.' There may be something to all of that. But if I thought that was it, I'd have said long ago, 'Mr. President, all we need to do is get someone in here and you can take speech lessons, and we'll keep hiring and firing speechwriters until we find one that's got what you need. If you don't want to scream and shout and curse at members of Congress, we can find somebody who can do it for you, and we can grant and withhold favors and money with the best of them.' But, you know, I don't know what needs to be done. Maybe it would just help if we started by explaining to the country what it is that's gone wrong."

A few weeks after Powell made those comments in a 1979 interview for this book, the President broke off from his normal routine, closeted himself for ten days with advisers at Camp David, and then made a national television address citing the energy impasse as an example of the breakdown in the nation's capacity to extract needed policy decisions from its fragmented political system.

The speech itself was well received, but the shake-up of the Carter Cabinet and staff which followed it (leading to the centralization of authority, which some of those already quoted had said was necessary) appeared to have confused the country as much as, if not more than, it steadied it.

There were suggestions from some of the Carterites that Carter's move came too late. Bo Cutter, who said that from his perspective as a budget builder for Carter, "the executive is precariously weak," argued that the only way to reverse the steady erosion of authority was "an immense exercise of will by a President from the beginning of his term.

"I think it would be extremely useful if a President began a term by saying to the people that 'I'm going to have four or five chats with you over the course of the next year . . . on my conception of power and how I'm going to use it in particular situations.' I'd try to explain, for example, that in the budget process the President is really the only person who can say that if you want restraint, you have to suffer the unpleasantness of restraining *particular* programs. . . . I'd talk about the use of the veto power, and I'd argue that its employment is not a sign that the system isn't working but a necessary tactic to assure that there will be a serious negotiation between the President and Congress on items where they disagree. . . . I have a feeling that it's like training a colt, which I do sometimes. If the President takes his knocks in the first year, he doesn't have to take them the next three years. But that will take a sustained exercise of will."

As Cutter well realized, such an approach would also bring inevitable charges that the President was trying to return to the days of Lyndon Johnson and Richard Nixon and inviting the calamitous consequences for the political system that their presidencies involved.

If such an approach is necessary to overcome the fragmentation of the post-Vietnam and post-Watergate political world, Jimmy Carter is certainly not the President to apply it. For the fact of the matter is that Carter was both a product and a victim of that political fragmentation—a point that Powell and Jordan, his two closest aides, well understood. "He could never have been nominated," Powell said, "unless the Democratic Party was as fragmented as it is. He was certainly not the insiders' candidate."

"If we hadn't had this fragmentation," Jordan agreed, "it wouldn't have been possible for Jimmy Carter to be elected President. I realize that."

And because he did, Carter's chief of staff was less critical than many —indeed, he was really full of praise—for the "opening up" of the system which had made so many people participants in national policy making and therefore rendered the President's job that much more difficult.

"It's amazing," Jordan said, "the change that's been wrought after the Sixties by the civil-rights movement. And that gave hope to other groups, like the anti-war movement, like the feminist movement, like the environmental movement. And there's a much keener sense today that a group of people can band together and effect a change in our country. . . . It's resulted in the fragmentation of our political system which makes the job of a mayor or governor or a President more difficult. But you can't argue with the basic premise or thrust of more people sharing in the power.

"I could make a splendid argument against fragmentation," he went on, "and for more discipline in the Congress and the party, but then basically you're arguing that real political power should be in the hands of the few instead of the many. I could make a practical argument that it would be a lot better if we had ten big-city Democratic mayors who could control their congressional delegations and deliver their votes to the President in the primaries and the general election. But that's a pragmatic argument. You can't make that on a moral basis. It would ignore the realities of life in this country today, try to turn the clock back and say that all these changes engendered to a large extent by the civil-rights movement had been bad for the country—when they've been good."

At the same time, Jordan said, what he has seen from the White House of the ability of mobilized groups, each pursuing its own legitimate interest, to frustrate the nation's ability to come to grips with complex problems like energy, convinced him "we can't keep on twenty or thirty more years like we have the last five or ten. While one of the great strengths of our country is our diversity, it can also be our great vulnerability, unless there's a sense of pulling together and focusing on the common good."

In the kind of period all of them perceived this to be, leadership—at least from the White House—had to take on a different character. Greg Schneiders said this as clearly as anyone.

"The nature of presidential power has changed drastically over the years," he said. "It's gone from being, in the beginning, principally institutional power, as defined by the Constitution, to being more a coalition of political power of the type that Roosevelt wielded, to what is now more the power of communication. Because of what has happened to the political parties over the years, and to the special-interest groups, and the resulting fragmentation, it is now more true than ever that the President can get things done only when he can develop the public consensus for action, and when he cannot, he will fail."

Because they put such heavy emphasis on the power to communicate as the *sine qua non* of successful leadership, the Carterites were sensitive to the charge that their own leader was seriously lacking in that regard. And they suggested that that particular ability should be given great weight in the choice of a President.

In a 1979 interview, Jack Watson said, "I think more so than ever before, the country needs people who have the capacity to articulate powerfully what are the essential problems and basic choices being faced. It is not enough to be competent as a problem solver, as an analyst. It is not even enough to be competent as a political negotiator, for example, between the executive branch and Capitol Hill. . . . You can have all of those things, and have them in abundance, and if you lack the ability to capture the essence of what is going on, in language that the people around the country can relate to and understand, you will not be successful. In some respects, the fragmentation of our processes requires this ability even more than it was required before."

Reiterating the point for emphasis, Watson said, "I'm suggesting that the glue that will hold us together, given the fragmentation that has occurred, is the ability to reach around and through the fragmented pieces to the body politic at large, and draw your strength and your support from them. . . . It is an absolute necessity for the political leader of our time and in the Eighties to understand how those messages can be conveyed."

Then, in what I took to be a very lightly disguised discussion of President Carter, Watson said, "Let's hypothesize a President who's very competent, who is a man of integrity, who is seeking at every turn of choice to make what he thinks are the right decisions. . . . Let's include in the hypothesis that he is a man who works very hard, who applies himself relentlessly to his task . . . who tries his best with very formidable personal powers of intelligence and analytical ability to gather facts, to assimilate facts and to make decisions. Let's assume all that. Let's assume that the man also has a reasonable measure of ability to deal in the governmental process, to do the political negotiating—not the best that the mind can imagine, but good skills, and skills that are improving. And finally, let's hypothesize that that man, with all those assets, for whatever set of reasons, is not finding it possible most of the time to do this articulation, to strike these chords in the public.

"I would say that single factor on a scale could balance out all the rest, and even tip it against his success."

Watson said that he recognized there was a danger of demagoguery in a man as gifted in communication as he said the presidents of the Eighties would have to be to succeed. "If the people make some mistakes, as we will from time to time, then we will elect some demagogues," he said. "Someone who is in a position of political leadership, with access to the media, and who is not constrained by high moral and ethical standards, can abuse that power."

In a separate interview, which served as an unplanned counterpoint to Watson's observation, Carter campaign aide Evan Dobelle said he thought the President's "premeditated" purpose was to wean the country away from the kind of leadership Watson was describing. The way he put it, Carter's purpose was "to try to get this country mature enough that people realize they're going to have to make decisions on their own and not listen to political leaders, because political leaders, under this Constitution, simply don't have the capacity to handle it all."

He said he learned of Carter's anachronistic view of the rhetorical aspect of leadership during the 1976 Florida primary. "I saw Jimmy Carter stand on a chair in shirt sleeves," Dobelle said, "and literally get an audience almost hysterical with an impassioned speech on senior citizens and the elderly. And when he left—I was standing by the car—I said, 'Governor, that was one of the greatest speeches I've ever heard from anybody.' And he said, 'No, it wasn't. I gave them expectations I can never match.' "

Whether anyone can match those expectations was the question troubling all the presidents' men, from Kennedy's heirs to Carter's, as the new decade began. Whatever their differences—and there were many—they shared the clear knowledge that the upheavals of the past twenty years, which they had witnessed at close range, had cut them and their contemporaries off from the comfortable certainties of the past. The Sixties had begun with the enthronement, beyond effective challenge, of what Godfrey Hodgson, in his book *America in Our Time,* called the consensus of "conservative liberalism."

"The ideology of the liberal consensus," as he called it, was inscribed in both the Democratic platform of 1960 and the 1961 Rockefeller Brothers Fund report called *Prospect for America.* The twin tenets of that consensus were the restraint of Communism abroad and the government-guided expansion and distribution of prosperity at home. It was, at its heart, a profoundly optimistic view of the world, rooted in the understandable euphoria of the generation which had climbed out of the Great Depression and defeated fascism and the dictators in World War II.

And then, as Hodgson wrote, a series of events occurred that "tore that consensus to shreds." The riots in the cities in the mid-1960s mocked the pretensions of welfare-state policies to deal with America's social problems. Vietnam showed the costs and the limitations of the containment policy. Inflation and the energy crisis undermined the belief that economic growth was guaranteed. "All these disappointments," Hodgson wrote, "combined to lay an impossible burden on the institution on which the consensus had counted to carry out that program, and to which everyone turned to put things right when it became apparent they were going wrong: the presidency."

Under the strain, the presidency cracked, and has gone through a period—from Kennedy through Carter—unparalleled in American history. After such a time, it was no wonder that the young people who had been drawn into politics by those five presidents were reeling a bit—and searching for their intellectual, programmatic and political bearings.

They—like hundreds of others their age—fell back and began to regroup in patterns that were unlike those of the previous political era. It is those groupings—or networks—to which we turn next.

NETWORKS

In politics men combine for great undertakings, and the use they make of the principle of association in important affairs practically teaches them that it is their interest to help one another in those of less moment. A political association draws a number of individuals at the same time out of their own circle; however they may naturally be kept asunder by age, mind, and fortune, it places them nearer together and brings them into contact. Once met, they can always meet again.

—*Alexis de Tocqueville,* Democracy in America

No lasting or potent reform is ever possible except as men can be roused from their disaffection and indifference by the prospect of a world more inviting than that in which they now apathetically reside. Our deepest need is not to propose specific reforms, but rather to create an intellectual and cultural atmosphere in which it is possible for men to attempt affirmation without undue fear that valid constructions will collapse through neglect, ridicule or their own inherent errors.

—*Kenneth Keniston*

The people we have met in the last three chapters are linked to each other in five circles by their ties to the five presidents who have occupied the White House in the past twenty years. Each of these circles forms a self-conscious network, based on a set of shared experiences, triumphs, tragedies and misadventures, especially vivid to those who were there. If past experience is any guide, those shared experiences in the early political lives of these young people will remain a strong bond among them as long as they are active. To one another, and to others outside their circle, they will always be, in a certain sense, "Kennedy people," or "Nixon people," or "Carter people."

But these are only a few of the networks that give structure and shape to the next generation in American politics. As the interviewing for this book developed, it became increasingly clear that there were many such networks which had been forged by the shared experiences of the Sixties and Seventies. When talking with a community organizer in Houston, for example, I would be told that I must by all means become acquainted with an organizer in Little Rock, with whom the first man had marched in Mississippi and demonstrated at the Pentagon.

When interviewing the director of one of the many "New Right" organizations, I was invited to sit in on one of the biweekly luncheons where he and his counterparts in similar groups—some of them with personal links going back almost twenty years to the founding of Young Americans for Freedom—meet to exchange ideas and gossip. A woman official in Minnesota, describing the "old girl network" in her state, tipped me off to the existence of a similar network in Washington, D.C., of which I had been unaware. A Mexican-American aide at the White House insisted that I talk to a particular parish priest in East Los Angeles, and he was right. A friend at a black think tank told me, again correctly, that almost all the up-and-coming black leaders of the country would be in Washington the weekend of the annual Congressional Black Caucus dinner.

The clustering of like-minded people is nothing new in American society. De Tocqueville noted early in the 19th century, in his classic *Democracy in America,* that "In no country in the world has the principle of association been more successfully used or applied to a greater multitude of objects than in America. Besides the permanent associations which are established by law . . . a vast number of others are formed and maintained by the agency of private individuals."

But the networks in which the coming generation of America's political leaders are involved are of a somewhat different character than those of their parents' and grandparents' generations. Many of those older networks were inherited; membership was acquired by being born in a certain place at a certain time, of a certain family, religion, race or political affiliation. They were handed down from generation to generation and thus served to stabilize the larger society.

Some of these traditional networks still play an important part in shaping the emerging political leaders. As was noted in the last chapter, the consciousness of being Southerners has been a vital force in forming the attitudes of many of Jimmy Carter's young aides. And as will be seen in later chapters, important networks have been formed by black and Hispanic leaders and by organizers of particular neighborhoods and communities.

But along with these vertical, or inherited, networks, there are networks of a different character—horizontal networks—shared by people who were brought together, often from widely dispersed locations and diverse backgrounds, by a particular historical crisis or cause. They may be activists in the women's movement, public-interest advocates, labor lobbyists or corporate public-affairs officers. But they tend to be people of a particular age who were drawn together by a particular challenge which, for the moment at least, was uppermost in their lives. The associations developed in that kind of struggle tend to be very strong, and to endure as common bonds for many years.

Where the crisis is large enough and the movement involves enough people, such an experience can unite a whole generation. Such was the case with the Depression and World War II. The leaders of the past quarter-century have characteristically been men who knew, as youths, the deprivation of the Depression, fought in World War II, came back to complete their education on the G.I. Bill and then pursued their political careers in the same pattern of onward-and-upward mobility that was established before they were 25. Since that experience was next to universal for young men of their age, it was the vital link in the broad consensus of that generation's view of the world.

The horizontal networks of this next generation are smaller and less universally shared. They are, in many respects, competing networks. They are networks of struggle, but not necessarily of triumph. But for those very reasons, the links among those network members may be even stronger than was the case with the wider and looser network of the Depression and World War II.

These new networks are already important. Hugh Heclo, the Harvard political scientist, said in his essay in the 1978 American Enterprise Institute book *The New American Political System* that the Carter Administration's political appointees came largely from what he called "issue networks of policy activists, environmentalists, consumerists, arms controllers and the rest." I believe that these networks and their rivals will become increasingly important in the Eighties and Nineties as their members compete not just for appointive positions, but for the top elective jobs as well.

In the next seven chapters, I have tried to look inside seven of the networks that I would guess will be of growing influence in the next two decades. They are dealt with separately, in an effort to focus on the special characteristics of each of them. But in real-world politics, of course, individuals are often tied into more than one network. It is possible, as we will see, to be both an important Hispanic leader and a prominent feminist, as Vilma Martínez is. A John Lewis has strong ties both to other blacks and to others working in community organizing. Raymond Momboisse runs a public-interest law firm, but he could also be considered a part of the neoconservative network.

To give an example of how those networks can intersect for one individual, consider the case of Jim Johnson, the Mondale aide we met in the last chapter.

He came to Washington from the University of Minnesota in 1965 as an officer of the National Student Association (NSA), where he was thrown in with the civil-rights activists of both races and with those who, two years later, would lead the Dump Lyndon Johnson campaign. Jim Johnson got his first briefing on that campaign from the ubiquitous Allard Lowenstein, then a Congressman from New York, in, of all places, Dar es Salaam, where he was an exchange student. Some friends, who were Peace Corps volunteers as well as alumni of NSA and the civil-rights movement, were meeting with the peripatetic Lowenstein. When Johnson returned to the United States, he joined a number of other young people we will meet in various parts of this book on the staff of the Kerner Commission, writing a report on the urban riots. From there, it was into the Eugene McCarthy campaign, which, for many of the activists, already had the air of a college reunion. The young woman who gave Johnson his orders when he was an advance man for McCarthy in the Oregon primary turned up ten years later as the manager of the successful New Jersey

Senate campaign of basketball star Bill Bradley, who, in turn, is one of the top early-book favorites for the Democratic presidential nomination in . . . perhaps 1992? Is there a chance that before they are 50, Jim Johnson and his National Student Association–Mississippi civil rights–Dump Johnson–Gene McCarthy–Kerner Commission–Carter-Mondale buddies will all join hands again in Bill Bradley's Cabinet?

Don't bet against it. But don't bet on it, either, because there are other, competing networks with equally plausible chances of coming to power.

Let us look at some of them.

5 · Organizers

ONE OF THE BASIC FACTS about America is the presence in our midst of a significant cadre of still-young men and women with up to twenty years' experience in the difficult and exacting work of organizing.

The task of the organizer is to convert the inert, latent power of large groups of people into an effective political force. The current generation of organizers first emerged in the national consciousness in the early Sixties, when white college students began going to the South in support of the black lunch-counter sit-ins and working in the West to help Cesar Chavez mobilize the Chicano farm workers. (Although they have been linked to the struggles of both the Hispanics and the blacks, the white organizers are distinctly different in background and are dealt with separately, for that reason, in this chapter.) Later, and in larger numbers, they mobilized on the campuses to oppose the war in Vietnam. Their techniques were borrowed in the Seventies by organizers working with different constituencies, including the handicapped and the homosexuals, and they have, indeed, been copied by political opponents on the Right, some of whom will be introduced in the next chapter.

In their more militant phase, some of the organizers became the fist-waving radicals of Students for a Democratic Society (SDS) and the obscenity-shouting Free Speech Movement. Frustrated by the Nixon Administration and frightened, in many cases, by the violence their own rhetoric sometimes unleashed, the organizers moved off campus in the early Seventies, hoping to build a more solid base in blue-collar communities, particularly in the older cities. They were on the scene when those same communities, responding to the independent resurgence of ethnic consciousness and identity, began to assert their claims against City Hall. Today, the marchers, demonstrators and organizers of the 1960s and '70s are scattered from agency headquarters and congressional offices in Washington to shabby walk-ups in San Francisco's South of Market district. But they remain in touch with each other, linked by a set of shared experiences and a dimly perceived but never-realized dream of a more open, responsive and just society.

Tim Sampson, 45, a bald, white-bearded organizer with the California Citizens Action League (CAL), one of the new community-based "economic-justice" groups, noted the contrast between today's situation and the time "when we started in the Sixties and few of us had any sense at all of continuity from the past. There was really very little of the organizing that had gone on in the Forties or Fifties that was accessible to us as a tradition. We didn't have teachers; for the most part, we had to invent it ourselves. But now, in the 1980s, we have had almost twenty years' unbroken experience with people organizing a variety of efforts. As young people come into this kind of work now, they have access to the developing technology and experience that we've had in organizing. . . . We should be very much ahead of the game."

Whether that proves to be the case, however, depends not only on the organizing skills of these young men and women, which are abundant, but on their reading of American society and psychology, which is more suspect. Sam Brown, one of the most successful organizers of his generation, said in 1979 that their success had been limited because "we've never tapped the American dream. We've focused on the grievances, but we've never drawn a picture of what the future would be like if those grievances were addressed." And for that reason, among others, the organizers have never achieved their potential.

It is not quite true that, as Sampson said, the organizers of the 1960s and '70s "did not have teachers." The tradition of mobilizing—or trying to mobilize—the common people against the big banks and railroads and corporations is an old one in American politics. At the end of the 19th century, the Populist movement sprang up around the country, with leaders like William Jennings Bryan and Ignatius Donnelly and "Pitchfork Ben" Tillman and "Sockless Jerry" Simpson, arguing for public ownership of utilities, free coinage of silver, the eight-hour workday and a host of political reforms. Mary Elizabeth Lease, a Kansas Populist, sounded a cry that echoed down the years when she told the farmers they should "raise less corn and more hell."

But while elements of the Populist platform were adopted and co-opted by other parties, its success as a distinctive movement was brief and limited. And even when, forty years later, the Great Depression created a climate for an overtly anti-capitalist political movement, the spiritual heirs of the Populists—people like Upton Sinclair—were no more successful. Under Franklin Roosevelt's patronage, union organizers did bring the trade-union movement into existence in the Thirties. But the outbreak of World War II put a quietus on home-front organizing efforts —and the postwar wave of reaction, especially the "Communist-hunting" forays of Republican Senator Joseph R. McCarthy of Wisconsin, had the effect of driving many of the organizers underground.

Thus, there had been a break of about twenty years—a full generation—when Sampson and his contemporaries began to revive the organizing tradition. And they had only one place to look for guidance, to a man named Saul Alinsky, who, in a real sense, "wrote the book" for this new generation of organizers.

Both Sampson and his social-worker father had studied at the University of Chicago, where Alinsky had taught, and the activist-sociologist was a friend of their family. Lee Webb, one of the early SDS leaders who has remained a focus for the organizers' network, recalled that when he went to Chicago in the early 1960s to begin SDS' first venture in community organizing, Ralph Hellstein of the Packinghouse Workers gave him a copy of Alinsky's *Reveille for Radicals* as a guide.

In that book and the later *Rules for Radicals*, the brilliant, abrasive criminologist-turned-community-organizer laid down the doctrine that, in various forms, provides the unifying theme of most of today's organizers. As a student, Alinsky had become fascinated by the methods which John L. Lewis used in the early years of the CIO to "organize the unorganized" in unskilled factory jobs.

In the late 1930s, Alinsky and a few friends used the same techniques to organize the Back of the Yards Council in Chicago, in a largely Polish-American neighborhood of angry, exploited stockyard workers and their families. Alinsky combined a radical political philosophy of redistribution of power and wealth with a sociologist's sensitivity to the underlying structure of the community. He forged what he called a "people's organization," which for years fought both City Hall and the employers. Later, he duplicated its pattern in a black community, Woodlawn, on Chicago's South Side and in a network of other cities around the country that was still expanding at the time of his death in 1972.

Preaching that "power and organization are one and the same," he asserted that "the ghetto or slum is not a disorganized community." The first task of the organizer, he said, is to identify that underlying structure of unions, lodges, clubs and churches. The second task is to find those "indigenous leaders [who] are in a very true sense the real representatives of the people of the community" and who are, more often than not, "completely unknown outside the community."

Because those indigenous leaders rarely have a complete set of skills and because most of them have been molded by the very forces that have kept their communities in thrall, Alinsky insisted that there was also a critical need for outside organizers to "analyze, attack and disrupt the prevailing power pattern.

"The organizer dedicated to changing the life of a particular community," he wrote, "must search out controversy and issues, rather than avoid them," and then "provide a channel into which the people can angrily pour their frustrations."

Alinsky's heirs are as diverse—and quarrelsome—as Freud's. But if one were to risk a generalization, their common history is one of a search for that elusive mix of issues, rhetoric and organization which might provide the leverage to move America toward that vision of a "democracy of individual participation" which was outlined in 1962 in the SDS Port Huron Statement as the manifesto for "this generation, bred in at least modest comfort, housed now in universities, looking uncomfortably to the world we inherit." That search had left them, by the end of the 1970s, fragmented and, in many cases, frustrated. The problems of war, racism and poverty proved far more intractable than they had supposed—and by the end of the last decade, many of them had turned back to the original Alinsky version of grass-roots organizing at the community level. And that is where we find them today.

To understand these organizers, it is important to understand the movements that nurtured them.

SDS began in 1960 on the University of Michigan campus, with a conference devoted to "human rights in the North." Historically, it was the grandchild of Upton Sinclair's 1905-born Intercollegiate Socialist Society. Its members had included Norman Thomas, Walter Lippmann, Paul H. Douglas and later, when it became the League for Industrial Democracy, Reinhold Niebuhr and Walter Reuther.

In its early years, SDS was not particularly radical. Tom Hayden, a University of Michigan alumnus who had been blooded in the Southern civil-rights battles, drafted the best-known portion of its manifesto. Kirkpatrick Sale, in his book *SDS,* described it as "unabashedly middle-class, concerned with poverty of vision rather than poverty of life . . . with the world of the white student rather than the world of the blacks, the poor or the workers. It was set firmly in mainstream politics, seeking the reform of wayward institutions, rather than their abolition, and it had no comprehension of the dynamics of capitalism, of imperialism, of class conflict, certainly no conception of revolution."

The ideology of the early SDS was a blend of romanticism and populism. It said that "politics should be seen positively . . . as the function of bringing people out of isolation and into community."

"The vision of making society somehow more responsive to its individual members," wrote Alan Adelson in *SDS,* "brought with it the idea of breaking down the size of governing institutions so that the people could be heard better."

SDS tried some experiments in off-campus community organizing in its early years. With financial help from the United Auto Workers, Hayden and his future codefendant in the Chicago Seven trial Rennie Davis directed a community organizing venture called the Economic Research and Action Project (ERAP). They worked in neighborhoods from Newark to Chicago, with mixed results, for about three or four years. But in part because it was a middle-class movement, interested in helping solve *other people's* problems, it proved to be rather easily diverted, first to help blacks in the civil-rights struggles in Mississippi and other states and then to the battle to end the war in Indochina.

It was in the middle Sixties that SDS became known as a radical organization. In a dynamic that is a familiar pattern for protest movements, the leadership and ideology of SDS became more and more radical as the struggle against the war dragged on from year to year. Teach-ins were followed by marches and demonstrations, and they in turn were replaced by acts of violence.

Michael Ansara was one of the younger-generation organizers who watched the transition—and did not like it. He was recruited for the movement at 13, when "walking down a street [in Boston] I saw three or four students picketing a Woolworth's in sympathy with the sit-ins in the South. I still don't know what happened. I said, It seems right to me that any American should be able to sit at a lunch counter and get a cup of coffee, and so I joined the picket line. And that was the beginning."

Ansara, like many of the other organizers, was a "red-diaper baby." His grandparents were Syrian-Lebanese immigrant peddlers in Lowell, Massachusetts, but managed to send their son, James, to Harvard. James Ansara was a leftist writer who joined the government in World War II "to help fight fascism" and in 1947, the year of Michael's birth, was fired by the State Department, under pressure from the House Un-American Activities Committee, as a security risk.

His parents, Michael Ansara said, "were so intimidated by the experience that I never heard a political discussion all the time I was growing up and had no idea of the background that I came from."

Nonetheless, his parents' values rubbed off on him, and he moved quickly from the civil-rights picket lines to disarmament campaigns and, as president of the Harvard SDS in 1966, Ansara was the instigator of one of the most famous anti-war incidents. Secretary of Defense Robert S. McNamara was invited to speak, under maximum-security conditions, on the Harvard campus. But when the lecture was over, a mass of demonstrators was waiting outside the building to block him from his car. Nervous Harvard officials led McNamara through an underground tunnel to safety, but the publicity given the incident furthered the public view that the anti-war agitators were no respecters of civil liberties themselves. The trend distressed Ansara, who said he joined SDS because "I really believed in the Declaration of Independence profoundly. It wasn't Marx at all; it was the Declaration of Independence and its vision that I wanted very much to put into practice." While his own ideology shifted to a more explicitly anti-corporate and anti-capitalist line in his SDS years, he recoiled against those who expressed "a mindless dogmatism and hatred for everything the country stood for, in a way that of course alienated a lot of people who otherwise might have responded to the ideals and vision the student movement had."

There were many in that time period whose hopes were betrayed by the dynamic of campus-based politics. The campuses seemed a tempting base for organizing mass movements, because the student population was bigger than it had ever been before. In the early 1960s, the postwar baby boom was beginning to swell the ranks of teen-age America. There were more Americans between the ages of 14 and 24 than ever before—27.2 million in 1960, fully 15 percent of the population. Almost 4 million of them were gathered at the colleges and the universities. There were plenty of students available. But Ansara was not the only anti-war organizer to learn an important lesson in the Sixties about the inherent limitations of student movements. Sam Brown had the same experience.

The organizer of the McCarthy campaign and the 1969 Moratorium and now, at 36, the director of ACTION, the federal agency that includes the Peace Corps and VISTA, Brown grew up in Council Bluffs, Iowa, the son of a prosperous shoe-store owner and Methodist lay minister. In high school he was three times the outstanding ROTC cadet, and he went off to the University of Redlands in California as a "sort of libertarian conservative, someplace to the right of Ayn Rand." His friends there included a black student from Watts and an American Indian, and in his second week on campus he was recruited for the civil-rights movement by Allard Lowenstein, who was there as a guest speaker. Brown began helping Chavez and the farm workers, but the really "radicalizing" experience (if one can use that term for a political organizer as circumscribed by convention as Brown is) came through a free-speech issue. In his freshman year, Brown wrote an editorial for the student newspaper questioning the ban on Communist speakers on the California campuses. Brown argued the classic John Stuart Mill free-market-of-ideas approach, and was astonished when the university administration reacted by censoring the newspaper. In response, he joined a group of students publishing an underground paper—which in turn became a target for the university. "We just found ourselves being driven further and further out," he said, "which is one reason, I suppose, that the part of me that is pragmatic and reformist makes me think that people get driven to craziness by having reasonable channels closed to them."

Throughout his career, Brown has played the role of the broker between those challenging establishment policies and the establishment itself, using his organizational talents for the former and his diplomatic skills on the latter.

Unlike the SDS leaders, he developed nothing that could be dignified as a political philosophy of his own, but worked instead on whatever project seemed important, with whatever means were at hand. In the summer of 1964, he joined with Lowenstein, Hayden and a host of others to organize the Mississippi Summer project that sent hundreds of student civil-rights organizers south in what became one of the great experiential links for the organizers' network. But he himself skipped Mississippi for San Francisco, where he worked, futilely, to derail the nomination of Barry Goldwater. He went east in 1966, first to Rutgers' Eagleton Institute and then to the Harvard Divinity School, and became involved in anti-war organization through the National Student Association. It was as chairman of the NSA supervisory board in 1967 that he helped expose its past links to the CIA. "One Sunday," he recalled, "I was sitting in the library of the Harvard Divinity School reading some obscure text in German, and the following Sunday I was on *Meet the Press,*" discussing the CIA revelations. From that point on, activism replaced scholarship. He lined up signatures of student-body presidents for an ad opposing the war, worked with Lowenstein on the Dump Johnson movement and became national volunteer coordinator for McCarthy. In the autumn of 1969, he led the Vietnam Moratorium movement which brought more than 250,000 people to Washington for a massive, peaceful protest of the war.

By 1970, Brown's renown as an anti-war personality was exceeded only by his frustration at the failure of the organizing efforts to end the hostilities. That spring, Brown and his colleagues closed down the Moratorium, convinced that President Nixon was using their opposition to build public support among "the silent majority" for continued bloodshed. Before heading off to Colorado to start afresh from the grass roots, Brown wrote an article for *The Washington Monthly* that became the definitive obituary for the campus-based political activism of the 1960s. "I am convinced," he wrote, "that it is not possible to build a successful peace movement simply on a student base. Not enough students have the stature, capacity or inclination to run a tightly disciplined peace movement which would be required to make them effective and keep them moving toward Middle America. Even if such an organization were possible, students alone would be unable to attract a majority of the American people to any politically effective peace position. . . . For one thing, I became convinced that there was a serious lack of long-term commitment among many students."

Had those words come from an older critic, they might have been dismissed; but coming from the young man who sent the McCarthy volunteers into New Hampshire and brought the anti-war marchers by the thousands to Washington, D.C., they could not be ignored. "If the conviction of young people has been a source of strength," he told them, "it has also been responsible for much of the self-containment of the peace movement. And the significant fact is not that active dissent began on the campus, but that it has largely stayed there."

There was one other attempt at national organizing in the 1960s which also deserves mention, because it too served a dual function: as a training ground for organizers, and as a frustrating learning experience which eventually turned those organizers back to the community. It was the National Welfare Rights Organization.

NWRO, headed by the late George Wiley, a former leader of the Congress of Racial Equality, was formed in 1966, in an effort to achieve for the poor in the Northern city ghettos a gain in economic rights comparable to the advance in legal rights the civil-rights movement had won in the South in the previous decade. Rather than espousing mass organizing, its theory was to mobilize welfare recipients in racially tense big cities in states that were of crucial electoral importance to the governing Democratic Party and, by planned demonstrations in welfare offices, to exert political pressure for passage of an adequate national income-maintenance program. That basic goal was never reached; and ironically, NWRO itself drew criticism from some liberals for lobbying against a Nixon Administration proposal that would have marginally improved welfare payments in most states.

The organization survived only five years, and at its peak, according to Frances Fox Piven and Richard A. Cloward in *Poor People's Movements*, "the national membership count did not exceed 25,000 adults. And it is our opinion that it had relatively little influence in the lobbying process to which it progressively devoted most of its resources." NWRO was more successful in agitating for changes in laws and regulations at the state and local levels and in mobilizing poor people to demand the benefits they had been losing simply through their own passivity or through the victimization of administrative caprice.

The organization had one important side effect. It coincided with Lyndon Johnson's War on Poverty and the displacement north of many young white organizers who were looking for a cause after their civil-rights experience in the South. "Perhaps three-quarters of all welfare-rights organizers were anti-poverty workers, many of them VISTAs," Piven and Cloward wrote. And many of them have remained active in organizing, even after the demise of NWRO.

Wade Rathke, now 32, went from draft-resistance counseling in New Orleans to a job as head organizer of NWRO in Massachusetts. "We did an excellent job of organizing that specific constituency," he said, "but every time we'd win a concession, we'd lose it in the legislature. Politically, we weren't in any better shape in terms of building constituency power, because even in Boston, only one out of seven people is a welfare recipient. So I was looking to building something that would have a majority constituency instead of a minority constituency."

Rathke's road took him to Arkansas, where he formed the Association of Community Organizations for Reform Now (ACORN). The group won a series of victories on welfare allowances, free school texts and property-tax relief. ACORN also became a significant local political force, electing almost half the members of the Pulaski County (Little Rock) legislative body. In the last three years, it has spread its organizing cells into seventeen other states.

Tim Sampson was also an NWRO organizer before launching the 10,000-member California Citizens Action League, which is now affiliated with ACORN. CAL's most successful campaign was called Electricity and Gas for the People (E&GP) and was aimed against the Pacific Gas and Electric Company (PG&E). It ended with the passage of the first state law reversing the normal rate structure and setting a minimal rate for a "lifeline" supply of power for small customers.

Many of the anti-war movement leaders also have made the transition from national and international issues to local causes—and with satisfying results. Lee Webb, one of the founders of SDS, now spends full time as the director of the Conference on Alternative State and Local Public Policies, which is a national network for the local organizing groups.

Webb's comments explain why so many of the organizers are "thinking small" these days. In his Boston student days in the early Sixties, he said, when he was working on the civil-rights movement, the massive turnouts for parades and rallies "gave me the feeling of actually being able to affect history . . . to start with nothing and make big things happen.

"But in the late Sixties," he went on, "we were up against this enormous war, this enormous establishment, the Pentagon, and no matter how many times we demonstrated or wrote letters or votes were taken, nothing seemed to change the direction of the monolith."

As Sam Brown retreated from the frustration of his anti-war efforts to Colorado, where he helped organize a successful move to bar the Winter Olympics from being held there, and later won election as state treasurer, so Lee Webb plunged into local politics in Vermont, backing candidates for the legislature and pushing legislation to ban throwaway bottles and provide state-paid dental care for youngsters.

At the end of the 1970s, Webb was saying that "liberalism in the U.S. made a fatal mistake by its overreliance since the New Deal on seeing the federal government as the major instrument of social change, and a strong presidency as the leading vehicle within this federal government. By 1970, I felt that instead of smashing ourselves against a wall of national politics and remaining deadlocked or stagnant, we could do a great deal by winning specific victories at the state or local level that could in fact become the national model."

At one of his national conferences, Webb said, "A new generation of state and local public officials and community leaders has emerged, represented in many ways by people in this room." Among them were mayors from Madison, Wisconsin, and Washington, D.C.; city-council members from Detroit and New York City; county officials from Florida, Missouri, New Jersey and Texas; state officers from North Dakota and Massachusetts. "The last few years," he said, "have been ones of enormous strides for progressives at the state and local levels."

In a similar effort to break out of "the isolation of the anti-war movement," former Harvard SDS leader Mike Ansara organized Massachusetts Fair Share, a citizens group claiming 23,000 dues-paying families and 45 organizers. Using what he called a mixture of "guerrilla tactics" and electoral strategies, Fair Share won some significant victories. It threw up picket lines to embarrass tax-delinquent businesses into paying their bills. It used a threat of mass picketing at a ceremonial occasion to extract a pledge from a Governor for action on auto insurance, and wound up with $55 million in rebates for city dwellers. It forced the phone company to give up security deposits on phones in low-income areas. And in its most important victory, Fair Share in 1978 was at the center of a broad political coalition that passed a referendum setting lower property-tax assessments for residential property than for commercial and industrial land and buildings.

"Most Americans," Ansara said, "have not really experienced being able to be effective politically. They tend to think that political history is made only by great men—Kennedys or Kings, maybe, but not ordinary people. A lot of what we are doing is challenging that notion and getting people over that tremendously debilitating sense of powerlessness and cynicism."

In the Seventies, the organizers turned their techniques to new constituencies. Karen Nussbaum, 30, was a University of Chicago dropout who was working as a clerk-typist at the Harvard School of Education in 1970 and found that she and her coworkers "were complaining all the time about the way we were treated on our jobs.

"Because of my experience in the peace movement," where she had been organizing demonstrations and marches for years, "I knew that you could start an organization to address a problem." And that is what she did. Beginning with the education school, Nine to Five, her organization of women office workers, expanded its base, by steps, first to all of Harvard, then to the city of Boston, and now has become a group called Working Women, The National Association of Office Workers, with active chapters in 13 major cities and an at-large membership in 40 states.

As its national director, working out of Cleveland, Nussbaum said she had found the techniques of the peace movement perfectly applicable to the new set of problems. "You develop an organization that speaks to the concerns of your constituency," she said, "and that's the way to solve problems."

The problems of women office workers range from unequal pay to sexual harassment to the oft-repeated pattern of the veteran secretary training one young man after another for a supervisory position, while she remains stuck in a job with no hope of promotion.

Nussbaum's organization invokes state and federal antidiscrimination laws, and presses business leaders to re-examine their own firms' personnel policies. But like all good organizers, she is alert for opportunities to stage some "guerrilla theater." The biggest breakthrough in Boston, for example, came when she heard about a lawyer's secretary who had been fired for insubordination.

"Her boss asked her to go out and get his lunch for him on a miserable, rainy day. She did it and brought it back, and then he buzzed her into his office again and said, 'You've gotten me corned beef on white. Don't you know that you can't eat corned beef on white? Go back and get it on rye bread.' And she refused. So he fired her for refusing to get the corned beef on rye.

"The next day," Nussbaum said, "we brought thirty-five members to picket his office, and the story was on the front page of the papers, and he was brought up before the bar association for unethical behavior. And we were launched."

While Working Women itself is not a union, it is seen by Nussbaum and others as the likely forerunner of a revived trade-union organizing push. Nussbaum, who served as president of a 500-member union of Boston office workers, chartered by the Service Employees International, said that she thinks "in the Eighties, you will probably see the massive unionization of clerical workers, because they are now the largest unorganized section of the work force." If she and her contemporaries do that, they will be repaying a historical debt, and closing a historical circle:

Alinsky drew *his* inspiration from John L. Lewis' success in organizing the unskilled factory workers. So it would be singularly appropriate if Alinsky's pupils led the breakthrough on this new organizing front.

Another of the organizing successes of the Seventies came from the homosexual community. Jean O'Leary, 32, who in 1979 wound up three years as co–executive director of the National Gay Task Force, which claims a membership of 10,000 homosexual men and women, was living in a convent in her native Cleveland during the height of the anti–Vietnam war organizing. While it was the confirmation of her own sexual nature that finally caused her to leave the convent, O'Leary said that she was also frustrated by the ban her superiors placed on her joining the anti-war marches.

"I remember walking onto campus and seeing all these hundreds of people organizing these mass rallies," she said. "I wanted to go to Washington and march with some of my friends. It was a movement that I *really* felt. I would go out of the convent at night to the organization meetings, but I never did make it to Washington. And that was one of the reasons I decided to leave."

When she arrived in New York in 1971, she quickly began organizing in the homosexual community. That was, of course, a difficult challenge, because, as O'Leary said, "the biggest oppression that we've always suffered has been our invisibility, our refusal to identify ourselves publicly. And we've not been able to organize because of that."

But that pattern began to change—and change dramatically—in the Seventies as "Gay Pride" and "Gay Power" marches were held in major cities. O'Leary said that the first time she walked into a meeting of a just-starting group called the Gay Alliance of Brooklyn "and there were two hundred people there who were admitting that they were gay, it was a fantastic experience."

But it is no longer an uncommon experience. According to her figures, the number of such local groups grew in the Seventies from fewer than 200 to more than 2,000. From the beginning, the movement has been involved directly in politics. O'Leary was elected as a delegate to the 1976 Democratic convention, and acknowledged gays have run for office in at least a dozen major cities.

The focus of the group has been on seeking legislation to bar discrimination against homosexuals in housing, employment and other areas of life. "We started in 1969," O'Leary said, "and it's just one decade later, and we have made major gains. We have forty cities that have passed civil-rights legislation. We have twenty-two states that have repealed or reformed their sodomy laws. We have federal legislation that's been introduced. We have had several meetings with White House aides and with the federal agencies on law-enforcement, immigration and similar problems."

As is well known, there has also been a strong backlash against the homosexuals in many areas, and protective legislation for gays was repealed in referenda in Dade County, Florida; Eugene, Oregon; Wichita, Kansas, and St. Paul, Minnesota.

But in a major test of strength in California in 1978, an initiative to close public-school teaching jobs to homosexuals was defeated in a popular vote, with such varied politicians as Ronald Reagan, Jerry Brown and Jimmy Carter all taking public stands against it.

With each passing year, the organizers of the gay community were persuading more politicians that the resources they commanded in campaign funds and volunteers were a tangible political asset, and gays were becoming part of the power coalition in cities from Washington to San Francisco.

To most Americans, one of the most unexpected sights of the Seventies was that of people in wheelchairs, or with white canes, staging sit-ins in the offices of government officials. The disabled and the handicapped, who had been passive and, in many instances, so isolated that they were practically invisible, also were organized for political action during the past decade.

Both Frank Bowe (a 33-year-old research psychologist, author and victim of deafness who is director of the American Coalition of Citizens with Disabilities) and David Pfeiffer (a 46-year-old political scientist and polio victim who is the former head of a similar coalition at the state level in Massachusetts) said it was no accident that the organization and militancy had developed now.

Until World War II and its medical advances in treating badly wounded servicemen, Pfeiffer pointed out, "most seriously physically disabled people died," because they were kept in bed and became victims of pneumonia and similar diseases.

Bowe estimated the number of handicapped people in the country at the end of the Seventies as 36 million, but pointed out that until the mid-Seventies the organizations that served them were one-dimensional, specializing in the blind, or the deaf, or the retarded, or those suffering from other particular afflictions. But the lessons of coalition politics were learned in the past decade so well, he said, that organizations of the blind were promoting letter-writing campaigns among their members in support of the deaf people's drive to increase the number of captioned programs on television. "They'll never see a caption," he said, "but they know that an advance in this entire area for civil rights is an advance for all of us. . . . And they also know, in a very practical sense, that if they do this, someday they will be able to go to those deaf people and get support for something for the blind people."

They also absorbed the lesson of the tactical use of militancy—particularly from the civil-rights organizers. "People just assume a handicapped person's going to be a nice guy," Pfeiffer said. "Well, we're just as human as anybody else. If the blacks could go to jail, if the women can go to jail, if the gays can go to jail, we can too. But most policemen won't arrest us. There are very few handicapped people who ever get arrested. So we decided, knowing this, that we'll use it."

Sit-ins and other tactics of civil disobedience became a standard lobbying technique of handicapped groups. They played some part—how much is a matter of debate even among the organizers—in the passage of tougher laws and regulations requiring schools, offices, transportation systems and other facilities to provide, as far as possible, equal and nonsegregated services for all the categories of handicapped people. As with the blacks and women and gays, the demands of the handicapped produced a backlash—particularly from budget-conscious officials who claimed the costs of the equal-treatment rules were prohibitive. Despite that strong backlash, the growing organized power of the handicapped was not lost on politicians.

While organizers like Rathke, Nussbaum, O'Leary and Bowe labored to build their national coalitions among people facing common problems, local communities were witnessing a rebirth of activism that may, in the long run, be of even greater significance.

It was fueled by the rediscovered force of ethnicity. The myth of the American melting pot had persisted and probably peaked in the postwar decade, with its mass migration to the suburbs. But when those left behind by that exodus looked around their cities, they found, to their surprise, that there were still Polish, Italian, Serbian, Croatian, Mexican, Cuban and, of course, black neighborhoods. As America neared its bicentennial, the "unmeltable ethnics," as Michael Novak called them, proclaimed their own cultural identity as a source of pride—and political power.

One reason the energy of the neighborhood movements has been relatively undiscovered is that they—and their leaders—are, by definition, local. John Kromkowski, the president of the National Center for Urban Ethnic Affairs, said that at "one time mayors and councilmen thought that going up [the political ladder] meant going out of the city. I think the politicians that are there today feel this is the most exciting, fulfilling human activity they can engage in."

But by 1980 there was at least one product of the neighborhood movement who was beginning to be nationally known. And as it happened, Baltimore's Barbara Mikulski epitomized, in personal terms, the energy, the drive and the self-assertive confidence that characterize this new source of leadership.

Mikulski, 44, had so much spirit packed into her chunky four-foot-eleven-inch frame that her body language was often as colorful as her vocabulary.

She grew up in the Highlandtown neighborhood of southeast Baltimore, attended Catholic girls' schools for sixteen years and lived at home with her parents until she was 27. "My mother and father had this old neighborhood grocery store," she said, "and the neighborhood was really our extended family. . . . If Bethlehem Steel was on strike, my father extended credit to the guys. In the middle of a snowstorm, if he didn't see Miss Sophie, who was a diabetic, he called down there to see if she needed anything, and if she did, I ran down the oranges."

Mikulski was an exemplar of what Novak called, in his 1972 book *The Rise of the Unmeltable Ethnics*, "network people." "The network people, among whom are the white ethnics," he wrote, "find it hard to think of themselves as atoms, or of their neighborhoods as mere pieces of geography. Into their definition of themselves enter their family, their in-laws, their relatives, their friends, their streets, their stores, familiar smells and sights and sounds. Those things are not, as they are for the atomic people, extrinsic. For the network people, these things are identity, life, *self*. It is not that the network people are attached to such things. They *are* such things. Take away such things, and part of them dies."

Novak saw the "new ethnic politics as a direct challenge to the WASP conception of America. It asserts that *groups* can structure the rules and goals and procedures of American life. It asserts that individuals, if they do not wish to, do not have to 'melt.' They do not have to submit themselves to atomization."

Two years before Novak wrote that book and the year before Mikulski began her political career, the 1970 census found that there were 9.6 million foreign-born people in the United States and another 24 million who had a foreign-born parent or parents. One of every six Americans was first- or second-generation, with the largest suppliers being Italy, Germany, Canada, the United Kingdom, Poland and Mexico. One out of five Americans reported a language other than English as his or her mother tongue. The ethnics were still concentrated in the cities of the Northeast, and like Mikulski's neighbors, many of them lived their lives on the ragged edge of poverty.

Mikulski trained to be a social worker; was influenced by the Christopher Movement ("You can change the world"); worked for Catholic Charities and the Baltimore welfare department, where her supervisor, the celebrated atheist Madalyn Murray O'Hair, "put me to the test about Catholicism" and introduced her to Michael Harrington's treatise on poverty, *The Other America*. In the mid-1960s, while she was in graduate school, she was drawn into the civil-rights movement and one of the community-action programs spawned by the War on Poverty. Working professionally with cases of child abuse and neglect, she began to see that "it was the structure, the very nature of the way government and society did business that did this" to people. While she was brooding about this problem, and about the growing tensions between blacks and her Polish neighbors in Highlandtown, a friend asked her to meet a man named Tom Fiorello who was fighting an extension of an interstate freeway through Mikulski's old neighborhood. "That conversation changed my life," she said. With others from her old neighborhood, she plunged into organizing SCAR—the Southeast Committee Against the Road. SCAR found allies in a group of middle-class preservationists in a neighboring section also imperiled by the expressway. They merged to form SECO—the Southeast Community Organization, one of the most successful neighborhood movements in America.

Mikulski "loved it. I felt like I'd come home. Not to demean my role in the civil-rights movement, but all of a sudden I was fighting for me and my own crowd, and that's a very different thing."

Through Joe McNeely, SECO's first paid organizer and an Alinsky disciple, Mikulski had her introduction to the principles of community organizing, many of them outlined in Alinsky's books.

Alinsky had written that "power is not only what you have but what the enemy thinks you have." Mikulski said that SCAR began with only about eight people "meeting seven times a week in groups under different names to create the illusion of power." Alinsky had warned that "a single issue is a fatal strait jacket that will stifle the life of an organization." As soon as Mikulski and her friends began to make progress on the highway fight, they moved on to other fronts—libraries, schools and other issues—applying Alinsky's dogma that "many issues mean many members."

Operating in Chicago, with its powerful Democratic political machine, Alinsky made the assumption that he and his Back of the Yards Council would perpetually be fighting City Hall. In Baltimore, where the Democratic organization was powerful but not quite that impenetrable, Mikulski came to a different conclusion.

"As we worked on all these issues," she said, "I became convinced that the answer was in politics. Every door we went to was a political door. . . . All roads led to either City Hall or the statehouse or Washington. And rather than being on the other side, banging on the door, I wanted to be where the action was."

In 1971 she plunged into a race for the Baltimore City Council and, against the odds, won. She served there until 1976, when she moved up to claim a vacant seat in the U.S. House of Representatives.

Earlier in 1976, the National Center for Urban Ethnic Affairs had published a study of Congress, documenting the gross underrepresentation of working-class, ethnic Catholics in its ranks. "A Protestant child of an upper-strata family occupational background has a 20 to 1 better chance of being elected to Congress in its lifetime than does a child of a Catholic ethnic family of working-class background," it said.

Mikulski was not only breaking ground in Congress but beginning to play a visible role in both Democratic Party politics and the ethnic-awareness movement at the national level. At a National Urban Coalition meeting in 1970, she had met Monsignor Geno Baroni, then director of the National Center for Urban Ethnic Affairs and now an assistant secretary of Housing and Urban Development. Baroni played a role in the neighborhood movement similar to that of Alinsky in community organizing or Allard Lowenstein in the civil-rights and anti-war movements; he was the older figure who drew many of the young activists into their roles.

In her speech at Baroni's conference, Mikulski capsulized her view of America: "America is not a melting pot," she said in a voice that always seemed too big for its source. "It is a sizzling cauldron. . . . Government is polarizing people by the creation of myths. . . . The ethnic worker is fooled into thinking that the blacks are getting everything. Old prejudices and new fears are ignited. The two groups end up fighting each other for the same jobs and competing so that the new schools and recreation centers will be built in their respective communities. What results is an angry confrontation for tokens, when there should be an alliance for a whole new agenda for America."

Widely reprinted and reported, those words were perceived as a stinging rebuke to the social policies of the Nixon Administration and made Mikulski a heroine in the Democratic Party. In 1973 she became chairman of the party's rules-revision commission and presided over the ticklish business of rewriting the "implied-quota system" which had been so damaging and divisive at the Democratic Convention in 1972.

Both on the city council and in the party commission, Mikulski said, "I learned something very important to my own development—how to broker conflict and persuade others to accept the trade-offs and compromises that are necessary for progress. When there were no credentials challenges taken to the floor at the 1976 Democratic convention, I felt like we had done a job."

Asked how this jibed with her earlier experience as a conflict-prone community organizer, she said, "Conflict is a technique. It's not a life-style. There's conflict any time there's an issue. But you don't use conflict continually and solely. You also have to ask yourself how you can organize to make things happen.''

Mikulski's restatement of the Alinsky doctrine from her new perspective as a professional politician is one that would be challenged by many of the purists of the movement. But she maintained that ''the community-organization mentality'' could be adapted to the work of a legislator. ''Community is not only based on your geographic location,'' Mikulski said, echoing another of Alinsky's dicta. ''It's a bonding experience . . . based on working for a common goal.'' In the House Democratic cloakroom, just as in the streets of her old neighborhood, people like to ''hang out,'' she discovered, and in that environment it proved possible to cement relationships and build strategy. A colleague of Mikulski's said that at the meetings of the ''steel caucus'' in the House (a group of members from steel-producing districts), it was Mikulski who tended to ask the key questions: ''What do we really want? What power have we got? Who do we use it on?''

Those were organizers' questions, and Mikulski said she came to feel that a ''kind of community'' sense of camaraderie and mutual commitment might be the best available substitute for the party discipline which no longer existed among congressional Democrats.

Mikulski's was not the only success story for the new breed of ethnic and neighborhood politicians. Another product of that movement, Gale Cincotta of Chicago, was instrumental (with help from Baroni and the Center for Urban Ethnic Affairs) in lobbying through Congress the first federal law exposing the practice of ''redlining'' by lending institutions—the boycott of ''declining'' inner-city neighborhoods. The fight against blanket denials of mortgages to ''high-risk'' urban areas used classic neighborhood-organizing tactics—including the type of imaginative, embarrassing confrontations that Alinsky had championed. Congress' 1978 legislation forbade discriminatory practices in the granting of mortgage money. Taking the redlining controversy one step further, activists in 1977 turned their attention to the same type of blanket denials by insurance firms. Homeowners had often heard the mortgage lenders' line ''If you can get insurance, we'll give you a mortgage''—only to find that insurance policies were also refused on a blanket basis. ''Insurance redlining is particularly severe,'' a study by the Michigan Department of Insurance found, ''because the individuals which it victimizes are powerless to reverse it.'' Wary of the power neighborhood groups had shown in the mortgage-lending fight, insurance firms quickly showed themselves receptive to activists' complaints, and Cincotta found they were ready to take steps to correct the situation. Insurance companies ''knew what we did with the banks and savings-and-loans—how we pushed it all the way,'' she told *National Journal* columnist Neal R. Peirce. "They felt it was coming. And they're scared to death of a lot of referral regulation.''

In some respects, the late 1970s saw the creation of a formidable interlocking network of locally oriented, change-seeking organizers. At HUD, Baroni was steering modest, but significant, federal grants to a couple dozen neighborhood-improvement groups. At ACTION, Sam Brown was supplying VISTA volunteers to ACORN and similar organizations. The Ford Foundation, with its $2.2 billion in resources, chose as its new president Franklin A. Thomas, 46, the president of the Bedford-Stuyvesant (Brooklyn) Restoration Corporation, a man who said, "I have a strong belief in community-based, neighborhood-based development.'' From Washington, the network extended out into every state and into literally hundreds of communities.

Yet as many of the organizers were the first to point out, it would be a mistake to exaggerate the potency and unity of the movement—or perhaps even to regard it as a movement at all.

Joe McNeely, the former Baltimore organizer who is now Baroni's deputy at HUD, said, "There is not a neighborhood movement. A movement means you have a clearly defined goal. The phenomenon is real and is being recognized, and it has some coherence, but it's too broad to be a movement.''

At its base, in the neighborhoods, there was a paradox, for the ethnic consciousness on which it rested had historically been a force for division as often as it had for unity. The old ethnic politics was regarded by many as an importation of Old World foreign-policy issues and rivalries into an American society that needed no additional divisions. To many, ethnic politics never rose above the level of crude ticket balancing of the kind familiar to the old-fashioned big-city machines.

"There is no use dodging the dilemma,'' wrote Michael Novak, the student and promoter of ethnic consciousness. "Not all ethnic groups desire to be integrated with others. . . . National culture is often more liberal than local culture.''

But Novak went on to argue that "in general, persons secure in their own families and neighborhoods are more likely to reach rational compromises than persons who feel total and unremitting threat. . . . The diminishing of anti-Semitic sentiment since the Second World War, the abatement of most inter-ethnic hostilities, the general rise of blacks in their own esteem and that of others, suggest that an ethnic focus does not carry all the dangers it once had. . . . Strongly ethnic families and neighborhoods are free to construct and defend their own distinctive ways of life, while recognizing that in a democratic and pluralistic society, many compromises and accommodations must be reached."

Whether or not the neighborhood movement has that benign a character, it is, by its nature, particularistic and somewhat inward-looking and, in that respect, not easily assimilated into a larger political base. There are few ethnic-neighborhood-oriented people who are also part of the more ideological and politicized network created by Lee Webb and his National Conference.

That is not accidental. The former SDSers like Webb and Hayden bring an ideology of socialism (or, as Hayden prefers, "economic democracy") with them to their work of organizing, and view the neighborhood movements as providing a vehicle for mobilizing a constituency for that program. While socialism is far from an alien concept to many of the European ethnics, there is also a great streak of conservatism in those neighborhoods, a desire to "get ahead" in a familiar American capitalist sense.

"Our people," Webb said, "tend to be more statewide in their focus, more strategic in their thinking. I think an awful lot of neighborhood politics is sort of the politics of pressure and influence . . . very oriented to street lights and zoning variances and development, highways, things that affect neighborhoods and particularly property values and home ownership."

There may be something more fundamental that separates the two groups. Neighborhood leadership is the outgrowth of the natural organization which Alinsky said was latent even in the worst of the slums. But that leadership may be uncomfortable with the confrontation tactics that are drilled into the outside organizers. Novak writes that "the tactic of demonstration is inherently WASP and inherently offensive to ethnic peoples." A neighborhood leader like Mikulski wants to be in on the bargaining process; an organizer like Ansara or Sampson is nervous about getting too close to those in power.

Often this tension is reflected inside the organizations and is visible in the social and age differences between the membership and the organizers. The organizers tend to be young (in part because only people with few family responsibilities can accept the minimal salaries organizers are paid) and well educated.

Steven Kest, who became ACORN's head organizer in Arkansas when Rathke began devoting most of his energies to the expansion of ACORN to other states, is a 28-year-old product of White Plains, a New York suburb, and Harvard. In interviews, both he and Rathke insisted they were not the leaders of ACORN, just the organizers. (In 1979, Kest left Arkansas to become ACORN's chief organizer in Connecticut.) They acknowledged that they controlled the hiring and firing of other staff members, that they remained in their posts while the membership-elected officers rotated into and out of office, that they selected the areas for organizing—but they insisted they were not the leaders of ACORN. That degree of self-effacement is perhaps an indication of the tension that exists between the ideology of empowering people to achieve their own goals and the organizational imperatives of giving direction and force to a movement.

Nor is that the only contradiction and dilemma the organizers must face. Although they are committed to building a coalition between the very poor and the blue-collar workers' families, they often find it difficult to build relationships with organized labor in their areas. Tim Sampson of CAL said, "When we get into coalitions with labor, rarely can labor deliver any people." The failure of labor to join a coalition with the organized poor was particularly conspicuous, he said, in the battle over rival plans to reduce the property-tax burden in California—a failure which ultimately let the issue be captured by the state's conservative movement in the form of Proposition 13.

Sampson made another point about the problems the changing shape of American neighborhoods creates for movements like his. It is a change that undermines Alinsky's basic assumption about the character of neighborhoods.

"I tell people we're going to organize a neighborhood," Sampson said. "Well, in the olden days in many cities you had in the neighborhood an infrastructure made up of churches, ethnic organizations, people who had been in the neighborhood a long time—some kind of connecting tissue. That's infinitely weaker now. People move around. Often, our first task in organizing is introducing people to their neighbors. Well, if our task is to create the infrastructure of the damn society, and we gotta do that in order to get a little social and economic change, that's a hell of a problem."

Perhaps for that reason, among others, the growth in the mass base of the community organizations has been very slow. None of them had signed up more than 25,000 families in an individual state—even a state as large as Massachusetts or California or Ohio. That would not be a significant limitation, if their focus were purely on remedying local grievances. But as Rathke, perhaps the most visionary and ambitious of the organizers, said in his ACORN manifesto, "All these [local] issues are mere manifestations of a much more fundamental issue: the distribution of power in this country. . . . You can win stoplights from here to eternity, which is what many community organizations around the country have excelled at, but unless your organizations address the question of who has the power to control what happens in a neighborhood, a city, a county or a state—and who *should* have the power to control what happens in these areas—then all your organization will achieve is a proliferation of stoplights in low- to moderate-income neighborhoods. Obviously, ACORN's goal is much more."

Aiming higher, Rathke has had ACORN involved in electoral politics from the beginning—with mixed results. While the organization elected many supporters to the Pulaski County legislature, it has had predictable difficulty holding them accountable to ACORN. According to Kest, after the chairman of ACORN's executive committee was appointed to the county planning commission, he changed his mind about a freeway ACORN had been fighting. Soon he was an ex-member of ACORN.

Despite such frustrations, Rathke has ACORN pointing toward politics on the national level, which is one reason he is pushing the organization into additional states. ACORN demonstrated at the Democratic mini-convention in Memphis in 1978 in behalf of a nine-point national platform. But with only 23,000 members nationally, even Rathke conceded that "it's probably five or six years away from being effective in national terms."

The gap between local organizing and national problems concerns many of the organizers. Sam Brown said the public distaste for "massive, anonymous" national programs dictated that "local government must be the fulcrum for a new progressive movement." He rejoiced in the fact that "eighty percent of the neighborhood groups have started in the last seven years. They represent a burgeoning chance to change long-term politics." But Brown also conceded that "without a national spokesman, it's pretty hard to gain attention."

The natural path to national issues and a bid for national power for the organizers comes from their ideological antagonism to business corporations. ACORN began challenging regional telephone companies, as an organizing tactic across state lines. Heather Booth of the Midwest Academy, a training school for organizers, was instrumental in forming the Citizens/Labor Energy Coalition, where liberal, labor, consumer and community groups joined to lobby against the oil and gas companies on the issues of deregulation and taxes. A similar coalition called COIN (Consumers Opposed to Inflation in Necessities) was formed to focus the anti-inflation fight on banks, corporate farms, hospitals and doctors and, once again, the energy companies.

The difficulty was that on those national economic issues, the organizers found the competition very tough—not just from their chosen enemies in corporate America but from neopopulist conservatives, who gave their own propositions a twist these organizers did not like.

That was most evident in the battle of the tax referenda in 1978. In Massachusetts, Fair Share and its allies showed considerable deftness and won a major victory in the "classification" initiative which blocked a significant shift of property-tax burdens from industry to homeowners.

In Arkansas, however, where ACORN placed an initiative for repeal of the sales tax on food and medicine on the ballot, it was defeated. It lost, Kest said, in part because the proponents were outspent by a wide margin and in part because the opposition forced them to concede that ACORN would seek what it called "a progressive tax package" in the legislature to replace the lost revenues rather than advocate cutbacks in services.

The clearest case of table turning, however, happened in California. Sampson's Citizens Action League mounted an early effort for property-tax relief, and in 1977 brought 2,000 demonstrators to the state capitol in support of a reform measure that would have granted the greatest relief to low-income families most squeezed by the rising valuations of their homes. But that measure failed to pass by one vote.

When conservatives representing the interests of large apartment-building and land owners took center stage with Proposition 13, CAL and organizations like it were caught in a terrible bind. Trapped between a fear, on one hand, that lost revenues would cripple programs of importance to the welfare poor and, on the other, the desire of many of its blue-collar worker families to cut taxes and "send the politicians a message," CAL simply abdicated on Proposition 13, "because we saw no advantage in alienating people in the organization" on either side of the question.

Long after Proposition 13 was passed, Tom Hayden was still puzzled as to how to react. "Proposition 13 is a legitimate grass-roots, populist revolt against the stupidity in government," he said, "but at the same time, it favors most heavily the large landowners, apartment owners and corporations, and the worst impact falls on the poor. It is in the nature of American populism, I think, to have this mixed blessing. It leaves organizations like ours in a kind of dilemma."

In 1979, Hayden began to recoup by organizing a movement in several California cities to impose rent controls on landlords who showed no inclination to share their property-tax savings with their tenants. But perversely, from the viewpoint of the organizers, the conservatives moved on from their Proposition 13 victory to an even more ambitious target: an amendment to the Constitution requiring a balanced federal budget except in times of national emergency.

The organizing impetus behind this movement came from the National Taxpayers Union, a group created and run by 33-year-old James D. Davidson. Davidson was, in most respects, the perfect antagonist for Hayden and his friends. Where they favored the open-shirt, blue-jeans look, Davidson affected a "young Jimmy Stewart" appearance, complete with white shirt, bow tie and banker's pinstripes. The son of a career government employee, he was a graduate of the University of Maryland and Pembroke College, Oxford, with a degree in medieval English. An intellectual and a bit of a snob, Davidson said he had "a strong sense that the

Vietnam war was a manifestation of the collapse of reason in politics." Feeling that the SDS and radical view that " 'Ho Chi Minh must be a good fellow since he is our enemy, and we shouldn't be fighting the war' was a very simplistic way of looking at things," Davidson took his protest in a totally different direction. He joined the campaign staff of Governor George W. Romney of Michigan, who in 1967 was one of the few Republicans vocally opposed to Lyndon Johnson's escalation of the war. But Romney's campaign collapsed before the first primary, and Davidson looked for other ways to curb what he saw as government's inherent tendency to blunder into actions with unintended and destructive consequences. With the help of a few "eccentric industrialists . . . troubled by the direction that politics takes," he founded the National Taxpayers Union in a Washington basement in 1969, and nursed it along. He worked with whatever allies he could find, joining liberal Democratic Senate staffers in helping kill the supersonic-transport-plane project, then enlisting the aid of A. Ernest Fitzgerald, the Pentagon "whistle blower" who made public the cost overruns on the C-5A transport plane.

In 1975 inspiration arrived, in the form of Maryland state Senator James Clark, who walked in one day with a resolution he had steered through his legislature calling on Congress to amend the Constitution to require a balanced budget. By 1979, the balanced-budget movement had become a national issue, and Davidson was frantically lobbying in the last half-dozen legislatures needed to call the first constitutional convention in American history.

His success could only make the left-wing organizers envious. Their only consolation was that as a group, they were almost as critical of the governmental bureaucracy as Davidson and his business friends. But their agreement on that point did not keep the organizers from recognizing that Proposition 13 and movements like it were a challenge to their whole strategy of assembling a coalition of the working class and the poor.

As Tom Hayden said, "We cannot dismiss it lightly. . . . It's the first time the right wing has been able to move from social issues to economic issues and start to channel the legitimate populist grievances of the low-income and the middle-income people into a campaign."

Michael Ansara said at the end of the 1970s that "at the moment, most of the choices are being defined by the Right. The collapse of the center is not producing a surging Left, but is producing both a kind of corporate Right and a populist echo of it. I don't think that Proposition 13 was an instrument of the corporations to shift capital out of the public sector and into the private. On the other hand, it echoes much of the corporate view of what the problem with the economy is: too many lazy and too inefficient public employees; big government spending fueling inflation;

social-welfare programs that have outlived their purpose, and so on. That is echoed in that populist movement.

"On the other hand," he continued, "we're still struggling to give birth to a popular movement that can fight for social and economic justice. We don't have one. A lot of us are trying to create a popular movement that's rooted in the day-to-day problems of a majority of the population, that can at least raise the crude vision of a democratic society . . . that really extends political democracy and begins to discuss economic democracy. But we're nowhere near even having that movement, let alone being able to figure out how that movement comes to power. I believe in being realistic. We're on the defensive, but it is possible for us to make great headway in that defensive struggle, because large numbers of ordinary Americans are desperately searching for answers to explain what is going on in their lives."

Tom Hayden said as the 1970s ended that "it's a fair question if our time is past." But he quickly answered that "I believe our time is coming . . . that the 1960s were only the birth crisis, the birth pang, of a generation of activists whose real impact is going to be measured in the future. We live in a time that will not let us retire or relax, because we live in a time of very profound change. . . . We were on the offensive for fifteen years, from the time of the first sit-ins until Watergate. . . . That is a rather long time for us to be on the attack against concentrated power, whether in the Pentagon, the corporations, the White House or the courthouse. It's only natural that there be a counterattack. But we are not defeated. Only regrouping."

6 · The New Right

TWO SCENES and two settings mark the transition of conservative politics in the past twenty years.

The first meeting was held in early September of 1960 at the secluded Sharon, Connecticut, family estate of author-publisher-columnist William F. Buckley, Jr. It was the first week of the Nixon–Kennedy presidential contest, and many of the ninety or so political activists who gathered at the Buckley estate could logically have been caught up in the dreams of that hard-fought contest.

Many of them were Catholics; many were conservatives. But they felt no enthusiasm for either John Kennedy or Richard Nixon. They were looking beyond both men to the time when someone they could really support might be the President of the United States.

On that weekend in 1960, they founded a conservative youth movement called Young Americans for Freedom. They adopted a manifesto called the Sharon Statement saluting the Constitution and its division of powers, the market economy, and the importance of achieving "victory over, rather than coexistence with . . . international Communism." And they went forth to tilt at their own favorite windmills.

The second meeting was held in the summer of 1979, in one of those Miami Beach hotel–convention centers which manage to be both tawdry and ostentatious at the same time. It was the annual convention of the International Longshoremen's Association, AFL-CIO, the tough dockworkers who came from something close to the opposite end of the social scale from the Buckleys of Sharon.

Their speaker was a good-looking 45-year-old Congressman and onetime pro football star, and he drew repeated cheers from the moment he opened his speech with the line that "ever since Herbert Hoover, a lot of Republicans have been advocating the economic equivalent of root-canal work for American labor . . . telling you that you'd really be better off unemployed every now and then." But the convention hall really went wild when he closed his speech with the oft-repeated line from John Kennedy's 1960 presidential campaign: "It's time to get this country moving again." No one was more pleased with the enthusiasm than the union officers who had decided to invite Representative Jack Kemp, a conservative Republican from near Buffalo, New York, as their speaker.

The Sharon conference was a refuge for young people who could find no place for themselves in the politics of 1960, who had suffered so many defeats already in their short political lives that the possibility of future success seemed to fade beyond the well-manicured hedges bordering the Buckleys' lawn.

By contrast, the self-confidence of the young conservative who took his doctrine of economic growth into the union convention was almost unbounded.

The transformation of conservatism in the past twenty years—the experiences that have reshaped the outlook of today's conservatives from that of their elders—is one of the remarkable changes in all of American politics.

It is not a simple story to retrace, for there are as many factions and feuds among the neoconservatives—or New Right—as there are among the organizers of the Left we met in the last chapter. Some of them, like Kemp, are people who grew up as Republicans and operate as Republicans today, seeking to remold their party's image and philosophy but not to abandon it. Others are former Democrats who have converted to the GOP. Some are still Democrats, but far more conservative in their thinking than they started out being. Others are people who have quit both parties in disillusionment and are operating as quasi-independent "movement conservatives," supporting candidates and causes that appeal to them and hoping for a political realignment that will bring a new "conservative coalition" to power.

There is dispute among them over who is entitled to identify himself as a "neoconservative" or member of the "New Right"—or even whether those terms are meaningful. In the context of this chapter and this book, the phrase really has only one meaning: It applies to conservatives who, by virtue of their age and experiences, are preaching and practicing a kind of politics distinctly different from that of their predecessors among the World War II veterans, the Nixon–Ford–Barry Goldwater–John Tower–Strom Thurmond generation.

There are, obviously, *some* continuing traditions (they could hardly be called conservatives otherwise) linking the younger generation with the older. On the issues involving national defense, for example, they seem every bit as committed to maintaining strong U.S. forces as did their predecessors who fought in World War II. But there has been an infusion of new doctrine—particularly in the area of economics. And there has been a development of new political techniques. And the combination of the changes in philosophy and political technology has produced something quite different and distinctive on the conservative side of the political spectrum.

One of the distinctive features is, quite simply, that it is possible now, as it was not a generation ago, to talk about conservative *thought* without causing snickers. There is, of course, a rich tradition of conservative philosophy, going back, in the Anglo-American context, to the economics of Adam Smith and the philosophy of Edmund Burke. But in the Thirties and Forties, when the minds of the World War II generation were being formed, the dominant economic theory was that of John Maynard Keynes and the dominant political theory was that of the New Deal. The intellectual reaction began with people like Friedrich von Hayek, whose book *The Road to Serfdom* was published in 1944. Discussing the New Deal efforts to manage the economy—on Keynesian principles—from Washington, and anticipating Britain's swing to socialism, Hayek argued that "the direction of economic activity" by the state inevitably means "the suppression of freedom." In making the argument that economic freedom and political liberty are inseparable, Hayek was harking back to a principle of 19th-century Liberalism. In its extreme form, that doctrine was converted in mid-20th-century books into the Libertarianism of Ludwig von Mises and Ayn Rand, who asserted that "man exists for his own sake, that the pursuit of his own happiness is his highest moral purpose, that he must not sacrifice himself to others, nor sacrifice others to himself."

In its purest form, that philosophy bordered on anarchism, but in the less exaggerated terms that Hayek used, it became a useful tool for criticizing the statism inherent in the New Deal and its postwar successors, Truman's Fair Deal, Kennedy's New Frontier and Johnson's Great Society.

Among those to take up and popularize the Hayek viewpoint was Bill Buckley, the organizer of Young Americans for Freedom and the publisher of the *National Review,* the magazine that, since its founding in 1955, probably has done more than any other journal to keep conservatism alive and respectable in America.

Ten years later, the *National Review* was joined by *The Public Interest,* begun by Irving Kristol and Daniel Bell and featuring such other academics as Nathan Glazer, Daniel Patrick Moynihan, James Q. Wilson, Robert Nisbet and Seymour Martin Lipset. Along with a similar set of scholars, published in *Commentary,* the magazine Norman Podhoretz edited for the American Jewish Committee, the *Public Interest* group brought something fresh to the conservative dialogue. Many of its leading spirits were

—and most still are—Democrats, Moynihan being the Democratic Senator from New York. But they were Democrats who were at odds with many of the tendencies in their own party, including the leveling aspects of the new liberalism. They disliked the use of quotas to enhance the position and influence of blacks and women. They were staunchly anti-Communist and believed, as ardently as the traditional conservatives, in a strong defense establishment. When the 1972 Democratic convention chose George McGovern, the candidate of those promoting quotas and promising sharp cuts in defense, they defected in droves. They used their social-science techniques to prove that many of the government programs aimed at improving the cities or remedying the effects of segregation had had perversely opposite effects from those intended—and that often they had tended to destroy communities which had a character and quality worth preserving.

Of no community were they more protective than their own academic community. And when the organizers of the anti–Vietnam war protests, the promoters of affirmative-action programs and even the mobilizers of Harvard's clerical employees began interfering with the decorum and routine of the intellectuals' own domain, the universities, all of their conservative instincts came rushing forth. They joined eagerly in protecting their own meritocracy—the meritocracy of the mind—against outside interference, whether it came from the SDS or from a federal bureaucrat wondering why their departments had so few black or women professors.

Though many of them had contributed ideas and service to the creation of the postwar Democratic New Deal variants, they now discovered that the extremely powerful welfare state, aiming to redistribute income and level social classes, had brought about a decline of authority and a weakening of the values and standards by which the works of the mind—indeed, all of life—should be judged.

Of all the critiques that have issued from these two sets of conservative thinkers, the most important—for the politics of the Eighties—is probably their critique of Keynesian economics.

That school of economics probably achieved its greatest success in the first half of the Sixties, when Kennedy and Johnson, guided by such Keynesian economists as Walter Heller and Arthur Okun, steered the economy through the longest period of unbroken expansion, with minimal inflation, of modern times. Between 1961 and 1965, the economy grew an average of 6.4 percent a year, with inflation averaging only 1.3 percent.

But the record since then, under presidents of both parties struggling to apply the same principles, has been anything but successful. There have been three major recessions, and inflation from 1966 through 1978 averaged 6 percent a year, with the average rising as the Seventies continued.

The United States began incurring serious deficits in the balance of trade in 1977, and the value of the dollar began to plummet. Worst of all, the productivity of American workers fell from its long-term secular growth rate of 3 percent a year to a near-zero rate in the late 1970s.

Clearly, something had gone wrong, and the economists who stepped forward to assert, with some confidence, that they knew what it was were members of a new circle in their profession. Where the Keynesians had emphasized the management of demand by government fiscal and monetary policies, these economists—now mainly in their thirties and forties—put their reliance on what they called a "supply-side" model of the economy.

Without becoming too technical, what this meant was that they emphasized those factors like investment and savings rates which they considered crucial to expanding supplies of those commodities—including energy—on which modern economies depend. Believing that the best way to hold down the price spiral and combat inflation was to increase supplies, they took a view of the role of government different from that of their predecessors. With a positive view of the efficiency of market economics harking back to the old conservative economists, they asserted that the best thing government could do for the economy was stay out of its way. That is something of an overstatement. They did ask government to assure a steady, slow growth of the money supply rather than the expansions and contractions which have marked the last decade. But in contradiction to their predecessors, they argued strongly that tax rates and regulatory costs should be steadily reduced, because those are—in their view—the main barriers to the saving, investment and innovation on which growth of the economy depends.

The economists who developed this new approach included Martin Feldstein of Harvard, Michael Boskin of Stanford, and Robert Mundell of Columbia. But perhaps the most important—in terms of political influence, if not academic standing—was Arthur Laffer, 40, of the University of Southern California.

In the late Seventies, politicians, who normally avoid economists' jargon as if it were contaminated, loved to throw in references—admiring or disparaging—to "the Laffer curve." The Laffer curve was a plotting of a graph of a basic theorem of Laffer's economics—the assertion that in any given political economy there are two tax rates that will produce the same revenue. One is a very high, almost confiscatory rate. The other is zero.

Between the two are a series of points—"the Laffer curve"—at which government can set the real tax rates. The trick, Laffer said, is to find that point on the curve which will maintain the greatest degree of incentive for saving and investment and still produce the revenues for the government-supported social programs that keep a "safety net" under those who need help from the state.

The crisis in the American economy, Laffer and the other "supply-side" economists argued, resulted from the interaction of inflation and progressive tax rates, which together kept pushing earners into higher tax brackets. In many instances, they argued, nominal increases in salary were "taxed" away by the combination of inflation and higher-bracket tax rates. In every case, they said, incentives were reduced; and the inevitable result was declining productivity, declining savings rates, declining venture capital, declining supplies—and therefore, more inflation.

The nuances of this theory and the rebuttals it has drawn from its many critics are beyond the scope of this book. What is significant for our purpose is how the availability of this theory seemed to energize the conservative sector of politics.

As James L. Sundquist pointed out in his book *Politics and Policy*, few ideas move directly from academia to the center of the political debate. The distance between the two communities, the difference in style and needs, are great enough usually to require middlemen. The middlemen broker the academic ideas and popularize them enough that they become accessible and useful to the politicians.

In the case of the new conservative economics, the broker was a journalist named Jude Wanniski. Wanniski has an interesting history. Now 44, he was born, as he said, "into a mixed marriage. A mixed marriage in the sense that my father was a red-white-and-blue God-fearing Roman Catholic and my mother's father was an organizer for the Communist Party in the coal mines, atheistic and Marxist. The two men were roughly the same age, because my mother was so much younger than my father. And from the cradle on, they were both struggling for my soul. From the time I can remember, I was having Adam Smith shouted in one ear and Karl Marx in the other."

Wanniski grew up in Brooklyn and, in large part to escape the din, went all the way across the country to the University of California at Los Angeles to take degrees in political science and journalism.

Like many of the other neoconservatives, he started out as a Democrat, campaigning door to door for Adlai Stevenson in both his presidential bids, and getting a good cuffing from his father when "I kicked the brand-new television set during the Checkers speech."

But working in Las Vegas, early in his career, first as a journalist and then as an urban-renewal administrator, Wanniski was struck by the contrast between the efficiency of the gaming houses, with their clear profit motive, and the waste and sloth of his government agency.

When he moved back east, first as a Washington columnist for the *National Observer* and then as an editorial writer for *The Wall Street Journal*, he found himself becoming more conservative (though he did not change his voter registration to Republican until 1978).

Wanniski met Laffer in 1971, when Laffer was serving on the staff of the Office of Management and Budget. A year later, when Wanniski had gone to New York to write editorials and Laffer was back teaching, they began to have conversations at 10 o'clock each morning, reviewing the economic and political developments. "Little by little," Wanniski said. "I began learning the supply-side model." And with the fervor of the convert, he began to believe that in Laffer's curve lay not only the explanation of the inexplicable gyrations of the Seventies but salvation for the Eighties.

Some of Wanniski's borrowed insights began showing up in the *Journal*'s editorials, but in 1977 he felt impelled to spell out the theory in a popular-audience book called *The Way the World Works*.

The book achieved a wide readership, but no one devoured it more avidly than Jack Kemp. The two men had met in 1976, when Wanniski wandered by Kemp's office and ended up spending the whole day and evening talking with the Congressman. During the nine months in 1977 he was writing the book, Wanniski said, he would drive to Washington almost every weekend, check into a hotel and then drive out to Kemp's suburban home with that week's manuscript and discuss it with him through dinner and on into the night. "Kemp was learning the model by having those Sunday seminars, and was also helping me argue out what I believed so I could get into the next week's work."

On the face of it, Jack Kemp was an unlikely student. He grew up a Republican small-business man's son in Los Angeles; quarterbacked the football team at Occidental College, where he majored in physical education, and then went into pro football, achieving stardom with the Buffalo Bills in the mid-Sixties. But when Kemp was playing for the San Diego Chargers, Herbert G. Klein, a once-and-future press secretary to Richard M. Nixon who was then the editor of the San Diego *Union*, introduced Kemp to Republican politics. He wrote some editorials for Klein, campaigned for Nixon and Goldwater and Ronald Reagan, and worked off-season as a Reagan aide. "I was innately an activist," Kemp said in an interview. "I was captain of just about every team I played for. I helped organize the union of professional football players and was elected president five times, and I had an interest in the issues."

An article in a 1960 issue of *Fortune* magazine on Hayek and his theories led him to explore conservative economics, and ten years later, when his playing career in Buffalo was ending, it was not difficult for local Republican leaders to persuade him to run for a vacant seat in the U.S. House of Representatives.

When Kemp came to Congress in 1971, most people viewed him as another jock-politician, like baseball pitcher Wilmer "Vinegar Bend" Mizell. But they underestimated the competitive drive that had made

Kemp a success as a quarterback. He pushed himself as hard to learn the issues as he had once studied the playbook and the opposition defenses; Wanniski, Kristol, Laffer and other neoconservative eggheads found him their most conscientious pupil.

Kemp broke into prominence, however, only after Ford's defeat in 1976 had opened the way for younger Republicans to come to the fore. Along with Republican Senator William V. Roth of Delaware, he began promoting support in Congress and around the country for an application of "supply-side" doctrine—an across-the-board cut of 33 percent in income-tax rates over the next three years.

Despite the misgivings of many of the senior Republicans on the congressional tax-writing committees and the open skepticism of many of the Nixon and Ford economic advisers, "Kemp-Roth" was adopted by the Republican National Committee as its main issue for the 1978 congressional campaign. Kemp led flying squads of Republican speakers across the country, arguing that just as a Kennedy tax cut had spurred the growth of the economy in the early Sixties, so Kemp-Roth could do again.

The difference was that inflation and deficits were both at low levels when Kennedy proposed stimulating the economy by a sizable tax cut. In 1978, with inflation the main concern, Democrats (and some Republicans) argued that Kemp's prescription made no sense and would only deepen the budget deficit. Democrats claimed the cloak of fiscal responsibility for themselves, and when Republicans gained only 11 House and 3 Senate seats that fall, some in the GOP blamed the meager results on "Kemp-Roth." "The Laffer curve," the joke went, "is shaped like a boomerang."

But Kemp was unfazed, conceding at most that the tax-cut campaign had been put together so quickly that its intellectual premises were not well understood. He noted correctly that many of the Republican challengers who scored upsets in 1978 had campaigned strongly on "Kemp-Roth," and went on to argue that the resistance to his message really displayed a generational cleavage within the GOP.

"The people who are of the orthodox Republican view that I equate more with Eisenhower and George Humphrey [Eisenhower's Secretary of the Treasury] and maybe the Nixon Administration . . . really hold to a static view of the economy," he said. "The younger politicians, the younger academics, the younger journalists, the younger staffers on Capitol Hill almost right down the line understand the dynamics of our conception. Other than Irving Kristol, I don't see many people over fifty-five who do so. So I think the resistance to these ideas is almost generational . . . and I think there definitely is as much ego and pride in it as there is intellectual content. They have spent a lifetime wrapped up in one model of the world and the economy, and suddenly that traditional economic model is challenged, and they don't like it. But in the face of the overwhelming case being made for the whole incentive-oriented economic idea, I can't understand how it could be anything other than ego."

The notion that Arthur Burns, the former chairman of the Federal Reserve Board and a leading economic force in the Eisenhower, Nixon and Ford administrations, would have to go back to school to take economics lessons from ex-quarterback Kemp struck some Republicans as ludicrous. But there was no question that among the younger academically inclined members of Congress, Kemp's ideas were having an influence.

Not all of the support for these theories came from Republicans. Representative Phil Gramm, a Texas Democrat, 38, came to the House of Representatives in the 1978 election, replacing a wounded World War II veteran who had served there for 32 years and who had, in fact, been the sponsor of the War Orphans Act under which Gramm, the son of a disabled veteran himself, had gone to college. The young native of Georgia studied economics because, in 1963, the year he had to decide his college major, "economists were number one in pay" of all the professions. He became a full professor of economics at Texas A&M at age 30 and, looking for new worlds to conquer, started writing guest editorials for *The Wall Street Journal* and the *National Observer* and making speeches as "an advocate of fiscal responsibility and free enterprise."

He ran unsuccessfully for nomination to the Senate in 1976, but bounced back to win his House campaign two years later, choosing to campaign both times as a Democrat because "I'd always been a Democrat . . . and I thought if the country was going to be changed, it had to be changed by the majority party."

But in terms of his views, Gramm sounds like a Kemp clone. "If you look at the history of Western civilization," he said, "the facts are pretty clear that man's progress is accelerated in periods when . . . we allow markets, which are impersonal and impartial, to allocate resources . . . There's never been an engine for destroying poverty like capitalism."

Gramm said he regretted that "the perception of the industrial revolution has been colored by poets and novelists . . . People were starving to death in the country. The people who came into the cities to work in sweatshops were entering the highest pay, the best working conditions that they'd ever had in their lives."

"I have to admit," Gramm said, "that deep down in my heart . . . I have to believe that unionism is difficult to make compatible with my basic sense of the importance of the individual. If you're working for me and you don't like the wages or working conditions, you ought to be able to quit and go somewhere else, but I don't think you should have the right to shut down my place of business or prevent others from working for me."

Gramm said he had to bend his philosophy a bit in his farm district to allow for government price supports for agriculture, but only because "no nation in the West has ever had competition in agriculture" and foreign markets were still restricted against American goods. "But it's a compromise position," he said.

Despite Gramm's statement that he was far from alone in his views among the younger Democrats in Congress, the greatest currency for these ideas was among the young Republicans. Among those who lent intellectual and political credibility to Kemp's movement was Representative David A. Stockman of Michigan, by anyone's reckoning one of the brightest new Republicans in the House. Elected in 1976, when he was not quite 30, Stockman succeeded a classic Old Guard conservative who had gone down in flames as one of Nixon's diehard defenders on the House Judiciary Committee. A protégé of Moynihan's when he was a student at Harvard, Stockman came to Washington as a staff aide to Republican Representative John B. Anderson of Illinois, probably the most eloquent of the older-generation GOP progressives.

Given his background, Stockman was expected to join that minority within the minority of progressive or Ripon Society Republicans. But instead, he moved to Kemp's side as an advocate of incentive- and market-oriented economics, less known to the general public but perhaps more effective than the fervent Kemp in persuading other opinion makers.

As Stockman said in the first chapter of this book, he was convinced that many of the old policy debates between liberals and conservatives had been mooted by the passage of the Great Society legislation in the Sixties.

"Not all the dire consequences emerged that Republicans were predicting," he said, "and not all the wonderful results occurred that the Democrats had promised. And as a result, everybody's had to become a lot more skeptical."

What was lost in the Sixties legislative rush, Stockman said, was "any differentiating principle as to what government ought to do or not do. Anything is fair game. And as a result, Congress has turned into a great political bazaar, where every imaginable interest group comes and presses its claim. It is merely a matter of expedience and logrolling and bargaining as to whether or not that claim is satisfied. I think we've got to step back and develop some kind of principle to differentiate which claims are valid."

For Stockman, a history major in college and a student of theology and ethics in graduate school, the search for that differentiating principle has taken him into the realm of economics. "Obviously, it can't give you the total answer in every concrete instance, but there is a tendency to define problems that allegedly need a government response or government solution that might not be problems at all. I think in the energy area we have that now. Obviously, we're in an energy transition; energy is going to be more expensive; we may be using different forms of energy than we did in the past, or at least different mixes. But it's not clear to me at all that this transition has to be guided and managed and dominated in a very detailed way by government bureaucracies and political decision making."

In what he called his "more market-oriented view of things, with a more minimal government role," Stockman has become a critic of the "moderate Republicanism" he embraced when he first came to Washington as Anderson's staff aide. "It's always had a kind of mugwump characteristic to it," he said, "accepting the major premises of the dominant Democratic ideology, but suggesting that it be done a little slower, or with a little more restraint, or with some gesture to the private sector . . . I don't find there's any intellectual substance in the moderate Republican view."

Critics of the GOP would agree with Stockman's observation that mainstream Republican economics has lacked much "intellectual substance." In pre-Depression days, Republican economic policy consisted largely of favorable treatment for business, coupled with a faith in the self-adjusting capacity of the business cycle. Calvin Coolidge's memorable assertion in 1925 that "the business of America is business" summed up the thought of a generation of Republicans. The present-day conservative view may strike some people as harking back to that type of *laissez-faire* philosophy, but it is notably more skeptical of the alliance with business. Stockman, for example, was one of the most vocal opponents of the Chrysler Corporation's bid for federally guaranteed loans in 1979. His willingness to see a major employer in his home state go into bankruptcy would have been regarded as heresy by some older-generation conservatives.

Politically, Stockman said, the Republican future must lie not in saving old businesses, but in putting its stamp on what he saw as the emerging issue: growth. "I don't think either party is going to gain control by promising to manage the system we have now better or more efficiently. If you go out on that platform, you're not going to excite anybody. The party that will control the 1980s is the one that puts a new item on the agenda that meets an emerging public demand and need. For the last eight years we've had no economic growth in this country. And I think the emerging demand of the public today is for a revival of economic growth, of income growth, of economic opportunities in the classic sense."

In political terms, what distinguished Kemp and Stockman and their allies from the older generation of Republican conservatives was their willingness to take "heretical" positions and to reach for a majority constituency in places where Republicans have not traditionally campaigned.

They were willing to say that tax cuts should precede budget balancing. They were prepared to accept, as necessary and desirable, many of the "safety-net" social programs Democrats had enacted over Republican opposition. And they were scathing in their criticism of their standpat elders, who questioned this new approach.

"The Republican Party has been running on a balanced-budget platform for forty years," Kemp said, "and a lot of Republicans say that what was good enough for our party in the past ought to be good enough for us today. They say that if the people are too stupid and ignorant to recognize that we're going to do what's best for them, come hell or high water, then so be it. And you know, it's usually been both—hell and high water—that we Republicans have had.

"I've grown out of my belief that government is the enemy and the Democrats are the enemy. I have come to realize that the real enemy is my own party, which hasn't been offering a real choice to the electorate. We're the ones who have said to the people, 'Don't come to our table for dinner. All we're going to do is tighten your belt.' "

So when Kemp took his message to the longshoremen's convention and similar labor and Democratic-oriented groups, he was not just pandering to those particular audiences. When he said that Republicans did not deserve their support as long as the Republicans were arguing that "raising the rates to balance the budget and slowing down the economy to fight inflation were more important than making sure that people have jobs," he was expressing his own deeply held view.

But with his new doctrine of growth and incentives, keyed to lowered tax rates and less regulation, Kemp was preaching a different message—one that he and others like him believed could make the Republicans a majority party in the Eighties.

Describing his longshoremen's speech, he said, "I went in there with both barrels firing and talked about the issues—growth versus no-growth, income opportunities versus income redistribution—and walked out to a standing ovation, and spent a half-hour signing autographs with Hispanic and black and blue-collar workers. I just got a call yesterday from Paddy Sullivan, the longshoremen's president from Buffalo, who said that in five days of speeches the only single standing ovation in the whole convention was mine, and how proud he was as a Democrat of my getting that type of response. We're going to get those guys."

As it happened, it was not just the enthusiasts like Kemp who were talking seriously as the Seventies ended about the possibility of bringing a Republican or a conservative majority to control of Congress and the presidency in the Eighties. That was also the dream and ambition of a new generation of conservative organizers and movement leaders, some of whom had been pursuing that goal since the founding of Young Americans for Freedom in 1960.

Representative Robert E. Bauman, 43, a Maryland Republican, was one of the founders of YAF and served as its second president. In 1979, speaking as chairman of the American Conservative Union, part of the network of New Right organizations, Bauman told a conservative conference in Washington, D.C., that historian Clinton Rossiter was wrong when he said that "conservatism is the worship of dead revolutions."

"He was dead wrong," Bauman said. "This conference has demonstrated again that conservatism is the liveliest, most energetic revolutionary force in America today. Ours is no dead revolution. It is the jubilant interment of the rigid corpse of liberal statism."

That euphoric claim was remarkable for one who had seen the conservative movement bounce from defeat to defeat over twenty years' time. Even before there was YAF, Bauman had been involved with the Student Committee for the Loyalty Oath, whose futile mission was to save the provision of the first post-Sputnik aid-to-education law that required any student receiving help from the government to swear in writing he was not a subversive. And in the summer of YAF's founding, many of the young conservatives, including Bauman, had banded together in a losing effort to make Barry Goldwater the vice-presidential candidate on the Republican ticket.

In the course of the next two decades, YAFers fought and bled in futile efforts to: keep the House Un-American Activities Committee going; support Moise Tshombe and the cause of secessionist Katanga province; block the nuclear-test-ban treaty and later arms-control agreements; prevent American companies from operating behind the Iron Curtain; build public support for the Indochina war through the wonderfully named Student Committee for Victory in Vietnam; pass a constitutional amendment for prayer in public schools; prevent U.S. recognition of China; preserve American control of the Panama Canal and a few dozen more losing causes.

Yet somehow, two decades after YAF's founding, these specialists in futility emerged as the key figures in a network of New Right conservative movements whose power could not be dismissed by anyone who had to contend with them in the arena of American politics. The Gang That Couldn't Shoot Straight had become a formidable force, and one with a degree of internal cohesion rarely found among the quarrelsome characters who are attracted to an ideological crusade.

No one was more delighted about the transformation than the man who was the spiritual godfather of the younger-generation conservatives—

Barry Goldwater. When I went to see the 71-year-old Senator from Arizona one morning in 1979, he said, "I wrote somebody this morning that history is like a wheel and if you stand in one place long enough, like I have, the same spoke is going to come by."

"You're talking about the swing to conservatism?" I asked.

"I don't like to use that term, even though I'm a diehard conservative," he said. "I know many people who would resent being called conservative who are now beginning to follow what we always called conservative philosophy. I look on it as a feeling of responsibility—to the Constitution, to national defense, to fiscal sanity. The American people are so fed up . . . a lot of them are ready to call a constitutional convention to require a balanced federal budget, which is way out past what this conservative would ever do. But they're finally fed up with the results of what we've had under both parties' presidents the last twenty years or more.

"The country is more hungry for leadership today than it's ever been in my lifetime," Goldwater said. "You have to recognize that since the days of Harry Truman and possibly Dwight Eisenhower, we haven't had any real leadership. I don't include Jack Kennedy in that, because we don't know. I have a hunch he might have provided it. But Lyndon Johnson couldn't tell the truth if his life depended on it. Nixon? I think it was the biggest shock of my life to suddenly realize in a flash, after knowing this guy like a brother, that he was a dishonest man all the way through.

"And today, the average American knows that he's not being told the truth about the energy crisis. They know that they're not being leveled with on our relations with other countries. So every time the President opens his mouth, whether he's Republican or Democrat, the average American says, 'Oh, bullshit.' That's it. And it shouldn't be. That's why I go back to old Harry Truman. As much as I disagreed with his politics, I had to admire the guy's willingness to stand up and say, 'Look, Mr. and Mrs. America, this is what's going to happen.' And by God, it happened. We don't see that today."

If the praise for Truman sounded strange coming from Goldwater, even more ironic was his singling out of that aggressive champion of presidential power as the model of national leadership. For almost three decades Goldwater had cast himself as a critic of the strong presidency. Sixteen years ago, his jibe at Lyndon Johnson was that he was "so power-hungry, if you plug him in the fuses blow." Last year, Goldwater was in federal court challenging (unsuccessfully) Carter's authority to terminate the U.S. security treaty with Taiwan.

But looking at the "precarious position" of the United States, both domestically and internationally, in 1979, Goldwater said, "It's going to take very strong, dynamic, honest leadership . . . to come out of it. . . .

If we merely substitute for Carter a Republican Carter, then we're little better off."

He was also clear in his own mind that leadership would have to come from people a good deal younger than himself. "The younger conservatives," he said, "are far more vociferous, but they are also far more willing to stop and study. Before they say anything, they know their ground. . . . The older conservative had a tendency to just get up and shoot off. These kids are far superior to what we were. . . . I think it's time we got some of these younger people into our leadership—just eradicate all the people my age and people ten years younger. Just get rid of them and let's start all over."

As Goldwater noted, the young people of the New Right are intellectually more confident than their predecessors. And they differ from their elders not only in some of the programs they are espousing, but in the backgrounds from which they come. While not all the movement conservatives, by any means, agree with the economic theories advocated by men like Kemp and Stockman, they share their view that conservatism can—and must—develop a blue-collar constituency.

To a significant degree, that reflects their own background. Bob Bauman was the son of a frequently unemployed vaudeville musician. Both his parents were Democrats. The same was true of Charles Black, another of the organizers we will meet later in this chapter. In fact, most of them have working-class backgrounds. Richard Viguerie's father began as an hourly worker for a construction company and worked his way into an executive job with a Houston oil firm. Paul Weyrich's father was a Racine, Wisconsin, hospital worker. Bauman, Viguerie and Weyrich are from Catholic families. Their friend Representative Mickey Edwards, an Oklahoma Republican, is the son of a Jewish shoe salesman. (Several of the other New Right figures are also Jewish, helping end the anti-Semitism that was part of the unlovely heritage of the Old Right.)

None of them bears any resemblance to the silver-spoon conservatives of the political cartoons, and none of them thinks of their constituency as being limited to the Union League Club.

David Keene is an example. His father was president of the Rockford, Illinois, labor council and once ran for Mayor as a Democrat. His mother was a United Auto Workers representative.

By 1960, when he was 15, his family had moved from Rockford to Fort Atkinson, Wisconsin, and it was there that Keene had his first political experience—handing out literature on primary day for John F. Kennedy. But in the next twenty years, Keene worked, in succession, on the campaigns or on the personal staffs of Barry Goldwater, Spiro Agnew, James

Buckley, Ronald Reagan and George Bush. He also sandwiched in a race of his own for the Wisconsin state Senate—a race which he lost.

He can remember "the exact moment" he became a Republican. President Kennedy was speaking at Madison Square Garden, on May 20, 1962, at a rally organized by the AFL-CIO and other unions to build support for the Medicare bill, then stymied in Congress. In one paragraph, Kennedy rebutted the charge that Medicare was the first step toward British-style "socialized medicine." "What they do in England is entirely different," he said. "In England, the entire cost of medicine for people of all ages—all of it: doctors, choice of doctors, hospitals, from the time you're born till the time you die—is included in a government program. But what we're talking about is entirely different."

And in the next paragraph, Kennedy said, "The fact of the matter is that what we are now talking about doing most of the countries of Europe did years ago. The British did it thirty years ago."

Listening out in Wisconsin, 17-year-old David Keene thought it a "very demagogic speech. First he said it was an outrageous lie that this would be like Britain. And then he said we were thirty years behind Britain. I just couldn't figure out how we could be both. I just got outraged by the whole thing, and decided that was that."

At the University of Wisconsin, Keene sharpened his debating skills in arguments with the predominantly liberal student-body activists and faculty members. He managed a losing congressional campaign against liberal Democratic Representative Robert Kastenmeier and took a semester off to work as a field organizer for Goldwater.

"You know," he said, "for most of the conservatives of my generation, the Goldwater campaign was the thing that got them involved. It did for us what the McCarthy and McGovern campaigns later did for the Democratic Party."

And then Keene made a point that is fundamental to an understanding of the generational cycles of American politics—and particularly the emergence as a major power center of the oft-beaten young conservatives.

"You almost need those things once in a while," he said, "even though they're electoral disasters, in order to revitalize the blood of the party. The parties really do die out if there's not something to bring new people in. It's only a campaign like Goldwater's that is emotionally exciting and ideological and nonestablishment that allows new people to come in. Otherwise, those people would never be considered, would never be given the time of day. And even if they lose, those people have gained the experience to go on, and many of them stay around for good."

That is what Keene and his friends have done. After the Goldwater disaster, he returned to the Madison campus, edited a rather respectable campus magazine called *Insight and Outlook,* wrote thoughtful literary-political essays on such subjects as the conservatism of Nathaniel Hawthorne—and despised the emotional polarization of the campus by the Vietnam war issue. "I enjoy debating," he said, "but there was no possibility of that in the late 1960s. I got up to debate a fellow who later sat on the Madison City Council, and he got up and said, 'When the revolution comes, people like you will be shot.' And walked out. It really was not fun, particularly there, when we had the National Guard out all the time and tear gas and everything."

Keene spent more time on national conservative politics, and in 1969 became chairman of YAF. He made three trips to Vietnam, each time finding cause for encouragement about the Saigon forces' chances of victory. He went back to law school. It seemed aimless, but it was not.

Organizations like YAF exist to nurture and train political talents. "That's what it was all about," said Keene. "That's what it was set up for. That's why Buckley and those people were so interested in it."

YAF has coexisted—and sometimes competed for influence—with the larger Young Republican National Federation. YRs specialize in producing convention tacticians; the federation's own conventions and officer elections have not infrequently been brutal political cockpits. Those who survive and flourish in that environment—people like Bill Brock, the Republican National Chairman, and Bill Timmons, who was the convention strategist for President Ford in 1976—are unrivaled as back-room players.

"They can count votes," Keene said of the YRs' alumni, "and they can do all those things, but they don't think about issues. YAF was set up to provide some place for people who wanted to combine political activity with thinking and writing. You can never gauge the importance of youth organizations at the time. They always look kind of silly to everybody else. You have to wait ten years and see what has happened to those people."

Organizations like YAF provide another service. They help place people. As Keene discovered, "There aren't that many people in this country that are involved in politics in any kind of operational level. And there are even fewer who know what they are doing. Once you are identified as being in that group, the opportunities are amazing."

Patrick Buchanan, the Nixon speechwriter, was a frequent speaker at YAF meetings, and he scouted the organization for talent. He mentioned Keene to Spiro Agnew, and Agnew invited him in for a talk. At 25, Keene became political assistant to the Vice President.

"That is the remarkable thing," he said. "It was easier for me to move from YAF to the Vice President's office or a presidential campaign than it would be to become a county chairman in the Ohio Republican Party. That would take thirty years."

As it turned out, working for Agnew was a mixed blessing, but after Agnew was forced to resign Keene dug himself out of the wreckage and went to work for James Buckley, then Senator from New York. In 1976, the year of Buckley's defeat, Keene was recruited into the Ronald Reagan presidential campaign, and when that was stymied in Kansas City, he was invited to help the Ford-Dole ticket in its ten-week struggle to avert disaster. In 1979, he bounced back again as the number two man in the George Bush for President campaign.

"I guess what you have to learn out of the whole thing," Keene said, "is that you shouldn't take it quite that seriously. First of all, politics is a game. It's a very serious game, and the stakes are very high. But the fact is that one guy, whether he's Richard Nixon or Barry Goldwater or George McGovern or Gene McCarthy or Ronald Reagan, his being the President is not going to make the difference between the end of the world and its continuance. And if you realize that, you can put it into a little better perspective.

"I find it very difficult to dig a trench and get into it," Keene said. "There's nothing to be gained from sitting there and shooting at each other. You say that to some people and they say you cannot be serious; you must just be a dilettante or a hired gun; that it doesn't matter to you. Well, that's not true. But the idea of civility has to be there. Civility is as important as anything else in our politics. And if it's not there, the other things don't matter."

Support for that view came from other young conservatives, among them Republican Barry M. Goldwater, Jr., of California, 42, who since 1969 has represented a portion of the San Fernando Valley section of Los Angeles in the House.

Young Goldwater said that he often found himself at odds with Republican Party activists in his home state, who wanted to turn every issue into a crusade. "I see the same zealots in the conservative wing of the party that I saw when my dad was running, the people who saw no grays, strictly black and white. They're here today and they're tough to deal with, because I don't happen to belong to that element. I happen to be a little more flexible in my approach to problems and, hopefully, a little more realistic. But there are still those elements in our party—in the conservative movement—that are very dogmatic and very much zealots."

The Congressman, who was headed for a career as a stockbroker until he got a taste of campaigning in his father's race for President, said that he thought conservatives were changing, not in their philosophy, but in their willingness to "address ourselves to some of the real gut problems and issues, rather than grand abstractions that the average person can't relate to." Goldwater himself had become a leader in Congress on an issue that was not part of the old conservative repertory—the issue of personal privacy and "big brother" government.

"What brought it to my attention," he said, "was taking a tour of the Los Angeles FBI office. They were showing me their information system, and they plugged in my administrative assistant's driver's-license number, and out came this ream of material from the computer. Here was a guy who'd never broken the law, and yet they had a whole dossier on him, from the beginning of his life to that day."

There was a time, I suppose, when J. Edgar Hoover was flourishing under the protection of his conservative friends in Congress, when that feat would have been applauded. But Barry, Jr., said he was "stunned by that capability. This man was a model citizen. Now, it occurred to me later that maybe they had acquired this because of his security clearance as a congressional employee. But nevertheless, their ability to acquire the information without his knowing about it was what bothered me."

Goldwater introduced privacy legislation and then, finding that then Representative (and now New York City's Democratic Mayor) Edward I. Koch had a similar bill, decided it was time for a practical accommodation. "Ed and I got together and married our bills, because we felt that by getting an extreme liberal and an extreme conservative together, we could bridge the gap." Passed by Congress in 1974, the Privacy Act opened federal files, for the first time, to Americans who want to examine their own dossiers and to challenge, correct or amend the material.

Goldwater saw the alliance with Koch as a practical way to achieve an important conservative objective. "The basic concept of privacy legislation," he said, "is the right to be let alone . . . to have a certain amount of assurance that you do control your own person, your papers, your effects, your home. . . . And I think there is a direct link to the conservative view of government. The more you ask government to do, the more information the government has to collect. They have to find out who qualifies to fit the mold of poor, teacher, student, veteran, etcetera, etcetera, so they've got to collect more and more personal information.

"I happen to think that I can make the defense of privacy in conservative terms," the Congressman said. "But I was very delighted to see that a liberal also sees privacy as an important value in his life, that a liberal and a conservative have a lot of things in common on this issue."

The stress that Keene put on civility and Goldwater on coalition building other conservatives would reserve for the acquisition of competent organization and political muscle. And many of them would assert that it is only in the last five years that they have begun to mobilize effectively to challenge their ultimate enemy, the liberal Democrats. That mobilization—more than any doctrinal contributions—has really been the hallmark of the New Right.

Paul Weyrich was a 24-year-old radio reporter when he came to Washington from Denver in 1966 to work for Senator Gordon Allott, a Colorado Republican. Recalling those early days in the Senate, Weyrich said, "I naively thought that every week Strom Thurmond and Karl Mundt and Carl Curtis got together and strategized about the best way to put forth conservative initiatives. I found out, to my bitter disappointment, that there was no such exchange. Senators who had the same views and who sat right next to each other on the floor would take some initiative with an amendment or something and never tell their closest friends about it. And as a result they would get twenty-three votes and say, 'Well, we tried and it didn't work.' Not only was there no communication within the Senate, there was no exchange between the House and Senate or between conservative Democrats and conservative Republicans."

That description may be an exaggeration, for in fact, at the leadership level, Senate Minority Leader Everett McKinley Dirksen of Illinois and House Minority Leader Gerald R. Ford of Michigan were meeting regularly in these years, and a broader group of party officials was conferring through National Chairman Ray C. Bliss's Republican Coordinating Committee.

But the initiatives that came from those leadership sessions were too much diluted by the call to intraparty consensus to satisfy real conservatives. And besides, few of the schemes went anywhere.

Weyrich and other young conservatives knew they wanted something more—and by chance, in 1968, Weyrich got a glimpse of what was missing. "Senator Allott," he recalled, "had a reputation for being a liberal on civil-rights issues, and in 1968 he was invited to attend a strategy session on open-housing legislation. He couldn't go, and I asked him if I could attend in his place. . . . And there, before my very eyes, was the coordination mechanism of the opposition. . . . I wasn't entirely stupid, and I would see these battles come up [in the Senate] and I would see the orchestration of them, but until that meeting I never understood the mechanics. They had the aides to all the senators there, and they had the authority to commit their bosses to specific strategies. They had the representatives of foundations, which could supply data on this or that. They had a legal group. They had the outside lobbying groups, and they could say, 'We need some pressure when we get down the line, and if they come up with this amendment, we want the whole country alerted.' And they had a couple of columnists who said, 'I can write something; just give me the timing on it.'

"It was one of the best meetings I ever attended," Weyrich said, "and it gave me a tremendous insight into how the opposition operated. I determined from that moment on that if I had any reason to be here at all, it was to duplicate that effort on the Right."

Building a parallel mechanism became the preoccupation of Weyrich and a small group of other young conservatives, and has been their main work in the past decade. Their efforts were slowed by frequent internal differences over tactics, by the organizational and personal jealousies that always plague such long-term ventures, and by the resistance of such older-generation conservatives as Dirksen, Ford and Bliss and such moderate Republicans as Senator Hugh Scott of Pennsylvania, who followed Dirksen as Minority Leader, to the emergence of a new power base in their part of the political spectrum. But the structure has been built.

The first step was to start a conservative think tank, capable of providing public-policy research on a timely basis for congressional debate and propaganda purposes. The Heritage Foundation was created in 1972 to fill that role.

Heritage carries a full load of activities traditionally associated with think tanks. It has published over a hundred studies on a variety of domestic and international issues, some written by scholars-in-residence at the Heritage Foundation; a quarterly magazine, *Policy Review*, is published under its aegis and boasts such contributors as Moynihan, Milton Friedman and Winston Churchill II; it organizes seminars for specialized audiences—often members of Congress—on topics of current interest; and it sponsors an internship program for students willing to work half time for Congress and half time for the foundation.

But that is only part of what the Heritage Foundation attempts to do. Possibly more than any other think tank, it operates on equal parts of research and timing. Of its staff of 32, 10 researchers assemble bulletins to answer requests from congressional offices for quick information on legislative issues. The research staff also anticipates these issues by preparing more comprehensive background reports on subjects of congressional concern. Finally, the Heritage Foundation includes a "resource bank" which acts as a clearinghouse "of people, ideas and facts important to the community and those organizations sharing the same traditional values." The bank works to focus the conservative intellectual resources of its network on the problems at hand. One of its tasks is to arrange for witnesses with conservative credentials to testify at congressional hearings.

In addition to his 1969 "awakening" at the hands of the opposition, Weyrich had been fascinated by the influence of the Democratic Study Group, the caucus of liberal House Democrats which had been founded in the mid-1950s by Eugene J. McCarthy and a handful of others and had become by the mid-1960s the dominant political force among House Democrats. The DSG staff, supported by contributions from affiliated House members, provided background memos on upcoming legislation, an informal but effective floor "whip" system and a vehicle for the liberals to shape their legislative strategy.

In preparation for the 1970 election, Weyrich and his friends—House and Senate aides—contacted Republican congressional candidates and offered help on speeches and information for their campaigns. Those who took the bait were urged to stop by on their visits to Washington and were given "a standard little number" by Weyrich and Co. on why Republicans needed their own version of the DSG. A dozen people who had, perhaps rashly, pledged to commit a portion of their staff allowances to that project were elected in 1972, and with the help of such young conservative incumbents as Representative Philip M. Crane of Illinois, the Republican Study Committee was launched. Two years later, a parallel organization was set up in the Senate, called the Steering Committee. The director of that committee is 44-year-old Margo Carlisle, an English and philosophy student who was drawn into politics by the 1964 Goldwater campaign. "Great strides have been made since this got started in 1974," she said, "just from people knowing each other and learning to lean on each other. If you say to me, 'Margo, I want to know something about the tax code,' I'll have you a tax expert within seconds, or just about anything else—the range of a particular strategic weapon and its cost, or whatever. . . . There was a time when it was considered absolutely freakish for someone with a Ph.D. to work in a conservative Republican Senator's office. And that's not so long ago. But one expert attracts another. It's a kind of stand-up-the-dominos effect."

The next piece of liberal machinery Weyrich and his friends copied was the campaign committee. There were many organizations, of both the Left and the Right, that were raising campaign funds for sympathetic candidates, but Weyrich noted that the "remarkably effective group which had been the point of the political operation" for the Left was the National Committee for an Effective Congress (NCEC). Rather than just sending money, NCEC supplied candidates with such specialized campaign assistance as polling and media advisers.

So Weyrich launched the Committee for the Survival of a Free Congress (CSFC) in 1974 to provide similar services for conservative office seekers. Weyrich now serves as executive director of that operation, which projects a budget of $1.5 million for the election year of 1980.

A team of ten regional directors around the country not only identifies attractive candidates in winnable congressional races, but actively tries to recruit conservatives who are willing to stump wholeheartedly for office. (Weyrich notes that conservatives on the ballot often run more out of a sense of civic duty—to get right-wing views into the political discourse—than with any hope for their own victory.) One of the more exacting standards CSFC uses to select candidates for its endorsement is a 12-page, 72-item questionnaire that puts to the test their dedication to conservative principles: The issues run the gamut from Medicaid-funded abortions for welfare recipients to new Pentagon spending to keep pace with Soviet weaponry.

At a CSFC training seminar for candidates and their staffs, the committee's five full-time Washington workers teach a detailed precinct-organization plan for turning out the conservative vote. Called the "Kasten plan"—after former Republican Representative Robert Kasten of Wisconsin, who first used the method in a state Senate race—it delegates responsibility for specific vote goals to a network of precinct chairmen as tightly organized as the urban machines of days past. As the campaign progresses, CSFC field operatives keep in close touch with candidates' staffers on applying the Kasten plan and interpreting polling data and historical vote patterns. Other "in-kind" services include paying part of the staffers' salaries, furnishing advice on relations with the news media and helping generate locally raised funds.

After the campaign season is over, CSFC and its companion operation, the Free Congress Research and Education Foundation—with its own $500,000 annual budget—hold members of Congress to rigorous standards of conservative performance with the Conservative Register, a detailed rating on as many as three hundred votes in each session. Broken down into categories of social, economic and defense issues, the register keeps a careful watch for fair-weather friends of the New Right movement—those who vote with conservatives on high-visibility issues but who leave the conservative fold on little-noticed matters.

Bit by bit and piece by piece, Weyrich said, "what we have sought to do is analyze what have been the component parts of the liberal success over the years, and then duplicate them, albeit on a smaller scale."

Financing all this was not easy. Members of the Joseph Coors family and executives of their Colorado brewery helped launch the Heritage Foundation and CSFC and subsidized the early staff efforts that led to the formation of the Republican Study Committee. Others emulated them. Under the sponsorship of about ten prominent foundations and individual donors, the Heritage Foundation currently operates on a budget of $2.5 million, and CSFC has a budget of $1.5 million in election years and $900,000 in nonelection years. But the sustaining infusion of cash into the New Right network has come as a result of its development of direct-mail solicitation as a principal tool of fund raising. Indeed, so successful has the New Right been in this respect that its opponents think it may have tipped the entire political balance in its direction.

To a remarkable degree, the story of that development is the story of one man: Richard A. Viguerie, now 47. Viguerie was a 28-year-old University of Houston Law School graduate when he was offered the job as executive director of YAF.

He found the barely one-year-old organization $20,000 in debt and immediately began making the rounds of the wealthy right-wing businessmen who had subsidized YAF's birth. "I found out real quick I didn't like asking people for money," Viguerie recalls. "I figured there had to be a better way to raise money. So I started writing letters. That seemed to work pretty good. So I hired more secretaries. I got a mimeograph machine. Just one thing pyramided on another, and after a year and a half, I said, 'Hey, where's this been all my life?' YAF relieved me of all duties except direct mail, and I said, 'This is for me.' "

While Viguerie was discovering his calling at YAF, the Goldwater campaign of 1964 was providing the first evidence in presidential politics that large numbers of conservatives were prepared to make small investments in the cause. The Goldwater campaign attracted 651,000 contributors and opened many eyes to the possibilities of a new kind of political financing.

It was in January 1965, two months after Goldwater's defeat, that Viguerie left YAF and formed his own direct-mail company. It has grown in the past fifteen years to a series of interconnected companies with several hundred employees and a battery of computers containing, as of 1979, the names and addresses of about 5 million conservative givers.

In 1978, Viguerie raised the stunning sum of $5.2 million for the re-election campaign of Senator Jesse A. Helms of North Carolina. But his most successful work has probably been done not on behalf of individual candidates but for the issues organizations that provide his staple employment. Groups like the Gun Owners of America, the National Right-to-Work Committee and the opponents of government-financed abortion use the Viguerie computer to mobilize members and financial support, and to bombard members of Congress and the state legislatures with their messages.

Viguerie is not overly modest about the weapons he has forged for the conservative movement. "We wouldn't be here without this technology," he said. "We just literally wouldn't be here. Without direct mail, the conservative movement as we know it today would not exist. We sell our magazine subscriptions, whether it's *National Review* or *Human Events* or *Conservative Digest*, through direct mail. We finance our foundations, our candidates, our causes, through direct mail. We also fight our battles through direct mail. A common-situs picketing bill would be law today were it not for direct mail." (That labor-backed bill, passed by Congress in December 1975, would have allowed a union to picket an entire construction site in a dispute with any single contractor on that site.) "Jerry Ford got 720,000 cards and letters [in late 1975 and early 1976] to veto that bill from Right-to-Work Committee mailings. We killed public financing of congressional campaigns through direct mail to the senators,'' and the same techniques played a key role in other congressional fights.

In the last few years, the Carter Administration, liberal congressmen and labor and liberal organizations have found it increasingly difficult to withstand the lobbying pressure of single-interest groups employing direct-mail techniques to mobilize their membership. A public-opinion poll saying 70 percent of the people favor gun control, for example, may not be as persuasive to a typical member of Congress as letters from two hundred constituents who say they are watching how the congressman votes on this issue and will work against him at the next election if he supports a gun-registration bill. The congressman views the poll figures as an abstraction, and suspects (correctly) that many of those polled will neither know nor care how he votes on gun registration. But the two hundred people who have been prompted by a computer letter to write him of their opposition are very real; they must be answered at once and dealt with at the next election if offended.

The power of Viguerie and the direct-mail technique has been enhanced by the fact that there is as yet no similar entrepreneur or facility for organization of the Left.

''I don't really fully know the answer why this is,'' Viguerie said, ''but one of the reasons has to be they haven't had a need of it. We had to invent it, because, without sounding like I believe in conspiracies, which I do not, it is just a fact of life that the major media in this country are dominated by people who have a left-of-center bias or perspective—whether it's radio, television, newspapers or magazines. Direct mail has enabled us to bypass the monopoly that Walter Cronkite and Katharine Graham have on the information that's fed to the American people. We can bypass the monopoly the Left has on the media and go directly to our people out there, which is what the special-interest groups do. They tell them when there's a vote coming up that concerns them. They tell them that Congressman X or Senator Y doesn't represent you in the area where you and I share a concern—gun control, abortion, whatever it is. We had to discover or invent direct mail, because as conservatives we would not be in business without it.''

Viguerie is a somewhat controversial figure within the New Right—as well as a much-feared symbol of conservative power among liberals in both parties. The costs of his fund-raising campaigns have been called excessive by some of his former clients, who complain that relatively little of the ''take'' reaches the supposed beneficiary. Personally, he is an intense, hard-driving man, whose impatience for victory for the causes he champions makes him scornful of what he considers irrelevant political inhibitions.

Viguerie and some of the others, like Paul Weyrich of the CSFC and Howard Phillips of the Conservative Caucus (who ran for the Democratic nomination for the U.S. Senate in Massachusetts in 1978), have tended, at times, to see the Republican Party and its officeholders as impediments to the conservative revolution they seek. The New Right never really trusted Richard Nixon, seeing him, at best, as a political pragmatist who might help their causes when it suited his interest. Viguerie, for example, said that he had defended Nixon for many years on the theory that "my enemy's enemy is my friend." But during the 1968 presidential campaign, when Hubert Humphrey began gaining and Nixon began waffling, "it hit me like a bolt out of the blue, hearing him on the car radio one day when I was driving into Washington, that the guy really is deceitful. He really is tricky. The truth is really not in the guy."

By 1972, Viguerie, like many of the others in the New Right, had adopted the view that Nixon's defense policies and his overtures to China were signs of fatal weakness in the anti-Communist ideology. So Viguerie helped Representative John Ashbrook of Ohio (another product of the Young Republicans and a New Right organization sponsor) in his abortive challenge to Nixon in the primaries.

By the time of Watergate, Viguerie, along with such New Right theorists and publicists as Kevin Phillips and William Rusher, had decided the Republican Party was probably dying. They thought of a new coalition uniting the supporters of George Wallace and Ronald Reagan under a new banner. Viguerie took on direct-mail fund raising for Wallace's 1976 campaign, and when Reagan resolutely insisted on keeping his challenge strictly within the framework of the Republican Party, Viguerie tried to promote John B. Connally, a Democrat-turned-Republican, as a write-in in New Hampshire. When that failed, he flirted with a third-party presidential ticket including himself for Vice President, but that too was stillborn.

Perhaps because so many of them come from working-class, Democratic families, there is a longing among many of the New Right politicians to slip away from the constraints of the Republican Party. Weyrich and Viguerie share the vision that at least in the House of Representatives, it might be possible to form a coalition of Republicans and conservative Democrats and seize control of that body by electing the Speaker and other officers. (Such bipartisan coalitions were formed in 1979 in the New Hampshire and New Mexico legislatures.) Weyrich said he believes such a coalition could come in the House of Representatives in the 1980s, were it not for what he called "the inordinate sense of loyalty to the Republican Party" of the older GOP House members.

His dream is shared by such New Right congressmen as Representative Mickey Edwards of Oklahoma City, a former staff member of Weyrich's House Republican Study Committee, who began political life as a Democrat, later became a national vice chairman of the Young Republicans and in 1976 became the first Republican in forty-eight years to represent his Oklahoma district, which is 75-percent Democratic in registration.

Edwards—who hired three blacks for his staff and found "my single biggest base of support is in labor-union households," despite the criticisms the AFL-CIO made of his record—is convinced that conservatism can prevail with blue-collar voters. His union constituents, he said, care less about "union-versus-management conflict" laws than they do about busing, gun control and taxes.

He has few disagreements with those Democrats who also represent "basically working-class, conservative people," but said he regards liberal Republicans as "totally meaningless in the spectrum of politics. There is no purpose for a liberal Republican. He is just a duplicate Democrat."

This attitude has been a source of real conflict within the conservative movement. Those who believe in ideology over party have felt free to endorse and underwrite primary campaigns against moderate-to-liberal Republican incumbents and to support conservative Democrats in districts where Republicans can rarely win, all in hopes of creating a conservative-coalition majority in Congress.

They are also bitterly critical of Republican leaders who, though conservative themselves, support the renomination and re-election of moderate Republicans, in hopes of achieving a congressional majority within the GOP. "I really think they're smoking something when they believe that," Weyrich remarked of such GOP leaders. "I don't believe it will happen in my lifetime, and I ain't very old."

The party regulars, including many conservatives, consider the theory of the new-party or new-coalition people either impractical or undesirable. David Keene, for one, said there would be too much sacrifice of "libertarian principles and economic freedom" in the proposed "alignment with rednecks and union members." While John T. (Terry) Dolan, executive director of the National Conservative Political Action Committee (NCPAC), predicted in the fall of 1978 that "a conservative takeover of the Democratic Party is clearly beginning to develop," his predecessor in that job, Charles Black, was skeptical. "There might have been ten or fifteen Democratic primaries where those guys [like Dolan and Weyrich] had an impact in the country in the last four years, but other than that, it's all inside the Republican Party," Black said.

Most conservatives took Black's view. Tom Winter, the 43-year-old editor of *Human Events,* the conservative weekly, said, "I would think most conservatives feel that the Republican Party with all its faults—and God knows it has them—still is probably the best vehicle for conservative expression." Sharing in the conviction that "liberal Republicans are a dying breed," Winter said, "If we ever really are going to implement a solid conservative program, it probably would be under a Republican President and a Republican Congress."

The general view was expressed by David Keene, who said that "during the next few years, conservative activists of an ideological but practical bent can be expected to dominate the GOP at all levels," and "as a basically conservative party in tune with the electorate on many issues, the GOP does have a future."

In 1979 the New Right leaders were scattered in their presidential preferences, with most backing Reagan, but others working for Connally, Bush, Crane or Tennessee Senator Howard H. Baker, Jr.

But these younger-generation conservatives had a strong sense that what holds them together as a group is more important, for the long term, than any current differences relating to tactical decisions or presidential candidate preferences.

All those mentioned here—and another dozen or so—began meeting regularly at Viguerie's office and other locations at the time in 1974 they were trying to derail confirmation of their old symbolic foe, Nelson Rockefeller, as Vice President. The meetings continued, even when they were supporting different presidential candidates.

And they were behaving not as a secret conspiracy, but as a serious political movement. Of all the differences the new generation of conservatives represent, probably none is more striking than their sense of openness and self-confidence.

As Weyrich remarked, "The highest badge of honor of the Old Right, if you will, was losing. It was a sign you were absolutely doing your job. If you won something, you had to examine whether you had perhaps done something wrong. The new guys have the attitude that it is possible to win. And psychologically alone, that is a tremendous advantage."

Weyrich noted a second difference—to which as a journalist I can attest: The new generation of conservatives is not secretive.

Weyrich recalled that when the Senate Steering Committee was being formed, "one of the original members said, 'We have to keep this group a secret, because if the media get hold of it, they'll crucify us.' Well, I immediately leaked the existence of the thing to the media, because I felt it would never succeed unless it was open and aboveboard. How can you possibly affect public policy if you're meeting in a closet?"

As a result of this psychological shift, the New Right leaders have won wide publicity (from the supposedly hostile media) for their tax-cutting and other initiatives, as well as for the candidates they support. And unlike their predecessors, who assumed failure and achieved it, they are remarkably upbeat about their prospects.

"At least," said Weyrich, "it has brought the conservatives into the position where we are now playing football on the same field where the liberals are playing. Before, we were playing baseball while the liberals were playing football, and the scores were always 38 to 9."

"I think," said Viguerie, speaking in the same vein, "that for the first time in our lifetime, we're going to see one gosh-awful fight between conservatives and liberals to see who's going to govern America. It hasn't been a fair fight up to now. The liberals have had things pretty much their own way. We haven't had leadership; we haven't had organization and structure. We've had a few men saying a few things, but we haven't had any leadership. And now we've got this leadership, and there's going to be a titanic battle here. And it can go either way."

7 · Labor and Business

SNAPSHOT 1: At the University of Illinois in the early 1960s his nickname was "Campus Vic," because he was a big wheel in every going organization: president of the Interfraternity Council, vice president of the student body, a gossip columnist for the *Daily Illini*—and not least, president of the Young Republicans. With that background, and a law degree from American University, it was not surprising that he was made director of administration for Citizens for Nixon-Agnew in 1968.

SNAPSHOT 2: Born six months after the Depression began to a near-bankrupt Yonkers, New York, jeweler, he was reared in a family devoted to Franklin D. Roosevelt. After graduating from Union College and Columbia University Law School, he began practicing law in New York City and soon became active, along with a young academic named Daniel Patrick Moynihan, in the Samuel J. Tilden Democratic Club in the Chelsea area of downtown Manhattan. When John F. Kennedy ran for President in 1960, he plunged into registration work as a volunteer and, after the election, was recruited by Robert F. Kennedy for the post of general counsel of the Federal Mediation and Conciliation Service. Later, he would work in the presidential campaigns of Robert and Edward Kennedy.

In the late 1970s, these two men were involved in two of the biggest lobbying battles in Washington—the first man in the fight over labor-reform legislation and the second in the struggle over oil-price decontrol.

It was an accident of history that made Victor Kamber, the Nixon-Agnew campaign aide, the chief tactician for the AFL-CIO in its unsuccessful effort to amend the labor law and crack down on anti-union employers who were frustrating the spread of unionism in the South. And it was a similar accident that made Herbert Schmertz, the second-generation Democratic activist, the head of Mobil Oil Company's aggressive drive to reduce government constraints on the energy industry.

What was no accident was that two people of exceptional political aptitude and inclination would find themselves involved in major battles for the minds of the American voters and their elected representatives while employed by giant labor and business organizations. The community organizers of the New Left and the direct-mail specialists of the New Right whom we met in the last two chapters may glorify the political power of the "little people" they are seeking to mobilize. But as we enter the final two decades of this century, much of the struggle for control of public policy is being waged by those massive agglomerations of economic power, the unions and the corporations, and the people they employ to direct their political strategies.

The struggle is not a new one, nor is their participation in it. A trade-union leader, Eli Moore, was elected to Congress from New York in 1834, and as early as 1908 the AFL was giving its endorsement and its campaign contributions to the Democratic presidential nominee, William Jennings Bryan. Twelve years earlier than that, big business had demonstrated its political influence in an even more dramatic fashion, assembling the biggest political war chest American politics had ever seen, to finance the election of the Republican nominee, William McKinley.

What is changing about business and labor's involvement in politics is not just the scale of the effort—the millions both sides spend in lobbying, political action, education and propaganda—but its sophistication. Kamber and Schmertz are far from unusual in finding their way from presidential campaigns to labor and business politics. Many other young veterans of political and governmental service have followed a similar path, bringing to the union halls and the corporate headquarters a far more skilled and subtle understanding of the tools necessary to influence policy decisions in the public sector. The development and testing of these techniques, on both sides of the struggle, clearly will be a major factor in the politics of the 1980s and 1990s.

For Herb Schmertz, the move from government to the oil business did not seem that dramatic. He stayed on with the Johnson Administration for a few months after John Kennedy's assassination, then set up a Washington law practice and in 1966 was hired by Mobil as a labor-relations manager. He began to blossom about three years later when he moved into the job of vice president for public affairs. The title itself is of fairly recent vintage in corporate life. Richard A. Armstrong, the president of the Public Affairs Council, a Washington clearinghouse for corporate political programs and a man with a quarter-century of personal experience in the field, said that it was not until the early 1960s that the term began to be used. Companies like Ford, Johnson & Johnson, U.S. Steel, Republic Steel, Minnesota Mining & Manufacturing, Monsanto, Chase

Manhattan Bank, Pacific Gas & Electric and Coca-Cola were among the pioneers.

In an ideal setup according to Armstrong, the public-affairs officer has authority over the Washington office and its lobbyists as well as the state government-relations, community-relations and inner-city-minority programs. He or she has a voice in the company's institutional advertising and its charitable giving as well—and serves as the political adviser to top management.

Schmertz does almost all these things—and does them with a budget and independence that have made him the envy of others. Mobil has become a major underwriter (about $7 million a year) of public-affairs and cultural programming on commercial and public television, and a sponsor of nationally broadcast "town meetings" from the John F. Kennedy Center in Washington. But what has made the company famous—and controversial—was its decision to spend about $1.5 million a year on regular, detailed and aggressively worded commentaries on the energy and regulatory policies of the U.S. government and the way those issues are reported in the American press and on television. Schmertz said the Mobil editorial advertisements—which run regularly in about ten of the country's most influential newspapers—are "a complete reflection of the kind of top management Mobil has . . . and their desire to participate in the dialogue, their willingness to put themselves and their views on the line for examination." The ads began in the early 1970s, as the energy issue was beginning to move into public consciousness, and accelerated after oil-company operations and profits became a matter of increasing controversy in the years following the oil embargo of 1973. "We had a very strong belief," Schmertz said, "that the energy policies of this nation were 180 degrees wrong; consistently wrong, aggressively wrong, intensely wrong. There was a sense of frustration that whether we were right or not, we were not getting our position across by putting out press releases and talking to reporters. The press was either ignoring the issue or misreporting it . . . so we concluded that the only way we could do this was through paid media. We still believe that. We still believe there is no hope for getting our story across any other way."

The ads, featuring explicit rebuttals and criticisms of statements by politicians and print and television journalists, have been enormously controversial. Congressional critics of Mobil have conducted investigations into the financing of the ad campaign and have subpoenaed what Schmertz called "a truckload of documents and backup materials." With some bitterness, the Democratic activist–turned–corporate spokesman said the "liberal Democratic congressmen and senators [involved] clearly didn't believe in the First Amendment insofar as it applied to a corporation. . . . There was clearly an attempt to intimidate us."

But despite the controversy, he said, "our perception is that on balance, it [the ad campaign] has been quite successful . . . in educating legislators and newspaper people on our positions and views." Mobil ads were frequently cited by both sides in the debate on energy issues. As the 1970s closed, other companies in highly regulated industries—energy and the airlines, for example—were beginning to run issue advertising of their own.

As the instigator and editor of the Mobil ad campaign, Schmertz became perhaps the oil industry's best-known spokesman. Therefore, there was understandable consternation and confusion late in 1979 when he took an unpaid six-week leave of absence to set up the television-advertising phase of the presidential campaign of Edward Kennedy, who, as a Senator and a candidate, constantly berated the oil companies in general and Mobil in particular for their alleged profiteering and monopolistic practices. Schmertz said he had "a long-standing personal relationship" with the Kennedys and denied there was any conflict of interest. But *Fortune* magazine expressed the skepticism of the business community when it asked in an editorial, "If Mobil's editor-in-chief thinks Teddy is presidential material despite his disastrous views on economic and energy issues, then why should readers of those Mobil 'editorials' think the issues involved are all that serious?"

A somewhat similar, if less-publicized, problem faced Vic Kamber when he moved from Republican politics to the labor movement. After his work on the Nixon-Agnew campaign, he joined the staff of a Republican Congressman from New York, Seymour Halpern, for several years, and then was offered a job by then Governor Nelson A. Rockefeller as the director of New York State's Washington office. At the same time, Robert A. Georgine, the incoming president of the building and construction trades department of the AFL-CIO and a man Kamber had met during his years with Halpern, asked him to join his staff as research director.

"I went to the Governor and I told him about my offers," Kamber recalled. "He said, 'Grab the labor thing, do it for a year as a Republican, and then you can go out and market yourself to anybody in the world, because there's no such thing as Republicans in labor.' "

Kamber took the advice, accepted Georgine's offer and became the "in-house Republican" at the labor federation's headquarters. His political skills were evident enough that by 1977, when he had been there three years, AFL-CIO President George Meany borrowed him from Georgine's staff to run the task force set up to lobby for passage of the labor-reform bill, whose principal purpose was to end some of the obstructionist tactics used to thwart union organizing efforts in the South. (In 1980, Kamber did move on, as Rockefeller had suggested, to form his own political-lobbying consulting firm, with several union clients.)

Just as Schmertz became frustrated with the oil industry's efforts to influence policy through press releases, so Kamber discovered in his work on the labor-reform task force some serious gaps in labor's approach to lobbying.

"We were a terribly effective force in elections," he said. "We could turn our people out—that one day. Our operation was phenomenal. It was like a political party, and in many cases better than either political party. . . . But we'd never learned how to translate that effectiveness to legislative politics. . . . We weren't succeeding in communicating with our people. We weren't building the kind of an effort that was needed to make an impact in Washington."

Kamber said that until the task force was set up, for example, the unions had not used one of the basic tools of contemporary legislative politics—the public-opinion poll—to guide their strategy. The task force commissioned a poll and discovered some disturbing facts. On the positive side, 8 out of 10 Americans believed that unions were a vital part of America, that they not only protected the interests of the workers but were in the forefront of the battles for education, health care and other social services. At the same time, similarly heavy majorities were disillusioned with labor's leadership, suspecting them of criminal ties, personal aggrandizement, illiteracy and being out of touch with the times.

The task force faced a problem: how to propagandize for labor reform without using labor's own leaders. As Kamber said, "Obviously the George Meanys of the world weren't being accepted by the American public." The answer was a modern application of a very traditional doctrine: coalition politics. Labor had been a key part of the Democratic Party coalition for two generations or more, but in the late Sixties and early Seventies it had been isolated from its coalition partners. The first great breach came over the Vietnam war: Meany and contemporaries, staunchly anti-Communist, supported the war effort and bitterly opposed the anti-war liberals, the churchmen and the student demonstrators who condemned the American involvement in Indochina. The disagreement spilled over into politics in the 1968 campaign, when labor ardently supported Hubert H. Humphrey while most of the anti-war liberals were with Eugene J. McCarthy or Robert Kennedy. The split became more aggravated in 1972, when the nomination of George McGovern left the AFL-CIO neutral in a presidential contest for the first time in its history. The federation withdrew from formal participation in Democratic Party affairs, charging that the new "reforms" in delegate selection discriminated against its members and in favor of the middle-class liberal "elitists." Many of the new constituencies in the Democratic Party were raising issues with which the Meany generation of unionists was plainly uncomfortable. The activist women, with their views on abortion and equal rights, antagonized them. So did the homosexuals and other "exotic" minorities. Even the old alliance between labor and blacks, so vital in securing passage of the landmark civil-rights legislation of the Sixties, was strained, as the affirmative-action policy in employment collided with the seniority principle so sacred to the unions.

When Kamber began courting support for the labor-reform bill from those groups, and proposing a public-relations campaign using their leaders—rather than union chieftains—as the spokesmen on the issue, it provoked what he called "a horrendous, crazy kind of battle" inside the AFL-CIO headquarters. "If you knew the infighting among staff people here about putting some of those names in a brochure, or getting someone to make a speech, you would not believe it," he said.

In the end, the campaign failed. Labor reform passed the House of Representatives in 1977 but fell victim to a business-backed filibuster in the Senate. As the campaign developed, Vic Kamber—the outsider—found himself going back into the history of the labor movement to try to understand the ferocity of the emotions that were triggered by this fight. What he found—what anyone would find—is that labor and business have shared a long and often bloody involvement in the struggle to mobilize the power of the government, political power, on their own side in the clash between workers and management.

Business got to government first. The nation's industrial expansion between the Civil War and World War I was spurred by the active assistance of pliant state and national governments to entrepreneurs large and small. To encourage construction of the railroad network across the continent, for example, the government did more than send federal troops to conquer hostile territory and protect rights-of-way; Congress also obliged the railroads in the 1860s and '70s with virtually interest-free loans and the gift of over 100 million acres of public land. If there was room for Washington's generosity, there was also room for railroad men to demonstrate their gratitude to cooperative politicians. The Crédit Mobilier scandals of the Grant Administration—a tangle of preferential stock deals and kickbacks to congressmen who looked out for the Union Pacific interests—epitomized business' early, unsophisticated methods of trying to win government favor.

The workingman's reaction to this coziness between business and government was predictably one of resentment. The first national labor organization, the short-lived National Labor Union founded in 1866, proclaimed that "there is one dividing line, that which separates mankind into two great classes, the class that labors and the class that lives by others' labor." But it was not until the financial panic of 1873 focused attention on the economic power of the railroads and their discriminatory rate structures that Midwest farmers and manufacturers forced the passage of the first regulatory laws through the state legislatures.

In 1887 Congress created the Interstate Commerce Commission, a weak first step (supported by the railroad barons themselves) but a crucial one in defining the role of the federal government toward private enterprise—establishing the responsibility of government to oversee industries where the free market had broken down.

Industrial relations in this era were marked by an obdurate refusal by business to recognize the right of workers to organize. In 1874, however, a tentative step toward collective bargaining was taken by Mark Hanna—the same Ohio industrialist who twenty years later would come to epitomize big-business–Republican ties. He set up direct negotiations, with an impartial mediator, during a miners' strike that year in Ohio's Tuscarawas Valley. But the contract did not hold, and business went back to blocking unionization by strikebreaking, labor spying and intimidation. Labor responded with greater violence, exemplified by the terror and assassination tactics of the "Molly Maguires" in the bitter 1874–76 anthracite strikes in Pennsylvania. The strikes spread in 1877, and government intervention took the form of state militiamen and, in some instances, federal troops being brought in to halt the strikes.

"The Great Upheaval" of 1877 (as the violence of that year is known) set the stage for labor's first full-scale entrance into third-party politics in 1878. Workers joined with disgruntled farmers to win fourteen seats in Congress and many local offices on the Greenback-Labor ticket. But their protest did nothing to halt the growth of the giant trusts—in oil, beef, tobacco, steel and banking—during the next two decades. The trusts bought their way in politics, moving their charters from state to state to find the most accommodating political climate. John D. Rockefeller, who shifted Standard Oil from Ohio to New Jersey, once remarked, "The ability to deal with people is as purchasable a commodity as sugar or coffee—and I pay more for that ability than for any other under the sun." Henry Demarest Lloyd, the author of the 1894 trust-busting tirade *Wealth Against Commonwealth,* said, "The Standard has done everything to the Pennsylvania legislature except refine it."

The interests of big business were cared for in a U.S. Senate that was so full of corporate apologists that in the 1890s it was given the sardonic nickname of "The Millionaires' Club." Until 1916, senators were not elected, but were appointed to office by their respective state legislatures—bodies where business exerted powerful influence. Journalist William Allen White wrote of that period: "A United States senator . . . represented something more than a state. . . . He represented principalities and powers in business. One senator, for instance, represented the Union Pacific Railway System, another the New York Central, still another the insurance interests of New York and New Jersey. . . . Coal and iron owned a coterie from the Middle Eastern seaport states. Cotton had half a dozen senators. And so it went."

During all this time, the labor movement was in turmoil, its organizing efforts beset by violence and accusations of anarchist influence, as in the Haymarket riots in Chicago in 1886. With charges of radicalism discrediting the idea of organizing unskilled laborers on a mass scale, P. J. Maguire, Adolph Strasser and Samuel Gompers launched the American Federation of Labor as a vehicle for skilled workers in the crafts, disdaining social activism in favor of material gain.

But even that kind of unionism encountered bitter resistance. Carnegie Steel Company broke an AFL union in the 1892 Homestead strike. Two years later, in the railroad strike that began in the "company town" of Pullman, Illinois, the federal government again showed where its allegiance lay. Over the objections of Governor John Peter Altgeld of Illinois, President Grover Cleveland, a Democrat, sent federal troops to help break the strike that had paralyzed America's railroads.

The zenith of big-business influence on elective politics came in 1896 through the efforts of Mark Hanna. Forging a Cleveland machine that soon became the foundation of Republican control of Ohio, the "Red Boss"—so nicknamed for the glow his factories and smelters gave the Cleveland sky—guided a young Congressman named William McKinley to the governorship and then to the Republican presidential nomination. Hanna saw in McKinley precisely the figure American industry needed to serve as "the advance agent of prosperity," a believer in sound money and in protectionist tariffs to shield American manufacturers from foreign competition. The election of 1896 put the vision of the new American industrialism up against the populist rhetoric of William Jennings Bryan, the Democratic nominee, and the Republicans and big business were the winners. McKinley mounted the best-financed campaign to that date, largely because of Hanna's skill at shaking down corporate boardrooms. Under Hanna's "systematic assessments," the Standard Oil trust alone gave $250,000 to the Republican ticket—a huge sum for its day. Although it endorsed Bryan's cherished idea of the free coinage of silver, the AFL declined to break its neutrality and support the Democratic nominee.

Although Bryan's populist platform was rejected at the polls, many of the issues he raised took root. Antitrust laws were strengthened, and Progressive Era state governments enacted workmen's-compensation, child-labor and wage-and-hour laws. The federal attitude toward organized labor changed drastically during the Progressive years. Instead of sending troops to break the strike, the Administration of Theodore Roosevelt intervened to mediate the crippling 1902 anthracite strike in Pennsylvania, establishing a presidential commission empowered to impose fair terms.

Still, the National Association of Manufacturers, which had been founded in 1895, kept up a steady drumbeat against "trade-union tyranny." When Mark Hanna's eminently respectable National Civic Federation invited Samuel Gompers to join as a labor representative, it was NAM executive John Kirby who declared he could not "in conscience wink at the great danger to the best interests of our common country that lies hidden in the endorsement . . . of these men and the doctrine they preach."

Although this was the era of trust-busting, highlighted by Roosevelt's prosecution of Standard Oil, it was business-as-usual for GOP fund raisers at TR's election time. Republican finance chairman George B. Cortelyou, the former secretary of the Department of Commerce and Labor, wrung campaign donations out of the beef, coal, paper and sugar trusts as skillfully as Hanna once squeezed out boardroom funds for McKinley (and as Maurice Stans would one day put the touch on the trusts' descendants for Richard Nixon). The duality of Teddy Roosevelt's attitude toward the trusts was summed up by the satiric "Mr. Dooley," a creation of Finley Peter Dunne: "Th' trusts are heejous monsthers built up by th' inlightened intherprise ov th' men that have done so much to advance the progress of our beloved country. On wan hand I wud stamp them undher fut: on th' other hand, not so fast."

The decade from 1906 to 1916 saw increasing labor involvement in politics and the start of the alliance with the Democratic Party. In 1906, the AFL's "legislative agent"—who had been lobbying in Washington since 1896—presented the President and congressional leaders with a "bill of grievances" calling for remedial legislation. When the Republican Congress ignored the demands, the AFL used the November congressional campaign to hold rallies and distribute voting records of the congressmen. "We will stand by our friends and administer a stinging rebuke to men or parties who are either indifferent, negligent or hostile," Gompers declared.

Despite the Tillman Act of 1907, which forbade corporate donations on the firms' own behalf to presidential contenders, businesses funneled money to William Howard Taft through the names of their officers. The AFL made a feeble gesture of response, raising $8,500 from 1,100 unions to finance pro-Democratic speaking tours by Gompers and other union spokesmen in the 1908 campaign. While insisting that labor would "be partisan to a principle, rather than a party," Gompers exploited the opportunity to contribute to the labor planks of the Democratic platforms of 1908 and 1912. Woodrow Wilson's Administration saw the creation of the Federal Mediation and Conciliation Service, the appointment of a United Mine Workers leader as Secretary of Labor, the establishment of the

Federal Trade Commission and the passage of the Clayton Antitrust Act—all goals of organized labor. On November 11, 1917, Wilson lent the American labor movement the legitimacy it had so long been denied by addressing the AFL convention in Buffalo.

But as the nation returned to "normalcy" under the Republican administrations of Harding, Coolidge and Hoover in the 1920s, American business returned to union busting—with no rebuke from Washington. Corporate public-relations specialists trumpeted in 1921 an "American Plan" for economic welfare, which coupled resistance to Bolshevism abroad with resistance to unionism at home. NAM vice president Charles N. Fay declared, "The welfare of business, especially big business, the product of intense individualism, necessarily means the *public* welfare. The two are inseparable." A politically subdued labor movement did not dissent. Gompers' successor at the helm of the AFL, William Green, said, "More and more, labor is coming to believe that its best interests are promoted through concord rather than conflict. . . . Unless management is efficient, labor standards cannot keep advancing."

Labor's political impotence was apparent. In 1924, when the Democrats nominated John W. Davis, who had been an attorney for the Morgan interests, for President, the AFL backed the futile effort to revive the Progressive Party. In 1928 and 1932, it was officially neutral.

While the organizing battles of the late Twenties brought even William Green to talk of "class war," it was not until the stock-market crash of 1929 signaled the onset of the Great Depression that such rhetoric reentered politics. Franklin D. Roosevelt flayed big business in the campaign of 1932, and stirred the nation with his first inaugural address: "Practices of the unscrupulous money-changers stand indicted in the court of public opinion, rejected by the hearts and minds of men. . . . The money-changers have fled from their high seats in the temple of our civilization. We may now restore that temple to the ancient truths."

Once in office, FDR created a regulatory network aimed at curbing the excesses of what he called the "private socialism of concentrated private power." While most businessmen denounced him, Roosevelt recruited a maverick financier, Joseph P. Kennedy, as the first Chairman of the Securities and Exchange Commission, to regulate the investment industry.

The Roosevelt years saw the cementing of labor's relations with the Democratic Party. New Deal legislation certified labor's right to collective bargaining and set up the National Labor Relations Board (NLRB) to certify union representation. Social Security and other welfare programs began addressing the problems of elderly and unemployed workers. The organizing battles of the Thirties finally cracked the industrial giants of steel and auto making and led, in 1938, to John L. Lewis' formation of the Congress of Industrial Organizations (CIO) as a more militant arm of labor. In 1936, a predecessor committee (with the same initials), operating within the AFL, formed a political adjunct called Labor's Nonpartisan League. Through it, Lewis raised $500,000 for contributions to Democratic candidates. Two years later, the CIO published the first organizing manual for precinct politics. In 1943, the CIO set up its Political Action Committee (PAC), which would become the prototype for hundreds of other union and corporation fund-raising units.

FDR's personal alliance with Lewis broke when the President refused to intervene in the Republic Steel strike of 1937, and in 1940 Lewis endorsed Wendell Willkie against Roosevelt's third-term bid. But other labor leaders expanded their influence inside the Democratic Party to the point that FDR, when preparing to switch vice presidents in 1944 from Henry A. Wallace to Harry S. Truman, instructed his aides to "clear it with Sidney." "Sidney" was Sidney Hillman, the leader of the Amalgamated Clothing Workers of America and CIO's PAC, whose intimacy with Roosevelt's political planning came to symbolize labor's ties with the Democratic Party.

By then the nation was at war, and Roosevelt had called off his campaign against big business. Wall Street bankers like Bernard M. Baruch, W. Averell Harriman and James V. Forrestal; captains of industry like Edward R. Stettinius of U.S. Steel, Walter Gifford of AT&T, John Lee Pratt and William S. Knudsen of General Motors—all were recruited for government posts in mobilizing the nation for war. Many of them stayed on in diplomatic and national-security assignments as the Cold War pressures demanded continued coordination of governmental and private economic decisions. The corporate world, led by defense industries that had to work in close conjunction with the Pentagon's planners, became a participant in setting national goals. Meanwhile, the growth of the regulatory and welfare apparatus of government, under administrations of both parties, posed problems for business that required an ever-larger presence in Washington and an ever-greater participation in politics. In a pattern that many found troubling, a "revolving door" shuttled people back and forth from business suites and private law firms to the offices of the Cabinet departments and agencies.

For labor, the postwar years brought fresh strife on the picket lines and a renewal of the restrictive legislation. The Taft-Hartley Act of 1947 sanctioned state laws forbidding union membership as a requirement for employment. A series of congressional investigations in the 1950s highlighted the problem of racketeering inside major unions. But when the AFL and CIO merged in 1955 under the leadership of George Meany and opened a headquarters just across Lafayette Park from the White

House, the presence of labor as a major force in government and politics was recertified.

The past twenty-five years have been a time of intense and growing competition between labor and business for influence on politics and public policy. And the people engaged in that battle today, on both sides, have learned much from the struggle.

It was late in 1952; Dwight D. Eisenhower had just been elected, ending twenty years of Democratic control of the White House. The President-elect called five former presidents of the Junior Chamber of Commerce to meet with him in Denver, and asked why business was not doing more to encourage its younger executives to take an interest in government. One of them was Thomas R. Reid, the man Dick Armstrong of the Public Affairs Council said "you would have to call the first public-affairs officer in the United States. He sold Henry Ford on the idea that he ought to have somebody on the staff . . . as a political adviser to Ford and the rest of the company." And in the mid-Fifties Ford set up an office of civic and governmental affairs and a network of regional offices, staffed by people with political or legislative experience.

Reid, insurance executive Bruce Palmer and others who had met with Eisenhower set up the Public Affairs Council (or, as it was originally called, the Effective Citizens Organization) in 1954 and, a few years later, began holding training programs for corporate executives on the political process. The idea spread to the U.S. Chamber of Commerce—formed in 1912 as a voice for small business—and in time, more than a million people were given some exposure to the rudiments of political organization.

"It's hard to understand how foreign an idea this was to the business community when we started," Armstrong said. "In Minneapolis, where I grew up, if you were a young executive, they told you, 'We expect you to be a part of community life here. This is part of your job. It will help you.' But in the same breath, they said, 'For Pete's sake, don't get involved in politics.' And the all-too-logical result of this kind of thinking was that in Minneapolis, the business community had marvelous control over the symphony orchestra. They could get you a room in a hospital. They could be sure that the library stayed open on the day after Thanksgiving. But at city hall, and the county courthouse and the state capitol, they were without influence or access. And this was the very time that the unions, through their part in the Democratic-Farmer-Labor Party, were gaining in power every day."

Armstrong said that when his own organization was getting started, it avoided publicity, holding its meetings in remote resorts, rather than Washington, to escape notice. "The reason"—understandable in terms of the history just recounted—"was that we were afraid this would be interpreted as an anti-union movement and . . . we wanted to be identified positively," he said.

In addition to their expanding contacts with Washington and grass-roots politics, businessmen found two other areas demanding increased attention. The urban riots of the 1960s forced many companies with downtown plants and offices to expand their programs for preserving and stabilizing their own neighborhoods. And in the 1970s, the upsurge of environmental and consumer legislation—not just in Washington but in the states as well—brought additional concerns. Major companies stepped up their monitoring and lobbying of state and federal governments. And they hired specialists in "issues management," politically savvy sociologists and public-opinion analysts who could help top management avoid the costs and embarrassments of suddenly being confronted with demands—like environmentalism and consumerism—they had not known their companies were going to face.

The results of these forces were the creation of the public-affairs department and the spread of political consciousness upward to top management and outward through the ranks of the corporate bureaucracy. The Business Council, formed in 1961, and the Business Roundtable, begun in 1972, brought chief executive officers of leading firms into direct contact with congressional leaders and executive-branch officials. At the same time, many companies began taking "political inventories" of their management, determining who was involved in either party and who had useful contacts with local officials, legislators or congressmen. (One major oil company, Armstrong said, decided to learn more about the political connections of its management when it fired an employee who turned out to be "the brother of a Congressman who was very important to them, and they had a hell of a time explaining it.")

But for all this growing sophistication, the corporations never abandoned the tool Mark Hanna had given them: the political contribution. In 1971, Congress made another of its periodic attempts to regulate campaign financing by tightening disclosure requirements; the Federal Election Campaign Act became effective on April 7, 1972. "The night of April 6," Armstrong said, "I understand every bank in town stayed open until midnight. One of our members came in with a suitcase—somewhere around $300,000 or $400,000. Just ridiculous." The break-in at the Watergate headquarters of the Democratic National Committee two months later—whose perpetrators were paid with illegally "laundered" corporate funds—raised the lid on the biggest political scandal of the century. Before Watergate was finished, 36 individuals and 19 corporations had pleaded *nolo contendere* or had been found guilty and fined or sent to jail for campaign-finance-law violations.

Watergate gave business another black eye; but ironically, the 1974 amendments to the Federal Election Campaign Act turned out to be a bonus for business. In 1975, the Federal Election Commission established by the 1974 law ruled, in a case involving the Sun Oil Company, that corporations, like labor unions, are entitled to use company funds to set up and administer political-action committees (or PACs), provided their accounts are kept separate from those of the corporation, that contributions are voluntary and that full disclosure is made of receipts and expenditures.

PACs had long been permissible for trade associations, and BIPAC (the Business-Industry Political Action Committee) was making campaign contributions in the 1960s. But the 1975 SUNPAC decision opened the floodgates. Between 1974 and the start of the 1980 campaign season, the number of corporate PACs grew from 89 to more than 800; trade-association and related PACs grew to over 825. Labor PACs, which had been legal since 1925, remained at about 275. In the 1978 congressional election, corporate PACs contributed $8.8 million; trade associations, $10.7 million; and other groups generally aligned with business, $3.1 million. This overshadowed the labor PACs' $9.4 million.

With the growth of business PACs came a new breed of political operative—the PAC consultants, exemplified by the Washington firm of Smith & Harroff, Inc. The partners in that firm are 33-year-old Mark R. Harroff, a product of an Ohio Republican family and a graduate of Denison University, and J. Brian Smith, from a family of Massachusetts Democrats and an alumnus of Loyola College in Baltimore. The two met as interns at the Republican National Committee, did a joint speaking tour of college campuses for Richard Nixon in 1972 and afterward formed a partnership, offering public-relations and campaign-consulting services to Republican candidates and congressmen and providing public-affairs counseling to a dozen major corporations.

Among the corporate services provided by Smith & Harroff to the Ford Motor Company was a motivational film used to encourage corporate managers to contribute to Ford's PAC. "A lot has changed since President Coolidge said, 'The business of America is business,' " says retired board chairman Henry Ford II in the film. "Today, government interferes with business at all levels. Regulations have had a dramatic effect on the operations—and profits—of the auto industry."

The Ford movie also dwells heavily on the threat posed by organized labor. Steve Stockmeyer, the executive director of the Republican Congressional Campaign Committee, says in the film, "There's no question that over the years labor has done the best job. They don't pussyfoot around. . . . They want total compliance and they go out and elect their friends." Representative John J. Rhodes, an Arizona Republican (and himself a Smith & Harroff client), says, "The minions of organized labor are at every door when the House votes. When a member beholden to labor comes in, they very blatantly give him thumbs up or thumbs down" on the pending vote. A Ford executive remarks in the film, "Most of 'em [the congressmen] are relatively honest, but they need help, and they remember who has helped. If Ford Motor Company doesn't help, why not just knock Ford around?"

Smith described the PAC phenomenon as basically "a self-defense mechanism" for business against the political influence of environmental, consumer and labor organizations. But neither he nor Harroff saw PACs as offering a long-term answer for business' political problems. Without the kind of effort Ford makes "to really educate their employees, really get them involved," companies are probably better off without PACs, Harroff said. In any case, Smith added, "I think the life of the PACs is limited. Sooner or later, there is going to be some action to restrict their growth. That is why we place a greater emphasis with our clients on developing their political communication and grass-roots organization, so they can have that kind of impact which, frankly, we feel is a lot more potent than giving dollars."

Just how potent those PAC dollars can be in influencing congressional votes is a matter of heated debate. "PAC contributions are contributions with a purpose," wrote Common Cause senior vice president Fred Wertheimer. "They are generally made by interest groups which have specific legislative goals and conduct organized Washington lobbying programs. They have a special investment quality." On the other hand, Robert Bauman, the New Right Congressman from Maryland whom we met earlier, argued during House debate on a 1979 proposal to limit the PACs' maximum contributions: "The growth of PACs has encouraged tens of thousands of people who may never have given to a candidate or party before to participate."

"PACs are growing," said his colleague, Representative Bill Frenzel, a Minnesota Republican, "because people like them. They find PACs a convenient way to participate in the political processes of the nation. They give to PACs in the same way other people give to campaigns directly." Critics of the PACs pointed to high correlations between interest-group contributions and House and Senate votes on issues of special importance to those groups. But when Congress Watch, a group associated with Ralph Nader, noted that 55 of the 58 Representatives who had received donations of $2,500 or more from oil-industry PACs in the 1978 election had voted with the industry on the 1979 windfall-tax issue, an oil executive replied, "Certainly, we take a look at the voting records of people we support. I'm sure everyone who makes contributions to political campaigns does. But we certainly don't buy votes in Congress that way."

Whether benign or malign, PACs have become the most efficient instrument since Hanna's "systematic assessments" for moving corporate money into politics. Their growth seems assured. Edwin Epstein, a University of California at Berkeley political scientist, noted at a 1979 American Enterprise Institute conference that only 22 percent of the corporations with reported assets of $100 million or more (and only 3.6 percent of those with $10 million or more) had set up PACs. "The market for potential PAC formation is virtually untapped."

How far that expansion will actually go is in doubt. As Armstrong remarked, "You still have a large section of the business community that is, by and large, apolitical, unmotivated, disinterested in the process." Even some companies that are deeply involved in issues do not rely heavily on PACs or campaign contributions. Herb Schmertz did not start a PAC at Mobil until 1979, because he thought "campaign contributions are vastly overrated." He bowed to the trend, he said, chiefly so that Mobil executives who were asked for contributions by politicians could say, "Look, I'm giving all my money to the PAC and the PAC is going to make contributions."

"There are two things in my opinion that influence legislators," Schmertz said. "If you can convince a legislator's constituents of the correctness of your position, that is a significant accomplishment"—and the purpose of Mobil's editorial-advertising campaign. "The other is, if he is not getting enormous constituent opposition to your position, you have a shot at him intellectually."

That attitude may sound suspiciously lofty, but it is not unique. Linda Asay, 42, is the director of government and public affairs for CPC North America, a division of CPC International, a multinational *Fortune* 500 food company, with sales of more than $3 billion annually. CPC has no PAC, and Asay has only one full-time Washington representative working with her as she divides her time between the New Jersey headquarters and the capital.

"I think it's important to remember when everybody is talking about PACs and the unholy influence of business on government that there must be an awful lot of companies like ours who really believe from a managerial standpoint in the delegation of authority, and really believe that people who are elected to do a job should be let alone to do it," she said. "Every single bit of our business is regulated by the government . . . but I can't conceive of a situation in which the management of our company would ever suggest going in and trying to stop something."

Asay herself is extremely knowledgeable about the workings of government. A graduate of Mills College and the George Washington University

Law School, she has worked on the staffs of former Representative Robert F. Ellsworth of Kansas and Senator Charles H. Percy of Illinois, for the National Governors Association and as executive assistant to former New York Attorney General Louis J. Lefkowitz.

With her background, Asay said, "I can see some naiveté" in the CPC approach. The idea of electing people and then "relying on them to run the government . . . worked a hundred years ago, but nowadays I think that's putting too much faith in the breadth of knowledge of members of Congress and their staffs. . . . You'd better get in there and tell them what your interests are, so they know what's important."

Another woman public-affairs director, L. D. (Dandy) Witty, 37, of the Clorox Company, is one of only four such specialists in the $600-million Oakland company. It has no Washington office, and until she was hired in 1975, it had no one even monitoring the variety of legislation affecting the chemical industry. Its PAC collects only about $10,000 per election, which, as she said, "is not a hell of a lot of money."

But Witty provided an example of how such a company can intervene successfully in the legislative process. When the Toxic Substances Control Act of 1977 was nearing final passage, the chemical specialty manufacturers—of whom Clorox is one—called on her for help. Democrat John Tunney, then a Senator from California, was a prime sponsor of the legislation, and "they needed someone [from a California company] that might have some sort of constituent relationship" with him.

The goal was quite specific: to persuade the twelve senators in a House-Senate conference that was adjusting differences between the versions of the bill passed by the different chambers to accept the narrower House definition of chemical mixtures.

Witty said she never talked to any of the senators. "But I did talk to the staffs of all twelve conferees, and it was very successful. But it was successful because we were taking them information that they hadn't had, not because we were putting political pressure on them. Hell, John Tunney didn't care whether the Clorox Company liked him or not. We're not his constituency. We're not any Senator's constituency. We happen to be a company in his state. But we were taking them information that demonstrated quite factually that the definition they were using was too broad, and they changed the three or four things we wanted changed."

Witty is an example of the kind of people being recruited in recent years for corporate politics. A political scientist from Vassar and the University of Texas, she worked for the Democratic National Committee; as a legislative-liaison person for the Department of Health, Education and Welfare; as an aide to liberal Democratic Representative Richard Ottinger of New York and for the city manager of Yonkers, New York.

It is not that unusual to find Democrats (or former Democrats) in corporate politics. Transamerica Corporation, a holding company with $7 billion in assets, named James B. Lockhart as its vice president for public affairs in 1979. Lockhart, a 44-year-old graduate of Boston University and its law school, received his basic political training as a lieutenant in the Daley organization in Chicago. When he left the Army in Chicago in 1963 (after serving there in the Judge Advocate General corps), he said, "Blacks were not accepted into major law firms or corporations, so I got an appointment as an assistant corporation counsel for the city of Chicago and practiced law at the same time—that was traditional. You gave the city about an hour's work [each week] and you practiced about twenty hours. The rest of the time you worked for the organization, and you gave back a part of your earnings—ten percent, to be exact."

Lockhart worked for the organization candidates. "I used to get out the vote—I thought that was more enjoyable than anything I'd ever done." His law practice led to a job with a Transamerica subsidiary, the Budget Rent-a-Car Corporation, where he became general counsel and senior vice president, before being brought to San Francisco as public-affairs chief for the parent corporation. While some of the operating subsidiaries in life insurance and entertainment had their own lobbyists, Lockhart said, the parent company was "just dipping its toe" into the whole political field.

Communications and old-fashioned lobbying remained a central element of corporate political action—and if the upsurge in PAC activity should be held in check by new limitations, business will have to return to these more established channels of political activity. In interviews, three professionals in corporate-government relations discussed that prospect.

Walter Howe, the 46-year-old vice president for government relations of the Weyerhaeuser Company, the forest-product corporation, was born in the state of Washington, grew up and went all the way through law school there and served for seven years as legal counsel and budget director of Washington's then Governor Daniel J. Evans, a Republican. He also served for two years as deputy director of the federal ACTION agency before joining Weyerhaeuser in 1974.

From its president, George Weyerhaeuser, on down, the company had been involved in politics, with a Washington office, state lobbyists and all the rest. Since the early 1970s, it had been spending about $5 million a year on institutional advertising, encouraging "the perception of Weyerhaeuser as a responsible steward of renewable resources," Howe said. Like Schmertz at Mobil, Howe had a fondness for sponsoring public-affairs programs on television, where Weyerhaeuser's identification as "the tree-growing company" would be seen by political influentials. The environmentalists began challenging its forestry practices with increasing vigor in the Seventies, and when Howe came, he said he found a demand from top management for "a stronger link" between the lobbyists and information managers and "the decision-making process of the company."

As an example of his work, he cited the battle over a 3,500-acre tract south of Tacoma, which Weyerhaeuser bought as the site for a deepwater port for shipping its products overseas. "It happens to be adjacent to a wildlife refuge," Howe said, "and it was clear that there was going to be a long and complex fight. After four and a half years and $4 million in studies, it is still going on. One of the things we did at the very beginning was to identify the environmental groups that would be most antagonistic to that sort of development and establish a dialogue with them. We have met with them once every couple of months over that period. There was much agony in the company about whether that was an appropriate way to proceed, whether it would shorten or lengthen the process, whether it would commit us to things we didn't want to do. I think in that process, clearly, we have been forced to do some things . . . that we probably wouldn't have done, that will make it even more environmentally safe. The environmental groups have very clearly articulated that they don't really want to see any development there . . . but that if anybody has to develop it, they know Weyerhaeuser will do it well. Three lawsuits have been undertaken by those environmental groups, and it remains to be seen whether some settlement will come, whether Weyerhaeuser will make certain concessions and the project will go ahead."

Howe said that while the outcome was still in doubt, he and his colleagues now felt the process was the right one. "Not only will the project be better," he said, "but if we had not done that, the degree of outcry and antagonism on the other side might have been sufficiently high that public attitudes might have made the project impossible to carry out."

And that led him to a larger point: "I think sooner or later, public attitudes and public perceptions really will be the primary determinant of public decisions. I think we're in a climate where no self-interest will justify a business decision. One of the real tests of the Eighties for business is whether we can identify with the public interest and articulate our policies in a way the public will accept as desirable. If you look at the array of issues coming at us—like health in the workplace—I don't see how any responsible or successful company can avoid that standard. If we can't identify the public interest on those sorts of issues, and respond to it, there's a legitimate reason for regulation."

That implicit acceptance of public opinion—political opinion—as the criterion for corporate decision making is a far cry from the 1920s doctrine of the NAM's Charles Fay that the well-being of big business defines the public's welfare. It is not a criterion all businessmen would accept—not by a long shot. But it is not unique, and it is shaping the approach to lobbying taken by many of the more progressive companies in America.

An example of this approach is the work of the Washington Business Group on Health (WBGH), which develops information in the health field as thorough as that of any government, labor or public-interest group and concentrates on effective communications at the top corporate and federal levels. Formed in 1974, the WBGH began with one corporate sponsor—the Ford Motor Company—and has grown to include 180 member firms which rely on its research on technical health-policy questions and its tracking of pieces of legislation as they work their way through congressional committees. (The group conducts no lobbying of its own, however, leaving such advocacy functions to its members or to another of its corporate-sector sponsors, the Business Roundtable's Task Force on Health.) The WBGH was founded and is directed by Willis C. Goldbeck, who is himself an example of the breadth of experience that newly active businesses draw upon: a former special assistant at the Department of Housing and Urban Development and a former congressional delegate to a United Nations conference on housing, Goldbeck is an advocate of medical and environmental planning that looks toward a future of increased government-business cooperation.

The treasurer of the WBGH's coalition of business spokesmen is Allan D. Cors, 44, the vice president and director of government affairs at Corning Glass Works. He cites the work of the WBGH as an example of industry and government's working together on the issue Howe had mentioned—health in the workplace. "The business community is recognizing," he said, "that we've got to get in early on these subjects instead of coming in so late."

Cors is a University of Cincinnati product. After graduating from law school there, he worked as minority counsel of the House Judiciary Committee and joined Corning in 1966. He is a Republican, as are the Houghtons, who founded and headed Corning. But, Cors said, the president of Corning, Thomas MacAvoy, is a liberal Democrat. However, in lobbying, he pointed out, he can use the names of Amory Houghton and Tom MacAvoy almost interchangeably, "because in the vast majority of cases, it really doesn't make a lot of difference" what the partisan affiliation of the business spokesman may be. His best lobbyist, he said, is a man named John Blizard, who is "a technical guy, an engineer with the company for thirty years" before being assigned to the Washington office to provide it with technical expertise on the energy and environmental issues so important to its business. "He's been a Common Cause organizer in upstate New York, a liberal-Democrat type, and has fitted right into the program quite well, because he's being called on by people on both sides of the issue on the Hill who want him to explain the technical aspects of what we're talking about."

Cors said that he thinks "the leadership in the business community is now convinced . . . that they can have an impact on the system. . . . Quite frankly, when I came to this company I don't think they really knew what they wanted from a Washington office, and I don't think most companies did at that time. . . . Through the years, there's been an awareness that they really can have an impact on the system. . . . There's been a dramatic growth in the company's willingness to pay for what they get back. I think the companies are putting better people here in general. . . . I think the professional in this business, the new hire, is different from the kind of guy that came into this job in the Fifties and the Sixties. He's a much more professional person, better educated."

Then Cors made a point, reflecting on the change in Congress, that was echoed by almost all the other business lobbyists—and those of labor as well. "Yes, there are still golf games, and there are still dinners and lunches," he said, "but at a dramatically reduced level. In the old days, the way you did business was you had a key chairman or subcommittee chairman or two that could really take care of you. They had enough stroke downtown [in the agencies] and on the Hill that if you had a good relationship with them, you had it made. And so I can understand why, maybe, there was a heavy emphasis on making that guy very happy, loving you as a friend. . . . But today it's just not on that level—the personal-relationship business. There are many people in government who really don't want that kind of relationship, for whatever reason. You've got to be able to deal with them on a very businesslike basis that requires delivery of good information."

Fortunately for the traditionalists, there are still some lobbyists of the old school. One of the most successful is a 40-year-old Washington lawyer named Thomas Hale Boggs, Jr. His father, Hale Boggs, was House Majority Leader at the time of his death in 1972. His mother, Lindy Boggs, was elected to succeed him and now represents New Orleans in the House. Tommy Boggs graduated from Georgetown University and its law school, worked in campaigns for his father and for Democratic presidential candidates, had a couple of government jobs, tried unsuccessfully for the House himself from a suburban Maryland district and settled down to head a Washington law firm that has grown to fifty members. Boggs's client list for his lobbying efforts includes Chrysler and General Motors, Ralston Purina, the makers of Mars bars and Pepsi-Cola, and the states of Louisiana and Alaska.

Boggs is renowned not only for his advocacy in congressional offices but for his indefatigable fund raising for the officeholders and candidates he likes. In 1978, he reported his own contributions of almost $25,000 to the Democratic Party and to thirty-five of its candidates. How many times as much he raised from clients and friends he cannot estimate. "One of the things I learned from running for office myself," he said, "is that the most distasteful part is raising money. Most candidates hate to ask people for money. . . . They really do. So I do it in most cases because I like the guys and know them—and somebody has to do it. There's no question about it: in some cases you do it because you owe them something. At least, you feel like you owe them something. It's not a *quid pro quo* by any stretch of the imagination, but . . . they've walked the extra mile for you—doing what was probably right for their districts and constituencies, but they didn't have to work as hard as they worked. And one of the ways you can help them is by raising money for their re-election."

Boggs said he sees an irony in the effects of the post-Watergate campaign-finance reforms. "In my opinion," he said, "money in politics is much more significant than it was ten years ago, even though the size of the contributions today is peanuts, compared to what they used to be. . . . Before 1972, a handful of people could basically finance your entire campaign. And the member [of Congress] felt he could vote for them once and against them two or three times, because they were actually friends. Now these members have to go to literally hundreds of people to raise the money they need to run. It's made them grateful for $500 contributions, and somewhat concerned that if they don't react favorably to the constituency that is responsible for a number of those contributions, they've got some problems. So it's really achieved just the opposite of what it was intended to achieve. It's made them totally dependent on the small givers who put $50 in a PAC and then watch the PAC closely. . . . And the PACs themselves have a hard time being professional—giving money to this liberal Democrat today and this conservative Republican tomorrow, or giving money to both sides in the same race, which was not unheard of in the past. The PACs themselves are becoming more ideological, and that's going to be an influence on the voting pattern of members."

Boggs also said that with the upheaval in Congress in the Seventies—the elimination of the seniority system, the weakening of the influence of the party leadership and the President, and the opening of Congress to public scrutiny—"external factors," including lobbying and campaign contributions, "now have a much bigger influence on members than they did before. What members of Congress want from a lobbyist . . . is information to make a judgment that appears to be the rational judgment for their constituencies. That type of lobbying is more like a political campaign. It's persuading them that it is better for them to be on this side of the issue than that, and giving them the proof—all the people in their district who think so. What you see more and more is a sort of mobilization of grass-roots lobbying becoming the function of the Washington lobbyist. . . . It's not at all unusual for us to sit around a table and look at a lobbying campaign and see the biggest expense is the polling. . . . They [the members] are much more influenced by what the local real-estate dealers think about a national issue, and that's what you've got to tell them."

Boggs said one other factor had increased the lobbyist's role: the growth of congressional staffs. "A lot of these fellows are very anxious to develop a particular area of legislative expertise, so they come to you or some other lobbyist and they assemble a whole roomful of facts and figures in some particular area, and then they get hold of their member to introduce legislation on it. And the legislation tends to be pretty sophisticated. It's a bill which a Harvard law graduate has spent six months developing for a member. The result is that you'll have five or six bills—sophisticated bills—in an area, and the bigger the volume, the more work for the lobbyists. A lot of times there will be five bills introduced, and the people involved don't know that there are four others, and you'll have five lobbyists working on a project which should just have one."

The offset to that, Boggs said, is the computerization of Congress—the installation, already under way, of information-retrieval systems that allow a member to "punch up" summaries of bills introduced and their status. One firm, he said, "has a computer service which we can plug in here, which basically does the same thing a computer does in a member's office. It's still embryonic, but five years from now it's not going to be embryonic."

A wide grin creased his face, and he played his fingers on an imaginary computer console. "That's going to be fun," he said. "Just sit here and tell a guy what to do. Here's what your constituents think. You don't believe it? How many phone calls you want? That's what it's going to be like."

Among labor lobbyists there is little disagreement about what is influential with the new-breed members of Congress. Bob McGlotten, 42, a lobbyist for the AFL-CIO since 1972, said that what is persuasive is a lobbyist's ability "to really know what the hell he's talking about, to give them the kind of argument they can go home and defend. . . . And that puts the lobbyist's feet to the fire, to be accurate and truthful."

McGlotten, a Philadelphian and a black, studied law and business administration at the University of Pennsylvania, became interested in labor relations, joined the staff of the Transport Workers Union and then went into a series of civil-rights jobs in the labor movement. In an old-fashioned, almost sentimental way, he said that the unions have "done more for the average working individual than any other movement or institution in our society. . . . I worked three years on the Child Health Assessment Program that passed the House yesterday," he said late in 1979. "I will not benefit from that, but there are a lot of youngsters out there in the street who will. . . . Similarly with the 1977 Social Security amendments that picked up domestics. . . . My name will never be associated with that, but I really feel good about it. There are a lot of things in our society that need to be corrected, and this is one institution that addresses itself to them."

McGlotten said he knew that when labor pushed such causes—and more expensive social legislation, like national health insurance—some of its critics in Congress said it was "out of touch" with its membership. But he would hear none of it. "Our membership is concerned about balancing the budget," he conceded. "But if you ask any one of our members, 'What would you like to do to balance the budget?' they will say, 'Don't cut out any of the social programs, the manpower programs, the anti-recession programs.' . . . And when you get down to it, there's nothing else left."

Others in the unions are less confident about there being no gap between labor's social agenda and the views of the membership. Vic Kamber said that "to a great extent today, members of trade unions are the middle class of America. They now have their color TVs, their cars, their kids going to college and their boats at their vacation places. And they are concerned about middle-class values while, to a great extent, the movement is still addressing itself to the social concerns of the lower economic people. There's not a building-trades union that pays the minimum wage, or double the minimum wage. How does the plumber who's making $11.50 an hour say, 'You've got to raise the minimum wage from $1.25 to $1.90'? I mean, the Congressman looks him in the eye and says, 'What do you care?' It's a dilemma for us."

What Kamber said was underlined by Robert F. Bonitati, 42, since 1975 the director of legislative affairs for the Air Line Pilots Association. Until the National Football League Players Association affiliated with the AFL-CIO in 1979, Bonitati represented the highest-paid constituency in organized labor: Its 33,000 members average $45,000 a year in salary.

Bonitati himself is a somewhat unusual labor skate. A native of Bridgeport and graduate of the University of Connecticut, he was working on the staff of the University of Tennessee when Republican Senator Howard H. Baker, Jr., recruited him for his 1966 senatorial campaign. He came to Washington with Baker, and later worked for the Republican Congressional Campaign Committee, worked as a private political consultant and served as a lobbyist for three different agencies in the Nixon Administration.

That background may explain, in part, why Bonitati said, "I sometimes get the impression that today's union leader is a bit out of touch with today's union member. They [the leaders] are supporting issues and causes that their membership would not. Labor hasn't had many gut issues, pocketbook issues, in recent years. And when labor espouses a variety of positions on social legislation, I'm not sure many of our members even care; they're often on the other side of the question. We're no longer talking for the poor and the downtrodden, although frequently labor goes to bat for the poor and the downtrodden—just by history and tradition."

At the very least, labor leaders have to make the effort to persuade their members that there is still some relevance in today's world for the platform and position inherited from the unions' more militant past. That is a fact the more astute younger officials recognize. Rachelle Horowitz, the 41-year-old political director of the American Federation of Teachers, comes from a background diametrically opposite Bonitati's. Born in Brooklyn, she became so caught up in the civil-rights movement while a student at Brooklyn College that she never did get her bachelor's degree. Instead, she became one of the white students in the sit-ins and freedom rides, worked with Bayard Rustin on the 1963 March on Washington and followed him into the A. Philip Randolph Institute, a focal point for black trade unionists. When she switched to the teachers' union in 1974, Horowitz said, "everybody else in the labor movement used to laugh at the teachers and the way we had to do things [in politics]. Before you could get them [the teachers] to endorse someone or work for anyone, you had to go through all the reasons why, and answer all their questions. Now the United Auto Workers and the AFL-CIO in Ohio have taken polls that show the same thing: Their members want them to present the issues—and not in polemical form, either—and the candidates' stands and let the members conclude for themselves.

"The modern trade-union member does read the papers, does watch TV and does not merely accept what the union says. The older members accepted it, because they had been through the wars of forming the union. If you were on the bridge with Walter Reuther, you said, 'Okay, if that's how the redhead wants us to vote, we'll vote that way.'

"But the modern union member joined an already-formed union, and his approach is 'What can the union do for me?' So we need a more reasoned approach. What was considered strange about the teachers' union only a few years ago is getting to be more typical of every other union. They're having to organize. It makes it harder."

In fact, labor has had a hard time organizing in the past quarter-century.

As numerous commentators noted late in 1979, when the late George Meany retired after twenty-four years as the only president the AFL-CIO had ever had, the trends were not encouraging. According to the Bureau of Labor Statistics, when the federation was formed in 1955, 34 percent of the nation's work force were union members; in 1979, it was 22 percent. Part of the problem was the transformation of the national economy from one centered on manufacturing (blue-collar jobs) to one centered on services (white-collar jobs). Some of the white-collar and public-employee unions have grown apace, but the industrial unions are largely stymied, and in fields like construction and mining there has been a resurgence of nonunion employment. The shift of jobs from the Northeast to the South and West has hurt the unions—particularly in the twenty states with "right-to-work" laws.

The ebbing of labor's strength has been a factor in its legislative defeats. Even in the liberal 89th Congress, which gave Lyndon Johnson his Great Society programs, the effort to repeal Section 14(b) of the Taft-Hartley Act—which authorizes the state "right-to-work" laws—failed. Kamber's effort to reform the National Labor Relations Act was killed by a business-backed filibuster in 1978. The New Right's letter-writing campaign, as pointed out in Chapter 6, helped kill the common-situs picketing bill in 1976.

Bob Bonitati was quite cold-blooded in his assessment: "The climate of public opinion has shifted in this country," he said. "The unions haven't quite kept pace with some of the changes that are taking place in politics on Capitol Hill. . . . The business community has. They have become aware of the fact that many members of Congress now have become professional politicians; getting re-elected is extremely important to them. They count those letters, they measure that pressure, and business-oriented lobbyists have taken advantage of that. They are usually in a better position to generate letters from back home, because everybody's got a secretary and a typewriter. Union members don't have that. . . . The power and clout that labor unions once had with their money is diminishing. In 1974, organized labor contributed 50 percent of the organized giving to candidates. In 1978, the proportion of PAC money that organized labor gave was down to 29 percent, and in 1980, I would venture to say that it's going to go down somewhere near 25 percent."

Some businessmen-politicians made the point that the financial measurements overlook labor's ability to mobilize voters at election time in far larger numbers than business can do. "The labor unions always have somebody in there stuffing envelopes, knocking on doors, making friends with the candidate long before he is the Congressman," Linda Asay said. "Business people, as a whole, send a check and then go have dinner with him after he's a Congressman." J. Brian Smith, whose company deals with some of the more politically active corporations, still said, "Business is about twenty years behind labor in its political sophistication. . . . Give me a storefront with a handful of volunteers in sandals and jeans and they will make more important political strategic decisions in a day than Mobil can make in two years. The corporations can't move. They don't have the flexibility to make decisions. They're just too bureaucratic."

Be that as it may, many unions are trying to emulate the corporations in the scale—and pragmatism—of their political-lobbying operations. In the first four years he was with the Air Line Pilots Association, Bonitati expanded its lobbying staff from himself and a secretary by adding two lobbyists, a speechwriter and two research assistants. A PAC that was nonexistent in 1976 "will contribute between $400,000 and $500,000 to the 1980 campaigns," he said. "Frankly, a PAC gives you lots of access that you normally don't have. I'm not sure it's a very good system, but those are the current rules of the game. A contribution gets you into the [campaign—fund-raising] receptions, where a good deal of the work is done. It's difficult to get in to see a guy at two o'clock in the afternoon, but at seven o'clock at night he's there with a drink in his hand and he's willing to talk to you. He's supposed to be friendly. . . . When I worked for politicians, I always knew that you were supposed to take care of your supporters. When somebody called or a letter came in, you checked: Is this a contributor? Those are your friends . . . and you're supposed to take care of your friends. That's part of the code, and I find you have to take advantage of it."

One of the biggest political war chests belongs to the United Food and Commercial Workers, formed in 1979 from a merger of the Retail Clerks and the Meatcutters. Its 1.3 million members contribute over $500,000 a year in voluntary funds, which are used for campaign contributions. A nickel a month of dues is allocated for registration and political-education programs, producing another $700,000.

The man in charge of spending that $1.25 million is 45-year-old Bill Olwell, who has been a union lobbyist only since 1978. "We're picking up the tools of the trade now," he said in 1979. "We're getting much more sophisticated in our propaganda . . . in our fund raising, in our education, in our research. We're doing polling. We're looking at the media as a tool to be used positively for us, rather than just always castigating the media for giving us a black eye. We've begun using advertising when we're on strike, appealing to the community for support by explaining our issues. And we're using it in organizing drives. We have two hundred organizers on the streets every day, as an international union, and probably another two hundred in the locals. . . . We believe we ought to be just like Exxon—sponsoring and giving our message on the CBS and NBC evening news."

It was striking that while corporations poured millions into shaping the public image of themselves, only two international unions in the late Seventies had launched television campaigns. The American Federation of State, County and Municipal Employees (AFSCME)—which had mushroomed to over 1.1 million members in the expanding public sector but then caught the brunt of the backlash of Proposition 13 against public employees and their salaries—began advertising itself as "the union that works for you." The International Ladies Garment Workers Union scored a public-relations coup by putting its message—"Look for the union label"—to a catchy tune that became a popular song.

But unions as a whole shied away from television. "I think our predecessors [in the movement] were afraid of the outside world," Olwell said. "They were very secretive people. They shunned the press; they shunned telling our story. They were afraid of the unproved, the unused; they didn't want to experiment very much. They had done it one way, and it was a winning way for them and they stayed with it. They stayed with it far too long."

Olwell himself had a personal history that set him apart from the older generation of unionists: His grandfather was a Western mine owner. A native of Seattle and a product of its Catholic schools, Olwell said, "I come from a Republican, upper-middle-class background. When the Mine Workers organized my grandfather's mines out there, he flooded them and never reopened them because he was so outraged that his people would unionize on him." Bill Olwell was working in a grocery store to supplement his G.I. Bill benefits while attending Seattle University, and "when somebody came along and told me I had to join the union, I got really kind of pissed off. I went down and joined, and then I went to every meeting and asked all the wrong questions. If I had to join, by God, they were going to show me what they were doing with my dues and what they were doing to earn my respect as a member."

The upshot was that "I really got sold on the union, and the good it could do," Olwell said. He became a business agent for a Retail Clerks local, then its president. Politically, he was active in the liberal wing of the Democratic Party in Seattle and in the anti-war movement. The union and political activities collided in 1968. Olwell, at 33, was president of the powerful King County (Seattle) Labor Council, and the building-trades leaders told him he would be ousted at the next election if he did not cut off his activities in the anti-war movement. "I was a proud peacock and there wasn't anybody who was going to make a deal with me on this issue," he said. "So they taught me how to count votes, because they dumped my ass big at the next election. I was stunned."

But Olwell remained active in his own union, became an international vice president (while still in Seattle) and finally moved to his full-time staff job in 1978. People in organized labor, he said, "have become a lot more tolerant in our disagreements. Let me give you an example. I'm gay. Everyone I work with in labor knows it. About fifteen percent of the people can't handle it, and I tolerate their intolerance. But ten or fifteen years ago, I couldn't have been here."

Of all the major institutions in America, organized labor has seemed the most resistant to leadership change. George Meany, a member of the World War I generation, extended his control to the end of 1979, and was succeeded in the presidency of the AFL-CIO by Lane Kirkland, 58, who was a merchant seaman during World War II. But even in the unions, the forces of generational change are beginning to be felt. Kirkland has a couple of pictures in his office. One was of the AFL-CIO executive council—the 33 union presidents who really control the federation—at the 1971 convention. The second was of the same group at the most recent biennial convention in 1979. Kirkland was in both pictures, of course. But only 9 of the 33 council members from the 1971 picture were still around in 1979. "We've got international-union presidents now," Kirkland remarked, "whose entire union careers have been since the merger in 1955. They have no memory of the AFL-versus-CIO fights—and it's very refreshing."

When Fred J. Kroll, the president of the Brotherhood of Railway and Airline Clerks (BRAC), went on the executive council in 1978 at age 42, he was the youngest person ever elected to the body. Kroll, a Philadelphian, had started out as an IBM operator for the Pennsylvania Railroad twenty-five years before, and was a part-time union officer by the time he was 19. He came to the union presidency in dramatic fashion. In the mid-Seventies, a group of young leaders in the brotherhood became increasingly restive and critical of the financial and administrative practices of then president C. L. Dennis, who had been in power since 1963. At a board meeting in the union headquarters in Rosemont, Illinois, in September 1976, Kroll and the other "Young Turks" pressed a resolution to monitor the union funds and strip some of the president's powers. The debate was just getting started when Dennis' son—L. E. Dennis—"broke into the room, beat me up and put me in the hospital," Kroll said. Two months later, the Dennises were forced out and Kroll was named president.

Kroll has put the union back on its feet financially, expanded its lobbying staff from three people to eleven, professionalized its research department and negotiated an agreement with the railroads for payroll deductions of voluntary political contributions that will increase its 1977–78 PAC size from $460,000 to perhaps double that sum.

"We're going more and more from the negotiating table into the legislative arena," he said, "because the airline and railroad industries are so heavily regulated by government. . . . And it's not like the old days where you could just go in and say to a Congressman or Senator, 'Joe, you're a friend of labor and here's what we want,' and Joe would say, 'Boys, you've got it.' . . . You've got to go in with a damn intelligent argument today and you have to sell these guys. They're not just going to roll over and vote for you."

Kroll's union has more white-collar than blue-collar jobs among its 200,000 members, and the average pay is between $18,000 and $22,000 a year. To grow, he said, "we have to change our style and change our image and work a hell of a lot harder. We have to address the so-called gangster stigma in unions. We've got to stress not only what we've done for our own members, but what we've done for society. We're making changes in our organizing department to bring in more women and minorities. You can't rely on the old way it was done of bringing a group of people into a back room of a bar and giving them a lot of old rhetoric. It just doesn't work with these people. You can't send the guy out with the beer belly and the T-shirt and the tattoos up and down his arm. The people we're trying to organize are better-educated and they've grown up in affluent times. I think we've got a tremendous educational job ahead."

Kenneth Blaylock, 45, who has been president of the 265,000-member American Federation of Government Employees (AFGE) since 1976 and a member of the AFL-CIO executive council since August of 1977, still has the traces of a North Carolina mountaineer boyhood in his voice. He joined AFGE (which had been formed in 1932) when he went to work as a plumber at Maxwell Air Force Base in Montgomery, Alabama, in 1954, and moved up from shop steward to local president to the national level. AFGE is set up as an industrial union, representing everyone from janitors to professionals in the hospitals, bases and sixty agencies where it is the bargaining agent. According to Blaylock, two-thirds of the white-collar workers and over four-fifths of the blue-collar workers in the federal government are covered by union contracts. Because pay rates and working conditions are still set by Congress and the executive branch, he too has taken his union much more into politics—expanding his legislative and political-education staff from three people to twelve. "Five years ago, we didn't even have a political-action committee," Blaylock said. "Last year [1978] we raised about $150,000, which is not a big amount, but it's a hell of a long way from nothing. We've got an intensive education program going on with our members, and we've used our computers to identify all our members—active and retired—in each congressional district. We're reaching the point now with our computer network that we can generate a hell of a lot of letters to any Congressman or turn out a good-sized group to have breakfast with him when he comes home. And we didn't have that even a year ago. Orrin Hatch [the Republican senator from Utah, one of the leaders in the filibuster that killed the labor-reform bill in 1978] is considered to be anti-labor and ultraconservative. Hatch has never voted against us on a pay issue, because we've educated him on the principle of comparability and where the pay levels really are in the private sector. And we've educated him about how many federal employees there are in the state of Utah. And our people out there are in touch with him. . . . The bottom line is [congressmen] relate to the people who are going to vote for them out there."

William Wynn, 49, the president of the United Food and Commercial Workers (UFCW) and the man who hired Bill Olwell for his job, is the leader of the largest AFL-CIO union but a man who says "I have never been inside a factory in my life." That is only the beginning of the paradoxes. When one sees him sitting in his luxurious Washington office, sipping coffee that has been served by a blue-uniformed black maid, gold rings and bracelet flashing as he lifts the cup, there is an initial impression of softness. But in fact, Wynn is one of the most aggressive and militant of the younger members of the executive council—and a major force in the future of the movement. His father and most of his other relatives worked at the Studebaker plant in South Bend, Indiana, and Bill Wynn "practically was raised" in the union hall of the United Auto Workers' Local 5. "My father, in the Thirties, would go to a couple union meetings a week. And my mother and my aunt were officers of the ladies' auxiliary. I would go down there and play basketball and Ping-Pong and box. Holidays—Labor Day, Memorial Day, Independence Day—were union picnics. It was a real tradition in our family."

When he finished high school, Wynn got himself a job at Studebaker, "but my father wouldn't let me take it. He said, 'No son of mine is ever going to work in a factory.' He was adamant." So instead, Wynn stayed on at the A&P, where he had been working part time; joined the Retail Clerks in 1948; became a business agent, an organizer and eventually a union officer. The Retail Clerks were apolitical in those years—"when I was an organizer, all we would say was 'You should register and vote,' but not another word." Its membership was conservative, and when its Republican president endorsed Lyndon Johnson in 1964, it was considered big news.

But Wynn had grown up idolizing UAW chief Walter Reuther; Wynn's political outlook was liberal, and his foreign-policy views diametrically opposed the AFL-CIO's support of the Vietnam war. His first move as president of the UFCW was to hire Olwell to construct what Wynn said "will ultimately be the best political mechanism in this country, one with members in every city in the United States." Two weeks after the union was formed in 1979, Wynn addressed the Americans for Democratic Action convention, telling that collection of anti–Vietnam war liberals he was there to reaffirm "the solidarity among progressives . . . really, a coming together again of leadership, after the separation which occurred as a result of the Vietnam conflict. . . . Disunity among ourselves is the greatest gift we could possibly bestow upon the forces of reaction . . . which have achieved not only massive new financing from corporate political-action committees, but also a new and highly dangerous sophistication for the spread of their dogma."

Wynn followed up that step by joining Ralph Nader, the consumer advocate, in an effort to revive the long-standing proposal (dating back to Populist days) for federal chartering of corporations "to correct the abuses of big business." Other, older presidents of some of the major unions who had found themselves to the left of Meany and Kirkland took up a similar stance. Jerry Wurf, the president of AFSCME, and William Winpisinger, the avowedly socialist president of the International Association of Machinists, prodded their colleagues in the AFL-CIO to adopt a more militant, anti-corporate stand. Douglas A. Fraser, the president of the independent United Auto Workers, quit the semiofficial Labor-Management Group which worked with government on wage-price policy in 1978 because, he charged, business' sabotage of the labor-law reform bill signaled the return to "class warfare."

Both Fraser and Winpisinger sought alliances with the New Left leaders on issues of energy prices and corporate power, and Fraser in his resignation letter said: "There's no point in pretending [labor and business] have anything in common on the broad issues of the day. . . . I would rather sit with the rural poor, the desperate children of urban blight, the victims of racism and the working people seeking a better life than with those whose religion is the status quo, whose goal is profit and whose heart is cold."

As they revived the more militant rhetoric that had marked labor-management relations through most of the previous century, all of these labor leaders were aware that their membership—watching and weighing their actions—was as far removed from them in age as they were from George Meany's generation. "The old World War II types that came to work for the federal government during the war or right after the war are all retiring now," Ken Blaylock said. "We're seeing a very rapid turnover in our membership." Fred Kroll said "about sixty percent of our membership is forty-four years of age or younger." And Bill Olwell remarked, "Our average age is unbelievable—it's under thirty."

Those looking after politics for corporations and unions are of two minds about whether their generation will see a period of intensified labor-management conflict or greater cooperation. They are equally uncertain about the future of their relations with government.

Linda Asay of CPC International said that as one who moved from government to business, "I don't understand why we have always tended to be at each other's throats. They're very similar institutions. The arguments over turf and jurisdiction of your committee or your group or your division [in the private and public bureaucracies] are not that much different." As for the demands that people like Wynn and Winpisinger were making of the corporations, she said, "I think those are the people who are going to be the saviors of the corporation. It's the critics of the corporations who are imbuing it with human characteristics, who are making demands and creating a public expectation that a corporation is supposed to be responding in a moral way, in a socially responsible way—really, having the good qualities that a human being would have. Senator Packwood [the Oregon Republican] is right when he says that if we don't start meeting those needs—like the need for day care, for job security and health protection—government will, of course. But meeting those needs may be the public-relations salvation of the corporation."

On a somewhat different level, Allan Cors of Corning saw increasing opportunities for labor-business cooperation on economic issues. As the maker of glass for color-television tubes, he said, Corning had gone to the industrial-union department of the AFL-CIO for help in lobbying for control of imports from Japan. "We've put together a very successful coalition of companies and eleven labor unions that we call COMPACT—the Committee to Preserve American Color Television. So when our guys go in [to a congressional office] to talk about television, there's a strong counterpart from labor there."

Cors said that in personal terms "it's been a joy to work with them. I don't think it will ever happen, but I could see myself working with a labor union someday. Most of our people think that if you get in bed with the labor unions, they'll somehow steal your eyes. But they're good; they're very good. And obviously they have a political clout that we don't have. We really represent management, but they represent people. They represent votes. If we come into a Congressman's office with the union representative, we can talk from the standpoint of political clout."

On the union side, there are examples of a similar pragmatism. "We look after the industries we represent," said Fred Kroll. "Profitable companies mean more jobs, and if there are more people at work, we have more members." So BRAC joined with the railroads to lobby against coal-slurry pipelines and to postpone cutbacks in the Amtrak railroad network.

Bob Bonitati said he thought that trend would accelerate. "As we go into the Eighties, you're going to find more unions concentrating on issues that are of concern to their members and to their particular industries. You'll find labor and industry frequently working together hand in glove on issues."

Labor and business did find themselves in a firm if unexpected alliance in late 1979, as Congress considered a case that seemed to set the tone for American industrial policy in the Eighties: the federal rescue of the Chrysler Corporation, the nation's tenth-largest industrial firm, from the brink of bankruptcy. In the effort to fashion a $3-billion plan of government loan guarantees, union concessions and new issues of stock—a plan that some critics saw as a precedent for future taxpayer-funded bailouts of mismanaged or unproductive industries—such longtime adversaries as the UAW's Douglas Fraser and Chrysler's Lee Iacocca teamed up to lobby the bill toward congressional approval. And Tom Boggs, the corporate spokesman, and Bob McGlotten, the AFL-CIO tactician, for once were acting in concert on Capitol Hill.

But those who foresaw hope for labor-management cooperation over the long run were decidedly in the minority among those interviewed. "The adversary relationship between business and government is likely to grow," Herb Schmertz said. "There will be more and more pitched battles between us and the environmental movement and the other groups whose policies are anti-business." And the business response, Schmertz said, will be increasingly aggressive. "Amongst the managers in their late thirties and early forties," he said, "you find a much greater perception of what is at stake. Most of the top managers of today were raised in the low-profile era. The managers that are coming along, the next generation, have seen the growing impact of government's role in their business, and they're more eager to take it on. In my own company, as aggressive as we've been in the last ten years, there is a generation behind us that is constantly pushing us to do more."

"What I see for the 1980s," said Jim Lockhart, "is more conflict, more interest groups and more selfishness among the interest groups. I think what that does is lead to more fighting, less harmony and less ability for groups to work together."

On the labor side, there were repeated expressions that the militancy of the younger workers would prod the leadership into stronger action. "What I'm seeing," Vic Kamber said, "is a throwback to what I read about happening back in the days of real struggle to create unions. Sure, we're middle-class today; sure, our people are making bigger bucks. But they don't see any opportunity to climb higher anymore. A lot of them out there feel that they're being pushed back and pushed down. And they're not blaming it on the welfare state or the woman who's having three babies while drawing a welfare check. That was the rhetoric of the Nixon era," said this onetime Nixon worker. "But that's not the evil, that's not the system that's killing us. It's corporate America up there. It's big business. Those are the boys that want to destroy us.

"There is a much greater militancy among the younger people out there," he said. "There's a greater desire to get up and flex our muscles and do the things that the radicals did in the Sixties—the kind of confrontation politics that the George Meany leadership held down. One of the biggest criticisms we had from our own people during the fight on labor-reform legislation was 'Why didn't you bring us to Washington? Why didn't we march in the streets? If the gays can march and the women can march, why didn't you bring a half-million of us to Washington to march?' Well, this institution didn't believe in it, but there are people who would like to close this nation down for a day—just strike it."

Ken Blaylock said the same thing of his government employees: "They're much more militant now. . . . I can remember in the AFGE conventions when to have gone on the floor to talk about a strike or a job action, they would have thrown you out as a flaming Communist. But it's been three conventions ago that we took the no-strike clause out of our constitution, and the problem I have today is sitting on certain groups that want to hit the bricks, rather than saying, 'Go get 'em.' It [a strike] couldn't be effective now, because it hasn't spread wide enough that there would be enough of them to protect each other. But I see that date coming, as the young people get more and more revved up.

"We're headed for some turbulent times," he said, aiming his comments not just at government but at the private sector as well. "When you look at the facts . . . free enterprise worked very well as long as they had slave labor in the cotton fields and child labor in the textile mills and as long as the coal miners were working for 50 cents an hour. But when the workers started organizing and saying, 'We want an education for our kids and a house like that one on the hill,' then they started having these confrontations. And then these corporations started going overseas chasing cheap labor and exploiting resources in foreign countries, and now those countries are waking up to that, just the same as workers here are waking up to it. If inflation goes screaming off the top and Congress and the Administration yield to the Proposition 13 mentality, you're going to build a climate where you're going to see federal employees on strike. There's no doubt in my mind. And personally, I live for the day."

There was also a clear sense that labor felt it had some scores to settle. "I think business has really missed a tremendous opportunity of sitting down and trying to work out its differences with labor," Bob McGlotten said. "We recognize the energy crisis and inflation, and we ought to be doing something about them together, instead of fighting with each other."

But for McGlotten and others, it was the business community's mobilization on the labor-law reform bill that really stuck in the craw. That measure, as labor saw it, was aimed merely at a handful of virulently anti-union companies, like the J. P. Stevens Company: The textile giant, whose tactics were reminiscent of the late 1920s in their efforts to block unionization, has been cited twenty-two times by the NLRB for labor-law violations. The only reason much of the corporate leadership would line up behind such a company, labor said, was that business in general still hoped to break the union movement.

"When the Business Roundtable and the NAM and the Chamber of Commerce got together and unleashed their dogs on labor-law reform," Bill Olwell said, "the fragile new spirit of cooperation was totally destroyed. We are angry, and we're not going to get mad; we're going to get even. It's going to get much rougher before it gets better. They crowed, and crowed, and crowed when they defeated us on the fundamental basics of labor law—the right to organize and be certified when the majority of workers want you to represent them. They beat us on that. And they are going to pay dearly."

If the Olwells and Blaylocks, the Lockharts and Schmertzes are right —if there is a new period of intensified labor–business–governmental conflict ahead—it will be no popgun war. It will be a multimillion-dollar battle, fought not just on the picket lines but in the legislative halls and the precincts as well, with all the weapons of modern political warfare in use. It could make this new round of the long-fought struggle one of the fiercest of them all.

8 · Public-Interest Lawyers and Reformers

DURING THE PAST DECADE there were only three people, other than elected officials, who turned up with any consistency on Americans' list of their most-admired men. The pollsters regularly found the Pope and Billy Graham—those symbols of religious faith and givers of hope—on the list.

The third was a man shy and prickly of personality, a gadfly and, often, a scold, not a source of reassurance. He was Ralph Nader, the consumer advocate. His struggle with General Motors over the safety of the Corvair, which reached an emotional climax at a 1966 Senate hearing in which the president of GM publicly apologized for the private detectives his company had hired to dig up dirt on Nader, had the elemental appeal of a David-vs.-Goliath battle. Nader pursued corporate wrongdoing, and the collusion of government regulatory agencies, with the single-minded passion of an abolitionist preacher excoriating the evils of slavery. And he became the symbol and magnet for a whole crop of similarly high-minded and intense young advocates, not all so selfless in motivation as Nader appeared to be, who created what they unblushingly called the "public-interest movement." Most of them were, like Nader, lawyers, exploiting what de Tocqueville had recognized more than a century earlier as the unique power position of attorneys in the American society.

"Democratic government," de Tocqueville wrote, "favors the political power of lawyers. When the rich, the noble, and the prince are excluded from the government, the lawyers then step into their full rights, for they are then the only men both enlightened and skillful, but not of the people, whom the people can choose."

De Tocqueville was talking about the advantage lawyers possess in the competition for public office, an advantage that continues unabated in our own time. But the lawyers who followed Nader's example were something different.

What they created—in the rapidly expanding network of public-interest law firms and movements—was a political force, not based on election to office, of a character quite without precedent in the previous history of the Republic. In barely a decade, the public-interest movement forced through sweeping changes in areas of law from the environment to public health to the penal code. It spurred basic changes in the administrative processes of government, and changes of similar sweep in the institutional processes of state and local government and the political parties. It also played a significant role in forcing the first presidential resignation in American history.

By the end of the 1970s, the public-interest movement had graduated scores of alumni into key positions in all levels of government. And it had bred a strong counter-reaction in the courts, in politics and in the legal community, which left its own future development in great doubt.

Whatever that future, there was no doubt that the men and women who were recruited, trained and toughened in its struggles would themselves have a significant and growing impact on the politics of this nation.

When one looks at who they are and what the pattern of their lives has been, one is struck by some of the distinctive characteristics of this network. More than any other group in this book, the public-interest advocates include a remarkable number of bright Jewish liberals, educated at the elite universities of the East. An extraordinary share of them (selected largely by their reputation among their peers) are the products of one particular institution: Yale Law School. Nader, who is of Lebanese extraction and a Harvard man, did not exactly clone himself in his recruiting efforts.

A sampling of the biographies of some of the people whose experiences and views we will be discussing suggests the pattern:

David Cohen, 44, the son of a Philadelphia clothing worker; graduate of Temple University; one of the few nonlawyers in the group; a union organizer; a lobbyist for Americans for Democratic Action and union groups, with a special interest in the fight against the tobacco companies on cigarette advertising; now the president of Common Cause, the self-styled citizens' lobby.

Paul R. Friedman, 36, the son of a government astrophysicist; a graduate of Princeton, Cambridge University and Yale Law School; after a one-year clerkship with the U.S. Court of Appeals in Washington, D.C., joined the Center for Law and Social Policy; since 1972, director of the Mental Health Law Project, which has played a key role in judicial decisions and legislation establishing the civil rights of mental patients, particularly those in confinement.

Mark Green, 35, the son of a Long Island lawyer; a graduate of Cornell and Harvard Law School; a "Nader Raider" for five years, with time out to help run two campaigns for former Attorney General Ramsey Clark;

now the director of Congress Watch, Nader's Washington lobbying organization.

Charles R. Halpern, 41, the son of a Buffalo, New York, judge and law professor; a graduate of Harvard College and Yale Law School; after a one-year clerkship with the U.S. Court of Appeals in Washington, D.C., and four years with a prestigious Washington law firm, cofounded the Center for Law and Social Policy and later the Mental Health Law Project; now director of the Institute for Public Representation; has played a key role in establishing rights for the mentally handicapped, as well as important work on consumer and environmental cases.

Benjamin W. Heineman, Jr., 36, son of a wealthy Chicago businessman and sometime public official; a graduate of Harvard College, Oxford University and Yale Law School; after a clerkship with Supreme Court Justice Potter Stewart, joined the Center for Law and Social Policy; litigated test cases involving the rights of the mentally handicapped; from 1977 to 1979, an assistant secretary of Health, Education and Welfare, before returning to private practice.

Joseph N. Onek, 38, son of a makeup editor on *Women's Wear Daily* in New York; graduate of Harvard College, the London School of Economics and Yale Law School; after a one-year clerkship with the U.S. Court of Appeals in Washington, D.C., and another year with Supreme Court Justice William J. Brennan, worked as a staff aide to Senator Edward M. Kennedy; organized a Nader-backed campaign challenging the management of General Motors; then joined the Center for Law and Social Policy, becoming its director; also a key attorney in cases involving poor people's rights to health care. From 1977 to 1979, a member of the White House domestic-policy staff, specializing in health legislation, and now deputy counsel to the President.

Michael Pertschuk, 47; son of a New York City furrier; graduate of Yale College and Yale Law School; one-year clerkship with a federal district judge in Oregon; staff aide to Democratic Senator Maurine B. Neuberger of Oregon; for 12 years, chief counsel of the Senate Commerce Committee, where he drafted dozens of important consumer laws; now chairman of the Federal Trade Commission, which he likes to call the "most active public-interest law firm in the government."

Anthony Z. Roisman, 42; son of an Oklahoma City businessman; graduate of Dartmouth College and Harvard Law School; after three years as a Justice Department tax lawyer and one year of private practice, formed one of the first public-interest law firms in country; a key figure in test cases developing "environmental impact" statements and applying them to nuclear power projects; chief staff attorney for the Natural Resources Defense Council; now chief of the Hazardous Waste Section of the Land and Natural Resources Division at the Justice Department.

Except for Mark Green, all of these people grew up in liberal Democratic households. "The area I grew up in, in all the stores I saw pictures of Franklin Roosevelt," said David Cohen. "Roosevelt was a heroic figure in our household," said Mike Pertschuk. When Ben Heineman was a senior at University High School in Chicago, he debated in the pages of the school newspaper the relative merits of John F. Kennedy and Richard M. Nixon with the son of conservative economist Milton Friedman.

Whatever political programming had been neglected in their childhood culture was supplied by their college years. Exceptionally bright, all of them were drawn to and influenced by teachers who reinforced their liberal views.

The role of the Yale Law School was not accidental. In the late 1920s, under Robert Maynard Hutchins and his predecessor as dean, Thomas W. Swan, Yale had become the center for the "realist movement," which held that "the rules of human action that we know as law are constantly changing, that no system of human justice is eternal, that law forms but a part of our ever-changing social *mores,* and that it is the function of lawyers, of jurists and of law schools to cause the statement and application of our legal rules to be in harmony with the *mores* of the present, instead of those of an outgrown past." Yale attracted such figures as William O. Douglas and Thurman Arnold, both to be key figures in the creation of the New Deal, and with the presence of such visitors as Harold J. Laski and Morris Cohen, did more than any other school to set the law firmly in a context of the social sciences. Three decades later, Yale's reputation may, as alumnus Halpern said, "have depended more on its faculty ghosts than the living teachers." But that reputation still attracted, in his time, such students as Edmund G. Brown, Jr., now Governor of California; Gary Hart, now Senator from Colorado; Eleanor Holmes Norton, now chairman of the Equal Employment Opportunity Commission, and dozens of Halpern's colleagues in the public-interest-law movement. Even though the word around Harvard in the early 1960s was that the Yale Law School faculty "consisted of old Turks and young fogies," it struck Joe Onek as a place that was "much more relaxed and socially oriented" than its counterpart in Cambridge.

"I applied to Yale," said Paul Friedman, "because it had a reputation at the time of being rather more interdisciplinary and nurturing a kind of innovative application of the law. . . . Yale was one of the few law schools that introduced a lot of relevant material from the behavioral sciences." In 1970, Friedman and several of his classmates undertook a project for Professor Charles Reich (whose book *The Greening of America* predicted a takeover of the nation by selfless youths) which became a full-scale survey of the public-interest-law movement for the *Yale Law Journal.* In approving tones, they wrote: "Keenly aware of the defects in our society, each of the lawyers we interviewed has made the existential decision to act to bring change. . . . Test-case law reform is a kind of interest-group politics which uses the courts as a vehicle. The great advantage of test-case litigation, of course, is that the appeal to legal principles short-circuits the political process, where the interests of unorganized poor or black people are rarely represented and often disregarded."

The desire to "short-circuit the political process" was obviously a reflection of the frustrations being experienced in the late 1960s and early '70s by liberal activists. As Halpern and others pointed out, the current crop of public-interest lawyers and activists are virtually all of an age; they were, almost without exception, born during the twelve years of Roosevelt's presidency. That meant they were old enough to see but, generally speaking, not to participate in the great legal victories that brought an end to racial-segregation laws. They were young enough to share the emotions of the anti–Vietnam war period but, for the most part, felt too old or awkward to be taking their protest to the streets. Peter Schuck, an early Nader lieutenant who has become one of the leading students and critics of the public-interest-law movement and is now, at age 40, teaching at Yale Law School, said its practitioners have "a world view that is profoundly liberal, activist and very hostile to conservative values."

As it happened, most of these liberal, activist and highly trained young lawyers came out of their clerkships at a time when the normal channel to influence—through the government—was not open or attractive to them. From the middle of the Johnson Administration, when the Justice Department began its prosecutions of anti-war protestors, through the end of the Nixon Administration, the Justice Department was not a hospitable place for them. On the first page of their 1970 *Yale Law Review* article, the young authors noted that "perhaps the most widely recognized way for a lawyer to serve the public interest in the past was by working for the federal government." But in their time, they said, "though there are certainly important differences among many of the agencies, critics say that they are at best demoralized and inefficient, and, at worst, the captives of a few powerful special interest groups."

Private practice was, for many of the idealistic, no more attractive. Halpern joined Arnold & Porter, the Washington law firm headed by two of the pillars of New Deal liberalism, Thurman Arnold and Paul Porter. But he found the firm representing the Tobacco Institute in its battle to delay and deflect government efforts to combat smoking as a public-health hazard. Arnold & Porter encouraged its lawyers to do *pro bono* work, but when some of the projects Halpern suggested were judged to involve potential conflict with corporate clients' interests, he went off to join Nader in the public-interest movement.

One of the other early leaders in that movement, who is now in the federal judiciary and did not wish to be quoted by name, said in an interview for this book that "it would be a mistake to think that we were more public-spirited and self-sacrificing than any other lawyers who had ever come along. If there had been a Democratic administration that we felt sympathy with, most of us would have gone straight into government and scrambled for career advancement just like everyone else. As for private practice, sure, we sacrificed income, but we handled cases in our public-interest firms that were far more interesting and important than we would have been allowed to handle in conventional law firms. I think almost all of us chose public-interest law because it was the most personally fulfilling work available at the time."

Support for the judge's view came from Tony Roisman, who sat back in his office in 1979 and calculated that "Sixteen years out of law school, I would be at least a middle-level partner in a Washington law firm, and that means that I would be making somewhere between $90,000 and $120,000 a year in salary and bonuses," instead of the $35,000 he was making as the top lawyer for the Natural Resources Defense Council. "That difference is made up in some way," he said, "and I guess for the lack of a better term, it's psychic income. Less nicely put, I guess it's just ego.

"Most of the people in the public-interest-law movement tend to be real egomaniacs," Roisman said, "which is why the public-interest-law movement is not a movement. We do not have a bar association, or meetings or conventions; we do not get together and periodically discuss policy. Everything is done on an *ad hoc* basis, because there is not one of us who is ready to submerge our thoughts to the group."

Roisman also maintained that there was "no guru" for the public-interest movement, but conceded that Nader was "a singular figure in all this." Nader, whose ego is probably proportional to his influence, built a network of at least twenty-one public-interest organizations from what began as a personal crusade for auto safety. Magnetic in his single-mindedness, he drew many of the recruits into this branch of law. He also used the press to publicize his causes as well as any individual to emerge in American politics in the past twenty years. Peter Schuck, who worked for Nader for a time before becoming director of the Washington office of Consumers Union, wrote of him in 1972: "Armed with preternatural energy, a fixed moral vision and a genius for political innovation probably unmatched since the creators of the first urban political machine a century ago, Nader is uniquely capable of seizing upon the vague, amorphous malaise that haunts so many Americans and fusing it into a laser beam of outrage, raw energy, in quest of a cynosure. A waggish former Harvard professor describes Nader as 'the Henry Ford of the crisis industry.' "

But Schuck, while admiring Nader, is also open-eyed about him and insists that he is best understood not as a unique creation, but as an expression of an American tradition of politically influential "agitators." "Harriet Beecher Stowe, Elizabeth Cady Stanton, Lincoln Steffens, Martin Luther King, Father Coughlin, Benjamin Spock and many other 'outsiders' have significantly influenced the terms upon which public issues, great and small, have been debated and resolved," Schuck wrote. "Nader is far more intimately and routinely involved in the nitty-gritty of conventional politics than most, if not all, these figures" and probably belongs "well within the ambit of conventional reform politics."

Lawyers, as de Tocqueville noted, have always enjoyed a privileged and influential position in American politics, and some of them have understood the social responsibility that went with their status. One of the earliest efforts in public-interest law came in 1876, with the establishment of the German Society of New York's legal-aid program for recent immigrants. It was not until 1920 that a National Association of Legal Aid Organizations was founded, with Chief Justice William Howard Taft as its president. Legal aid, as it was then understood, really meant private lawyers' providing part-time free or subsidized assistance to individual clients on problems that more affluent citizens hired those same lawyers to handle. It was not until the 1930s that policy-oriented public-interest law began. The models on which the public-interest advocates of the past decade have built were provided by the American Civil Liberties Union (ACLU) and the NAACP Legal Defense and Education Fund, Inc. Both organizations had been around for a considerable time—the NAACP since 1909 and the ACLU since 1916—before they developed the elements that make up the modern concept of a public-interest advocacy. Those elements include fund raising from a broad membership base, supplemented by court fees and foundation aid, to support a full-time salaried staff of high-quality attorneys. The concept also involves the rejection of "service" cases for individual clients in favor of the selective intervention or initiation of litigation that offers the opportunity to challenge or establish broad principles of law. While the ACLU did most of its work as an *amicus* in civil-liberties cases, the NAACP developed a strategic approach of initiating suits that step by step changed the way the United States dealt with minorities. As both the NAACP and the ACLU increased their activities in the late 1950s and early 1960s to consolidate the civil-rights advances in the South, more and more foundation support was attracted.

Several factors, in addition to Nader's personality and proselytizing, made the last half of the 1960s the breakthrough period for the public-interest movement. As the leadership of the civil-rights cause became more black than interracial, the energy of socially conscious white advocates was seeking new channels of expression. Lyndon B. Johnson, as part of his War on Poverty, launched a massive new program of legal services for the poor, which, while oriented primarily toward client service, also had elements of public-service law. Government-subsidized poverty lawyers challenged welfare systems, education financing and other governmental programs and forced significant increases in state and local spending on social programs. In personal terms, the poverty lawyers, many of them young, pricked the conscience of their contemporaries in conventional law firms.

Tony Roisman, for example, was happily practicing law with a private firm in Washington when his wife, also an attorney, went to work for the just-starting Neighborhood Legal Services Corporation. "It was clear that she was getting as much enjoyment out of what she was doing as I was getting," he recalled, "and because she was in law reform, the appellate work where they were taking the cases that were making new law, her work had the additional element that she cared how it came out. In my work, I didn't care how it came out." It was his wife's example, Roisman said, that led to his forming a public-interest law firm the next year.

Lyndon Johnson also adopted the consumer cause, for which Nader and a few members of Congress had been pressing, and showed that consumerism could be good politics. In the first three years of his presidency, Congress passed the Truth in Packaging Act, the Child Safety Act, the Truth in Securities Act, the air-pollution-standards law and the Auto Safety Act. Mike Pertschuk, who had become General Counsel of the Senate Commerce Committee just in time to catch this wave, noted that in 1968 the committee chairman, Democratic Senator Warren G. Magnuson of Washington, rolled to re-election on the slogan "Maggie Keeps the Big Boys Honest." "Congress tested the water and found that nobody got punished for helping the consumer," he said.

Pertschuk also noted another development of the 1960s that augmented the movement: the rapid growth in the size of congressional staffs. "When I came to the Commerce Committee in 1964, there were six people on the staff. When I left in 1977, there were over a hundred. You had a lot of younger people drawn into legislative work," he said, "and in a sense, they formed a counterweight to the private-interest lobbyists. They had a certain independence and probably represented a more public-interest-oriented force on Capitol Hill than the elected members, who were somewhat dependent on the special interests for campaign contributions." As the case of Joe Onek illustrates, there was easy movement from congressional staff to public-interest law firm, and close communication and collaboration between young friends on both sides of that particular street.

But the final ingredient for the activation of the public-interest movement probably was provided by Richard Nixon and the election of 1968. "The Vietnam war and Watergate," wrote David Cohen, the president of Common Cause, the largest of the public-interest organizations, "were as important to the development of the public-interest constituencies as the Depression was for the Roosevelt constituency. . . . The fracturing of the Roosevelt coalition—its last hurrah was the 1968 Hubert Humphrey campaign—led to the start of a new mix in our political system. Organized constituencies began to form in support of long-neglected issues. The consumer and environmental movements are the most obvious examples. They became involved in both issue and candidate politics, but at arm's length from the established political parties."

Indeed, the founder of Common Cause was John Gardner, a nominal Republican with impeccable establishment ties, who had quit as Secretary of Health, Education and Welfare in Johnson's Cabinet because of the war. Under Gardner's leadership, Common Cause played a major role in translating popular discontent with the war into Capitol Hill lobbying efforts to cut off funds for military operations in Southeast Asia. While Gardner coupled his policy criticism with continual exhortations to both parties to encourage more able candidates to seek public office, he drew frequent criticism from both Democratic and Republican leaders. In 1971, three years after he had quit the Democratic administration, the Republican National Committee charged that Gardner had become "a purveyor of the radical Democratic line on virtually every major issue."

"Until people had experienced some of Nixon," Cohen said in an interview, "I'm not sure that an organization like this could have attracted enough moderate and liberal Republicans" to give it the credibility older liberal lobbies lacked. As it was, Common Cause was launched in 1970 and rode the tide of Vietnam and Watergate to a peak membership of 315,000 dues-paying members by 1974.

"As the [public-interest] movement grew," Cohen said in a 1978 speech, "its participants discovered that the tired old political system had ossified. It couldn't bend. Government had become an insider's game."

Increasingly, public-interest advocates focused on "the process questions," the ways in which the government made its decisions—or avoided making them. Drawing largely on an educated, middle-class constituency with a modernist, managerial outlook ("You're more likely to get a plant manager for IBM than a plant manager for Ford involved in Common Cause," Cohen said), the new-breed advocates lifted the curtain on long-unexamined Washington practices. In the first survey Common Cause took of its membership, the issue of "institutional accountability" ranked in importance just behind Vietnam and the environment. And when Nixon in 1970 vetoed a campaign finance "reform" bill, the stage was set for the accountability questions to take priority.

A comprehensive review of the substantive accomplishments of the public-interest movement in the past ten years is far beyond the scope of this chapter. While still engaging only a tiny fraction of the legal profession, the public-interest movement has been institutionalized in several hundred organizations. Its impact is seen in altered laws and practices in dozens of major fields. On issues ranging from airline "bumping" of passengers to maternity leaves for women employees, from lawyers' advertising and fee setting to air-quality degradation, from the Alaska Pipeline construction to broadcaster-license renewals, to say nothing of the rights of children, the elderly, homosexuals, the handicapped, prisoners and mental patients, the force of the public-interest advocates has been felt. On the process questions, Common Cause has helped change federal laws on campaign financing, income disclosure for elected and appointed officials, secret meetings, recorded votes, lobbying and similar questions, not only in Washington but, literally, in one or more respects, in every state and many of the cities. As Mark Green has written, "Richard Nixon, for one, can also attest to the influence of this new bar, for it was William Dobrovir's milk-fund lawsuit that first got hold of White House tapes; Common Cause forced the Committee to Re-Elect the President to produce a list of previously secret campaign contributors; Tax Analysts and Advocates initiated the attack on the president's questionable tax deductions; Public Citizen's Alan Morrison persuaded a federal court to rule Archibald Cox's firing [as Watergate special prosecutor] illegal; and the Tax Reform Research Group successfully brought suit to get the IRS to release its list of 99 'enemies' warranting special tax attention."

Green claimed, with some justification, that "the impact of these public-interest lawyers has surpassed the muckrakers at the turn of the century, whose success lay largely in exposure of ills. The new muckrakers first expose but then lobby concern into law and ensure that the new laws do not lie idle."

As might be imagined, this kind of success breeds controversy, among both practitioners and observers of this political technique. The argument starts with the very label "public interest," whose appropriation by a particular group of policy advocates strikes some people as being the height of arrogance. Defensively, perhaps, many public-interest-movement people use a definition of "public interest" that derives from economic theory, rather than an ethical claim. Peter Schuck, for example, uses the term to refer to "an organizational entity that purports to represent very broad, diffuse, noncommercial interests which traditionally have received little explicit or direct representation in the processes by which agencies, courts and legislatures make public policy." Contrasting them with groups of varying ideologies that are "organized around the common professional, occupational or political ties of their members," he said, "the public-interest group, in contrast, is organized around a status or role which virtually all persons in the community are thought to share in common—the status of consumer, citizen, taxpayer, member of the biosphere."

David Cohen, using a similar approach, said public-interest groups commonly seek "common, collective or public goods that do not exclusively, materially or selectively benefit their members. Open meetings, clean air and freedom of information are all examples of collective goods."

The public-interest advocates go one step further in trying to deflect criticism, by denying the claim of special virtue for their position. "Use of the term public-interest law," Charles Halpern wrote, "does not imply a claim that the side represented by the public-interest lawyer is always right as a matter of law, policy or morality. Rather, public-interest law rests on the conviction that the public interest is more likely to emerge, and the legal process to function more effectively, if all sides to a dispute are represented." Despite the purported modesty of their claims, the public-interest advocates have drawn criticism for moral arrogance. Chief Justice Warren Burger attacked the "young people who go into the law primarily on the theory that they can change the world by litigating in the courts."

Nonetheless, the organized bar, with its conservative flavor, has been generally hospitable to the new practitioners. Its leaders, for the most part, have conceded that there were gaps in the adversary system, and that by providing representation for those who lacked either the financial resources or the direct, personal and financial interest in an issue, the public-interest advocates have helped, as Justice Thurgood Marshall said, "move us a little closer to the ideal of equal justice for all."

The more interesting—and important—debate, in judging the likely future role of the public-interest advocates in our politics and government, concerns not the propriety of the movement's existence but the nature and limitations of its contribution.

There is general agreement that the greatest impact of the movement has come when it focused scrutiny on the governmental decision-making process. Common Cause's assault on secrecy and seniority in Congress and on campaign-finance practices did correct what David Cohen calls "serious distortions" in the power and influence wielded by some in the political system. In challenging the procedures used by many government regulatory agencies, the environmental lawyers have often brought stinging criticism of those agencies from the most conservative judges. Citing a case in which the court found an agency's regulations "at best vague and at worst disingenuous," Tony Roisman said his role was like that of the little child who pointed out that the emperor had no clothes. "If the crowd decides that they don't like nudity, are we to blame because we said that he was naked?" he asked. "Absolutely not."

The complaint has been made with increasing frequency that the process changes forced by the public-interest advocates have thrown a monkey wrench into the system. A Congress freed from the "tyranny" of strong committee chairmen has found it harder to hammer out agreements on complex issues. Fulfilling every requirement of the environmental laws has slowed the development of many needed energy projects. There are trade-offs involved, but the argument can be overstated. As Joseph Onek said, "It bothers me a lot that so many people now criticize public-interest lawyers for their ability to slow up decisions. I don't disagree with that. It cannot be a rational system where it takes twenty years to make a decision on siting a nuclear power plant. Whether you are pro- or anti-nuclear, twenty years is too long a time. But the thing that bothers me is that many of the people who are making the criticism are the same people in corporate law firms who lived by that process for years. Every anti-trust lawyer will tell you that if he can hold up a case for ten or twenty years, by that time nobody cares. But now that delay is being used by others, and their ox is being gored, they don't like it."

A more troubling question for many of the public-interest advocates is whether their characteristic focus on process questions is adequate for the challenge they now face. "It's all quite nice," said Charles Halpern, "to approach problem solving through a fairly sophisticated understanding of political processes and institutional interactions. That kind of focus enables you to diffuse ideological disagreements. But it may not be enough." In the case of Common Cause, the nonideological approach enabled John Gardner to bring disillusioned liberal activists into an organization much of whose financial support and leadership came from the headquarters of corporate America. But as David Cohen conceded, it is difficult to sustain that coalition when "you try to get accountability talked about in ways that reach beyond the integrity" of the public official, or to focus Common Cause's lobbying power on issues like energy or inflation, where the economic ideologies of its leaders and members are not necessarily in agreement.

Ben Heineman said that public-interest litigation "is a very important consciousness-raising device," more effective in directing political attention to an issue than marching or demonstrating. But as a way of bringing solutions to social problems, he added, "I think it's a very limited tool. . . . When you're talking about major social change . . . there are obvious limitations."

Some of those limitations have to do with the role of the judiciary in America, but some have to do with the absence of real ideology in public-interest law. "If there is an overall criticism of public-interest law," said Charles Halpern, "it is that it's insufficiently ideologically grounded and smacks too much of the *ad hoc* solution. Too much of the master ideology of public-interest lawyering stops at the point of presenting different viewpoints and letting a decision maker decide. It leaves public-interest lawyers rather at sea when they leave that world and take on roles that are defined in different terms."

Peter Schuck, the insider critic most respected by the public-interest advocates, has enlarged on Halpern's point to make the most significant attack on the kind of public-interest advocacy pioneered by Ralph Nader.

"Having invoked the 'public interest' *ad nauseam,*" Schuck wrote, "Nader seems convinced that he knows what it is. But what in fact is the 'public interest' and where does it lie? Given the existence of a freely elected government with an independent judiciary and a body of duly enacted law, at what point are we justified in concluding that particular policy outcomes are 'not in the public interest'? . . . Are the revealed preferences of voters entitled to the same respect in the legislature as those of consumers in the marketplace?"

Schuck argued that Nader (like other public-interest advocates) "can ignore these moral issues because he has rejected the role of decision-maker and assumed the more comfortable role (particularly for a lawyer) of advocate. The advocate's role is comfortable because it relieves him of the dread responsibility for making difficult choices among alternatives. . . . The advocate can vigorously advance those values he happens to cherish, secure in the knowledge that the moral burden of adjusting the claims of his values with the claims of competing values will fall upon others."

But in the late 1970s, some of the public-interest advocates found themselves in exactly the place where Halpern and Schuck said they would be most uncomfortable. The Carter Administration was the first since the emergence of the movement to recruit large numbers of public-interest advocates into the executive branch. And many of them felt—at least initially—uneasy in their new surroundings.

Sitting in the Executive Office Building in 1979, Joe Onek recalled, almost nostalgically, that it seemed "particularly easy and virtuous" to go into court on behalf of needy clients, caring only that "you do your best for them." In an important case he filed against the District of Columbia General Hospital, alleging inadequate care of its patients, "we were quite successful in getting more money" for its budget. "But the one thing that was interesting in retrospect is that I never spent much time worrying whether the money we would get was best spent helping D.C. General Hospital or whether, from the point of view of poor people in the District, there might be some other more desirable expenditure. That isn't what a lawyer thinks about.

"Of course," he added, "in this job" (he was then a member of Carter's domestic-policy staff), "it's just the opposite. You're always asking whether $5 million here wouldn't better be spent somewhere else. There was a certain ease to being a lawyer, with your position staked out, and a certain dangling feeling in what I'm doing now."

Across town, while he still occupied his HEW assistant secretary's office, Ben Heineman said that his old work litigating "seems like an eminently rational process, compared to the sort of entrepreneurial manipulation of myth and symbol which unfortunately occupies an awful lot of government time."

The preference for the relatively "clean" adversarial role of the lawyer over the "dirty" mix of propaganda and trade-offs that became their lot as government officials was expressed by others besides Onek and Heineman. It may reflect a distaste for nitty-gritty politics natural to members of a profession which de Tocqueville characterized as being the American aristocracy. Some public-interest advocates, like Charles Halpern, did not go into government, in part because "I didn't really feel I had the answers to some of the hard problems that were going to be addressed. And since I didn't feel I had the answers, why should I go in and be the person who does all the balancing?"

But scores of public-interest advocates made the opposite decision. Mike Pertschuk, in 1979, estimated there were "at least thirty-five to forty people" he had brought to the Federal Trade Commission "who have had some full-time, substantial background in public-interest organizations of one kind or another." Probably close to one hundred alumni of the movement occupied key policy-making jobs on the White House staff and at the Justice, Interior, Agriculture, Transportation and Health, Education and Welfare departments, as well as in many of the specialized agencies and regulatory commissions.

And their presence made a difference. Carol Tucker Foreman, now 42, the former executive director of the Consumer Federation of America, was named Assistant Secretary of Agriculture for Food and Consumer Services. The consumer lobbyist was not only the first woman in that post but the first person whose experience had not been in one of the land-grant colleges or food-processing corporations. "The food-stamp and other feeding programs add up to about two-thirds of the budget for this department," she noted, "but as far as I can tell, my predecessors spent an awful lot more of their time speaking to industry groups, eating lunch with lobbyists and generally making sure that business got along well with the Department of Agriculture than they did running the feeding programs. . . . I bring a whole different set of concerns to the job. I don't eat lunch with lobbyists and business people. I meet frequently with consumer representatives. And I have involved myself in the intimate details of the food-safety-and-quality service and the food-and-nutrition service."

Her approach to her job was also different from her predecessors'. "The habit of the food-and-nutrition service," Foreman said, "was to bring a package of regulations over here and say, 'Please sign these; they have to be at the Federal Register this afternoon.' Well, I asked the agency to develop option papers on every single major issue. In the end, I reviewed about a hundred option papers, sometimes accepting theirs, sometimes asking them to draft new ones. I admit I'm meddlesome and a nitpicker. But I guess one of the things that people are so upset about is that government never really changes. And I'm not sure that you can make it change, unless you get that much involved in the detail of what's happening."

If controversy is one measure of the degree of change that is taking place, then Carol Tucker Foreman and Mike Pertschuk were two of the most successful public-interest people to move into government, for they were both enveloped in controversy. Business kept up a barrage of criticism of their work. The meat-packing industry accused Foreman of indulging her personal biases when she warned against nitrites in bacon or bits of ground bone in processed meats. An alliance of breakfast-cereal, candy and toy manufacturers, with help from the advertising industry and broadcasters, attacked Pertschuk for his long involvement in the effort to regulate television advertising aimed at children. Pertschuk's opponents tried to obtain a court order in 1979 barring him from the FTC's deliberations on the issue because of his earlier "emotional" statements in favor of limiting "kid-vid" commercials; to defuse the controversy, he voluntarily withdrew from the inquiry early in 1980.

While defending themselves as best they could against such attacks, the public-interest alumni in government sometimes found themselves being shelled by their own former comrades who had stayed on the outside. In a celebrated 1977 incident, Nader demanded that his longtime ally and former chief lobbyist Joan Claybrook resign as head of the National Highway Traffic Safety Administration because of what he called "a failure of leadership and a failure of nerve" in her job. Claybrook stayed put, and many of her former colleagues rallied to her defense. David Cohen wrote a public letter reminding everyone that "public-interest advocates are not the public-interest movement's insiders in government. We should not expect public advocates to jump through our hoops any more than we would want veterans from industry to jump through industry's hoops."

But in fact, it did make a difference to the movement to have friends on the inside. Charles Halpern said he still marveled at the fact that Jim Moorman, the environmental lawyer with whom he had once gone, hat in hand, seeking Justice Department help in the possible settlement of the Alaska Pipeline case, was now sitting behind the desk as Assistant Attorney General for Lands and Natural Resources in the same office where they had been coolly received.

Tony Roisman, looking at the environmental area from the viewpoint of the outside advocate, saw "a significant difference that they [the alumni] have brought in substantive outcomes." Others, like Paul Friedman, the mental-health advocate, were more guarded. But all of them agreed that in terms of access to the decision makers, the late 1970s had brought them light-years closer to the center of power. "When I came to this city in 1970," Mark Green, the Nader lobbyist, said, "I did a study of the anti-trust division, and Richard McLaren [then the Assistant Attorney General in charge of antitrust] wouldn't see us. He called me a 'yellow journalist.' Today, without undue difficulty, we can speak to Cabinet secretaries and sub-Cabinet officials and almost invariably get an audience for our views. With friends in high positions in government, it's obviously helpful to get my opinion implanted in that agency."

That is an important change, because the public-interest movement has been going through a transformation from a reliance on litigation as its basic weapon to a much wider variety of political tools, including monitoring of administrative decisions, legislative lobbying and direct political action.

Mark Green said that "unless you're dealing with a *Brown* v. *Board of Education* case, which is rare, the amount of time spent in getting a particular decision in the courts can have a bad cost–benefit ratio in terms of social change. There are a few exceptions, but I find I have more influence as a lobbyist than I did as a litigator."

Often, the two go hand in hand. Tony Roisman told the story of how his wife, Florence, who has her own public-interest law firm, learned one day that a Senate committee had voted 8–5 to kill a particular subsidized-housing program. "Three of the senators who voted to cancel it would have been normally expected to be friends of the poor," he said. "So Florence came back to her office, picked up the phone and called three legal-service lawyers who ran statewide programs in the three states where these people came from. This was a Friday afternoon. They, in turn, called their clients who belong to poverty groups, community-action groups and so on. And they started calling the senators.

"On Monday morning, she got to her office and got a call from one of the senators' staff people: 'Florence, hi! This is Bill So-and-so. We've decided we'd like to have the committee reconsider the vote of last Friday, and we'd like to get from you the exact wording that we ought to use.' She helped them out, and went to the markup session. This Senator stands up and moves to reconsider and the other two senators who voted wrong move to second it, and the vote is 8–5 the other way. So she saved probably $250 million of housing, because she was there and knew what to do."

As this anecdote suggests, politicians are sensitive to the impact of the public-interest network. And the network has become increasingly politicized. Environmental and consumer issues have fueled any number of political careers, including those of Jimmy Carter and Walter Mondale. As Governor of Georgia, Carter took a strong stand against "excessive" dam building by the Army Corps of Engineers. He used his 1972 opposition to the Sprewell Bluff Dam on the Flint River to good effect in his 1976 presidential campaign literature, and won the near-unanimous endorsement of environmentalists. Mondale, as Attorney General of Minnesota, gained a reputation as a champion of consumers. When he reached the Senate, he sponsored legislation like the 1966 Fair Warning Act, requiring automakers to inform motorists of potentially hazardous defects, that won praise from Naderite consumer-advocacy groups. Such upwardly mobile young elected officials as former Mayor Neil Goldschmidt of Portland, Oregon, now the Secretary of Transportation, Governor Bill Clinton of Arkansas and Governor Bruce Babbitt of Arizona have followed the public-interest-law path to political office.

Instead of the arm's-length relationship appropriate to their roles as attorneys suing government on behalf of private clients, many of the public-interest advocates have become increasingly and intimately involved with the political and governmental process.

Common Cause has so far not made political endorsements, but its issue advocacy leaves little doubt about which elected officials should be supported or scorned. Mark Green at Nader's Congress Watch said in 1979, "We are becoming more political. Still nonpartisan, but more political. In the past, we have been very weak in [congressional] district organizing. We have been top-heavy in Washington with lawyer-lobbyists. We are now spending substantial resources creating Congress Watch locals in swing districts around the country, so we don't simply have to exhort their consciences or their intelligence but appeal to their sense of self-preservation as well. . . . Not to be political in Congress is to be self-defeating."

In 1979, Nader suggested that there might be more to the grass-roots organizing than just an attempt to buttress the lobbying impact of his organization. He said in a series of interviews that he believed the country was ready for a new political party, if not in 1980 then certainly by 1984. He said the new party would focus on "the overriding issue of our times—corporate power"—and on achieving what he called "the expansion of citizen access to all branches of government, the mass media and corporate decision making."

Paul Friedman provided a clear example both of the transformation and of the tensions associated with it when he outlined the changes the late 1970s brought to the Mental Health Law Project. "Up to now," he said in 1979, "we've been basically a litigating project, using the courts to try to articulate basic rights. . . . But the rights we got declared in the federal courts have been picked up and recognized in some very important federal legislation, which bars discrimination on the basis of mental handicaps and provides due-process protection and a policy of 'mainstreaming' wherever possible in education. So now there's a federal statutory body of law to enforce. We've just brought a skilled person, a lawyer who's been working within HEW for a number of years, here to try to ply her trade from the outside, to become a voice for patients' rights in administrative decision making and to present the patients'-rights point of view before hearings on Capitol Hill.

"Our funding has begun to change, and it's caused a lot of anxiety and reservations among our board members. We were originally entirely private-foundation-funded, and then a few years back we got a very small and discreet grant from NIMH [the National Institute of Mental Health] to produce a model legislative guide for reform of civil-commitment codes at the state level. Last year, we got our first significant federal grant to provide technical assistance for [mental-health patients'] protection and advocacy agencies in HEW Region Two. This year we have a grant to service twenty-two of those agencies in four of the HEW regions. So at this point, close to half our budget is federal money."

Friedman said he was "feeling my way" through the risks of co-optation inherent in that degree of dependence on federal funding. But there is no easy escape from the dilemmas that arise for a litigating agency that is transformed into a service adjunct of a government bureaucracy.

The problems raised by the increasing politicization of the public-interest movement are compounded by uncertainty over the future receptivity of the courts to pleas for social-policy change.

Probably no aspect of public-interest advocacy has been more controversial than the charge that its practitioners have encouraged courts and judges to usurp policymaking from the elected legislators and executives. That is particularly the case when activists themselves sit on the bench.

Perhaps the most unusual judge in America is Justin C. Ravitz, 40, of Detroit, an avowed Marxist who has said that he regards himself as being part of the "system of injustice" in the United States. Ravitz was elected in 1972 to a ten-year term on the Detroit Recorders Court, a trial court handling criminal cases. In his eight years on the bench he has won the respect of the legal community, but has made few converts to his own ideology.

Ravitz, like many others in this book, made a big U-turn in his own thinking in the course of the Sixties. A native of Omaha and the graduate of a business college, he came to Washington in 1962, eager to "become a guerrilla and go to Vietnam and fight Communism." As a step in that direction, he took a job with the Central Intelligence Agency reading dossiers on people seeking admission to the United States. Boredom drove him back to academic life, and, after graduating from the University of Michigan Law School, he joined a black activist, Kenneth Cockrel (who will surface again in Chapter 11), in a new law firm.

They were not public-interest advocates of the kind we have been discussing. They were criminal lawyers, specializing in the defense of poor people in trouble with the police.

It was a time of turmoil in Detroit, with tension running high between the residents of the city's ghetto and a police department under heavy pressure to reduce the level of crime in the city. Ravitz and Cockrel won acquittals for their clients in several highly publicized cases. "The more I probed into the workings of the city," Ravitz said, "the more socialism came to make sense to me. . . . The institution of the criminal injustice system affected me deeply, but so did the civil-rights movement, the anti-war movement . . . and the way the whole society was organized."

Despite his local fame, his election to the bench in 1972 came as a surprise to the organized bar, and his actions in his early months as a judge did nothing to diminish the controversy. At his swearing-in ceremony, he remained seated while everyone else stood and recited the pledge of allegiance to the flag—an act of protest, he said, against the Vietnam war, and because he did not believe the United States provided "liberty and justice for all."

Because he wanted to "alter the atmosphere in the courtroom that makes people so uptight they are afraid to assert their rights," Ravitz removed some of the "symbols of authority," including the American flag. He frequently neglected to don his judge's robe. The Michigan Supreme Court ordered both the flag and the robe restored, and his response was to wear a robe that is more tatters than threads, unbuttoned, over his open-necked sport shirt and to place the flag behind a partition where it can barely be seen.

"It pissed me off," Ravitz said of the Supreme Court order, "because they're talking about all these false trappings that don't mean a damned thing and they ignore so many things of real substance."

Some of his critics made the same point about his own resistance to the norms. But they conceded that on questions of substance, Ravitz had succeeded often in making a point.

His conduct of his courtroom was judged both firm and fair, with a poll of prosecutors and defense attorneys rating him close to the top of the twenty judges on that bench. While removing some of his own badges of authority, he required courtroom guests to rise when the jury entered, "because the jury represents the people."

He has been perhaps the most vigorous of all the judges in pushing prosecutors to induce drug dealers brought in for trial to testify against the higher-ups in the world of heroin trafficking. At the same time, he forced the prosecutors to bring in anyone arrested for arraignment within twelve hours, by threatening to order the release of any prisoner held in jail without formal charges for a longer period of time.

He dramatized the problem of white-collar crime by threatening to sentence a supermarket executive to a day in jail for short-weighting meat, and by ordering that the president of a corporation found guilty of polluting a stream be placed on probation for two years, with a contempt citation hanging over his head if the offense was repeated.

Ravitz said such action "gives a glimpse of how the institution [of the courts] could be used to serve our collective needs, rather than just the needs of the wealthy few." But noting the frequency with which he has been reversed on appeal, he said the "dual standard" of justice, for the rich and poor, is too deeply ingrained to be changed by one judge.

"We have an economic and social system that is criminogenic," he said. "It causes crime. With unemployment and racism, with the glorification of greed and violence and competition on television, there's going to be crime." The Constitution's Bill of Rights "promises a lot of things that are illusory abstractions," he said, while the Cuban constitution, in his judgment, "guarantees those things that ought to be guaranteed in any society that really cares about human beings—dignified employment, free and equal education and recreational opportunities, medical care."

Ravitz said he would not seek re-election in 1982—not because he thought he would lose, but because "I don't think we're going to take over this institution in the foreseeable future, and I have no particular interest" in simply administering it as it exists.

That such a person was even part of the judicial branch was disturbing to some Detroiters. But judicial activism is not a new phenomenon. In a sense, it is inherent in the American system. Not only are judges given the power to interpret the Constitution, they are left free to choose which of several competing legal principles they will invoke in making a particular decision.

For most of our history, that broad discretionary power was used for conservative ends—to challenge and restrict legislation aimed at "correcting" social or economic inequalities. But with the government expanding the range of its involvement with people's lives in the 1960s and '70s, the opportunity increased for public-interest advocates to persuade the courts that certain classes of individuals were suffering discrimination in their access to those newly proclaimed rights.

Federal District Judge Frank M. Johnson wrote in a 1976 *Texas Law Review* article, "As governmental institutions at all levels have assumed a greater role in providing public services, courts increasingly have been confronted with the unavoidable duty of determining whether those services meet basic constitutional requirements."

Johnson was perhaps the prime exemplar of the activist judge. Locked in a bitter dispute with Alabama Governor George C. Wallace, Johnson, at one time or another, took under the custody of his court the desegregation of Alabama's schools, the apportionment of its legislature, the assessment of its property taxes and the treatment of its mentally ill and its imprisoned criminals.

Judge Johnson may have been forced into an extraordinary number of roles by Wallace's obduracy, but he was far from unique. From Boston to Los Angeles, judges found themselves imposing their judgments on elected officials and the public on matters of social policy, and even making detailed administrative decisions for school systems and other public services. Their interventions won the gratitude of those whose interests were being protected, but only at the cost of angry complaints from others in the same community.

Much of the judicial activism was sanctioned and encouraged by the Supreme Court during the two decades Earl Warren was Chief Justice, and it conceivably could be given new force by some of President Carter's appointees. While Carter had not, at this writing, made any Supreme Court nominations, he elevated Frank Johnson to the circuit court and gave another circuit-court judgeship to Patricia Wald, a former partner of Friedman and Halpern in the Mental Health Law Project.

In 1979, Carter named Joseph W. Hatchett, the first black member of the Florida Supreme Court, to the Fifth U.S. Circuit Court of Appeals, thus installing a former NAACP Legal Defense Fund activist on a bench that has jurisdiction over desegregation compliance in six Southern states. A 1977 nomination to the District of Columbia's Court of Appeals went to John M. Ferren, who had litigated public-interest cases as head of the community-service department of the Washington firm of Hogan & Hartson and had set up neighborhood legal-services offices in Chicago and Cambridge. A 1979 appointment to the U.S. Court of Appeals for the District of Columbia went to Ruth Bader Ginsburg, a Columbia Law

School professor and a leading advocate of women's rights and the Equal Rights Amendment. In another appointment to that same prestigious bench, Carter selected Abner J. Mikva, a five-term Congressman from Illinois with a record of liberal activism on tax reform, government regulation of business and handgun control. (Vigorous opposition from the National Rifle Association to his gun-control advocacy helped make the Mikva nomination the most controversial of Carter's presidency, although Mikva was finally confirmed by a Senate vote of 58–31.)

But as on so many other questions, Carter seemed equivocal, and many judicial officials, led by Chief Justice Warren Burger, were trying to roll back the tide of judicial activism. The uncertainty of future judicial policy was illustrated by the differences expressed by two young men, both former members of the board of Common Cause, who were chosen by Carter as U.S. attorneys.

Michael H. Walsh, 38, of San Diego, is a graduate of Stanford and Yale Law School and a former White House Fellow. Walsh moved to San Diego to work in the public defender's office and later, while in private practice, headed California Common Cause's successful 1974 campaign for passage of an initiative that dramatically tightened the lobbying, campaign-contribution and conflict-of-interest codes.

Walsh said in a 1979 interview that he neither expected nor desired any reduction in the role of the judiciary. "I think there will be a continuing impetus to take to the courts those questions that are stalemated elsewhere in government," he said, "and I am not frightened of what that means for the courts. Even with its backlog of cases, the judiciary is not in bad shape, compared to other branches of government. It has been relatively immune to charges of corruption or incompetence, and its decisions still carry a great deal of authority."

Quite a different view was expressed by another alumnus of the Common Cause national board, Richard Blumenthal, 34, the U.S. Attorney in New Haven. Blumenthal followed the familiar path from Harvard College to Yale Law School, with a short detour through *The Washington Post* and a White House staff job. He said in 1978 that he expected to see "less and less resort to the courts" on issues of social policy, "mainly because I think judges are more and more reluctant to take on that role. I think the American judiciary is now swinging the other way. The Supreme Court maybe reached out too far during the Warren era, although obviously my sympathies were very much with what was done in the Warren era, and I think they made a lot of good law. But I think there's a sensitivity to reaching out too far, and I see it in judges when I talk to them in chambers. The feeling is that American judges have taken too much power unto themselves, and I think the judges are fearful of that view spreading too widely."

Many of those conflicting pressures came to focus, late in the 1970s, on the person of Rose Elizabeth Bird, the 44-year-old Chief Justice of the California Supreme Court. That bench, which had probably been the most prestigious among the fifty states, was by 1979 without challenge the most controversial—and largely because of the first woman member in its history.

Bird was raised in genteel poverty by a widowed mother, who worked in Long Island factories to support her two sons and a daughter. "I think she was fearful that I would get caught in the same way that she had," Bird said, "and so I think I became rather single-minded in terms of my education." She went through Long Island University on a full scholarship and worked as a secretary for a year to save enough money to go on to the University of California at Berkeley for graduate work in political science. She won a Ford Foundation fellowship for a year as a staff aide in the California Legislature and "decided to go to law school because, after looking at the legislature, I could see really graphically that lawyers ran everything in government."

She went to Boalt Hall, the Berkeley law school, and after a year's clerkship on the Nevada Supreme Court, she became the first woman hired in the Santa Clara County public defender's office, where she worked for eight years and taught at Stanford Law School as well.

Bird had known Jerry Brown slightly at Berkeley, when they both lived for a semester in International House. But he was "fresh out of seminary, quite serious and withdrawn." It was more her own interest in politics than any bond to him that caused her to volunteer in Brown's 1974 gubernatorial campaign.

When he won, much to her surprise she was offered a job in the Brown Cabinet. "First, he asked me if I would become head of the resources department," she said, "and I said, 'I don't know anything about resources or the environment, so it's crazy. It's a ludicrous idea.' But he had some idea that resources were sort of Mother Earth, and Mother Earth was a woman, and if you needed a woman in the Cabinet, resources would be the place. So I said to him, 'Well, it seems to me that what women really do in our society is cook and raise children and work. A much better agency, if you're looking for one, is the one that contains agriculture, industrial relations, consumer affairs and those things.' " So Bird became secretary of the Agriculture and Services Agency—a catch-all post—in the first Brown Administration. In that job she proved herself a tough administrator, as demanding of her subordinates as she was of herself. She also wrote and successfully lobbied through the legislature the landmark California Farm Labor Act, which brought collective-bargaining procedures to the fields which had seen decades of bitter strife between growers and their workers.

Despite this achievement, there was genuine shock in 1977 when Brown named her to the prestigious California Supreme Court, not just as one of the seven judges, but as the Chief Justice.

The Commission on Judicial Appointments held days of televised hearings before approving her selection on a 2-to-1 vote. Some colleagues on the court—who had harbored their own ambitions for the Chief's seat—were even more irreconcilable, snubbing their new leader in every way possible. In her own hard-driving style, she quickly curbed the discretionary role of the court's administrative staff, firing those longtime aides who would not adjust to a Chief Justice who was reluctant to delegate much of her own authority. In selecting lower-court judges for temporary assignments to appellate panels, including the Supreme Court bench, Bird went out of her way to give recognition to women and minority members.

While her style and approach were distinctly disturbing to colleagues accustomed to the old ways, Bird insisted she was really an "old-fashioned" person. She contrasted herself with the Governor who appointed her, saying that Brown "in a way personifies a generation that has been a little cynical, that sort of goes with the flow, that is suspicious of any kind of philosophical underpinnings because they believe they set limits, rather than giving you a kind of stable foundation.

"I tend to think of myself as a little more old-fashioned," she said—and particularly in her conception of the judiciary. What disturbed her, she said, was that the insulation of the courts—"the mystery and symbolism that lend them authority"—was being eroded, and "it's going to be much more difficult to maintain a judiciary that is nonpolitical." Pressures are growing on judges, backed by threats of retribution at the polls, to "stop being so independent and do what we want done. That goes against the whole symbol of justice as a woman with balanced scales and her eyes blindfolded.

"I feel that the courts are the most fragile branch of government," she said. "We are the last aristocratic part of a democratic system. Having served in both the legislative and executive branches of government, I have a view of the courts as a much more limited and restricted kind of institution. And one of the problems that we face right now is that because we have such stagnation in the executive and legislative branches, an awful lot of the very difficult political decisions are thrown into the courts. And to me, that's very dangerous, because I think that the most important role of the courts within the system is the protection of the Bill of Rights, and that, by definition, is an unpopular role. If the court is going to defend the individual against the state or the minority against the majority very often, it's going to be unpopular. But we can't make too many unpopular decisions and remain a viable institution within the system. And I think when the courts have to start taking over the schools and running them, or decide whether the Concorde can land here or there, and a lot of other questions that rightfully belong in the legislative and executive arenas, it's dangerous.

"Courts make a decision in a closed room—in our case, with seven people. Nobody gets to listen to what we say. Nobody else is called and asked what they think. There is no attempt to search out and find all the different viewpoints. We are limited to the arguments in the briefs, and the specific issues of the case as it's brought before us. Well, in a society in which people are part of the social compact, they like to have a say in what happens and how the laws impact on their lives. And if you have too many of the decisions being made in your society by a body that is basically private and aristocratic, people are not going to accept those decisions over the long haul."

Bird made those observations in the course of a long interview in 1978, and events since then have served to underscore her warning. She and her court have both been consumed in controversy. Under California law, she was required to stand for approval in the first election after her appointment. Conservative groups, still simmering over her role in drafting the California farm-labor bill and her nomination as Chief Justice, mounted a major campaign against her. She barely survived at the polls in November 1978, winning a 52-to-48-percent majority. On election day, the *Los Angeles Times* reported that the court had deliberately withheld reporting a decision in which Bird had voted to overturn the state's mandatory-sentencing law for crimes involving the use of a gun—a decision that might well have angered enough people to defeat her. Bird argued in her opinion that the legislature had been guilty of unconstitutional interference with a coequal branch of government when it sought to bar judges from granting probation to criminals who had used guns.

At Bird's request, the state Commission on Judicial Performance—a group of judges and attorneys empowered to monitor the performance of the courts—began its first public, televised hearing in the summer of 1979 on the circumstances surrounding the issuance of that opinion and several others, whose timing also had been questioned.

The hearing did nothing to enhance the standing of the court. Instead, it depicted an assemblage racked by personality conflicts and imputations of political motivation. Bird had a particularly antagonistic relationship with Justice William Clark, a former top aide to Brown's predecessor as Governor, Ronald Reagan. Clark was as conservative in his politics as Bird was liberal, and she accused him of inserting language in his opinion on the gun case for the purpose of embarrassing her—a charge that he denied.

At one point Bird told the commission that the proceedings were undermining the judicial process. "We're dealing with very delicate china here, and I feel we have thrown very delicate china into the Laundromat."

After a month of hearings, the investigation was aborted when another justice believed to be hostile to Bird, Democrat Stanley M. Mosk, refused to testify and challenged the constitutionality of the public proceeding. A panel of seven state judges, sitting in place of the Supreme Court, upheld his contention, and the investigating commission ended its work with a brief report saying that it would not recommend filing of misconduct charges against any of the justices.

Later that summer, Mosk told the American Bar Association convention that the independence of the judiciary was gravely threatened by such occurrences. "There is no more pathetic sight," he said, "than learned judges cringing in front of an aggressive investigative commission which is in turn pandering to an assaultive press."

While Bird and her colleagues began the new decade trying to repair the damage to their institution, public-interest lawyers across the country were pondering what lies ahead for them. The mass migration of activist lawyers into government at the start of the Carter Administration, coupled with a shift in public mood, at least temporarily cost the movement leadership and momentum. Common Cause's membership slumped to about 210,000 people—a drop of more than one-third from its 1974 peak—in January 1979, before bottoming out and making a slight recovery. To the shock of Nader and his allies, Congress in 1977 rejected a bill for creation of a federal consumer-protection agency, which had been the main legislative goal of that branch of the public-interest movement. The defeat was part of a broad backlash against "over-regulation," which put Pertschuk and many of the other newly recruited regulators very much on the defensive. In 1979, Congress sharply restricted FTC investigations into the funeral industry, agriculture cooperatives and insurance and used-car sales practices, and curbed the agency's financing of public-interest advocates' participation in its own proceedings.

But interestingly, just at the point when the public-interest advocates were beginning to doubt their own potency, they acquired some imitators whose tactics were indeed a form of flattery. Business groups in many parts of the country chartered their own public-interest law firms to use the same techniques for a different set of goals.

One of the first and most influential was the Pacific Legal Foundation, launched in 1973 by two career lawyers for the state of California, Raymond Momboisse and Ronald Zumbrun, with the backing of the California Chamber of Commerce.

The two lawyers were defending Ronald Reagan's reforms of the state welfare system against challenges from public-interest and legal-aid lawyers, representing welfare recipients. They concluded that "the state was at a tremendous disadvantage," Momboisse said, because "the opposition had the ability to throw tremendous manpower into the litigation." So they quit their government jobs and, with business backing, organized a Sacramento and Washington, D.C., law firm to intervene in such disputes on behalf of a conservatively defined public interest.

Taking what it called the "free-enterprise" side of the argument, the foundation moved into a wide variety of disputes—on issues ranging from land use to pesticide controls to "reverse discrimination" in hiring to nuclear-plant siting—and won a significant number of victories. The lawyers took particular delight in using some of the public-interest movement's favorite weapons—such as environmental-impact-statement requirements and open-meeting laws—to frustrate the strategies of the movement alumni in government. "Our job," said Momboisse, "is to keep them honest," as in the case where they challenged an Environmental Protection Agency order to Los Angeles County to cease dumping sludge in the ocean, on the ground that EPA had not considered the environmental impact of forcing the county to create a landfill for the refuse. While still outgunned by the traditional public-interest firms, Pacific Legal Foundation had grown to eighteen lawyers and a $1.5-million annual budget after six years, and had spawned at least sixteen similar groups in locations from Atlanta to Denver and from Boston to Kansas City.

While both the old and new kinds of public-interest firms continued to recruit young lawyers, some veterans of the movement expressed fear about the changes they saw. "It's becoming more bureaucratized now," said Paul Friedman, "and it's losing its sense of mission. When we began here, we thought we'd be at it for a year or two. Now I have a certain number of friends saying, 'You're still there? What are you going to do when you grow up?' I don't know of any good answers for that."

In a similar vein, Mark Green said that "unlike the antiwar movement, which had leaders but no institutions, I think the public-interest-law movement has created institutions which will survive its original founders. Agency officials, the White House, Congress and the media all need people with legitimate credentials who can speak to issues from a financially unbiased point of view. And that is true whether Ronald Reagan or Ted Kennedy is President. But on the other hand, there's a lack of animating passion of the kind that I gather marked the labor movement forty years ago, so I can't say we will survive another forty years."

Of more immediate concern at the end of the 1970s was the financial future of the public-interest movement. Foundation support had gradually been diminishing, and court rulings were undercutting the hope of gaining large enough fees from legal victories to finance the losing cases. Congress was balking at providing direct support of public-interest representation at congressional hearings and regulatory-agency forums.

The public-interest movement suffered a heavy blow in the autumn of 1979 when the Ford Foundation, which had supplied $21 million in funds as the largest backer of the advocacy organizations during the previous decade, said it was terminating its grants to the ten advocacy law firms it was regularly funding. While the foundation said the decision was consistent with its policy of pushing grantees toward self-sufficiency, Nader said the act was a form of retaliation by the corporate world. "If no one else comes forward," said Herbert Semmel of the Washington-based Center for Law and Social Policy, "public-interest law will be nothing but a shadow of itself in two years."

"I think we've reached a very critical juncture," Tony Roisman added. "All the easy, general principles have been established, and now we've got the hard cases. A lot of federal agencies are genuinely trying to implement the law. The duty is now on those of us who say we represent the public to make a record, to prove on the merits that we're right. And that is extremely difficult. It requires expertise that no lawyer has. It requires economists, marine biologists, engineers, doctors, accountants to make the case. And that costs money."

The other great question mark was leadership. "I don't see people coming along with the unique talents of a Ralph Nader," said Peter Schuck. His comment appeared to dismiss the possibility that the many Nader protégés who had gone into government at the end of the 1970s might emerge to take new and broader responsibility on the outside. Dozens of successful Washington careers had been built by in-and-out lawyers, who moved with ease from the concerns of their private clients to their governmental responsibilities and then back again, gaining new insight and skills on each round trip.

Might the same thing happen with the public-interest lawyers and serve to benefit both the government and their outside constituency? "I won't deny that people are beginning to talk about that," said Joe Onek in 1979, "but there are few answers. Some [of the public-interest advocates] will probably go into conventional law firms when they leave government [as

Ben Heineman did in 1979]. Some will teach. I think quite a few may go up to Capitol Hill as committee staff directors and so on."

Charles Halpern said he thought the disparity in salaries would be a problem. "People who are making $50,000 a year in government have a lot of trouble cutting back to $35,000 in the public-interest law firm," he said. "And there may be a psychological problem for people in their forties or fifties doing what public-interest lawyers do. I have trouble picturing myself at age fifty-five holding a press conference to denounce the latest outrages of the Supreme Court."

Perhaps because he had been at it longer than many of the others, Mike Pertschuk was more optimistic about the durability of the movement. "I think you can speculate that when this [Carter] Administration goes out of office," he said, "you'll have many of the old leaders coming back to the public-interest movement. I think the prospect of a substantial number of these people opening up corporate law firms is unlikely. You will have them going back outside with the increased prestige and knowledge and experience and responsibility their years in government have given them. If Ronald Reagan were elected President, I think you would have a very formidable public-interest movement again in this city."

9 · Women

FOR MORE YEARS than anyone can remember, the University of Texas has been an incubator of talent in both football and politics. The same competitive drive for dominance and prominence that has characterized the Longhorn football teams has marked the politicians, from Tom Connally and Sam Rayburn to John Connally and Bob Strauss, who have come off that campus. Imbued with the Texas spirit, a steady stream of ambitious, gifted and successful candidates, organizers and behind-the-scenes advisers have shaped American government, at every level, for decades.

So it was hardly remarkable that at the end of the Seventies you could find Texas graduates—the oldest of them 41—serving as Mayor of Austin, as the top political organizer for the fastest-growing union in the AFL-CIO and as one of the senior assistants to the President of the United States. The only surprising thing was that these three Texans were not alumni, but alumnae—Carole McClellan, Betsey Wright and Sarah Weddington.

They were part of a transformation of American politics and government from the domain of dominant males to a forum where females were —if not yet nearly equal in numbers and prominence—at least moving up at a rapid enough pace that their increased power in the next two decades could no longer be in doubt.

The successful breakthrough that women have achieved in recent years in overcoming the legal, psychological and cultural barriers to full partnership in this democracy is probably the single most important change in the leadership pool of this nation. Almost overnight, the range of people who can be considered for the policymaking jobs in the public sector has been doubled. It was not until 1920 that women were even allowed to vote in the United States, and their use of the franchise grew very slowly after the formal right was acquired. As late as the 1950s, the University of Michigan Center for Political Studies' surveys indicate, there was a gap of 10 percentage points between male and female turnout rates, but that gap declined to a reported 1.4 percent in 1978. At the end of the 1970s, only five women had served as governors, 13 as senators, 88 as U.S. representatives, six as Cabinet members and none as justices of the Supreme Court. All those numbers seem certain to take quantum leaps in the remaining years of this century.

The arrival of women in political and governmental leadership posts is part of a much broader—indeed, massive—movement of women into the entire job market. According to Census Bureau estimates, between 1945 and 1978 the percentage of women employed outside the home rose from 35 to 56 percent. Two-thirds of the women between the ages of 20 and 64 are employed at any given moment, and at least 90 percent of them will be employed at some time in their lives.

The massive transformation of the American economy implied in those figures is matched by the massive transformation of the American family. By the end of the Seventies, only one family in six matched the stereotype of the previous generation—a working husband, a wife with no employment outside the home and two or more minor children. More and more women are facing life on their own—voluntarily or otherwise. One marriage in three ends in divorce; one woman in four never marries; one woman in nine is widowed. (Those statistics apply to the women in this chapter. Three of them have been divorced, two have never married and two have been widowed.)

With a social change of that dimension, it was inevitable that there would be controversy—much of it pitting women against women. Two of the major battles of the Seventies saw women taking the lead on opposing sides. One concerned the Equal Rights Amendment, a proposed addition to the Constitution barring discrimination on the basis of sex. Polls showed majority support from both men and women for its passage, but activist female opponents of the measure managed to stymie it short of ratification by the necessary three-fourths of the state legislatures.

An even more emotional struggle was raging between feminists' demands for access to abortions for women of all incomes and a countermovement determined to protect the "right to life" of the fetus. In angry and sometimes violent confrontations, the two groups of women battled for control of that sensitive area of public policy.

Because the emergence of women into leadership roles in this society has been so striking and pervasive, there is difficulty in isolating the phenomenon for discussion in a book like this one. Women figure in almost all the chapters in this book, because there is hardly any significant new leadership network that has not been influenced by women and does not include women.

There is an obvious arbitrariness in a scheme that puts Barbara Mikulski, Carol Bellamy, Vilma Martínez, Eleanor Holmes Norton and Anne Wexler into separate chapters, when all are self-proclaimed feminists and all have played a significant role in what is now a highly developed national network of women leaders.

But it still seemed important—because of the overriding significance of the emergence of women as a major leadership resource—to collect the stories of some women leaders in this chapter as a way of illustrating that basic phenomenon.

Feminism has arisen as a major movement only twice in the history of this nation. In both instances, it appeared during times when American society was addressing discrimination in general and racial discrimination in particular. The first feminist movement began shortly after, and as an outgrowth of, the abolitionist sentiment of the 1840s and culminated in the passage in 1920 of the amendment guaranteeing women the right to vote. The second feminist movement, that of the 1960s and '70s, came in the wake of the civil-rights protests.

In both periods, there was tension between those in the movement who sought a sweeping redefinition of women's roles and those who were more narrowly focused on gaining specific rights. The suffragettes of sixty years ago won the franchise for women, but the women's movement did not last into the 1930s. In more recent times, reformers have succeeded in winning equal-pay-for-equal-work laws, but have been able neither to ensure their consistent enforcement nor to satisfy the more committed feminists, who perceive that such laws do not strike down the stereotypes of "women's work."

In the early decades of this nation, when America was an agrarian society, women were in many ways "full partners" in the operation of the farm. But with the clustering in cities came the distinction between male bread-winners and female bread-bakers. As these sexual divisions became entrenched, the public relationship between men and women grew more formal and "Victorian."

During the 1830s, American women found a political cause in the antislavery movement. Often their husbands were also abolitionists, but abolitionism had much to recommend it as a women's cause. It dealt with ethical and basically religious questions, and religion was a legitimate province of women. The founders of the American feminist movement—Lucretia Mott and the Grimké sisters, Sarah and Angelina—were Quakers and abolitionists, trained in the rhetoric of emancipation.

The early feminists had their inspiration in a book by a Briton, Mary Wollstonecraft. Her *Vindication of the Rights of Woman,* published in 1792, drew an explicit connection between the American Revolution and a women's revolution. The abolitionists learned a great deal from her application of the concept of natural rights to the problems of a hierarchical society; and the feminists learned the important—if not always pleasant—lesson from the abolitionists that rights were not transferable. Indeed, the suffrage movement was sparked—unintentionally—by the shortcomings of the abolitionists.

Elizabeth Cady Stanton was married to abolitionist Henry Stanton, and they spent their honeymoon at the World Anti-Slavery Convention in London. That body voted to exclude female delegates. Stanton met other women abolitionists there, and their shared anger at their own treatment spurred the efforts that resulted, a decade later, in July of 1848, in the Women's Rights Convention in Seneca Falls, New York.

For that gathering, Stanton—who had been confined to her household duties as wife and mother—drafted with Lucretia Mott and others a "Declaration of Rights and Sentiments," proclaiming women's rights to own property, to obtain a divorce, to have access to educational and professional opportunities and, of course, to vote.

The Seneca Falls convention was important not only in setting the feminist agenda, but also for mobilizing people like Lucy Stone and Susan B. Anthony, who carried the program into the political arena with their organizing efforts. In 1860, Anthony's work persuaded the New York Legislature to pass several of those reforms, but the next sixty years were required to make those gains common across the nation. In the early 20th century, under the leadership of women like Jane Addams, the feminists once again broadened their agenda to include prison reform, prohibition, sex education, tax reform, pure-food laws, free libraries, public transportation—and international disarmament. Once again, the common thread was a sense that these were "moral" questions, where women were believed to have a natural superiority.

The second burst of feminism has come not so much from ideological as from sociological sources. World War II was a boon to the women's movement, for the simple reason that it brought large numbers of women out of their homes and into the workplace. During the war, some 6.5 million women took jobs for the first time, an increase of more than 50 percent. The number of female unionists quadrupled, and the efforts of "Rosie the Riveter" and her counterparts were praised by male officials, who were grateful for their help in the war effort.

But the wartime gains were inherently fragile, and the 1950s saw a "baby boom" so great that Philip Wylie could magnify public fears about "mom-ism" capturing America. It was a time of value conflicts. Society was pressuring women to return to their conventional roles, but was critical of the female dominance of the family. At the same time, more and more women were breaking out of the traditional pattern. By 1960, 40 percent of all women held jobs, twice as high a percentage as in 1940.

And the women's ranks were growing in both numbers and skills. By

1960, women had attained a numerical majority in the country—one that has been steadily increasing ever since. They were outliving men by an average of 6.5 years—and that number too has continued to rise. More of them were living outside of marriage—either spinsters, divorcées or widows. And they were better educated, with a doubling in the percentage who held college degrees.

Nonetheless, the most obvious kinds of discrimination persisted. Women's earnings did not budge above 62 percent of the male average, working women were still largely consigned to the clerical jobs and their unemployment rates were higher than men's.

The first harbinger of feminist discontent came in the form of a special supplement to the October 1962 issue of *Harper's* magazine. Entitled "The American Female," the supplement contained a series of articles —mostly by women—about working-class women, women and the New Frontier, divorce, education and male–female relationships. The foreword said that "an extraordinary number of women [were] troubled by some of the same problems that bothered the Women's Rights agitators of the past" and were re-examining "the roles as wives, mothers and members of the human race. . . . Crypto-feminism, it would appear, is a mass movement. This is something new on the American scene."

The next year, 1963, the "crypto-feminists" went public with Betty Friedan's book *The Feminine Mystique,* which was immediately heralded as the manifesto for a new movement. Friedan focused on "the problem that has no name," which she defined as the lack of fulfillment for contemporary women.

Noting how the wartime workers had been herded back into the kitchens and bedrooms, she said, "Fulfillment as a woman has had only one definition for American women after 1949—the housewife-mother. As swiftly as in a dream, the image of the American woman as a changing, growing individual was forgotten in the rush for the security of togetherness. Her limitless world shrunk to the cozy walls of home."

Friedan's message was stamped on thousands, perhaps millions, of minds as the young women of the 1960s—particularly those on the college campuses—were drawn into the civil-rights and social-protest movements of that decade. Once again, as with Elizabeth Cady Stanton, they found that they were second-class citizens even in the eyes of fellow reformers. Stokely Carmichael, the leader of the Student Non-Violent Coordinating Committee (SNCC), was blunter than most when he said, "The only position for women in SNCC is prone." The authors of a feminist resolution at a 1966 SDS convention were pelted with tomatoes. Understandably resentful, some women activists became overtly antimale, forming semiserious organizations like SCUM—the Society for Cutting Up Men. But most of them went into organizations aimed at achieving a new definition of equality for women.

Friedan formed NOW—the National Organization for Women—in 1966. Two years later, the Women's Equity Action League (WEAL) came along. And in the early Seventies, two more major organizations, the National Women's Political Caucus and the National Women's Education Fund, were started with the aim of encouraging more women to participate in elective politics.

Betsey Wright, who ran the last of these organizations for several years, is a good example of the cultural dynamic that has produced this generation of women leaders.

"I came to feminism through politics, rather than the other way around," she said. Wright was born on July 4, 1943, in Alpine, Texas, and, as she says, "was named for the one woman in American history that the family was familiar with"—Betsy Ross. Her father was the Democratic county chairman, a liberal in a conservative, rural community. "By the time I went off to the University of Texas at Austin," she said, "I had done more nitty-gritty political work than most people my age had ever had an opportunity to do." At the university, "I learned that I wasn't alone, that there was a whole peer group of other Texas liberal Democrats." Wright became president of the Texas Young Democrats and after graduation "served for several years as seasonal liberal labor, working from campaign to campaign."

It was her treatment by the liberals that made her a feminist. "As soon as I graduated, I became associate director of a state voter-registration drive," she said. "I was told that the titular director of the project was to be an attorney, that he wasn't really going to be involved, but that I surely understood that they couldn't have a woman be named the director."

In subsequent years, Wright noticed that while her liberal and labor allies "may have considered me absolutely critical to any kind of campaign that came down the pike, they didn't take care of me between campaigns the way they did young men, and they didn't pay me the way they did young men." It was the same experience the early feminists had had with the abolitionists who barred them from their meetings.

"The culmination," she said, "came in '72, with the person that McGovern had sent in to manage the Texas campaign. I was one of only two Texans on the professional staff of that campaign, but not a day went by with this man, when I tried to talk to him about some of the political factors we had to consider, that he didn't ask me about my hormones or when was the last time I had been laid. That crystallized my feminism. I struck back. I was very angry, I was very depressed and I was very hurt. And when I came out of it, I was a fighting feminist."

A year later, she was hired through what she calls "the Wellesley network"—a group of McGovern supporters and feminists, many of them Wellesley College graduates—as executive director of the newly formed National Women's Education Fund. That organization has been a major training center for women candidates and officeholders.

One of the lessons "we've tried to make women understand," Wright said, "is that it's only the rare district which is going to elect a woman to the city council or the legislature or Congress whose primary identification is feminist and women's movement. . . . The district may be overwhelmingly in support of ERA and its ratification, but it probably is not a very high priority to the voters in that district. What she has to do as a candidate is find out what those priority concerns are and build her message on them. Otherwise, she never makes a link with the voter, and she never gets elected to vote on ERA. . . . But even the women who are getting into office today who haven't come through the movement are getting there because the movement has opened those doors, and put the pressure on to break down the barriers to them. . . . The gains are there, and they're encouraging, but it's very slow. We're still talking about only ten percent of all of the elected officials in this country. . . . We're not so far beyond tokenism, but the overwhelming number of women in office are supportive of women's issues and women's rights, and it transcends whether those women identify themselves as liberals or conservatives, or Republicans or Democrats."

While expressing satisfaction with the women's side of the equation, Wright said in a 1978 interview that she feared "we're still pretty far away from having men being comfortable working with women in coalitions. I consider myself to be a political operative," she said. "Before I was in the women's movement, it seemed to me that I was pretty good for a political operative, and now I'm pretty good for a female political operative. I don't like that. I am as good a political operative as any male around, and that's what I want recognized."

Wright gained the recognition she sought when, in March of 1979, she was hired as director of political action by the AFL-CIO's second-largest and fastest-growing union, the American Federation of State, County and Municipal Employees (AFSCME). Ten months later, she left that job "for personal reasons" and began searching for a new position "where I can practice politics in a male-dominated environment." But at the outset of her search she was finding it "difficult to get out of the stereotype of being just a feminist politician."

Other women found their recognition by doing what Wright and her organization encouraged—running for office in their hometowns. Her fellow Texas alumna Carole McClellan is typical of them. McClellan, 41, grew up in a family of lawyers; her father, Page Keeton, was dean of the University of Texas Law School, and she and her brother "were the only kids on the block who had bedtime cases, instead of bedtime stories, read to us." There were no artificial barriers created in her mind about aspirations and expectations. As a high-school senior, she ran for student-council president. The boy she had asked to be her running mate for vice president had his father call the elder Keeton, a fellow faculty member, "to tell your daughter she shouldn't be doing it; she ought to be doing it the other way around." Carole's father did not even pass along the message, and she went ahead to win the presidency.

McClellan married a University of Texas classmate, taught school while he earned his law degree, spent a few years with him in Washington and then moved back to Austin with four young children. Blessed with that extra energy or adrenaline that so many successful politicians seem to have, McClellan volunteered to run the Travis County Democratic headquarters. "I just took the kids and diapers and everything else and really got into precinct work and the nitty-gritty of politics, which I had not done before."

It was a good time for women in Texas politics, for the role models were abundant. One of the outstanding Texas women of the older generation, Federal Judge Sarah T. Hughes, had administered the oath of office to President Johnson on November 22, 1963. Johnson's wife, Lady Bird, had become the first First Lady since Eleanor Roosevelt to expand the limits of the semi-independent policy role of that office—making both social legislation and environmental beautification her personal concern. One of Johnson's most talented assistants was an ebullient, tough-minded Texas woman named Liz Carpenter, a former journalist and born politician.

And the Texas Legislature in the late Sixties included two more outstanding women. One was Barbara Jordan, a black lawyer from Houston, whose intellect and organ voice would later capture for her a national audience, first as a member of the House Judiciary Committee during the impeachment proceedings against President Nixon, and later as the keynote speaker of the 1976 Democratic convention. Jordan left politics—at least temporarily—in 1978 to teach at the University of Texas.

The other standout legislator was a deceptively fragile-looking lawyer from Corpus Christi named Frances (Sissy) Farenthold. Inside four years, she would organize the most potent "reform" caucus, the "Dirty Thirty," that that roughneck body had seen in years, and in 1972 she would run ahead of the incumbent Governor and Lieutenant Governor before losing in a runoff for her party's nomination for the state's top office.

When Liz Carpenter was asked what explained the tenacity of a Sissy Farenthold and some of the other soft-spoken Texas women, she had a ready reply. "Living in the same house for forty-five years is the source of Sissy's courage. You can fight tigers if somebody cares about you." Warming to the theme, she went on: "We were shaped by our Southern grandmothers, all of us—strong women who came to the frontier packing their classical libraries and their John Wesley Bibles; that's all within the storytelling memory of all of us. We have the true grit of the frontier and the style of the Southern woman, who makes it more tactful, somehow, and softer."

Carole McClellan was Liz Carpenter's kind of woman. McClellan made her first race for public office in 1972, gaining election to the Austin school board. In 1977, after serving as the first woman president of that board, she jumped into the contest for Mayor.

"Being a woman was a downer all the way in that election," she said. In an Austin newspaper interview, she added, "A woman has a real problem if she comes on too soft as a candidate. You know, you're not tough enough for the job. But if you start hitting directly on the issues and speaking hard and tough, then you turn off some of the thirty-to-forty-year-old women. For other people, it was 'She's a nice lady, but isn't it a shame that she's leaving her husband and four kids alone,' which was totally untrue, but that's what everyone assumed if you were out running for office. It's not just a problem with men. It's also a problem with how women view other women running for office."

McClellan managed to overcome those problems in her first race, and after two years in office she breezed to re-election in 1979 with over 78 percent of the votes—the widest margin in Austin history. (A quiet divorce in 1979 proved to be no issue in the campaign.) A skillful conciliator, she won support of previously skeptical businessmen by pushing a downtown-renewal project. Despite her role as leader of the successful referendum fight to continue Austin's participation in a Texas nuclear-power project, she was able to maintain most of her original backing in the liberal and university communities.

While she was luckier—or more skillful—than most, McClellan's problems were typical of those confronting women office seekers and officials. As Susan and Martin Tolchin wrote in their 1974 book *Clout: Womanpower and Politics*, "The very texture of American politics—its folkways and byways—militates against women's entry into the mainstream. The smoke-filled rooms, bourbon-and-branchwater friendships and all-night poker games exclude women from the fellowship and cronyism that seal the bonds of power."

Surveys of women candidates find that fund raising is a particular barrier, in large part because most of them are outside the channels not just of political power but of financial power as well. "Men are not accustomed to giving large sums of money to women they don't know well," one woman member of Congress commented, "and the women don't have the money to give."

The discrimination does not end once the election is over, the Rutgers Center for the American Woman and Politics reported in 1977. On the findings of a survey of women officeholders in New Jersey on different questions, "proportions ranging from 50 percent to 78 percent . . . complain that they are not taken seriously, are stereotyped in their characteristics, are regarded as sex objects, are excluded from the 'old boy network,' are not consulted on pending issues, are discriminated against in committee assignments, are asked to do clerical work and domestic chores, are asked to assume an unfair share of the work load, are subjected to opposition to their programs and ideas because a woman has initiated them, are expected to prove their competence while that of men is taken for granted, and are sometimes avoided or ridiculed by male constituents."

How much of this discrimination is reality and how much is perception cannot be measured, of course. But in politics, perceptions are often as important as realities. And there is little question that the barriers to women's acceptance have been heightened by the views they—and others—carry about women in politics.

Public-opinion surveys suggest a growing willingness to consider women for public office. The percentage of respondents believing the American people would support a woman for President rose from 37 percent in 1937 to 73 percent in 1975. In the latter year, the affirmative responses for Governor, Mayor and member of Congress all topped 80 percent. But as recently as 1972, a Virginia Slims poll showed that 63 percent of the women believed most men are better suited emotionally for politics than are most women, and majorities thought the men had more of the stamina and aggressive drive it takes to succeed.

In the face of these obstacles and attitudes, it is not surprising that women candidates and officeholders represent a kind of elite group—high in social and economic status and accustomed to success. A 1976 survey by the Rothstein/Buckley political-consulting firm found that the average woman candidate was white, Protestant, middle-aged, with at least one college degree, married, with grown children, employed at about $20,000 a year and enjoying a family income of about twice that amount.

And despite all that has been said, women candidates do have certain advantages. Most of those surveyed said they thought that being a woman was an advantage in gaining press publicity and voter identity. They also said it helps in recruiting volunteers (many of whom, of course, are fellow females).

Women are very slowly increasing their numbers in elective office, with the most visible progress coming at the state and local levels. In 1979, in cities with a population of 30,000 or more, there were 60 women mayors, up from 10 a decade earlier; their ranks included Lila Cockrell of San Antonio, Jane Byrne of Chicago, Margaret Hance of Phoenix, Dianne

Feinstein of San Francisco, Janet Gray Hayes of San Jose, and Helen Boosalis of Lincoln, Nebraska. The number of women in state legislatures rose from 305 in 1969 to 770 in 1979, but they still filled barely over 10 percent of the seats. And at higher levels, women once again became scarce. In the whole country in 1979, there were 17 women in Congress (fewer than in 1962), 6 women lieutenant governors, 6 women state treasurers, 10 women who were secretaries of state, 2 women governors and about a dozen women in minor state elective offices.

One of those who have made it into that select circle of elected officials is Joan Growe, 45, the second-term secretary of state of Minnesota. A divorcée, she became involved in politics through the League of Women Voters and the anti-war movement, and gained election to the state legislature in 1972. Two years later she sought the party endorsement for secretary of state, survived challenges both at the endorsing convention and in the primary and went on to beat the Republican incumbent. Remarkably, despite Minnesota's reputation as a progressive state, Growe was the first woman elected to statewide office in her own right. Twenty years earlier, the widow of a man who had served as secretary of state for some thirty years was appointed his successor at his death, was elected once and then was defeated.

But as the earlier experiences with the abolitionists showed, liberalism is no guarantee against sexism. In the 1950s, in Minnesota, the promising congressional career of an independent woman named Coya Knutson was ended, after two terms in the House, when her jilted husband ran ads in their hometown paper headlined "Coya Come Home." The voters obliged by sending her home—but not to him.

If it seems surprising that a state where leaders of both parties have often been in the forefront of the battle for civil rights and civil liberties would not have elected women to major office, Growe said, there was an explanation. "I think that there is today and has been for years a subtle idea from the men in politics that, 'Boy, this is our little world, and we hold this power.' I think men feel terribly, terribly threatened about having a woman get involved, because it complicates things. People who have power are generally hesitant to share it, and they're particularly hesitant to share power with people who they figure don't understand the rules of the game."

To combat the "old boy network" of which so many women speak, Growe and women legislators, party officials and friends in business organized "an 'old girl network' . . . to pass on the informal information about job openings and things that are happening . . . and to give moral support or assistance if we see one of the women getting a raw deal somewhere." Inside a year, they found they had 1,000 members on their mailing list. Similar networks have sprung up in many other state capitals, and there is a flourishing one in Washington, D.C., which has been used to recruit women for many jobs in the Carter Administration. In Washington, as in most places, the women's network cuts across party lines to include both Republicans and Democrats.

Like many other elected officials, Growe thought of herself as a politician first and a feminist second. "I just didn't think about it," she said. "Feminist issues were not necessarily my issues when I ran for the legislature. I was a supporter of the Equal Rights Amendment, but almost everyone in my area was. It was a well-educated, sophisticated Republican area. . . . Abortion was not my issue. I happen to be a Catholic, and so I had never dealt with the abortion question; I chose not to, because I'm not totally comfortable with it. I'm just now learning to say, 'Yes, I support freedom of choice' and then not say any more."

Growe said she was not certain "what brought me to be an out-and-out feminist. Until I made my own race, I would have said, 'I've never been discriminated against,' and I would have meant it. Living in a fairly wealthy suburb, you tend not to see a lot of things. But with my involvement in a field that was mainly male, even though I think I have been treated extremely well by my party, it is just that over and over again I have seen how much more difficult it is for women. I think a lot of the male politicians would just like to write us off. They would like to bury us, because they can't deal with us. We don't come in a neat package. You can't address women's issues and please all women."

Growe learned that last fact herself because Minnesota, even though a progressive state, is one of the centers of anti-abortion organization. Despite a four-year record as an active party campaigner and a full-time administrator of her office, Growe was challenged for endorsement for a second term by an anti-abortion, anti-ERA candidate, who received one-third of the convention votes. The experience solidified her feminism.

"Getting challenged not on the job I had done as secretary of state but on my role as a woman made me angry," she said. "And I decided to confront it. There was a lot of disagreement among my advisers, but I went before the convention and I said that I do play a unique role because I'm a woman, and it is a difficult challenge at many times, but it's one I accept, and I want you delegates to know I am concerned about women's issues and I will continue to speak out for women's rights."

The incident was emblematic of a transformation in Growe's personality from the "mousy" woman old friends had known in her suburban-housewife stage to the confident politician of today, a transformation that is not uncommon among the emerging women leaders. In 1978, Growe not only surmounted the convention challenge but, in the fall election, was one of the few Democratic incumbents to survive a major Republican comeback that gave the GOP the governorship and both Senate seats for the first time since 1940. As the 1980s began, she had more political options open to her than perhaps any woman in Minnesota political history.

If Joan Growe is an unlikely rebel, then Barbara Bailey Kennelly, the secretary of the state of Connecticut, is a totally implausible one. She is a daughter of the late John M. Bailey, Democratic National Chairman in the early 1960s and, for more than twenty years, the Democratic party chief in Connecticut. Her husband is James J. Kennelly, a former Speaker of the Connecticut House of Representatives. When she ran for secretary of the state in 1978, she was a newcomer to state politics, but hardly a novice.

Kennelly, who is 44, took her own path to politics. Speaking of her childhood, she said, "People always thought we sat around the dinner table talking politics. We didn't. If you knew my daddy, you knew he didn't tell. If you behaved, he'd take you to the national conventions with him. But he never encouraged it. . . . After I married Jim, he wanted to go into politics, but it was not me at all. I did volunteer work and got very interested in human services. Eventually I became president of two of the largest human-service agencies in town. I came to realize that where the action and power and money were was in City Hall. So I backed into politics; but once I was here, I loved it."

Kennelly was appointed to a Hartford City Council vacancy in 1975, then led the field in both the primary and the general election. She carved an independent course as an "urban Democrat," a term she said she prefers to the "liberal" label, because "the liberals are so damn used to losing." Hers was a pattern of shifting alliances—sometimes working with Nicholas Carbone, the former "boss" of the city council, and sometimes opposing him; sometimes with the neighborhood groups seeking more aid from the city and sometimes with the alliance of taxpayers and businessmen trying to hold down city spending.

She demonstrated her independence most vividly in the summer of 1978 by doing something her father would never have sanctioned—challenging the established powers and procedures of the Democratic organization at its endorsing convention.

Kennelly was not supposed to be slated for secretary of the state. The job was being vacated by a Jewish woman, and in keeping with the balanced-ticket traditions of Connecticut politics it should have gone to a person of the same background, as a complement to the Italian and Irish Catholics and the one black already on the slate.

But the daughter of the old boss proved she was a woman with a mind of her own. Without the approval or clearance of her father's old ally and protégée Governor Ella Grasso, she put together her own skillful floor organization and alliances and snatched the endorsement from more favored candidates. In November, she was elected handily.

Conservative in her personal style and a devout Catholic, Kennelly is far from the stereotype of the typical feminist politician. But she is a woman who had a strong personal sense that this was the time and place for her.

"I figure," she said, a few months before her victory in the statewide race, "that I'm starting a little late, even. You gotta have a little attraction —you know, a little pizzazz, a little movement—and as you get older it gets tougher. I don't worry about the men. But we've got some young women in the legislature that are fantastic. And I think you'll see them running younger and younger for state office. It was kind of now or never for me."

Traditionally, many women have come to public office by the painful route of widowhood. Of the 101 women who have served in Congress since 1917, 40 took over seats held by or campaigns begun by their late husbands. Many of them, like former Senator Margaret Chase Smith of Maine, surpassed their husbands in reputation.

Olympia Snowe, 33, is a variation on that pattern. She was married the year she graduated from the University of Maine. Her husband, Peter Snowe, was a businessman and a state legislator, and as she said in a 1978 campaign speech, he had "the incredible foresight to encourage" her to learn as much as she could about both those aspects of his life.

When she was widowed in 1973 at the age of 26, she ran in a special election to complete his term, "even though I'd never given myself to thinking of running for public office at all."

But the interest in politics had been there. Her parents—who died before she was 10—had run a Greek restaurant in Augusta, the state capital, and "people who knew my mother said that they're not surprised that I got into politics." As a political-science major, she worked two summers as an intern in the Maine Governor's office. "I was hoping to go to Washington when I graduated to work in a government capacity of some sort," she said, "but instead I got married."

In her three campaigns for the legislature—twice for the state House of Representatives and, in 1976, for the state Senate—Snowe, who has a vivid, outgoing personality, relied heavily on door-to-door campaigning. She earned a reputation as a serious, hardworking legislator and was named chairman of the Senate health committee in her freshman year.

The campaign for Congress in 1978 was a more difficult challenge, but Snowe had some advantages most women candidates lack. While serving in the legislature, she had also run a district office for Republican Representative William S. Cohen, who in 1978 was vacating his House seat to make what proved to be a successful run for the Senate. The Cohen and Snowe campaigns were closely linked. As one of the few women candidates with a good prospect for gaining a House seat in 1978, she received unusual financial support from both Republican and women's groups and raised a campaign budget of $210,000. Snowe defeated Maine's Democratic secretary of state, Markham Gartley, a Vietnam war veteran.

In conservative Maine, Snowe did not, she said, run as a "feminist politician." She had supported the Equal Rights Amendment in the Maine Legislature and also backed the Supreme Court decision on abortion rights for women.

But knowing her constituents, she spoke up for women's rights on the basis of her own experience—not because of a feminist ideology. "All my life," she said, "I've had many ups and downs. I've had to be independent and I've had to gain confidence to do what I had to do for myself." And that quality of independence commended itself to the voters of Maine.

As was shown in the previous chapters on the organizers and the public-interest lawyers, each movement's success has bred countermovements using the same tactics and fighting for the same constituency. When the organizers of the political Left went into blue-collar communities, seeking to build coalitions around tax issues, they brought forth a neopopulist conservatism symbolized by Proposition 13. Similarly, when public-interest law firms showed that litigation could expand the rights of the indigent, prisoners, mental patients and other groups dependent on the government, the lesson was not lost on farmers or businessmen. They sponsored their own public-interest firms, which often found themselves opposing their counterparts of the Left in court.

But in no area of American life has there been a more massive and emotional counterattack than that which the "women's movement" has drawn from other women. The battles over the Equal Rights Amendment and abortion have pitted women against women in the legislatures, the courts and the streets.

This chapter would not be complete without portraits of some of the conservative women who are on the other side of the barricade. We start with another widow, who happens to be one of the most successful women politicians in the country and who rather revels in the fact that "I am shunned by the women's movement."

Faith Ryan Whittlesey, 41, was elected to the Pennsylvania Legislature from Delaware County, outside Philadelphia, in 1977. "I ran for what was known as a safe Republican seat against six men in a Republican primary, and received approximately fifty percent of the vote," she said. "I was also pregnant at the time with my third child. The child was delivered—a ten-pound boy—two weeks before I was elected. So I was not only a lady candidate in a conservative, Catholic district, but I was a pregnant lady candidate."

The daughter of an Irish immigrant to Hoboken, New Jersey, Whittlesey is about as tough and outspoken a politician as one could ever meet. "To call a man tough, politically forceful and strong-minded is considered a matter of praise," she once told a Philadelphia newspaper interviewer. "But if these same attributes are seen in a woman, she is called arrogant, ruthless and lacking in compassion. A woman is supposed to be weak and submissive. I won't play that role. I wouldn't be where I am today if I did."

Whittlesey is a conservative true believer, converted from her early liberalism, she said, by her experience in two bureaucracies. After graduating from the University of Pennsylvania Law School and finding "it was not fashionable in those days to hire women lawyers," she taught English "in a blackboard jungle" in South Philadelphia for five months. "I saw before my eyes the failure of the liberal solutions. In my classroom, probably eighty percent of the students were emotionally disturbed. Those were the children of the welfare families. Vast sums of money had been poured into these families for how many generations without success. Money was obviously not the solution to the personal problems of these people."

Later, as an attorney for the Pennsylvania welfare department, Whittlesey said, "I saw the undermining and sabotage of elected officials by the bureaucracy. I saw how government attracts mediocrity and promotes it. There were people devising solutions to our social problems who had no understanding of where the money came from or what were the overall goals of our society."

Possessed by a zeal to stop what they saw as unconscionable waste, Whittlesey and her advertising-executive husband plunged into politics in Philadelphia in the mid-1960s. He managed several campaigns and ran unsuccessfully for the legislature himself in a Democratic district. Then they moved to Delaware County, believing it a place where they could find political success. In 1972, Whittlesey became the candidate and her husband "marketed me," as she put it.

"Together, we worked at nothing else. Didn't go to a movie for four months, didn't have any social engagements; we did nothing but ring doorbells." They also mounted a sophisticated, self-financed media campaign, something new in Delaware County races. And she beat the candidates of a Republican organization—the Delaware County "War

Board"—which had built a reputation as one of the strongest (and most corrupt) surviving Republican machines in the country, but which, the Whittleseys knew earlier than most people, "had ridden the registration edge for many, many years and had become fat and sloppy."

"We set out literally to beat the machine, and we did," she said. What she could not anticipate was that in her first term in the legislature, her husband, beset by business problems, would commit suicide, leaving Whittlesey on her own with three small children.

Quitting politics was one option she did not consider, she said. Having built a personal organization as a maverick challenger in 1972, Whittlesey was able to hold on to her legislative seat in 1974, when the collapse of the Republican Party nationally and in Pennsylvania wiped out virtually every other GOP officeholder in Delaware County.

By 1975, the now-chastened machine knew that its only chance of surviving in power was to ask the onetime rebel to run for the key job—in terms of patronage and power—of county commissioner. "I was in Harrisburg when the call came. I said yes, and cried all the way back in the car, because I knew what I was getting into," she said. "I said yes because it was my obligation to do what I could to save the party."

Whittlesey won—and in her first act after being chosen as chairman of the County Commission (since renamed the County Council), she fired 300 patronage holders. For four years she ran a county government with a budget of $62 million and over 2,000 employees. More exceptionally, she labored mightily to revive a political organization that still has many of the characteristics of a machine.

"Am I a boss?" she said, repeating the question that had been put to her. "In the sense that I believe in party discipline, I am. I know that without the imposition of party discipline we cannot maintain an organization which can deliver votes on crucial issues and for candidates at any given time. That is not a fashionable position in these times, and that's why I take tremendous abuse. In suburban counties like this one, people glorify the idea of independence, and they criticize the city of Philadelphia and its machine. But in the legislature, the money goes flowing to the city of Philadelphia, and the suburban counties, who are glorifying the idea of independence, are on the short end of the stick, because we can't move our votes as a bloc."

Whittlesey argued that she was justified in challenging the machine because "it had abused its power" and had become corrupt and arrogant. But claiming that it has "internally cleansed itself," she mourns that she and the others now running it cannot impose the discipline on its candidates that their predecessors did.

Unionization has limited her patronage powers. And the difficulty of controlling the nomination process, she said, makes it ever more likely that "people with selfish financial interests, or the princes of the media, the perfect plastic candidates, will take over. I say often that I feel like I'm putting my finger in the dike."

Nonetheless, Whittlesey ran the county government in her own fashion, installing young business managers with one hand and swatting the Democratic opposition with the other. With like-minded allies around the state, like Philadelphia GOP Chairman William Meehan, she has built up a power base that must be reckoned with by statewide candidates. She failed in a bid for the Republican nomination for Lieutenant Governor in 1978, but the man who beat her, William W. Scranton III, had a name that made him almost a certain winner.

Her position as a woman political boss involves a series of contradictions of which Whittlesey herself is painfully aware. "Politics is a closed fraternity," she said. "The smoke-filled rooms are filled with men. I was certainly not invited in. I fought my way in.

"I sympathize with many of the goals of the women's movement," she said, "but they choose not to associate with me, so that's where we are. I find myself in those closed rooms filled with men, but I'm never invited to the women's movement's functions, because I am a conservative.

"That's all right, because I have never been at ease with women. My best friends, from the earliest years, were boys and men. To this day I get frustrated at women's groups, because they can never seem to figure out where the power is. Consequently, they spin their wheels doing so many things that never get them anywhere.

"I have views on abortion which are generally in line with their views, but I don't buy their whole agenda, so that doesn't suit them. You have to be with them on every issue right down the line. I am not a supporter of increased government day-care operations. I think the problems of ERA are greater for married women than the gains, and I've stated those positions publicly.

"So I don't feel at home with either group," Whittlesey said. "I've made it on my own, and I guess it's just going to stay that way."

The leaders of the women's movement obviously cannot claim ideological unanimity on the "women's issues"—not with someone like Faith Ryan Whittlesey around. But they tend to minimize the size of the opposition. Betsey Wright, for example, argued that "the overwhelming proportion of women who seek public office tend to be liberal, progressive and feminist, because for those who are anti-feminist and conservative, running for public office is a contradictory action, by and large. Their orientation is that the women's role is in the home and the men's place is to make the decisions."

But Whittlesey is not the only woman politician who rejects that contention. State Representative Donna Carlson, 42, of Mesa, Arizona, is a conservative Republican and the national chairman of an organization of conservative-minded state legislators called the American Legislative Exchange Council. Carlson said that in 1979, "at least fourteen of the seventeen women in the Arizona Legislature would be classified as moderate to conservative. There were four or five militant feminists elected the same year I was [1974], and there's only one of them left. They were kind of one-issue–type candidates, and I think perhaps talked about women's issues too much."

Carlson said that her own gender "is irrelevant to me" as a legislator. "I'm not there to represent women alone. I'm there to represent the taxpayer. I consider the feminists to be selfish individuals. They want their issues, and they want them passed into law, and they want the taxpayer to foot the bill. It's as simple as that. I have found that if there is any discrimination against women in politics, it is the extremist feminists discriminating against the conservative women."

Carlson, an engineer's wife with five sons, became active in politics as a volunteer in the 1964 Goldwater campaign. When she moved to Arizona with her family in 1966, she indulged her interest by taking a job as a mail-and-message runner for the Arizona state Senate. Later, she worked as a secretary for three state senators, one of whom was vice chairman of the appropriations committee. "I had to take the minutes on some of the state-agency budget hearings, and I just was a little shocked at how easily they spent the taxpayers' money. . . . It hit me when I was typing up the reports and the figures: 'Hey, this is my money.'

"I thought that what we needed was more conservative Republicans, and when there was a vacancy in my legislative district, I decided to try my hand at running." Carlson said that her entry into elective politics "really wasn't that much of a change in the balance between home life and a career, except that I was getting paid less as an elected official than I was as a secretary."

She deliberately avoided assignment to such committees as education, health and welfare, because "most women end up there," and instead went onto judiciary, commerce and the committee handling city and county matters. But there has been one women's issue on which she has been highly active: the ERA fight. She was coordinator of the Stop ERA committee in Arizona, one of fifteen states that stymied ratification for seven years.

Probably few things were more frustrating for the feminist politicians in the 1970s than the emergence of an active and effective band of anti-ERA lobbyists, under the leadership of Phyllis Schlafly of Alton, Illinois, a veteran conservative organizer. The Equal Rights Amendment was approved by Congress in 1972 with bipartisan support, was endorsed by both parties' platforms and presidential candidates and—for a time—sailed smoothly toward ratification in the legislatures. But as the number of additional states needed for ratification dwindled, the issue was taken up by the New Right, and with Schlafly's female troops out front, strong pressures were applied to wavering legislators. Rival groups of women, advocating and opposing ERA, packed legislative hearing rooms and threatened retaliation at election time.

But while polls showed majorities of both men and women favoring ratification, the opponents' skillful lobbying tactics stymied the amendment three states short of the thirty-eight needed for ratification, forcing proponents in 1978 to obtain a three-year extension of the ratification deadline from Congress.

But the emotions of the ERA fight were mild compared with those engendered by the battle over abortion. In 1973, the Supreme Court ruled that state laws could not interfere with the right of a woman to obtain an abortion for any reason within the first trimester, or twelve weeks, of pregnancy. For "the preservation of the life or health of the mother" the state may "regulate" abortions—usually simply requiring that they be performed in a hospital—within the first twenty-four weeks of pregnancy.

Subsequently, Congress affirmed that legal abortions for needy women could be financed, like other medical procedures, from Medicaid and other federal funds.

The twin decisions were hailed by feminists and civil libertarians as affirming woman's "right to control her own body" and to determine for herself whether to reproduce.

But for many other women and men, the exercise of that discretionary choice violated a moral principle—what they called the "right to life" of the fetus.

No sooner were the policies enunciated by the court and Congress than they came under violent and unremitting attack. Over the next seven years, in state legislatures and Congress, the anti-abortion activists successfully lobbied and applied pressure to candidates in order to reduce—and in many cases, virtually eliminate—public funding of abortions for needy women. Their protests often spilled over into physical threats and intimidating actions against the physicians and patients at legal abortion clinics. But their main objective, still unrealized at the end of the decade, was the passage of a constitutional amendment to reverse the original Supreme Court ruling.

Like any movement, the "right-to-life" campaign served to politicize new people and bring them into the ranks of the activists.

Elizabeth A. Sadowski, one of the leaders of the annual "right-to-life" march in Washington, marking the anniversary of the Supreme Court decision on abortion, may not have been typical of the group, but she offered some clues to their background.

A handsome, fortyish woman from Freehold, New Jersey, she said flatly that "nothing in my upbringing ever prepared me to do this" sort of political work. "I'm a housewife and the mother of three children. That's my bag. That's what I do. I take care of my children, my husband. But when this issue of abortion surfaced in this country, that was the dividing line for me from a society that I didn't want to live in. I just could not exist in a society that could legalize the killing of unborn children. I didn't need a priest to tell me. I didn't have to go to the Bible. I just had a gut reaction, and so I jumped in."

Sadowski and her husband called a meeting of "pro-life" people in Freehold, when the Supreme Court decision came down, and "we were really thrilled to have something like thirty-five people come around. . . . We started an educational campaign, showing 'the infamous slides' wherever we were asked." The slides showed medical photographs of aborted fetuses at various stages of development and had a shock effect on many viewers. "I don't apologize for them anymore," Sadowski said. "I mean, if you're going to sell potatoes, you have to show a potato. Well, we're selling the idea that this is the killing of unborn children, so we had to show unborn children."

In short order, she and her husband took over the organization of a county "right-to-life" group, including chapters in fifty towns. "And then I was elected to the board of New Jersey Right to Life and the board of national March for Life, and that last few years I've given just about all of my time to it."

The intensity of the involvement with this issue has made Sadowski politically sophisticated. She was part of a lobbying effort that persuaded the New Jersey Legislature in 1977 to pass a resolution calling for a constitutional convention to adopt an anti-abortion amendment to the Constitution. Convinced that ERA proponents were also pro-abortion, she organized and became state director of an anti-ERA group called "New Jersey Majority Women" and worked successfully for an anti-ERA vote in a 1975 state referendum.

Unflinching in her zeal for the cause, she walked brazenly into the "enemy camp" and won a delegate's seat to the 1977 International Women's Year convention in Houston, the only one of forty-five New Jersey delegates to oppose ERA and abortion. She was not pleased with what she saw there. "You scratch away all the rhetoric about women's rights, and you really find a lot of very unhappy women. And you find a lot of self-pity, which I don't find in my movement. And you also find in the feminist movement a lot of man-hating. You really do."

Sadowski was interviewed for this book on the day of the 1979 March for Life in Washington, and she was exultant at its success. "It's the best thing we do," she said. "Let's face it, it's a media event. We're getting very good at that. We learned from the other side how to stage these things." When she was asked if she "enjoyed the experience of becoming a political activist on this issue," she demurred at first, and then said, "Well, I do have my days." Then she caught herself. "It's not all a bed of roses, as they say. I mean, I'm not in this to enjoy it. It's a serious business. But I love the people I meet. I really do. They're a great group of people."

When she was asked if she was "at all tempted to stay in politics beyond this one issue," she gave an answer any professional politician would have envied. "I don't think of myself as being in politics," she said. "I just think of myself as being a spokesman for the unborn, because they have no one to speak for them. I will only stay as long as the unborn do not have their rights. When they have their rights, that's when I quit."

In the next breath, she was saying that two allies in the movement from North Carolina had been elected to the legislature in 1978—"just sweet little Southern girls, real little Miss Americas, you know. And when they called me election night, I just couldn't believe it."

Might she do that herself? "Well," said Liz Sadowski, "I'm not ruling it out completely or saying that I just wouldn't do it. I'm just saying that until the rights of the unborn are pinned down, I'm going to do everything I can for them."

Earlier, she had remarked that she had never worked outside her home after her marriage. "When I got married, that was it. My husband said no. And I didn't work."

For a person of that background, Liz Sadowski had come a long way.

If there was any one woman who was forced to examine—and cope with—the conflicting forces produced by the women's movement, it was Sarah Weddington, the 35-year-old assistant to President Carter and White House specialist in women's affairs. She is another of the remarkable Texas women, daughter of an itinerant Methodist minister and a college-teacher mother, the oldest of three children. Raised with the feeling that "I could do whatever I had the capacity to do," she began as a teacher and quickly found that "I was better at things where I relied upon myself for success than on other people, like students. I tried to teach *Beowulf* with every visual aid I had been taught, and the kids still wanted to talk about who they were going out with on Saturday night. I found I didn't handle that as well as some other things. So I decided to go to law school."

That decision brought her to the University of Texas at Austin. Having worked her way through McMurry College, with high honors, she sped through law school in twenty-seven months, supporting herself as a clerk-typist for the legislature, a sorority housemother and a medical-records librarian. She finished in the top quarter of her class and was invited to interview at a leading Dallas law firm. It was not a reassuring experience. "They spent most of the day telling me that their wives were not really quite ready for them to have women partners, although women secretaries were another thing; telling me that the only way you could really train a young lawyer was to cuss him out, and they couldn't cuss me because I was a lady, so they really couldn't train me; telling me that they felt that I would have to leave early to cook supper, and lawyers have to work late; and a lot of those things that I do think tended to make you feel that you'd like to hit them."

That last phrase is about as strong an expression as Sarah Weddington allows herself to use. A lady to her fingertips, she manages to combine a first-rate lawyer's mind with the tact of the minister's daughter.

Her first job turned out to be a three-year assignment with one of her law professors, on the staff of the American Bar Association's special committee on ethics, which drew up the model code of professional responsibility.

During that time, she volunteered her services as a lawyer for a group of women who wanted to set up an abortion-counseling service in the university community. One of the patients of that service became the plaintiff in *Roe v. Wade,* the landmark case in which the Supreme Court set forth its basic doctrine on abortion rights. Sarah Weddington was 27 years old, and making her second courtroom appearance anywhere, when she argued that case before the justices. The calm professionalism of her performance is still the subject of comment among Supreme Court observers, but her coolness did not surprise her friends at all.

"In manner and appearance," said one woman friend from Austin, "Sarah is the straightest person you ever met in your whole life. You have to punch her in the ribs if you're going to tell her anything funny. She's unique. She always seemed to be eighty-five years old, even when she was twenty-five."

Her involvement with the abortion cause led Weddington into other women's issues, and while practicing family law with her former husband in Austin, she began lobbying in the Texas Legislature on women's issues.

"I was sort of outraged," she said, "at how difficult it was to see the representatives and how lightly they seemed to take our causes and how difficult it was to find someone in that body who really had a deep, genuine concern for the issues."

In 1972, she and "five or six women friends were sitting around a few days before filing deadline, saying that the only way that women's issues would really ever be dealt with was to have women in elective bodies. I was eligible to run in Austin, had no children, was in private practice, had fairly minimal income requirements, could afford to campaign and was interested in government." So she ran and won. For the next four years, she was a leader in the small reform bloc in the legislature and the sponsor of successful legislation on equal credit rights for women, strengthened rape laws and a variety of social measures.

After turning down job offers from the Carter Administration in two other departments, Weddington accepted the post of general counsel in the Agriculture Department in 1977. Her reasons were, as usual, eminently practical. She was—and is—interested in a future statewide race in Texas, and she knew that "the issues I was almost exclusively identified with in the public mind were basically women's issues. So this was an opportunity for me to learn an area that was obviously important in Texas life and politics, to have the administrative experience of running an agency with 350 people, and of learning something about Washington politics."

Her political education proved to be greater than she bargained for. After a successful year at Agriculture, she was drafted onto the White House staff to replace the outspoken Margaret (Midge) Costanza as assistant for women's issues. Costanza had worn out her welcome by publicly criticizing President Carter's well-known opposition to publicly financed abortions for poor women. So Weddington, the lawyer who had won the court fight for abortion rights, was called in to aid the President who opposed that very stand. As if that were not enough, a few months after her arrival the President fired former Congresswoman Bella Abzug as chairman of his women's advisory committee, provoking a resignation by about half the membership of that panel.

Weddington's performance under the cross-pressures of that job was a model of professionalism, even if it was inherently one that brought her criticism from women more militant than she was. "My job," she said, "is helping the President keep his own commitments to women's issues."

In the wake of the blowup with Abzug, the fiery New York feminist, Weddington felt a special responsibility to prove that her quieter methods of persuasion would yield results. In her Texas days, she recalled, "I just didn't personally feel comfortable in some of the marches" that militant feminists organized at the state capitol. "But what was useful about them was that after they were over, even the legislators who reacted very negatively to the women in the marches would come to me and say, 'Now, Sarah, what in the world was all that about?' And because I had a personal rapport with them and they respected what I said, I could then explain what the issues were."

Sitting in the White House, where she was promoted to the senior staff and given broader duties in 1979, Weddington said, "I think one thing that women need to learn is to give each other flexibility to work in the way they work best wherever they are. We can't all be in solidarity now, when some of us are on the inside and some are outside. The women's movement will have to use a greater variety of techniques than when we were all on the outside trying to get in."

In a broader context, too, Weddington was arguing that flexibility should keynote the next stage of the women's movement. "The agenda for the Eighties," she said, "has to be one of expanding options. We are really trying to arrive at a time when every woman has every option for her life. The option to be a wife and mother, to be honored and respected, and not penalized, for it. The option of combining family with work responsibilities outside the home. And the option of an emphasis on the professional part of one's life."

In very similar terms, California Chief Justice Rose Elizabeth Bird expressed her own version of "feminism":

"I believe strongly that both men and women should have the freedom to be themselves as individuals. And part of the way you make that possible is that you bring about equality between the sexes in terms of what possibilities there are for them in life—in terms of education, careers and pay. I don't think that's a feminist issue. I think basically it's an issue involving how you view human beings.

"I think the ideal world would be one where people would have the freedom to be whatever they want to be. That means if they want to be a housewife, and stay home and raise children and cook, that they should feel satisfied with that, not feel that somehow they're not living up to whatever the role or the fad is at the moment. And if they want to go out and be head of the bank and have no family at all, they should have that liberty. In the same way, if men want to stay home and have a wife go out and earn the living, you should feel free to have that as well."

When that degree of freedom—and equality—has been attained, perhaps the women's movement and the debates it has stirred will no longer be relevant. But for the rest of this century, both the women and the issues they are raising seem certain to be increasingly important in our politics.

10 · Hispanics

As INDIVIDUALS, they are vivid, talented—and obviously on their way up: Henry Cisneros, the 33-year-old San Antonio city councilman, whose skills have made him an intimate and adviser of officials in the last three national administrations; Vilma Martínez, the 37-year-old San Antonio native, president and general counsel of the Mexican-American Legal Defense and Education Fund (MALDEF), appointed to the ambassadorial selection commission by Jimmy Carter and to the University of California Board of Regents by Jerry Brown; Robert García, the 47-year-old Puerto Rican sugar-mill worker's son who had been in Congress only one year when he landed the chairmanship overseeing the vital work of the 1980 census; Alfredo Duran, the 44-year-old survivor of the Bay of Pigs Brigade who, as chairman of the Florida Democratic Party, became a key figure in President Carter's 1980 fight for political survival.

These, and dozens like them, are clearly destined to play an increasing role in the leadership of the United States in the 1980s.

It is only as a group that the estimated 12 million Hispanics in the United States are hazy and hard to define. When the mass media of the United States "discovered," toward the end of the Seventies, that they were the "hidden minority" in our midst, there was laughter in the *barrios*—and bitterness. Only the smugness of the Anglo majority could explain the belatedness of the discovery of a population this size, some of whose ancestors had been in America long before the first English settlers arrived in Virginia.

But even more significant than the tardiness of the press in turning its attention to the Hispanics, their potential and their problems was the fact that Hispanics themselves, as the 1970s ended, were still preoccupied with defining and identifying their community.

At a round table of several Hispanic leaders convened for the purposes of this book by Louis Nuñez, the 49-year-old staff director of the U.S. Civil Rights Commission, I asked what was the most significant fact to stress about Hispanics in the United States and the leadership emerging from that group. The point they all focused on was what Carmen Delgado Votaw, past president of the National Conference of Puerto Rican Women, called "the groping for unity among the diversity in the community."

Nuñez himself, a New York–born Puerto Rican, said, "you do not have in the Hispanic community a recognized cadre of national leaders. If you asked people who are the top five black leaders, you would probably get an 80- or 90-percent consensus on names like Vernon Jordan or Benjamin Hooks or Andy Young. If you ask who are the top five Hispanic leaders, you would probably get a 5-percent consensus.

"A man like Cesar Chavez," Nuñez continued, "is probably the best-known Hispanic in our country. But the fact of the matter is that the Hispanic community is an urban population, and the idea that it's totally a farm community, or migratory farm workers, is a myth."

Nuñez is, of course, correct. Despite the powerful hold on the national imagination that Chavez, the charismatic farm-worker organizer, developed with his fasts, his marches and his boycotts, the Bureau of the Census estimated that 85 percent of all Hispanics lived in metropolitan areas, with over half the population in central cities; only 5 percent of the Hispanics worked on farms, and that percentage is declining all the time.

But it is not just the lack of identified national leadership that keeps the Hispanic community out of focus, if not out of sight. The Hispanics are several groups—not one—sharing a common experience only in variants of the Spanish language and Spanish culture. Of the estimated 12 million, almost 60 percent—about 7.2 million—are Mexican; 1.8 million are Puerto Rican; 700,000 are Cubans; 900,000 are Central or South Americans and about 1.5 million are of other (unspecified) Hispanic backgrounds.

The histories, immigrant experiences and economic standings of the different groups vary tremendously. The Puerto Ricans have been American citizens from birth, and have concentrated their continental residence chiefly in New York, Boston, Philadelphia and Chicago. The Cubans came under "privileged refugee" status and have concentrated in Miami and southern Florida, with another pocket in New Jersey. The Chicanos (a term for Mexican-Americans that is widely used but still occasionally resented) are spread across the U.S.–Mexican border from Texas to California, with an unknown number of entrants, estimated at 3 to 6 million, among them.

The statistical portrait of Hispanics, to the extent that it exists, shows a community that is still significantly victimized by poverty and discrimination. The qualifying phrase is important, because the Census Bureau has acknowledged serious problems in obtaining an accurate count and description of the Hispanic-origin population. Because many of those missed by the census are likely to be poor, including those residents who are in the United States illegally, official figures probably conceal an even bleaker reality.

According to the March 1978 census estimates, almost one-sixth of the Hispanics had completed fewer than five years in school. Only 3 percent of the Anglo population was similarly limited. Fewer than one-fifth of the Hispanics were in white-collar jobs. The median income of Hispanic families was about two-thirds that of Anglo families. Almost two-fifths of the Puerto Rican families and more than one-fifth of all Hispanics lived below the poverty line, while only 9 percent of Anglo families were in similar straits.

And yet there were significant variations within the Hispanic community that made it hard for it to function as a cohesive whole on economic and social issues. In income, education and job status, the largely urbanized Cuban-Americans approached or exceeded the levels of non-Hispanic whites. Many of those who came to the United States after Fidel Castro's revolution were middle- or upper-class, well educated and business-oriented, and others became prosperous in Miami's "Little Havana." Even among the Chicanos, about one-fifth of those surveyed in 1977 reported family incomes of over $20,000—far from the poverty line. The Census Bureau's 1978 calculation of median family incomes in the United States reflected Hispanic groups' economic variations: Among all U.S. families the median income was $17,640; among Cuban-Americans, it was $15,362; among Mexican-Americans, $12,835; and among Puerto Ricans, $8,282. (Black families, by comparison, had a median income of $10,879.)

There has been a broadly supported effort to put aside these differences, at least for the purpose of gaining support for bilingual and bicultural programs in the schools, but even that cause is opposed by some Hispanic leaders. Other issues—immigration, welfare, poverty programs—scatter Hispanics across the ideological landscape. There is agreement that their numbers entitle them to a larger voice in government—but disagreement about what those numbers really are.

In 1979, several magazines proclaimed the Hispanics "the biggest minority group" that will emerge in America in the Eighties. One magazine asserted that by 1990, "California will become America's first Third World state."

Those claims are viewed with skepticism—and some concern—by many Hispanic leaders. Joseph Aragón, President Carter's former White House assistant, worried that Hispanics would "undercut our credibility" by claiming gains that are unlikely to materialize.

"We're making a terrible, terrible tactical mistake," he said before leaving the White House in 1978. "We're not about to take over the damn world, you know. This kind of millennium everybody is talking about is setting up a very high set of expectations for us that there is no way we will fulfill. We're not going to turn out to be a 20- or 22-million population in this country. It's going to be more like 14 million or 15 million, and the black population is far larger than that. We're not going to get all those new congressmen or state officeholders, either. We don't have that many registered voters, and we seem to have a real problem with registration. Our geographical base is getting more diffused, and that means most of our new officeholders will have to win in non-Hispanic constituencies."

Diffused. Divided. Disunited. Hard to define. Their numbers uncertain—perhaps exaggerated. All the things these Hispanic leaders say about themselves are probably true. But to any open-minded observer of the American scene, all of those barriers to influence seem likely to be overcome in the years just ahead by the sheer talent and tenacity of individual Hispanics.

Consider, for example, Henry Cisneros and Vilma Martínez, the two Chicanos mentioned earlier. They are part of a people that is older than this nation, some of whom held land grants from the Spanish and Mexican governments that were confirmed by the United States in the Treaty of Guadalupe Hidalgo, which ended the Mexican War in 1848. That same treaty welcomed Mexicans in the annexed territory as American citizens. But the history of the next century was one of efficient dispossession and disenfranchisement of the Chicanos. Most of the millions of more recent migrants from Mexico have also been confined to the lower rungs of the American economy, with available evidence showing Chicanos lagging in every measure from education to income to job status to voting participation.

But in the past two decades, they have begun to escape the confines of past prejudice and poverty and to claim their place in the leadership of American society.

Vilma Martínez began school in San Antonio knowing no English. She found "it was a battle every step of the way" for the education she craved. "I barely got through the first grade, because I didn't understand anything the teacher was saying, but fortunately my grandmother had spent time with me teaching me in Spanish, so I knew I was going to be able to catch up ultimately."

Each stage seemed to bring its own struggle. After the eighth grade her counselor wanted to send her to the vocational high school, but her father insisted she be allowed to enter the academic school. In the twelfth grade, Martínez had to fill out her application to the University of Texas alone; the counselor was "too busy" to help. Despite her straight-A average, advisers at the university told her, "Don't get your hopes up" for law school.

"I was washing dishes in the biochemistry lab at the time," she recalled, "and the man I was working for said, 'Vilma, don't be stupid. They're discriminating against you.' " So she wrote off on her own to Columbia and was admitted to its law school.

After graduating, she became a civil-rights lawyer for the NAACP Legal Defense and Education Fund and helped write the proposal that led to the creation of MALDEF, a parallel organization for Mexican-Americans. Despite her role in its creation, she encountered opposition from "a lot of Mexican-American men who thought that this organization should not be headed by a woman." Her experience of discrimination from those who are themselves the victims of discrimination was not an unusual one, but the record she has made since becoming president of MALDEF in 1973 has stilled most of the criticism.

Her fellow townsman Henry Cisneros is the grandson of a Mexican revolutionary who, forced to flee his own country, arrived in San Antonio with 18 cents in his pocket to take up his trade as a printer. The grandson went to Texas A&M and thrived on what he calls the "meritocracy" of that conservative, military-oriented school. "If you could run far enough, study hard enough, do your military chores and basically toughen up in a kind of macho way, you'd get advanced," he said, and Cisneros could do these things. As cadet sergeant-major he was chosen in 1968 to attend a national youth conference at West Point, and from a *Time* magazine he read on the plane he learned a new word, "urbanologist," that was being used by Daniel Patrick Moynihan. "I decided that's what I wanted to be." So he took a master's degree in planning at Texas A&M and, at 21, came home to San Antonio as assistant director of the Model Cities program. From there it was more education, at George Washington University and Harvard, a White House Fellowship with Elliot Richardson at the Department of Health, Education and Welfare, and a final return home, where he has been serving since 1974 on the city council, a political apprenticeship that he hopes will lead to his election as the city's first Hispanic Mayor.

The upward mobility suggested by these stories is characteristic of this generation of Hispanic-American leaders. It is one reason why that leadership is less well known and less clearly identified by Anglo Americans than that of the blacks. "In terms of the dominant white community in America," pollster Louis Harris wrote in a 1979 study, "Hispanics have suffered most of all from being ignored."

This problem was very much on the minds of the Hispanic leaders Louis Nuñez assembled for the round-table discussion of this chapter. In addition to himself and Carmen Delgado Votaw, the president of the InterAmerican Commission of Women, those who were able to accept his invitation included Raul Yzaguirre, the 41-year-old president of the National Council of La Raza, whose $2-million-a-year budget makes it the largest Hispanic technical-assistance and advocacy organization; Paquita Vivo, 44, a free-lance writer and past president of the National Conference of Puerto Rican Women, and Paul Sedillo, 45, the director of the Secretariat for Hispanic Affairs of the National Conference of Catholic Bishops/U.S. Catholic Conference. All endorsed Votaw's view that the "groping for unity" was the preoccupation of the Hispanic leadership. Sedillo, "an eleventh-generation New Mexican," said that it was only in the 1970s that he saw "the beginning of a coalition or understanding between the Northeast and the Southwest" centers of Hispanic population—essentially between Puerto Ricans and Chicanos. "There's a new Hispanic leadership that's coming up that doesn't have all the old prejudices" which divided Cubans from Chicanos and Puerto Ricans from both, he said.

Acknowledging that there has been competition among Hispanics for jobs, influence and government funds, Nuñez said that despite "the very distinct views of the world" held by those separate subgroups, there is "among the emerging leadership a recognition that all of the Hispanic groups put together are a relatively weak force in our society; but separated, they're no force at all. If we want to make an impression here in Washington . . . and get a kind of recognition that this is an important component in our total society, it's going to have to be as one group. It cannot be as four or five groups, no matter what everyone would like."

That political reality, Nuñez said, has been reinforced by the spread of the Hispanic population from their previously separated bases. "There are Puerto Ricans in every state of the Union," he said. "There are Mexican-Americans in every state of the Union. There are Hispanic communities growing in every large city in America. Either they can spend a lot of time fighting each other, or they can try to develop programs and projects of mutual benefit and support."

Alex Mercure, the Assistant Secretary of Agriculture for Rural Development in the Carter Administration, who came up as an educator from Rio Arriba County, New Mexico, a famous local political fiefdom, said that there was "fragmentation and a very heavy struggle for leadership positions" among the Hispanics. But that, he said, "is probably true of any kind of community." With the infusion of more and better-trained young people into leadership, he said, "there's an increasing development of spheres of influence."

There is also a growing organizational structure within the Hispanic community, whose history and relationships can perhaps be fully comprehended only by a 50-year-old veteran like Herman Gallegos, the chairman of the board of the San Francisco–based Human Resources Corporation. Gallegos, who has moved from neighborhood organizing in a San Jose *barrio* with Cesar Chavez and Saul Alinsky to a directorship of the Pacific Telephone and Telegraph Company, can explain how CSO (the Community Service Organization) evolved into MAPA (the Mexican-American Political Organization) or delineate the tensions between PASO (the Political Association of Spanish-Speaking Organizations), LULAC (the League of United Latin-American Citizens) and the GI Forum.

But perhaps the best perspective on this organizational jumble was provided by Vilma Martínez, who said, "As a lawyer, I know quite well that the legal statuses of Mexican-Americans, Cuban-Americans and Puerto Ricans—not to mention all the Central and South American folk—are very different. And the potential legal tools available to each group vary. But I ain't no dummy, either, and the political reality is that we are increasingly becoming, as Hispanics, more politically sophisticated. We're beginning to learn to put aside our differences, to learn that there are issues on which we have varying opinions and on which we should stay out of each other's way, but that there are other issues on which we should stand united."

When asked for an example of the kind of distinctive issue that has the potential of unifying or coalescing Hispanics, the one that is almost automatically mentioned is that of bilingual and bicultural education. It is an issue that will grow in importance in America just as surely as the number and influence of the Hispanics will increase in the next two decades.

"When I look at the issue of bilingual education in this country," said Vilma Martínez, "it's clear to me that all of us want it." That is an overstatement. It is an issue that touches all of the Spanish-speaking communities and the different income and class strata within them. For many of those who are succeeding in the American economy, it is an assertion of pride in their heritage. For those who are on the margin, it is often held out as a practical device for cutting the school-dropout rate that is one of the main barriers to advancement through the same public school system which has served earlier immigrant and minority groups so well.

But there have been squabbles before congressional committees between Puerto Rican and Chicano groups over the geographical division of bilingual-education funds—an example of the fact that even a "unifying" issue can prove contentious within the Hispanic communities. And some Hispanic leaders reject the concept in its entirety.

One of them is Albert Bustamante, the first Chicano Presiding Judge (chief executive) of Bexar County (San Antonio), who argued that bilingual education "has proven regressive, because it has placed an additional burden on a child who is an orphan in two languages."

Bustamante, 45, is a migrant worker's son, the oldest of eleven children in a family that annually followed the harvest from Corpus Christi north to the Willamette Valley in Oregon. "I didn't start school until I was nine years old," he said, "and then I couldn't read or speak a word of English, and my Spanish was a sort of in-between dialect." After years of struggle, he managed to graduate from Sul Ross College, his last semester financed by a $250 loan from the school janitor. He taught and coached in the San Antonio schools, and eventually took a job as a constituent-service aide to Democratic Representative Henry B. Gonzales, then, as now, San Antonio's Congressman. In 1971 he ran for the county commission himself, defeating Albert Peña, a liberal Democrat who, in Bustamante's eyes, "had polarized the community, pitting Anglo against Mexican-American." Bustamante, who called himself "a moderate who hugs the middle and can go either way," built a following on constituent service and local projects. In 1978 he won the top countywide office as a fiscal conservative, but with strong support in the West Side Chicano community.

His position on bilingualism drew criticism from Chicanos, "who said if you're against bilingual education, you're against the Mexican-American." But Bustamante stood his ground. "I think it's a great program," he said, "but it should be taught as a foreign language, and the emphasis placed on our native tongue, which is English. . . . The teachers and administrators who want to keep their jobs say it's a beautiful thing to learn two languages. Sure it is. But I'm for bringing about a system of education that will help a child to live within the business climate that we have in this area of the country. And that is English."

That Bustamante could prevail at the polls with his well-known position on bilingual education was evidence that some Hispanic parents and students were not as dogmatic on the issue as most of the spokesmen for the community. But bilingual education is much more a bone of contention between the Hispanic leaders and the majority Anglos than it is a matter of debate within the Hispanic community.

Alfredo Duran, the Florida Democratic chairman, was defeated for the Dade County (Miami) school board in 1974, after serving two years by appointment. "I had sponsored a five-year, $52-million bilingual-education budget for the 200,000 schoolchildren of Hispanic heritage," he said, "and the whole theme of the opposition was the bilingual-education program. It was probably one of the bitterest school-board elections that ever happened—really, a very bigoted race. And I lost by about eight thousand votes."

Congress passed the Bilingual Education Act in 1967, authorizing experimental programs designed to find out how to help students, mostly Hispanics, who lack skills in English. Seven years later, the Supreme Court upheld an interpretation of the 1964 Civil Rights Act requiring schools to do something to "rectify the language deficiency" of these students. Although the high court did not require bilingual education as the remedy, HEW has been pressuring affected school districts to begin such programs or face a potential loss of all federal education funds.

Critics of bilingual education claim the evidence does not indicate that the programs work. In theory, they are supposed to provide Spanish-language instruction in mathematics, science and social studies until the child is proficient enough in English to join his or her Anglo classmates. But some studies have suggested that the programs not only do not improve overall academic performance, but tend to maintain the segregation of the Spanish-speaking in their own classrooms. The sharpest critics claim they are chiefly a job-security program for Spanish-speaking teachers and a muscle-flexing exercise by the emerging Hispanic political leaders.

But Vilma Martínez, who has litigated several of the court tests of bilingual education, said, with more than a little impatience and passion in her voice, "Let me tell you what I think bilingual education is. It is the use of the only learning tool a child has, which is Spanish-speaking ability, to train that child in English and to make him or her competitive in our society. . . . The only thing we can fight for legally now is that kind of transitional aid, and I think before we get into a discussion of anything else, goddamn it, let's give transitional bilingual education a chance to turn around the 80-percent dropout rate in Texas and the 60-percent dropout rate in California, which has produced in my community a disenfranchised, uneducated group of people."

For those like Martínez who have fought their own battles for education in English-speaking schools, the arguments against bilingual instruction evoke nothing but bitterness.

Gonzalo Barrientos went to school in the South Texas town of Bastrop, while his migrant-worker parents spent the harvest season in the labor camps. When he started school, there were three separate school systems in that little town: one for Anglos; one for blacks; one for Mexican-Americans. Like Vilma Martínez and Henry Cisneros, he had parents who pushed him hard. "They kept telling me, 'You're just as good as anyone else.' And they pushed me to be in the band, to play trumpet, to run track, to take debate"—and, after graduation and an early marriage, to go to the University of Texas.

Barrientos began his career as a community organizer, working, at various times, for the Urban League, the federal anti-poverty program and the National Conference of Catholic Bishops/U.S. Catholic Conference. In 1972, he tried for election to the Texas House of Representatives, led in the first primary, but was beaten by 1,000 votes in the runoff, when "my opponent really strapped it on me about my being a radical revolutionary, Cuban-trained infiltrator and a lot of other racist stuff."

In 1974 he tried again, and once again was forced into a runoff against an Anglo candidate. But this time he took his door-to-door campaign "right into the lion's den"—to the wealthy, conservative areas of Travis County. "In some cases, they would slam the door and say, 'Hell, I ain't gonna vote for no damn Mexican! Get out of here!' And in other cases, you could almost see the people's little gears turn and say, 'Why this little fellow knows how to speak English. He might be all right.' That time I won, by ninety-four votes, and that's how I came to be known as 'Landslide Barrientos.' "

Barrientos was the first Chicano to represent Austin in the legislature, and when he was asked, four years later, about what he had been able to accomplish, he said, "Very little. Very little. My priorities are certainly not the same as most of the other folks here in the legislature. . . . I was able to arrange for nearly $1 million worth of scholarships at the University of Texas for disadvantaged students. . . . But it's so frustrating when you come in and you're lobbying for, let's say, bilingual education, and you go up to some fellow from East Texas and say, 'Can you help us out on this bilingual-education bill? It's good for kids, and it's not only good for Spanish-speaking kids but English-speaking kids. It's a two-way street.' And he says, 'Barrientos, I'll tell you one goddamn thing. If you want to talk Spanish, boy, you go back to Mexico, you hear?' And this crushes you, you know. Good Lord, the mentality."

It is not just language that sets the Hispanics apart from other emerging leadership groups in this society. There are also powerful religious and cultural forces that shape their distinctive approach to national policy.

Estimates are that about 90 percent of the Hispanic-Americans are Roman Catholics; and conversely, Hispanics make up about 28 percent of the Catholics in the United States. And yet, as Paul Sedillo pointed out at our round table, for two hundred years before 1970 there was no Hispanic-American bishop in the Church. Even now, of the 350 bishops in the American Catholic Church, only nine are of Hispanic origin, and only one of them is an archbishop. Not only was the Church hierarchy exclusionary; it was, until recent years, insensitive or negative toward self-help efforts among its Hispanic parishioners.

"The Church culture," said Raul Yzaguirre, "was summed up in the slogan 'You pay and you obey.' You come to church, you listen, you don't participate. And unfortunately, it permeated our lives and affected the way we acted."

When individuals tried to escape from the passivity that kind of religion inculcated, or organized in behalf of the oppressed, they were, more often than not, disciplined by the Church.

Herman Gallegos recalled that in the days when he and Chavez were starting their organization in the San Jose *barrio*, "there were only a few rebel priests . . . who would identify with us, but they were important because they were symbolic that we weren't Communists." In those days, James Cardinal McIntyre of Los Angeles prohibited Catholic interracial councils. "I remember going to my hotel room with a priest who was a very dear friend," Gallegos said, "and we had to celebrate the Mass in a hotel room, because he was *persona non grata* because he was working in such militant ways. And the militancy really amounted to nothing more than going to our meetings and offering a few prayers, or counseling those of us who were organizers that we wouldn't go to hell because we had gone to a Protestant church to ask their membership for support on something."

As we enter the Eighties, while tensions remain, there are areas where the Church has undergone a remarkable transformation from being what Henry Cisneros described as "part of the colonial system" to an active partnership in the political self-realization of the Hispanic community. "Today," said Herman Gallegos, "many of the priests who have gone through organizing schools understand not only their role as priests but as organizers, as technicians in bringing about change."

Father Juan Romero, 42, the pastor's representative of St. Alphonsus Parish in East Los Angeles, is such a priest. Born in Taos, New Mexico, where his family had lived for almost four hundred years, he spent the early Seventies in San Antonio, as executive director of the PADRES, an organization of Chicano priests started at the beginning of the decade. (PADRES is the acronym for Priests Associated for Religious Education and Social Rights.) One of its objectives is to increase the influence of Hispanics within the Church, but the larger purpose is to link the Church more closely to the forces of change within the Chicano community. "We are holistic in our approach," Father Juan said, "and don't make great dichotomies between heaven and earth and this life and the next life. . . . Some of our guys took some training in Chicago with the Industrial Areas Foundation, a Saul Alinsky organizing school, and we knew that if we wanted to help empower the Hispanic community that the Catholic Church had to be an important institutional base."

When Father Juan came to East Los Angeles in 1976, he joined an Alinsky-trained organizer, three priests and three nuns who shared the view that "part of our ministry is to help discover and form key leaders, to be a teacher and mentor to them, so that the ministry will be multiplied through them. At first there was hostility among the people, but we did a lot of the kind of old-fashioned pastoral visiting that had fallen into disuse. Previously when we came around we usually had something to sell or something to give or something to sign them up for. So this was a new experience for the lay people here, when we came to their home and asked, 'What are the things that concern you, that bother you?' We were really asking them what their self-interest was, without using that jargon.

"The next step was house meetings in which we asked people who their networks were, who else they knew that was interested in this problem. We asked them to help organize house meetings, trained them how to run them, and what was really happening was we were trying to flush out potential leadership and issues. When we had our leaders, they were strung together like rosary beads—that's an analogy we used—not only within a parish but in a federation of twenty-two parishes. People felt good about coming together, knowing they shared a self-interest in the betterment of the community."

The product of all this is called UNO, the United Neighborhoods Organization, and when it had its first formal convention in October of 1979, over five thousand people turned out at Los Angeles' Shrine Auditorium. Even before that, however, UNO had taken the lead in a campaign that forced auto-insurance companies to reduce their rates an average of 38 percent for the East Los Angeles *barrios,* saving residents of the community an estimated $13 million a year.

In talking to many of the emerging Hispanic leaders, I heard frequent suggestions that the social policies this community would seek as it gained increasing influence would be, in many respects, innovative. There is acute consciousness among the Hispanic leaders that theirs is still a deprived community. "We have to be certain at all times," said Herman Gallegos, "that it's a better life for the many and not just the good life for the few." Sitting in his sunny study in a handsome restored Victorian mansion in San Francisco, he said, "When you meet someone like myself who has a nice office and a nice suit and a decent income, it's too easy for people to say, 'Well, see, they're making it.' And that's not true."

At the round table, Raul Yzaguirre said, "We tend to forget the obvious . . . that we have been and we still are an oppressed minority." But in the very next breath, he added, "The fact we have been an oppressed community gives us values and a way of looking at the world and a creativity" that others may lack.

"We don't fit neatly into the existing categories," he said. "We have a more humanistic way of approaching life and a more communal way of solving problems. That is part of our Indian heritage."

Paul Sedillo remarked that when his father had a stroke and was very ill, "my brothers and sisters and I never thought of sending him to a nursing home, because this is a responsibility of ours, of caring for our own."

Sedillo then asked his colleagues: "Is it additional AFDC [Aid to Families with Dependent Children, the main federal income-support program] programs we're looking for? No," he said, answering his own question, "we're looking first of all for the human dignity."

Carmen Delgado Votaw, a feminist as well as a Hispanic activist, agreed. "There's no question that if the Hispanic community participated more in social-policy making," she said, "you wouldn't look at the traditional welfare systems in the same way."

Raul Yzaguirre, probably the most militant of those present, said his organization "had a conference just to deal with that issue—the welfare issue—in Albuquerque. We brought in a lot of welfare-rights activists, and to a person, they were for doing away with AFDC and the welfare system that currently exists in this country. Doing away with it. It blew my mind. A few were people who were actually dependent on the system —actual welfare mothers—and they were saying, 'It's best if we do away with it. It's ruining our communities. It's ruining our extended-family structure. It's ruining our sense of values, and we'd just as soon not have anything as to be brought into this terrible system.' "

Albert Bustamante made it very clear in his victorious race for county judge in San Antonio that he believed "we're not in the Sixties, when money was available for every type of social reform and innovation. I think we have gotten fat and lazy throughout this country," he said, "and we've allowed ourselves to continue a runaway type of approach to government, with no controls. . . . We have tremendous waste in the poverty programs. I was the only one that raised my voice at the county level against the waste and mismanagement of the poverty programs. No accountability. No fiscal control. . . . We'd be better off if we gave the poor $4,000 a year instead of all this bureaucracy that we've given them."

Bustamante is, like most other Hispanics in elective office, a Democrat, but as his rhetoric suggests, that does not mean he is a conventional liberal. Among the Hispanic politicians, there appears to be much more willingness to mix private and public resources, entrepreneurial initiatives and social motives, in a single blend.

That was true even of Robert García, 47, the Puerto Rican sugar-mill worker's son who represents the South Bronx, one of America's most poverty-ridden regions, in the House of Representatives. "There are parts of my district that are absolutely devastated," he said, "as bad as anything in Berlin in 1945." But the Assembly of God church begun by his father—a late-starting "Holy Roller" minister—in a storefront in the South Bronx survives today as a two-story red-brick structure "with nothing but rubble around it," the cleared ruins of abandoned, vandalized slums. "You talk to the people of the South Bronx and you're going to find many people who—in spite of the adversity, in spite of the tremendous odds, in spite of everything—have been able to raise families and bring forth young people who are making a contribution," García said.

Coming from that kind of neighborhood, García was an ardent supporter of federal urban-aid and anti-poverty programs, and, more openly than anyone else, criticized the conservativism of some of his Hispanic colleagues from the Southwest.

"Ed Roybal [a Congressman from California] and I are the only two who vote liberal, for the most part," he said. "I look up at the board in the House and see how some of the others are voting on these programs, and I can't believe it. When there's so much need, I don't see how anybody can be voting against these programs that are so important to poor people, when the overwhelming majority of our people are really living at poverty levels."

García was cruelly disappointed, in 1979, when the New York City Board of Estimate rejected the Charlotte Street project that was to have been the first step in a federally subsidized redevelopment program for the South Bronx. A member of the House Banking, Finance and Urban Affairs Committee, he began asking the financial officials who came to him for help on legislation what they were prepared to do in turn to help his community. "I'm hopeful," he said, "that I can get the financial institutions that really have the money and power to come in. All I need are one or two successful projects. I think from that point on we can take off on our own. I think we'd get enough private money in so we wouldn't have to worry about the government's help."

Gallegos, the onetime community organizer, concurred, saying it was clear to him as the 1970s ended that "we've got to begin to look at the private sector, the corporations and the foundations" for support of Hispanic causes. He said he was concerned that "we've had really no influence and no involvement with respect to the top 500 corporations . . . and out of the 150,000 trustees that govern the 26,000 grant-making private foundations, as near as we can tell, there are only three Hispanics."

Driving me around the West Side of San Antonio one afternoon, Henry Cisneros said he was working in local government because "I'm a strong advocate of the use of city authority as an integral part of a development process that really doesn't get all hung up on the distinction between what is private and what is public. . . . The whole liberal agenda of the Sixties was necessary for that period of time," he said, "but we allowed ourselves to get trapped into an income-maintenance, social-program mentality that had 'Give me' as its slogan. The action in the next years is not going to be in welfare; it's going to be in economic development for jobs and income.

"Those other approaches," he said, "have not bred a kind of independence and self-reliance. But when you start talking about jobs and income, then the potential becomes almost limitless. You begin talking about family stability, kids with aspirations, professional careers and all the good things that come from having stability in a neighborhood."

As he drove, he broke off his thoughts from time to time to point to a park that had been built in formerly flooded bottomland, or a street of freshly painted homes, or new curbs and sidewalks, or a new high school. All of the projects had been promoted by COPS (Communities Organized for Public Service), another of the Church-related organizations, begun a few years before UNO was launched in Los Angeles.

"Unlike all previous liberal efforts, and all efforts to politicize based on ideology or personalities, this one was based on the only lasting institution in the Mexicano community, the Catholic Church," he said. "And it has done a tremendous job of focusing on real needs. . . . After all the government programs, after all the dollars, after all the ordinances and the laws, what it finally boils down to is a certain spark in the people of individual initiative and energy. COPS has awakened that spark and opened the possibility in people's minds that we can do something about these problems."

He spoke about his hopes for the future: a mixture of residential, commercial and industrial building to bring jobs close to a community still plagued by 20-percent unemployment; a new technical-training center to provide employers with a skilled work force. The dream began taking form in 1979 when Control Data Corporation, the computer manufacturer, decided to locate a major plant in San Antonio and to hire and train from the local community. Cisneros led the San Antonio delegation, including representatives of COPS and the business community's Economic Development Foundation, in the negotiations with Control Data. "I would like to prove in San Antonio," he said, "that the American system can do what it is supposed to be able to do—to spread its benefits to more and more people; that in fact, by targeting our manpower programs, by attracting industry to high-unemployment areas, by putting the dollars to develop the infrastructure, by education, by family stability, by guiding our economic development, blurring the lines between public and private, we can make the system work."

In a different arena, Alex Mercure, the 49-year-old New Mexico–born educator who became an assistant secretary of Agriculture in the Carter Administration, gave another clue about how the values of the Hispanic culture might influence social programs.

Mercure said that he had learned, from a survey of the first fifty families to participate in a small, state-sponsored "self-help housing program" in New Mexico, that a year after they moved into their new homes, every one of the families had increased its income by more than 25 percent—"in a lot of cases with the same employer. I concluded that what had happened was that this guy had learned some carpentry skills, he learned some cement work, he learned a little basic electricity and plumbing, and all of a sudden he was a lot more useful to his employer than he had been when his only work was to turn on the irrigation system."

So in his Washington job, he persuaded Congress to try a similar program for federally subsidized rural housing for families with a cash income of only $2,400 to $6,000, helping them buy a home they had helped build, rather than just renting them quarters at a subsidized rate. Under this program, he said, "any appreciation in the value of the house, beyond the recovery of the government's subsidy, accrues to the family, so that that low-income family benefits from inflation the same way most of us do. That's one example," Mercure said, "of some very significant changes in the character of our old programs. It de-emphasizes the rental subsidy, which is a kind of public charity, and emphasizes the buildup of family resources and self-reliance."

If Hispanics appear to be absolutely in the mainstream in their eagerness for economic advancement, there was one unresolved issue as the 1980s began that was seen by the emerging leaders as uniquely threatening. That was the issue of immigration.

For several decades, large numbers of Puerto Ricans had moved back and forth between their island home and New York and other Northeastern cities, seeking relief from the crushing unemployment of the island. That two-way traffic had contributed to the educational and economic problems of the community, but it did not raise any immigration law-enforcement problems, because the Puerto Ricans could claim American citizenship wherever they were.

But in the 1960s and 1970s a similar, massive traffic developed across the border from Mexico, which also faced serious unemployment and an exploding birthrate. And the illegal immigrants—or "undocumented aliens," as they were euphemistically called—created a problem which Joseph Aragón, Carter's former Hispanic adviser, said "has potential for a tremendous amount of damage domestically and internationally as well. It can prove to be a divisive issue even within the Hispanic community," he said. "I was very surprised to find some of my friends who live in the Southwest border towns, who I've always considered to be strong community grass-roots people, saying that they were afraid of the increase in illegal immigration and they felt threatened by it. . . . There was a tremendous backlash building up over this issue in the Southwest, and many Hispanics are threatened, not only on the economic level, because their jobs might be taken by someone else, but also at the civil-rights level, because they feel the backlash might cause repressive measures to be taken by the government, and there could be violent vigilante activity as well."

The illegal immigration *was* threatening to many Anglos, in part because its dimensions seemed so hard to gauge. It clearly was raising barriers to cooperation between Hispanics and blacks, and between Hispanics and organized labor, because of the fear both groups had of aliens' competing for jobs and holding down wages.

There were strong—and growing—pressures to "crack down" on the illegal immigration by increasing the strength of the undermanned border patrols or fencing the boundary between the United States and Mexico. But the American government, pressured by Hispanic organizations and seeking access to Mexico's oil and gas riches, resisted creating such a "tortilla curtain."

Caught in the crossfire of these conflicting pressures in the first thirty months of the Carter Administration was Leonel J. Castillo, the first Hispanic to head the Immigration and Naturalization Service. The son of a Galveston dockworkers'-union organizer, who came to San Antonio for college and found himself labeled a "Communist" for helping blacks picket a segregated movie theater, Castillo had been elected controller of the city of Houston before accepting the appointment from Carter. Fascinated by computers, he spent much of his time at the immigration service trying to modernize its outdated record keeping. But his main need was to dodge the crossfire of criticism from fellow Hispanics, who feared he would "sell them out" to secure his own position, and the Anglos—including many in his own bureaucracy—who assumed he was in his job only to take care of "his own people."

Castillo resigned before the end of Carter's term without solving the problem, and illegal immigration remains a major hurdle for the Hispanic community and for its relationship to the larger U.S. society.

An equally imposing—if not larger—barrier is the historical discrimination that has kept Hispanics from exercising power in the American political system. Except in New Mexico, where Hispanics have been part of the government since the first territorial secretary, there is gross underrepresentation of Chicanos in legislatures and major offices. In New Mexico at various times during the 1970s, Chicanos held the governorship, the lieutenant governorship, the attorney general's office, one of the two Senate seats and one of the two House seats. In 1979 Chicanos held 28.8 percent of the state legislative seats—approaching, but not equaling, their 40-percent share of the population.

But in the other Southwest states, the picture was very different. The percentage of state legislators and of citizens looked like this in 1979: Arizona, 11.1 percent of the legislators, representing almost 19 percent of the population; California, 6.6 percent for 15 percent; Colorado, 7 percent for 13 percent; Texas, 10.5 percent for 18 percent. In 1979, there were no senators and only 6 representatives from a national population of more than 12 million.

In many of those states, the Anglo majority has manipulated districting lines or forced at-large elections in order to diffuse the political power of Hispanic communities.

Much of Vilma Martínez' work at MALDEF has involved filing reapportionment and redistricting cases. In Texas, MALDEF joined the Republican Party in suing to end at-large legislative elections and won a decision forcing single-member districts. The effect has been dramatic. Gonzalo Barrientos had to struggle to win a narrow victory in his second try for at-large election in Travis County; since districts were created in his first term, he has had no serious challenge for his seat. Similarly, in San Antonio, Chicanos went from 1 seat to 5 on the 11-member council when districts lines were finally drawn.

While Chicanos have sporadically ventured into political separatism (most recently in the 1969-born La Raza Unida Party, which took control of Crystal City, Texas, but failed to establish a statewide base), for the most part Hispanic political energies have been channeled through the Democratic Party. The 1960 Kennedy campaign was particularly important for the younger generation of Hispanic leaders; almost everyone interviewed for this chapter mentioned a personal involvement in that effort. But these people also noted that it was not until Carter ran and was elected sixteen years later that Hispanics were recruited in sufficient numbers for the campaign and Administration to make them a visible presence close to the highest levels of politics and government. Joseph Aragón, who appears to be the first Hispanic appointee to have had an office in the West Wing of the White House, credited Carter with being "the first President to really make for us dramatic advances in terms of participation in government." Before leaving his job to return to private industry in 1979, Aragón counted at least seven presidential appointees at the level of assistant secretary or higher and a number of ambassadors who were Hispanics.

Republicans, however, have not ignored the Hispanic community, as they tended for years to ignore the blacks. President Nixon implemented the Bilingual Education Act and, in 1972, courted Hispanics with appointments and economic-aid programs. Both President Ford and Ronald Reagan had Hispanics on their staffs and campaigned for Hispanic support—with some success. And in the 1980 campaign, there was even a Mexican-American candidate in the GOP race: self-made millionaire businessman Benjamin Fernandez.

"We are not a monolith," Vilma Martínez said. "We are developing a middle-class community. There is a strong and vibrant tradition of helping yourself and a conservative work ethic within my own community, and Republicans are making an overture to that element."

Nonetheless, almost all those interviewed predicted that the Democratic Party will continue in the 1980s to be the main channel of Hispanic political energies. Louis Nuñez came to the federal government during the Nixon Administration. But he said that "Ninety-five percent of the political leadership of the Hispanic community is very much into the Democratic camp."

Alfredo Duran offered perhaps the most interesting explanation of that phenomenon—based on his own remarkable history.

Born in Havana in 1936, Duran fled Cuba when Fidel Castro came to power in 1959, and joined the anti-Castro movement in Miami. He was part of the brigade that went ashore at the CIA-sponsored Bay of Pigs invasion in 1961 and spent twenty months in a Castro prison before the United States could arrange to have the survivors of that aborted effort released in 1963.

Many of the veterans of that attempt were bitter that the United States had failed to supply air cover for the mission or to back it up with U.S. forces. "Many Cubans had the concept at that time that they were used by the American government," Duran said. "But I had the concept that I used the American government to try to get rid of the dictatorship in Cuba, and if we failed in that purpose, it was our fault."

Nonetheless, he conceded that "I was one of the few Cubans who was very active in the Democratic Party" when he came out of the University of Miami Law School in 1967 and began to get involved. "The majority of the Hispanics at that time were registered Republicans. They felt that Nixon was going to send the Marines into Cuba and get rid of the dictator. But today the majority of Cubans are registered as Democrats."

When I asked Duran what he thought had brought this change, he said there were several explanations. First, he said, "Cubans are generally liberal; the social legislation in Cuba was very advanced before Castro; health care and education were always free." Duran came from that tradition: His stepfather was president of the Cuban Senate, and his father-in-law, Dr. Carlos Prio Socarrás, was the last constitutional President of Cuba.

"As a new immigrant to this country," he said, "I started to develop an identity, not only as a Cuban but as a Hispanic-American. I started identifying my needs with those of the Mexican-Americans in the Southwest and the Puerto Ricans in the Northeast. I saw that if there was a Puerto Rican Harlem and if there was absolute poverty in the Southwest, there was surely a possibility that our Little Havana area here [in Miami], which today is basically a cute ethnic place to go and enjoy yourself, might become a Cuban Harlem in the next generation."

The passage of time, Duran said, has convinced him and other young Cubans that "the issue of Castro is essentially an issue for Cubans to deal with. I think after Castro they may be able to evolve into a social democracy of some sort. . . . The younger Cubans here in America are becoming a little bit like the American Jews. They have a commitment toward the preservation of Israel, and yet they do have a life here in the United States. We have a commitment toward returning to the democratic processes in Cuba, but we also have a life here, and many more of us are beginning to feel that our quality of life will be much better with the Democratic Party type of programs."

Duran has not had an easy time as an American politician. In addition to the school-board race he lost on the bilingual-education issue, he also lost a 1970 bid for the City Commission. His election as chairman of the state Democratic Party in 1976 came through a coalition of blacks, Hispanics and urban liberals, and he joined the Carter campaign early enough to have some influence at the national level during the late Seventies.

Yet he and other Hispanic leaders were painfully conscious of the interlocking handicaps which limit their political power.

For one thing, there is a tradition of boss control in heavily Hispanic communities. In Texas' Rio Grande Valley counties, Anglo bosses maintained power by the ability to "deliver" votes from a subservient Chicano community whose members were totally dependent on the Anglos for their precarious livelihood. In Alex Mercure's native Rio Arriba County, New Mexico, Emilio Naranjo maintained power for twenty-five years as "a kind of rural counterpart of Mayor Daley," to use Mercure's phrase, by his control of patronage, welfare and other benefits.

Equally debilitating has been the Anglo politicians' skepticism about the size of the Hispanic community and the Hispanic vote. When the 1980 census was being planned, Hispanic leaders organized an unprecedented effort to reduce the size of the universally acknowledged "undercounts" that had occurred in 1970 and 1960. Fortuitously, Robert García found himself after only a year in Congress the chairman of the subcommittee on census and population, the most strategic position from which to monitor the 1980 enumeration. "They tell me," he said in 1979, "that in 1970 they had a 7.7-percent undercount for blacks. I would venture to say that it was probably double, maybe even triple that figure. They will not even guess what their undercount was for the Hispanic community. [Census officials said it was probably no greater than the 7.7 percent for blacks.] Well, this is not only vital for drawing legislative-district lines and congressional-district lines; it also affects how much we get from every fiscal-aid program. There is political clout and billions of dollars at stake here. You know, we have many noncitizens in my district—I don't call them illegal aliens; I call them noncitizens—and in districts through Texas and the Southwest and California. They use the trains, they use the schools, they use the hospitals, and that's the way it should be. But we need help to provide those services; we need those people counted."

Through organizations like the Southwest Voter Registration Project (SVREP) in San Antonio, run by 36-year-old William C. (Willie) Velásquez, the Hispanic community struggled to improve its poor statistics on registration and voting.

According to Census Bureau estimates, in the 1976 election, 68.3 percent of all whites were registered and 60.9 percent voted; 58.5 percent of all blacks were registered, and 48.7 percent voted. But only 37.8 percent of all Hispanics were registered, and only 31.8 voted.

SVREP's estimates on 1976 were a bit less bleak, but its study of turnout in the 1978 Texas elections, where Democrats, with overwhelming support in the Chicano community, lost both the senatorial and gubernatorial races, dramatized the political cost of low turnouts. SVREP said that barely more than a quarter of the *registered* Chicano voters came to the polls. The number of registered Chicano stay-at-homes was about 30 times as great as the margins by which their favored candidates lost.

Velásquez, a union organizer's son who joined in the farm workers' struggle, said that he believed those abysmal rates are the result of the fact that most Chicanos "have never won anything, so they don't have a goddamn thing" to show for their participation in politics. "People are not going to vote if you have no chance of winning, and they intuitively don't feel they can win."

In Texas, Velásquez said, his organization late in the Seventies switched to a very locally oriented strategy, combining registration and redistricting drives, in an effort to increase the number of Chicano county commissioners.

"Take a county that is 30 percent Chicano," he said. "The registration rate right now is 20 percent, and the turnout of them is 30 percent. They elect nobody. Now redistrict that county to give each of the four county commissioners 25 percent of the population. Put all the Mexicans in one precinct. Then they will get out and vote. And the county commissioner they elect, he's important. He's got a full-time, paid job, and he's got a road crew. He can put in a park. He can fix a street, put in a light. And every one you elect, you've added to the cadre of people at the local level who know something about politics."

Using this strategy, Velásquez said, Texas had elected 80 Chicano county commissioners in 1978, with a 30-percent increase targeted for 1980. "In Crockett County," he said, citing one of those where the strategy was used, "we got 93.6 percent of the Mexicans registered to vote; 97.5 percent of them turned out. We won by 34 votes and have half the county commissioners."

In Miami, Alfredo Duran said he had been struggling with the same problem. In Dade County, about 20 percent of the registered voters are Hispanics (as against about 33 percent of the total population), "but the lines for election districts have been drawn in a way that there's no district that has ten percent of the registered Hispanics." So there are no Cuban-Americans on the county commission or in the delegation to the legislature, and, Duran said, there will not be until a redistricting measure is passed.

It was clear from what they and others said that the political enfranchisement of the Hispanics is going to be a long struggle. "One hundred years of exclusion cannot be overcome by what Willie Velásquez is doing of late," Herman Gallegos said.

Yet there is no doubt the "sleeping giant" is awakening.

"It's clear for me and for many people," said Vilma Martínez, "that the time to act is now. I think the actions that we're engaging in probably will not produce results commensurate with our actual numbers. But I think clearly there will be results. To have no representatives, and now to have twenty, in the Texas statehouse is a very significant change. Any national politician who is smart recognizes we are the bloc of potential new voters."

Whatever the future immigration patterns, the Hispanic community will outpace the growth of most others, because it is, as Louis Nuñez pointed out, "by far the youngest community in the United States." The median age is 21—nine years below the national average. The 1978 Bureau of the Census estimates were that 42 percent of the Hispanics in the United States were under 18, and only 4 percent were over 65.

How far and how fast the increase in Hispanic political power will come is a matter of conjecture. Alberto Bustamante and others have proved that Hispanics can win with help from Anglo voters. There are growing resources of strength for such candidates, not just in numbers but in dollars as well. Bustamante mounted a $100,000 campaign in San Antonio, and his largest backer was Frank Sepulveda, a millionaire Chicano produce dealer. Carmen Delgado Votaw and others made the point that through such events as the Congressional Hispanic Caucus Dinner, the growing middle class is being educated "to support our own organizations and people."

There will undoubtedly continue to be competition for leadership places within the Hispanic community. But equally, there will be competition from Anglo leaders of both parties for the support of Hispanic voters. Both Hispanic causes and Hispanic leaders will become more prominent in American politics in the Eighties—a trend that will be accentuated by the growing importance to the United States of the resources of Mexico and Latin America.

On both the domestic and the foreign fronts, Hispanic-American leaders seem ready for those challenges.

11 · Blacks

THERE ARE, I SUPPOSE, as many ways to approach the subject of the next generation of black leaders in America as there are black leaders. And there are a great many black leaders, with constituencies ranging from the millions down to one. One approach, perhaps as valid as any and more provocative than most, is to look at them through the eyes of four men, of descending seniority, whose experience has given them exceptionally good vantage points from which to survey the field.

Clarence Mitchell, 69, came to Washington just before Pearl Harbor and for almost forty years was the NAACP's man on Capitol Hill. He saw segregation end in the nation's capital and played such a key part in the passage of every civil-rights measure now on the books that he came to be called "the 101st Senator."

Louis Martin, 68, a street-smart and successful Chicago newspaper publisher and politician, was the deputy chairman of the Democratic National Committee and the top black politician in the Kennedy-Johnson years. He was part of everything from John Kennedy's effort, just before the 1960 election, to speed the release of Martin Luther King, Jr., from a Birmingham jail to the appointment of Robert C. Weaver as the first black Cabinet member. At the end of the 1970s, Martin was recycled into a new environment as the ranking black assistant in Jimmy Carter's White House.

Eddie N. Williams, 48, a former journalist, State Department official and university administrator, has been since 1972 the director of the Joint Center for Political Studies in Washington, D.C. The JCPS is both a major source of scholarly research on issues affecting the black community and a principal training agency for black elected officials seeking to expand their managerial and political skills.

Vernon Jordan, 45, has moved through the ranks to positions of increasing power in the network of nonelected black officials. From a job as Georgia field secretary of the NAACP in the early 1960s, he became director of the Voter Education Project of the Southern Regional Council —the main agency for the registration drives in the first years (1965–70) the Voting Rights Act was in effect. He then headed the United Negro College Fund and since 1972 has been the $75,000-a-year director of the National Urban League, which runs about $19 million a year worth of education, training and social-welfare programs. He was the chairman of the Black Leadership Forum, whose fifteen members comprise something of a directorate of the power centers in the contemporary black community.

Excerpts from interviews with Mitchell, Martin, Williams and Jordan provide a kind of kaleidoscope of impressions about the emerging black leaders—starting from the basically upbeat generalizations of the oldest of the quartet of senior spokesmen, and coming down to the more focused (and more ambivalent) comments of the youngest.

Clarence Mitchell: "I think they have a broader outlook and understand the forces that are loose in the world a little bit better than the people of my generation. . . . I am impressed by the realism with which they are beginning to face up to their problems. . . . They staged a lot of demonstrations and resisted the government when they thought government was not doing the kind of thing it ought to do. And now many of them *are* the government in their communities. . . . And I think they think in broader terms than just doing certain things for blacks alone. I think they realize there are a lot of other people who are at a disadvantage, and something has to be done for them as well, if we're really going to make substantial progress. . . . And I'm impressed with the way they try to surround themselves with capable people."

Louis Martin: "In the decade of the Sixties, black America was consumed with correcting wanton abuses of civil rights and denials of the right to vote. And that cause excited not only the sensitive leadership but the masses of blacks. And you had these fantastic marches all over the place, and finally the President and the Congress did respond. . . .

"The Seventies have been considerably different. The focus is on economic opportunity and jobs. And we're developing an entrepreneurial class and an economically alert group. When I went to the University of Michigan in the early 1930s, I knew only one black who ever went to the business school. I was there last month surrounded by about 125 black students and alumni of that business school. . . . In Chicago we have seven black banks, where in the Sixties there was not a single one. . . . A lot of the black entrepreneurs are not doing much in politics at the moment, but they are becoming the ones our politicians can go to for money. . . . And that gives the politicians greater freedom. . . . And you've got the black mayors now, who just weren't there in the Sixties. . . . The mayors are practical operators. None of them are ideologues. They've got a problem and they've got to solve it. . . . But they also have contracts to give . . . and that's meant a great deal to the economic aspects of black life. . . . Black America is learning that we have got to find a way to create permanent jobs and become producers as well as consumers. . . .

"We cannot go on the next 25 or 30 years like we were in the last 25 or 30. . . . We've got to get into the mainstream . . . and I think we've got the kind of young leaders coming up who recognize that the competitive forces in this society cannot be escaped."

Eddie Williams: "There is no doubt the agenda is going to be economic . . . and a great number of blacks still look to the government as the employer of last resort, and for them there will still be a need to reform welfare and protect the right to education. . . . But if you really want to talk about the new leadership . . . more and more blacks are getting business degrees, and the corporations are snapping them up. . . . And my close friends who work for the energy companies articulate the same things that their bosses articulate. . . . So we're moving into a period where a significant number of blacks will be taking a countervailing point of view on some of the major economic issues. . . . I mean, the rub-off theory will apply. You move to the suburbs, you also take on some of the characteristics of the suburbs. You move more into the economic mainstream, you're going to take on more of the traits of that particular mainstream.

"Politically, the black population will continue to provide the base for most black elected officials. . . . In a conservative climate, black candidates have a hard time establishing—or holding—a white political base. . . . But the black elected officials are very intelligent, well-trained individuals. . . . The aggressiveness, the ability to organize, the inclination to want to lead that were all part of the civil-rights movement . . . have equipped them for office. And on the whole, they are deeply committed to the cause of civil rights, although they are sometimes frustrated as to how to manifest that in a political system where they have broader interests to represent. And they get more frustrated when their constituents don't understand that just because you were a marcher, a protestor, a civil-rights activist the day before the election, the day after the election you really enter a new world in which you need votes to carry out your notions. . . .

"So there are sometimes some tensions between the so-called civil-rights leader in a community and the political leader in the community. . . . Just the decentralization of black leadership makes it difficult to accomplish anything. Instead of 1 or 2 people who will set the standard, you now have to deal with 15 or 20, not all of whom are even speaking to each other at a given time. . . .

"One thing I'm greatly disappointed about is that we have not applied the successful organizing techniques of the civil-rights movement to what we most need today—a black voters' crusade. We just do not have the registration and turnout we need, because we are not using the techniques that worked in the 1960s to touch the spirit, the mood, the race pride and translate that into political mobilization."

Vernon Jordan: "I really think there are five new leadership classes in the black community. One of them is the black elected officials. In 1965, in the eleven states of the old Confederacy, there were only 70 elected black officials; in 1979 there were nearly 2,300 in the South alone. The vast majority of the political leadership came out of the civil-rights movement. . . . Politics was the next logical frontier. And now you're beginning to get a proliferation of black leadership, which I happen to think is healthy . . . and also a transformation of that leadership, because the issues take on a very different context in government than they had in the purity and morality of the civil-rights movement. . . . And sometimes that causes great frustration. I mean, we've seen black mayors, with strong support of the downtown business establishment, break strikes by public employees' unions in Atlanta and New Orleans. . . . We've had black people turn out black elected officials based on their performance, and I happen to think that's healthy. . . .

"My second new leadership group is those blacks who are managing multimillion-dollar public and private entities, basically white institutions. That's a brand-new phenomenon. Black guys are presidents of state colleges, running state and federal agencies; now Frank Thomas is running the Ford Foundation. . . .

"The third group is those black people who are in corporate America, basically because of affirmative-action programs. . . . That's a new leadership group, because they come out of business school on the basis of equality with their white peers, and they work in these companies, and then, after five o'clock, they're available to serve on the boards of the local YMCAs, NAACPs, Urban Leagues, Boys' Clubs, bringing their own perspectives and skills. . . . Those are my natural constituents, and I've got to figure out a way to get them involved. They care, but what gets in their way is they're so busy being a success and closing this deal or that deal, it eats into some of their time.

"The fourth new leadership class is the new community people who have come out of the Model Cities program, the antipoverty program, all those Great Society programs that required that poor people be brought into the decision making. That meant that black institutions, like white institutions, have gone through a process of democratization. The old leaders of the black community—the head of the NAACP, the local preacher, doctor, lawyer, school principal, head of the Urban League—who made all the decisions for everybody—have had to open up and let Miss Sally Jones, who is the president of the Joe Louis Improvement Association, into the inner circle. Some of them are strong, dynamic, community-oriented people, and they learned a lot about how to operate politically on those community-action-program boards.

"The fifth group is the new black entrepreneurs, who are profiting from the minority-purchasing programs. They're different from the traditional black businessman, who was the undertaker, or poolroom or café operator, or who had the local black newspaper. They're doing business with everybody in the white community as well as the black, and it exposes them in ways they never would have been exposed before.

"I reject out of the hand the notion that there's a chasm between these middle-class blacks in government, industry or business and the masses of the black people. Most of us are first-generation educated . . . and so we got kinfolks on welfare, kinfolks in the ghetto. . . . Historically, in the black community, middle-class elitist blacks have given leadership to the movement. Frederick Douglass, Booker T. Washington, W. E. B. DuBois, Walter White. . . . Martin [Luther King, Jr.] was a middle-class man. Whitney [Young] was a middle-class man. . . . But as we begin to permeate all of these structures where heretofore we were excluded, some things will take a normal course. . . . So I'm not taking any chances on it. I tell these young college graduates, 'You've got the responsibility to make sure that chasm does not become a fact. You've got to reach back and help the poor.' . . . Because it is so easy to forget. But that is not a racial phenomenon.

"Despite the fact that we don't have a Martin or a Whitney or a Roy [Wilkins] anymore, I think black leadership is stronger and has more depth. There are black people around now who really know something about energy . . . who've become experts in certain techniques of management. There was a time when Clarence Mitchell was the only guy on Capitol Hill. Now we're developing a whole cadre of kids who understand politics, government, the media, management. . . . I see ex-SNCC kids [the Student Non-Violent Coordinating Committee] working for big corporations, wearing white button-down shirts; no more jeans, no more beards. . . . But you've also had a great strengthening of community groups at the local level.

"It all means there's a lot more competition within the black community. A Jesse Bell runs against Dick Hatcher [for Mayor of Gary, Indiana].

A Marion Barry takes on a Sterling Tucker [for Mayor of Washington, D.C.]. Blacks competing with blacks for positions of real power. That's progress, in the truest sense of the word."

The themes that emerge from these four sets of comments are the dominant themes of this examination of black leadership. There is a strong sense of optimism, which at first glance appears to be at odds with the doomsday rhetoric many black elected officials use in lobbying for more governmental programs. ("You've got to recognize," said Louis Martin, "the historic political game in black America is simple: You play upon whatever guilt the white man may feel about the way he's treated blacks. There's nothing wrong with that. You give the white man hell and he deserves it.") But the rhetoric probably conceals a deeper reality.

The optimism is based on a sense that the dedication and commitment that characterized the civil-rights movement have been translated into other areas of leadership, including politics and government. That confidence is bolstered, to some degree, by the contributions that the anti-poverty programs of the 1960s have made to local-level leadership and, more significantly, by a recognition that the vast educational gains of the past twenty years have tremendously enriched the substantive and managerial skills of the younger generation of black men and women.

But there is also an awareness that the greater variety of opportunities now open to talented blacks has meant, in part, a fragmentation of leadership. Many of the best-trained and most skillful leaders have been attracted into business. While blacks in government increasingly emphasize the managerial over the ideological approach to their jobs, the greatest material rewards for good managers may currently be found not in the black-run city halls or government agencies, but in big white-controlled corporations or in the growing number of black-owned firms that both government and private procurement policies have spawned.

Material rewards are important, because the economic agenda has replaced the legal-rights agenda for most blacks, both individually and collectively. Within the political arena, competition between blacks is increasing, and a certain nervousness can be detected—probably greater than many black leaders will acknowledge on the record—that the pursuit of both financial and political success may be drawing black leaders away from a primary concern with the mass of blacks still suffering severe effects of discrimination. And there is certainly concern that the political mobilization of the long-disenfranchised black masses, which moved at high speed in the last half of the 1960s, has now stalled well short of the point at which blacks can command the attention of all politicians—white and black—that their unmet needs deserve.

Nonetheless, black leaders had achieved a position of power and prominence at the end of the Seventies unrivaled in American history. In the 1976 campaign and in office, Jimmy Carter acknowledged his debt to Martin Luther King, Jr., in a way no American President had ever done to a black, saying that without the work of the slain civil-rights leader, it would have been impossible for a white Southerner to seek the highest office in the land. Whenever Carter's credentials were challenged—as they often were—it was King's father and King's disciple Andrew Young to whom Carter turned for support. Blacks achieved more positions of influence in the Carter Cabinet and sub-Cabinet than ever before. And when Andrew Young resigned as the Cabinet-level Ambassador to the United Nations in 1979, in a controversy over U.S. policy in the Middle East, the leaders of the often-quarrelsome black organizations showed they could unite in support of their most prominent spokesman.

In this book, we can deal with only a portion of this wide spectrum of emerging black leaders, principally those who are in politics and government. While their private-sector contemporaries—in business, foundations and educational institutions—may manage resources of incalculable long-term consequence, it is the men and women who are involved daily with public-policy decisions who are likely to determine, in the years just ahead, the impetus blacks give to the direction of our government.

What is extraordinary—and difficult to remember in the 1980s—is that there have been only two brief periods in the long history of this nation in which more than a handful of blacks occupied elective office. One was in the decade of Reconstruction. And the other has been in the past fifteen years. From the time they were imported as slaves, the majority of blacks in the United States have lived in the South. And for most of our history, they have been systematically deprived of political rights in that region. It was not until the Reconstruction program of 1867 abolished the white governments in the Confederate states and gave power to the rulers of the five military districts spanning the Confederacy that blacks were allowed to vote.

While records are scarce, there are estimates that more than 700,000 blacks were enrolled as voters in the first year of Reconstruction. Blacks won a majority in the South Carolina Legislature, high executive-branch posts in several other states, fourteen seats in the House of Representatives—and Mississippi had two black Republican senators.

But Reconstruction ended in 1877, when Southern Democrats resolved the contested presidential election between Rutherford B. Hayes and Samuel J. Tilden by swinging their votes to the Republican Hayes in return for his promise that federal troops would be withdrawn from the South and civil authority—meaning white authority—restored. Within a few years, black officials virtually disappeared from public office in the South, soon to be followed by the newly enfranchised black voters. Southern legislatures vied in devising new voting requirements—ranging from affidavits of good character to poll taxes to interpretation of the Constitution—which eliminated black voters, and Southern Democratic parties adopted rules barring blacks from their primaries. By the end of the 19th century, the influence of blacks in Southern politics was virtually nonexistent.

The reversal of that pattern began in 1944, when the Supreme Court ruled the "white primary" unconstitutional. For the next twenty years, gradual steps were taken at the federal level—the outlawing of the poll tax in 1964; civil-rights laws in 1957, 1960 and 1974 expanding the Justice Department's authority to intervene on behalf of disenfranchised blacks —which nibbled away at the problem. But in 1964, Tennessee and Florida were the only Southern states where as many as half the voting-age blacks were registered to vote. The percentages in other states ranged downward to Mississippi's 6.7 percent.

The turnaround accelerated in 1965. That year—after television showed a shocked nation the violence that greeted blacks marching from Selma, Alabama, to Montgomery to demand the right to vote—Congress passed legislation allowing federal registrars to go into the South to enroll voters. More than a million blacks were added to the voting lists in the first five years the federal registrars were at work. And with black voters came black officeholders. In 1970, when the JCPS issues its first report, there were 756 black elected officials in the South. By 1979, that number had risen to 2,768. Louisiana and Mississippi, formerly among the states with the lowest percentage of black voters, now lead all the states in the number of black elected officials.

Outside the South, where barriers to voting had never been as high, there was also a significant increase in the number of blacks gaining public office. The non-South totals rose from 1,104 in 1970 to 1,839 in 1979. The growth there was fed by two forces: the increased concentration of blacks in center-city urban areas and the court rulings requiring one-man, one-vote reapportionment and single-member legislative districts. The number of blacks in the House of Representatives rose from 2 in 1950 to 4 in 1960 to 12 in 1972, when Andrew Young of Atlanta and Barbara Jordan of Houston became the first Southerners in the Congressional Black Caucus, to 17 in 1979. In 1967, Richard C. Hatcher of Gary, Indiana, and Carl Stokes of Cleveland became the first blacks to win the mayoral chairs in major American cities. By 1979, the number of black mayors had climbed to 191, including such major cities as Los Angeles, Detroit, Newark, New Orleans, Birmingham, Richmond—and Atlanta.

Atlanta held special significance because for a century it had been, as

Mayor Maynard Jackson, 42, said, "the largest center for black private higher education in the world." Four associated black colleges, Atlanta University and the interdenominational Theological Center drew the brightest black youths in the country. "From W. E. B. DuBois to Martin Luther King, Jr.," Jackson said, "you name the leaders, they've all touched those brick pathways one way or another."

Atlanta was also the home of one of the oldest black political organizations in the country, the Negro Voters' League. It was founded in 1947, when there were probably only five hundred black voters in the whole state, by Jackson's grandfather John Wesley Dobbs, a railway mail clerk and grand master of the Prince Hall Free and Accepted Masons. Dobbs was the Republican cochairman of the Voters' League. He and his Democratic counterpart, a lawyer, Colonel Austin T. Walden, encouraged blacks to overcome the barriers to registration and met in private—usually on election eve—to decide which white candidate to support. "When they opened the door," Jackson said, "they literally spoke for the black community. They would produce the ticket, and that's the way 96 or 97 percent of the black voters went."

Maynard Jackson grew up in that kind of political atmosphere, graduated from Morehouse College in Atlanta and took a law degree at North Carolina Central University. He went through the sit-ins at North Carolina and came home to take a job with the Emory University Neighborhood Legal Services Center, part of the network of anti-poverty law offices created by the Great Society.

The next steps are best told in his own words: "Martin Luther King was shot and killed on April 4, 1968. My daughter Brooke was born on April 8, and the next day we buried King in Atlanta. So I went from the hospital to the grave. I was very much influenced by King, and I became convinced . . . that there had to be a method, a strategy to carry on the civil-rights movement. Although imperfect, the best available nonviolent means of changing how the masses of people lived was through politics. I thought I would begin to make a move toward politics, but I thought it would be gradual. Less than two months later, on the night of June 4, 1968, I sat in front of a TV and watched Bobby Kennedy shot to death. The next day, June 5, the last day you could qualify to run for the U.S. Senate, I resigned my job with the legal-services center. I borrowed $3,000 for the qualifying fee, and with twenty minutes left in the qualifying period, I qualified to run against Herman Talmadge. I lost that race, but I carried Atlanta by over six thousand votes against him. The next year, I ran for Vice Mayor, the president of the board of aldermen, and I won that race against the longtime, powerful chairman of the finance committee. I served for four years, and in 1973 became Mayor. I was re-elected in 1977. So that's been the background. And I continue my belief today that although imperfect, politics remains the best available nonviolent means of changing how the masses of people—black and white—in America live."

While others may tell their stories with less conscious drama than Jackson, there are hundreds of young black activists who made the same transition from civil-rights and/or antipoverty organizing to electoral politics.

John Lewis, 40—from 1977 through 1979 the director of domestic operations at ACTION, the federal agency for volunteer service—was renowned for his physical courage in the 1960s, when courage was anything but rare among the civil-rights leaders. Lewis was a 15-year-old on a farm in Pike County, Alabama, "preaching practice sermons to the chickens," when King organized the bus boycott in Montgomery, fifty miles to the north. "We watched it on television," Lewis recalled, "and it was just an amazing thing. We had been told over and over in our own schools that black people will never stick together. And here were fifty thousand black people, primarily poor people, organizing car pools to share rides, using church buses, broken-down station wagons and cars, rather than ride on segregated buses. It gave all of us what Jesse Jackson calls a sense of somebody-ness."

Four years later, Lewis began his own civil-rights work while a college student in Nashville. He organized sit-ins, joined the original group of Freedom Riders seeking to desegregate bus depots across the South, became chairman of SNCC, delivered a speech at the 1963 March on Washington whose militancy made older civil-rights leaders nervous, then went back to Mississippi for Freedom Summer in 1964. Along the way there were some forty jailings and uncounted beatings. On "Bloody Sunday" in Selma in 1965, at the start of the march that produced the voting-rights bill, John Lewis was hospitalized with head injuries.

In the 1970s, Lewis took over from Vernon Jordan the task of running the Voter Education Project from Atlanta. When I asked if the shift seemed strange to him, he said, "I saw it as . . . just a natural transition, another step down a long road. . . . I felt that if hundreds and thousands and millions of new black voters were added to the registration lists, it would change the whole national and international climate."

In 1977, he tested himself at the polls in a special election, seeking the Atlanta seat in the House of Representatives left vacant when Andrew Young went to the United Nations. Lewis finished second in a twelve-man field, but lost to a white rival in the Democratic runoff. His campaign brochures had dramatized the path he had climbed with a pair of photographs: one showed him being shoved into a police wagon; the other showed him dining with President Carter.

"I don't think any of us were naive," he said in 1979, speaking of the time when the first picture was taken, "but we had a great deal of faith in the political system and in the national government. . . . We felt somehow that the American system was just, and that if we pressed hard enough and long enough, and kept our means consistent with our ends, it would respond. And I don't think we have changed our outlook on political change and social change; it's what it was 10 or 20 years ago."

A classmate of Lewis' at Fisk University (doing graduate work in chemistry) and a predecessor in the chairmanship of SNCC was Marion Barry, 44, now the Mayor of Washington, D.C. Barry was sent to Washington in 1965 "to raise funds, not hell," as Milton Coleman wrote in *The Washington Post,* but the latter proved much more agreeable. He took on the police, the white business establishment and, frequently, federal authorities, even while running Pride, Inc., a job-training program funded with antipoverty dollars. But as self-rule came to the District of Columbia, Barry diverted his energies to politics, gaining the school-board presidency in 1971, a City Council seat in 1974 and the Mayor's chair in 1978.

"For a long time," he said in 1979, "those of us in the movement were rather reluctant to get involved in electoral politics. . . . But you can only struggle with direct action so long until you just get burned out. . . . And eventually you learn that it's better to make policy than try to influence policy. It's one thing to sit here and sign an executive order; it's another to come in here and try to get somebody else to sign one for you."

Perhaps the most remarkable story is that of the Ford brothers, John, Harold and Emmitt, three of the 12 surviving children (there were 15 in all) of a Memphis mortician. All twelve Fords went through Tennessee State University in Memphis, where most of them were involved with SNCC and were active in the sit-ins, stand-ins and other civil-rights demonstrations.

Their political saga began in 1969, the year after King was murdered in a Memphis motel. John, the eldest of the political Fords (others are doctors, lawyers, teachers), had been in Chicago for several years, studying and working. His extracurricular activities ranged from Jesse Jackson's Operation Breadbasket to service as a South Side precinct captain in Richard J. Daley's organization. Inside five years, the three Ford brothers had pulled off a coup that caused old-pro Daley to tell them in 1976, "You handle your politics right."

In 1970, they pooled their talents and elected Harold Ford, now 35, to the Tennessee House of Representatives. In 1971, John, now 38, won a seat on the Memphis City Council. When each of them was well entrenched, they risked a three-Ford parlay. In 1974, Harold Ford ran for the U.S. House of Representatives, John for the state Senate and Emmitt, now 37, for brother Harold's seat in the Tennessee House. All three won, and five years later they were still in place. In 1979, John's old seat on the city council was taken over by a fourth brother, James, now 31, expanding a family dynasty that may be unrivaled in the country.

John Ford describes the difference between the black agendas of the 1960s and today as clearly as anyone: "We came up in the turbulent Sixties right in the mainstream of the civil-rights struggle, when we were on the outside looking in. All we wanted to do was get into the lunch counters or the movie houses or be able to drink from the same water fountains. But once we got that, we saw that was really insufficient. We saw that the real name of the game was economics. That was the only cure, the only way of becoming equal. And we knew, as brothers, as a family, that to become a part of the mainstream, we had to get into it by becoming more politically astute and more financially sound."

Becoming "politically astute and financially sound" is the keynote for the younger generation of black activists. What is striking about many of them is their emphasis on developing managerial skills and then applying them to an ever-broader range of problems. As they do so, they are discovering leadership roles for themselves that a few years ago did not exist.

Marian Wright Edelman, 41, the director of the Children's Defense Fund, is the daughter of a South Carolina Baptist preacher who named the youngest of his children for singer Marian Anderson. Possessed of a keen mind and a driving energy which sends her sentences out in nonstop torrents, she went through Spelman College in Atlanta, the sit-ins and Yale Law School and found herself, in 1964, running the NAACP Legal Defense Fund office in Jackson, Mississippi. ("That's where the need was," she says, "and once I got pushed down a courtroom steps, there was no chance I was not going to go back there.")

"It became very obvious, even during the first year," she said, "that you could not confront social problems narrowly. You could not send a child off to desegregate a school without looking at all the backup needs that family had. You have to deal with the human problems if you're going to make it work."

From that point on, Edelman's special mission has been to meet the "backup needs" of the victims of poverty and discrimination. While still in Mississippi, she became involved with the Head Start program at the local level, then started making trips to Washington to protect it from its political enemies. In Washington, she learned that while traditional civil-rights groups mobilized effectively for the passage of headlined legislation, "nobody was paying any attention to its implementation, to the very specialized advocacy that really addresses how bureaucracies work or don't work." Edelman put together funds for a euphemistically named Washington Research Project and began, she said, "to pester and pester and pester the bureaucracy." Her work ran the gamut of programs—health, food, school and antipoverty issues.

"It was very clear by the late Sixties," she said, "that anything that had just poor and black people as clients had a shrinking constituency. . . . We had to figure out how to reach old issues through fresh handles." The first efforts led to passage by Congress of a comprehensive child-development act, which enlisted self-interested support from a coalition including women's groups, day-care-center operators, church groups, labor groups and educators, as well as welfare mothers and traditional civil-rights organizations. The bill was vetoed by President Nixon, but the elements of a new "coalition for change, built on a concern about children" had been brought together.

"I can be accused of being tactical," Edelman said, "because I was a civil-rights lawyer. But when we attack a problem like unjustified school suspensions, we find that black kids are disproportionately hurt, even though far more white kids in actual numbers are suspended."

The Children's Defense Fund was formed in 1973 to do public-interest advocacy on issues ranging from school desegregation to dropouts and suspensions to health care to housing to corrections.

Its creed represents what Edelman has learned in her twenty years of struggle: "I am extremely result-oriented. I am concerned about making things work. I am so tired of establishing new principles, either in legislation or through litigation that people neither know about nor care about. . . . We have a working rule in this office that we will bring no suits unless the issue is important to people at the community level, they know about it and have a built-in monitoring capacity to take it through the next steps."

She has become extremely pragmatic in her tactics. When the goal was to force local authorities to separate children from adult criminals in jails, "the clear solution was to have church ladies all over this country, wives of local bank presidents, and Junior League members go and look at their police lockups occasionally. Their calls on the local sheriff will stop the jailing of children in America quicker than anything I can do through fifty-state legislation."

Edelman has also put her emphasis on staff expertise, including one data analyst of whom she says, "I'd fire twenty people rather than lose him." When a delegation of civil-rights leaders went down to the Office of Management and Budget one recent year to protest a recommendation that the annual civil-rights survey of federal school aid be ended, as an economy measure, Edelman took her data analyst along. "He had a wonderful argument, while all of us sat there and watched him humiliate the deputy director of OMB on OMB's own procedures. And we walked out and some civil-rights type said, 'Jesus, we didn't even have a chance to mention justice once.' And that was right; that was beside the point. It was won on technical grounds."

The best counterpart of Edelman in government is probably Eleanor Holmes Norton, 43, another Yale Law School graduate, who has won wide praise for transforming the federal Equal Employment Opportunity Commission (EEOC) from a bureaucratic nightmare with a backlog of over 130,000 unprocessed complaints into an effective and innovative government agency. Norton, who had previously gained a reputation as a crack administrator at the New York City Commission on Human Rights, had a half-joking answer to the question of why she puts such emphasis on managerial skills.

"Unfortunately," she said, "the world is run by lawyers, and we are trained to stop things. But I got fascinated by what it takes to run things. I was bothered by the fact that leadership was viewed as talking—not doing. Most civil-rights agencies had a bad reputation for ever producing results. And when I realized how unrun government really was, I saw there was a real risk that it would be run out of business. Administration is like exercise," said the petite jogger. "You master administration so you can get what you want out of the system."

Norton grew up in a middle-class family in still-segregated Washington, D.C., and did her civil-rights apprenticeship as both a demonstrator and a lawyer in Mississippi.

"The genius of the civil-rights movement," she said, "was that it threw up a set of leaders who understood the times precisely. There is hardly a better instance in American history of that. . . . The essentially neo-Gandhian pacifist tactics were really exquisitely suited to a moral issue. . . . But civil rights is no longer a moral issue today. It is a political issue, and an economic issue, and people are going to respond in a different way. . . . With their newly acquired power, blacks have to think in a far more complicated fashion about what their strategies need to be. . . . And I think black people are making that transition."

For Norton herself, that transition has involved two seemingly disparate elements: feminism and management. She was among the earliest of the prominent blacks to identify with the women's movement, recognizing, as she said, that "there are few easy analogues," but recognizing also that there is a "need for an alliance" between two groups whose wages lag almost equally behind those of white males.

As for the managerial emphasis, that seemed to her both logical and inevitable in a society which found itself in the situation of the United States in the Seventies. The civil-rights movement of the Sixties, she said, completed the thirty-year process of giving legal definition to "a society based on rights." Then, in the Seventies, that society suddenly came up against a set of forces—inflation, resource scarcity—which sharply curtailed its economic expansion.

"At that point," she said, "something like becoming middle-aged occurred, and we had to work for what we'd always just enjoyed. It's like, somehow, I began to jog last year and I didn't jog ten years ago. I am the same weight that I was ten years ago, but I have a feeling I wouldn't be if I didn't do more than I did ten years ago.

"For the first time," Norton said, "government cares about management, because the taxpayers are not going to fork up money automatically each year when measured against inflation. But the mentality to manage does not have generational antecedents in the bureaucracy. My agency may be the best example of it, and yet it was in perhaps the worst trouble of any agency in the federal government. [That was] because the agency was born in the Sixties, when the emphasis was on the development of rights—not on managing the agency or even the implementation of those rights."

Norton said she knew there were inevitably going to be conflicts among black leaders because of this change in the environment. And she linked that conflict to the finding in a 1979 Louis Harris survey that blacks' confidence in both the leaders of traditional civil-rights organizations and black public officials had declined sharply in the Seventies.

"Civil-rights leaders will lose much of their reason to be," she said, "if they are not continually trying to expand rights. But because I've been in government now since 1970, I've seen that most of the fundamental rights depend on systems that are not working very well. I mean, look at the sorry state of the welfare system. So I think that in order to keep a backlash against rights from occurring, you have to make certain that the programs set up in the name of these rights are in fact effectively managed."

Norton's own emphasis was on the affirmative-action programs in employment. And she was operating in terms of a sophisticated economic strategy, aimed not just at "helping people get hired and promoted generally throughout the society," but at moving the victims of past discrimination "from leftover jobs in declining industries into the more lucrative growth industries."

A man who had already found his way there was James A. Joseph, 45, who in 1977 left his post as vice president of Cummins Engine Company, a *Fortune* 500 multinational, to take what he clearly indicated would be a temporary assignment in the federal government. Joseph had already had a remarkable variety of experiences since coming out of Opelousas, Louisiana. The Baptist minister's son and Yale graduate was commander of an Army medical detachment, a college chaplain and teacher of theology, a foundation administrator and a business executive. He had rejected what he regarded as "marginal, showcase black jobs," like director of black-studies programs in academia, and when Andrew Young sent his name to the Carter transition team, "I told them I would not consider an assignment in an area in which blacks have traditionally gone," Joseph said.

The job he was offered was anything but traditional: Undersecretary of the Department of the Interior. As Joseph noted, "it is kind of interesting" that ever since the undersecretary's job in the Cabinet departments had been designated as a top management post, a black had never been in that job. That is exactly why he wanted it.

"Blacks who are concerned about the plight of the black community," he said, "have to take that concern into nontraditional institutions and try to deliver nontraditional resources. I firmly believe that one of the mistakes we have made is that we have articulated the problems of black and poor people in a language of civil rights and tended to focus on the marginal institutions of social service, rather than the more fundamental institutions of social change. . . .

"Coming from the foundation world to Cummins, one of the things I noticed was that the decision Cummins made about where it locates a plant could have far more impact on a community than a million-dollar foundation grant. . . . And when one looks at the federal budget and sees where it's expended, the specialized programs . . . that deal with black problems . . . only touch the surface. So I believe that blacks have got to get in on the policy analysis and decision making which determine where all the federal resources go . . . and make an effort to ensure that those resources are used to benefit all of the people." Joseph mentioned his hope that his presence and influence might help minorities get a better opportunity for the jobs, contracts, leases and facilities the Interior Department distributes. But he also said, "I think my first responsibility to the black community is to demonstrate that as a black, I can perform my job as effectively as anybody else."

The implications of Joseph's comments are amplified in the views and the career of a younger black man, 39-year-old George Dalley, who was the Deputy Assistant Secretary of State for International Organization Affairs until 1979, when he was named as a member of the Civil Aeronautics Board. Raised in Harlem by Jamaica-born parents who worked as a cook and a maid to send their two sons to an integrated private school, Dalley found in the civil-rights movement something that "gave me as a Jamaican . . . a pride and identification with black people, a recognition that this was a struggle in which we were all involved." He went to law school at Columbia, thinking he would become a civil-rights lawyer, but courses in international law turned his ambitions toward the Foreign Service. "I and other blacks who came up through the Sixties recognized that we should take advantage of our greater opportunities and try to blaze trails in places we hadn't been before,'' Dalley said. As it turned out, he took a long excursion through the byways of black domestic programs before coming back to his original interest in foreign policy. Each step, however, expanded his concept of what leadership might entail.

The first stop was the Metropolitan Applied Research Center (MARC), a black-run ''think tank'' in New York City founded by social psychologist Kenneth Clark ''to do some long-range planning and strategizing about . . . the next phase of the civil-rights movement. Clark recognized,'' Dalley said, ''that beyond demonstrations . . . there was going to be a long-term need for building institutions in the black community to sustain the progress that was being made in the mid-Sixties.''

Very quickly, however, MARC found itself preoccupied with the ill-fated experiment in school decentralization that was attempted in New York in response to the civil unrest of that period. Trying to train local school-board members and build links between schools and communities, Dalley saw ''the bright promise of decentralization . . . turn to ashes. In poor communities, it never involved the parents or the ordinary people in a meaningful way. What it did was to involve the poverty hustlers, the people who started making $20,000 or $25,000 a year in the anti-poverty program and were looking for ways to maintain their affluence on the public payroll. . . . I'm a strong believer in integration, and in New York City, decentralization slowed the tendency toward integration.''

Through a friend, Dalley learned about an opening on the staff of the House Judiciary Committee. He was assigned to a subcommittee monitoring civil-rights enforcement in the Nixon Administration and learned an important aspect of bureaucratic policies. ''We always had these long dances, and they [the administration officials] would try to convince us that they really were upholding the very letter of the law. We knew very well they weren't, but we weren't very effective trying to force people to admissions. Then we started networking with disgruntled people within the agencies, who started giving us chapter and verse of what wasn't being done, and that gave me my first recognition of the importance of building those networks.''

Another lesson came when Dalley moved onto the staff of Representative Charles Rangel, the Democratic New York Congressman from Harlem. ''Charlie was chairman of the Congressional Black Caucus for two years,'' Dalley said, ''and we became increasingly aware that in order to be effective, we had to have positions on the full range of legislation, from agriculture to foreign assistance. We were not going to be able to negotiate on urban policy or small-business policy unless we knew enough to know where we wanted to trade votes in other areas. So we started systematically to become more and more involved in foreign policy.''

The impulse that began with the need for coalition building and informed vote bartering was furthered by the arrival of members like Andrew Young and Cardiss Collins (of Chicago), who had a strong interest in African policy. Soon the caucus was asserting itself on Angolan policy, meeting with Secretary of State Kissinger, conferring with the African ambassadors. After working on the Carter campaign in Harlem, it was natural for Dalley to be given a State Department appointment, as one of the Andrew Young protégés in the international-organization section.

It is not, perhaps, that difficult these days for smart, sophisticated blacks like Jim Joseph and George Dalley to make their way to appointed leadership positions in institutions and on issues previously closed to minorities. It is more remarkable to find black elective officials traveling a similar path.

Jim Joseph does not have a black constituency to whom he must justify the work he does on the Outer Continental Shelf, nor is George Dalley up against a political rival who would debate his statement that "the real challenge of the next twenty-five years is going to be how the United States engages with the needs of the developing world."

Dalley is honest enough to concede that "when I go back to Harlem and talk about human rights and the work I am doing, the general question I get is 'When are we going to deal with human rights at home?' When people are hurting domestically, they are concerned about their own condition."

But he insisted "there is a linkage. So long as you're willing to ignore the South Bronx, then you're not going to be morally outraged about Calcutta or about the starving children in Africa. And I think that folks in Harlem do recognize that. They're interested in foreign policy."

A measure of the black community's concern for foreign policy came in August 1979 in the furor over Andrew Young's contacts with the Palestine Liberation Organization and his subsequent resignation from his post as the U.S. Ambassador to the United Nations. While united behind Young, black leaders quickly split into two camps, with some making well-publicized visits to PLO leader Yasir Arafat while others condemned "ill-conceived flirtation with terrorist groups."

Through the uproar, there was a new sense of blacks' participation in a major foreign-policy debate. As Young himself told the 1979 Congressional Black Caucus dinner, "We're supposed [in the eyes of some critics] to be confined to civil rights. But . . . it is nowadays impossible to deal with the problems of inflation and unemployment in a strictly domestic context. . . . Unemployment is directly related to our relationships to Africa."

As if to confirm that basic contention, a knowledgeable black foreign-policy specialist, Donald F. McHenry, was chosen as Young's replacement at the United Nations. And the linkage was visible far from Washington or the United Nations as well.

Across the continent, in Los Angeles, another young black man who had an early interest in foreign policy (reflected in his degree in Near Eastern studies from UCLA) expressed the same view. Robert C. Farrell, 44, is every inch a practical politician, deeply enmeshed in urban problems as a second-term member of the Los Angeles City Council.

"I have an orientation toward the Third World," he said. "At one time, I wanted to go to the Middle East for the U.S. government. I wanted to be an Arabist, but that did not come to pass. But," he said, "Los Angeles is a world center, and by moving on the foreign circuit here, with the consuls general, I think indirectly I'll improve some options for people in South L.A. Perhaps they will understand that part of their responsibility is investing resources in minority banks and minority businesses and minority communities. I think they don't understand the minority community well, and by being a representative of that community and not coming off perhaps as a person who fits their stereotypes, maybe I can help them understand it better."

Bob Farrell is certainly not anyone's stereotype of a black city councilman. The former Freedom Rider said, "I represent the kind of black community leaders of the future who are really process-oriented, who understand that the real delivery system in the United States, both public and private, does not depend on the spectacular things that come about rarely but on the quiet but significant pattern of routine activities that we take for granted every day."

When he was asked—as the representative of a black working-class area—what his main objective was, he said, without a moment's hesitation, "Rationality and order in the black community, based on the integration of federally funded, state-funded and private programs into a clearly understood community-plan framework. . . . I'm not saying that I don't go out and scuffle for as much as I can get, so I can have a consistent flow of press releases for those who see this as an indicator of the effectiveness of a local official. But to me, the real investment has to be in some brainpower focusing on the process so that, as we look to the 1980s, we can begin to deliver a more effective pattern of services that people can take for granted, almost as a right." Then, quoting a line that has become popular since actor Ossie Davis used it at a Congressional Black Caucus dinner, Farrell added, "Like we say, at this moment of history, it's not the man, it's the plan. It's not the rap, it's the map."

The substance behind this rhetoric is a five-year capital-planning process, including roads, lighting, housing, parks, recreation, police and fire services and other basic elements of the urban infrastructure, that was approved by the city council in 1978. In his 1979 re-election campaign,

Farrell had to defend himself against criticism that "the alley is filthy, there are potholes in the street, and you tell me you're sitting downtown talking about a plan that is not going to be in place until way later." But Farrell argued that progress is built into understanding the process—"and not something magic that some individual brings you because you're nice." And he made his argument the basis of a winning campaign.

Farrell also organized his staff to obtain the kind of expertise his planning- and process-oriented approach required. His office was put together by Beverly Hawkins, a Ph.D. who later won a White House fellowship, worked for Joseph at the Interior Department and went, on his recommendation, into an executive post at Cummins Engine. A later top aide was a graduate of Stanford and Harvard Law School—"not the normal kind of person you have working as an aide to an L.A. city councilman," Farrell said.

Then he said something that touched on a sensitive point: the whole question of class-consciousness in the black community. There had been some criticism in the district, it seemed, because the Farrell aide "doesn't live in South L.A. He lives in an area," Farrell said, "where you tend to find fellows who are out of Harvard maybe five or six years and doing okay in life."

While Farrell defended this decision in the specific case, he confessed to disquiet about the pattern. "We have this phenomenon of our best and brightest moving out," he said. "The family works hard; the children get a good education; and as they begin their upward mobility, they move to one of the neighboring areas. . . . If you go into certain parts of my constituency, you'd look around and say, 'My gosh, all of those millions of dollars went into South L.A. and I can't see any benefits.' Well, of course not. The benefits are in the minds and bodies of the people who attended those classes and went through all those training programs and had that broad exposure. And many of them have moved out of the community."

The area west of Farrell's district, between the University of Southern California and the airport, is a sizable step up on the socioeconomic ladder, so much so that its Congressman, 46-year-old Julian C. Dixon, said it "has been tagged as the 'gilded ghetto' in Los Angeles. It's primarily a bedroom community," said Dixon, who represented much of the same territory for six years in the California Assembly before coming to Washington in the 1978 election. "It is a district where they really believe that good neighbors come in all colors. They are very proud of their integration pattern. In the last census it was about 44 percent black, 50 percent white and about 4 or 5 percent Asian. It's a middle-class district, with a lot of homeowners. Thirty-three percent of the people in the district work for the government in one form or another—city, county, state or federal. So, a large number of government employees, a large number of professionals, a lot of schoolteachers, some entertainers. It's a very comfortable district to represent."

Dixon's is the kind of area where the upwardly mobile people from Farrell's district move. And he has no doubt that their concerns are different from their poorer black neighbors' to the east. They are, he said, "more concerned with the social, economic issues than with the racial issues. Most of the people that live in the district have grown up in an integrated community, work in an integrated community, so there are very few issues that the cutting edge is whether you're black or white. . . . The adjacent area [which includes the district Farrell represents on the city council] is Congressman [Gus] Hawkins' district. The concerns in Hawkins' district are a lot different, in the main." Hawkins was the prime sponsor of the so-called Humphrey-Hawkins bill to make the government the employer of last resort for jobless citizens. That bill, in diluted form, was passed before Dixon came to Congress, but he said, "Anyone who is black has concerns for the poor and for strong social programs. But I also have concerns for a lot of 'middle-class' issues that maybe, if you come from a completely impoverished area, you wouldn't have."

I asked him what his constituents were concerned about. "Most of them," he said, "are homeowners or live in moderate- to high-income apartment dwellings. . . . They are definitely interested in police protection. Their kids are victims of juvenile gangs, and so they want strong enforcement of the laws that relate to the juvenile-justice system."

It was no accident that Dixon made that area of legislation his specialty in the Assembly. Nor was it an accident that the law he shaped was one that "got tougher with young people that committed serious crimes, while we decriminalized the status offenses" like truancy or curfew violations that are most likely to involve middle-class kids.

The other big issue in his district, Dixon said, is education. And he gave me as clear a description of the political geography of the school issue in a major metropolitan area as one is ever likely to hear. "If you look at the school system in Los Angeles," he said, "it's always moving west. The people who live in Jefferson High School district—which is in Gus Hawkins' district—are physically going to school at Crenshaw [in Dixon's district] because they feel that education is better. The people who are domiciled in the Crenshaw district, they're going to Pacific Palisades and University High School. And the white folks who live in University and Pacific Palisades are moving their kids into a private school. You can see the migration, and they avoid a lot of the direct conflict by busing their kids west."

The conflict Dixon is talking about is class conflict, and it is one of the most sensitive subjects in the black community. I asked Dixon how his community had reacted to Proposition 13, the 1978 move to slash California's property taxes, which was opposed by most liberals as a threat to social-welfare programs. "I was opposed to Proposition 13," he said, "and it failed in my district—but only by about three percent of the vote. . . . People are becoming very self-interested. A person who lives in my area who has a home that he paid $90,000 or $100,000 for is very concerned about property taxes. A lot of blacks voted for Proposition 13 in my district, because they're working people and their problems are not the same as those who are more interested in the welfare programs and whether or not there's going to be a cost-of-living increase in them."

Dixon, who was exceptionally candid in discussing these facts of life, was asked whether he thought that the growing political power of the black middle class would or would not be used in the years ahead to help blacks in poverty.

"That's an interesting question," he said. "I think as blacks become more integrated into the political system, it becomes a lot tougher in some ways." He pointed to the example of Wilson Riles, the California superintendent of public instruction. "Yes, he is black," said Dixon, "but no, he cannot exclusively represent black interests. He was criticized recently because of his vote on the Board of Regents [of the University of California system]. Their statistics show that there are more kids entering college who are not passing the basic English test and are taking what they call remedial English. A resolution was offered to require another year of high-school English for admission. A lot of people thought that would be discriminatory against blacks and other minorities. But he voted to do that. A lot of blacks criticized him for doing something that would jeopardize young black students' getting into four-year institutions."

Many black officials go out of their way to deny that there are important class divisions within the black community—sometimes even while claiming a proletarian identity for themselves. Mayor Marion Barry of Washington, D.C., for example, made a point in an interview of stressing the significance of "my election as a symbol of what can happen with someone who didn't come out of the traditional background of black leadership. I've traveled more distance than most." Most elected black officials, he said, came from middle-class backgrounds, with parents who were preachers or professionals. His parents were meagerly educated Memphis working people, he said, and while he had several college degrees in chemistry, "I think I understand a wider range of people and a wider range of problems. I feel just as comfortable sitting in a poolroom talking to a guy who's an ex-junkie or an ex-convict as I do talking to the President of the United States."

But when Barry was asked about analyses in Washington newspapers showing that in the three-man Democratic primary in which victory was (to use the old phrase) tantamount to election, he had run best in the more prosperous wards with large and growing white populations and worst in the old, black and relatively poor sections of the city, his response was defensive. "It is true," he said, "that I did terribly well in certain parts of Wards 1, 2 and 3, where you have a younger, white professional. . . . But my base is much broader than it's been characterized. I had senior citizens. I had all kinds of people." Then Barry stressed that even though "I knew from all the data that I shouldn't spend much time in Anacostia [the poorest black section of the city] because it traditionally has the lowest voting percentages, there was always that urge to go spend a day in Anacostia, or in this public-housing project. . . . There's just a gut reaction to go where the most problems are."

Barry cited Atlanta's Mayor Maynard Jackson as a black leader with a more conventional background than his own. But Jackson also rejected outright any talk of class divisions in the black community. Although he broke a strike of predominantly black city sanitation workers during his first term, he said, "I don't think there's going to be in the foreseeable future the forgetting of a common bond. White America won't let black middle-class America forget it is black. There will always be the reminders. And simple political pragmatism teaches that you never forget your base."

The facts that lie behind this argument are not readily available, and there is more dispute than agreement on how to interpret them.

Part of the problem is that black progress tends to be measured against white status. The Census Bureau and most other students of demographic trends have not really looked at the black community except in comparative terms. The statistics that are available suggest that since World War II, blacks have moved—much more slowly than whites—up through the income, occupational and educational levels, and are now more evenly distributed across the status spectrum.

For example, in 1953, 32 percent of all black families made less than $3,000 a year (in 1974 dollars). This proportion fell to 14 percent in 1974 and less than 10 percent in 1976. Meanwhile, the share of black families making $15,000 or more (again, in 1974 dollars) rose from 2 percent in 1953 to 19 percent in 1974 and by 1976 was well over 25 percent. The number of middle-class blacks was very nearly equal to the number still poor.

Thus, black society in America has moved in the past twenty years from the point where it was virtually classless to the point where the beginnings of class consciousness and class conflict were expectable. In the past, to be black was almost automatically to be poor and undereducated. Now the variations are much greater.

In 1978, a respected black sociologist at the University of Chicago, William Julius Wilson, published *The Declining Significance of Race.* Wilson provocatively argued that "economic and political changes have gradually shaped a black class structure, making it increasingly difficult to speak of a single or uniform black experience. . . . As we begin the last quarter of the Twentieth Century, a deepening economic schism seems to be developing in the black community, with the black poor falling further and further behind middle- and upper-income blacks."

Wilson's argument was criticized, both for its interpretations and for its implications. But whatever the merits of these broad arguments, the evidence is accumulating that a split of some significance is growing in the ranks of black political leaders. Almost all of them are still committed personally and politically to the traditional liberal agenda of programs aimed at relieving the effects of poverty and discrimination that still plague many blacks: manpower training and public-service jobs; welfare reform; subsidized housing and health care. But as they themselves move into the political and economic mainstream of a society that is relentlessly middle-class, the emerging black leaders have begun to focus on economic-development strategies that are certain to increase the social distance between successful and unsuccessful blacks.

That does not, by itself, mean any lessening of the effort to improve the standing of the black community as a whole. As Vernon Jordan pointed out, much of the past leadership of black causes has come from an educated elite within that society. That tradition continues today, as exemplified by two generations of the Coleman family.

William T. Coleman, Jr., 60, has never held a long-term full-time government job. His longest periods on the public payroll came in 1948, when he spent a year as the first black law clerk on the Supreme Court, and almost 30 years later, when he served almost two years as Secretary of Transportation in the Ford Administration. But in between, in private practice and in a series of part-time assignments, he has had a major role in changing the legal and social history of this country. As a young lawyer, he coordinated the research and was one of the signers of the brief of the NAACP Legal Defense and Education Fund in *Brown v. Board of Education,* the 1954 Supreme Court case that declared school segregation unconstitutional. He argued and won the case that ended Florida's ban on interracial marriage and won the protracted and controversial challenge to the whites-only policy of Philadelphia's Girard College. He was a counsel to the Warren Commission investigation of the assassination of President Kennedy and has served on innumerable other commissions for the city of Philadelphia, the Commonwealth of Pennsylvania and the nation.

A plump, pleased and prosperous man, now practicing law in Washington, D.C., after working most of his life in Philadelphia, Coleman has passed on both his preference for private-sector law practice and his sense of social obligation to his children, two of whom are also lawyers, and one of whom, Lovida H. Coleman, Jr., 31, was serving in 1979 as the special assistant to the Attorney General of the United States, Benjamin Civiletti.

She was there, her father said, "against my recommendation. I've tried to keep them in the private sector, but she's having a lot of fun, and she's young enough that if she gets out of there in the next year or two, I think it will be a good experience."

Lovida Coleman graduated from Yale Law School (a small act of rebellion against the wishes of her Harvard-trained father), served a clerkship with a circuit-court judge and in 1976 took a job with the Washington law firm of Williams and Connolly, from which she was recruited in 1978 for her Justice Department job.

While working for the Carter Administration, Coleman suspended her political activities—which centered on the recruitment of young blacks for the Republican Party. Republicanism was the family tradition, but for a time in the early Seventies, she had rebelled against the Vietnam war and the Nixon Administration and had been a Democrat.

But, she said, "You can't have a party own a minority and expect people from that group to have a real voice. And I think that's happened to blacks in the Democratic Party. The party thinks they have no place else to go, and so they don't make the effort they used to make to articulate good policies that would benefit a broad range of people."

Believing that, Lovida Coleman said she viewed her work in the Carter Administration as both nonpolitical and noncareer. She had absorbed the lessons of her father's career and planned her own to match. "I would like to feel there will always be long periods of my life when I practice law, and then I like the idea, for particular periods of time or for particular purposes, of working in government—but not as a career person."

It would be a very doctrinaire person indeed who would argue that the pursuit of private careers in the business and professional sector was an abdication of public responsibility for people like the Colemans.

But there was greater concern about the tendency of some black elected officials to be pulled toward the business community, as the area which had both the resources and the motivation to satisfy their needs.

Marion Barry, for all that he had talked about the tug of Anacostia and the housing projects, became known in his first year as Mayor principally for the push he gave black-owned businesses obtaining municipal-service contracts in the District of Columbia—and for accepting a preferential interest rate on his own home mortgage from a local savings-and-loan, until adverse publicity forced him to give it up.

While their "formal" agenda has not changed, relatively few black officials are still actively trying to mobilize mass support for direct efforts to redistribute wealth and power downward to the lower class.

Consider, as examples of the emerging and the declining styles, State Senator Sanford Cloud of Hartford and City Councilman Kenneth V. Cockrel of Detroit.

Cloud, 35, the son of a Hartford auto mechanic, went off to the University of Arizona "so I could play golf all year and major in business administration," with the alternative career possibilities of becoming a golf pro or going into the men's-clothing business. Instead he went to Howard University Law School, clerked at the prestigious Washington corporate-law firm of Covington and Burling and then returned to Hartford to join the law department of the Aetna Life and Casualty Company. In 1976, before establishing a private law practice of his own, he won a seat in the state Senate, where his most notable accomplishment was joining an *ad hoc* coalition of Republicans and other urban Democrats in holding up the Governor's budget to force an increase in welfare and urban aid. The only black in the state Senate, Cloud is viewed as a "liberal" in Connecticut politics, which means that he favors introduction of a state income tax. His philosophy, he said, is that jobs are basic to everything else. "If a man or woman has a job, the person's going to be in a position to provide decent housing for the family, and raise the children in an environment which is more conducive for those children to be prepared to learn in the educational system."

The Great Society programs of the 1960s, he said, had one good effect: "Your community-action agencies and Model Cities programs . . . generated a larger middle class of blacks . . . who had some opportunities to run and administer programs at salary levels that they probably would never have had the opportunity to receive in the private sector during those years. And now in the Seventies, those same individuals are getting opportunities in the private sector because of skills they acquired in those nonprofit, poverty-type organizations. As to the masses outside of the citizen-participation mechanism, I'd have to say that the benefits were quite limited."

Cloud himself has followed the pattern he described and has found his way into the corporate world, heading a new section on housing and economic development in the law department of Aetna, where he began his legal career. "The corporate leadership in this town is probably the most progressive in the country," he said, "and I see a career right there."

Kenneth V. Cockrel, 42, a member of the Detroit City Council, has a much less benign view of corporate power. The son of a Ford assembly-line worker, Cockrel spent his early years in a converted Army barracks outside Detroit, used to house blacks who moved from the South to work in factories during World War II. Ever since he came out of the Air Force in 1959, he has been looking for ways to organize the people he sees as victims of the American economic system. In the 1960s, while working his way through Wayne State University, he became active in such short-lived movements as the League of Revolutionary Black Workers and the Dodge Revolutionary Union Movement (DRUM). These were avowedly Marxist-Leninist groups that Cockrel says "went through a period of wildcat strikes attempting to develop community support for the in-plant struggle."

Greater success and notoriety came as a defense attorney, who always seemed to be first on the scene during the years of tough Detroit police tactics following the Twelfth Street riots of 1967. He was an outspoken critic of the STRESS team, the special tactical squad of police working in ghetto areas, and assailed one judge as "a racist monkey . . . a honky dog fool." He also outraged the establishment by bringing his social philosophy into the courtroom. As the *Detroit News* noted in a profile of Cockrel, when defending a man who had murdered his foreman, "Cockrel in effect put the factory itself and the assembly line in particular on trial." He introduced expert testimony on the "dehumanizing effects" of the factory environment and not only won an acquittal for his client on grounds of temporary insanity but later forced Chrysler to give him back pay and rehabilitation assistance.

In 1972, a white partner in the law firm, Justin Ravitz (whom we met in Chapter 8), who shares Cockrel's political views, was elected to the Detroit Recorders Court bench. A year later, firebrand Cockrel had attained enough respectability to be honored at a Detroit NAACP banquet. And in 1977, Cockrel was elected to the city council, after a campaign in which he said, "I'm not here selling the collected works of Karl Marx. . . . I'm talking about jobs for people."

But Cockrel's approach does not incline him to favor tax abatements and other incentives for private industry to locate or expand within the city. After one 8–1 council vote, in which he was the lone holdout, he said, "I am just philosophically opposed to the utilization of public resources to enhance the profit-making potential of private entrepreneurs. . . . I'm opposed also to our taking steps [to lure industry] that have the effect of reinforcing the exploitation of working people who happen to be in other parts of the state or country." Rather, he has been pushing (so far unsuccessfully) for a feasibility study of a city takeover of Detroit Edison, the utility company.

Cockrel said that "what's important about my being on the council" is not whether he prevails on any particular issue but "the extent to which it can be used to facilitate the external organization of this independent socialist force" he has been seeking for the last twenty years. Late in 1978, he and his colleagues organized a group called the Detroit Alliance for a Rational Economy (DARE) at a convention with about two hundred people. Although far from being a mass movement, it has been pressing issues—particularly energy, health and environmental issues—that Cockrel said "emphasize the mutuality of interest that working people have irrespective of race and sex."

In that respect, he is unusual among the black elected officials in addressing directly a concern that many of them share: the seeming letdown in the mobilization of the black community during the 1970s.

During the Sixties, when the registration drives were vigorously pushed, black voter registration in the South went from less than half the white rate to a near-parity. But nationwide, black registration hit its peak of 66 percent in 1968 and had declined to 58 percent eight years later.

The actual turnout of black voters shows an even bleaker trend, running consistently from 11 to 15 percentage points behind the white turnout rate, which itself has been declining. In presidential years, the percentage of eligible blacks actually voting dropped from 59 percent in 1964 to 49 percent in 1976. In congressional elections, it dropped from 42 percent in 1966 to 37.2 percent in 1978.

It was in response to that trend that all the major black organizations united in 1979 under the leadership of Eddie Williams to launch "Operation Big Vote," an effort to increase black registration by 20 percent in forty-one targeted metropolitan areas and to achieve a turnout rate of at least 75 percent in those areas. Some black leaders thought the drive was overdue.

John Lewis put it most bluntly when he said, "I think there's a tendency on the part of national black leadership today to come and literally beg the President of the United States or members of Congress for help. I think there should be more effort to go out and organize—to *mobilize* the black community and to try to pick up that coalition that existed during the Sixties."

Lewis, who spent more than six years in voter-registration work, called current black voting figures "a shame and a disgrace. One thing Dr. King tried to do before he was assassinated was to build a coalition with other groups that are left out—Chicanos, Native Americans, low-income whites. I don't think anyone is working on that agenda today."

Lewis may be overstating the case. As he noted himself, the VISTA volunteers his own government agency sent into the cities focused their efforts on mobilizing the poor to demand services from their elected officials.

But the concern is real—and merited. In Washington, Marion Barry said, "You don't find the community or neighborhood activist working on civil rights as I was. There are not many of them out there now." In

Memphis, John Ford remarked, "There are younger people who are turned on to politics, but in a different way. I don't think they really understand it as we do who were caught up in the sit-ins in the early Sixties. It's a new era today. The things they were brought up in—this hippie movement, this 'Give me what I want' movement—were somewhat different, and I think if they're not careful, they're going to miss the boat."

Perhaps the most poignant expression of this concern came from Eddie Bernice Johnson, 46, a remarkable woman who went from a career in nursing to four years in the Texas House of Representatives and then in 1977 began running the Dallas regional office of the Department of Health, Education and Welfare. From her high-school days in Waco as a volunteer for the YWCA, Johnson has always been one to take responsibility. She was never what she called "a screaming marcher; my way was always to attempt to talk about problems and attempt to work out and negotiate solutions. My objective was always to attempt to open doors and not close them, open up avenues of communication and not create more barriers."

Through long years of maddeningly slow progress in the 1960s, Johnson became a prime resource for the Dallas black community. "I guess my involvement started with voter registration," she said. "That was back when we had the poll tax in Texas. I always did read a lot and I felt that the only real power that minorities had for change would be through the electoral process, so I would walk from door to door and shopping center to shopping center to help register voters. . . . Later, we brought the suit for reapportionment, and I walked from door to door and business place to business place, getting petitions signed and trying to help raise money to bring the suit for single-member districts." When the suit was successful and the new districts were drawn, Johnson was the chairman of the citywide black caucus to screen potential candidates—and also its choice as a candidate. She defeated three black males in the primary for her first nomination, but was never opposed again.

"The thing that I feel has aided me in achieving the little I have been able to achieve," she said, "has been my willingness to be out there with everybody at all hours, day or night, and just giving it whatever seems to be necessary to get it done. I think that was something that was probably built into me from my childhood: being reliable, following through on what you start—a belief that if you don't give up, good things are possible.

"But I see men, especially black men, becoming more and more threatened by the women's movement, by seeing black women coming onto the scene and offering perhaps a little better image of leadership. . . . When you look at Dallas, there's just not that much black male leadership emerging in terms of . . . trust, reliability, taking stands and holding them, win or lose. You see a little bit more of the what's-in-it-for-me kind of thing, and it troubles me.

"I made up my mind before taking this job [with HEW] that I would not feel comfortable, nor would I feel that I would be doing justice to my own community, if I just broke my ties there. I knew within myself that if I did completely, there would be a void. . . . When issues came up, unless I called the meeting and did the follow-through, almost single-handedly, it was just not going to happen.

"I realize that I can do only so much as an individual. But I have told my story over and over to different groups of people and pleaded and begged . . . but even in this last election, we couldn't get a black headquarters open. We didn't have a headquarters in the black community to generate interest and get the black vote out until I sat down with the group, in my usual fashion that they've depended on me to do for the last seven or eight years, and got it open. And even at that point, when I was at work and really governed by the Hatch Act [which prohibits government employees from taking part in partisan political activities], I was still getting calls about 'How do we do this?' or 'How do we call for that?' So I sat down at night and wrote down outlines of things that needed to be done. It's almost like needing Mother around. . . . But I refuse to believe that it takes me. I really think that what it takes is to have a few people get involved and have one or two successes."

A few months after that interview, in mid-1979, Johnson did take a new job, as executive assistant to the administrator of the Health Services Administration in Washington. Although the job permitted visits to Dallas with some frequency, her move was also, she said, an affirmation of her belief that "there is new leadership coming along."

If success stories are the key, they should not be scarce in the next decade for blacks. Particularly economic success stories. Louis Martin noted that the Carter Administration had boosted the amount of government contracts set aside for minority enterprises from less than $1 billion in 1976 to over $3 billion in fiscal year 1980. That means not only profits but jobs going into the black community.

Eleanor Holmes Norton, while conceding that affirmative-action programs "will not help people without skills," nonetheless predicted that the 1980s will be a "golden period" for trained and educated black youths. "The Labor Department predicts there will be something approaching a labor shortage in this country by the mid-1980s," she said. "I do not expect the country to fill this shortage by going around the world looking for immigrants. I expect it to look inside. And that is when the rising education levels of blacks, and affirmative-action programs that guide employers to nontraditional labor sources, will really pay off."

If Norton is right, the change should be dramatic, for it is difficult to overstate the educational gains that blacks have made in recent years. Between 1960 and 1978, the percentage of young black people (25 to 34) with at least a high-school diploma jumped from 33 percent to 73 percent, while the comparable percentages for white youths went from 61 to 85 percent. Another way of putting it is that in those eighteen years, young blacks overcame more than half their education disadvantage when compared with whites.

For those blacks who have not only an education but a political bent, the opportunities will be greater—but so will the competition. The best example of that may be found in Memphis, where the Ford brothers' political dynasty is the object of jealous attention from other black politicians.

Dedrick Withers, the grandson of a black lieutenant in Boss Crump's Memphis machine, was only 22 years old when he upset the white incumbent, a local labor leader, and won the Democratic nomination for a seat in the Tennessee House of Representatives. When he took office, he was the youngest black elected official in the country. In 1979, at the ripe old age of 27, he was taking dead aim on the congressional seat held by Harold Ford, and was contemplating a challenge to Ford as early as 1982.

Withers is nothing if not brash and bold. His first campaign headquarters was his Volkswagen Beetle, which his opponent arranged to have the police impound four days before the primary. He won that race by 188 votes, and his victory, he said, came from "a part of my district called White Haven. You can imagine what that was like. I was viewed as a Black Panther because I was young and long-haired and all that. So when I walked door to door in White Haven I got spit on, and had dogs sicked on me, and all that. But along with that, I got welcomed into some homes and had an opportunity to sit down and talk with them. And I believe that those who ended up voting for me realized I wasn't anybody who was interested in burning their house down and killing them.

"One man sicked his dog—a Doberman pinscher—on me, and I just went up the tree. He came out to the tree, and I said, 'Well, sir, you just take your dog away and I'll go on about my business.' And he said, 'Well, nigger, if you got the nerve to come up here, I got the nerve to sit down and talk with you.' And we ended up in his living room talking."

Withers made the point that "Malcolm X once said that we are unique in America because we can choose whether to try to change this country by taking up the bullet or taking up the ballot. We do truly, genuinely, have an opportunity through this system—to change it with the ballot. I believe that. I really believe that."

In that belief lies the hope that the blacks' economic gains—which seem certain—will be broadly shared and not selfishly hoarded.

SHAPES OF THINGS TO COME

Since the days when the fleet of Columbus sailed into the waters of the New World, America has been another name for opportunity, and the people of the United States have taken their tone from the incessant expansion which has not only been open but has even been forced upon them. He would be a rash prophet who should assert that the expansive character of American life has now entirely ceased. Movement has been its dominant fact, and, unless this training has no effect upon a people, the American energy will continually demand a wider field for its exercise.

—*Frederick Jackson Turner*

Perhaps the most provocative and influential essay ever written about the evolution of the society and politics of the United States was Frederick Jackson Turner's paper "The Significance of the Frontier in American History." Delivered originally to the American Historical Society in 1893, it was a persuasive argument that the clues to the development of America's governmental structure, its social customs and its democratic institutions lay in the existence of an open frontier, ever available for settlement. "The frontier promoted the formation of a composite nationality . . . the nationalization of the government . . . the evolution of democracy . . . and intellectual traits of profound importance," he wrote.

When the 32-year-old University of Wisconsin historian delivered his essay, the superintendent of the Census had but recently noted the closing of the last frontier, an event which Turner was sure marked the end of the first period of American history.

In a sense, the Census judgment was premature, and not just because Alaska, with its vast lands, and Hawaii were yet to be added to the Union. Throughout the span of almost a century which has followed the official "closing" of the frontier, Americans have continued to move on to new frontiers—both literally and figuratively speaking.

As a strictly amateur historian, I share Turner's belief that it is the people at the frontiers of the American experience who continue, in our time, to forecast and, in a sense, to determine the emerging character of the nation, its government, its laws and its politics. For that reason, the next chapters, the concluding section of this book, deal with some of those who are exploring the outer edges—the growth areas—of American society and culture.

We begin with two chapters focusing on the geographical areas of most rapid population increase—the suburbs, the West and the South, in that order. These are the places to which Americans have moved by the millions in the past twenty years, and from which, as a direct result, more and more of our leaders will be drawn in the remainder of this century.

As Turner suggested, these frontier areas have bred distinctive types of leaders. Of course, they differ from each other as individuals, but they also display some common characteristics which make them easily distinguishable from their counterparts in the older, more established or declining sectors of the country.

We look at the politicians of suburbia, the West and the South principally in terms of those common and distinctive traits—including their shared preoccupation with the environmental and economic issues that are the direct by-products of growth itself.

Then, in Chapter 14, the focus switches to that man-made frontier of television. It is almost a cliché to say that this is the "television generation" which is about to take over the country, the first generation in our history reared from infancy in front of the orthicon tube. Its members proclaim themselves different from their book-reading parents. But in what ways? And how has the communication revolution, which has established television as the principal source of the nation's shared knowledge of itself, changed politics and government?

From that question, we turn in Chapter 15 to an exploration of the frontier of ideas and look at some of the idea brokers who are important to this oncoming generation of American leaders. The focus is on two groups. The first is the private political pollsters who interpret the vague murmurings of the public for those who seek to lead the nation. Their own perceptions—and prejudices—inevitably shape the view of reality adopted by those leaders, suggesting to some that there is a national malaise and to others that an opportunity is just waiting to be seized. Along with them, we meet three young journalists of print and television who, by virtue of their following among the public and among the politicians, deserve to be considered influential forces for the future of our politics.

The following chapter discusses the newest members of an unofficial academy which plays an enduringly important part in American government and politics. These are the "new pros," the junior partners of that bipartisan establishment which always seems to have someone ready to be Secretary of State or assistant to the President, to carry the toughest bills in the legislature or to make the hardest budget choices. Even among these "pros," who will never be far from the center of action, no matter who is in power, there are important signs of the new-frontier psychology at work—in the suburban reformer turned political operative, for example, or the son of a show-biz couple now shaping foreign policy.

Many of these younger politicians are impatient with the past. But the irony is that even in their impatience for change, this next generation is harking back to one of the oldest and most important American traditions. As Turner wrote of 17th- and 18th-century Americans, "In spite of environment and in spite of custom, each frontier did indeed furnish a new field of opportunity, a gate of escape from the bondage of the past. And freshness, and confidence, and scorn of older society, impatience of its restraints and its ideas, and indifference to its lessons, have accompanied the frontier."

That statement is no less true of the next generation of America's leaders, exploring their own frontiers.

12 · Frontiers I and II: Suburbia and the West

THE UNITED STATES is no longer a nation of immigrants. It is a nation of migrants. Immigration peaked in the decade of the 1910s and has been declining ever since. But the restless movement that Frederick Jackson Turner noted in his essay as the distinguishing characteristic of Americans has accelerated, not diminished, since the "closing" of the frontier almost a century ago. The "new frontiers" of American society—the suburbs, the West and the South—which have become the destination for the tides of internal migration are playing an ever-more-important role in the reshaping of American politics.

As suburban population swelled, largely at the expense of inner cities, congressional representation since World War II has given suburbia increasing political clout. In 1970, a man who began his political career as a Western suburban Congressman, Richard M. Nixon, was sitting in the White House, and a suburban county executive from Maryland—Spiro T. Agnew—was "a heartbeat away" in the vice presidency.

A decade later, Richard Nixon had been replaced by Jimmy Carter, a symbol and leader of a "New South" no longer isolated from the mainstream of American politics by the issue of racial segregation. And Spiro Agnew had been succeeded by Walter F. Mondale, a resident of the tiny town of Afton, a suburb of Minneapolis–St. Paul, Minnesota.

The shifts of the past twenty years will become even more visible and important as we move into the 1980s. The 1980 Census is expected to show that the population center of the country has, for the first time, moved west of the Mississippi River. And if projections are correct, the 1980 Census will also shift enough House seats to the South and the West that, for the first time in history, they will control the majority in both houses of Congress and in the Electoral College.

Within these regions, the greatest areas of growth have been the suburbs and, lately and dramatically, the nonmetropolitan areas. During the 1950s, the suburbs grew five times as fast as the central cities of the nation; during the 1960s, the differential was 4 to 1 and in the 1970s, central cities were losing .4 percent of their population each year while suburbs swelled by 1.5 percent annually. As a result, the proportion of Americans living in central cities has declined from 32.8 percent in 1950 to an estimated 30.9 percent in 1975, while the suburban share has risen from 23.3 percent to 42.1 percent. An additional seven House seats are expected to be lost by the cities to suburban districts in the reapportionment following the 1980 Census.

The bare statistics conceal the amount of individual movement that has taken place. Between 1975 and 1978, for example, the South gained an estimated 1 million people through net in-migration. But that was the result of almost 5 million individual moves—2.9 million people moving into the region and 1.9 million moving out. Americans are extraordinarily footloose. The Census Bureau estimates that the average individual changes residence every five years. (And it is not unusual for people to find political careers in areas far removed from their homes. For example, two young conservative Congressmen discussed elsewhere in this book, Representatives Robert K. Dornan and Jack Kemp, have, in effect, switched places. Dornan was born in New York and built his political career in California; Kemp did just the opposite.)

For three-quarters of a century, after the Civil War, there were three main streams of internal migration in the United States. One was the east-to-west movement of which Turner wrote in his famous essay. The second was a movement from the country to the city. And the third was the flow of population from the South to the North.

Since the end of World War II, two of those three main patterns have been reversed, with dramatic effect on the nation's political geography. The east-to-west flow has continued and accelerated, with almost 5 million people migrating to the West in the past twenty years. But the migration from rural to urban areas, which was spurred by the industrial expansion during and following both world wars, slowed to a trickle by 1970. During the past decade, while the flow from center city to suburb has continued, something over 2 million people moved from metropolitan areas to less-developed counties. In part, this was a spillover from the cities, as a search for space drove people into ever-longer commuting patterns. But a significant part of the movement represented the development of large-scale "retirement areas" in previously rural areas from the Southwest to the Ozarks to Florida.

In some ways, the most dramatic reversal has been in the North–South flow. Even after World War II, the South retained its role as an exporter of population. There were growth states like Florida, but they were more than offset by such steady losers as Mississippi and Arkansas.

But by 1977, every Southern state could claim net in-migration for the decade, and the gains for the region as a whole were probably closer to 4 million than 3 million people. In the closing years of the decade, the South was attracting more people than the West for the first time.

The migrants are not a cross section of the population. While retirees seeking warm climates, lower housing costs and lighter taxes are an important stream, the highest mobility rates are generally found among people in their twenties. Jeanne C. Biggar of the University of Virginia said, in a 1979 study for the Population Reference Bureau, that the median age for migrants to the West in the three previous years was 25.8 and for migrants to the South, 24.5. About one in five of them is a person in a professional job, and about one in seven has gone beyond four years of college—both well above the national norms. What is true of the South and the West is also true of suburbia. While some of the older, inner-ring suburbs of the Northeast have themselves developed pockets of poverty and the social problems that go with them, the gap between central city and suburbs is still significant. The past decade has seen a major shift of new-job location from city to suburb, increasing the market for technical, white-collar and professional employment in suburbia.

Thus, the expansion of the South, the West and suburbia has meant a transfer to these areas of people and money, of education and expertise—that is, of all the ingredients of political power in a society like ours. But it has also meant a transformation of politics in both substance and technique.

The substance has changed because of a conflict inherent in the very migration patterns that have brought new power to these areas. The main reason for moving—cited by more than half the people in a Census Bureau survey—is either the search for a job in an area of economic expansion or the transfer of an existing job in that area. But the next-most-important motivation is the quality of life—climate, cleanliness of air, access to recreation and, of course, the avoidance of both the environmental and the social problems of the areas being left behind.

Given the mixture of motivations of those who are swelling their populations, it is not surprising that almost all the growth areas find their politics dominated by the two sides of the "growth question" itself—the individual and collective gains to be realized by encouraging new capital, new jobs and new people to move into the area vs. the dangers to the environment, the community values and the amenities of life that can result from that kind of accelerated growth.

Nor is it surprising, given the mobility of the people who have fueled the growth of these areas, that the style and structure of politics in these areas are a good deal less rigid or predictable than those of older, declining political centers—thus making it easier to enter politics from a variety of backgrounds and to advance at a more rapid pace. Among the cross section of "growth area" politicians in this chapter and the next are people who were running major suburban counties at 26, and who were elected Governor at 32 or Senator at 34. It is also easier to change parties —as many of these people did at least once and one man did three times in a still-incomplete political career—or to ignore parties entirely, as many of them do to the maximum extent possible.

While partisanship is not important, other qualities are. In an atmosphere where people like to feel removed from the crass conduct of the city machines, the politicians display a conspicuous concern for public and personal ethics and appear to scorn patronage in all its connotations. In communities where private-sector managers congregate, a "professional approach" to government is highly prized. Most of the politicians in this chapter have fought their way through to their own resolution of the two sides of the "growth question," and have developed techniques for communicating their approach through the mass media to voters who may have few other links to their elected officials.

This pattern and style of politics has been noted by students of suburban politics from the 1950s onward. It is also, and increasingly, the dominant pattern of politics in the growth area of the West. And, as will be seen in the next chapter, it is now showing up with increasing frequency in the South, replacing the politics of race which dominated that region for a century before, and a century after, the Civil War. With the South, the West and suburbia all practicing this kind of politics, it is rapidly becoming the dominant politics of the nation—with consequences both healthy and dismaying. An exploration of these changes begins in the place where they first appeared—in the suburbs.

It began for Carolyn Whittle, a pretty White Plains, New York, homemaker and mother of two young children, one evening in 1973. "I had just finished testifying to the Common Council on behalf of the Sierra Club against that awful elevated highway they wanted to put through here, and some friends of mine said, 'Come with us, we want to go to the Democrats' slating meeting,' " she recalled. "The next thing I knew I was running for the county legislature."

Whittle was 28 then, and had migrated, first with her parents and then with her husband, from Seattle, Washington, to Cairo, Illinois, to the Chicago suburbs, to Wisconsin, to the Boston suburbs and, less than two years before, to Westchester County, the classic suburb north of New York City between the Hudson River and Long Island Sound.

She was, in many respects, a typical suburban homemaker. Her husband, a management consultant, traveled extensively in his work, "so I have become involved in politics." In Wisconsin, she worked for Eugene

McCarthy; and in Massachusetts, she helped elect Representative Robert Drinan, a liberal Democratic priest, to Congress. "I got involved in the environmental movement strictly for personal reasons," she said. "Right after the birth of my son, I got this awareness that things were going wrong with the air and water around us, and I wanted to do something about it." She began researching the use of chemicals as highway de-icing agents and became a volunteer lobbyist for the Audubon Society in the Massachusetts Legislature, eventually persuading that body to control substances that could pollute ponds and harm wildlife.

"When I was uprooted—when we were transferred to New York—I immediately wanted to get involved with an organization that was doing the same kind of thing, so I organized the Sierra Club for Westchester, Rockland and Putnam counties, and began working on the environmental issues, transportation, water pollution and the rest.

"But it was almost an accident that I became a candidate. They had never elected a woman *or* a Democrat from my district, so it wasn't that they were giving me such a prize. The party gave me $100 when I was nominated, and they manned the polls on election day, but in between I was completely on my own.

"I started with six of my close friends, women I had met at the League of Women Voters and the YWCA—places where newcomers congregate. They had coffees for me in their homes, and I met their friends."

Soon there was a headquarters staff of seventy-five women volunteers, and Whittle could begin contacting voters. Her literature emphasized purely local concerns—a proposed highway that would cut off Battle Hill from the rest of the city; the feasibility of closing an incinerator that was a source of air pollution; the need for a county consumer agency.

"At first," she said, "it seemed just hopeless. The district had a 4,000-vote Republican registration edge, and I was running against a real dynasty. My opponent's grandfather had been Mayor of White Plains, and Henry R. Barrett III had been in the county legislature for six years himself. But he did no research and he did no work. He didn't even discover I was a newcomer until two weeks before election day—too late to exploit that issue. I shook 11,000 hands and won by 98 votes, and here I am. We always had this image of David and Goliath, and we were shocked when Goliath fell so easily."

Carolyn Whittle was not unique in upsetting the political odds in Westchester County in 1973. On the same day she ended the Barrett dynasty, Alfred B. DelBello, then the 36-year-old Mayor of Yonkers, became the first Democrat elected as Westchester County Executive. DelBello was no newcomer, but a third-generation Yonkers lawyer. Four years before, after four years of service on the city council, he had been the first Democrat since Depression days to win the Yonkers mayoralty. He came into a city hall wracked by scandal and threatened by bankruptcy, and demonstrated the kind of politics that has since become his trademark. He went outside for a city manager and other key appointees, overhauled the bureaucracy, aggressively sought federal aid, cleared a $15-million debt and produced the first balanced budget in twelve years. At the same time, he pushed hard for slum clearance, housing, parks and environmental, manpower and consumer-protection programs.

During the eight years that DelBello was getting his basic governmental training in Yonkers and for eight years before that, Westchester County was being run by a remarkable Republican County Executive named Edward G. Michaelian. Michaelian was one of the inventors of what is now called "urban county government," a development that has lifted this largely rural relic of the past into an active role in today's political structure. What had been a stagnant, patronage-dominated level of government—concerned only with rural road maintenance and running the county poor farm, the home for the elderly and the jail—became in the hands of Michaelian and others like him a mechanism for overcoming the fragmentation of jurisdictions within metropolitan areas and delivering a wide variety of social services.

During Michaelian's time, too, Westchester Republicans appeared to be securely in the saddle. For much of his era, the Governor (Nelson A. Rockefeller), the Lieutenant Governor (Malcolm Wilson) and several Republican state chairmen all called Westchester their home.

But beneath the surface, the GOP grip was weakening, there as in many other areas. Democrats moving out from New York City were cutting the Republican registration lead. A Conservative Party was drawing strength from the opposite flank. In 1973, when Michaelian stepped down, there was a three-way Republican primary, and the lingering bitterness helped DelBello squeeze out a 3,000-vote upset. Four years later, in 1977, he was re-elected with a 60-percent landslide, while Whittle was winning her third two-year term in the county legislature.

In those four years, DelBello launched a wide variety of human-service programs: senior citizens' discounts at more than two thousand stores; a consumer-protection agency; a women's center to furnish free vocational and personal counseling; mobile recreation vehicles; a county art gallery and theater; outreach programs aimed at dropouts, potential food-stamp beneficiaries and others.

But at the same time, he maintained the county's AAA bond rating during all the period of the New York City financial crisis and provided modest relief for property-tax payers.

For Whittle too, there have been accomplishments, even though she says she has learned "it takes two or three years at least to see a program come to fruition": the consumer-affairs office was part of her original platform; a "meals on wheels" program is operating in White Plains; shelters have been built for bus patrons, without the expenditure of public funds; a pilot project in solar energy has been started; instead of the massive elevated highway against which she campaigned, the city has installed a computerized traffic-signal system to move cars through its streets.

But it has not all been smooth. A county solid-waste-disposal program, which was one of DelBello's top priorities, was still locked in controversy five years later. There were sharp tensions between him and the board of legislators, not only because of its Republican majority but because his managerial style left the legislators frequently complaining about lack of consultation. And despite DelBello's personal success, his arm's-length attitude toward the Democratic Party left many of its leaders frustrated at their inability to build on his strength.

On the last point, DelBello, like many other growth-area politicians, is unapologetic. Conceding that his relations with the Democratic Party organization have been "difficult," he maintained that "a New York City patronage-type Democrat couldn't be successful here. You have to have a lot more openness in style, a moderate posture, certain liberal positions, some conservative—you mix it up, so you can't be typed. It's not a question of whether you're liberal or conservative but if you're committed and competent and capable of performing. And that has nothing to do with patronage."

From the first, DelBello has been adamant on the question of patronage. "The patronage system as it used to operate is no longer relevant," he said. "Giving jobs to a few of the faithful is just not meaningful. Sure, some low-level jobs you'd give to the people you know, rather than those you don't know. But not the supervisory, managerial jobs."

When DelBello took office, he went outside Westchester to fill his top four jobs—the commissioners of hospitals, transportation, corrections and finance. The "professional approach" impressed many voters, but it left a party that was savoring victory for the first time in two hundred years wondering why none of its stalwarts was qualified for these $35,000-to-$40,000-a-year jobs. And the questions grew louder as Republicans continued to dominate other county offices during the DelBello years.

The kind of social and environmental concerns that motivated a Carolyn Whittle to enter politics are far from uncommon in suburban settings. In Dade County, Florida, a transplanted New Yorker named Harvey Ruvin has been involved in the same struggle for the last eight years as a member of the county commission.

Ruvin, 43, was, like Carolyn Whittle, an activist in the anti-war movement and the environmental battles of the Sixties. In 1968, Ruvin knocked on the doors of all 1,500 registered voters in North Bay Village, a tiny suburb of Miami consisting of three man-made islands in the middle of Biscayne Bay, and was elected Mayor. His first move was to call Buckminster Fuller, the visionary planner whose writings he had long admired, "to get some advice on his concept of floating-island situations." In three days of talks in New York, which, Ruvin said, "had more influence on my thinking than anything in my whole life," Fuller convinced him that "since the depth of the Bay is only about six feet there, you're not about to be able to float any sort of land mass." But he also persuaded Ruvin that the issues of growth and the environment—which had prompted Ruvin to become president of the Dade County Audubon Society—were even more important than he had realized.

Two years later, lawyer Ruvin represented the Key Biscayne taxpayers' association in a referendum on a county ordinance allowing a short-term moratorium on building in areas like Key Biscayne, where existing zoning laws threatened serious overcrowding and environmental damage.

The effort produced 20,000 signatures to place the initiative on the ballot, and it was approved by a 3-to-1 margin. When the county commission took no steps to implement its provisions, Ruvin in 1972 decided to run for the commission himself, as an independent candidate. He campaigned on a "good news/bad news" platform. "The good news is that if nothing is done, by 1980 everybody will be drinking raw sewage. The bad news is that at the rate we have been growing, there won't be enough of it to go around."

Created in 1956, the Metro Dade County government has broader powers and responsibilities than most area governments, and is strengthened by the fact that more than half the population it serves is outside the incorporated cities, in the suburban growth belt.

In Ruvin's first year on the board, it won public approval of a $700-million "decade of progress" bond issue for mass transit, waste disposal and other basic services needed to accommodate a growing population.

In 1974, it adopted a land-use plan creating special zoning districts where development would be limited to protect the basic ecological system, particularly the natural water-retention-and-recharge area west of Miami toward the Everglades. Ruvin reports broad acceptance of what were once controversial growth-planning strategies.

"I think there is a general consensus even in the building industry that this was needed," he said. "The worst proposals we're seeing now from developers are better than anything that was proposed before, because the developers, I think, are beginning to realize that the amenities—the open space and the uncrowded kind of living—are salable items. People are not complaining about them, because they can make them features of their projects.

"I think we've struck a pretty good compromise," he said, setting a theme that one can hear time and time again from successful growth-area politicians. "We want growth, but we want to make sure that that growth is healthy. And we define healthy growth as being timed to the provision of all the services that are needed to support it and consistent with the carrying capacity of the land. Obviously, South Florida is a very desirable area, and we can't put up a gate or a fence. But we don't want to see people coming in at such a rate, as was happening without the safeguards, that it would eventually destroy what they were coming here to enjoy."

It is no accident that the political machines which grew up and flourished in almost all the old urban centers have failed to take root in suburbia. In the cities, population was compressed, neighborhoods typically had a clear ethnic base and there was generally a prevailing party preference or ideology. In a small sphere and with an ordered daily routine, political information could be disseminated through close human contact; threats could be made, favors dispensed and people's political behavior monitored. This system of space and time naturally gave rise to an ordered system of brokerage politics, based on mediation of conflicts by explicit hierarchies or machines.

The suburbs are based on significantly different space and time dimensions. These areas grew wildly after World War II, which had imposed a moratorium on housing growth while it disrupted many lives. Changes in technology—television, the commuter roads, the second car—increased personal time and space and societal distance, so the social networks and politics itself became more diffuse. Suburbanization was seen by many as an escape from ethnicity into cultural homogeneity, so nonpartisanship and political independence assumed positive values.

One of the few places where an effective political machine run by an old-fashioned boss survived in a predominantly suburban setting well into the 1970s was in Essex County, New Jersey. Perhaps because the city of Newark still contained over one-third of the county's more than 800,000 people, and perhaps because New Jersey's state governmental structure still provides strong patronage incentives for solid vote-delivering blocs, the pre–World War II Democratic political machine maintained its sway in Essex County until 1978, guided for the last decade by a boss named Harry Lerner. In 1978, it was overthrown by a most implausible figure, even for a growth-area politician, a 26-year-old man named Peter Shapiro. In 1969, he was suspended from Columbia High School in Maplewood for distributing anti–Vietnam war literature. Nine years later, he was running the county government as its first elected County Executive.

Shapiro, whose father is a surgeon and whose mother runs a bookstore, is an exceptionally bright and handsome young man. He went to Harvard, became managing editor of *The Harvard Crimson* and worked in the Washington bureau of *The Wall Street Journal* only long enough to decide that most journalists were "frustrated" and most Washington politicians "mediocre." Armed with these insights, he returned to New Jersey, worked briefly for the state Department of Transportation and then, in 1975, filed for the state Assembly, challenging the Democratic incumbent to a primary fight in a district that was regarded as an organization stronghold.

"All of the good anti-machine Democrats told me, 'You're crazy. You can't win in this kind of district.' And I said, 'This is where I live, though.' Perhaps if I had known more, I never would have started," he said.

But Shapiro went out on the same kind of handshaking campaign that won for Whittle, DelBello and Ruvin, and, catching the organization asleep, won the nomination by 191 votes. At 23, he was sworn in as the youngest member in the history of the New Jersey Legislature, and soon won recognition as its most productive freshman legislator. He sponsored successful bills to provide low-cost "lifeline" utility rates for the elderly, to permit generic drug prescriptions, and to mandate tenant rebates and anti-redlining laws. But he also supported creation of a state income tax, abortion rights for women and decriminalization of marijuana—issues which, he noted, "are not considered to be conventionally politically helpful . . . in a district which is dominated by blue-collar Catholic voters."

Nonetheless, he was easily re-elected in 1977, the same year a group of anti-organization "reformers," led by the League of Women Voters, finally succeeded in forcing a referendum on creating a new form of county government. The new government would be headed by a County Executive, with powers great enough to challenge Lerner's authority as the boss of the county.

Under the old system, as Shapiro was later to remark, "the power structure in the county was very similar in a sense to Communist China under Mao Tse-tung. The party chairman was the one who ran the show. The elected officials were more or less window dressing." Although Lerner, who owned a cab company and insurance firms in Newark, did not hold public office during most of his time as county boss, "he was," Shapiro said, "involved in the most minute level that had to do with any appointment, any compensation, any contract that went through the county. And the county was basically structured to do only that.

"The Democratic chairman of almost every one of the towns and every one of the Newark wards had a job on the county payroll," Shapiro said, and usually in a position that gave Lerner knowledge and leverage in a vital area. "The East Ward chairman was a tax commissioner. The Central Ward chairman was the assistant registrar of mortgages and deeds. The South Ward chairman was a county freeholder. The North Ward chairman was an assistant county counsel. The West Ward chairman was the secretary of the board of tax appeals. The Irvington chairman was the county undersheriff. The Maplewood chairman was the assistant county purchasing agent. The East Orange chairman was the warden of the county jail. The Bloomfield chairman was the superintendent of public works. Every single one of them down the line."

In 1977 Shapiro was the only Democratic officeholder to support the new county charter, and he campaigned as hard for its passage as he did for his own re-election to the legislature. When it passed, he was the logical "reform" candidate for the newly created post of County Executive, and in 1978 he won another hard-fought primary against Lerner's candidate by 2,800 votes out of 82,000 cast. In predominantly Democratic Essex County, the general election was relatively easy, and Shapiro breezed in with 61 percent of the vote. He was aided in the campaign by an appearance from his Harvard classmate Robert F. Kennedy, Jr., and by the discovery by Shapiro campaign researchers that his Republican opponent had never registered to vote until a few weeks before the June primary.

Before Shapiro took office, Harry Lerner resigned as Essex County Democratic chairman, and a few months later was indicted along with three others in the old government on federal racketeering, bribery and extortion charges.

That sounds like the end of a modern morality play; but for Shapiro it was, of course, just the beginning of the task of creating a new government and meeting the needs of an urban county with as many problems as any metropolitan area in the country. After a year in his job, he had learned what Al DelBello and others had found before him: "It's tough—tougher than I expected." The remnants of the old machine successfully resisted his attempt to install one of his own allies as the county Democratic chairman. Nurses, welfare workers and vocational-school teachers went out on strike, at different times, in an effort to pressure him for higher spending. More broadly, Shapiro said, the bureaucracy that had been created in the old system of feudal political baronies proved very resistant to his efforts at modern, centralized management.

If one asks what it is about the suburban politicians that makes substantive success so difficult for them to achieve, one approaches the heart of a paradox that is of growing importance for all of American politics. As the successful suburban-style politician has been copied in other growth areas, notably the West and South, the characteristics of the breed have become better known—for good or for ill—not just in their own jurisdictions but increasingly in national politics as well.

This is a kind of politics, as Ann Lennarson Greer and Scott Greer say in their study "Suburban Political Behavior: A Matter of Trust," that depends more on "value representation" than on issue representation. Jimmy Carter's 1976 presidential campaign was as much an expression of this style as were the races of Carolyn Whittle and Harvey Ruvin. It is a highly personalized approach, depending on the establishment of a relationship of confidence between the individual vôter and the individual office seeker. As long as the candidate appears to be open, honest, accessible and hardworking, his constituents are likely to be tolerant—as Shapiro noted his were—of the instances in which his votes deviate from their predominant beliefs. What they most seek and cherish in their politicians is a sense of professional competence and independence. And for many of the politicians, the easiest way to communicate those qualities is by doing what DelBello and Shapiro have done in their own ways—rejecting the patronage policies and political discipline of the old machines. Suburbia is the incubator of the anti-politics politician who is coming to be such a factor in our lives.

Representative Christopher J. Dodd (a Democrat and one of the Peace Corps alumni mentioned in Chapter 2) represents a largely suburban district in Connecticut. He made a point in an interview of saying that until he decided in 1979 to run for the Senate in 1980, "I had not set foot in the doors of the Democratic state headquarters. I just didn't have any reason to.

"What I have done, in a sense," he said, "is become my own institution. I have my own volunteers, my own political people. I've become a bit more sophisticated, maybe, but each one of us—the newer people, who were so critical of the power structures—has created our own little power structures."

Dodd then referred to the accoutrements of the modern suburban politicians—the district offices to handle constituent problems with government; the mobile vans that tour the shopping centers to make it even easier for constituents to receive that kind of aid; the frequent town meetings, where the officeholder reports on his activities and answers constituents' questions.

"Call it what you want," he said, "but basically it is the old spoils system, only this time it's not jobs or contracts we're handing out, but constituent service. I reach out to people. I think it's a worthwhile thing to do, and I do it because I feel it's important to maintain accessibility.

But I also know that the political spin-offs are most positive. Going back every week, going to a lot of these events, sitting down and listening to personal problems, I suppose one could argue that it detracts from your legislative or governmental responsibilities to some extent, but I feel it's important today in the total concept of public service."

The same ambivalence that Dodd expressed can be found among other suburban politicians in the House, who are struggling to balance the "independence" that suits so well the political climate of their constituency with the need for a degree of party discipline for Congress to be able to function.

In the "Watergate election" of 1974, Democrats won 21 previously Republican suburban districts. While Dodd was gaining his House seat in Connecticut, Representative James J. Blanchard, now 38, was taking over a House seat in Oakland County, Michigan, a suburb of Detroit. Like Dodd, Blanchard was a Democrat by inheritance and conviction, adaptable enough to feel at home both in the United Auto Workers hall and with the solar-power advocates or environmentalists. Like Dodd, he quickly discovered that attentive care to constituents' services was the key to political security in Republican territory, and he plastered the district with billboards advertising his phone number ("If I can help you, let me know") and cruised the district's shopping centers in his mobile office.

Blanchard became a prime House sponsor of the "sunset bill," which would require regular review and reauthorization of existing federal programs. It was the legislative equivalent of the zero-based budgeting which became a favorite of managerial-minded suburban politicians like DelBello and Whittle—a way of demonstrating to the taxpayers the officeholders' concern for the efficiency of government. It was, not surprisingly, strongly supported by Common Cause, the archetypal suburban, nonpartisan, good-government organization of the 1970s.

Dodd and Blanchard, like many others in the big Democratic freshman class of 1974, had served no apprenticeship in public office before coming to Congress. But perhaps because of their inherited Democratic leanings, they were soon identified by their elders as more "organization-minded" than most of their contemporaries, and both were made "assistant whips" (that is, given part of the responsibility of corralling the independent-minded newcomers behind the party leadership's program).

It was no easy task. After four years in the House, Blanchard pronounced himself frustrated with having to deal with "the anti-politics people" who, he said, "refuse to come to grips with this system and make it work."

"It's hard, it's awfully hard," his friend Chris Dodd echoed. Acknowledging that his criticism could be made of himself as well as others, Dodd said, "There are so many people here who don't want to feel they have to be responsible to the leadership. They see themselves as being leaders in their own right. Unless we get to the point that some people are willing to be foot soldiers while others are leaders, I really question the ability of this institution to come to grips with the problems that face us."

The question whether these individualistic, autonomous politicians can make the institutions of government work was one of the largest questions being asked about American politics as the Eighties began. And it was complicated by the growing awareness of the sharp regional differences that persisted—in some cases in heightened fashion—between the frontier areas and the older regions of America. Those differences come into clearer perspective as one moves from suburbia to the politicians of the frontier West.

If there is such a thing as a quintessential Western politician, Republican Senator Alan K. Simpson of Wyoming could play the part. The son of former Governor and Senator Milward L. Simpson, he graduated from the University of Wyoming and its law school, and served fourteen years in the state legislature. The reason for that long apprenticeship was not that Simpson was lacking in ambition, but simply that he wanted his three children to grow up in Wyoming. In 1978, when the youngest of them was 15, Simpson ran for the Senate and won easily. At 49, the balding, six-foot-seven-inch-tall Senator looked and talked like a cowboy—relaxed, funny, direct, blunt, profane and ingratiating. In a Washington drawing room he was likely to break up a serious discussion by suddenly performing one of his Cheyenne bar tricks—flipping a silver dollar in the air, catching it just above the floor with the heel of his cowboy boot and sending it up over his head into his opposite hand.

In his essay, Frederick Jackson Turner wrote that "the most important effect of the frontier" was an environment that is "productive of individualism." If individualism characterizes the politics of today's suburban frontier, then it is even more pronounced in the West. "What's funny about Wyoming politics," Simpson said one day during his first year in the Senate, "is you get elected and you're not known as Governor This or Senator That, the way you are in the bigger states. You're known as Al or Teno or Ed or Dick or Malcolm. And there is no awe connected with your effort. You walk down the street and they say, 'Hey, Al, for God's sake, I see you voted for the Education Department, you dumb son-of-a-bitch. What did you do that for?' And you say, 'Well, would you like to know?' And you tell 'em."

If nonpartisanship is the style in suburbia, it is even more so in the West. "Guys walk in the door here," Simpson said, gesturing around his

Senate office, "and you never know whether they're Democrats or Republicans, nor is that any entryway into public office. Ed Herschler [the Democratic Governor] is probably as conservative as many Republicans I know, but he believes in protecting the environment, just as I do. He and I were in the legislature together, sat next to each other for six years, and when we sponsored a bill we'd get it passed, because he'd work his troops and I'd work mine. We work well together now."

But as Simpson readily conceded, the happy picture of a first-naming, never-mind-the-party-label, all-pals-together politics did not mean there were no strong clashes of opinion or of interest. "The real one," he said, "is industry versus the environmentalists. And that's very shrill."

The environmental issue is one of the few in American history that have moved from the West to the East. In the 1950s and 1960s, environmentalists fought to stop the Hell's Canyon Dam in Idaho, to reclaim Lake Washington in Seattle and to save Pyramid Lake in Nevada. The Sierra Club in California raised basic challenges to the exploitation of public lands and the degradation of air and water quality. In the 1970s, environmentalism became a national issue, but the battle continued to be fought more bitterly in the West than anywhere else. There was one simple reason for that—a truth that Turner had recognized.

The fact was this: The West is rich in sunshine and space, in minerals and energy sources. But it is painfully short of water. The sunshine and the space have attracted millions of migrants; the resources—including two-thirds of the nation's coal reserves and 87 percent of its uranium—have drawn industry like a magnet. But west of the 100th meridian water is scarce, and the struggle for its use as bitter and bloody as any religious or racial war in history.

There is nothing new about this fundamental fact. Historian Walter Prescott Webb said, "The heart of the West is a desert, unqualified and absolute." Upstream and downstream states battled for years in court over the division of the Colorado River waters; farmers and cowmen had fought the same battle earlier in history.

But in the postwar years, the flood of migrants, greater in scale than the West had ever known before, brought developers into the battle against the agricultural interests and the environmentalists. And then, in the Seventies, the depletion of domestic oil supplies, and the staggering increases in overseas-petroleum prices, triggered an industrial rush to bring the coal and uranium of the West to market, which added an even more controversial element to the struggle. Western politicians, Republicans and Democrats alike, erupted in rage against Carter Administration policies which they saw as aiming to force them into mining their rangeland and cropland while, illogically (from their point of view), compelling them to put millions of additional acres into protected wilderness areas and (worst of all) attempting to cut off some of the water-storage and reclamation projects on which the West depended for the preservation of its most precious commodity.

In the late 1970s, "sagebrush rebellions" broke out against absentee control from Washington—and more than one Western politician argued that the West had replaced the South as the most put-upon region of the country.

If the West was virtually united against the Carter policies (as the 1976 election returns showed), it was anything but united within itself over how to resolve these tensions. Thornton Bradshaw, the president of the Atlantic-Richfield Oil Company, told Lou Cannon of *The Washington Post* in 1979, "All regions are conflicted. But the West is the most conflicted of all."

Alan Simpson said much the same thing about his own state of Wyoming, which was experiencing all of the counterpressures typical of the region.

It is also, Simpson said, what makes Wyoming politics "totally different" from what it was in his father's time. Milward Simpson, who was Governor from 1955 to 1959 and Senator from 1962 to 1967, "made a statement once," his son said, "that as far as he was concerned he'd just put a big fence around Wyoming with a dodge gate, so you could get out but you couldn't get back in. That was the attitude in the Fifties. In the Sixties, our Republican and Democratic administrations went out to lure industry into Wyoming. And now we're just hanging on tight, knowing they're coming anyway."

From 1970 to 1977, as the energy crisis spurred the exploration and exploitation of Wyoming's mineral resources, its population grew by an estimated 22.2 percent. There were bitter disputes, within the state, over wilderness areas, timber policies and the diversion of water to coal-slurry pipelines.

When I asked Simpson how a Wyoming politician operates in that kind of cross-fire, he answered in a way that once again, as with so many of the suburban politicians, emphasized the importance of personal qualities over specific ideology in growth-area politics.

"They hired me on, I guess," he said, "for my common sense, and that's not a laudatory or pompous statement. I say to them, 'Look, pal, I'm as ambivalent as you are, but I'm going to go out there and sort through the stack as best I can and come to what I think is a reasonable decision. And they are willing to take that statement, instead of saying, 'Wait a minute, Simpson, that's evasive.'

"But I don't skirt the issues," he said. "I have taken a pretty firm stand that I do not favor any further wilderness areas in Wyoming. We have twenty-three percent of them now, some of them sitting on what the geological data indicate may be a world-class oil field. That stand has placed me at odds with the environmental movement. But I also say I want SO_2 scrubbers on the coal, and that I want to ship our coal to Arkansas, instead of processing it in Wyoming, in order to protect our air. So I come down specifically on the issues as they come along, and then they have to run around guessing whether I'm a conservative or a liberal."

Simpson said he believed that if the federal government adopted what he called a "realistic" coal-leasing policy on the 50 percent of Wyoming's land it owns outright (another controversial issue), "then America will use Western coal to get out of the energy crunch. And that will mean a lot of development for Wyoming." (Delayed for years by environmental concerns while the Interior Department formulated land-use regulations, coal leasing was to resume in 1980 under procedures which Simpson and some others thought too protracted to encourage swift development of mineral reserves.)

Simpson contended that the state is ready for development, despite what many point to as the past mistakes in such coal "boom towns" as Rock Springs. "We have the best mined-land-reclamation law in America, so good the federal government doesn't even mess with it. We're not West Virginia. We have no cliffs and holes. We have housing laws, community-development authority, mineral trust funds and highway-development funds, all financed by the severance tax. We have an air-quality act, a water-quality act, a plant-siting law, a state land-use plan —I was the sponsor of that bill, and got an incredible amount of emotional flak. But we're ready. We have it all there, ready to go."

If Simpson represents the optimistic pole of political opinion about the chances of the West's meeting its challenges, then Democratic Governor Richard D. Lamm of Colorado, 45, probably is at the other pole. "I feel that this country is very future-blind," he said in a 1979 interview. "It's very myopic. . . . The political process in this state and in this country allows you to have all the foresight of the lookout on the *Titanic*."

Ironically, Lamm's own career constitutes something of a refutation of his argument. He is part of the postwar Western migration. A native of Wisconsin and a graduate of the University of Wisconsin, he was assigned by the Army to Fort Carson, Colorado, in 1957 and knew that Denver was the place he wanted to practice when he got his law degree from the University of California in 1961. Active in the civil-rights movement, Lamm was elected to the legislature in 1966 and promptly distinguished himself by sponsoring one of the most liberal abortion laws in the country. He became increasingly identified with environmental issues and, with

Sam Brown and other activists, led the fight for a 1972 referendum that kept the Winter Olympics from coming to Colorado in 1976. Lamm capitalized on the momentum of the Olympics victory to win his first term for Governor in 1974, hiking more than eight hundred miles around the state in a Western version of the door-to-door campaigning so many of the anti-politics suburban politicians favor.

As a legislator and as a gubernatorial candidate, Lamm had spoken and written with unusual eloquence of the dangers of unrestrained growth. "Increased population," he said in a 1969 article in the *Denver Post,* "is not only not an unquestioned blessing, but it may in fact be counterproductive to the amenities we are accustomed to. . . . Historically, 'selling Colorado' has meant more smog, more water pollution, more regimentation, more governmental control, less open space, less parks and recreation, less quiet."

In 1979, when Denver's air pollution was rated the worst of any city in the nation, *Denver Post* columnist Kenneth T. Walsh said Lamm "seems to have been proven correct on many issues that are pressing and vital today."

But Lamm himself was inclined to look on it as a lost decade. Like so many of the other "new politicians" of these growth areas, he had found the task of translating his policies into action far more difficult and frustrating than he had expected.

As a reformer, he had little claim on the loyalty of his own party, and the opposition Republicans who controlled the legislature were disinclined to give him much help. An effort in his early months in office to cut off funds for completion of an interstate-highway leg provoked a fearsome battle—and later Lamm was forced into an awkward compromise. In other areas he made even less headway. "The irony is," he said in 1979, "that we were closer to success on some of the things I fought for ten years ago than we are today. I missed passing a major land-use bill in 1969 by one vote. Hell, I wouldn't come near that close now."

While still arguing that what his state needed was "a dose of reality therapy from somebody who can show us that there is a lot of value in smaller and simpler life-styles," Lamm was ready to concede after five years as Governor that he had not found a way to administer that therapy. Echoing the theme of good management heard from so many of his suburban counterparts, he said, "Essentially, I make my mark by running government well and by handling crises. Leaders aren't leaders nowadays. I am essentially an umpire, a mediator. I call the balls and strikes as they come across society's 'plate,' and the different factions and groups and special interests decide who wins and who loses."

The final irony is that after five years, Lamm had become more of an umpire than an advocate even in environmental disputes. Because he supported some new industries entering the state—including a controversial uranium-mining company—he was denounced by some of the environmental activists who had been his original supporters.

"The first election [for Governor], it was a bunch of insurgents and environmentalists and quality-of-life people, Common Cause members, outsider groups that really put on a passionate crusade," he said. "This one [his re-election in 1978] was a very professionally run campaign by an incumbent Governor, a professional. It wasn't a Holy Crusade anymore."

Lamm may be one of those rare politicians who understate—rather than exaggerate—their own successes, for he emerged not only as a respected and potent political figure in his own state, but as the West's most effective advocate in its battles with the energy and water policies of the Carter Administration. Yet, as we will see in the next few pages, there are examples which suggest that efforts to plan and channel growth may not be as foredoomed as Lamm, in his gloomier moments, seemed to think.

There is, however, a special challenge in the frontier tradition for those who pursue such policies. "The tendency" of the frontier, Turner wrote, "is anti-social. It produces antipathy to control, and particularly to any direct control. The tax-gatherer is viewed as a representative of oppression . . . [and] individual liberty is sometimes confused with absence of all effective government."

Those tendencies were evident in the West in the 1970s, when the federal government (which owned almost half the land) was serving not just as tax collector but as landlord, regulator, inspector and—in Western eyes—maiden aunt. Western states in the Seventies sent to Washington several New Right senators whose platform amounted to an injunction to the federal government to keep "hands off."

One of the most outspoken of those senators was Orrin G. Hatch of Utah, a 46-year-old Republican lawyer whose literary credits include tracts titled "Sinking Bureaucratic Hooks Into the Public" and "The New Slavery." After coming to the Senate in the 1976 election, Hatch quickly became a favorite spokesman for New Right groups across the country and an indefatigable fund raiser for their candidates.

But in one of those ironies in which the West abounds, Hatch's constituents back home in Salt Lake City were nurturing the political career of quite a different kind of politician. Ted Wilson, 41, was the one member of the Kappa Sigma fraternity at the University of Utah who was "inspired and excited" by John Kennedy in 1960. Wilson spent seven years as a teacher before a friend of the Kennedy family, Wayne Owens, was elected to the House and took him to Washington as his assistant. When Owens was defeated in a bid for the Senate in 1974, Wilson came home and, the following year, defeated the 64-year-old incumbent Mayor. In his first five years as Mayor (he was re-elected in 1979), Wilson has taken the city through a transition to a new council/mayor form of government. But his main challenge has been to try to channel the growth that made the 1970s the most turbulent decade in Salt Lake City's history since the Mormon pioneers came into the valley behind the Wasatch Range.

"Some of the people in my community are just absolutely turned on and excited about the growth that is taking place out here," Wilson said. "I'm turned on and excited, but I'm also a little fearful that we're losing what has made Salt Lake City great: that it is a nice, quiet community where growth has been slow enough that things have kind of fit in place. I'm trying to see us not be quite so excited."

Wilson found his first allies in that effort among the neighborhood organizations, whose members "have seen a freeway come in and chop out homes, who don't like that high-rise going up next door and who don't want to see another hospital expand and take out more homes or a park.

"The growth push," he said, "comes from the downtown business community, from the developers and from the labor unions that see it as the way to more jobs."

During his years in City Hall, he said, the lines of communication had begun to open and a degree of consensus develop. "People are beginning to ask whether we are paying more taxes just in order to bring in more people. They are beginning to distinguish between the kinds of companies we want to attract and those we don't. The conflict is still there, and in some ways it is sharper, because the anti-growth forces have grown beyond that neighborhood base. But the understanding of the issue is certainly greater now."

A few hundred miles south, in Albuquerque, New Mexico, 40-year-old Mayor David Rusk, the son of former Secretary of State Dean Rusk, was facing similar battles over the growth patterns of his city. On the local level, David Rusk has been almost as controversial as his father was during the first turbulent Vietnam years. In his first eighteen months as Mayor, Rusk was confronted with two recall efforts, the firing of his former campaign manager from a major city post, and bruising battles with the real-estate developers. But he rode through them with the same serenity that so infuriated the elder Rusk's opponents during the Vietnam war debates in countless congressional hearing rooms.

David Rusk's presence in Albuquerque was the result of an improbable chain of events. He was on his way toward an academic career—with most of his course work completed for a graduate degree in economics at the University of California at Berkeley—when a research project at the

Library of Congress brought him to Washington in the summer of 1963. He volunteered to help the staff arranging the great civil-rights march of that August, and from that experience he was offered a job with the Washington office of the National Urban League, where he worked for almost five years. Late in the Johnson Administration, he joined the Labor Department's manpower-training administration, and he stayed there under the Nixon Administration until 1971, when the veto of a major manpower-training bill led him "to the rapid conclusion that the time had arrived for me to leave Washington." He and his wife sat down with an almanac and rated all the cities with a population over 100,000 where they might live, putting Albuquerque at the top. Rusk went there to work for the city and county government, under an "executive interchange" program, and designed, on the local level, a successful job-training program of the kind Nixon had vetoed for the nation. In 1974, after only three years in town, he ran for Mayor and managed to finish fourth in a field of thirty-three candidates. Encouraged by that showing, he left the public payroll, went into the insurance business, was elected to the legislature in 1976 and, a year later, won the mayoralty with 47 percent of the total vote in a field of four, including the incumbent Republican Mayor and a Democrat backed by the old-line organization.

When Rusk became Mayor, Albuquerque had grown from 35,000 people in 1940 to 340,000 people, and it had expanded its confines from 12 square miles to 92. It had a decaying downtown area deserted by merchants, and heavy unemployment in its Hispanic and other minority populations. "We're growing at a rate of three percent a year net," Rusk said. "We will obviously double in population within a generation, and we don't want to double in size. So the whole effort is to become less of a suburb and more of a city in our patterns of growth. I am also stressing more and more use of public transit to reduce the area's almost total dependence on the private automobile," he said.

Rusk has pursued his strategy with flair and an almost reckless defiance of political risk. In an effort to lure people back into the city's decaying center, he sponsored thirteen consecutive "Downtown Saturday Nights"—ethnic and arts festivals with subsidized entertainment. To lure people out of their cars, he invested heavily in a "grid system" of buses, designed to make that form of public transportation easily accessible to everyone.

Albuquerque's geographical sprawl was based on developers' desires to tie into city water and sewer service, rather than provide their own. Seeking higher-density use of land already within the city boundaries, Rusk tried to make the tie-ins more costly and less attainable.

Rusk forced the pace of change faster than many of his constituents were ready to accept. The "suburbanites" in the affluent Albuquerque

Heights (the word is in quotation marks because they actually lived within the expanded city borders) thought it was fiscal folly to subsidize buses and downtown revival. The city council blocked some of his more ambitious plans, and voters turned down a tax hike that would have kept the experimental bus service going. Rusk's mass-transit director (his former campaign manager) fought so bitterly with the city council that he was finally forced to resign. Two groups of irate citizens circulated petitions for Rusk's recall, but came up well short of the number needed to obtain such a referendum.

Still, after two years in office, even his critics conceded that Rusk had changed the direction of his city's future. Bus ridership was up and growing. Downtown was showing signs of revival, with two major new office buildings, new apartments, four new art galleries and an old movie house being converted into a performing-arts center.

The city's outward expansion did not halt, but higher water and sewer rates went into effect, and a new policy was adopted of charging developers for the total capital cost of their hooking into the system. With help from the federal government, Albuquerque acquired strategic park and mountain acreage to preserve its natural setting and prevent it from becoming one giant housing tract.

Rusk remained a controversial character, but his view of his job did not change. "I think people can see that preserving the kind of environment that made most of them want to move to Albuquerque *is* the key to our future economic development. I think that if we can develop in ways which preserve the sense that Albuquerque is a civilized island in the midst of an undeveloped sea, we will maintain the values of the Southwest and yet benefit from the richness of urban life—with downtown restaurants, theaters, galleries and movies—and be a place where the cultural currents as well as the winds are at work."

From the early days of the West, the "lawman" has been a central figure. As soon as the days were past when there was "no law west of the Pecos," law enforcement became the path to political power. And as the pressures of growth have brought new problems, that pattern has become even more predominant.

Two of the current crop of Western governors, Bruce E. Babbitt of Arizona and Robert F. List of Nevada, demonstrate the way in which the explosive growth of the postwar period had given new emphasis and direction to that role of politician-lawman. Though List is a rather conservative Republican, a product of the same Young Republican movement which bred so many of today's New Right leaders, and Babbitt is a rather liberal Democrat, a veteran of the Selma voting-rights march and a former War on Poverty worker, both of them came to the leadership of their states from the attorney general's office. And their similarities are more striking than their differences.

Bob List, now 44, grew up in the state capital of Carson City when it was a small town of about 2,500 people (it now has 27,400 residents) and after graduation from the University of California's Hastings Law School came home to practice. When he was 30 he was elected district attorney, and four years later he challenged the incumbent Democratic attorney general, Harvey Dickerson, a twelve-year veteran whose father had been Governor—"a real institution in the state," as List says.

"But the office had gotten sleepy. The lawyers were allowed a part-time practice, and most of them were either young fellows just out of law school, attempting to get their feet on the ground and get enough private practice built up that they could afford to go at it full time, or they were fellows who were on the other end of the pipeline, coming down off good careers and looking to build up a little retirement they could draw. The turnover of the average deputy was about a year or eighteen months, and salaries were $10,000 or $12,000."

List ran in 1970 on a platform of "building an aggressive, highly professionalized legal office with good personnel." It was the same sort of managerial approach that worked well for other politicians in suburban growth areas. But it was especially effective in a state whose population jumped almost 30 percent in the first seven years of the past decade, whose personal income in constant dollars increased almost 50 percent and whose leading industry was legalized gambling, which presented obvious problems of law enforcement.

List became the first Republican to win the attorney general's job in eighty years, and as promised, he eliminated the part-time private practice; created antitrust, consumer-protection and criminal divisions and "generally took the office out of the last century."

He also struck up the sort of arrangement with Democratic Governor Mike O'Callaghan that typified the nonpartisanship of the growth areas. "Many attorneys general who find themselves in that situation [having a Governor of the opposite party] have been at war with their governors," List said. "I approached it from a contrary point of view. I approached it from a professional standpoint, that I would treat the Governor, although we were of opposite political parties, as I felt a lawyer should treat a client. We were both there to serve the people, and I respected his confidences; I didn't try to upstage him or undermine him or embarrass him. If I picked up on something that one of his department heads was doing that was out of line, I would pick up the phone and call Mike, rather than have a press conference."

The arrangement worked so well that when O'Callaghan stepped down in 1978, he all but openly endorsed List as his successor.

List's approach to the growth issue sought to avoid Colorado-style confrontation by devising subregional strategies to meet the needs of the state's three distinctive geographic areas. In western Nevada, the Reno–Carson City–Lake Tahoe area, "where we have blue skies, abundant water, hunting, fishing, skiing and a small-town atmosphere, the challenge," List said, "is how we're going to limit or manage its growth. In Las Vegas, which has been a boom town for twenty-five years, there's a real need to diversify industry, because our gaming monopoly has been broken by New Jersey, and other states will follow. In the rural counties, we need economic diversification—not big, dirty smokestack industries, but alternative places of employment."

Bruce Babbitt's strategy in Arizona was similar. He is a native Arizonan who grew up in the Sputnik era, when all red-blooded American males who made good grades became scientists. He studied geology at Notre Dame (John Sears, the Nixon-Reagan strategist, was a classmate and friend) and geophysics in England. When the Sputnik spell passed, he went to Harvard Law School. Having grown up in a "very conservative small-town environment . . . where Democrats and Republicans were all alike," and having been a student in England during the Kennedy years, Babbitt found the mid-1960s a time of excitement and political redefinition. As a law student, he went south to Selma for the 1965 march to Montgomery that finally produced the voting-rights bill. After graduation, he worked for two years as an OEO poverty lawyer in Texas, before coming home to join a Phoenix law firm.

In 1974, he and a few other "young lawyers who had been chafing for the chance to lay a few on the establishment" decided their time had come, and Babbitt announced for attorney general.

When I asked Babbitt why "it all came together in 1974," he said, "Two things, I think. Arizona had been essentially a one-party state since Senator [Barry] Goldwater arrived on the scene in the early 1950s, and it was afflicted with the inevitable cycle where a party achieves total dominance and sows the seeds of its own corruption and destruction. Secondly, the source of in-migration to Arizona changed in the 1960s from older people from the Middle West to a lot of younger people from California and all over the country. And a lot of the new people were saying, 'What the hell's going on here?'

"The attorney general of Arizona had always been a sort of lawyer for the governing establishment. His job was really analogous to being a corporate lawyer for IBM—to facilitate what the board wants done. It was a very reactive, passive kind of role. The system had gotten terribly corrupt. No law enforcement, no regulation, some overt political corruption.

"I ran a campaign which said, in effect, 'If you elect me, you're electing a law-enforcement official. The attorney general is going to be sitting out there blowing the whistle on everybody.' And it sold very well."

Babbitt was able to use his election as a mandate for passage of legislation strengthening his authority. "We dusted off the antitrust laws," he said, "and got a really great antitrust operation going. We went into prosecution of white-collar crime. We put some of the crooked insurance companies into receivership, mailed out 300,000 checks to citizens who'd paid too much for bread. We sued the hell out of the liquor companies for price-fixing, and that resulted in my participation in the Don Bolles death-plot prosecution. [Bolles was an investigative reporter fatally injured by a bomb planted in his car. Three men—a wealthy building contractor and two small-time hoodlums—were convicted of the crime.] We sued the construction companies that sold asphalt to the state. We simply created a state-level prosecution system for organized crime and white-collar crime that had not existed before."

In March 1978, the death of the incumbent Governor elevated Babbitt to that office, and he was elected to a full four-year term that November. "I'm identified as an environmentalist," he said. "My wife and I are active, outdoor people. Backpackers. I've written a book about the Grand Canyon. We've had our kids in the woods camping from the time they were eight months old. But I have made it quite clear to the electorate that I'm pro-growth. I am pro-growth simply because I don't believe that in a democracy you can do much about growth as a state policy. You've got to talk about birth control if you want to eliminate growth.

"The real issue is: 'Can you avoid the mistakes of Southern California? Is it possible to grow in an orderly way, to have a modicum of land-use planning, to utilize your water resources properly, to have some really stringent approaches to air quality, to have a state policy of preserving open spaces and parks, rather than just have your state growing wild?' "

Babbitt said that in Arizona at least, "the trick is to stay out of the rhetorical battles. Leave the labels behind, because the minute you pick them up, you're in real trouble. If you say you're going to have a comprehensive state land-use plan, you've lost. On the other hand, you can get support for a bill relating to the identification and protection of wildlife habitats. Nobody objects to that. Nobody objects to a master plan for state-owned land—and that's an enormous component. If you take air quality as a separate issue, people who are choking on smog are willing to address it.

"With these issues," Babbitt said, "you're no longer looking at marshaling legislative majorities based on Democrats or Republicans. On any issue, what you must do is assemble a public coalition. For example, on the air-quality issue, in Arizona there's an enormous tourist industry. With a careful effort to contact all the innkeepers and resort people and get them to identify their interest in this program, you've got a real chance. If you're willing to view hunters who kill animals as environmentalists, all of a sudden you've expanded your environmental base on lots of land-use issues from 5 percent to 30 percent of the population."

Babbitt's incremental approach appeared to be working. In 1979 the legislature approved most of the recommendations from a task force studying the controls that were needed on use of state-owned lands in the urban areas near Phoenix and Tucson, and created a single agency to handle all water-management questions. By halting all private development on state land, Babbitt was able to swing the developers' lobby behind a far-reaching proposal to change from sale to lease of state land for commercial purposes, a measure that will channel back to the public some of the profits that population growth and economic development normally put into the speculators' pockets.

"Henry George would have been proud of us," Babbitt said, invoking the name of one of American history's foremost economic reformers. It was fitting that the spirit of Henry George—who, leading the "single-tax" movement of the 19th century, advocated a tax on speculators' increases in property values to eliminate all taxes on industry and labor—should have been recalled by this planning-oriented Governor of the modern Western frontier.

More than eighty years ago, Frederick Jackson Turner said that among the intellectual traits the frontier encouraged was "that practical, inventive turn of mind, quick to find expedients."

It might be that Babbitt's inventive pragmatism can show others how the frontier can be developed—and still saved.

13 · Frontiers III: The South

THE WALLS OF the state capitol in Columbia, South Carolina, still bear the scars of Union cannonballs, loosed against the building during Sherman's march northward from Georgia—an enduring monument to the "lost cause" of secession.

On January 10, 1979, a slim, solemn, bespectacled man of 46 named Richard W. Riley took the oath as Governor of South Carolina and said, "We gather today on the south steps of this historic statehouse, and we begin this administration looking south. Nothing could be more symbolic of our future, because we live in times when an entire nation is looking south—looking south for new spirit, looking south for new energy, looking south for new leadership."

No one could be more symbolic of that leadership than Dick Riley. The son of a former Democratic state chairman, a Furman University graduate whose parents went there before him, a Greenville lawyer whose Navy service was on a Charleston-based minesweeper, the son-in-law of a leading lawyer and politician from the Pee Dee section of the state, Riley is steeped in the traditions of South Carolina. But in the sixteen years before he was elected Governor, he was part of a continuing revolution—involving reapportionment, constitutional revision, conflict-of-interest laws and desegregation—that has transformed the character of South Carolina politics.

If the changes in the politics and politicians of suburbia and the West have altered the balance of national politics, then the changes in the South have had even more dramatic consequences. It is not just the fact that Jimmy Carter, a native of one of the most conservative counties in Georgia, reached the White House, in large part because Southern black leaders vouched for his credentials to skeptical Yankees—though that is remarkable enough. It is also the fact that a new generation of Southern politicians—typified by Dick Riley—is shaping the growth of a long-slumbering region in ways that are setting national patterns on such issues of the future as nuclear-waste disposal, coastal-zone management, early-childhood development and the revitalization of small towns. After a century of economic and political subjugation, the South is once again providing leadership for the nation.

The key to the transformation of Southern politics has been the virtual demise of the race issue. For almost a century after the end of Reconstruction, the organizing principle of politics in the old Confederacy was the suppression of the black vote and the elimination of any competition for the allegiance of blacks, which would have given them influence on the social and economic policies of the region. That principle was rendered inoperative—broken to bits—by the civil-rights demonstrations of the early 1960s and the response of the federal government, particularly the Civil Rights Act of 1964 and the Voting Rights Act of 1965.

In barely a decade, the South went through as complex and dramatic a political upheaval as any in American history. In broad outlines, there were three phases.

First came a period of resistance, led by segregationist Democrats, of whom former Alabama Governor George C. Wallace was the most important. When the Republicans in 1964 nominated Barry Goldwater, an opponent of the new civil-rights legislation, as their presidential candidate, many of the Old Guard segregationists in the South responded by shifting their support and efforts to the dormant Republican Party. By 1968, when Richard M. Nixon and Wallace (a third-party presidential candidate) divided 68.9 percent of the Southern presidential vote, the region's long-dominant Democrats were being badly squeezed.

But the election of 1970 signaled a sharp turnaround and the beginning of a second phase. Registration of blacks had accelerated, under the new federal laws, between 1965 and 1970, and in that year's gubernatorial elections a set of moderate Democrats, who appealed to voters of both races, came to power across the South from Florida to Arkansas. As a result, many of the candidates who had ridden the Goldwater, Nixon or Wallace coattails were defeated in the early Seventies.

By the middle of the decade, the third (and, so far, last) phase of the new Southern pattern was established. It is a pattern of intense competition, but devoid of the polarization of the race issue. Democrats appeal openly for black support, as a key part of their coalition, by emphasizing programs for education and economic development. At the same time, they address the concerns of the growing white middle class for the costs and inefficiencies of government. The result is a blend of policies neither overtly liberal nor conservative.

Their Republican opponents, having put last-ditch segregation behind them, also seek black votes, but build their electoral coalitions largely on the younger, more affluent and more independent whites of the South's expanding metropolitan areas, emphasizing their criticisms of the regulatory and tax burdens imposed by distant bureaucracies.

The result has been the creation of a kind of politics with its own regional flavor, but also with distinct similarities to that of the other growth regions—suburbia and the West.

The Southern politicians coming to power today have seen a more dramatic alteration of the fundamental social customs of their region than their contemporaries anywhere else in America. They have lived through a time that took character and courage—and an exceptional degree of self-discipline. Dick Riley needed those qualities more than most, because during his Navy service he developed a severe arthritic condition in his back called rheumatoid spondylitis, which has left him permanently stooped. "I had light fever and very serious pain for about a fourteen- or fifteen-year period," he said, "without taking any kind of medicine; nothing—not even aspirin. It was just kind of a covenant I made with myself because I was kind of determined to face up to it."

That sort of quiet courage made political issues which intimidate most politicians seem easier to face. "I went to Columbia," Riley said, speaking of his election to the legislature in 1962, "knowing of many of what I considered to be weaknesses in the state system, things that had kind of disgusted me in a quiet way for years. I was considered to be a reform person from the very first day. That used to shock my father quite a bit." Ted Riley was described by his son as "a real fighter, but just in another era. I had a lot of his good political friends say to me, 'Dick, I love you to death and am going to vote for you and support you, but please, next year, try to do something that I can tell people we're proud of.' "

What Riley did in fact was push a series of reforms which have changed the face of government in South Carolina. In the state House of Representatives, he took on the issue of reapportionment—which, he recalls, "was kind of an un-American thing to do." At first, only 2 of the 16 members of the committee supported one-man, one-vote reapportionment. But eventually that principle was accepted and became one of the major agents of political change, providing representation for blacks and encouraging the growth of the infant Republican Party. When Riley moved to the state Senate, he joined the group struggling for constitutional revision. Article by article, they went through the state's charter, gradually bringing it into the 20th century. At Riley's urging, the revisions were brought to referendum serially, and were accepted, on their individual merits, "in my conservative area of Greenville . . . and throughout the state," where wholesale revision might not have been.

As Governor, Riley has continued his campaign against what he calls the "good-old-boyism" of the legislature. In his first year, he fought a bitter struggle—surviving fifteen filibusters in the state House of Representatives alone—for a bill aimed at breaking the legislature's control of the Public Service Commission and the conflicts of interest that arose from it. What finally emerged, though less than Riley sought, shifted the appointive powers from the legislature to a merit board chosen jointly by the legislature and the Governor; it barred members of the legislature from being appointed to the utility-rate-setting commission and it banned them from appearing before the commission in rate cases.

Fulfilling another campaign pledge, Riley signed legislation financing a statewide kindergarten system, lowering the compulsory school-attendance age from seven to six and creating a new program for gifted and talented students.

His governmental approach is based on the belief that "it's not inconsistent to believe in strong management of state government and to be concerned about poor people or uneducated people. By letting business people know you understand business management, you can get them completely in tune with you, and then you can talk about the needs of public education, and they'll be right with you on it, so long as they understand you're not talking from a vacuum, but have an appreciation for sound management principles."

Riley is an example of what Terry Sanford, the former Governor of North Carolina and now president of Duke University, called the "liberation of our leaders."

"I don't think it's odd at all that you see leadership coming out of the South," Sanford, now 63, said in 1979. "My contention has been that there's been great leadership there all the while. But as long as our leaders were burdened with having to take certain stands on the race issue, they were all discredited as true leaders in the nation's eyes—even a Bill Fulbright. [Former Senator J. William Fulbright of Arkansas, longtime chairman of the Senate Foreign Relations Committee, was passed over for appointment as Secretary of State in 1961 because he had been required by the home-state political climate to vote against all the civil-rights bills of the 1950s.] My generation—those who came out of World War II—were beginning to be able to shake loose from it in the early 1960s, but as late as 1972, when I lost to Wallace in my own state's presidential primary, the race issue was still there.

"I think it's gone now. I just don't see it anywhere. And now our leaders can address themselves to the real problems of our states. Almost all these governors are putting education at the head of their list. And they are addressing issues we always thought were beyond the realm of accomplishment—how you accommodate your industrial development to the quality of life. That question simply wasn't something we thought about. Our leaders are still conservative fiscally, and that's probably a good thing. But they can look at people's problems without the blinders of that race issue, and they can look at the mistakes made in other parts of the country, and they can think creatively and they can dare to do the unusual things that we never would have tried."

The change of which Sanford spoke has been astonishing. In his landmark study *Southern Politics in State and Nation,* published in 1949, V. O. Key, Jr., wrote that "whatever phase of the Southern political process one seeks to understand, sooner or later the trail of inquiry leads to the Negro." He argued that the subjugation of blacks was the unstated premise of virtually all the political institutions and strategies of the South. But in their updating of Key—*The Transformation of Southern Politics,* published twenty-seven years later—Jack Bass and Walter DeVries asserted that the "political liberation" of Southern whites was a fact. They quoted Andrew Young's somewhat cynical review of the change that had occurred. "It used to be," Young told a conference of the Association of Southern Black Mayors in 1974, "that Southern politics was just 'nigger' politics: who could 'outnigger' the other. Then you registered 10 to 15 percent in the community and folk would start saying 'Nigra.' And then you got to 35 to 40 percent registered, and it's amazing how quick they learned how to say 'Nee-grow.' And now that we've got 50, 60, 70 percent of the black votes registered in the South, everybody's proud to be associated with their black brothers and sisters."

The half-mocking tone of Young's recital may be appropriate, but there is no question that the passage of the Voting Rights Act of 1965 had a tremendous impact. As was noted in Chapter 11, more than one million blacks were enrolled as voters in the first five years after its passage. (In South Carolina, one of the few states to keep voting statistics by race, nonwhite registration increased from 37.3 percent in 1960 to 51.2 percent in 1966; in the same period, white registration went from 75.7 percent to 81.7 percent.)

By 1970, the South was ready to elect a new set of governors—Reubin Askew in Florida, Dale Bumpers in Arkansas, Jimmy Carter in Georgia, John West in South Carolina—who drew support from the newly enfranchised blacks and looked beyond the race issue for their programs. In the early 1970s, while Wallace still held sway and Nixon was pursuing his "Southern strategy," there were still pressures on young, ambitious candidates in some campaign years to send sympathetic smoke signals to the segregationists. Democratic Senator Sam Nunn of Georgia, who may well be the most influential legislator of the younger generation, succumbed to those pressures in his first statewide race.

In 1972, when he was only 34 years old and his political experience consisted of four years in the Georgia House of Representatives, Nunn was elected to the U.S. Senate. That year, Georgia politics was in an uproar. Nunn won an upset victory in the Democratic primary over the interim Senator named by then Governor Carter to fill the seat left vacant by the death of Senator Richard B. Russell. In the primary, Nunn drew his support from a diverse group of anti-Carter Democrats, ranging from black state Senator Julian Bond to segregationist Lieutenant Governor Lester Maddox. As if the pro-Carter-vs.-anti-Carter split were not serious enough, the Georgia Democrats were shell-shocked by the success of George McGovern's backers in flooding the delegate-selection caucuses and ousting longtime Democratic powers from the national convention delegation. Forced to run on a ticket headed by McGovern and facing a strong right-wing Republican opponent—then Representative Fletcher Thompson, Jr., who would enjoy the coattail help of Richard Nixon—Sam Nunn grabbed for the strongest available source of support: George Wallace.

He flew to Alabama in mid-campaign to receive Wallace's endorsement, and publicly condemned Carter for refusing to nominate Wallace for President at the Democratic convention. "George Wallace represents the real views of Georgians," Nunn said. He echoed Wallace's rhetoric in his attacks on "judicial tyranny," his denunciation of school-busing orders and his calls for referendum elections on federal judges every six years. The crypto-Wallace campaign was enough to counter Thompson's effort to alarm whites with charges that Nunn would receive the black "bloc vote."

Seven years later, comfortably ensconced in the Senate and looking forward to a career of growing national influence, Nunn reiterated his opposition to the busing orders but otherwise dismissed the 1972 campaign as "reflecting the special and very difficult circumstances for a Democratic candidate in Georgia that year."

As Nunn, like his predecessor Senator Russell, acquired commanding respect inside the Senate, particularly on issues of defense and national security, the memories of that first campaign faded—in the minds of others. Were Nunn to run for President someday, as Russell once tried to do, "the issue" would probably not block his way. Whether Nunn himself had forgotten his past was another question, however. His Georgia contemporary Jody Powell observed in 1979 that the full benefits of being "liberated" from the "exclusive preoccupation with race—politically, socially, economically and in every other way—probably flow more to the generation of Amy [Carter, the President's daughter] and Emily [Powell's daughter] than they do to me and my generation. When I was in school," Powell said, "the schools were still segregated, and you'd be a fool to believe that for my generation the problem has been completely solved. But the next generation has really experienced a dramatic change."

Yet many of those governing in the South by the end of the 1970s had thoroughly assimilated the change. When Dick Riley was asked, for example, if he had found the change in his state at all hard to handle during a career in public office that began in 1962, he said, "I was *never* comfortable with the situation in the South as far as blacks were concerned. That's not new to me. That wasn't something I picked up when I ran for the House. I had that feeling all along. . . . I had tremendous black support in the campaign [for Governor], and I stated that I was going to make my administration representative, and yet have the best governor's staff in the country. I have six executive assistants who all have direct access to the Governor's office. Of those six people, two are black, two are women, and they are very, very competent people."

Another Southern Governor inaugurated in 1979, Arkansas's Bill Clinton, now 34, was only 11 years old when Governor Orval Faubus defied federal authorities and forced President Eisenhower to send in paratroopers to enforce the desegregation of Little Rock Central High School. Clinton, living in Hot Springs, never attended an integrated school until he went east to Georgetown University, to Oxford on a Rhodes Scholarship and to Yale Law School. But he says he knew as a youth "my state was on the wrong course, and I wanted to change that." Noting that Faubus had been viewed as a populist politician "before any of this race stuff got hold of his administration," Clinton argued that "had it not been for the race crisis, I believe that the New South could have begun in Arkansas thirty years ago."

He is not the only one who sees the current period of Southern politics as an opportunity to do what should have been done long ago had not the race issue held the South in check.

Kirkman Finlay, 44, the Mayor of Columbia, South Carolina, the state capital, is a grandson of the city's onetime Episcopal bishop, an iconoclast who marched with the suffragettes and integrated his diocese's churches and conventions in the mid-1930s, "twenty-five years before other people were even thinking about that kind of question in the South," his grandson says. It was in the family tradition, then, for Finlay himself to serve as campaign manager for a black Episcopal priest who ran for the city council in 1970. And it was no surprise that Finlay's wife served on the faculty of a predominantly black college in Columbia. With that background, he was able to win 30 percent of the black vote against a black opponent in the three-way race for Mayor in 1978, a vital part of the winning coalition which also included the leadership of the business community and the Democratic Party.

Joseph P. Riley, Jr., 36, the Mayor of Charleston, South Carolina (and no kin to the Governor), had a similar coalition in his campaign when he was elected in 1975. Riley had spent six years in the legislature, and quit to "practice law and be a good family man.

"But," he said, "I was very concerned about the polarization that existed in our city; in the 1971 Mayor's race, the black and white communities were split. When I was elected to the legislature [in 1968] I began to work with the black community. No one with an open mind and an open spirit, in the late 1960s, when George Wallace and his crowd, under the guise of states' rights, were preaching racism—no one could have gone to a meeting in a black church and not been moved. Once the top was lifted, it just became very easy to be involved and recognize the problems segregation had brought to the South. And at the same time, you couldn't help but perceive what wonderful results could occur in a South where bigotry and racism had been laid to rest.

"Because of my work with the black community and their respect for me," Riley said, "I was able to get about 80 or 85 percent of the black vote, notwithstanding a black candidate opposing me. And the white business leadership supported me, because they recognized that for the community to move forward, its leadership had to be one the black community respected."

With a 45-percent black population, there are six blacks and six whites on the Charleston City Council. "I worked very hard on keeping the city council working together, getting black people involved in boards and commissions; worked very hard on affirmative action; and to an extent, the black community feels very good about their city government now. We got an All-American City award on recognition of citizens' participation," Riley said.

As he talked, it became clear that much of his emphasis had been on projects of particular concern to his black constituents: a housing-rehabilitation program for a ghetto area; opening of storefront police headquarters with community-relations specialists, in a program that cut the center-city crime rate 15 percent; a controversial projected hotel/convention center project, which would provide 950 new jobs "right in the heart of the city" and a minority-contracting program that directed 44 percent of a large economic-development grant to black businessmen.

But the real feather in Riley's cap was persuading composer Gian Carlo Menotti to bring his Spoleto Festival to Charleston in 1977 and subsequent years, "putting our citizens in the front row for the very best that the cultural world has to offer.

"I don't think any mayor could want anything better for his city than that," Riley said, "and I have told our citizens that this was the final proof to me that the civil-rights movement liberated the white South as much as the black South. The Spoleto Festival could not have come here. There would have been no legitimacy to an effort to bring what we feel is the world's most comprehensive arts festival to a segregated Southland. And I remind people of that when they say my administration has been too interested in the black community."

It would be Pollyannaish to pretend that there is no resentment toward the politics of a Joe Riley. When I first talked to Riley in 1978, he told me about one of "the saddest moments" of his life as Mayor.

"We have a Hibernian Society that is one of the oldest in the United States. Since my name is Joseph Patrick Riley, my family and I have been members for a long time. My father was president one time. Well, a year ago I heard that a black county council chairman was not being asked to come and sit at the head table. So I went to see the president. But this was just a few days before the dinner, and my name was in the program to respond to the toast to the city. So I reluctantly went, telling myself that this was a mistake, that they just weren't thinking. So this year they didn't ask him again, and so I didn't go. It was a tough thing. There was an article in the paper, and I got a kind of snide cheap shot from the speaker, who was John Connally, who made a remark that it was my fault for not going."

In 1979, when I talked to Mayor Riley again, I asked him about the Hibernian Society situation. "I was in a quandary," he said. "The black chairman of the county council had retired and been replaced by a white man. In 1978, when I refused to attend, they said the dinner was open to everyone. So I decided [in 1979] to take a black guest—a very distinguished black businessman. There was some controversy about it in the community, but he was treated courteously and it went very well.

"There was kind of a funny aftermath to it," Riley said. "President Carter gave a judicial appointment to a South Carolinian [Falcon B. Hawkins] who was a member of the Hibernian Society, and the question was raised at his confirmation hearing about whether it was a segregated group. And the fact that I had taken a black as my guest was cited in his defense by our Senator, Fritz Hollings."

Riley also mentioned one other fact in our conversation. He was unopposed for re-election as Mayor in 1979.

That a man like Joe Riley would be Mayor of Charleston, South Carolina, the city where the Civil War began, may come as a surprise to those whose impression of the South is still shaped by the television scenes of police battling civil-rights demonstrators. But for the younger generation of white politicians in Dixie, reality is not the battles of the past but the registration figures of the present.

The best witness on that point I found was yet another South Carolinian, Representative Butler C. Derrick, Jr., 44, a lawyer and a Democratic member of the South Carolina Legislature for six years before coming to the House in the 1974 election.

Although Edgefield County, where Derrick lives, has only 16,000 people, it is a political hotbed, which has produced ten South Carolina governors. Derrick grew up in that atmosphere of political talk and graduated from high school in 1954, the same spring the Supreme Court ruled school segregation unconstitutional.

He went off to the University of South Carolina and then to the University of Georgia Law School. And looking back, he said, "quite frankly, I don't remember very much progressive thought in that area. I think we were pretty much the products of our families and our times. When I came back to my hometown [to practice law], I was criticized by many people for shaking hands with black people on the main street. The first time I campaigned [in 1966, when he lost his first bid for the state legislature by 180 votes], I was the first candidate that spoke before black organizations and went to black homes and sought their votes. I received rather substantial criticism for that, too.

"But things began to happen in the South when the blacks gained the vote. That's when discussions got practical. Twenty-two percent of the registered voters in my [congressional] district are black, and I sought the black vote. When I was in the state legislature, I appointed the second black person ever to serve on a school board in South Carolina. And by the time I finished my tenure in the legislature, I can say that there was not a board or commission in my home county where blacks were not represented—and substantially, not just piecemeal."

When Derrick was finishing his first term in the legislature and "making some of these changes," as he said, "it was very much an issue. And for the first time I can recall in my home county's history, we had a serious Republican candidate for the state House of Representatives—although I did beat him right handily, I might add."

Coming from a rural and rather conservative county, Derrick said in 1979 that the race issue may not be present "on the surface, but it is underlying. . . . To deny that it exists is not being fair." He said that in his opinion, "the existence of a strong Republican Party in South Carolina is a result of *Brown v. Board of Education* and the Civil Rights Act of 1964."

Republican Senator Strom Thurmond, who is from the same South Carolina county as Derrick, led the exodus of former Democrats who broke with their party on the civil-rights issue, becoming first an independent and then, in 1964, a Republican. When Derrick graduated from law school in 1965, Thurmond offered his fellow townsman a job as his administrative assistant. "I probably went to a Republican organizational meeting one time," Derrick said, "but that's as far as it went." He turned down the job and declined to switch parties, although "I had a lot of advice from people back then, telling me that the Republican Party was the wave of the future in the South and that as a practical matter, it would be good for me to be a Republican.

"A great percentage of my contemporaries in my state are Republicans," Derrick said. "A lot of them went Republican back in the Sixties. All of a sudden, because of the race issue and other things, it became the socially acceptable thing to do. You know, if you had a college education and you belonged to the country club, the next thing that you did was join the Republican Party."

What Derrick describes was certainly part of the process feeding the growth of Republicanism in the South in this generation—but only a part. The emergence of two-party competition has transformed Southern politics as much as the enfranchisement of the blacks—and the two phenomena are not unrelated. Barry Goldwater, in 1964, used his opposition to federal civil-rights legislation to carry five Deep South states, including South Carolina, with a vote pattern paralleling that of Thurmond's independent "State's Rights" presidential candidacy in 1948. Goldwater's "Southern strategy" was adopted and expanded by Richard Nixon in 1968 and 1972, even though his Administration was carrying out more school-desegregation orders than any previous government.

But the black enfranchisement following passage of the Voting Rights Act of 1965, the landslide defeat suffered by Goldwater, the later discrediting of the Nixon Administration and the rise in the 1970s of a new generation of Democrats able to draw votes from both blacks and whites have forced Southern Republicans to reject a strategy of last-ditch segregationism with which some of them had never felt comfortable. Thurmond, in his seventies, put blacks on his senatorial staff, supported blacks for the federal judiciary, enrolled his young daughter in an integrated public school and actively campaigned for black votes. And younger Republicans in the South have found more durable bases for establishing their political identity—whether it be one of inheritance or one of recent adoption.

Lamar Alexander, 40, the Governor of Tennessee, is a Republican by long tradition. An eighth-generation East Tennessean, he was born in Blount County, a Unionist stronghold in the controversy that split the state at the time of the Civil War. "When I was in high school," he said, "I just assumed I'd always be a Republican because that's the way things were in the Union part of the state. But I tested my Republicanism some. . . . I was awfully impressed with what you'd call the Kennedy movement. I guess I thought about being a Democrat, but two or three things brought me back. There was a family tradition. I thought we needed a two-party system. And to get ahead in the Democratic Party, you had to stand in a long line. The Republican Party was wide open."

Alexander did a law-clerkship for Judge John Minor Wisdom, one of the Eisenhower appointees to the Fifth Circuit who made that bench a key agency for the advancement of civil rights across the South in the 1950s and 1960s. Alexander was a top aide in the 1966 and 1970 campaigns that made Howard H. Baker, Jr., the state's first Republican Senator since Reconstruction and Winfield Dunn the first Republican Governor in fifty years. Defeated in his first bid for Governor in 1974, Alexander came back to win handily in 1978.

Like his political mentors Wisdom and Baker, and true to his family tradition, Alexander identified himself with the cause of desegregation. But he received only 10 or 12 percent of the black vote in his two campaigns. His hopes for change in that area are modest.

"Our politics in Memphis, which is where one out of five Tennesseans live, are dominated by racial considerations," he said, early in his term. "I thought a Republican Governor with black support could open new avenues of opportunity and keep things from being so polarized, but I've not had any great success with that yet." His main hope, he said, is that by increasing the number of blacks in state government, he can help provide "additional leaders . . . who are not so much rhetoricians—which has been the way you get ahead in the black community so far—as managers. . . . That would be the best thing I could probably do."

W. Henson Moore III, 41, the Republican Congressman from Baton Rouge, Louisiana, is at the opposite end of the traditionalism scale from Alexander. "My great-great grandfather was a Democratic Lieutenant Governor of Louisiana," he said, "and I was the first Republican in my family." The elements that entered into his switch of party and his election to Congress are typical of the complex of forces that has been feeding the growth of Republicanism in the South. In 1964, Republicans won 16 House seats in the old Confederacy. Going into the 1980 election, they held 31 seats, with three of those gains coming in Louisiana.

Moore's story—like so many others—is a mixture of social mobility, conservative ideology and political opportunism. His wife was the catalyst for the change. "She fell in with a group of women who were very interested in current events, good organizers, and she joined this Women's Republican Club in Baton Rouge, and became a registered Republican six months before I ever changed. Men are much more hesitant to change parties; they fear it's going to interfere with their careers, or bring dishonor on the family or something. A woman is much more impetuous and just does what she thinks is right."

The Moores switched in 1969; but long before that the Congressman had become an apostate Democrat. He cast his first presidential vote, in 1960, for Richard Nixon and in 1964 had his first taste of actual campaigning through Democrats for Goldwater.

"If you study the people who are registering Republican," he said, "they are basically younger people, and they are tending to register ideology. Most of my contemporaries that I went to high school and college with are now registered Republicans. I think as the years go on, the philosophical differences are becoming clearer. They perceive Carter and McGovern and the Democrats before them as being weaker on national defense. And they perceive that the Democrats are the ones who are creating the expensive social programs, increased taxes, deficit spending, inflation and more government regulation. The other thing you'll find is that almost all the people I know that have joined the party and are active in it are doing it for one reason only: to build the two-party system. We have felt that Louisiana Democratic politics was rotten to the core."

Moore was elected to Congress in 1975 under circumstances that emphasized the ideological issues which he says are becoming dominant. In the September 1974 Democratic primary, a young television sportscaster named Jeff LaCaze upset incumbent Representative John Rarick, an unabashed right-winger and segregationist. In November, Moore and LaCaze ran such a close race that the courts ordered a new election to settle the outcome. And in the special election, Moore was able to focus attention on his opponent's strong support from organized labor and his near-unanimous black vote, thus mobilizing conservative Democrats who had previously backed Rarick. Moore won the special election by 11,000 votes and has been gaining strength ever since.

Many of the Republicans' Southern victories in the 1970s came in races like Moore's, where blacks joined with other urban and progressive groups, including organized labor, to nominate a liberal candidate in the Democratic primary. But the avowed liberal often lacked enough support in the whole electorate to win a general election. Thus, most of the congressional victories won by Republicans in the South, and such important statewide contests as the 1979 election of Representative David Treen as Governor of Louisiana, have come in contests between "non-racist conservatives," as the *National Journal* called them, and moderate-to-liberal Democrats.

Moore contended that his state has had less "nigger-baiting and racial cleavage than most," and claimed that "so far as the growth of the Republican Party is concerned, it had nothing to do with it. In my own congressional district, I spend a lot of time bringing blacks into the party, and every politician is basically doing his best to attract the black vote."

Then Moore made an observation about a change in black politics which was discussed in an earlier chapter, but which is important here as a clue to the thinking of the new generation of Southern Republicans.

"The interesting thing," he said, "is that as long as the issue was civil rights—as it was from the time I started in 1964 until sometime in the Seventies—the blacks were all unified. They would pick the candidate who stood most for civil rights, in their belief, and they would stick with him. That was admirable of them. There was a black vote you could trust; you knew where they were going and what they were going to do.

"Now, since the days of civil rights are over—they won—the question is basically patronage or economics. And now the blacks are beginning to splinter and factionalize, just like whites would do. If one or two black groups back one candidate, then the other black groups figure there is going to be nothing in it for them to do the same thing, and so they are beginning to splinter off.

"Republicans are moving into that breach and are dealing with these splinter groups," Moore said. "Before, our Republican candidates got zero black votes. Now we are picking up anywhere from 10 to 18 to 24 percent of the black votes in the last three elections in Louisiana. We are picking those up by going to the splinter groups and saying, 'You are on the outs, and the other groups are on the ins, with that fellow. So you come with us and you'll be on the ins with us.'

"Blacks," he concluded, "are becoming an even more important force by virtue of the fact that they are available to more than just one candidate."

Across the state line in Mississippi, a young man named Trent Lott faced an interesting decision in 1972. He was 31 years old and for the last four years, since graduating from the University of Mississippi Law School, he had been working in Washington as administrative assistant to one of his state's Democratic representatives, William Colmer, the chairman of the House Rules Committee. Colmer, who was fifty years older than Lott, had come to Congress in the 1932 election and had stayed around long enough to be one of the linchpins of the conservative coalition of Southern Democrats and conservative Republicans which, for most of his tenure, was the *de facto* operating majority in the House. Now Colmer was retiring, and he wanted Lott to have his seat. Lott was ambitious to succeed his mentor, but he had one problem: Trent Lott had decided that he was probably a Republican.

"In Mississippi, when I was growing up [as the son of a schoolteacher mother and a sharecropper father who moved south to Pascagoula to become a wartime shipyard worker], there weren't two parties," Lott said. "Everybody was a Democrat, and there was no word 'Republican.' There was just 'damn-Republican'—one word.

"I guess 1964"—the year Goldwater carried Mississippi—"was the first time that we really started thinking, 'Gee, maybe we are Republicans,' " Lott said. After that election, House Democrats stripped the seniority from one Mississippi Congressman, John Bell Williams, who had openly supported Goldwater over Lyndon Johnson, and threatened to remove Colmer from his chairmanship. "A real sour taste started to develop in the mouths of Mississippians," Lott recalled.

But it was not until he came to Washington in 1968 as Colmer's aide that he discovered he was really a Republican. It did not take long. "I came in April of 1968 and by August of 1968 I was a Republican," he said. "Working with Mr. Colmer, I saw he was much closer, if the truth be known, to Jerry Ford [then the House Minority Leader] than he was to the Speaker. He worked with the Republicans and was a very important part of the old Republican–Southern Democrat coalition." The turning point came when Lott went to a meeting of the Burros Club, the organization of administrative assistants to Democratic congressmen. The speakers were Ray Blanton, then a member of the House and later Governor of Tennessee, and Lawrence F. O'Brien, the former White House lobbyist and Postmaster General. "I remember turning to a fellow sitting next to me, another administrative assistant to a Democrat from Mississippi," Lott said, "and I said, 'You know, I don't agree with a word those guys have said—either one of them, but particularly Larry O'Brien. I am not a Democrat.' "

By 1972, it was far easier for Trent Lott to explain to old friends in Mississippi why he was running as a Republican than it would have been to explain why he was making his debut on a ticket headed by George McGovern. "Most of my predecessor's supporters, who had been Democrats all these years, initially went for the bushes," he said, "but most all of them wound up supporting me.

"Race was not a part of it, as far as I was concerned," Lott said, noting that his district is less than one-fifth black and that the heavy presence of military facilities and defense contractors had pushed cities like Biloxi and Gulfport toward racial moderation.

In his four terms in Congress, Trent Lott has moved with surprising speed into the leadership of his party, confirming Lamar Alexander's observation about the lines being shorter on the Republican side. In 1979 he was elected Chairman of the House Republican Research Committee, and he is talked about as a future contender for the Minority Leader's job. But his rise has been less spectacular than that of Thad Cochran, another Ole Miss graduate, who ran for Congress from Jackson in 1972 and six years later became the first Republican Senator from Mississippi since Reconstruction days.

Like Lott, Cochran, 43, considered himself "an independent-minded Democrat." While practicing law in Jackson, he had served as director of Citizens for Nixon-Agnew in 1968, so his partisanship was far from rigid. But when the incumbent Congressman stepped down in 1972, Cochran put aside thoughts of running, at first, because he could not see any practical possibility of winning the Democratic nomination.

"Then a friend called up one day and asked if I had thought about running as a Republican," Cochran said. "And I laughed, because I certainly had not. But I began talking informally with some of the Republican hierarchy there in the state to see if I was acceptable to them and they were acceptable to me. And I was surprised. I had thought that they were probably still operating their politics down there in the Republican Party on the illusion of returning to racial segregation and some of the other political nightmares that we had already gone through. But I was assured that they realized I was going to be actively pursuing black votes as well as white votes, and not trying to represent just one segment of the society down there."

Running against a McGovern-led Democratic ticket, Cochran was able to argue that "the Democrats have sort of turned their back on Mississippi, so we have an opportunity to vote our conscience. We are not shackled to past political loyalties." He was aided by the presence in the race of a black independent candidate who drew off 8.8 percent of the votes, which might otherwise have gone to his Democratic opponent, and Cochran won with 47.9 percent of the total vote. A similar circumstance in 1978, when black civil-rights leader Charles Evers ran as an independent and received 22.8 percent of the vote, helped Cochran win his Senate seat with 45 percent of the total. Cochran himself has campaigned for black votes and has—like almost all the new-generation Southern politicians—run his office on a color-blind basis.

When I asked him if the time was past that anyone—Republican or Democrat—would "refight the battles of segregation," he said, "I hope that is behind us. I see no evidence that it's a political issue. I know of no candidate who tries to get elected by returning to the old race-baiting rhetoric that we had become so accustomed to hearing down in Mississippi and throughout the South in the Fifties."

And then Cochran told a story that may explain more than anything else why politicians his age have put that issue in the past.

Cochran was attending law school at Ole Miss when James Meredith was the first black admitted to its undergraduate college. When the federal government sent troops to campus to ensure Meredith's safe admission to classes, Cochran said, "it was almost comical the way the leadership in the state pretended it could resist. I recall seeing a large number of highway patrolmen assembling there on campus, under the leadership of Governor [Ross] Barnett and Lieutenant Governor Paul Johnson, and they had these police dogs in crates in the back of the cars. And I recall sitting out on the steps of the law school and one of our professors, John Fox, said, 'Oh, I'm glad to see they brought the dogs. When the tanks come over that bridge onto the campus, they're going to get out there and say, "Now, dog, go bite that tank." '

"It was ridiculous, pretending these highway patrolmen on the side of

Mississippi could frustrate the efforts of the United States Army to see that James Meredith was enrolled. And it was quite sad, frankly, to walk around the campus after the battle and see the broken concrete benches in the grove there in front of the old Lyceum building. And the tear gas that was used to cut down the riot hung in the air, it seemed, for days. And the large numbers of troops that had to be flown there . . . It was kind of embarrassing, really."

If today's Southern politicians have moved beyond the race issues that have been dominant in the past, what kind of politics are they entering? It appears that the emerging politicians of the South have much in common with those who have come to power in the other growth areas, suburbia and the West.

They are young. The ten discussed in this sampling, chosen for the promise that has made them successful in public office, range in age from 34 to 46.

They are well educated. Most of them have graduate degrees in law or other studies. They bear out Terry Sanford's contention that the commitment to education which began in his generation of Southern leaders will be accelerated in this new generation. Trent Lott, one of the most conservative in the group, said that "the one area where I used to argue the most" with his predecessor and mentor, Bill Colmer, "was on education. He grew up in an era when there was no federal aid to education, and instinctively, he was opposed to it. I, on the other hand, being the son of a schoolteacher and having worked for the University of Mississippi after I graduated from undergraduate school, had a very pro-education attitude. And I felt that a state like Mississippi had a tremendous need for a better educational system, which included federal assistance to get the job done. We just don't have the resources to do it ourselves."

Both Riley and Clinton were elected as governors in 1978 on platforms stressing pledges for full funding of statewide kindergarten programs, reduction of class sizes in elementary grades and other measures to improve the laggard educational systems of their states.

The new Southern politicians are as media-oriented as their counterparts in suburbia or the West. Lamar Alexander worked as a journalist while continuing his education and, after his defeat in his first try for Governor of Tennessee, stayed in the public eye as a political commentator for a Nashville television station. Trent Lott noted that his predecessor, who served for thirty years, "didn't really communicate very much" with his constituents. By contrast, he said, "I do five thirty-minute television programs a month, I do a weekly radio program, I do a weekly newspaper column that's carried in from 12 to 19 papers. I do three newsletters a year, plus a questionnaire, and I've averaged going home twice a month."

Travel is nothing new for these Southerners. More than half of them went out of state to school, in some instances deliberately testing the temptations of the bigger world against the familiar charms of their home states.

"I wanted to make sure that I wanted to stay in Tennessee," said Lamar Alexander, "kind of operating on the theory that if I never got out, I'd never know whether I was happy in Tennessee. So I went to New York University, which is the last place you'd go to enhance your political career in Tennessee. I worked for Bobby Kennedy one summer in the Justice Department. I worked for a big law firm in Los Angeles one summer. Then I worked for Judge Wisdom in New Orleans. And then, after all that, I determined that I wanted to live at home, so I came back."

The new Southern politicians have also demonstrated a good deal of political mobility. Except for Alexander, all the Republicans in this chapter started adult life as Democrats; Alexander, as has been noted, flirted for a time with becoming a Democrat, and Butler Derrick thought, at least momentarily, of joining Strom Thurmond's Republican Party. But the ultimate in political mobility is probably represented by Kirkman Finlay, the Mayor of Columbia. When he was at Harvard Law School at the beginning of the 1960s, he was on the board of governors of the law-school Republican club, giving vent to "something of a conservative streak" by campaigning for Massachusetts' Republican Senator Leverett Saltonstall in Scollay Square. In 1964, back home in Columbia, he ran unsuccessfully for the state House of Representatives as a Democrat, because "I did not think the Republican Party in South Carolina had arrived at the point [on race-related issues] I probably thought they should be."

In 1974, when he ran for the Columbia City Council, it was as a Republican, because "I felt that a lot of the liberal policies were just not focused on making government work, and also the people who were asking me to swap over at that time, I thought, represented the new leadership of the Republican Party in South Carolina—the Ford-Rockefeller wing of the party, as opposed to the Reagan wing." That guess proved wrong, and "in the spring of 1977, I announced to the world that I was a Democrat again, and ran for Mayor in 1978 as a Democrat and was elected. The Democrats welcomed me back. The defense I've always given to that inconsistent history is that Winston Churchill swapped parties three times and each time it was a matter of absolute conviction. I think you have more fun being a Democrat," said this man who ought to know, "and ultimately that's an ingredient in whatever you're doing."

Whether Democrat or Republican, the new generation of Southern politicians tends to emphasize the same set of managerial and reform issues that loom so large in suburbia and the West. "The most important idea I probably brought back from Harvard," said the itinerant Mayor Finlay, "was the concept of polycentric problems. What causes a lot of our frustration with government is that people tend to run off and solve one problem without understanding its implications for other problems. The hardest issues are always the polycentric problems."

Like their counterparts in other growth areas, the Southern politicians see conservative fiscal policies and sound management as a precondition for gaining public support for the social-welfare programs they espouse.

That was a point Bill Clinton made in talking about his own career in the state of Arkansas. On paper, Clinton is about the last man one would expect to be elected Governor of Arkansas. All his higher education was out of state. While at Yale, he was a volunteer campaign worker for the senatorial campaign of Joseph D. Duffey, later president of Americans for Democratic Action, and for the presidential campaign of George McGovern. He is married to an ardent feminist who has kept her maiden name, Hilary Rodham, and her own law practice in Little Rock.

But Clinton, in person, is all-Arkansas, with a slow drawl and a shy smile and an autobiography ("I was born in a little town called Hope . . . and my natural father was killed in a car wreck about three months prior to my birth") that is so down-home it sounds made up. And he learned something that he has never forgotten from watching McGovern's self-destructive campaign. "I was for him for, God knows, a long time before he was well known, and ironically, I always thought he had a chance to win the nomination. What was so disturbing to the average American voter was not that he seemed so liberal on the war, but that the entire movement seemed unstable, irrational," Clinton said. "The average person watching it on television in some small town in Arkansas, the kind of person who is the backbone of my support there, had the unsettling feeling that this campaign and this man did not have a core, a center, that was common to the great majority of the country.

"In Arkansas," Clinton said, "there's probably a hard-core thirty percent that is always going to vote for the more conservative of the two candidates. But the election can still be won by a more progressive candidate if you can persuade people you've got a center core they can understand and relate to and trust."

Clinton said he had trouble with that "center-core" electorate because of his stands on some social issues, such as his support of the Equal Rights Amendment. But economic conservatism is more important than social conservatism, he said. And Clinton endorsed the prevailing desire for keeping property taxes down and financing expanded government services only to the extent possible in a state with the lowest per-capita state and local taxes in the nation. Further, as attorney general, he intervened time and again in electric, gas and telephone utility-rate cases, playing the populist line against the power companies.

On the surface, the populist Democrats like Clinton seem at the opposite pole from the conservative Republicans like Moore and Lott and Cochran, who stress their criticism of the expanding role of the federal government. Similarly, in the West, liberal Democrats like Dick Lamm and Gary Hart seem poles apart from such conservative Republican senators as Orrin Hatch of Utah and Malcolm Wallop of Wyoming. But in reality, the voters in the frontier growth areas of the South and the West appear equally receptive to either appeal, and the candidates use the issues as almost interchangeable means of certifying their own independence. It is almost as though the important thing to the voters is not whether a candidate is anti–utility company or anti–big government. What is important is simply that the candidate place himself on the voters' side against some of the big, unresponsive bureaucracies that have had such a major impact on their lives.

In the South, as in suburbia and the West, the politicians seeking ways of demonstrating their independence put great stress on displaying their personal openness and honesty. (Henson Moore, Lamar Alexander and Dick Riley made full financial disclosures long before it was required of them. Alexander also adopted the favorite populist trick of walking the length of his state.) And like their counterparts in other growth areas, the new politicians of the South have also had to come to terms with the issues created by growth itself. Dick Riley made national news in 1979 by refusing to let low-level radioactive wastes from the Three Mile Island nuclear power plant near Harrisburg, Pennsylvania, which was shut down by a reactor accident, be added to the nuclear burial grounds near his father's hometown of Barnwell, South Carolina. Later, working with Governor Robert List of Nevada and Governor Dixy Lee Ray of Washington, he forced the federal government to impose stricter standards on the transportation of these wastes through populous areas.

Riley was certainly not unique among the younger Southern politicians in arguing that the push for energy and economic growth should not always have priority over concerns for public health and the "quality of life." His fellow South Carolinian Butler Derrick broke one of the cardinal rules of old-style Southern politics when he came out against a major public-works project in his own district. (For the older generation of Dixie congressmen, there was never a contradiction between denouncing "federal encroachment" in one speech and claiming credit for bringing in a military base or a public-works project in the next.) When Derrick was elected to Congress in 1974, work was already under way on a $299-million Savannah River dam, designed to produce 300,000 kilowatts of electric power. The dam was criticized by conservationists in the area, because most of the 59,000 acres it would flood were a wildlife habitat. Others questioned whether the benefits were worth the cost of construction. But Derrick took the position in his first campaign that "it's an ongoing project and so I'll support it." In 1977, President Carter included the Richard B. Russell Dam on his "hit list" of wasteful water projects and, after first trying to halt construction, agreed to a compromise calling for a review of their merits. Most members of Congress predictably defended their own projects, but Derrick said he agreed there should be a review. "My administrative assistant came in here," he recalled, "and when I told him what I was going to do, he looked at me and said, 'Well, I think it's the right decision, but are you prepared to go home and practice law if it's the wrong decision politically?' And I said, 'Yes, I am.' " Derrick commissioned a three-month study by a member of his staff, a Budget Bureau analyst and a team of specialists from the Library of Congress, and then made public a report that concluded, surprisingly, that the economic justification for the project was lacking and it ought to be stopped. "I didn't know what the reaction would be," he said, "but I rather expected it to be on the minus side. But what I found out in the polls that I've taken is that there were about 65 or 70 percent of the people who had an opinion, one way or the other, and they kind of split down the middle. Half of them thought I'd made the right decision, and half of them thought I'd made the wrong decision. But most of that half that thought I'd made the wrong decision respected me very much for the way I'd made it. And so, politically, it has come out very much a plus."

The battle over the Russell Dam was a skirmish in a still unresolved struggle over the character and shape of the South's future growth. With the region's population increasing by one million people a year, the Southern governors in 1972 created the Southern Growth Policies Board to monitor and advise on that crucial process. In 1974, as an offshoot of that continuing board, nineteen Southerners, under the chairmanship of Jimmy Carter, were named to a Commission on the Future of the South. The report of that commission outlined a growth strategy for the region aimed at protecting both its agricultural lands and its seacoast and focusing its commercial and industrial development on the medium-sized metropolitan areas and smaller urban centers. H. Brandt Ayers, editor and publisher of *The Anniston* (Alabama) *Star,* has been one of those most assiduously promoting this planned-growth strategy. In his book *You Can't Eat Magnolias,* Ayers held out the hope that if the South refused to "ape the Northern model [of skyscrapers alongside slums], or abandon our cities to development by random fits of the real-estate economy," it might show that the "easy graces of the small-town South could be partially re-created in large Southern urban centers."

That, of course, is easier said than done. But there are examples which suggest that growth does not have to be destructive of amenities. In Fort Lauderdale, Florida, one of the fastest-growing cities in the state, Mayor E. Clay Shaw, Jr., 41, a former Democrat who switched to the Republican Party during Barry Goldwater's 1964 campaign, has shown in three elections that careful planning can be good politics.

"Working through our planning-and-zoning board," he said, "we've actually been able to rezone the entire city and have almost cut our potential population growth in half. There are areas where a conservative has to be practical, and in areas where [local officials in other cities] have completely let supply and demand rule the question of zoning, they've ended up with some very bad problems. I view the ownership of private property not only as a basic human right, but also as a basic responsibility.

"I was responsible for passage of the shadow ordinance, which met with a great deal of controversy . . . and a great outcry from some property owners. I was looking at a photograph of our beach line one day, taken about midafternoon, and I noticed there were large shadowed areas where the hotels were casting their shadows across the beaches. And it dawned on me that if that kind of development continued, the beach would end up in complete shade after four o'clock in the afternoon. So I got an ordinance drafted and passed requiring them to set their buildings back from the property line one-half the height of the building."

As Mayor, Shaw also started a massive reforestation program which added almost 9,000 trees to the city. "I don't think it's any compromise for a conservative to be in favor of planting trees," he said, "or planning our future growth."

It would be fatuous to pretend that because they share a distaste for the racial politics of the past, a concern about education, public ethics, good management of government and keeping control of their region's future growth, the new politicians of the South are birds of a feather. They are not. Rather, they are competitors for control of a region whose political future is, more than almost any other part of the nation, up for grabs in the Eighties and Nineties. In 1972, Richard Nixon, backed by all the Republicans in this chapter, swept every Southern state. In 1976, backed by such Democrats as Dick Riley and Bill Clinton (both early supporters and Carter chairmen in their states), Jimmy Carter carried every Southern state except Virginia. He was able to capitalize on the region's pride in him as a native son and also its embarrassment at having succumbed to Nixon's "Southern strategy." But the new candidates in the South, whether Republicans like Thad Cochran or Democrats like Butler Derrick, are building bases of their own—biracial bases—rather than hanging on the coattails of some national candidate.

The fierce competition is raising the quality of the candidates both parties are offering at the state and local levels within the South. But the question that must be raised about these talented newcomers is similar to one that was confronted with their suburban and Western counterparts: Will their individual political skills be directed to any goal broader than their personal ambitions and agendas? Does their arrival on the scene mean a further fragmenting and dispersal of the nation's leadership, or can it be—if not immediately, then eventually—a help in finding that elusive national consensus which seems to have been lost in the Sixties?

Thus far, the evidence is contradictory. Some Western and Southern politicians are finding a measure of success in bridging the environment-vs.-development controversies; others are failing and feeling frustrated. Most Southern politicians are representing and leading their whole communities, not playing off whites against blacks. But there are many observers who see the regional divisions that have always been present in American politics growing sharper since the new leaders have begun to appear on the scene. Kevin Phillips popularized the phrase "the Balkanization of America" in a 1978 article in *Harper's* magazine. Many Western politicians were convinced that the first modern administration headed by a Deep South president was indeed waging what they called "a war on the West." Members of Congress from the Northeast and Midwest organized to redistribute the flow of federal funds from the growth areas below the Mason-Dixon line to the declining "Frost Belt" —and the Southern states mobilized for battle. While there were tentative efforts to build cooperative relationships between the center cities and their surrounding suburbs, most of the suburban politicians found it easier to deplore the cities' problems than to help tackle them.

The first set of growth-area politicians to gain the presidency and vice presidency, Richard Nixon and Spiro Agnew, proved unworthy of the nation's trust. The next set, Jimmy Carter and Walter Mondale, found themselves frequently on shaky ground in their first three years in office. But despite the troubles these growth-area products encountered in Washington in the Seventies, the inexorable forces of population movement and political competiton seem certain to give their suburban, Western and Southern counterparts an ever-greater role in national affairs in the Eighties and Nineties.

From its beginning, America's history has been shaped on its growth frontiers. And that will be no less true of its future.

14 · Frontiers IV: Television

THE TIN WOODMAN'S NEPHEW was sitting on the couch of his congressional office surrounded by piles of newspaper clippings. A beeper on his belt brought him periodic messages from the Republican cloakroom, warning him of impending votes. On the closed-circuit television set in the corner of his office, split-screen cameras showed him both participants in the debate taking place in the House on an agricultural-appropriations bill.

"I'm such a McLuhan creature," said Republican Representative Robert K. Dornan of California, "that I'd rather watch the debate on the screen than be on the floor of the House. I really believe I see more this way."

If there is one institution that has changed American politics since World War II—and changed both the politicians' and the voters' perceptions of reality—it is television. What began as an expensive experiment in the decade after the war has become the ubiquitous companion, teacher, interpreter and entertainer for millions.

In 1948, when the junior members of the current Congress were infants, there were 190,000 television sets in use in the United States. Today, the number is approaching 100 million. Over 97 percent of American households have at least one set, and in the average home, TV is viewed more than six hours a day. The Federal Communications Commission estimates that the typical viewer, between ages 2 and 65, will have spent more than a decade of his life watching television.

Television has become, in one generation, the most used and the most trusted source of information on the events and personalities of the political world. It is, among other things, the place where elections are won and lost, where political careers or even presidencies are born and die. Richard Nixon's career was born in the televised Hiss-Chambers hearings and saved in the televised "Checkers speech." It was "ended," or so it seemed at the time, in his televised "last press conference" in 1962 and, definitively, 12 years later, in the televised impeachment hearings of the House Judiciary Committee, which left him no option but to make his televised resignation speech.

All of the new generation of political figures have had to learn something of the marvelous and mystifying techniques of television. Almost all of the successful ones have employed consultants to instruct them in this new art of survival. They have had to learn to apply in practice what students of communication and public opinion understand only imperfectly in the realms of theory: how the flickering electronic image on the orthicon tube affects the judgments and emotions of human beings watching the pattern of shapes and colors.

What is unusual about Robert K. Dornan is that he is pure television politician—or at least, as pure a form as has yet manifested itself in public office. He is, to an exaggerated degree, what all of his contemporaries are somewhat.

Dornan, now 47, was a teen-ager before he saw his first television set and, in that sense, is somewhat removed from the younger "television generation," who had the tube as a companion from the time they left their cribs. But before he was elected to Congress in 1976, he was that quintessential television creation, the talk-show host. Ask him the difference between what he was doing then and what he is doing now, and he says, in his nonstop delivery:

"We're all in this together. I mean, it is the exact same profession. All trying to seek beauty, truth and justice . . . to save the free world from Communism . . . and make these United States a social paradise, get every black kid reading and get him a job. We're all heading in the same direction, but we're on different sides of the camera, different sides of the microphone. . . . Now, the difference is—a newsman can implement a crusader's conscience by ferreting out foul play and malfeasance . . . [but] the Congressman is more the cutting edge. . . . But it's still all the same profession."

Dornan is the son of a New York Hell's Kitchen Irishman who made money in autos and haberdashery and supported FDR until the third term. His mother—"a political zealot of the General MacArthur school," as he called her—had been a *Ziegfeld Follies* girl, and her sister was married to the late Jack Haley, the Tin Woodman in *The Wizard of Oz*. In the 1940s, the Dornans moved to Hollywood, and it was there—after five years as an Air Force pilot—that Bob Dornan's political/media career bloomed.

When he was a child of 5, his father had taken him to the White House and let him sit on the edge of Roosevelt's Oval Office desk. On his 17th birthday, his lifetime friend Michael Casey recalls, he and Dornan spent the evening talking about how Dornan could get to Congress. In 1960, the excitement of John Kennedy's campaign "hit me like it did a lot of other displaced East Coast Irish Catholics," Dornan said.

Dornan's circle, which included such Hollywood figures as Uncle Jack Haley, Ronald Reagan, George Murphy and Irene Dunne, was caught up in the anti-Communist crusades of the motion-picture industry and the conservative movement. Dornan, who says he was "always pitting myself against JFK," at least mentally, became a young favorite of the Hollywood Right. To "make it" politically, he decided, "I'm probably going to have to establish a background in media." First a celebrity; then, perhaps, a Congressman.

He tried movie acting, but was less than a spectacular success. The break came when former cowboy star Gene Autry hired Dornan as the host of a talk show on his Los Angeles television station. For two years there, and three more at another station, Dornan was on the air up to four hours a day, five days a week, interviewing guests lined up by Michael Casey, who served as producer for the program.

Dornan found that he was ill at ease asking bland, neutral questions, so the format became one of free-swinging debate between the host and left-wing antagonists like Jane Fonda and Tom Hayden. By the time the incumbent in the congressional seat Dornan had long coveted got around to retiring in 1976, Dornan was a media hero to Los Angeles conservatives and a man who could trade words with anyone. The campaign was expensive and vituperative, but Dornan came to Washington. He brought with him his boyhood pal and talk-show producer Casey, now cast in a new role as congressional administrative assistant. But politics held less charm for Casey than for Dornan, and he went back to television as a producer for Warner Brothers in 1979.

When Dornan was asked, toward the end of his first term in the House, what he had learned from the years on television that stood him in good stead, he said, "From a pragmatic standpoint, I learned the importance of news; that to win a battle, and not let anybody know about it, is nothing."

In saying that, he capsulized the wisdom of the new generation of television politicians. When asked to describe the main differences between the people who entered Congress in the last few elections and those who came in the 1950s and '60s, almost every member of a bipartisan round table of senior House members said that their juniors are products of the TV revolution. "They tend to play the outside game, rather than the inside game," said Democratic Representative Lee Hamilton of Indiana. "They are darlings of the media," agreed Republican Representative John Rousselot of California.

At a similar session, a bit later, with some of the newcomers to the House, there was general agreement on that proposition. "Certainly I understand the media, to a larger extent, and how it impacts contemporary society," said Democratic Representative John Cavanaugh of Nebraska. "I grew up with television; they did not. Many of the older members fear television and the mass media; I do not. And so I'm more comfortable with that acceleration of information, as we say, and the use of it, than they are."

Virtually all contemporary politicians use television as an advertising medium, and they use it in increasing amounts. In the 1976 presidential campaign, Jimmy Carter and Gerald Ford reported combined television advertising expenditures of almost $17 million. They do so in the face of some evidence questioning whether the TV ads do significantly change voting decisions. One study—admittedly controversial—by political scientists Thomas Patterson and Robert McClure said only 4 percent of the voters in the 1972 presidential election acknowledged being influenced by TV ads. The politicians spend money on television for the same reasons that makers of commercial products advertise. Their own research tells them that consumers or voters pick familiar, favorably recognized products. And besides, they feel compelled to match what the competition is doing.

But because expenditures on television advertising are limited—either by statute or by the problems of fund raising—the competition between politicians now focuses largely on their skill in injecting themselves into "free media," particularly television news programs.

The clamor for attention is nothing new in politics, of course. Ever since the invention of the printing press, office seekers have been wracking their brains for ways to get into the papers. That competition has not eased—as any Washington reporter wading through his daily stack of press releases can testify.

But the exertions the politicians make to break into the television news are much greater—for two quite sensible reasons. A typical half-hour television news show, whether local or national, can deal with far fewer stories and personalities than that day's edition of the newspapers. The familiar comparison is that the scripts of the network news shows contain fewer words than are found on the front page of *The New York Times*.

The second reason the scramble for television time is so frantic is the size and importance of the audience. Since the early 1960s, studies by the Roper organization show, television has been the single most important source of news, and the gap between television and the second-most-important source, newspapers, has been steadily growing. In 1978, 67 percent of the public rated television its most important news source, and more than half those surveyed said they relied only on television. Similarly, the reliability rating of television is extremely high, with 47 percent of the public in 1978 calling it the most believable medium—more than twice the credibility newspapers enjoyed.

Dornan has been relatively sparing in his use of television as a campaign advertising medium. In 1978, television accounted for only $34,000 of a campaign budget of almost $300,000.

But he is indefatigable in "working the media." A major issue for him in his first session in Congress was the battle over the B-1 bomber, which was built in his district. Ultimately, the fight was lost, but not until every one of the people in Dornan's district had an opportunity to see how hard he had fought. "On December 6 [1977]," he recalled, "we turned it around. I didn't go over to somebody's office and have carrot stalks and champagne. I came back here, closed the door, got on the phone and did fourteen radio interviews and five newspaper interviews. I remember the late Bill Ketchum [a Congressman from a neighboring district] was mad as hell at me, because the B-1 actually flew out of his district. He came up to me and said, 'What the hell are you doing taking credit for all this B-1 stuff, when I have been working on this?'

"And I said, 'Hey, Bill, I live in L.A., where all the stations are. I didn't cut into any of your action. You didn't call any of the stations. You were articulate on the floor; so was I. But I can't help it if [columnist] Mary McGrory calls me the B-1 leader, as a freshman. I went in and worked the news media.' "

"Working the news media" is something almost all the younger-generation politicians do, but rarely as uninhibitedly or imaginatively as Dornan. He had been in Congress only two months when a group of Hanafi Moslems took over several buildings in Washington to dramatize their grievances with the government. Dornan whizzed to the scene—and into the news—with an offer, quickly rejected, to trade himself for the hostages.

When congressional Democrats were trying to pass a Carter Administration bill for election-day voter registration, Dornan arranged to have some false Virginia identification cards made in California, and called a press conference to show how easy fraudulent voting would be under the proposed law. What put it on television was the impudence of having the fake credentials bear the name and picture of the bill's prime sponsor, Democratic Representative Frank Thompson, Jr., of New Jersey.

Thompson was apoplectic, and the incident helped solidify Dornan's reputation in the House as an impassioned debater and uninhibited partisan, whose talent for attracting attention has not been matched by the solidity of his day-to-day legislative work. Dornan, like many others of his generation, is less concerned with his reputation among his congressional peers than in playing the media game that can help him follow JFK's path—at least as far as the Senate.

By no means was Dornan California's first successful show-biz politician. In his hometown, Baxter Ward went from television anchorman to Los

Angeles County supervisor. A constituent of Dornan's, a onetime radio sportscaster named Ronald Reagan, became famous enough as a movie actor and television host to be twice elected Governor of California. Reagan has spent the last six years of his life broadcasting political commentaries when he was not running for President, and running for President when he was not broadcasting political commentaries. For him, as Dornan suggests, the trip from one side of the microphone to the other has been a very short distance indeed.

California likes celebrity senators. The man Dornan hopes to succeed, Republican Senator S. I. Hayakawa, was, in a certain sense, a "television creation." It was the television news coverage of Hayakawa's tiny, tam-o'-shantered figure defying the student protestors at San Francisco State College during the Sixties that made this quiet semanticist into a public figure—and stirred his appetite for public office. Earlier, back in 1964, show business claimed its first Senate seat when Californians sent movie star/dancer George Murphy to Washington. Murphy helped break the ice. "They asked me," he recalled, " 'What has a dancer to do with politics?' I said, 'I'm a citizen first of all, and I was a damn good dancer, and I think it's an honorable tag. So what's your next question?' "

Murphy thought good entertainers were naturals for politics, because they must be "sensitive to people, quick on their feet and know how not to bore an audience." He worked with Dornan in several of the Hollywood anti-Communist crusades, watched him on television and found him "a very bright young man."

He had only one suggestion: that Dornan curb the high-pressure tactics which made him, in Murphy's view, "almost too eager for general consumption." Putting it in his terms, Murphy said, "I told him to stop belting out the song, and just sing it. I'm old-fashioned, I guess."

It may be that the Pacific Coast, the modern-day mecca for mobile Americans, is particularly prone to TV politicians. There, even more than in the rest of the country, the constant, restless wandering of the citizenry has thwarted old-fashioned political organization on precinct, ward and district lines. Political parties are weak across America, but on the West Coast they are almost nonexistent. There is, instead, the "machine" politics of the new generation—based on the television set that literally accompanies families to the beach or the mountains, that rides with them in their vans, that dominates the living room or the den and is never left behind when they move.

A thousand miles up the coast from Santa Monica and one year after Dornan was elected to Congress, television news commentator Charles Royer was elected Mayor of Seattle. He told his viewer constituents, in his formal announcement, that he had decided, after seven years on the air, "it is time for me to stop trying to get some of the worst people out of politics, and time to start trying to get some of the best people in."

"My training," Royer said, "is in journalism. And it is good training for government. . . . Reporters are people whose job is to try to find the truth. To try to be fair in the telling of it. Reporters spend most of their time listening to people. People who have been damaged by government, or angered or hurt by it. Or disappointed by it. People with ideas government won't listen to. That is my experience. Listening to people. Caring about people. And communicating with people. Explaining government to people. That's good training. It has given me the philosophy and the skills which are not common in government. They are the skills we need in government, the philosophy we need in government."

As Dornan had his models in Reagan and Murphy, so Royer had his in Tom McCall of Oregon, who, during the 1960s, rose from Portland television commentator to two terms as Governor and now is back again where he began, doing TV commentaries.

Royer, 40, is as serious-minded as Dornan is frenetic, and he built his credibility and familiarity in a more low-keyed manner than did the fast-talking Californian. But he still found it "kind of presumptuous really to think I could be Mayor of Seattle after having lived there seven years."

Nonetheless, prominent Democrats began talking to him about that possibility in 1977, and after first telling them, "I would look unhinged if I tried to do that," Royer began testing the idea in his own mind and trying it out on friends. The more he thought about it, the more plausible it seemed: "I had a good feeling about government; I had a good sense of what our problems were . . . and some vision of what the city ought to be, which is a hell of a start on a campaign. . . . And having covered a lot of campaigns, I figured I could win."

It all crystallized one evening when Royer was out making a speech with his KING-TV associate and close friend Don McGaffin. As McGaffin recalled:

"Charlie and I had a dog-and-pony show. We'd be invited to make speeches in tandem. We'd take turns making fun of each other. People seemed to enjoy it. One night, we'd been invited to speak to a large Democratic precinct group. We hadn't had any dinner, but we'd had a couple of drinks. I covered myself with glory by bringing my Bloody Mary to the speech. We had been unable to agree about a subject to talk about, and we found ourselves on the stage with people staring. I said I would therefore like to announce that my friend is a candidate for Mayor of Seattle. The place went crazy. People were screaming, shouting. Charlie was absolutely pale. He said he would like to thank Don McGaffin, who'd probably just cost him his career. But in fact, he said, he did plan to become a candidate."

In the subsequent campaign, Royer confirmed his belief that "the television exposure helped a lot." Voters, he found, "pretty much knew the name and hooked it up with some sort of experience they had on television with a guy who was talking about government and seemed fairly sound." On the other hand, he noted, seven years of commentaries on current issues gave him the equivalent of a public record, and his opponents were quick to comb through those past commentaries in search of useful issues.

Still, he won the race against several opponents with experience in city government, took over and immediately "found out I really didn't understand the press. . . . The first thing I saw when I got into office was that the press sees only a piece of the huge flow of information that runs through government. . . . And so I thought I would rectify that by having absolutely open government—making everything available to the press. Which was naive."

Royer scheduled briefing sessions in which he and his aides would discuss anything—and even open their files to the press. But at the first one, television camera crews arrived "and it turned into a guarded question-and-answer session. So I said no TV cameras, and there was a huge flap. I should have known my own brethren in television better. And I should have known that it's not my job as an elected official to lead the press or try to do the press's job. My job is to do my job."

In that, Royer receives—and gives himself—mixed grades. Despite his belief that journalists are shrewd judges of people, he admits to "making some mistakes in hiring people." A former colleague, now covering him, said after Royer's first two years that the commentator-Mayor still seemed to be searching for "two-minute solutions" to the city's problems, formulas for complex issues that could be expressed in the confines of his old air time. On the other hand, the man who had never even had a secretary in his old job "found out I'm a pretty good administrator," and managed to overcome the fears that Seattle would simply fall apart in a TV commentator's hands.

The charge that television promotes politicians who can beguilingly pledge "two-minute solutions" to complex problems is one of the critics' major indictments of the medium's effects on contemporary politics. It is not an open-and-shut case. There have been notable instances, from the Army-McCarthy hearings to the Watergate hearings, in which the willingness of the television networks to carry hour after hour of testimony and argument allowed the American public to sit in judgment on high officials and on issues of the utmost importance.

There have been televised documentaries—on drug abuse, malnutrition, migrant workers, the environment—that have put neglected problems on the national agenda in a way that no politician could ignore.

Whatever their limitations (and no one is more aware of them than television journalists), the nightly national news shows have brought millions of Americans whose hometown papers carry only a meager diet of national and international news a better perception of that broader world than they would otherwise have had.

In the past decade, public broadcasting networks—both radio and television—have greatly enriched the available supply of public-affairs programming, lingering longer on discussions of a particular topic and providing more live coverage of political and policy debates than the commercial networks can do.

It is a rare person who would claim that Americans would be better informed if an edict banished television from their lives. But the view of some young politicians that television tempts them to oversimplify issues to the point of distortion cannot be easily dismissed.

A case in point is Democratic Representative Timothy E. Wirth of Colorado, 41, who earned his Ph.D. at Stanford and seemed headed for a career in education administration when a stint as a White House Fellow and the shock of Kent State turned his thoughts to politics. Wirth won a House seat in the Denver suburbs in 1974 in a campaign in which TV spots consumed more than half his $140,000 budget. His most effective tool was the classic gimmick of the "empty chair" debate against an incumbent he said refused to face him. In 1978, facing a serious test against a challenger who said Wirth was being "tricky" in presenting himself to the voters as a fiscal conservative, Wirth used another TV spot which became something of a classic. Three Hollywood actors, filmed in detective-story dramatic lighting in what appeared to be a lavish lawyer's office, are representing what the unwary might take to be the challenger's campaign committee. "The question is," the boss asks, "how can we beat Tim Wirth?" His two assistants have some ideas: "Call him a big spender. . . . Let's tie him in to the White House. . . . He doesn't care about people." "No," the boss finally says, "Tim Wirth is clean." In desperation, one assistant proposes, "Let's say he tricks people." "How can you prove that?" asks the boss, shifting in his chair. The rejoinder: "Who said anything about proof?"

Wirth thinks that spot, plus another in which his opponent's support of deep tax cuts was lampooned as a carnival barker's fast-talking spiel to the yokels, probably saved his career. But he worries about the fact that "we are in a television age which demands thirty- or sixty-second solutions. This is a time of increasingly complex issues, and the people of my generation are not frightened of dealing with complexity and ambiguity. Our education has given us the analytical tools for doing that. But how do we communicate that to the people we are supposed to be representing? It has become increasingly difficult to impart information to the American people about energy, or taxes, or transportation, or air pollution, because the primary medium is television. . . . The frustrating thing is that all of us know how to use it, but we've got to handle these issues in the same time span and format that television news handles a fire. In fact, they'd much rather have thirty seconds of a fire than thirty seconds of 'talking heads,' so how do we ever communicate on these issues?"

It is not a question that is easily answered. But the specialists in television communication—the modern politicians' media advisers—are not defensive on the subject. They point out—and rightly—that politics has always exploited both simplification and illusion.

Long before television, William Jennings Bryan and Huey Long were using the speaking tour to provide their constituents with something television also achieves: a thin veneer of information and a broad dissemination of a particular point of view. Bryan and Long learned what could be gained by spreading their rhetoric evenly across a broad geographical area: a solidified base of support. The same speech, as they rightly supposed, was likely to produce the same reaction as often as it was repeated.

But Bryan's and Long's fiery oratory would have to be remade for television. The medium simulates immediacy and intimate experience; while Bryan and Long may have done very well in the open air, in a living room they would seem loud and obtrusive.

A pamphlet published by the National Association of Broadcasters as a guide to candidates for "campaigning on TV" emphasizes the desirability of the understated, comfortable image on the screen.

"You undoubtedly are aware that television is an intimate medium. . . . When standing, maintain a relaxed stance. . . . Move slowly, but naturally. You might even sit on the edge of the table at times—to give you that natural, relaxed air.

"Any talents you may have as a flowery orator must be replaced with friendly, informal conversation. . . . Keep always in mind that no matter how far from the camera you may be, it still is possible to take a close-up of your face. Since you have no way of knowing when a close-up is being made, act as if one is being taken at all times."

That guidebook is little more than a paraphrase, in prescriptive form, of the description of television's characteristics found in Marshall McLuhan's pioneering book *Understanding Media*. It was McLuhan who defined television as a "cool medium" and said, "The success of any TV performer depends on his achieving a low-pressure style of presentation." In 1960, he predicted that TV "would inevitably be a disaster for a sharp, intense image like Nixon's and a boon for the blurry, shaggy texture of Kennedy."

Since then, we have been blessed (or cursed) with an ever-growing number of politicians with blurry, shaggy images, including the current President of the United States, who cultivated a hairdo that increased his resemblance to John Kennedy. That look—open-eyed, soft-voiced, sincere—has become the dominant look of American politics. But it is not just the style which TV has dictated. It has also altered the structure of our politics, for reasons which McLuhan best explained.

"With TV," he wrote, "came the end of bloc voting in politics, a form of specialism and fragmentation that won't work since TV. Instead of the voting bloc, we have the icon, the inclusive image. Instead of a political viewpoint or platform, the inclusive posture or stance. Instead of the product, the process."

In his shorthand fashion, McLuhan has touched on many of the changes being described in these three chapters on the "frontier" politicians, and one can see those changes perhaps more clearly through the television camera lens than through direct observation. Television, as much as any single force, has undercut the role of the political parties, eroded the stable alignments of the past and drained politics of its ideological content.

"Instead of the product, the process," McLuhan said, simply reinforcing the characteristics of the growth-area politicians, their emphasis on a professional *approach* to problem solving and their commitment to ethics in government. They ask to be judged on the *way* they do their job, on how accessible, responsive and accommodating they and their staffs are to constituent requests. They are distinctly less eager to be judged by the *results* they obtain; indeed, when government comes under criticism as balky, expensive, intrusive and inefficient, the younger politicians often jump to the head of the protestors' parade, rather than attempting to defend the institution of which they are a part.

"Instead of a political viewpoint or platform, the inclusive posture or stance," McLuhan said. "Instead of the voting bloc, we have the icon, the inclusive image." The growth-area politicians operate as political entrepreneurs, not as subordinate parts of political organizations or parties. They do not inherit their party labels, or their party's voting bloc, nor do they confine their own political solicitations to that bloc. Their door is open to everyone—and so, frequently, is their mind. Their ideology is sandpapered away to leave visible only a few broadly acceptable traits—of which the most important is that frontier quality of independence which Frederick Jackson Turner so exalted. "That dominant individualism, working for good and for evil" of which he wrote in 1893 is still visible on the frontiers of American politics, especially as seen through the television lens.

Not all these characteristics can be found in all the frontier politicians.

But some of their campaigns show just how clearly these traits can be transmitted as television images.

A particularly interesting example of that type of campaign was provided by Robert Squier, a highly regarded television adviser and political strategist for Democratic candidates. Squier, 46, is both a product and a shaper of the media age of politics. "I have always been emotionally a Democrat," he said, "or at least since I saw my grandfather cry when we heard on the radio that Franklin D. Roosevelt had died. I knew I was a Democrat because it was the first time that I'd ever seen that powerful man I felt so close to show any emotion.

"Later, when I was at Boston University, Joe Welch [the lawyer in the Army-McCarthy hearings] became my hero when I watched him on my TV set take on the people who had made life miserable for my professors. That experience gave me intellectual confirmation of emotions I'd almost been born with as a Democrat."

Thus shaped by one radio news bulletin and a televised Senate hearing, Squier became a media adviser to Hubert H. Humphrey and Edmund S. Muskie in their unsuccessful campaigns for the presidency. But he really came into his own, beginning in 1974, when he began working with candidates of his own generation. They were not "professional politicians." They were "young enough to go do something else if they lost." They reminded Squier of Jefferson and the Founding Fathers, and, he said, "Bob Graham is a good example."

Graham, elected Governor of Florida in 1978 at the age of 42, was a millionaire developer who had served for twelve years in the state Senate from Dade County (Miami). When Squier was hired by Graham in 1977, "he had zero recognition statewide—zero." His chances of winning seemed doomed by the fact that the front-runner in the race, Attorney General Robert Shevin, was not only thirty-two points ahead of him in the polls but came from the same county and the same relatively liberal constituency that Graham himself had as his base.

"One of the most difficult things I had to prepare him [Graham] for," Squier recalled, "was that he could probably get into the runoff, but he would probably lose his own senatorial district. That was very hard for him to accept. It was unthinkable in the old way of looking at politics for a man to lose his base by a two-to-one margin and yet go all the way. But now campaigns are much more sophisticated."

Squier explained that the combination of personal mobility and communications technology had altered the old structure of political organization. "People used to get their political information about candidates through a long, complicated chain which ended when someone in the neighborhood you knew was hooked in somehow with the political group or party you generally associated with. Where you lived had more to say than anything else about how you hooked into that chain. Because the person you knew in the block or neighborhood was hooked into the ward organization, and the city organization and the state organization. What TV has done is to short-circuit that whole system, so that now, instead of waiting for that chain reaction to take place, you get your information directly from television. And as people began moving more and more from district to district and state to state, it was only TV that could bring them that information. The old chains [of political communication through party organization] were broken."

By the time he signed on with Graham, Squier had won a reputation that allowed him to become much more than the man who filmed the television ads for the campaign. "I will not work in a campaign in which I am not a senior member of the strategy board," he said. "In the Graham campaign, there were really four of us, and I was really the designer. I designed the campaign and everyone else executed it."

The basic concept of the campaign was "workdays." Graham announced, eighteen months before the election, that instead of traditional stumping, he would work at one hundred different jobs on one hundred different days in all parts of the state to "learn what the people of Florida want in their next Governor."

He did just that—going out with the telephone linemen one day, the sponge fishermen another. He was a hospital orderly, a waiter in a Cuban restaurant, a Tampa cigar maker, an equipment manager for the Miami Dolphins and a garbageman. The spectacle of a wealthy businessman-legislator doing these jobs was fascinating to the mass media, and Graham reaped the kind of publicity that speechmaking and handshaking could never have brought him. But, as Squier explained, there was much more to it than that.

"He had to attach himself to another part of the state in order to have a chance to win, and in our case no one saw that's what Bob was doing. People thought 'workdays' was a gimmick, and didn't see that it had anything to do with the northern part of the state." North Florida is rural, conservative and less affluent. It is more akin, in its Baptist beliefs and Protestant ethic, to Mississippi and south Georgia than to Miami.

"What we were doing," Squier explained, "was making him the candidate from upstate. We attached him to the concept of work, which was more closely akin to the thinking of the people in that part of the state than anything they knew about Bob Shevin, the liberal lawyer candidate from Dade County."

I asked Squier where the idea had come from, half expecting him to acknowledge that it was a variant on the theme of "walking the state" to win election. In 1970, a then unknown state Senator named Lawton M. Chiles, Jr., had scored an upset victory for a U.S. Senate seat by virtue of the publicity he won by covering Florida, end to end, on foot. In the next ten years, dozens of other candidates, from Maine to Colorado and from Iowa to Tennessee, seized on Chiles's gimmick, with generally successful results.

But it turned out my supposition was wrong. "In the case of workdays," Squier said, "we had tried it once before. It had had an out-of-town trial." In 1974, Squier had served as a consultant on a project financed by the National Committee for an Effective Congress to aid liberal Democratic challengers for House seats. One of his clients was Tom Harkin (the Iowa Congressman in the round table of Vietnam war veterans in Chapter 2). Harkin was trying, for the third time, to overturn an entrenched Republican incumbent.

"Harkin was the first guy I saw doing workdays," Squier said. "When I went into the campaign he was doing workdays as a kind of learning experience for himself, almost unconnected to the communications end of his campaign. I proposed that they bring workdays to the center of their campaign. . . . We built all the media around workdays, and he won.

"I didn't do it again until I met Graham, because I didn't find the right set of circumstances. But it suited Graham. His father was a man who worked his boys hard, and he had done some of those jobs as a boy."

Graham himself told me in a separate interview that he had tested the water before meeting Squier. "I was speaking to a group of high-school teachers on civic education a few years ago," he said, "and one of the teachers challenged me to try it. So I did teach civics for a semester, and I learned how hard it is to do well."

So when Squier told him of his Iowa experience and proposed the workdays strategy, Graham was receptive. "We tried it for about ten days, with no publicity, just to be sure he could handle it physically," Squier said, "and he did fine."

Squier took me down to the basement of his town-house office on Capitol Hill and showed me several of the commercials that had "moved Graham philosophically" in the voters' perception from the "millionaire Miami liberal" Squier said he had been when the campaign began.

He explained that the TV scenes were not really from Graham's workdays. Rather, after Graham had done a series of workdays in an area, Squier would send out a film crew to shoot Graham back on the scene of his previous "jobs."

The coworkers' reaction, on film, was uniformly enthusiastic. "You will be elected Governor," said a woman at one site. "If you stay with what you're saying right now, working with the common man, the man that votes, the middleman that's putting the taxes out, we're going to put you in there."

"Her reaction," Squier said, "was unbelievable. She didn't care what his politics were or anything else about him, except that he'd done the work he said he would."

A co-worker on a telephone-repair crew, in another commercial, found a way of telling the people watching a TV ad that it was not just another TV ad: "I really like him," he said of Graham. "He's getting out, he's finding out, you know, about the working people and what they're doing. So many times you see a man on TV, but you don't really get to know him or meet him or find out what type of person and so on. He's got the right idea."

Squier said several times that Graham "passionately and fiercely" believed that "workdays was not just a strategy for winning a campaign but of educating a man to be Governor"—a view that Graham himself confirmed when I talked to him. And there was a commercial making that point, too.

"I think a campaign ought to be a two-way street," Graham told the viewers. "I think a person ought to come out of the campaign a better person to serve in the office they're seeking. . . . Workdays offer a constant personal growth and education. You do find out more about people and their problems, and what makes this state tick, than you did when you began."

In another commercial, Graham asked himself what he had learned, and the lessons seemed rather unexceptional: "I've learned that the people of this state are very independent [that favorite frontier word again], that they want to have as much control of their own lives as possible and that they see things in government they recognize aren't working very well."

In his pioneering essay on TV, McLuhan said that "anybody whose appearance strongly declares his role and status in life is wrong for TV. Anybody who looks as if he might be a teacher, a doctor, a businessman, or any of a dozen other things all at the same time is right for TV."

Knowingly or not, Squier had devised a format in which Graham came on the screen in all of those guises, and another ninety-seven besides. And Graham had the kind of appearance which McLuhan, two decades earlier, had sensed would be right for this medium—a round, full face that was pleasant to look at but without any striking or distinctive features. After Graham's victory, an aide to Robert Shevin told *The St. Petersburg Times,* "He [Graham] had the good sense to realize that you must be fuzzy and soft on the issues, that you can't project rough, jagged edges. The voters have no sense of Graham's past—just warm, fuzzy images of him in a sport shirt, working hard and looking sincere."

Squier paid his client perhaps the highest compliment when he said, "I wish I could clone him."

Since both the candidate and the media adviser had vigorously denied that workdays were just a campaign gimmick, I asked Squier for an example of something he *would* consider a gimmick. Graham's campaign, according to press reports, had also featured "Graham Cracker" campaign buttons, ties with the outline map of Florida stitched on them and the Harvard-educated candidate singing his campaign song, "Bob Graham Is a Cracker."

But Squier found his example of gimmickry in something Harkin's opponent in the original Iowa workdays campaign had done "when he realized that workdays were working in that race. He tried to neutralize it by putting on an engineer's cap and riding the engine of a train for three hours to make it look like he was working. That was a gimmick. You know, he still had his dress black shoes on."

Squier told me that another reason he quickly established rapport with Graham was that both of them were admirers of the late V. O. Key, Jr., the student of Southern politics. In his last book, *The Responsible Electorate,* Key wrote: "If politicians perceive the electorate as responsive to father images, they will give it father images. If they see voters as most certainly responsive to nonsense, they will give them nonsense. If they see voters as susceptible to delusion, they will delude them. If they see an electorate receptive to the cold, hard realities, they will give it the cold, hard realities. Voters are not fools. The electorate responds about as rationally and responsibly as we should expect, given the clarity of the alternatives presented to it and the character of the information available to it."

Paradoxically, the chief criticism of the younger politicians, especially those from the growth frontiers who have learned to use television so well, is that instead of giving the voters "the cold, hard realities," they are giving them "warm, fuzzy images" in their campaigns. By obscuring the difficult choices and emphasizing the comforting generalities, they are, the charge goes, contributing to the public's cynicism about politics and government.

It was in this context that I asked Squier if he really believed that working 100 different jobs was the best reason Bob Graham had to give the people of Florida for electing him Governor. He was, after all, a successful businessman, a much-honored twelve-year veteran of the legislature and a leader in battles for tax reform, environmental legislation and greater education aid. A campaign might have been built on his record in those fields, rather than his day on a shrimp boat or a concrete mixer.

Squier claimed Graham's way was better. "He said, 'I'm not going to do what most politicians do—just spend the campaign making speeches at you. . . . I'm going out and do something completely different. I'm going to work a hundred jobs. I'm going to go out and gather the golden fleece, and if I gather the golden fleece, then you owe me some consideration.'

"He gained permission to run for Governor by doing that," Squier said, "and by the time we were finished, we had almost changed the thing around to the point where if you hadn't worked a hundred jobs, you hadn't bought the ticket of admission to the race."

I told Squier that—in less metaphorical language—Bob Dornan and Mike Casey had expressed the same feeling about Dornan's years on a four-hour-a-day Los Angeles television talk show: that it was a necessary "ticket of admission" to running for Congress.

"Really," he said. "That's fascinating."

15 · Opinion Makers and Takers

IN THE MIDDLE OF the third year of his presidency, Jimmy Carter suddenly canceled a nationally televised address, suspended his schedule and withdrew from his involvement in the daily decision making of the government. He retreated to Camp David with groups of advisers for a searching ten-day reassessment of his Administration and of the condition of the nation he was attempting, with fitful success, to lead. When he returned to Washington, he quickly removed or reassigned half the members of his Cabinet, recast the White House staff and announced —to a startled world—that he was making a fresh start.

If Carter's behavior seemed astonishing to millions, the man who was least surprised was 29-year-old Patrick Caddell, who held no title in the government but served, on a retainer from the Democratic National Committee, as the President's personal pollster. For months, Caddell had been monitoring and reporting to Carter on the steady decline in public confidence in his leadership. He linked that decline to broader data showing a deepening of the decade-old public doubts about the capacity of all American leaders and institutions—and a growing pessimism about the future of the country. Late in 1978, he wrote a draft of a 1979 State of the Union speech in which Carter would have addressed that "national malaise," but the draft was rejected. In April of 1979, as Elizabeth Drew later reported in *The New Yorker,* Caddell spent several hours with First Lady Rosalynn Carter, warning her that unless the trend in his polls was reversed, Carter's presidency was doomed. He spelled out the same warning to the President in a new memo. And it was to these urgings that Carter finally responded in his dramatic actions of that July.

If there was any doubt in anyone's mind about Caddell's role in the upheaval, it was erased by the speech that Carter gave when he came down from Camp David to begin the shake-up of his government. The opening section of the speech was an almost word-for-word copy of the State of the Union address Caddell had drafted six months before, and its key phrases and ideas were barely changed, in fact, from a speech that Caddell himself had delivered in 1975.

This was not the first instance of a pollster's guiding a President, but it was the most publicized. And the reaction suggested that some voters and some journalists, at least, found the situation disquieting. "Why don't we just elect Caddell and save the other guy's salary?" one letter writer suggested. "I hate to think that this country is being run by a 29-year-old kid," said another.

The influence of polls and pollsters has been a source of controversy for two generations now, ever since magazines and newspapers began using survey research techniques to measure attitudes toward candidates, public officials and issues. There was both anger and glee when the published polls went spectacularly wrong in the presidential elections of 1936 and 1948. But with increasingly sophisticated techniques being employed by the opinion samplers, the challenge since then has not been to the accuracy of the polls so much as it has been toward the propriety of their use. And that criticism has grown as an industry has developed in the past twenty years to provide private and continuous monitoring of public opinion to those in leadership positions in this society.

In their own defense, the pollsters cite the obvious fact that as long as there have been leaders, those leaders have had advisers. Every king had his counselor, every president his confidant. This is not an age of philosophy, but those who are seeking to provide leadership are not oblivious to learning or immune to instruction.

Quite the contrary. Most of them have spent years in the classroom, from kindergarten through graduate school, and most have not abandoned the habit of reading or listening or learning. Recognizing that this is a time of political transition, they are seeking guides on their journey into the unknown. And the fact that they turn to pollsters for some of that advice is both inevitable and appropriate at this stage of American life. Politics, like everything else from ice-cream making to lovemaking, has become in large part an application of high technology and expertise. When America was about to step into space and open a new perspective on the world, it did not send poets or philosophers to record the experience; it sent pilots and scientists. Thus, the soil samplings of our political terrain are left to people as adept with numbers as are the space scientists in their hardly more mysterious realm.

I have chosen five of the political pollsters and demographers—the "number crunchers," as one of them labels the group—to discuss in this chapter. They are Democratic pollsters Caddell and Peter Hart, Republican pollsters Richard Wirthlin and Robert Teeter, and political demographer Michael Barone, the principal author of *The Almanac of American Politics*.

In the wonderfully American way, the work of the pollsters is given weight, in part, because it is very expensive. A typical statewide poll in the late Seventies might cost anywhere from $8,000 to $40,000. "One of the things I always say to a client," Peter Hart remarked, describing the meeting where he presents his voluminous findings and the strategic implications he draws from them, "is that unless you're into illuminated manuscripts or rare-book collecting, this is the most expensive book you're ever going to buy. And it's amazing, when they've paid X dollars for it, how they listen!"

Some of the pollsters are plainly uncomfortable with the influence they have—or at least, the influence that is attributed to them. Wirthlin defined his role as "advising on how to allocate campaign resources—time, money, volunteers—rationally," and said it mainly consisted of "outlining options and the consequences of decisions that are made. There are times when I place myself in an advocacy position," he said, "but that isn't the rule."

Teeter, on the other hand, said that "it bothers me" that when Republican officeholders "want to think through some problem that they have, there is a propensity to call me or call Dick Wirthlin. We tend to be more their mentors than is healthy. Regardless of how scrupulous we try to be in separating our roles as reporters of research data and as advisers, I'm afraid our advice often takes on the mantle of research findings."

And Caddell, whose exercise of influence has been most notable, said he was "more and more concerned that technicians like myself have helped really to distort the political process. I think we have exacerbated the leadership problem tremendously by teaching people how to survive. We have made them think of followership, rather than leadership—finding out where the public is and what you do to protect yourself."

As in the space program, the decision in politics seems to have been that scouting is the work of the young.

The oldest of our five "number crunchers" is Wirthlin, who is now 49; the youngest is Caddell, who is 30. Teeter is 41; Hart, 38; Barone, 36. But their advice is not confined to their own contemporaries. Among them, they have been the principal sources of public-opinion analysis and campaign advice for virtually all the major presidential contenders of the past ten years. Caddell was the chief pollster for both George McGovern and Jimmy Carter. (He had to leave the McGovern campaign briefly just before the 1972 California primary in order to take an often-postponed swimming test, so that he could graduate on schedule from Harvard College.) Peter Hart has played the same role for Vice President Mondale and in 1979 became chief pollster for Senator Edward M. Kennedy's presidential campaign. Teeter was one of the pollsters in President Nixon's 1972 race and had top responsibility in that area for President Ford. Wirthlin has been the chief source of public-opinion analysis for Ronald Reagan's national campaigns and worked in conjunction with Teeter on the 1972 and 1976 presidential elections. Among them, they have worked on hundreds of senatorial, congressional, gubernatorial and mayoral campaigns in the past decade.

That they have gained this degree of influence at their relatively young ages is only in part an accident. They are not the pioneers in the craft, but a second generation. Wirthlin is a former partner of Vincent P. Barabba, who left the polling field behind to run the 1970 and 1980 censuses. Barone's work in the *Almanac* builds on the political demography of an earlier census director, Richard M. Scammon. Both Caddell's and Teeter's early careers were influenced by the teaching of Walter DeVries, a Michigan and North Carolina author, pollster and political scientist. Hart's first job was given him by Louis Harris, who was John F. Kennedy's pollster. While all of their mentors remain active and involved themselves as the 1980s begin, the pupils have, in terms of influence, outdistanced their teachers. The reason may lie in Hart's observation that "it's very hard to be able to understand two different generations. . . . It's not the technology; it's just a question of understanding what's going on."

There is certainly no rigid formula for gaining that understanding, as the biographies of the five "number crunchers" demonstrate. Wirthlin and Teeter are refugees from academia; Barone, a nonpracticing lawyer. Hart has been a pollster all of his short adult life, and Caddell, from puberty onward. It is interesting that all five of them either worked for or voted for Democrats their first time out, but Wirthlin and Teeter now confine themselves to Republican clients, while the others (Barone is vice president of Hart's polling firm, as well as one of the authors of the *Almanac*) serve Democratic candidates.

Taking them in descending chronological order, Wirthlin was born and raised in Salt Lake City, the son of a Republican meat-and-poultry dealer who, after a lifetime of service, became the Presiding Bishop of the Church of Jesus Christ of Latter-Day Saints (the Mormons). When Dick Wirthlin was 19 he served a mission for the church in Switzerland, and he came home to study economics at the University of Utah and the University of California at Berkeley. After finishing his Ph.D. at Berkeley, he became chairman of the economics department at Brigham Young University. It was there, in 1964, that he was asked to use his knowledge of statistics and his ready supply of graduate students to do survey research for two Utah candidates—David King, a Democrat running for the House of Representatives, and Mitchell Melich, a Republican running for Governor.

"At that time," said Wirthlin, "I wasn't as partisan as I've later become. I would have been classified as a liberal Republican, but a ticket splitter. I was clearly conservative in terms of the economics department at Berkeley, but I taught Keynesian economics, and quite frankly, I was a somewhat controversial figure at BYU, because I was considered a liberal. In 1964 my mother was the Republican National Committeewoman for the state of Utah, and I gave a dollar and my name to an ad in the newspaper for a group called Professors for Johnson. I had a delegation from my family to contend with on that, wondering how I would dare use the Wirthlin name for that purpose."

As it happened, both the local candidates Wirthlin helped in 1964 were losers, but his work was praised, and two years later he polled for a number of Republican winners in the Mountain States.

The following year, he took a sabbatical to explore the potential for his avocation, and in 1969 joined Barabba in forming Decision-Making Information (DMI), a political-analysis firm combining polling with census data. Since then, the firm has handled sixty to seventy campaigns each election year. Wirthlin's own politics have shifted further right ("I just found the Keynesian theories I'd spent a good deal of my life understanding did not fit the real world of stagflation and political decision making that I came to know"), and he has become the principal pollster for Reagan and other conservative Republicans.

A similar position for the moderate-to-progressive Republicans is occupied by Teeter, the president of Market Opinion Research Corporation (MORC) in Detroit. Teeter grew up in Coldwater, Michigan, the son of a local businessman–big shot who was, at various times, Mayor, president of the Rotary, president of the Chamber of Commerce and president of almost everything else in town. Bob Teeter was president of the student body at Coldwater High School, but he drifted through Albion College and graduate school at Michigan State University without having much of an idea of what he was going to do. In 1960, the 21-year-old Teeter cast his first presidential vote for John Kennedy, because "I really didn't like Richard Nixon." But in 1964, he asked his father, a staunch Republican and a delegate supporting Michigan Governor George Romney, to take him along to the GOP convention in San Francisco, and it was there that Steve Stockmeyer, now director of the Republican Congressional Campaign Committee, offered Teeter a job as an advance man for Romney's re-election campaign. While teaching at Adrian College, Teeter continued to help part time in Romney's Lansing office, and in 1966 he became a full-time campaign staff member. When that race was over, Frederick P.

Currier, Romney's pollster, asked Teeter to join his firm (MORC) to handle the expanded work load of Romney's planned 1968 presidential bid. While that campaign was no more successful than Wirthlin's debut, MORC's work was praised. And just as DMI expanded through the West and the conservative wing of the party, MORC expanded through the Midwest and East and the moderate wing of the GOP. (In the Seventies, their spheres began to overlap, at least geographically.)

Hart, the third of the quintet, was born and raised in Berkeley, where his father teaches English at the University of California. His political influences are on the maternal line—a socialist grandmother who "started out with Teddy Roosevelt and the Bull Moose Party and was very close to Norman Thomas and Eugene Debs" and a mother who was "a good liberal for Adlai Stevenson in 1952 and 1956." Hart went east to Colby College in Maine; was hired out of school as a $75-a-week coding-department drone by pollster Lou Harris; worked brief stints between 1968 and 1971 for John J. Gilligan's unsuccessful Senate campaign in Ohio, the Democratic National Committee, pollster Oliver Quayle and, once again, Lou Harris before setting up his own firm in Washington. While Kennedy was Hart's first presidential contender, he has handled the polling for dozens of moderate to liberal Democratic candidates across the country.

Barone, Hart's associate, grew up outside Detroit. His father was a physician and his mother an apostate Catholic, and both were FDR Democrats who became ticket splitters—for Eisenhower in the 1950s and for Romney and Nixon in the 1960s. Barone was the kind of precocious kid who memorized political statistics as easily as he did Tigers batting averages, and all through private school in Detroit, Harvard and Harvard Law School, he would be shown off by his friends as "this guy who can tell you the exact population and presidential vote of your hometown." The attraction of John Kennedy made him a Democrat, and his decision was strengthened by the discovery he made, while working summers for the party in Oakland County, Michigan, during the mid-Sixties, that "you had all these very different worlds, really, in the different suburbs within three or four miles of my parents' house.

"I'd grown up in a homogeneous suburb and met nothing but kids from professional and business backgrounds in my school. And you know, in the Democratic Party you meet Jews, you meet Catholics, you meet Polish people, you meet blacks, you meet liberal intellectuals, you meet labor-union people . . . and that really reverberated for me." In 1972, after law school, Barone put his fascination with the varieties of political communities—"why the $30,000-house neighborhoods in Birmingham, Michigan, are a lot more Republican than $30,000-home neighborhoods in Berkley, Michigan"—to broader use. With two other Harvard graduates,

Grant Ujifusa and Douglas Matthews, he wrote *The Almanac of American Politics,* a compendium of voting and population statistics and mini-profiles of the 50 states, the 435 congressional districts and their elected officials. The biennial editions of the *Almanac* have become the "bibles" of American politicians and political journalists.

Caddell, the last of the quintet, is also something of a prodigy. The son of a Coast Guard career officer, Caddell was born in South Carolina, but grew up in Jacksonville, Florida. A Catholic, Caddell found himself one of the few John Kennedy supporters in a mock election in grade school in 1960; later, when his father was transferred to Falmouth, Massachusetts, the family would go to Otis Air Force Base to see Kennedy land for his vacations on Cape Cod.

As a 17-year-old Jacksonville high-school student, Caddell, intrigued by the television networks' ability to do early projections of election winners, took on as a project for his mathematics class the design of a similar sampling system for Jacksonville. His polling in a special election proved so accurate that he was given publicity in the local papers. The story was noticed by Frederick H. Schultz, then seeking election as Speaker of the Florida House of Representatives and now vice chairman of the Federal Reserve Board. Schultz brought Caddell to Tallahassee as a personal aide and threw him into polling races for his allies in the legislature. Caddell also used his statistical skills to solve some thorny redistricting problems in a Jacksonville–Duval County consolidation proposal. When the special elections were held in the new districts, he did the polling and projections for television station WJXT and proved himself at least the equal of the network computers. Schultz had enough confidence in his skills to invest in a polling firm Caddell and two Harvard classmates started while still undergraduates, and the firm was working for Democratic candidates from Florida to Ohio before Caddell himself was old enough to vote. In 1972, a Florida supporter of George McGovern told Gary Hart, then McGovern's manager, about Caddell, and at a meeting in Miami, "Gary asked us if we'd be interested in helping them. Of course, we were committed to McGovern at that time anyway, because of the [Vietnam] war," Caddell said, "so we very nonchalantly said yes. But inside, we were jumping up and down."

Caddell rode the roller coaster of the McGovern campaign as well as anyone could, and emerged from the ruins with his reputation intact—and a useful contact with Jimmy Carter. They met in June 1972 when McGovern visited Carter at the Georgia Governor's mansion. "We sat up in the kitchen until really late in the night," Caddell recalled. "We talked about my college thesis on the changing politics of the South and a lot of other things." Despite that meeting, Caddell gave a quick brush-off to Carter aides Hamilton Jordan and Jerry Rafshoon when they tried to make the case to him, at the Miami Beach convention, that McGovern should choose a Southerner (presumably meaning Carter) as his running mate. But by 1975 he had agreed to help Carter with some polls in Florida for his March 1976 primary contest against George Wallace, "and we just began to hit it off, more and more." Caddell has remained Carter's personal pollster, but his firm, Cambridge Survey Research, Inc., has also polled for dozens of other Democratic candidates, as well as doing contract polling for many corporate clients.

Perhaps because of his youth and his spectacular rise to the top of his field, Caddell has attracted more charges of opportunism than his colleagues and competitors. When a memo he wrote for Carter immediately after the 1976 election was leaked to the press in 1977, it appeared that Caddell had turned against McGovern and the liberals who had given him his start in national politics.

"Traditional liberals in the Democratic Party," Caddell wrote Carter, "in many ways are as antiquated and anachronistic a group as are the conservative Republicans. However, because of their representation in the establishment, the media and in politics, they have a weight in public affairs far greater than their numbers. They have been openly hostile in the past to Governor Carter, not only because he has a different set of national priorities but also because of differences over style and approach. This wing is composed of individuals such as Ted Kennedy, George McGovern and Mo Udall. For these people, there is little risk in challenging an incumbent President, coupled with an overwhelming desire to do so." A page later, he also warned his client President about the threat from the "articulate and politically ambitious Young Turks"—among whom was Gary Hart, the man who had hired Caddell for his first national campaign.

Caddell defended himself against the charge of opportunism and maintained his professional and personal relationships with McGovern and Hart. But he readily conceded that "my view of politics has changed enormously. My view of the country changed," he said. "Judging the public attitudes . . . between 1972 and 1976, I felt a deep psychological crisis. . . . There seemed to be a tremendous void between the public and its leadership. . . . I felt the country was in deep trouble . . . that we were a very goal-oriented country without any goals. . . . It struck me that more than any one single issue, dealing with that problem of healing the country was critical. . . . At one point I was more of a defined ideologue than I probably am now, because I came to feel that unless we could deal with these larger questions, the specific problems couldn't be addressed."

In a speech to a Democratic issues conference in Louisville in 1975, the speech that anticipated both the language and the concepts of Carter's mid-1979 address, Caddell sought to analyze the causes of what he called "a crisis of confidence in the political process and the future of the nation.

"Americans always believed that their country fought only just wars, and that we did not lose wars like other nations. Then came Vietnam.

"Americans always believed that every President would at least try to provide moral leadership—that whatever was wrong with the man, the office itself would right. . . . Then came Nixon and Watergate.

"Americans believed that we had learned to control the economy. . . . Then came double-digit inflation, eight-percent unemployment and the energy crisis.

"Americans always believed that this country was ruled by the ballot, not the bullet. . . . Then came Dallas and all the horror which has followed. . . ."

The result, he said, was that instead of the traditional belief that "Americans were a chosen people," there had come a "pervasive pessimism . . . and the result of this pessimism is alienation. . . . Americans increasingly feel that the system will not work. They are uncertain about what is happening to them and untrusting of the basic institutions to solve their problems."

As a youth of 25, who had idolized Kennedy, been on campus at Harvard when anti-war demonstrators "trashed" Harvard Yard and forced the suspension of classes; as one who had been close at hand when McGovern tried—and failed—to make Watergate an issue, Caddell perhaps felt the disruptions of the past decade more acutely than the other "number crunchers," none of whom was actively involved in the protest movements of the Sixties.

But he was certainly not alone in sensing the impact of those events, or the creation of what he called "a new era of politics." Bob Teeter said, "I don't think that anybody who didn't live through it could begin to realize what kind of a period 1963 to 1976 was, and how really rough it was on the country."

The journalistic cliché was that after that time of upheaval, and with the pressure of recurrent waves of inflation, the country was becoming more conservative. But oddly, the Republican pollsters did not see that as an accurate description of the turn-of-the-decade mood.

Dick Wirthlin, personally the most conservative of the quintet, said that "it's very difficult from a pragmatic political point of view just to make a blanket declaration that we're moving in a more conservative direction. Many of the conservative policy alternatives, such as balancing the federal budget, lowering taxes, limiting government programs, generally now garner more support from the electorate than they did five or ten years ago. Our experience indicates that people are also more comfortable giving lip service to the amorphous ideology of conservatism. But when you come to some specific issues, they frequently opt for the liberal choice. . . . Overwhelmingly, they want a reduction in welfare spending, but overwhelmingly, they favor food stamps . . . and aid to dependent children. . . . They want a smaller federal budget, but at the same time they want America to be strong militarily vis-à-vis Russia. . . . And they favor national health insurance, which would be one of the most expensive governmentally run programs we could have. . . . Americans do want to take care of the needy, and they are clearly more liberal on the life-style issues, like the use of drugs, the ERA, abortion, gay rights and their attitudes toward marriage. . . . So ideological trends don't always present a nice, neat picture, even if the combination of ideology and partisanship is usually the best predictor of the candidate a voter will support."

Teeter also expressed skepticism about the "conservative tide," saying, "I'm not sure that the people have changed as much as the problems. When the problems are property taxes, crime and public-employee strikes, the reactions are what we call conservative. . . . But when the problems are fair housing and getting black kids an education, those same people look more liberal. It has always been and still is a centrist, pragmatic country."

Peter Hart said that "when I look at the polls, I do not see ideology. I just don't see it as a Right–Left politics. I just don't see people making their decisions that way." But Hart also pointed out that the *values* which have become uppermost, as distinguished from the issues positions, are, in fundamental respects, conservative values. "The thing that I see is the sense that voters want a certain amount of order and stability," he said. "They want a sense that their lives can be planned."

Expressing the same thought in somewhat different words, Caddell said—a year before Carter's 1976 election—that the two strongest instincts among the voters were "a desire for change, born not of ideology but of pragmatism" and a "desire for a restoration of basic values, of the things which people believe made America great." He also emphasized a point made by several of his colleagues: that despite the seeming increase in "nonnegotiable demands" from the interest groups surrounding government, the people were "exhausted emotionally" by the violent confrontations of the previous decade and were eager for accommodations in the national interest.

As they looked to the 1980s, all five of the "number crunchers" focused on one particular segment of the electorate, which they judged would dictate the next major turn in American politics. They were the "baby boom" contingent, the people born between 1945 and 1955 and now between 25 and 35 years old. "It's a huge group," said Bob Teeter, "and they're just sitting out there," uncaptured by any party or personality, any issue or ideology. There are over 41 million of them, according to the Census Bureau. They are better educated and more affluent at their age than any previous generation. But they are notably less involved in politics. In the 1976 presidential election, only a shade more than 50 percent of them turned out to vote; even fewer—only about 35 percent—turned out for the 1978 congressional elections. A survey Dick Wirthlin took in 1979 showed their level of interest in the 1980 election to be only about two-thirds as great as that of voters in their fifties, and said the probability of their turning out in equal proportions was even more negatively skewed.

"In the past," Teeter said, "when people were going through the marriage and householding process—in their mid to late twenties, or whenever it is—they began to gravitate to one of the political parties, or at least, to a pattern of voting behavior that remains pretty constant throughout their life. Most often, that was the party of their parents. But this is the group that has come into the electorate [or avoided coming into the electorate, in a lot of cases] after '64 or '66, and they look today just like they looked when they turned twenty-one. They tend to be apolitical. That's where turnout is lowest; it's where alienation toward government and politicians is highest. It's where party identification is lowest."

When I asked Teeter why he thought this group had remained outside the political culture, he said, "Their first experience in the political process as eligible voters came against the background of what they thought was a miserable performance on the part of the system. I mean, we assassinated two or three national leaders; we got into a crummy war; then we had a whole bunch of riots, and then we had Watergate, and then we had a recession. And nobody has ever been able to convince them that somebody's election would change it."

All of Teeter's colleagues agree with that basic description, and all of them contribute, from their own data, elements of the portrait of this group. It is not a group that can be labeled as Democratic or Republican, or as liberal or conservative *on the issues*. Partisanship and ideology are not controlling their political behavior. "They're all over the map," said Dick Wirthlin. "They're up for grabs, in a political sense." Decline of partisanship is an "across-the-board phenomenon," Wirthlin added, "but the younger voter is less partisan than your older voter, partially because he hasn't had the set of experiences that build the political value structure that leads to a partisan preference."

Wirthlin's data showed that in 1979, among the 25-to-35-year-olds, there were as many who denied any degree of party preference (20.5 percent) as called themselves strong Democrats (14.1 percent) or strong Republicans (6.2 percent). Other surveys confirmed Wirthlin's point, showing similar slackening of partisan identification in this age group. But among the older voters, according to Wirthlin, the ratio of partisanship to nonpartisanship ranged from 5 to 3 all the way up to almost 3 to 1.

What is distinctive about this group is their broader set of values. They are distinguishable in the surveys both from those who are older and those, just barely in the electorate, who are younger. "They're more Democratic in their voting behavior," Wirthlin said, "than any other age group, and very liberal." But "liberal" in this context reflects more their social attitudes than their economic views. "They don't have the heritage of the Depression," Michael Barone pointed out. On the contrary, those who are voters in this age cohort tend to be people of some affluence (and the nonvoters, as Bob Teeter noted, are, conversely, largely non-college-educated). "The gas-station attendants aren't voting," Barone agreed, "and the young marketing experts and the equal-employment-opportunity enforcement officials are. They've got as high incomes as anybody, and lesser financial obligations than the thirty-fives to forty-nines." Barone said that was why he thought so many of the younger members of Congress—Democrats as well as Republicans—voted in the late Seventies for reductions in business and personal income taxes and for lower capital-gains taxes, defying the predictions that they would be critics of such "conservative" economics.

It is in their social values that the members of the "baby boom" cohort display their liberal—or perhaps more accurately, nonconformist—character. "The social and cultural views that came out of the mid to late Sixties," Pat Caddell said, "had to do with life-styles, music, dress—all kinds of things that, politically, we normally don't pay much attention to." The "rebellion" of the college-educated young people was not directed just against the Vietnam war, Lyndon Johnson and Richard Nixon. It was also directed against the standards which large bureaucracies—academic, military or political—sought to impose. And in that dimension, they are still rebels.

"They're just alienated," Teeter said. "Every place they go, they have to deal with some kind of huge, complex structure that they can't function within as an individual. They hate to shop at Sears, because it's a big chain. Their job is much less important to them than it used to be—and much less satisfying—because they're probably in a big company. If they're in a union, it's a great big union, and they think the guy who runs the union is as bad as the guy who runs the company."

In using their affluence to flee from this rigid structure (which also includes the structure of the two-party system), the 25-to-35s, both Teeter and Caddell noted, attach great importance to their private life—especially their leisure time.

"They've become inner-directed," Teeter said. "Their value system is different. Their job is much less important to them than it used to be, and their recreational pursuits are more important. Their quality of life is important to them; their home is important. But they live in condominiums, apartments, trailer courts and subdivisions. There aren't any community organizations that have brought them together, but they may be terribly interested in the cocker spaniel–raising club of America, or the cross-country skiing club, or racquetball, or square dancing. . . . They'll drive all weekend to go to a dog show."

In a separate interview, Caddell picked up the description, almost as if he had been hearing Teeter instead of reading similar data. "They tend to be much more liberal on social issues," he said, "and some are much more conservative on fiscal and economic issues. . . . They put enormous priority on their leisure and their leisure goods. But they tend to trade down in terms of brand names. Trade names [like party names, one might insert] don't seem to carry the same values they did for my father, for instance. And they're the people who really like foreign cars and small cars."

Peter Hart said that on some of the life-style questions, "when you look at your data, it's almost like looking at two different countries." In a 1978 survey for the Department of Transportation, for example, Hart found the "baby boom" generation far more ready than older Americans to believe the energy crisis would force them to make changes in their life-style, including the way they heat and cool their homes and the way they travel to workplaces or stores. They were more willing than their elders to consider forming car pools or riding buses, to favor the reserving of highway lanes for such mass transit and to accept the need for higher taxes for these forms of transportation. On the other hand, reflecting their recreational interests and opposition to bureaucracy, they were among those most adamantly opposed to gasoline rationing or weekend gas-station shutdowns.

Because their own life-styles are very important to them, the 25-to-35s put great stock in an attitude of tolerance toward the individual's taste in such matters. The pollsters found a fascinating illustration of this in the 1976 voting, when, as Caddell said, "from the beginning of the primaries on, they were a great problem for [Jimmy] Carter. . . . In that twenty-five–to–thirty-five age group, we just didn't run as well as we would have expected. They were clearly the most liberal group within the population, and yet we couldn't get the kind of support you would have assumed, as the Democratic nominee. They were people who reacted, in a lot of ways, against Carter's image—the Southern Baptist, preacher, moralist kind of thing."

Michael Barone, commenting on the same phenomenon, noted that the campaign ads for Jerry Ford (on which Teeter, of course, collaborated) exploited the "life-style" question by "practically saying that the President doesn't mind if his kids smoke pot. They were not so crude as to say that in so many words," he said, "but that was the message they gave. You know, one of the Ford kids would say, 'Dad's a little different, but he understands us.' And in my judgment, he carried California on the basis of that. I think a lot of Californians just asked themselves, 'Who would I rather have as a father: Jimmy Carter, with his Baptist B.S.—from their point of view, that is—or Jerry Ford, who is kind of tolerant?'

"I also think," Barone said, "that's why they had all the blacks in the ads: not to get black votes—they knew they weren't getting black votes—but to get a message to younger voters that this was a man who was basically a tolerant person and who's always believed in equal treatment for blacks."

Their view of the present—and particularly their focus on this key segment of the electorate—shapes the five men's view of the likely direction of American politics. They do not see that future dawning tomorrow. Rather, they agree with Peter Hart's estimate that "we're in a transitional period"—a shift not only of generations but of moods. "We're just due," Bob Teeter remarked, "for an in-between period. You don't go from Vietnam, Watergate and recession to another New Frontier in one jump. The social distance is just too great. . . . We may go through a couple of presidents, or even three, before the country is looking again for a strong, dynamic leader who has some clear goals for the country. I thought Ford was a good President for this period, and even though Carter has thrown out all of these initiatives, when it's all over his Administration will not be one of new direction or great innovation. The country was ready for a certain kind of period, and it's going to go through that period, and it's not going to make a lot of difference who is President."

But eventually, Teeter said, the massive, unmobilized "baby boom" generation of voters will be mobilized by someone—or something. "I can't believe we're going to run a generation through their electoral lifetimes without them becoming political," he said. "I just don't believe it. . . . One of these years, you're either going to have an idea, or an issue, or a candidate come along that will create a majority coalition . . . a coalition that would last quite a while." But Teeter said he thought it unlikely that that would occur in 1980. "We're going to have to get down into the forty-year-old and younger candidates before we're really going to see a new direction for the country," he said. "Historically, majority coalitions have been built more by bringing new people into the electorate than by getting voters to switch parties. Now, for the first time since 1932, we have a large-enough group outside the active electorate to build a majority coalition if they come in—these young people, usually those with less than a college education."

Wirthlin agreed that the kind of election that might activate the "sleeping giant" generation "almost takes a crisis or a clash of strong interests in a society, and I don't see any of those on the near horizon. If we can't control inflation, if the burden on the middle class becomes more heavy than it is now, if there is an across-the-board reduction in our standard of life, then I would see the possibility of an '82 or '84 realignment. And I think the change will come primarily from the economic issues. . . . I can see a revolt of the middle class in '82 or '84 or '86 . . . and the possibility of the formation of new parties at that time . . . and in any case, that's the time clearly that we're going to have a new generation of leaders who have been conditioned by their own experiences."

Who these leaders will be, or what they may be like, is obviously of special concern and interest to these men, who function as their political guides. Caddell, who thought he had discerned the needed qualities in Jimmy Carter in the mid-Seventies, had a professional obligation—as the President's pollster—to maintain even at the end of the decade that his judgment had not been wrong.

When we recall that Caddell's sense of what the country sought was "nonideological change, linked to a restoration of traditional values," the things that he said "struck me about Carter" are significant. "He had a great sense that there was a psychological problem among the people of the country that had to be addressed. He wasn't an ideologue in any sense. He did not hesitate to approach complicated problems, and it was hard not to be impressed by his intelligence. And the symbols of who he was—a Southerner, a farmer, a family man, a religious man—all those things appealed to me."

Without withdrawing any of those judgments, Caddell conceded in a speech halfway through Carter's term that it was not working out as he had hoped. His analysis was that the President had "not come to grips with the dichotomy between being leader of the society and being leader of the government." As leader of the society, Caddell said, Carter needed to maintain a certain distance from the political threat and barter that dominated Washington, and speak to and for the mass of citizens who felt outside that interest-group struggle, who were weary of confrontations and who wanted a sense of national goals.

Instead, Caddell implied, Carter had been drawn down by some of his conscientious habits into what he called "the hard currency of government—dollars and decision memos." Small-scale battles were filling the vacuum left by unattended large issues. "Carter understood what the country wanted when he was campaigning," Caddell said, "but he has lost sight of it under the avalanche of government decisions."

The other "number crunchers" were less charitable in their assessment. Peter Hart in 1979 said, "I really thought we might get to this new age with Jimmy Carter, but it's clear the period of transition will continue as long as he is President. . . . He's a 'remainder man,' and a remainder man can't be a leader."

The Republicans were, understandably, critical. "Carter's inability to cope with the process of government" has cost him dearly among those who thought he would make the bureaucracy more efficient, taxes more fair, Wirthlin said. "I still think," said Teeter, "that the single greatest reason Carter got elected was that he was perceived as a Christian man who would bring those qualities to government. But the problem is . . . he does not appear to be competent to handle the job . . . and that will never work for anybody."

The descriptions of the kind of leader the country needed reflected the views—and perhaps the biases—of the speakers. "We need somebody," Hart said, "who's going to prick the boil and get us out of this lousy transition period." He said that might be Ted Kennedy, but also saw the danger that Kennedy could "raise hopes and expectations so high . . . they might rebound into cynicism."

Barone offered a variety of names, all of them Democrats, because, he said, "the Nixon years gave Republicans a bad name for people of my generation. . . . I think they alienated a generation of political leadership." But when that view was challenged, Barone readily conceded that conservatives "may be recruiting some younger people, and they are on the initiative right now . . . in terms of introducing new political ideas. . . . I wouldn't be surprised at all to see them win a lot of elections in 1984 and 1986."

On the Republican side, predictions were more cautious. "People are definitely looking for a change," Wirthlin said. "I think a candidate has to point to the prospect of change, but not overpromise. He has to be perceived as being able to get things done. He has to be perceived as trustworthy and as competent. He has to be perceived as caring and sincere . . . and he cannot be viewed as a 'classic liberal' or a 'classic conservative.' If a candidate can portray to the electorate the prospect that he will induce change that will modify the system in a direct measurable fashion, that's the man who's going to receive political support. Now, that change can take the form of an expensive national health-insurance program *or* a reduction in property taxes: That's the frustration, and that's the inconsistency of these present attitudes."

Teeter put it this way: "The person's ability as a communicator is all-important. Secondly, he's got to be someone who has an idea about how individuals can function in a big, complex society. He's got to demonstrate his own religious-moral-ethical feeling about the tenor of his own life, whether it's as a reborn Christian, environmentalist, self-help, self-improvement, get-in-shape or all of those things together. . . . The people that are going to emerge as the strongest leaders from that generation are not going to be the slickest politicians. They're going to be the ones with an ability to communicate that central idea of the integrity of their own lives."

In that context, several of the polling consultants expressed misgivings about what they saw or had seen among their contemporaries in politics. "I think one of the problems we face," Pat Caddell said, "is that politics has become a real profession, and we have helped make it that. I am struck by the fact that in my own generation, many of the best people are not in the political process. What we need in the 1980s are some people who are willing to spend some time in that process, who go into it with some sense of purpose and some concern for the country, on a very short-term basis, and who don't see their own political survival as the essential element of their existence."

In making that comment, Caddell returned to a theme he and others had raised earlier in this chapter: the concern that their own data-interpretation skills had conditioned their clients in this generation of politicians to follow, not lead, the country.

"In the Eighties," Dick Wirthlin said, "the system will be able to react even more sensitively to public attitudes than it does now. And maybe it's gone too far already. Maybe that's part of the problem. Maybe the fact that politicians know as quickly as they do, and as accurately as they do, where public opinion lies has provided a cause for some of the instability."

What they all seemed to be hinting was that they—like the American public—yearned for leaders whose horizon extended beyond the latest poll, or even the next election. Teeter made the point explicitly in talking about his reactions during the 1972 Nixon campaign.

"I don't like to sound like an elitist," he said, "but I used to say that one of the biggest problems with the Nixon Administration was that he put a whole bunch of people in responsible positions who were bright, competent individuals, but who had absolutely nothing in their background or education or experience that gave them the perspective to have the jobs they had. I used to go to meetings at the White House, and I often got the feeling as I'd sit through the meetings with Dwight Chapin and Bob Haldeman and Jeb Magruder and three or four of those types, 'Jesus, I'm not sure any of these guys could pass History 101. They seem to have no perspective or background on what it is we're involved in here. *None*.' "

The work of providing an after-school education or perspective to politicians often falls in our society to journalists, who may or may not be better equipped than the pollsters for the task. But if there are any of the next generation who are esteemed not only for their political insights, but for their willingness to deal with the historical and moral dimensions of politics, they would probably be cartoonist Garry B. Trudeau, television journalist Bill Moyers and columnist George F. Will. Moyers, 46, Will, 39, and Trudeau, 32, have vast audiences, and particularly avid followings among politicians. When Trudeau's comic strip, *Doonesbury*, disappeared for a few weeks from the Washington newspapers, bootleg photocopies were made in the White House and other departments, and episodes were read over the nightly television news.

Although both Moyers and Will have worked in government, and Trudeau has made politicians his favorite subject matter, all of them keep their distance from the daily concerns of politics. In the manner of the subtle moralist rather than the polemicist, they juxtapose ideals and realities, letting their audience see for themselves where the inconsistencies arise. Their wisdom, and the setting for their work, is to be found in the small towns, or in the small towns of the mind—towns which they have sought out or made for themselves. Moyers' America is Richmond, Indiana; Lawrence, Kansas; Cascade, Idaho, and Mathis, Texas. Although he ranges the world, Will seems most at home in the Illinois college town where he grew up and the suburb where he resides. Walden Commune is Trudeau's spiritual home; New Haven is just where he lives. His photograph on the cover of the *Doonesbury Chronicles* pictures him sitting in the Commune house with his cartoon characters.

Perhaps all three of them would agree with Dorothy after the experience of Oz: Truth is in your own backyard, in yourself and in those around you, and not necessarily in the Emerald City—or in Washington, D.C. They are of the political world, but a bit detached from it—which may be one reason why the politicians who are their contemporaries turn to them for perspective.

That separation has been a pattern of their lives. Trudeau was the artistic young man in a sports-minded prep school. George Will was a professor's son who seemed to care for nothing more serious than the fortunes of the Chicago Cubs. And Bill Moyers was a small-town Texan, an ordained Baptist minister among the Ivy Leaguers and Catholics of the Kennedy Administration.

Moyers was born in 1934 in Marshall, a town in East Texas, at a time when "Texas was a state as close to the frontier" as any in America. "Its politics were the politics of personal persuasion," Moyers said, "and they had everything to do with opportunity. It was all wide open. Texas was free of ideological divisions, which meant that you didn't have to take a lot of intellectual baggage with you. Personal character and hustle were what made you successful. Most of the people who were running things in Texas had started poor and started young."

Moyers did the same. From the age of 14 he worked as a reporter on the Marshall paper, under a publisher who assumed he was grooming in Moyers a future editor. But Moyers had larger goals. As a sophomore at North Texas State University in 1954—before he transferred to the University of Texas—he sought and gained a summer job on the staff of Senator Lyndon B. Johnson. Johnson, said Moyers, "liked those who had to make it, like himself, with no expectations of anything being handed to them." Six years later, when Moyers was teaching theology at Baylor, Johnson called him back to help with the 1960 campaign.

Moyers entered the Kennedy Administration through his connection with the Vice President, but unlike most others in Johnson's entourage, he soon managed to gain standing in the Kennedy circle as well. He joined Sargent Shriver in creating the Peace Corps and eventually became its deputy director. At the same time, he made himself useful on political chores. He was an advance man on the Kennedy trip to Texas in 1963. When word of the assassination reached Austin, where Moyers was preparing for that evening's Kennedy appearance, he chartered a plane and reached Dallas in time for Johnson's oath taking. He remained at his side, as press secretary or domestic policy coordinator, for the next three years.

Those years were a period of perplexity and difficulty for Moyers. He had found common bonds with the Kennedy people, despite their regional and religious differences, because, he said, "all of us were basically indebted to the New Deal, living with the constant image of Roosevelt and Truman." But with Johnson's ambitious finale to the New Deal, embodied in the Great Society legislation of 1964–66, Moyers felt "it was time for a new approach. We arrived at the tail end of this quarter-century of New Deal liberalism that did wondrous things but finally played out. We wound up without a war to fight. The last war was over for us. The landscape was different."

Unfortunately, the landscape that emerged was Vietnam, and that war troubled Moyers deeply—"shocking" him, "benumbing" him. Inside the White House, Moyers organized a small anti-war clique to attempt to influence Johnson. He was blocked in a bid to become the National Security Adviser. In December of 1966 he left the White House to become publisher of *Newsday*, the Long Island daily—a step that Johnson, his patron and mentor, persisted in believing, until his death, was an act of personal disloyalty.

Under Moyers, *Newsday* expanded in circulation and influence and won two Pulitzer Prizes. But his greater impact as a commentator began in 1971, when he shifted to public television and began a program called *Bill Moyers' Journal.* The "television essay" was a new form of expression. Moyers said in a Public Broadcasting Service profile that this new genre "marshals pictures and impressions and often needs only a modest amount of narration. You aim to produce an essay that is not verbal but is visual—a picture essay, not a written essay. If you were to take out the word 'literary' from the dictionary definition of 'essay'—'an analytical or interpretive literary composition usually dealing with its subject from a limited or personal point of view'—you would have the definition of a television essay as I perceive it." Moyers stayed with public television until 1976, when he went to CBS to produce documentaries. In 1979 he returned to public television and the editorial freedom it provided.

Moyers' acclaim as a television essayist has been almost unanimous. He has won at least fifteen prizes for his work, which has ranged from lengthy interviews with leading political and intellectual figures to studies of social phenomena from ghetto arson to 20th-century homesteading.

Throughout, the quality of his vision has been enhanced by the fact that his personality recedes as he reports. "Moyers," said the television critic of the New York *Daily News,* "goes in quietly, never intruding, always the curious outsider blending into the background; he dresses like a native, not a newsman. When he leaves, townsfolk must turn and ask, 'Say, who *was* that unmasked man, anyway?' "

George Will's approach to his role as a shaper of opinion has been equally understated. His father was a professor of philosophy at the University of Illinois in Champaign, where George was born in 1941. His mother was a high-school teacher and later the editor of a children's encyclopedia—"word people," said Will, "from way back," and apolitical Democrats who may have voted occasionally for Norman Thomas. George Will was, by his own admission, "a late bloomer intellectually," not really interested "in anything except the National League until about my senior year in college," when he moved from being sports editor to editor of the Trinity College paper in Hartford.

He went through a "college liberal period," when he was cochairman of Trinity Students for Kennedy, but began his intellectual journey to conservatism while a student at Oxford, which he attended after Trinity. "It was in Britain," Will said, "that I began to see how a state fueled by unclear ideas about egalitarianism and a sort of reflexive, trendy, intellectual anti-capitalism could suffocate the social energies of a country, could condemn a lot of people to a frustrating future, by stamping out, in a nation where they needed it most, social mobility. And I became a quite thoroughly ideological capitalist."

At Oxford, Will's circle of friends included some students of the free-market economist Friedrich von Hayek, whose influence on the younger generation of conservative politicians was discussed in Chapter 6. "It was a mad, intellectual atmosphere," according to Will; "insanely right-wing; deliciously, wonderfully libertarian; anarchist almost. Some guys there had started a publication in Chicago in which they once ran a review of a book by an Italian jurisprude who was arguing for private courts. You would have thought that was quite enough to satisfy these right-wingers. But no: In one obscure footnote he committed the error of saying it's all right for the state to own the lighthouses. So my friends pounced on this as the thin edge of the communist wedge."

This latent skepticism about the free market as a political panacea was heightened when Will came back to America. Working toward his Ph.D. at Princeton, and shaping a dissertation on the First Amendment, he became a disciple of Leo Strauss, the University of Chicago political philosopher, who argued that government was both the most necessary and most perilous of institutions. As Moyers turned away from classic New Deal liberalism in the late Sixties, Will rejected the emerging brand of free-enterprise conservatism. "The great conservative mistake," he said, "is to elevate free enterprise into a political philosophy. It disparages the political role; it disparages political institutions. It says that market forces ought to allocate wealth, opportunity, happiness and justice and that the outcome of markets is justice—which I do not believe."

Will launched a teaching career at Michigan State and the University of Toronto, but in 1970 cast it aside to come to Washington to work for Gordon Allott, a Republican Senator from Colorado. "It was," he explained, "like the swallows going to Capistrano. I just had so much fun in the Senate." Others found the period traumatic, but for Will, "it was terrific. I got here just as everything was going to hell. Bad times are always fun. I came in January 1970. April 1970 was Cambodia, and May was Kent State." It was a time of almost frenzied effort by opponents of the Vietnam war to bring it to a conclusion, but Will plunged happily into his first assignment—to "help organize the filibuster against the Cooper-Church amendment" to terminate funds for ground-combat operations in Cambodia and Laos.

While the voters of Colorado appeared indifferent to Will's contributions (they voted Allott out of office in 1972), more discerning people noted the sudden improvement in the quality of the Senator's speeches that coincided with Will's arrival on the scene. Will began serving as Washington editor of William Buckley's *National Review* and, with the encouragement of Meg Greenfield, then its deputy editorial-page editor, became a regular contributor to the op-ed page of *The Washington Post*. He also had a close brush with the Nixon White House.

"When Haldeman and all those guys got fired and Alexander Haig was brought back in," Will recounted, "Haig called me and asked if I would come work for him at the White House. I thought very seriously about it. If he had said right away, 'Come do it; let's save the country,' I'd have done it. The luckiest thing that ever happened to me was that he was slow in calling back. One of his assistants called from Camp David about two weeks later and said, 'The General would like to see if you're still interested.' I said, 'Well, I may still be interested, but he'd better read what I've written in the paper on Watergate.' " Will had written that Nixon should consider resigning, and Haig "never called back."

Instead, Will began doing a syndicated column for the Washington Post Writers Group and later for *Newsweek* magazine as well. He broadened his subject matter from Washington politics to the manners and mores of the American people. Some of his most-quoted columns concerned the names fast-food franchises give their products, the perils of child-rearing and the effects of lifelong addiction to the Chicago Cubs. In the preface to his 1978 collection of essays, *The Pursuit of Happiness, and Other Sobering Thoughts,* he wrote: "I have made it an aim of my life to die without ever having written a column about which presidential advisors are ascending and which are descending. I write about the 'inside' of public life in another sense. My subject is not what is secret, but what is latent, the kernel of principle and other significance that exists, recognized or not, inside events, actions, policies, and manners." In 1977, Will won the Pulitzer Prize for distinguished commentary.

Two years earlier, the Pulitzer Prize for editorial cartooning was awarded, for the first time, to a comic-strip artist, Garry Trudeau, the creator of *Doonesbury*. As Moyers broadened the scope of television journalism and Will expanded the subject matter of a political column, so Trudeau erased the artificial boundary as to where and how an artist could comment on politics in a newspaper. All three men have created categories of commentary appropriate to a new political generation.

They share a distaste for celebrityhood. Will has spoken with scorn of those for whom "politics is nothing but the pursuit of the swiftly darting spotlight." Bill Moyers has written that "the real heroes I know are anonymous," and has said that "the real thing we have to distinguish in this society is the difference between celebrities and leaders." Trudeau offered another example of this horror of celebrification. While responding to all factual queries, he declined, very politely but very firmly, to be interviewed for this book. His dislike of publicity is notorious. One of the few major profiles of Trudeau, appearing in *Time* magazine in 1976, reported: "Once he hid in his bathroom for four hours to avoid a Baltimore

Sun reporter." Trudeau himself said, "I don't like celebrification. Everything I have to share I share in the strip."

Garry Trudeau was born Garretson Beekman Trudeau in New York City in 1948. He grew up near Saranac Lake in upstate New York, the son of a doctor. His parents divorced when he was 12 years old, and he entered the jockish St. Paul's School in Concord, New Hampshire, where he was president of the Art Association—for which, one of his friends said, "Garry took a lot of grief." In 1966 Trudeau enrolled at Yale, and wrote first for the Yale *Record,* the campus humor magazine, and later for the Yale *Daily News,* where, in his junior year, he launched *Bull Tales,* a comic strip satirizing college life. It caught the eye of the founding partners of the Universal Press Syndicate, who talked Trudeau into a twelve-year contract. For its national appearance, *Bull Tales* was christened *Doonesbury* after one of the strip's leading characters. The name comes from "doone," meaning "out to lunch"—the prep-school nickname for Trudeau's college roommate, Charles Pillsbury, who also lent the second half of his name.

Trudeau's method of operation is thoroughly journalistic. He turns up at Senate hearings, and he reads press releases and government documents. He even travels to other countries, most notably with President Ford on his 1975 trip to China. Many of Trudeau's characters seem drawn from real life, even though he insists the prototypes provide only "creative reference points." The Reverend E. Scott Sloan, the activist priest, bears a resemblance to William Sloane Coffin, formerly the Yale chaplain; Uncle Duke is clearly based on *Rolling Stone* journalist Hunter S. Thompson, though Trudeau says he has never met Thompson. Many readers have seen in Congresswoman Lacey Davenport the character of Republican Representative Millicent Fenwick of New Jersey, but Ms. Davenport appeared two years before Fenwick was elected to Congress. During the early stages of the 1980 presidential race, Trudeau's sympathetic portrait of John B. Anderson's struggling Republican candidacy helped boost the Illinois Congressman's popularity on college campuses. The saga of Michael Doonesbury's lonely life as an obscure but earnest campaign staffer culminated in Trudeau's celebrated definition of a dark-horse candidate's advance man—"He's the one who gets out of the car first."

For a comic-strip artist, Trudeau works dangerously close to his deadlines. He delivers strips only two weeks ahead of publication, while the industry norm is a six-week lead time. Because of its topicality and its high level of political comment, some of the five hundred newspapers that run the strip place it on the editorial page, rather than with the other comics. Unlike his politically inclined predecessors Walt Kelly of *Pogo* and Al Capp of *Li'l Abner,* Trudeau does not always rely on allegory to make his points. The world of *Doonesbury* is peopled with real as well as fictional characters. Sensitive newspaper editors—and, no doubt, John Mitchell—were not amused when Mark Slackmeyer, Trudeau's beat disc jockey, finished an on-the-air profile of the former Attorney General with the words "Guilty! Guilty! Guilty!" A few years later, the same character offered his listeners a coupon—"just like the ones the gun nuts use"—so that they could send for information about congressional ethics violations. The coupon was printed as the last panel in the strip, and included the address of Speaker of the House Tip O'Neill, down to the zip code. The Speaker's office was flooded with coupons, and he didn't think it was funny either.

Despite the differences in their ages, all three of these commentators saw their lives transformed in the decade of the 1960s. Moyers entered the decade as a teacher and came out, via the White House, as a publisher about to become a television journalist. Will began the Sixties as a pro-Kennedy college student and ended them as a Senate staffer supporting the Vietnam war. Trudeau went from being a teen-age preppie to a precocious syndicated cartoonist.

Trudeau is part of the college group which Dick Wirthlin characterized as the "most liberal" in American history. In a 1979 graduation address at the University of Pennsylvania, Trudeau tried, half kiddingly, to describe his own collegiate experience. "It was as a sophomore," he said, "that I first became acquainted with the vagaries of the U.S. Criminal Code. My main interests were, in order of priority, a steady supply of recreational drugs, a 2-S draft deferment and overthrowing the Nixon Administration. In pursuit of these, I became, at least in my own estimation, the model of lawlessness. My specialty, like that of every other undergraduate of the day, was civil disobedience, and none of my roommates is ever likely to forget the time I tried to explain Thoreau's famous essay on the subject to four hyperventilating state troopers."

In one early strip, a pensive Zonker Harris tells Michael Doonesbury, "They say it's very pretty in Ohio this time of year. They say it was a very pretty day exactly two years ago at Kent State." The two friends pause in silent thought. And then Zonker says, "Have a nice day, John Mitchell."

Trudeau's youthful identification with the causes of the Sixties is indicated not only by his condemnation of Richard Nixon and his associates but by his creation as a sympathetic character of Phred, the sometime Viet Cong terrorist turned United Nations diplomat. He has also made the feminist cause his own. He annually invades his own privacy by appearing at a benefit show and sale of his original cartoon panels to aid the National Women's Political Caucus. One of his strongest characters is the feminist Joanie Caucus.

And yet even in the area of politics where he has been most involved and supportive, Trudeau is quick to catch the ironies. Joanie Caucus, the admirable feminist manager of a day-care center, just ups and leaves her own child to her unbearable husband. Mark Slackmeyer is blaring his nonnegotiable demands at a university president (who strongly resembles Kingman Brewster), but when "President King" offers not only to turn over his office to Mark but show "where I keep my brandy and cigars," Mark can only put his head on the president's desk and cry. At one point in Trudeau's version of the Watergate hearings, the Senate investigating committee opens the floor "to innuendo and hearsay." A television newsman, reporting on President Nixon, says, "He went on to condemn television commentators for 'the vindictive leers and sneers directed at the great office of the presidency.' Most reporters present agreed the President was being his usual, asinine self."

If Trudeau maintained his distance, through irony, from identification with activists of his own generation, then Will found them mainly an object for intellectual scorn. In a 1978 column and commencement address, he turned on the student protestors of the Sixties as "sandbox revolutionaries," whose "radicalism was a pseudo-political manifestation of a culture of passivity." He argued that the "radicalism" of the Sixties "was confined to a small minority of the privileged minority who were students," among whom, Will said, "posturing passed for ethical action."

The significance of the Sixties' upheavals, Will said in an interview for this book, was "on another level. The sheer disorder and violence on campuses sensitized people to what may be the fundamental conservative insight, which is that society is a fragile creation and that it's not easy holding it together. . . . In the little foreword I wrote for my book, I tried to say that men and women are biological facts, but ladies and gentlemen suited for self-government are social artifacts. In each generation there's a twenty-one-year race to civilize them, and we were losing that race in the Sixties because a generation swallowed a decadent, romantic, liberal view of the world which took away standards and inhibitions."

It might be expected that someone with George Will's views would be rather critical of the young politicians who are the products and exemplars of that decade. But if one can judge by his work, Garry Trudeau, who was closer to them, is more skeptical. No one has been more scathing in his denunciation of what he perceives as the hypocrisy of that model of "new politics," California Governor Jerry Brown. Trudeau also ridiculed a fictitious Congressman who, in an effort to demonstrate his responsiveness, tells his constituents, "I want your views, your thoughts on how my vote should go." "Whatcha askin' us fer now, Ed?" asks one constituent. "Yew always voted any way yew dang pleased before! Yew done voted for that fool war fer eight years without askin'!"

By contrast, Will is almost gentle. "My sense is that the caliber of politicians is better today than it was ten years ago. They have a better sense of the complexity of things, a sense that there are ideas at stake, and a very wholesome sense of the connectedness of things."

Bill Moyers said that he too found the younger politicians "better than I was when I was their age—bright and sophisticated and savvy and intelligent, and committed to the public interest. The confounding part of it," he confessed, "is that one day I will meet one of them who calls himself a Democrat and a liberal and come away admiring of him or her, and the next day I will meet one who calls himself a Republican and a conservative and come away equally admiring."

Moyers and Will share an insight that Trudeau, if he believes it, has never found occasion to voice. The two essayists have perceived and communicated an understanding that politics and government are serious vocations, deserving of respect. Although Moyers was a Carter sympathizer, and perhaps a supporter in 1976, and Will was skeptical from the start, both saw him as evidence of the popular conceit that government is easy and leadership a commonplace quality. "There is a difference between politics and government," Moyers said. "Jimmy Carter's great discovery has been that it is one thing to run for office and another thing to govern the country." George Will, in a 1979 column making the same point, implicitly chose Moyers' former mentor as the contrasting model to the Carter presidency.

"This is a big muscular nation, full of muscular 'factions,' " he wrote, "and the nation cannot be governed by other than muscular politicians. It can't be governed by someone who is not good at—let us use the honorable phrase—'wheeling and dealing.' And over the long haul of a presidency, no one can do that well who despises it, who doesn't actively enjoy it, even relish it."

Will's fundamental difference with most conservatives stems from his belief that the art of government is as noble as it is exacting. "I think," he said, "I'm the most conservative person writing in America—I mean that quite seriously—in the sense that most American conservatives are classic 19th-century liberals, who share in spades the heresy of liberalism . . . the worship of markets . . . the belief that government is easy and that society is based on a natural tendency to cooperation and harmony. . . . Where conservatism has most damaged itself and most damaged the country is by joining in a reckless, profoundly dangerous attack on the political vocation, the dignity of government."

In his column, Will gently rebuked his friend Republican Senator John Danforth of Missouri for advocating term limits for all federal elective officials. "In government," Will wrote, "as in other serious enterprises, knowledge is cumulative. Government is as much a profession as law or teaching; it is a learned activity and an increasingly complicated one."

On the last point, Moyers gave independent corroborative testimony. He said that in large organizations in both the private and public sectors, "there is a feeling now that leadership is no longer possible on the grand scale and it is not possible for single individuals to cut the wide swaths through history that have been cut before. There is a general perception that the real heroes are the people who can make committees work, and that takes a different kind of talent and skill. You have to be more collegial and accept being more anonymous."

Moyers and Will are in agreement on one other point of fundamental importance. The challenge of leadership—or as Will defined it, "having a longer time horizon than those you represent, and inflicting pain on them and getting away with it"—is more difficult in this period. And the readiness of the people to accept leadership has been diminished.

"It is very hard, once you are affluent, to see the need for discipline or sacrifice," Moyers said. "I am not sure we understand and appreciate, as a people, the need for this to be a commonwealth. I'm not sure if this generation can relate 'my place' to 'the other place,' 'my interest' to 'the other interests' and achieve what the founders of this country called the common interest. Nobody is addressing that very well." In a similar vein, Will said, in a column written on the eve of the nation's bicentennial, that "the Republic's most pressing task is to demonstrate that political habits of restraint and moderation are compatible with an economic and cultural ambience that celebrates instant gratification of immoderate appetites."

In those terms, these three most influential of younger-generation commentators are all conservatives—conservatives in stressing the fundamental importance of character and of the conservation of values. Garry Trudeau said in his 1979 Pennsylvania commencement speech: "As we enter into an age in which only uncertainties are fixed, addressing this problem [of self-interest vs. public interest] has become increasingly more frustrating. . . . Taking a stand has come to mean deciding which trapdoor will support the weight of your convictions the longest. . . . We have overlooked the insistence of a previous generation that reputation be built on moral precepts. As we respond to fame and power for their own sake, all too often the questions by which we judge a man's character are no longer asked." One of the *Doonesbury* characters asked in a 1975 comic strip, "The 'new post-Watergate morality' . . . What exactly is the '*new post*-Watergate morality'? I mean, I feel the same way about bribery and extortion as I did a year ago."

As they looked about America, the three commentators saw much that struck them as false and pretentious and, in their fashion, made it material for both comedy and criticism.

Some of the funniest moments in Will's essays occur when he confronts popular culture—or rather, when popular culture confronts George Will. He seems thoroughly out of place at an Elvis Presley concert or in a Baskin-Robbins Ice Cream shop. One of his unsung heroes is the man who walked out of Burger King rather than call a ham-and-cheese a "Yumbo." "His principles are anachronisms, but his prejudices are impeccable." Will himself is plagued by the fact that his favorite ice cream "bears the unutterable name 'Hot Fudge Nutty Buddy.' There are some things a gentleman simply will not do, and one is announce in public a desire for a 'Nutty Buddy.' "

Trudeau too depicts this desensitization. Michael Doonesbury, after ordering a Coke in a fast-food restaurant, watches as a pop-eyed, salivating man orders "a Big Mickey, a Tall-Boy, a Burger Prince, three Slurp Shakes, two Bozo Burgers, six Fries, and four Creamie Cole-Slaws!" But for Trudeau, as for Will, the desensitization becomes malevolent when it enters the sphere of morality. An American plane bombs South Vietnam, and Phred, the Viet Cong guerrilla, cries, "You heartless air pirates! I hope you can live with it! I hope you can live with all the destruction and carnage you've brought to my little country!!" And in the insulated cockpit of the bomber, the two pilots are heard to say, "Didja hear the Knicks took two?—Hey! That's great!" Moyers describes the poverty and diseases in a Chicano *barrio* in Texas, where people have been taught, according to one *barrio* worker, a "gringo lie": "And he pointed to the little three-year-old girl, standing barefooted beside her mother. In her right hand she gripped a plastic Santa doll."

All three of these commentators keep their eyes on the young, as the best measure of the health of the American culture. George Will said in the introduction to his book: "At the end of the day, we are right to judge a society by the character of the people it produces. That is why statecraft is, inevitably, soulcraft."

In stressing America's need to perceive what Will called "the wholesome connectedness" of the generations, they marvel at the capacity for growth and understanding Americans of all ages seem to exhibit at most unlikely moments. The young boy in Trudeau's Fritters, Alabama, is one wise citizen. When President Nixon comes to Fritters—to speak where he is assured of a warm reception—the boy who has read up on Watergate asks the crucial question: "Pop, you mean believin' in America is the same thing as believin' in President Nixon?"

No poll was needed to determine the answer to that.

16 · New Pros

WHATEVER MAY CHANGE about politics and government in the United States in the remainder of this century—and enough has been said to suggest the likelihood of such changes—there is one factor that will probably remain constant. A high percentage of the decisions that determine our future as a nation will be made by men and women whose basic commitment is not to any partisan cause or ideology or party, but to the process of politics and government itself.

They are the "new pros"—the younger-generation heirs to a bipartisan tradition of public service symbolized, in various ways, by such Democrats as William B. Benton, Chester Bowles, James F. Byrnes and Clark Clifford, and by such Republicans as Henry L. Stimson, John J. McCloy, Elliot L. Richardson and the Dulles brothers. Many of the "new pros," like their predecessors, are part of the bipartisan foreign-policy "establishment," legatees of those who provided continuity to America's international policies from Lend-Lease days to the fall of Saigon.

But there are others, deeply involved in domestic politics, on White House staffs and in Congress, state government and city hall, who are equally "pros" in their approach to their responsibility. Although some of them have held power under regimes of both parties, they operate closer to the firing line of elective politics and are subject to the hazards of that game. But like such predecessors as Thomas G. Corcoran or Bryce Harlow on the White House staff, Elmer Staats or Charles L. Schultze at the old Budget Bureau, Robert A. Taft or Richard B. Russell in the Senate, Jess Unruh or Nelson A. Rockefeller in state government or Richard J. Daley in city hall, their personal skills are such that they are never far from the center of action, whether they or their party are up or down at any given moment.

Some of them are careerists in government or politics. Others are, by choice or by political or economic circumstance, "in-and-outers"—travelers between the private and public sectors. Some of them are in elective politics, subjecting themselves to the hazards of the polling place. All of them, whether elective or appointive officials, career people or "in-and-outers," have careers that are fueled by personal ambition, the energizing force of all politics. But they are distinguishable from others who may at any given moment have greater power and reputations by their constancy, their durability and their belief that the process of politics and government is ultimately more important than any particular election or policy fight.

Much of the reputation of government will depend in the future—as it has in the past—on the competence of the mid- to top-level civil servants, who provide continuity in the direction of public agencies. There are those around Washington who argue that part of what the public perceived as the decline in the performance of government in the Seventies was the result of a generational turnover: Passing into retirement from the top levels of the bureaucracy were most of those who were recruited during the twelve years from the start of the New Deal to the end of World War II—a time when government service was seen as a challenge and an opportunity by many of America's brightest youngsters.

The 1965–75 period, by contrast, was one in which much of young America was at war with—or at least, at odds with—its government. Those who were not out demonstrating were in many cases casting skeptical and worried eyes at what passed for policymaking in Washington. But it would be easy to overstate the effect of that disillusionment. When the federal government launched a Presidential Management Intern program in 1978, designed to give the top graduates of the nation's professional schools of public policy and public administration a two-year introduction to the civil service, it received 921 applications for the 250 spots. I met one evening with several of those who had been selected as interns, basically to explore what made them interested in working for a government whose reputation for competence, efficiency and even candor had been so battered while they were in school.

Helen Rothman, 29, of Atlanta and Georgia State University, was the oldest of the group. As an undergraduate at the University of Illinois, "I was out there [during the Cambodia–Kent State protests] with my candle in the nighttime marches, standing up facing the National Guardsmen across the street, and all that kind of thing," she said. A psychology major, she began teaching mentally retarded adults and counseling mentally disturbed patients in Fulton County, Georgia, facilities. "And that's where I really got involved in a firm commitment to federal service. . . . I wanted to get into some more of the decision making, because I could see that the government can do so much good and so much bad for the average citizen."

Justine Finch, 22, of Dayton and the State University of New York at

Stony Brook, went as an undergraduate to a small Quaker school (Earlham College, in Indiana), studied economics and found that most of her classmates were "either into vegetarianism, extreme individualism or were going into business." None of the three appealed to her, "so I thought I'd direct my attention toward social services as a way of helping people and . . . came to the conclusion that perhaps the best place for me was in some federal agency."

Paula Nuschke, 26, of Monterey was regarded as "a radical" at Scripps College in California. Like Finch, she found "profit-making enterprises . . . very boring," so after graduation she came to Washington and worked in a congressional office ("very institutionalized"), for Ralph Nader ("incredibly noninstitutionalized") and then for the United Nations. After "just going plop from one to the other, I suddenly realized that the reason I'm interested in government and have been for so long is because it's the only place where I perceived a really fundamental change is needed. So I said, I'll go to graduate school [at George Washington University] and study it. And out of that I fell into this program."

Sean O'Keefe, 22, of Wyckoff, New Jersey, and Syracuse University, was the son of a military officer and part of a family long active in Louisiana politics. As an undergraduate at Loyola of New Orleans, he was involved in student government, "and I guess the most important thing I learned . . . was that there is an incredible need for administration, an incredible need for institutionalization, if you're going to make it work. In the late Sixties and early Seventies . . . there was all nondirected energy [on the campuses], but where did it go? . . . Much as the lifetime of a university student is four years, a political administration may be only eight. A lot rests on the strength and character and capabilities of the people who are there for life; they are the ones who are actually able to move the bureaucracy."

There was a rather touching naiveté to the blend of altruism and nascent professionalism with which these young people spoke of their future careers in the federal government. As fresh recruits to the civil service, they were, at the same time, somewhat critical of the inertia and make-work, the lack of enterprise and weakness of direction they found in the bureaucracy. But their comments were mild compared with those from another round table of a different sort of "new pros": nine political appointees to key line and staff jobs in the Carter Administration. The motivations expressed by these people—mainly in their thirties—were similar to those voiced by the younger civil-service interns. One of them, Si Lazarus, an associate director of the President's domestic-policy staff, said, "You don't have to be ashamed to say that you find public service meaningful, even though it may be out of favor this week, and you don't have to be ashamed to say you find it fun." But Lazarus also said, to general head nodding, that "a number of us in this room identify somewhat with the popular mood of concern about the size and lack of productivity of the government, and feel that we're trying to make the government work better and respond in some sensible way to these concerns."

In the course of the discussion, it became clear that their concerns focused on the interlocking relationships among three bureaucracies: the staffs of the executive agencies, the congressional subcommittees and the interest groups—the so-called "iron triangle" of Washington.

As far as the executive-branch bureaucracy was concerned, the problem these political appointees saw was the lack of incentives for ingenuity and efficiency. Donna Shalala, then the assistant secretary of HUD whom we met earlier in Chapter 2, complained that "if you want to maintain your budget in an agency at a certain level, there's no incentive for coming and suggesting ways of delivering those precise services in different ways. Cost-conscious budget managers for the President will take advantage of your initiative, and they'll simply take the rest of the money off to someone else who didn't show that ingenuity.

"I went to the Hill this year without an increase in my budget," Shalala said. "My choice. And I told the Secretary I didn't want an increase, and everybody yelled and screamed and jumped up and down and said, 'You've got to take an increase the way everybody does, 'cause when you get to the Hill you've got to take a cut.' The Hill paid no attention to the fact that I went up without an increase; they just gave me the same cut they gave everybody else. And I went up and I argued that I hadn't asked for an increase. And they said that was just dumb."

"They'll take the minus," said Theodore Lutz, then director of the Washington-area Metro system, "and never give you the plus."

As for Capitol Hill, where the number of congressional staff employees has grown from 10,721 in 1969 to roughly 18,500 in 1979, Pat Swygert, the general counsel of the Office of Personnel Management, said, "When you look at the proliferation of committees and staffs and buildings . . . I don't think the hard choices are going to be made there."

Frank Raines, then associate director of the Office of Management and Budget, said that if the goal is more manageable government, "the first thing to do is to knock off about half the staff on the Hill, since they have to justify their existence by fooling around with these little programs." "They got into this business of creating subcommittees," Lutz said, "in order that all the freshman and sophomore Democrats could have their own chairmanships. Each one was authorized thousands of dollars for staff, and each staff has to produce a bill each year, so they can get their invitations to go out and speak to the lobby groups that support the extension of Title 10 of the act—it's always Title 10. . . . If you want to be a big person in town, you've got to have something to create action. And so we end up generating more government."

Lutz's reference to the role of the interest groups evoked a wave of agreements. John White, a former Defense Department official now deputy director of the Office of Management and Budget, said, "The disturbing part is that each group not only wants its program, it wants it mandated so that next year no one can question that priority; they want to peg their program to grow every year." And Raines noted the irony that state and local elected officials increasingly have formed their own interest groups, with their own professional staffs, to lobby in Washington, and those staffs too quickly develop "their own agenda," which may or may not reflect the views of the governors, mayors, state legislators or county officials they are supposed to represent.

"This is the craziness," he said, "when you've got a bureaucracy that represents elected officials here in Washington, and our bureaucracy has to maneuver around them to find out what their membership really wants."

When I took the same question up to Capitol Hill to a round table of senior congressional staff members, there was more agreement about the overgrowth of the Capitol Hill bureaucracy than one would have expected. Richard Conlon, executive director of the House Democratic Study Group, was one of the dissenters. He denied that the House was overstaffed and said it was "a very healthy trend" that "being a professional on the Hill is a legitimate career and one that is the equal to being part of any administration." He ascribed the criticism from the executive-branch appointees to their disappointment at the "lack of reverence" for them that their predecessors had received from understaffed members of Congress who, in the 1960s, Conlon said, had had to go "hat in hand" to the executive branch for even the most rudimentary information on what was happening in the agencies and programs Congress had created.

But that was not the general view. Gary Hymel, the assistant to Speaker of the House Tip O'Neill, said "there's a lot of truth" in the comments of the executive-branch officials. "The proliferation of subcommittees . . . really has confused the power," he said. John McEvoy, staff director of the Senate Budget Committee, said the "radical expansion" in the size of congressional staffs had had all of the effects described by the executive-branch officials—and more besides. "A lot of the staff I see on the Senate side confuse whether they're really working for a Senator or are the assistant secretary of this or that," he said. "And they're confused whether the congressional role is to make laws and oversee, in some general way, their implementation, or whether it's to write down the inside details of programmatic execution." McEvoy also argued that, in the Senate at least, surplus staff members find themselves competing with each other for the time and energy of their senators, so "the members' attention is getting increasingly fractured and they forget why they're here. . . . They try to become experts on everything their staff can think to put in front of them."

There was a good deal more; but the overall feeling after the three round tables were completed was that the country might be seeing something new: a breed of professional or semiprofessional senior government official rather disturbed and skeptical about the size and habits of the very bureaucracies of which he or she was a part. To the extent that these people can themselves be considered leaders, their influence is not likely to be on the side of preservation of the *status quo*. To the extent that they are the agents of the elected policy makers—their arms and legs and hands and eyes—they are looking for leadership that might challenge what they see as the rather sprawling, ineffectual character of the government.

But they are not passive during that wait. They are engaged. And so are many others who share their commitment to a life in politics and government—not just a brief passage. In the course of the interviews for this book, I came across dozens of people I put in my own subjective category of "new pros"—people with an exceptional degree of devotion to, or aptitude for, the complex challenges of governing. Many of them found their way into other chapters of the book, as part of one or another of the "networks." But rather arbitrarily, I have held out a number of them for this section. They represent both sexes, both parties and all levels of government from city hall to the White House. By introducing these brief portraits in chronological order, from a 50-year-old to a 29-year-old, I hope to suggest some of the varieties of people and views that will be part of our political future.

Anne Wexler

In 1968, Anne Levy Wexler, Skidmore class of 1951, wife of Westport, Connecticut, ophthalmologist Richard Wexler, mother of two sons, did something outrageously impudent. She challenged John M. Bailey's control of the Connecticut delegation to the Democratic National Convention. It looked like a classic mismatch. Wexler had been working at the local level in Democratic Party campaigns since 1952, but she had been very much in the mainstream, supporting all the nominees from Adlai Stevenson ("the best articulator of what I believed of any politician I've ever known, before or since") to Lyndon Johnson. Rebellion was something new for her. But by 1966 "I was extremely angry at Johnson" because of the Vietnam war. "I was beginning to see some of my friends' children either going to Canada or going to jail . . . and I just thought the war was wrong." So she signed up with Eugene McCarthy and went off to fight John Bailey, who was backing Hubert Humphrey with his accumulated power as the longtime state Democratic chairman and the national Democratic chairmanship as well.

Wexler got McCarthy 9 of the 44 Connecticut delegates, which was about nine more than anyone had expected. She got something more for herself—a political education. "I came out of that crazy liberal tradition," she said a decade later, "where there are only good guys and bad guys and everything was a life-or-death kind of issue. . . . John Bailey was the toughest negotiator I ever dealt with, but also the fairest. It was absolutely like pulling teeth to get Bailey to give his word on anything; but, boy, once he made a deal, he never broke it—never.

"John Bailey taught me early on that the guys that you are fighting with on one issue are going to be your allies on the next. And that you've got to make your case and fight your fight as hard as you can, but you don't burn your bridges."

Because she has adhered to that philosophy and become almost as skillful as her antagonist-turned-mentor had been in his time, Anne Wexler finds herself, at age 50, one of the two women and one of the few "outsiders" on the senior staff of Jimmy Carter's White House. Her job has been to orchestrate interest-group support for the Carter legislative and diplomatic initiatives. Unlike many others, who denounce the "single-interest" groups and let it go at that, Wexler is seeking to shape the new force to her own—or the President's—purpose. "I have great sympathy for the people who are beginning to understand the scope of the power they have in some of these single-interest groups," she said. "After all, it's what we did in 1968 [with the peace movement] very successfully. Hell, it's been going on for years. And they're the same kind of people we were."

Because she could recognize a bit of her own past self in the ardent advocates of today's causes, Wexler had unusual success in persuading them to join in coalitions useful to her President and her party. She was, in effect, teaching them the same lessons John Bailey had taught her on the shortsightedness of bridge burning.

Along the road from suburban rebel to White House pro, Wexler has had her own liberal education in the vagaries of electoral politics. In 1970, she managed the losing Senate campaign of Joseph Duffey, to whom she is now married. In 1971, both of them decided to back Senator Edmund S. Muskie of Maine in his losing bid for the Democratic presidential nomination, but they also went down in flames in the 1972 general election with George McGovern. Jimmy Carter was her first winner in a dozen years.

But Wexler also has played a signal role in the transformation of the

Democratic Party as an institution—a role about which she is, in retrospect, more than a little equivocal. One of the smaller prizes she extracted from Bailey in their 1968 negotiations was a seat for herself on the convention rules committee, where she and like-minded liberals framed and managed to pass the resolution that led to the creation of the McGovern Commission on Democratic Party delegate-selection reform. Wexler was a prime lobbyist for the new rules, designed to get the people who were on the streets demonstrating in Chicago in 1968 into the convention hall as delegates in 1972. It worked, "but not in the way we thought it would," she said. "The lesson we've learned is that you've really got to feel passionately and strongly about an issue before you use the political system. So what you've got now is strong participation from the Left and the Right, and the center is sort of out of it. . . . And all the primaries have just destroyed the grass-roots political structures. The result has been really tragic in that way."

Between campaigns in the early 1970s, Wexler worked for Common Cause, and she has come to have second thoughts about the campaign-finance "reform" law that that organization helped lobby through Congress in 1974.

By providing a public payment to the presidential candidates, she said, "it makes you and me the subsidizers of the commercial networks, because that's where each candidate spends most of his money." And by barring any private contributions to the general-election campaign, "what we've done is basically kill the capacity of people to participate in elections. It's awful. If you lived in a little town someplace, there was no local headquarters you could go to, nor could you go organize one if you wanted to, because there was no money to pay for it . . . and you could not raise the money to rent the telephones or print your own literature or anything." (Such restrictions on grass-roots activity were eased in 1979 by campaign-finance-law amendments—which had bipartisan support in Congress—allowing for the purchase of bumper stickers, lapel buttons and the like.)

Wexler said she still felt "we did the right thing" in the delegate-selection reforms, "because if we ever found ourselves in a situation like we found ourselves in in 1968, we could really do a great deal more [under the new rules] than we did then."

But now, she said, "it's the center we have to worry about. Those are the folks who should be voting and participating, and they're not. We have to go back and start over again, and let people work at the grass roots again, and give them a feeling of association with their elected officials—the way I felt when I was raising money and licking envelopes and working in Westport. But I don't even know if all those things John [Bailey] and I thought were important—electing Democrats at the local level, having a Democratic Governor and legislature—whether those things are important to Democrats anymore."

They are still important to Anne Wexler, and because this onetime suburban party envelope-stuffer was one of the few people on Jimmy Carter's White House staff who remembered from one day to the next that all politics is really local politics, she was enhancing her reputation as a "pro" while many of her coworkers were dismissed as hopeless amateurs.

Richard G. Lugar

In the state of Indiana, which has a rich tradition of robust political characters and unrelenting partisan wars, Senator Richard G. Lugar, a 48-year-old Republican, is considered something less than a vivid political personality. But he is smart, he is tenacious, he is ambitious and he is organized—and that combination marks him as a political figure of far-greater-than-average long-term influence.

Indeed, he has already been at the game longer and more effectively than most of his contemporaries in the GOP. It began for him, when he was 8 years old, in Indianapolis, "listening on the radio with my dad to Wendell Willkie's nomination and keeping the score sheet by states." Later in that summer of 1940, his parents drove over to Elwood for Willkie's acceptance speech and brought young Richard home souvenirs of that great day for Hoosier Republicans. "I was fortunate," Lugar would say much later—when, on his second try, he had made it to the Senate—"to have parents who were very eager for their children to succeed and made every opportunity available to them. I could even imagine as a teen-ager what it was like to be there at a convention, or on the podium giving a speech."

He had his chance as the keynoter of the 1972 Republican convention, chosen for that honor by Richard Nixon. By that time, Lugar had won his share of prizes. He had become an Eagle Scout; had graduated first in his class from Denison University; had won a Rhodes Scholarship and two more degrees from Oxford University; had served as an intelligence officer on the staff of Admiral Arleigh Burke, the Chief of Naval Operations; had been elected first to the Indianapolis school board and then as Mayor of Indianapolis and, in 1969, had put through a merger of Indianapolis and Marion County governments which was the largest such consolidation in history. More equivocally, as it turned out, he had won the informal title of "Nixon's favorite Mayor," by making Indianapolis a laboratory and showcase for general revenue sharing and what Nixon liked to call "New Federalism."

Throughout this copybook career, Lugar disciplined himself to extract useful lessons from his setbacks. He lost twice in tries for high-school office, but became co-president of the Denison student government. In 1974, when he tried for the Senate, his links to Nixon and his role in the previous Republican convention were of no help, and he lost in the Watergate tide. But two years later, he bounced back to win a Senate seat by the largest margin ever achieved in an Indiana election.

Serious, intense and immaculate, Lugar sometimes seemed almost too eager to please. To encourage colleagues to drop by his desk in the Senate, he kept a supply of hard candies handy for those who might like a snack. But such gestures at fellowship were just that—gestures; Lugar's real strength was that of the plugger on whom others could depend to get the job done. He made himself the ally of Senate Minority Leader Howard H. Baker, Jr., of Tennessee, organizing Republican opposition that killed Carter Administration proposals for labor-law reform and revision of election laws.

Lugar also made himself the GOP's spokesman on urban issues. Having pushed through city–county consolidation in a political maneuver exquisite in its artistry, and having seen Indianapolis prosper in a way that was rare for cities of its age and region, Lugar could argue plausibly that the answers to many urban ills did not require intervention from Washington. "Most people in the country," he noted with the sadness of an Eagle Scout discovering there are lots of Tenderfoots, "have not been willing to take the political risks or the effective political action that was required" to save the cities. "Rather than noting that every metropolitan area in this country is a viable entity, if you put together the pieces in the right structure, people have preferred to say that there are a lot of nonviable entities, and that the federal government alone can give them the sustenance they need annually to stay alive.

"It was a convenient accommodation," Lugar said, with the air of a man used to rejecting such temptations. "People in the suburbs felt in that way that they really would not be involved in the scrapes of the inner city. People in the inner city really did not want to be involved in diluting any of their newfound political power with the suburbs. So it accommodated everyone, with the federal government picking up the tab with printing-press money.

"Now, one can say at this point that we should have learned that throwing money after problems doesn't solve anything, or that the federal government, if it does this, creates inflation, which causes greater ravages for city budgets and all that. But the mayors and people involved in city government haven't learned that at all, because the pain of trying to solve it at the local level, or through the state governments, has always been too great."

If Lugar were an Oxford don, he might have left it there. But he was also a political pragmatist, who knew, among other things, that Republicans regularly lost state and national elections by their inability to win big-city votes. Gerald Ford lost New York State and the presidency in 1976 in part because a year earlier, during the city's fiscal crisis, the New York *Daily News* had run a headline: "Ford to City: Drop Dead."

So in 1978, when renewal of emergency fiscal relief for New York City was mired in a Senate committee, it was Lugar who came up with a compromise that saved the legislation. It did not violate his principles, he pointed out, because it reduced the size of the long-term guarantees by one-quarter, and required both the state and the city to accept much stricter budgetary discipline as a condition of receiving the loan installments. It was a "bail-out" which put most of the burden on New York's back, which is where Lugar thought it belonged. But it also won him a grateful and admiring profile in *The New York Times,* with a headline reading, "Fiscal Conservative Is Hailed." Somewhere between the static-filled broadcast of Willkie's nomination and the Senate, Richard Lugar had figured out that you don't tell 7 million voters to "drop dead."

WINSTON LORD

Winston Lord, 43, the first of a group of early-fortyish foreign-affairs specialists we are going to meet, is about as complete an embodiment of the enduring American foreign-policy establishment as one can find. That establishment is bipartisan in makeup and operation, but liberal Eastern Republican in tone. Lord's mother, Mary Pillsbury Lord, was a New York liberal Republican, co-chairman of the 1952 Citizens for Eisenhower and, later, Eleanor Roosevelt's successor as the U.S. Delegate to the United Nations Human Rights Commission. Winston Lord came out of Yale and the Fletcher School of Law and Diplomacy at Tufts to spend fifteen years in various diplomatic assignments, almost perfectly divided between Democratic and Republican administrations. His governmental career was capped (at least for now) by service as special assistant to Henry A. Kissinger on the National Security Council staff and as director of the policy planning staff of Kissinger's State Department. After the 1977 change of administrations, Lord became president of the Council on Foreign Relations.

Yet at one point in this almost-too-perfect biography, when he had been a Foreign Service officer for 4½ years with rather interesting assignments, he was threatened with the job as "the No. 4 man in the political section of our embassy in Kuala Lumpur"—a fate he managed to sidestep by a quick lateral move to the Defense Department's Office of International Security Affairs, where Kissinger found him waiting when he came to Washington.

Into this well-ordered life, as into others less programmed, the Vietnam war and all that surrounded it came as something of a shock. Lord was at Kissinger's side on all his negotiating trips to see the North Vietnamese in Paris and Hanoi, to say nothing of nine trips to China and six to Russia. "It was a very painful period for me," he said, "as it was for almost all of us. But particularly in my position. Like most people, I was a full supporter of the war for a good part of it . . . but then the Tet offensive really had a major impact on me personally. . . . I never got to the point where I thought—nor do I now—that what we were doing was immoral, in the sense that we had bad intentions. . . . My problem was that it was not being conducted in the right way, and it was ripping our society apart. . . . So within the Administration, I guess I was rather dovish. What made it painful was that there were people I was working with closely who resigned over some of the same issues I felt strongly about. I searched very hard in my mind and decided that . . . Kissinger and Nixon were trying to wrap it up honorably. There were some things I disagreed with tactically. But I decided to stay in."

As a man who is plainly more comfortable dealing with issues than with emotions, Lord has come to see that some of the rips in the cherished bipartisan consensus on foreign policy which had been inculcated in him both at home and at school were inevitable. "Even without Vietnam," he said, "you would have had, after two decades of global leadership by the United States, both intellectually and materially a fraying of the consensus. The American people were wearying of supporting the kind of commitments around the world that we'd built up. Both the financial drain and the psychological drain on the American people and the Congress would have begun to undermine this consensus. People would have started saying that allies ought to do more. They would have started saying it's ridiculous to treat the Communist bloc as a monolith. The other centers of power would have become obvious, and so would the role of economics and resources. . . . Vietnam accelerated all this, brought it to a head, and then Watergate greatly complicated our adjustment."

But in Lord's world, at least, people were, by the end of the Seventies, adjusting. "I think we're recovering from it. In the late Sixties and early Seventies, people weren't even talking to each other. There were scars, and they're still there . . . but now, I think, it's much more civilized. People are going to remain on friendly terms even when they disagree. We don't have that kind of passion we had then, which I think is good."

Now that foreign policy is by way of returning to the "gentlemen's game" that it had been before Vietnam unleashed all those disturbing passions, Winston Lord is worried about what he sees as the "excessive" reaction to some of the perceived problems of the Vietnam period.

Not that the problems were wholly imaginary. "I think, in fact, the executive had too much power in the late Sixties and early Seventies," Lord said. "I say that as someone who feels that the policy of the Kissinger era basically was damn good. . . . But I do think that the executive branch during that period was not checked enough by the Congress. . . . I think there was an excess of secrecy, for example. . . . I think Nixon, the White House and Kissinger to a certain extent were overly secretive. I think their concern to keep some of the issues and some of the negotiations secret was justified. But some of the methods used were excessive, and we paid a price for it."

One of the methods was wiretapping, and Lord's phone was one of fourteen tapped in 1970 in a campaign to snuff out "leaks." Morton Halperin, then a colleague of Lord's, filed a civil suit against Kissinger for the taps, but Lord opposed it, Halperin said, arguing that it was "understandable" that people with access to sensitive information would be subject to such procedures. To his friends, that suggested exceptional tolerance on Lord's part; to his critics, it implied that his ambition was so great that he would not cross Kissinger on any account.

Lord's own view, he said, is that the counterreaction to the Kissinger period has been excessive, particularly where Congress is concerned. "I think Congress is getting into the kind of detail [in foreign policy] that I think is unjustifiable—specific human-rights amendments, whether aimed at the Soviet Union or Turkey. . . . Congress certainly ought to be fully informed; they ought to have a chance to discuss strategy and options at a fairly early period, so they can help shape general lines of policy. But they shouldn't get into day-to-day tactical amendments."

While waiting for another turn of the electoral wheel that might bring him back to government, with greater responsibilities, Lord offered judicious support to the Carter Administration and judicious criticism. He endorsed the Panama Canal treaties and SALT II, the recognition of China and the Camp David Egyptian–Israeli agreement—all essentially, in his view, extensions of Kissinger policies. "What I think they're missing, what I think Kissinger was better at, is articulating a strategy, giving a sense of priorities and showing how the pieces fit."

Making "the pieces fit" was as important to Winston Lord as fitting in comfortably himself. And he was skillful at leaving the impression that a proper government would understand that the two went together, hand in hand.

David L. Aaron

If Winston Lord can be said to have been born into the world of diplomacy, the same cannot for David L. Aaron, 42, the deputy assistant for national security affairs in the Carter Administration. His parents were in show business—his father, a musician with Les Brown and other of the 1940s big bands; his mother, a dancer and choreographer of nightclub shows. "We lived in the shadow of Columbia Pictures, and I went to Hollywood High School," Aaron said, "and the first interest in foreign relations came from seeing movies like *Flying Down to Rio, Intrigue* and *Foreign Correspondent.* As soon as I got out of high school, I went to Europe, and worked for six months, but at that point, I thought I was going to be a nuclear engineer. . . . It's a wedding, I guess, of my romantic impulses about foreign places with my interest in technology that's led me to be involved with the security part of foreign policy."

Aaron studied at Occidental College in Los Angeles (where he was a football teammate of Representative Jack Kemp) and the Woodrow Wilson School at Princeton, entered the Foreign Service in 1962 and, after an initial posting to Ecuador, had a series of assignments relating to NATO, nuclear weapons and the SALT negotiations. In 1972, he moved from the Arms Control and Disarmament Agency, where he had worked for almost four years, to Kissinger's National Security Council staff. In 1974, he went to work for then Senator Walter F. Mondale and, through him, came back to the White House as Zbigniew Brzezinski's deputy.

Aaron is not a risk taker, in personal or political terms, and he thinks he knows why. "I was traumatized a little bit by seeing friends of my parents' in Hollywood who were victims of McCarthyism, people who had been blacklisted and driven out of their professions. I was personally very reluctant to get associated with political movements and, philosophically, very, very skeptical about absolutist political philosophies."

Aaron wrote a column for the school paper called *The Beat Scene* about the Hollywood coffeehouses, but stayed out of the drug culture himself. He gave money to the civil-rights movement, but "I just didn't have time to march." When he entered the State Department, it was a time when "if you were interested in making a mark . . . the thing to do was go to Southeast Asia. But I didn't want to go near that with a ten-foot pole.

"When it came to the war," he said, "it took me a while before I felt it was not a desirable thing. To be frank, I maintained throughout the whole time that if we could have prevented North Vietnam from taking over . . . and had had an independent and relatively free South Vietnam, I think that was the right policy objective. . . . It simply turned out to be something we couldn't do at a price to us and to the country concerned that was acceptable. And when I came back from France in the fall of 1967 [after a NATO assignment], I could see suddenly what had been done to this country by the war, how it had polarized people."

Polarized but *not* traumatized people, Aaron insists. "I don't feel responsible for Vietnam. I was not involved. I find the people who now are less inclined to use the instruments of power in foreign policy are usually those who were, in fact, directly involved in applying that power in Vietnam, and feel guilty about it or feel that it was wrong. Those are the ones who are affected, and those tend not to be people of my generation. . . . I don't think my generation has been traumatized by Vietnam to the point of being unwilling to face the realities of power or being unwilling to use it." In fact, Aaron is depicted as one of those inside the Carter Administration who argued for "showing the flag" in the Persian Gulf after the 1979 upheaval in Iran, and for firmness in dealing with Soviet and Cuban intervention in Africa.

"There are some people on both ends," he said, talking about the older-generation hard-liners and soft-liners, "who say that because of Vietnam we've got to do twice as much as we did before, and some, I suppose, who were traumatized by it. But by and large, I think that the people of my generation are sensible about the fact that you've got to use power from time to time, have to stand up in certain situations."

The difficulty, Aaron said, is that "the American people aren't as clear as to what our role has to be in the world. They see something like China fighting Vietnam and they wonder what their sons got killed for. There is a pulling back on the part of the American people, and much less willingness to be militantly engaged, if you will, in world affairs. But there still is a great willingness to be involved, and defining that involvement is more subtle and difficult. It isn't just a 'crusade in Europe'; it isn't just 'containing Communism'; it isn't just 'paying any price and bearing any burden.' It's paying some prices and bearing some burdens, and not others, and it's a damn difficult political job to explain. It's very difficult to simplify and dramatize the issues. Some things have caught on. Human rights, for example. People are drawn to it, because it does express something good about this country, and it is relatively easy to understand, even if it's not easy to carry out. But it's one of the few things that have caught the public imagination.

"But," Aaron said, "I'm pretty optimistic. I think this is a terrific country, and I consider myself a fortunate person. I sometimes think what would have happened if I had been born in Europe. How many people are there in the chancelleries, or in Downing Street, or in the Elysée, whose father was a jazz musician and whose mother danced in nightclubs and put on floor shows? I mean, that would just never happen in those countries."

Samuel M. Hoskinson

When I asked David Aaron if his belief in a broad consensus on foreign policy among the specialists of his generation extended to the people who might be sitting in his seat in the next Republican administration, he said, "I tend to suspect that you find in the Republican Party a little bit more of the attitude that in order to prevail, we've got to dominate [potential enemies], and I think there's a little less sense of accommodation in their attitude toward international problems."

Samuel M. Hoskinson, 42, is an example of that tendency. In 1979, he made a move that was a mirror image of Aaron's 1974 shift from Kissinger's staff to Mondale's. Hoskinson moved from being Brzezinski's staff specialist on intelligence and Middle Eastern affairs to being the issues director of John B. Connally's presidential campaign. (As the Connally campaign was nearing its end in 1980, he became a senior analyst for a firm doing contract research for national-security issues.) Republicanism was nothing new to Hoskinson, however. He grew up in "a good, strong Republican upper-middle-class family" in the Chicago suburb of Riverside, where his father was an insurance man. The summer he graduated from the University of Iowa, he went to the 1960 Republican convention in Chicago, happily organizing "spontaneous demonstrations" for both Richard Nixon and Barry Goldwater. Toward the end of his graduate work in international relations at Georgetown University, he found a part-time job as a night "watch officer" at the CIA, "monitoring events on the other side of the world while the rest of Washington was asleep." After a brief, unsuccessful try as a trainee at the Chase Manhattan Bank, he came back to the CIA as a political analyst. It was Alexander M. Haig, a classmate in the Georgetown graduate school, who brought him from the CIA to the National Security Council staff in 1969, as a specialist in Middle Eastern and South Asian affairs. He returned to the CIA in 1973 and stayed there until 1976, when he returned to the White House to help the NSC set up a system for closer monitoring of intelligence activities, as part of the "reform" in that area. "So at the end of the Ford Administration, I was still sitting there," Hoskinson said, "and much to my surprise, Brzezinski came along and asked me to stay on in a similar kind of function and also resume some of my former interest in the Middle East."

The decision to leave government in 1979 "involved a lot of soul-searching"; but Hoskinson had been a Connally fan since 1972, when he served as chief of staff for the retiring Treasury Secretary on a tour of eighteen countries that Nixon asked Connally to make, as his personal emissary, on Air Force One. Also, Hoskinson said, he was "distressed" about what he regarded as a "certain naiveté" in Carter's personal approach to foreign policy, and what he regarded as Carter's tendency to improvise foreign-policy decisions on an "*ad hoc,* issue-by-issue basis" rather than managing it on clear, conceptual lines.

Beyond these personal criticisms, however, he expressed somewhat different concerns about the changes in the way in which foreign policy is conducted than the other "new pros" in this field. "It's no longer possible to have within the U.S. Government a discreet decision-making process. The leaks start with the first position paper . . . and people begin to fight it out in the press long before it ever gets to the President. . . . And then when he makes his decision, from the assistant secretary level on down, they all call in their own favorite journalist and tell him five thousand reasons why they disagree. You can't make effective policy that way. It forces it into smaller and smaller groups, meeting in secret, without notes, and that means the staff experts can't be there for support, and it also means implementation is jeopardized."

When I asked Hoskinson why he thought this had developed, he said, "It's a rebellion against authority, and nothing's been done to tighten this up. I'm a firm believer that disciplinary action by the President, like firing someone on Monday morning, might help. . . . But it began really with Vietnam . . . with the Ellsberg case [the Pentagon papers] and the young people in the streets marching around the White House, and it's gotten worse.

"A lot of people who came into this [Carter] Administration suffered from the Vietnam hangover," he said. "I never had a sense of guilt myself about the use of power. But many people saw Vietnam essentially as a misuse of American power, and they have a fear of themselves, really—a fear that we might create another massive tragedy like this in the world. They have a fear about using the instruments of power in traditional ways, and also a kind of moral reaction, which leads to this extreme emphasis on human rights."

Like Aaron, Hoskinson said he was immune to the "Vietnam hangover. I've long had this kind of *Realpolitik* approach. I come out of the intelligence community, so I'm aware of some of the seamier sides of life and human nature. The use of power has never frightened me . . . and during those Vietnam years I was so obsessed with another problem even more important—the Middle East—that I didn't have a hell of a lot of time to sit around and worry about it, quite frankly. I didn't have a deep crisis of conscience."

Despite the seeming similarity of their views, Hoskinson rejected Aaron's contention that there was a bipartisan consensus on foreign policy. "We can all agree on certain motherhood issues," he said, "but beyond that, I think it's been a myth for a long time. . . . There are vastly different approaches and perceptions of how to deal with the Soviets, for example." To meet the challenge of the Eighties, when Soviet "nuclear strategic parity . . . will present a much more variegated challenge to us," Hoskinson said, "you have to have a change of people in key places. That will come if John Connally becomes President or another Republican. And I think you'll find more people like me in any Republican administration, from the assistant secretary level on up. But you've got to have that first. The people with the Vietnam hangover just aren't going to get over it in time. It's scarred them, I'm afraid, permanently, and some of them are good people."

Douglas Bennet

Douglas J. Bennet, Jr., 42, the administrator of the federal Agency for International Development (AID), is part of a rather remarkable network of men and women whose talents were encouraged and directed toward public service by one of the "old pros," Chester Bowles—sometime adman, price controller, Congressman, Governor of Connecticut, Democratic Party activist and Ambassador to India. Bowles had a special eye for promising young people and, over a quarter-century, launched more than a dozen of them into distinguished academic and public-service careers.

Bennet is a kind of second-generation Bowlesian, his father having worked for Bowles in the World War II Office of Price Administration. Bennet had sailed through Wesleyan University and the University of California at Berkeley, studying medieval Russian history, and was well on his way to a Ph.D. in history at Harvard and a scholarly career when, as he says, "I began to have an urge to do something else." So he headed out to India for two and a half years, serving first on an AID mission and then as Bowles's assistant. When he came back, he picked up the degree and then came to Washington, working first for Vice President Humphrey, then for Missouri Senator Thomas F. Eagleton, for the Muskie for President campaign and for Connecticut Senator Abraham A. Ribicoff. After making an unsuccessful try for a Democratic congressional nomination in Connecticut (he lost to Christopher Dodd), he became the first staff director of the Senate Budget Committee, under Muskie's chairmanship, and spent three years launching what was probably the most important new element of congressional decision making in the postwar period: a formalized budget-review process. In 1977, he was recruited as Assistant Secretary of State for Congressional Affairs—the department's top lobbying job—and in 1979 moved onto the hot seat at AID.

Even after three years in the executive branch, Bennet still talked like a congressional man. "I think," he said, "there is a fundamental difference between the branches. There is much more room for creativity on the Hill. There is a trade-off, because there is less requirement to deliver results. But the Hill lives on new ideas. The premium is on individual entrepreneurship. Now, that, just realistically, can't be true in a bureaucracy, which is much more stable. Setting up the Budget Committee staff was a remarkable experience," he said. "We thought we were sort of a Green Beret outfit up there—really an elite corps. Here [in the executive branch] you don't have the latitude for selecting your troops. The troops are here, the system is here and it's a question of making it work. . . . One of the amazing things about bureaucracy is how it takes up its own time. Its own internal crises and tensions and disagreements absorb an enormous amount of energy. If you're an optimist you can say that this is a self-correcting process that produces a generally good result, but it certainly does slow down innovation and risk taking and flexibility. My experience tells me that Congress is much more flexible as an institution. There, one or two people that really want to make a change in directions can do it—for good or for ill."

As we have seen, Bennet's strictures about bureaucracy are widely shared. But his view on one aspect of the bureaucratic world differed sharply from Hoskinson's perception. That was on the matter of secrecy. Where Hoskinson feared the consequences of taking too much of the internal debate to the public, Bennet's view was that the public—and Congress—were too often being kept at bay.

"Bowles's vision and Humphrey's vision of how you mobilized support in the public is very different from what I see now," Bennet said. "I think that most people that I know in government today feel basically defensive about the public. Their instinct is generally to be reluctant to take a case to the public, to lay the facts out to them and rely on their ability to make sober judgments. . . . And maybe that's realistic. The public is much bigger. The government is much bigger and more centralized, and maybe we're trying to do more than is humanly possible. And a lot of our leadership goes for very short-cut, manipulative techniques, and those may have turned the public off considerably. But I think that unless the country has leadership and institutions that are prepared to focus on the hard realities of a few policy objectives and mobilize the public to deal with them, I think the whole thing becomes just mush."

Bennet said he recognized a paradox in his own position. In arguing that Congress was the more flexible and innovative branch, but asserting that the key task was mobilizing public opinion on a few key issues, he seemed to be putting on Congress a burden it cannot carry. "There are so many voices there [in Congress]," he said, "that it obviously has trouble providing coherent leadership. So what you need is an executive branch that's prepared to offer a hypothesis of public policy that Congress could then work on and refine and help the people understand. Some people would say there is a big element of abdication in that concept of leadership. There are people who believe that the way you lead is to arm-wrestle and prevail. You wrestle with the Congress and you wrestle with the public. You figure out what's good for the country and, by God, you make it happen. But I guess I've developed a more organic view of the process by which this society can be led, and it requires offering a hypothesis that everyone can examine, and it requires reassuring people a lot. Implicit in it is the assumption that you don't go any faster than the public wants you to go. But I'm pretty sure I'm right about this. It's not just that the strong-arm leadership is distasteful. It doesn't work."

DAVID R. OBEY

A clear echo of Bennet's view comes from one of the most influential of the younger members of the Congress, Representative David R. Obey, a 42-year-old Wausau, Wisconsin, Democrat. A full-time, professional politician and legislator since he was elected to the Wisconsin Legislature in 1962, Obey is, in his own words, "an institution man," noted both for his acerbic criticism of the performance of the House of Representatives and for his indefatigable efforts to improve it.

Talking in 1979, he said, "The problem is that it's so hard to put together a majority in Congress for doing anything beyond the immediate and symbolic, because so many people are afraid that if they vote for anything you could call a policy, it won't work. There aren't that many good ideas around on energy and the economy," said Obey, reiterating a complaint heard often in this book from liberal Democrats like himself. "Congress is as confused as everyone else. The President needs to lay out the options of policy and force us to choose. Otherwise, we will continue to run off in 435 different directions."

Obey describes himself as "kind of an odd duck" in a House where the turnover was so great that, at the start of the 1980 session, he ranked 138th in seniority among the 435 members with only his eleven years of service. "I got into politics early enough so that I shared the approaches and the style of a lot of people older than I am," he said. Obey has come to appreciate the craftsmanship of the legislative process, of the coalition-building give-and-take in the House, he said, admiring such mentors as Richard Bolling, the senior Democratic Representative from Missouri. "And yet chronologically, I'm the same generation as the young guys just now coming into the House," Obey said. "I've had a foot in both camps, but I think I've adjusted to it, and come to enjoy it now."

The tension in the current Congress is between the inclination of its predominantly young members to pursue primarily their own political interests, on the one hand, and the institutional need, on the other, for a degree of discipline and cooperation in order to produce a legislative product. Obey understands those tensions in both generational and personal terms.

As a hot-blooded parochial-school student in Wausau, he was a constant truant, who was asked to change schools after decking a nun who had hit him. Politics provided an outlet for that excess energy and ego. He began as a Robert Taft Republican, dropping leaflets (while still in junior high) for the Ohio conservative from his bicycle and wagon at about one-quarter of the homes in Wausau during the 1952 Wisconsin primary. A high-school teacher named Art Henderson (whose picture is on Obey's office wall) encouraged him to study the career of Republican Senator Joseph R. McCarthy, the anti-Communist demagogue who was then at the height of his power, and McCarthy made Obey a Democrat. By the time he finished work for a master's degree in political science at the University of Wisconsin, politics and the Democratic Party were the places where "a pretty screwed-up kid . . . finally found a place where I felt at home and belonged."

Obey came to Congress in a 1969 special election, filling a vacancy created when Melvin R. Laird became Secretary of Defense in the Nixon Cabinet. As the first Democrat to win that Wisconsin district in this century and the youngest member of the House (he was 30), he was the object of special attention from the press. But inside the House, Obey was a new boy in an institution that still revered seniority—and he didn't like it "a damn bit. Hell, when I came," he said, "the House was not an enjoyable place to be, unless you were one of a very select few. You really felt humiliated most of the time. I sat on the Public Works Committee the first eight months, and of the senior members, only John Blatnik [the longtime Democratic Congressman from Minnesota] managed to recognize that I existed. The others wouldn't even talk to me."

Given a seat on the Military Appropriations Subcommittee (where Laird had been influential for years) to help him with re-election, Obey showed he was still the rebel. As Mary Russell of *The Washington Post* wrote, George Mahon of Texas, the chairman of the subcommittee and its parent Appropriations Committee, "made it a custom for members to stand when high-ranking generals and admirals appeared to testify. Obey refused. The chairman sent a staff member to inform Obey that he expected him to rise with the others. Obey told the chairman to go to hell."

That kind of reputation could have killed a man's prospects in the old House; but as it happened, Obey's rebellion was just a foretaste of the revolt against the seniority system that transformed the House in the mid-1970s. By the time the big wave of rebels arrived, Obey was well on his way to impressing his elders as a conscientious, effective legislator, interested in making the institution work and not just in indulging his personal whims. In addition to his Appropriations Committee seat, he was named to the House Budget Committee and the Democratic Steering and Policy Committee. Later in the 1970s, Obey worked on special task forces that proposed realignments of committee jurisdictions, spearheaded the effort to tighten the House rules on use of campaign funds and office accounts and other "ethics" questions, and was elected chairman of the Democratic Study Group, the caucus of liberal Democrats.

Obey is convinced that the tide of history that has swept over the

House cannot be rolled back. Never again will a handful of unchallenged committee chairmen and a Speaker impose their will on the other 420 members. But, he said, "the dispersal of power has gone so damn far now, with all the subcommittees and their independent staffs, that everybody gets a piece of the action, and the place is so disorganized and decentralized we can hardly get anything done. . . . The new members have a different value structure, too, which means less caring about the party, less belief in programs, even less willingness to take risks. None of them want their margins [of re-election] to drop below sixty percent. And you have these special-interest groups, with their damn PAC [political action committee] contributions, just picking them off, one by one, so there's damn little glue left to hold people together who essentially see themselves as political loners."

When Obey was asked what chance he saw for rebuilding a functioning legislative body from this sort of anarchy, he was not pessimistic. "I think that all could be turned around significantly if we were lucky enough to find somebody running for President who really could articulate a sense of mission for the country. And you might also get some better results than any of us anticipate as this tremendous turnover [in House membership] slows down. . . . As they gain experience and get a couple of elections under their belt, they'll decide they don't have to throw away votes on every damn issue in order to come back. I think you may start getting a better operation in Congress."

But ultimately, Obey said, Congress would be no better than the voters who elect it; "so a hell of a lot depends on the country itself—how much they want to be indulged and how much they want to be led. Today, every damn little group that you can think of wants the government to say, 'Okay, you can quit holding your breath, you can quit stomping your feet; we'll do what you want.' People have to get over expecting that."

And then Obey recalled a colleague from the Wisconsin legislature, "old Ben Riehle," who was debating an opponent before the teachers' association. The opponent was for higher teachers' pay, more state aid for schools, more scholarships. But he was against a tax increase. "And old Ben got up, and the teachers were mad at him because he had voted for less of an increase in faculty salaries than the education community had wanted and he had voted for the tax increase. And he leaned on his cane and said, 'I want you to remember one thing. I may not have voted for everything you ever wanted, but I voted for everything you ever got. And I didn't do it ten minutes after I told you I was going to cut your taxes.'

"The last few years," Obey said, "people haven't been willing to listen when you said that kind of thing. But this last year, things have finally gotten so damn bad they are willing to listen again. They may scream like hell, but more of 'em are listening. And that's a hopeful sign."

MATTHEW NIMETZ

The official biography of Matthew Nimetz, 41, reads like another of the classic biographies of the American establishment: B.A., 1960, Williams College, *summa cum laude,* valedictorian, president of Phi Beta Kappa Society; Rhodes Scholar to Oxford University, M.A. with first-class honors in philosophy, politics and economics, 1962; LL.B., Harvard Law School, 1965, president of the *Harvard Law Review* and *magna cum laude,* as the highest-ranking graduate of the class; clerk to Justice John Marshall Harlan of the Supreme Court, 1965–67; staff assistant to the President of the United States, 1967–69; associate and partner in Simpson Thacher & Bartlett, a top Wall Street law firm, from 1969 to 1977, with time out in 1974 to serve as executive director of New York Governor Hugh L. Carey's transition task force; from 1977 to 1979, counselor of the State Department, the Secretary's top lawyer and a policy adviser; and since February 1980, Undersecretary of State for Security Assistance, Science and Technology.

When that proposition was put to Nimetz, he demurred. "I grew up in Brooklyn; went to local public schools, not a prep school. I feel quite an ordinary American." Ordinary, maybe; but extraordinarily bright. Like Michael Barone, he had a mind that could not stop memorizing. "Being Jewish, the Arab-Israeli war interested me," he said, "and I remember I memorized all the prime ministers of Egypt when I was nine years old. They changed them every few months then, and I thought it was odd that they all had the same last name—Pasha. I didn't quite realize it was an honorary title." As for the rest of his achievements, he said it was quite simple: "I like plunging into the most competitive areas. I think it's a matter of temperament. Trying for the big leagues and seeing if you can make it." At a certain point, the credentials become so overpowering that the effort seems minimal—like a Reggie Jackson homer. When he was finishing his clerkship with Justice Harlan, he thought "I would like to spend another year or two in Washington." So he wrote a one-page letter to fellow Brooklyn lawyer Joseph A. Califano, Jr., who was running Lyndon Johnson's domestic-policy staff at the White House. "There was no pull," Nimetz said. "He called me down for an interview, checked with some of my professors at Harvard. It was the classic thing. The *Harvard Law Review* and a Supreme Court clerkship open doors in government."

Perhaps because he found so many doors open to him, Matthew Nimetz took a more tolerant view of the activities of the outside interest groups that try to influence public policy—in foreign affairs as in domestic—than almost anyone else I talked to. As one who will probably be an insider/outsider all his life, he held the opposite of the professional bureaucratic attitude decried by Douglas Bennet.

"I think I have a sense of the limits of government, more than most," he said, "and I do think the most dynamic aspects of our society come from outside. I'd venture to say that if you look at the period since 1960, most of the innovative things in American society have come from leadership outside the presidency and outside government: the civil-rights movement, the women's movement, the antiwar movement, the environmental movement—all those things which have changed our society most.

"They reflect a deep commitment to certain ideas or needs. In foreign policy, I've dealt with all the ethnic groups that come down and lobby us, and although it drives us wild at the State Department—especially the career people—it's a healthy aspect to our society that those groups can express themselves. . . . In any event, it's inevitable. In a mass society, people, in order to avoid alienation, do find association in groups very meaningful. And I think the system does respond fairly well, when a group starts pushing beyond the natural boundaries of its influence. The ethnic groups that are most powerful are the Jewish groups and the Greek groups. And both lost last year on major issues [the lifting of the Turkish arms embargo and the sale of warplanes to Egypt and Saudi Arabia] because they got to a point where they were fighting something that clearly was in the national interest."

As one who served as the White House staff liaison to the District of Columbia police during the period of protest in 1967–68, when "we literally didn't have the faintest idea what was going on five or ten blocks from the Capitol," Nimetz said he expects the wounds of that period to "last a generation. Some of that antagonism will spill over into other areas," he said, and make it harder to lead the country. "I think we have not reached a new consensus on foreign policy, and it will not be easy. In order to reach accommodation around the world, there will have to be a gradual giving up of what we used to call sovereignty, and I think it will be very hard to persuade the American people to do that. . . . I think the gut reaction of Americans will be negative.

"Let me give you an example," he said. "I work on the Mexican illegal immigration problem. From a purely American point of view and under international law, we could just close our border. It is *our* border. And yet the turmoil that would create in Mexico, and the difficulties in the Hispanic community here, make it very difficult to take a step like that. The migration issue is the perfect example of our need to adjust to the Third World. Every month, maybe a hundred thousand people walk across that border. It's the Third World moving in. There are hundreds of issues like that where we have to make accommodations, and it's hard for our people to understand. We have to fight for our position in the world, and yet be prepared to make these accommodations. Because it's not just the United States adjusting itself. Everyone is. China has adjusted its concept of sovereignty with regard to Taiwan. The Soviet Union has adjusted its concept of sovereignty to allow us to photograph its missile sites and check its telemetry data. 'Interdependence' is a word I hate to use, because it's such a catch-all. But we are involved in a web of relationships in which you have give-and-take. And it's going to take good leadership to persuade people at home these adjustments are in our best interest and represent the best deal we can get."

BARNEY FRANK

Barney Frank, 40, is a Democratic state Representative from Boston and that rarity at the end of the 1970s, a practicing liberal politician who was not seeking a euphemism to describe his faith. "By the time I was fourteen," he said, "I was a very partisan liberal Democrat, and I still am, notwithstanding the fact that I endorsed Republicans up here for the Senate and the governorship in the last election." Frank endorsed incumbent Senator Edward W. Brooke in 1978 because he thought there should be at least one black in the Senate, and he endorsed state Representative Francis W. Hatch, Jr., for Governor because Edward J. King, a conservative, had won the Democratic nomination, and if there is one thing Barney Frank cannot stand, it is a conservative Democrat. Both his candidates lost, but that too is a way that liberals prove they are keeping the faith.

Barney Frank acquired his faith in a "newspaper-reading" family in Bayonne, New Jersey, where dinner conversations were so spirited, the children learned to talk fast. Twenty years later, a spectator sitting between Frank and his older sister, Ann Lewis, a leading feminist and aide to Democratic Representative Barbara Mikulski of Maryland, would find his head swiveling as if he were at a tennis match. Few sentences were finished without interruption.

Frank is one of those people whose weight can fluctuate as much as fifty pounds in a single year, but his appearance is consistently unkempt. One year his campaign poster showed a characteristically disheveled photograph of the legislator with the caption "Neatness Isn't Everything." In his case, it certainly is not.

What Frank does have is one of the quickest political minds in America and the nerve to follow his own instincts—on a one-liner or an endorsement or a piece of legislation. He came out of Harvard College in 1962, having done volunteer political work every campaign year; spent the summer of 1964 with the civil-rights workers in Mississippi; and in 1967 was settling in to write his Ph.D. dissertation on the Massachusetts Legislature when he was asked by a friend to work in Kevin White's race for Mayor of Boston. He joined the campaign five weeks before election day, "and after about three weeks, it became clear to everybody but me that I was probably going to be working in the administration. I remember one guy asked me to go to lunch with him and he said, 'Look, I'll be honest with you. I can see the way things are shaping up around here. You're going to have a big job in the next administration, and I'm going to be supportive of you, and I want you to remember me.' And I walked out of there stunned, and said, 'Jesus, I'm an academic. I'm going to write a thesis. My God, this has never happened to me before . . . especially since I was from out of town.' "

But the instinct was right. He worked as White's right-hand man in the city administration for almost four years before going back to Harvard to write his dissertation. When he tried, "it really became clear to me that I was temperamentally much better in politics than academics. I think quickly, and if we all have fifteen minutes to react to a problem, I'm going to do very well. If we then get another two weeks, I'm not going to improve very much, so my competitive advantage will have diminished if not disappeared. I am much better at doing a lot of things quickly than doing a couple of things over a long period of time."

Armed with this insight, Frank became administrative assistant to then U.S. Representative Michael J. Harrington, and in 1972 was elected to the state legislature—both positions where the premium is on a short attention span.

Asked in 1979 if he was "the last liberal left," Frank said, "No, but there aren't a lot of us. It reminds me," he said, "of Kennedy's line about how he became a war hero: 'The Japanese sank my boat.' I became the leading young liberal by a process of elimination. There were twenty guys in front of me, and all of a sudden three went to the bathroom, and two of them heard their mother calling them, and there I was."

Frank became active on the national level in Americans for Democratic Action, the organizational link to the flickering memories of New Deal liberalism. And he found contemporary applications of traditional liberal doctrine. One prime goal was to combat what he called "the corrosive effect of the interstate competition for industry, which keeps us from adopting progressive policies at the state level." As the New Dealers had used that rationale to promote a national minimum-wage law, Frank argued that the same problem today requires passage of a uniform national welfare payment and a labor-reform law that, by facilitating union organization in the South, would reduce the drain of jobs from the Northeast and Midwest.

"Forty years ago," Frank said, "federalism was a progressive thing. [Supreme Court Justice Louis] Brandeis could say, 'It is one of the happy incidents of the federal system that a single courageous state may, if its citizens choose, serve as a laboratory and try novel social and economic experiments without risk to the rest of the country.' Well, my amendment to that is: Yes, but the rats have now become mobile, and they say to us in Massachusetts, 'If you try that novel experiment, I'm moving to New Hampshire.'

"In the forty years since Brandeis wrote, the economy has become national, but the political system hasn't, so business can play the states off one against the other to reduce its own environmental, consumer and social-policy costs."

At the state level, Frank said, his main goal was even less traditional for a liberal: curbing what he saw as the excesses of civil service. In this, he reflected a criticism of the bureaucracy that was expressed not only by the federal program managers quoted earlier in this chapter, but by many of the community leaders met earlier in this book. "We have to make it possible to fire people," said Frank. "Otherwise, with inflation pushing their salaries up and the constraints we've got on public spending, the level of services to those who need government is bound to decline.

"The climate is tough for liberals," he said, "and all you can do these days is try to hold the line and cut down the rate of erosion. And hope for a better day."

Peter C. Goldmark, Jr.

Peter C. Goldmark, Sr., has gone into the history books as the inventor of the long-playing record, the first practical color television set, the videotape cassette and dozens of other artifacts that are part of the communications revolution of the past generation.

Peter C. Goldmark, Jr., 40, the executive director of the Port Authority of New York and New Jersey, has no comparable achievements in his record. But there are many of his contemporaries in his own chosen field of public administration who think he will come close to that mark.

When he was 28, he wrote, anonymously, some of the most influential and controversial words of the Sixties. As a staff member for then Mayor John V. Lindsay of New York, Goldmark sat up all night, with fellow staffer Jay Kriegel, and wrote the introduction to the Kerner Commission report on the urban riots. That was the report which said, "Our nation is moving toward two societies, one black, one white—separate and unequal. . . . What white Americans have never fully understood—but what the Negro can never forget—is that white society is deeply implicated in the ghetto. White institutions created it, white institutions maintain it, and white society condones it."

Early in 1979, more than ten years later, the still-young Peter Goldmark quoted these words back to me, from memory, and said, "I would argue that that is, ten years afterwards, the most coherent and insightful and comprehensive statement by whites in America about the black-white problem. And that summary is a fairly radical piece of work."

We were sitting in a magnificent office, complete with private dining room and bathroom, on the sixty-seventh floor of the World Trade Center, with floor-to-ceiling windows looking down on New York Harbor and the Statue of Liberty. It was one of the perks of the $77,194-a-year job Goldmark has held since 1977 as the top official of the Port Authority, the interstate body which runs the basic transportation facilities of the New York metropolitan area and, increasingly, is a prime agent in the region's struggle for economic survival.

Goldmark's climb to that lofty perch began in a classic attitude of rebellion. "I had a very strong reaction against the pressure which came from my father to go to graduate school, to get interested in science and math." Young Peter was, instead, a government major at Harvard, and despite a distinguished academic record, he declined to seek anything beyond a bachelor's degree. Instead, he taught for two years at the Putney School in Vermont, then came to Washington looking for action. He found it in the just-starting Office of Economic Opportunity, the antipoverty agency, but when his boss left to join the Lindsay Administration's budget office, Goldmark followed along. He stayed with Lindsay until 1970, spent four years as secretary of human services in Massachusetts and came back to New York as director of the state budget office during the height of the New York City fiscal crisis. In managing the $12-billion state budget, while leading the effort to provide interim financing to save the city from bankruptcy, Goldmark showed himself almost as innovative in his own chosen field as his father had been in his. His latest position provides new opportunities for him to test his management skills.

Looking back and looking down from his present perch, Goldmark can see the mistakes of the 1960s urban programs as clearly as anyone. "We tried to do too many things at once," he said, "rather than some things well. . . . It was that old bugaboo about being comprehensive. Because of the way the American political system works, we were trying to spread every program dollar like butter across the whole piece of toast. We didn't go after providing jobs the way we probably should have—really focus our efforts on that. . . . I think a lot of the money and effort we spent on physical redevelopment of the cities was wrong; it was misdirected and wasted. And I think all of us—and I certainly include myself—had a very exaggerated idea of what the government bureaucracy could do in delivering health services, child care and all the rest."

Still, Goldmark said, he was both "an optimist and an interventionist," which was why he had taken the job of managing the Port Authority: to see if its $839-million annual budget could be used as leverage for the economic development of a region where, he said, "we let the private sector and the public sector get out of equilibrium. I really don't hold with the new conservatism that says government can do nothing more useful than stand aside for the market forces. I think there are ways to do things, and some of them require more direct and forceful government intervention than we've had. I just don't think you attempt to do it everywhere at once through traditional policies and structures."

But, Goldmark said, letting his mind roam beyond the Atlantic horizon, "if the Defense Department can employ two million people . . . and AT&T can employ a million, why can't we have a TVA for jobs, whose mission will be to do public works? We need $50 billion worth of public works right here in New York and New Jersey."

But, as he continued to gaze across the harbor, he said, "I'm very scared about this country, and where we are in relation to the realities of the world. I'm one of the generation that absorbed its picture of reality from Cy Vance and John McCloy and those people. That picture is best characterized for me by the countries of the world standing in a line, with the United States at the head of the line, something like the Pied Piper, and Ecuador and Pakistan, say, elbowing each other to see who's going to be seventeenth or eighteenth in the race to be as democratic as we are, and as rich. But now we know that the world not only can't afford to have other people like us, because we won't survive; it may not be able to afford to have *us* be like us. We know we're not going to have 6 percent of the people consuming 40 percent of the world's energy twenty-five years from now. We can't have a world where we put as much fertilizer on our golf courses and cemeteries each year as India uses in its total agricultural production. So the picture we grew up with was wrong. And I'm scared that we're going to be the dinosaur in the briar patch. But I'd like to try to be one of those—because it's the most interesting thing to spend your energy on—who try to make our institutions do the things that ought to be done to come to terms with those realities that are going to shape the world for the next twenty-five years. I'm not telling you that I'm high on confidence we can do it. I just think it's better to assume you can, and try to do it."

Newt Gingrich

Some people would say that it is close to inevitable that anyone whose boyhood ambition was to be a paleontologist would wind up as a Republican Congressman from Georgia. But if that was his fate, destiny stuttered, because Newt Gingrich, 37, traveled a circuitous path from fossil collecting to Capitol Hill.

Gingrich, an extraordinarily intense young man, is a blend of seemingly contradictory impulses. He is a former professor of history who defines his political role as that of a "modernizer," a conservative who, as a graduate student at Tulane University, led a demonstration in defense of the school newspaper's right to print a nude photograph of a faculty member, and who backed Nelson Rockefeller in Louisiana because of Rockefeller's support of civil rights. In his freshman year in Congress, he became the leader of a back-benchers' movement which set as its notably immodest goal the achievement of a Republican majority in the House in the Eighties.

Gingrich, who was born in Harrisburg, Pennsylvania, and migrated to Georgia as a child, was 15 when his stepfather, an infantry officer, took the family to visit a friend who was stationed near the World War I battlefield of Verdun. The host was a survivor of the Bataan death march, "and the combination of every evening talking about the Japanese prisoner-of-war camps and every day seeing the field where a hundred thousand men were killed in battle—I guess it was a catharsis," Gingrich said. Instead of studying fossils, he took up studying history, convinced that in political action was "the critical path for the survival of my culture. I went to my sophomore English teacher and said I wanted to do a paper on the balance of world power as a way of training myself." Never one for half measures, Gingrich turned in 180 pages of prose—and, incidentally, announced to the bemused teacher that his new plan was to "go to Georgia and create a second party and run for Congress."

After studying at Emory University and Tulane, he did just that, losing twice by agonizingly small margins, first in the year of Watergate and then in the year when Jimmy Carter was leading the Democratic ticket in Georgia. Finally, in 1978, Gingrich achieved his ambition.

He had no more than arrived when he began talking up his next crazy scheme—to achieve the majority Republicans had not won in the House since 1952. "I'm not up here [in Washington] to do anything that's essentially personalistic, or that's built around short-run Band-Aids," he told anyone who wondered why he was not just working at securing the suburban Atlanta seat he had struggled so hard to win. "My friends and I are trying to figure out strategically what we have to do in this country in the next ten years to build a majority. And that kind of strategy has to be based on increasing the range of controllable resources, rather than building the name and image of a single Congressman.

"I guess one of my reactions to the whole period from Kennedy through Nixon, and reinforced by Carter, is that we have to rebuild the institutions, including Congress and the political parties, if we're going to govern this country and keep it a free society. The world is just too complex now to have randomly chosen president-kings who may or may not be competent."

Gingrich's effort in his first congressional term was centered on building a cohesive Republican challenge to the ruling Democrats on the basic question of the size and shape of the government's budget. A believer in some of the neoconservative economic theories of deep tax cuts and spending discipline, he argued that the absence of a clear Republican alternative had not only kept the GOP from majority status for more than a generation, it had deprived the country of something vital.

"I am a Republican," Gingrich said, "but I think the greatest failure of the last twenty years has been the Republican Party, not the Democratic Party. The Democratic Party has attempted to do what the governing party should do—govern. But it failed. And when it failed, there was nobody there to take up the burden. And I think that in order for this civilization to survive, at least as a free society, we've got to have a more rigorous and cohesive sense of an alternative party."

That view was so unusual in a politician of Gingrich's age that the freshman legislator drew much more than his share of attention. He said that he knew the conventional wisdom was that he should look after his constituents' needs and his own re-election and let someone else save the free society—at least until he had a couple or three terms under his belt. But Gingrich said that "the dearth of strategic vision in this party is so enormous that it's the old story: a one-eyed man, even if he's nearsighted, has huge advantages." Gingrich's special advantage, aside from his compulsive energy, may have been his sense of history—another quality that is in notably short supply among many of the self-centered politicians of his age.

"I grew up in Pennsylvania," he said, "before my stepfather was assigned to the South. And the great Republican tradition which my family identified with in Pennsylvania was the 1856-to-1912 tradition that was very progressive. It was the party of industrialization, of economic growth. It was the party of the full lunch pail. And that party was very activist. That was the party that created the land-grant colleges and built the transcontinental railroad. It had a vision which it was willing to impose upon the society.

"But for the last fifty years the Republican Party has been hypnotized by Franklin Roosevelt, and its entire vision has been to stop what he began.

"So I'm a modernizer who is suggesting that we leap back an entire span and claim our own heritage again. I think we can do that," Gingrich said, "but even if I weren't confident of that, I'd still be working at it. I believe in institutions. I believe in the Republican Party and the House of

Representatives, and I think strengthening the one will strengthen the other. If all I were going to do is bail out the ship while it keeps sinking, I would just as soon quit and get on the life raft. But I'm not ready to quit."

Tom Quinn

When Jerry Brown was setting up his administration after winning the governorship of California in 1974, he named Tom Quinn as chairman of the state Air Resources Board, a semi-obscure agency charged with enforcing California's environmental laws. It was not a bad job, but it was not the kind of job most people expected Brown to give the man who had been the manager of both his successful statewide campaigns (for Secretary of State in 1970 and for Governor) and, seemingly, his closet confidant during that period. The speculation was that either Quinn and Brown, both strongheaded individuals, had had a falling-out or Quinn had lost favor because Brown had barely held on to beat Republican Houston Flournoy in what most thought would be an easy race. But the rumors proved to be wrong. Quinn, with backing from the Governor, made the Air Resources Board job the center of nationally publicized energy and environmental battles, and remained Brown's political strategist, both in his landslide 1978 re-election campaign and in his two bids for the Democratic presidential nomination.

In short, Tom Quinn, at 36, has become something new in the political scene: an environmentalist-politician. James A. Farley ran the Post Office Department, but he did much more than that for Franklin D. Roosevelt. J. Howard McGrath and Robert F. Kennedy ran the Justice Department for Presidents Truman and Kennedy, but also looked after their political needs. But Quinn is the first to combine environmentalism with politics in this fashion.

Like those predecessors, Quinn is an Irishman with a well-earned reputation for being a tough adversary in a close-quarters scrap. He was born in Los Angeles, where his father was a wire-service reporter and editor and his mother was the first woman lawyer in the U.S. Attorney's office. The first political debates he can remember hearing were at the dinner table in 1952, when his mother was an ardent Stevenson supporter and his father a dedicated Eisenhower man "who couldn't understand how anybody could be for anybody named Adlai." Tom Quinn wavered in his own political faith until he went off to Northwestern University to study journalism. "I became a liberal and a Democrat," he said, "from being around Northwestern, where there were so many people active in the Young Americans for Freedom and all those other right-wing groups." After graduation he did radio work in Chicago for a time, then headed back to California for a series of news-service, radio and television assignments in Sacramento and Los Angeles.

In 1969, when he was 25 and bored with his work, Quinn filed as a candidate for the Los Angeles Board of Education. He lost, but in the course of the campaign got to know Jerry Brown, who was running successfully in the same election for the junior-college board of education. "We got to be friends," Quinn said, "and later that year when he decided to run for Secretary of State [in 1970] he asked if I would get involved." And involved he has been ever since.

Quinn symbolizes a style of laid-back, hard-boiled politics that is, if not unique to California, particularly flourishing there. His approach is seemingly low-key to the point of nonchalance. He smiles a lot. But he has proved himself a very tough bargainer, whether dealing for Brown with old-line machine politicians in the Eastern presidential-primary states or negotiating with oil-company attorneys on the terms for a pipeline permit. His approach to politics is highly pragmatic. He did his best to deny Brown's opponent in 1970 television exposure, fearing the comparison would help the Republican, and in 1974 did just the opposite, knowing that Brown would emerge with an advantage from television debates in that race.

His policy views are a similar tossed salad. Quinn said in an interview that he thought he had stayed "more liberal" than some of his 1960s radical friends from Berkeley, "most of whom are now living with 2.3 kids in the San Fernando Valley and working as the number one insurance adjuster in their company." On the other hand, he said, "If I hadn't felt at the time that the passage of Proposition 13 might be a serious problem for Jerry [Brown], I guess I could have voted for it. . . . It was totally logical to be for Prop 13. In my case, I was going to save $2,000 a year on my property taxes, and I knew my kids were not going to be affected in terms of their education, and everything would work fine. The only thing that's affected me are the reductions in the public-library hours."

On the other hand, he said his work on the Air Resources Board has made him "much more suspicious of large corporations. I really believe that most large corporations are operating in a fashion that's detrimental to the interests of this nation, particularly the multinationals, whose interests are no longer tied exclusively to those of this country."

That suspicion colored Quinn's approach to his regulatory job and provoked bitter battles over refineries, pipelines, industrial plants and automobiles—and their adverse impact on the environment. While his industry critics saw Quinn as a man who adopted extremist environmental positions, either to satisfy himself or to serve Brown's political needs, his own view was that business had time and time again shown its ability to adapt to regulations whose imposition it had fought.

And from that, he drew his conclusion: "I think that there is enormous irresponsibility on the part of many large corporations, but that irresponsibility was created and condoned by the government. We [in government] wrote the rules of the game, and they learned to use those rules to make their profits."

The solution that Quinn saw was this: "*We* must rewrite the rules" and push the corporations into doing "what *we* believe should be done in the social good."

As a politician, Tom Quinn had learned at an early age to play by the rules. As an environmentalist, he wanted to rewrite the rules to produce the outcome he wanted.

That seemed like a paradox—and it was. Exactly the kind of paradox a Jerry Brown could appreciate.

Janet Brown

Janet Brown, 29, a press secretary in the office of Republican Senator John C. Danforth of Missouri, is one of those rare creatures, a fourth-generation Washingtonian. It is a group whose habits and customs are not well known; ironically, avoidance of politics is their norm.

"No one in my family has ever been involved in government in any way," Brown said. "I think it's fair to say that's true of the majority of native Washingtonians. In order to survive half a generation in this town, it's probably wiser to steer clear of quadrennial political vicissitudes."

Even after taking her own apprenticeship in government as a White House aide in the final year of the Ford Administration, she was on the verge of following the family pattern by getting a law degree. She decided instead on graduate study at the Kennedy School of Government at Harvard, but only after "almost kicking myself and realizing that for five years I'd been fighting the notion that this was what I really wanted to do . . . because almost none of the friends that I had when I was growing up had gone into government and almost none of them can even stand to say the word."

When I asked this youngest of my candidates for the "new pro" category why she disagreed with her friends' judgment about government, she said, "It really bothers me that there's this perception of government as something else. Government involves the whole country, and whether you like it or not, you're part of it. So it seems silly to have this built-in antagonism."

But Janet Brown's introduction to government was almost entirely fortuitous. A Republican, more because of the "neighborhood aura" in her part of Northwest Washington than for any other reason, she spent two years at Wellesley and then took a degree in American civilization at Williams without having any real idea where she was headed. As a temporary expedient Brown was coaching athletics at a girls' school in 1973, and "the end of the field-hockey season coincided almost perfectly with the 'Saturday Night Massacre,' " when Attorney General Elliot L. Richardson resigned to protest Richard Nixon's firing of Special Prosecutor Archibald Cox.

On a hunch, she wrote to Richardson asking for a job. After receiving a polite turndown from the former Cabinet member, who was on his way to a fellowship at the Woodrow Wilson International Center for Scholars at the Smithsonian Institution, she spent several months as a paralegal at the Washington law firm of Covington and Burling, "so that I could go to law school and be my father's daughter from then on." Then, with no additional prodding on Brown's part, Richardson called to offer her a job as a research assistant for his book *The Creative Balance*.

For the next two years, she took a quick cram course in every area his career had ever covered—which was, of course, virtually the entire range of state and federal government. When Richardson was finished with her, he sent her on to Vice President Rockefeller's staff, for a "crash project" drafting President Ford's 1976 State of the Union address, and from there she was recommended to the White House Domestic Council staff. There, among other assignments in the last year of the Ford Administration, she became the action officer on Indian problems—or, as she put it, "Domestic Council Indian chief . . . because that was perceived by everybody else as a giant no-win situation, and no one wanted to have egg all over their face when the Indians came to call.

"There were issues that were tying up dozens of people at Justice and Interior and infuriating the Indians, and I came into the middle of the whole thing, saying, 'Hey, guys, I've got no authority to do anything, but I'll be glad to talk to you.' And I came to realize that if you were honest with them, and forced them to stop the bluster and tell you what the problem was, the problem could always be reduced to something that was fairly handleable.

"One of the best relationships I had with anybody," she said, "was with a headman from the Sioux tribe in Rapid City, South Dakota, whose name, if you can believe it, was Chief Louis Bad Wound. The scariest-looking person I've ever met in my life. But we developed a wonderful relationship, where he'd call me and give me the official version, and then he'd give me the real version, and I'd get on the phone to Justice or HUD, and just by talking to the right guy and saying, 'Let's not make a big deal of it; let's just see if we can get someone to go over and fix the problem,' we'd get it done. Where if he called directly, they probably wouldn't even put his call through. To me, that's what the whole process is about; but it worked so well that the last day I was there he called, really upset, and said, 'Hey, Brownie, you no can leave. Who I'm going to call?' And I said, 'Louie, I got a name for you. Get a pencil. Eizenstat. E-I-Z-E-N-S-T-A-T.' He almost died, but I figured, 'Here's my legacy to the new Administration.'

"I've been lucky so far," she said after coming back from her post-White House Harvard studies and just before starting her job with Danforth. "I've never followed anybody in any of the jobs I've had. I've always been the first one in that position, and I've always been the youngest in the office and one of the very few females. So for me, it's been an experience of working with people and trying to do something that's going to help people. It all sounds terribly Crusader Rabbitish, but there's nothing else I've encountered that gives you the feeling that maybe you can make a difference.

"One woman in our neighborhood who had known me since I was a small child had the gall to tell the FBI when they were doing my security check for the White House, 'Why are you checking on her? You should just be grateful she wants to work for you.'

"I'm not anywhere near the stage where anyone in the country would feel a whole lot better about the government from knowing what I was doing. But I really do believe in the percolation theory on this. If you break government down into individual components, I sincerely believe that the individual can make a difference. Sometimes it's just a simple question of trying to do a job well, as opposed to not well, which is what happens quite often in government.

"I'll never forget when someone asked me at the White House, 'Why are you rewriting that memo? You know the slop that passes for standard fare around here.' And I remember being really irritated, and just turning to him and saying, 'Which doesn't mean we have to make it unanimous, does it?' "

No more than any of the other people who have paraded through the pages of this book does Janet Brown carry a money-back guarantee that she will stick with the difficult work of government and politics long enough and effectively enough to make her impact felt.

But her disdain for mediocrity and her impatience with the *status quo* typify to me the spirit that she and her contemporaries bring to the challenge.

Like many of the others I met in writing this book, she made me feel better about the future.

17 · Conclusion

THIS BOOK WAS CONCEIVED essentially as a large-scale reporting project. It was an effort to draw a portrait of a generation poised on the brink of taking power. There were no obvious models for this particular kind of journalistic history, so I relied on the techniques used every day in reporting less ambitious topics.

What this has meant is that the portrait has been sketched largely in the words of the book's subjects. They were asked to describe the experiences that had propelled them into the political process and to discuss the attitudes and outlook they have toward themselves, their predecessors, their colleagues and rivals, their country and its government.

It was probably best to leave that task largely to them, for they, after all, are the ones who are going to be running this country. But there are some personal impressions I have gained from this intensive two-year dialogue with these leaders which have changed my own thinking about the political future of America. I am not reluctant to set down those impressions—for whatever insights they may give the contemporary reader and whatever amusement they may provide those who in time will write the history of the final two decades of this century.

The question young Bill Scranton asked himself way back in the first chapter—"What are you going to be in that process?"—is, ultimately, the question facing all of the men and women of his generation. They sense—and correctly—that they are about to claim their inheritance of leadership and responsibility. But they do so at a time when the institutions of government have been badly weakened and when public confidence in the nation's leadership has been eroded. We have gone twenty years—a full generation—without a "normal" presidency. Dean Rusk, the former Secretary of State, made the observation that those now taking power, like his son David, the Mayor of Albuquerque, had "seen this country through fifteen pretty rough years, beginning with the assassinations . . . the agonies of Vietnam—because whatever one thinks of Vietnam, it was an agony for everybody—the extraordinary events of Watergate, followed by a recession, unemployment and inflation." But unlike their parents, Rusk said, "they've never seen this country with the sense of élan and confidence we have when we all seem to be moving in the right direction. . . . So if you find some among them who are discouraged, maybe a little cynical, there's a reason for it."

But Rusk went on to say that he did not find "despair and cynicism are by any means the prevailing attitudes. I find them informed and responsive to the new problems. And I find that most of them are in the mood to take at least a piece of the action and try to do something about it."

If there is anything that gives one hope about the passage of power that will take place in this decade, it is that those who are about to inherit that authority seem unintimidated by what they have seen and what they will face. If they are questioning, as they are, their own role and their own beliefs, they are not paralyzed by indecision. Rather, they accept the ambiguity as a condition for survival—and for effectiveness—in such an age of transition. They have done their part, until now, by keeping the dialogue open.

Despite the upheavals that conditioned the outlook of this generation, they are, in almost every instance, aware of and attuned to the values they inherited. The question of what they, in turn, will impart to their successors is the more critical—and less answerable—matter. For most of their adult lives, these men and women have been testing the political and social system and asking hard questions of it. More than any other age group in this society, they have asked insistently and repeatedly: Does this policy make sense? Is this program needed? Why this secrecy? Why this war? Why this discrimination? Why this regulation? Why this human and economic waste?

The questions they have asked have been—for the most part—the right questions. But now they are at the point in their lives when they must, in the natural rhythm of nations, begin to offer—and to test—their own answers.

The changing of the guard is a ceremony as old as civilization, and one that is subject to endless rehearsal and repetition. But for each shift, the reality is unambiguous, and it is unique. One moment they are at rest, spectators on the sideline of history. And the next, they are maintaining the guard on which the security of the future depends.

For these men and women, the moment of responsibility is nearly at hand.

I did not begin this project with any thought as to whether its message would be upbeat or downbeat, optimistic or pessimistic about the prospects of seeing these people take power. The changing of the guard was inevitable and therefore worth examining. But I could not have said with any honesty whether it was something to be anticipated with eagerness or with dread.

At the end of the project, I find myself distinctly hopeful about the coming change. There is impressive quality in many of the people I met for the first time, or came to know far better than previously, in the course of wandering through their ranks. As with young people of every generation, a disproportionate share of their time early in their careers has been spent in preparation and in seeking promotions. They have not yet been tested in the hardest tasks of governing a nation over a long period of time.

But the best indication of their quality is what they have achieved in their twenties, thirties and forties. They have been at the center of the movements that are the most significant of their time, movements that have altered the social and political and institutional fabric of this nation. As Tim Sampson pointed out, they have had, in many instances, a twenty-year course in organizing to achieve change and are only now beginning to occupy the leadership positions where those skills can be most effectively employed.

To be sure, the sampling in this book is hardly a cross section. The effort was made, within each of the networks of new leadership that have been described, to identify those individuals who were regarded by their peers as the best exemplars of the kind of talent to be found in that particular area of American life. In most of the networks, there was a fairly high degree of consensus, and most of the selections were guided by those peer-group judgments. But of course I added my own crotchety criteria, seeking to avoid the overpublicized, the hacks and the nakedly ambitious. There are almost certainly some identifiable future presidential prospects who are missing from this book. And I am arbitrary enough to confess that I do not mourn their absence for a moment. Sufficient unto the day is the inevitability of having to write about them.

So, in a certain sense, this is a stacked deck—a selection of people, highly regarded by their peers, who also pass my personal test as being something other than pompous asses, young fogies or overly precocious pups. But the group could be expanded fivefold or tenfold without diminishing the quality. There is a lot of talent coming along.

We are reaping a rich reward as a nation for the investment we have made in the past two decades in our education system—particularly our system of public education. A reference to the educational background of almost all the people in this book was included quite deliberately. There are, as always, a crush of Harvard and Yale alumni—and of Rhodes scholars. The meritocracy still reigns. But because there has been so much doubt about the performance of the public schools in this country in recent years, especially in our urban centers, it was reassuring to see that public education remains, for many of our next leaders, what it was for earlier generations—the pathway to knowledge of, and participation in, a larger world. Nothing touched me more in all the interviewing than the stories of those people who have moved in their own lifetime from being outcasts of this society to being contributing leaders. A Vilma Martínez, who could not even speak English when she began first grade at a San Antonio public school, went through sixteen years of public education in Texas, took a law degree at Columbia, a big-city university in what has become a depressed neighborhood, and is now an eloquent advocate for social justice, heard by the President, and helping to select this nation's ambassadors.

She illustrates another lesson of this experience, and one that we can count as both an achievement and a blessing for this country. The success in the past twenty years of the struggle against discrimination is beginning, like the investment in education, to repay us rich rewards in the widening of the leadership pool. It is remarkable to think that in 1960 no Catholic had ever served as President, no black had served in the Cabinet or on the Supreme Court, and both Hispanics and women were notable by their absence in decision-making posts.

All of these groups are still underrepresented in our leadership. But having won major battles against the legal and social barriers blocking them from the mainstream of American life, they are coming on—and fast. There is no way to know who specifically will be running this country in 1990 or 2000, but it is certain that the leaders will have a vastly different look—a far greater mixture of races, religions and sexes—than they have today. And a good thing, too—not simply because it will make us feel better about ourselves, and make our government more representative than it has been. The simple fact is that when everybody competes, and not just male white Protestants, the people who emerge with power have to be that much better equipped to do their jobs.

This optimism about the people who will be taking over this country is a rather new sensation for me. In my newspaper reporting, and in a previous book, *The Party's Over,* I have been persistently part of the chorus of doomsayers about the declining health of American political and governmental institutions. This is not the place to repeat all of those observations. But neither is it my intention to recant them. I think the decline (some would say demise) of an effective two-party system has been terribly destabilizing to our politics and debilitating to the functioning of our national government. George Reedy's decade-old description of "the twilight of the presidency" has unfortunately proved to be an accurate summation of the decline of that central office in our politics and government. The Congress has so decentralized and bureaucratized itself that it all too often appears hog-tied. The fragmentation of authority has encouraged the competition of organized interest groups and has carried many essentially political questions into the courts. And the courts are institutionally less equipped to find broadly acceptable solutions for these problems than the executive and legislative branches would be—if they were healthy. The burdening of the judiciary with these disputes has damaged its legitimacy, as Rose Elizabeth Bird testified from her own experience, thus weakening that third branch of government.

In all of this process of bulldozing and battering the institutions of our politics and government, the instruments of destruction have most often been wielded by the very same young people who are described in this book with such admiration. They pushed through the "reforms" in delegate selection and campaign financing that contributed to the weakening of the party structure. Their demand for substantial equality with more senior members of the House and Senate overthrew the old authority structure in Congress, dispersing power so widely that it has become difficult for them to legislate on controversial issues. The activists on the Left helped drive Lyndon Johnson from power, and the activists on the Right nearly denied nomination to Jerry Ford—with the result, in both cases, being the election of a President from the opposition party whom they found even more distasteful. These activists also are the ones who have pushed the courts of the land further and further into the political thicket.

So the admiration expressed for them here is highly paradoxical. If there is a way of rationalizing it, it is this: Across the spectrum, my impression is that their ultimate aim is not to destroy, but to change. Much of what they seek to change is practices and policies that have cried out for alteration. It was surely no mistake to take to the streets to protest segregation. If the Vietnam war was not immoral, as they claimed, it was surely unwise, and the protests they organized against it helped push American policy back toward sanity. It was not wrong for them to be affronted by the spectacle of a senile committee chairman's stalling needed legislation, simply because he had never had an opponent at home and the seniority system kept him in power as long as he had strength enough to hold the gavel. Nor were they in error in thinking that unreported, under-the-table campaign contributions came close to being bribes.

Those who organized for Eugene McCarthy in 1968 and Ronald Reagan in 1976 were giving voice to widespread and legitimate dissatisfactions with the performance of the presidents then in power. Those who sued and sued and sued government agencies were protesting genuine abuses of law and administrative process.

What can be criticized is not the motivation on which they acted, but their inability to foresee the unintended consequences of some of the changes they managed to bring about. But that is a failing from which no one is immune, and it is particularly and historically the shortcoming of youth. What is encouraging now is the extent to which they have begun to identify and correct their own previous misjudgments. An Anne Wexler now understands, far better than she did a dozen years ago, the institutional values of the old Democratic Party coalition. A Jack Kemp and a Newt Gingrich realize that the opposition party must struggle to achieve a cohesive program of its own, not only to test the wisdom of the government's policy, but to be prepared for its own return to power.

In Congress, a Jim Blanchard, a Dave Obey and a Norm Mineta see very clearly the consequences of the dispersal of power. They understand the urgency of rebuilding an acceptable form of leadership discipline. Public-interest lawyers like Joe Onek are learning, from their governmental responsibilities, that the public-policy problems are not ended by a court edict—they just begin there. And civil-rights advocates like Marian Wright Edelman have begun to operate on the understanding that they can ignore the bureaucracy only at their peril. The young men who helped make Jimmy Carter President confess that the same fragmentation of authority which made his victory possible has impeded his ability to function in the presidency. And everywhere, there is an overriding concern about the seeming disappearance of the fundamental American consensus and the political immobilization of the broad center of our politics.

The prediction I would like to make is that the next two decades will be as much a period of institutional rehabilitation and repair as the last two decades were a time of disparagement and destruction of the machinery of our government. There is sufficient understanding of the task that needs to be done, among those same young people who were busy in their twenties and thirties with the crowbars and bulldozers, to make that prediction come true. Given leadership, the parties, the Congress, the presidency and the courts can be set up to work again—and state and local governments can attain a level of competence they have not shown before. To me, as a devotee of those institutions—a thoroughgoing conservative when it comes to the structure of our democracy—that would be the fulfillment of a dream. But whether it is realized or not, the exercise of writing this book has impressed on me a lesson of which others too may need reminding. Institutions are human artifacts. What is fundamental is the people who create them and lead them. They give life to the institutions and determine how well they function. The institutions cannot create their own leaders. But the leaders can create—or perhaps it would be more accurate to say re-create—the institutions the country needs.

But are these leaders? Or are they just individuals gifted in acquiring the credentials and the badges of authority in which this rich society abounds? On that crucial question, the jury is still out. While many of them have proved themselves highly effective as organizers outside the formal structure of governmental authority, most of them are still relative novices inside the system.

Much of the question about their leadership potential turns on the issue of how comfortable they are with the exercise of power. The pervasiveness and the fervor of their anti-bureaucratic sentiment was striking. The complaints about bureaucracy were not limited to the conservatives, and they did not sound simply like campaign oratory, whether coming from them or from liberal Democrats like Barney Frank, Donna Shalala and Frank Raines.

The products of the "baby boom" have lived their whole lives in educational, military, business and governmental bureaucracies, where their records, their careers and, metaphorically, their hopes, dreams and very souls were spun out on punch cards from the computer. As Bob Teeter pointed out, they are all rebels against that kind of mass culture and huge institution. At a level much more fundamental than their reason, they yearn for a world where things are smaller, simpler and freer than they have known. The bipartisan drive for deregulation of the economy and decentralization of government decision making is a secular force that seems almost certain to gain momentum as this generation takes power.

But it is pure romanticism to think that in the next twenty years America is going to return to the pattern of the self-sufficient family or the self-contained community. Government will become larger, not smaller, overall, and so will the scale of enterprises, be they farms or corporations.

So the challenge to the young people will not be to abolish bureaucracy or escape from it, but to tame it and to lead it. And there were some moments when I thought I heard them saying that that was a task from which they might shrink. Most of them have spent much of their lives, at this point, on the outside, lobbing bricks—real or verbal—at the establishment. In those movements, as Dick Celeste pointed out, authority was so decentralized, the command structure was so loose, that even local leaders could "do their own thing." As they have entered the formal structure of government, many of the next generation have continued to "do their own thing." The Congress is composed of 535 individual political entrepreneurs. The man in the White House as this decade began was an even more successful example of the self-starting, self-motivated, self-contained political entrepreneur.

None of these individualists—whether products of our growth frontiers or from elsewhere—is eager to accept the discipline involved in any hierarchical power structure. Chris Dodd may be right when he said the House of Representatives needs pawns, not just knights and bishops. But he said it just before he left the House to run for the even more individualistic Senate. And it is not clear where the volunteers for pawnship will be found.

What was equally puzzling—and disquieting—was the sense I occasionally had that some of these young people might be as uncomfortable giving orders as most of them are in taking them. It may be just a stylistic trick, a part of their characteristic "cool," but many of them felt called upon to deny that their love of politics had anything to do with the pursuit of power for power's sake. There is no harm, I suppose, in their striking such an attitude, as long as they know it is a pose. For leadership *is* the exercise of power, and leadership is what the country will demand of this generation.

It is reassuring that there are obviously some first-class administrators in this group, and some of them, like Alfred DelBello and Eleanor Holmes Norton, have made good management almost a first principle of their political lives. But a relative handful of this generation have had an opportunity as yet to fill important elective executive positions—and those are the jobs from which leadership normally comes in this society.

There is a second aspect of leadership on which this generation has yet to establish its credentials, at least in my view. Leadership, as Dean Rusk stressed in our conversation, has traditionally meant a mixture of inspiration, dedication and education. His is a call to citizenship in the broadest sense: "In the present mood of the country one has to ask, 'Where have all the citizens gone? Where are those who begin to think of themselves as citizens of this great Republic, whose own special interests or concerns cannot succeed unless this nation thrives and flourishes?' "

Rusk's own model of an exemplary leader in a democratic society is George Catlett Marshall, the disciplined career soldier who, by dint of character, molded the largest army in American history, and, later, mobilized public opinion for the economic rehabilitation of war-ravaged Europe and the creation of the military alliance which, thirty-five years later, is still keeping the peace in that vital portion of the globe.

By this high standard, one must search a long way for those of this next generation in public office who offer promise of a similar performance. The public men and women of this generation—whether elective or appointive officials—are people who pride themselves on their openness, their responsiveness, their accessibility. They are attuned to the public mood—and the public-opinion polls—sometimes so sensitively that they mistake the turning of a leaf for the roar of a hurricane.

But the question that can fairly be asked of them is: When have they moved ahead of public opinion, and used their intellectual, political and rhetorical skills to prepare the nation—or the segment of it that is their constituency—for the challenge they can see looming ahead?

The instances are rare, and came chiefly before their acquisition of public responsibility, during the days when they were challenging law or policy from the outside, rather than shaping it from the inside. It may be that leadership of that exalted character comes only in time of crisis; but it is nonetheless sobering to realize that none of the challenges of this past decade has brought forth from this immensely talented and well-educated set of men and women a speech or set of speeches which illuminated the public's understanding and helped to move a nation. Probably the last such speech from anyone in this age group was Martin Luther King's address at the civil-rights march in 1963. Seventeen years is a long time between drinks of inspiration.

That is especially true when one realizes that there have been so many instances in which the people have turned, almost in desperation, to their leaders for enlightenment. The young men and women of whom I have written have greater confidence in the use of the mass media than did their predecessors. But so far, they have applied their skills largely to the advancement of their own political careers, and for no broader objective. The constitutional crisis called Watergate provided no single speech that proved a catharsis for the nation—though Barbara Jordan came close during the House Judiciary Committee proceedings which, ironically, served only as a prelude for her premature retirement from politics. Neither the energy crisis nor the long, debilitating war against inflation and declining national productivity brought forth anyone who was able to clarify their causes or crystallize public sentiments into a call for action.

All this I find disquieting, for words are the weapons of political leadership, and for the most part these young people have been firing blanks. It is all well and good for a Gary Hart to proclaim, as he did in the slogan of his 1974 Colorado Senate campaign, "They had their turn. Now it's our turn." But "they" found the means to rally a nation in the Great Depression and in World War II, and those whose turn is at hand have yet to give evidence of being able, once in power, to move this country.

The final question one can expect to be asked at the end of this kind of book is the most difficult of all: Which of these groups is likely to take command in the coming political struggles? In whose hands is the power likely to reside? The answers are as diverse as the people who have filled these pages.

In a certain sense, the patterns are obvious. Power is flowing to the South and the West and the suburbs, because that is where the great tides of migration are moving. That is why two chapters were focused on the politicians emerging in those areas. Power is growing for those skillful in using (or exploiting) the mass media, which is why we looked at some of them.

Power remains with business and labor—the corporations and unions—even if they waste it in warring on each other. But power will be shared for the first time with large numbers of blacks, ethnics, Hispanics and women—and we have looked at some of the prospects for leadership in those groups.

What is uncertain is whether power will be exercised for most of the rest of this century by those whose shaping experiences have come within the political Left or Right, those who have been "insiders," like John Sears or Stuart Eizenstat, or "outsiders," like Tom Hayden and Richard Viguerie.

My guess is that those who are "outsiders" today will likely remain on the fringes of power, and not at the center, for the balance of their political lives. I came away from my discussions with the people who are community organizers skeptical that they have the capacity to do much more than get stop signs into neglected neighborhoods. That is an overstatement, of course. As recounted in that chapter, they have mobilized effectively on some state tax and utility-rate issues. But two things were striking about them and their movement. One was the narrowness of their popular base. In a time of strong economic discontent, they have been able to recruit probably fewer than 100,000 people in the whole country with their mixture of confrontation tactics and semisocialist rhetoric. It may be that those in power will provide them an issue of much broader organizing appeal—if not another Vietnam war, perhaps a runaway nuclear reactor. But I do not see them mobilizing mass support with their present package of issues. Because the second impression I had about the former SDS and welfare-rights organizers is their genuine discomfort with the idea of exercising real power. The organizers themselves—as evidenced by the interview with Wade Rathke—go to extraordinary lengths to deny the obvious fact that they are the leaders of the organizations they have brought into being. That denial may be necessary for them to preserve the mystique of their present "people's movements," but it almost certainly forecloses any mass expansion of their influence.

I have the same feeling about Richard Viguerie and the organizers of the New Right movements. They have found issues of greater emotional impact than their opposite numbers on the Left: Opposition to abortion, to gun control, and even, to my amazement, to the return to Panama of control of the Panama Canal Zone have mobilized more people "outside the system" than utility-rate reform or redlining. But the real breakthrough for the New Right organizers has been in technology. They have outstripped the rest of the political world in the exploitation of computerized direct mail for fund raising, campaigning and grass-roots lobbying. They have exploited their breakthrough with great skill. But if there is one thing that history teaches, it is that technology is likely to be imitated. Already, labor and corporate lobbyists are emulating Viguerie's computer lists. By the end of this decade, if not sooner, the kind of power that he supplies for the New Right will be available to others across the political spectrum, and the advantage he and his friends have gained will be seen to have been temporary.

The more interesting competition, I expect, will come between those who have moved into conventional politics and government from stage right and from stage left. One is forcibly struck by the marked increase in the intellectual self-confidence of young conservatives, not only in comparison with their predecessors of the past but, dramatically, in contrast to the floundering on what was once the Left of the political spectrum.

That is a complete reversal of the situation that prevailed when I came to Washington in the mid-Fifties, and for twenty years before that. I have traced, in the chapter on the New Right, some of the sources and reasons for this intellectual invigoration of that sector of the spectrum. And I have inferred, in the comments of the young people who got their starts in the campaigns and administrations of Presidents Kennedy, Johnson and Carter, the sense of a growing intellectual vacuum on their part.

I would simply add here that, contrary to the conventional wisdom—that American politics operates in a middle ground, a foggy miasma of vague beliefs, devoid of issues—I have long felt and still believe that, as conservative philosopher Richard M. Weaver said, "ideas have consequences." It is doubtless true that the American voters are pragmatic, not ideological. They are seeking plausible leadership with practical ideas for solving problems. But the ideas are an important—indeed, vital—ingredient in that mix. From 1932 to about 1966, the Democratic Party was the marketplace for policy ideas in American politics. That is where academics, intellectuals, authors, commentators and all the middlemen of policy—lawyers, journalists, campaign and government staff people—went for stimulation and argument. Lyndon Johnson killed the Democratic idea factory, first by exhausting its inventory in the rush of legislation that formed the Great Society, and then by antagonizing both the professors and the students, as well as many of the intellectual middlemen, with the Vietnam war. When they turned over the White House to Richard Nixon in 1969, instead of restoring that idea factory, the Democrats expended their energy on "reforming" their delegate-selection and convention rules. These were matters of consequence to some of the new constituency and leadership groups, but they were only tangentially connected to the emerging problems of the nation. Then the Democrats concentrated on bringing Nixon to judgment for Watergate. Those influential in the majority party became experts on apportionment and impeachment, but neglected to think seriously about inflation or productivity or the costs of bureaucracy.

The Republicans, meanwhile, stepped timidly at first and then with increasing boldness into the arena of ideas. To start the process, they had to borrow some renegade Democratic brains like Daniel Patrick Moynihan and Irving Kristol. But when they saw that they could survive thinking, they began to recruit and develop intellects of their own, and they have not stopped.

It will be surprising to me if there is not a significant political reward for the party that leapfrogs the opposition in the realm of policy ideas. At some time in this decade, the Republicans will probably have a chance to test their policies from the White House. As in Great Britain, the public frustration with inflation and laggard economic growth will tempt the voters to experiment with a leader who offers hope of a bigger pie for everyone to share. And as the Seventies ended, young Republicans were on the verge of stealing that "franchise of hope" from their Democratic counterparts.

In this respect, the greatest imbalance in this book may be the disproportionate number of Democrats who are found here. It is the result not of political bias, but of the fact that in 1978 and 1979, when the interviews were being collected, young Democrats—and *not* young Republicans—staffed most of the positions in the national, state and local governments of this country. The Republicans were out there—in lesser numbers—and they are in this book. But you had to search for them.

My last observation takes me in a somewhat different direction. Intellectual vigor and self-confidence is one barometer of future political success. But it is not the only one. There is also that hard-to-define but important sense of "being connected" to one's time. The notion that there are networks of people, on the verge of power, who are linked to each other by shared experiences during their formative years is the central concept of this book. And the fact is that most of those networks involve people who think of themselves as Democrats. That is not primarily because Democrats now and in the recent past have held most of the political power in the country; on the contrary, most of the new movements and their networks were formed in opposition to those in power. Rather, it is because, for whatever reason, the young people who are Republicans held themselves aloof from those experiences and therefore are outside those networks.

The shaping experiences for this next generation of American leaders were the civil-rights struggle and the war in Vietnam—or more precisely, the effort to end the war in Vietnam. The Peace Corps, the War on Poverty, the forced resignation of a President affected many careers intensely, but reached fewer people. For some conservatives, the Goldwater and Reagan campaigns or the "right-to-life" movement have had a comparable emotional impact. But when it is reduced to its essence, the set of rallying points for most of the generation's leaders centers on the moments of protest: Mississippi in 1964, Selma in 1965, and Washington in the anti-war demonstrations from 1967 to 1969. And few Republicans were there.

It was those activists of whom Dick Celeste, the Peace Corps director, spoke when he offered this possibility:

"I wouldn't be surprised if, some time in the next few years, there is a meeting somewhere that no one person calls, that the Ford Foundation doesn't finance, and that is not a Democratic or Republican party convention. But it will be a meeting that brings together several hundred folks of this generation who have exercised some small piece of leadership already, who share in common a degree of frustration, of being perplexed, of being baffled, bothered, eager, determined, and who come together feeling, 'Hey, we've been together before; let's get back together again. What in the world is happening, and how do we really have an impact on it?' Where that leads and what it means, I can't say. But I have a theory that probably if twenty or thirty people are prepared to go to work in the next few years and say, 'All right, let's put a hundred names on a piece of paper; any one of these hundred names represents the first President of our generation that we're going to elect,' they can do it. And it will be the first list of names that really has black people on it, really has women on it, really represents a cross section. But if those twenty or thirty people—some of us in the public arena, some of us in the private arena, corporate life, academia—really say we're committed to make this happen, probably we could make it happen."

He may be wrong, and so may I, when I suggest that the lack of those spiritual and emotional bonds—those network links—to the shaping experiences of this generation may ultimately deny the New Right the long tenure in power that its intellectual energy would otherwise be likely to earn it.

In some areas, they have already shown that they can adopt or adapt the techniques of their opposition and beat them at their own game. Paul Weyrich and his friends in the New Right have played successful copycat to the liberal lobbies. Conservative public-interest lawyers are winning court tests from liberal public-interest firms that showed them how to use the law for their own purposes. The corporation PACs have dwarfed labor's political treasuries.

Where it is a battle of intellect or of organizing technique or of money, the conservatives will do very well. But there is wisdom in George Will's admonition to his fellow young conservatives that they make a fundamental mistake in attempting to reduce politics to a series of economic propositions, and in suggesting that they have no higher aspiration for government than to let the market allocate resources efficiently.

Politics is more than that; it is also a way of defining and achieving positive goals for a people and a nation. Young Bill Scranton was right when he said, "I think a lot of politics is intuitive. It's not the square in-boxes and square out-boxes. A lot of it is off the wall. And that's the charm of politics."

In the coming competition, the country will benefit from having people who are as disciplined mentally as David Stockman, and as off the wall as Barbara Mikulski.

It may well be that, as Mikulski said, "The United States has hit forty and is in a mid-life crisis. We've discovered there are limits on what we can do, and that's caused a tremendous anxiety, with people trying to nail down everything they can right now. There's no sense of the long term, no readiness to build coalitions, no sense of compromise or consensus.

"But," she said, "we'll come out of that and we'll find our way. Other people at the bottom are going to come up, like I did, with new ideas. We'll find a way to express our anxieties and to deal with them, not with a master plan, but with a lot of initiative at the neighborhood, local and national level. The energy is there—waiting to be tapped."

On that last point she is certainly correct. The further down one digs in American political life—in age and in levels of government—the healthier it looks. There may be cynicism and apathy at the top, but down below there is energy and commitment—the Janet Brown faith that, damn it, it doesn't have to be second-rate and it won't be around here.

Of all the people in this book, probably none has paid a higher price to help change this country than John Lewis. He was physically beaten repeatedly in the civil-rights marches, beaten politically when he ran for Congress, battered in the bureaucratic wars in his three years in Washington.

"These are peculiar and strange times that we live in," he said, when we talked in 1979, "because we've gone through so much in the past two decades. I think there's a feeling that we've lost the steering wheel, we've lost a sense of purpose, we've lost a sense of direction as a nation and as a society. If we get very far into the Eighties without that and without a revival of spirit, then I have a sense of despair, really, about the future of the American society as a viable republic.

"But I think out of all of that, out of all the ashes, a new temple can be built. I don't think the election of a new President can build our temple. It's possible that a new force or a new personality can come along to give us this sense of what we are and what we should be as a people and a nation. But I have this strange feeling—out of my religious training, I guess—that we were blessed with a John Kennedy and a Martin Luther King and a Robert Kennedy, and we may not be good enough to be blessed with that again."

"We may just have to make it on our own?" I asked him.

"That's sort of my gut reaction," he said.

And it is mine.

But thinking about the people I met in writing this book, I feel some confidence that this generation has not lost its sense of direction or its capacity for leadership. On the big questions they have faced in their adult lives, their instincts have been more right than wrong—and more right than those of many of their elders.

I think they have a crack at turning the country around. And the competition to do so should be fascinating in itself. It will be worth staying around to watch.

Acknowledgments

IN THE COURSE of writing this book, I was aided by numerous individuals who gave generously of their time, encouragement and advice. Elizabeth McKee, my agent, was very helpful in suggesting ways to develop this basic theme into a publishable manuscript. My editors at *The Washington Post*—particularly Ben Bradlee, Howard Simons, Dick Harwood, Bill Greider and the late Larry Stern—were generous in arranging leave time for me to work on this project. The members of my family—Ann, George, Josh, Matt and Mike—bore the disruptions of an author's life with their usual good grace.

My greatest debt is to the more than three hundred people who took time from their schedules for the rather lengthy interviews that provided the raw material for this book. Most of them are in the text, but a few were dropped for reasons of space, and my gratitude to them is even greater.

I particularly appreciate the contributions of those who participated in the six round-table discussions cited in the text. The members of the panel of senior civil servants were H. Patrick Swygert, Donna Shalala, Matthew Nimetz, John White, Simon Lazarus, Theodore C. Lutz, Frank Raines, John Callahan and Sarah Weddington. In the round table of senior members of Congress were John Rousselot, Barber Conable, Morris Udall, John Brademas, Lee Hamilton, Elford Cederberg, Jack Edwards, Gillis Long and Clarence Brown. The young members of Congress in their round table were Norman Mineta, David Stockman, James Blanchard, Jim Johnson, Butler Derrick, Edward Pattison, John Cavanaugh, Jim Leach and Timothy Wirth. The members of Congress who took part in the Vietnam veterans' panel were Michael Barnes, Leon Panetta, Don Bailey, David Bonior, Tom Harkin, John Cavanaugh, Albert Gore and Tom Daschle. Members of the Hispanic leaders' round table were Louis Nuñez, Carmen Delgado Votaw, Raul Yzaguirre, Paquita Vivo and Paul Sedillo. The panel of presidential management interns included Helen

Rothman, John Hall, Justine Finch, Paula Nuschke, Mark Kerrigan and Sean O'Keefe.

Various sections of the manuscript were read by scholars, journalists and experts in their various fields of study. Their insight and expertise helped me avoid many errors, of both fact and judgment; however, those judgments in the text are finally my own, and any errors should be ascribed solely to me. My thanks go to James Sundquist, Richard Scammon, Robert Rutland, George Reedy, Dan Fenn, George F. Gruner, Stephen Hess, Lou Cannon, Edward Walsh, Martin Schram, Nick Kotz, Joe McNeely, Geno Baroni, Gail Bensinger, Robert Phelps, Kirkpatrick Sale, Mary McGrory, Michael Novak, Joel Kromkowski, Joel Stern, Richard Mooney, John Robert Starr, Al Hunt, Saul Friedman, Suzanne Weaver, Alan Baron, Charles Halpern, Peter Schuck, Ann Inskeep, Mickey Wiesenthal, Bernie Shellum, Chuck Bailey, Susan Tolchin, Jean Kirkpatrick, Fred Cusick, Molly Ivins, Noel Epstein, Bo Byers, Dan Morgan, Lee Lescaze, Kemper Diehl, Vernon Jordan, Eddie N. Williams, William Raspberry, James Cole, Beau Cutts, Tom Johnson, Richard Willing, Joel Kotkin, Joe McFadden, Daniel J. Evans, Didi Corridini, Jim Barrows, Mort Pye, David Kraslow, Elizabeth F. Shores, John Siegenthaler, John and Jan Stucker, Jack Nelson, Jack Burby, H. Brandt Ayers, Jack Bass, William Small, Tom Brokaw, Paul Duke, Bill Prochnau, Charles Patrick, Robert Hooker, Patrick Caddell, Peter D. Hart, Michael Barone, Robert Teeter, Richard Wirthlin, Garry Trudeau, Stewart Huffman, Harvey C. Jacobs, Joseph L. Rauh, David Burke, Jack Kole, Gary Hymel, John McAvoy, Richard Conlon, Alan K. Campbell, Gene Russell, Pat Jones, Ed Salzman, Robert Healy, Donald A. MacGillis, Hal Gulliver, Haynes Johnson, Murrey Marder, Don Oberdorfer, Jim Hoagland and Frank Swoboda.

I am also grateful to Mark Hannan and his staff of *The Washington Post*'s research department, to *Congressional Quarterly*'s library staff, and to the Joint Center for Political Studies' research department for their able assistance.

The final manuscript was typed with speed and skill by Olwen Price, Michael Slevin and Julia Lee; they also provided transcriptions of taped interviews, with the assistance of Connie Gray, Ednamae Storti, Joanne Flanders and Fran Boyle. The Oral History Research Office at Columbia University provided additional assistance in transcribing tapes, and I thank that project's associate director, Elizabeth B. Mason, for her conscientious help.

Finally, I want to pay tribute to the three young people whose work is visible on every page of this manuscript. M. Victoria Kiechel, 26, was the researcher on this book from April 1978 until September 1979, when she left to become a Rhodes Scholar at Pembroke College, Oxford. Vicky brought with her from Yale University a scholar's feel for American history and a writer's gift of expression. She plunged bravely into the chilly areas of demographics and voting statistics and was helpful in arranging most of the interviews for this book.

When Vicky left, her work was taken over by Christopher W. Colford, 26, a product of Duke University and graduate school at Harvard who had sharpened his journalistic skills on *The Berkshire Eagle*'s editorial page. Chris was a major collaborator on some of the late chapters—such as "Labor and Business"—and was an invaluable participant in much of the rewriting and editing that spilled over from the autumn of 1979 to the spring of 1980.

Most of all, I am indebted to Jonathan Coleman, 29, a graduate of the University of Virginia, who was the editor of this book. From the very first meeting in which we discussed the general concept until the last galley proof had been cleared, he gave this book the kind of attention that an author hopes for—and rarely finds. He challenged, prodded, argued and fought. His concern was constant—and occasionally, at least, he was right.

The three of them made me feel that publishing, journalism and Medieval English studies may be in good hands in the next generation too.

D.S.B.

Bibliography

I. Books

Adelson, Alan, *SDS*. New York, Charles Scribner's Sons, 1972.

Alinsky, Saul D., *John L. Lewis: An Unauthorized Biography*. New York, G. P. Putnam's Sons, 1949.

———, *Reveille for Radicals*. Chicago, University of Chicago Press, 1946.

———, *Rules for Radicals: A Practical Primer for Realistic Radicals*. New York, Random House, 1971.

Auerbach, Jerold S., ed., *American Labor: The Twentieth Century*. The American Heritage Series (Leonard W. Levy and Alfred Young, eds.). Indianapolis, Bobbs-Merrill, 1969.

Ayers, H. Brandt, and Naylor, Thomas A., eds., *You Can't Eat Magnolias*. New York, McGraw-Hill, 1972.

Barnet, Richard J., and Müller, Ronald E., *Global Reach: The Power of the Multinational Corporations*. New York, Simon and Schuster, 1974.

Baskir, Lawrence M., and Strauss, William A., *Chance and Circumstance: The Draft, the War, and the Vietnam Generation*. New York, Alfred A. Knopf, 1978.

Bass, Jack, and deVries, Walter, *The Transformation of Southern Politics: Social Change and Political Consequence Since 1945*. New York, New American Library, 1977.

Brooks, Thomas R., *Toil and Trouble: A History of American Labor*. New York, Delacorte Press, 1964.

Bryce, Herrington J., ed., *Small Cities in Transition: The Dynamics of Growth and Decline*. Cambridge, Mass., Ballinger Publishing Company, 1977.

Cloward, Richard A., and Piven, Frances Fox, *Regulating the Poor: The Function of Public Welfare*. New York, Pantheon Books, 1971.

Croly, Herbert, *The Promise of American Life*. Indianapolis, Bobbs-Merrill, 1965.

de Tocqueville, Alexis, *Democracy in America*, Phillips Bradley, ed. New York, Alfred A. Knopf, 1945.

Drucker, Peter F., *The Unseen Revolution: How Pension Fund Socialism Came to America*. New York, Harper & Row, 1976.

Epstein, Edwin M., *The Corporation in American Politics*. Englewood Cliffs, N.J., Prentice-Hall, 1969.

Friedan, Betty, *The Feminine Mystique*. New York, W. W. Norton, 1963.

Greenstone, J. David, *Labor in American Politics*. New York, Vintage Books, 1969.

Harrington, Michael, *The Other America,* rev. ed. New York, The Macmillan Company, 1971.
Heilbroner, Robert L., *Beyond Boom and Crash.* New York, W. W. Norton, 1978.
Hodgson, Godfrey, *America in Our Time.* Garden City, N.Y., Doubleday & Company, 1976.
Hofstadter, Richard, *The Progressive Historians: Turner, Beard, Parrington.* New York, Alfred A. Knopf, 1968.
Josephson, Matthew, *The Politicos: 1865–1896.* New York, Harcourt, Brace and Company, 1938.
Key, V. O., Jr., *The Responsible Electorate: Rationality in Presidential Voting, 1936–1960.* Cambridge, Mass., Belknap Press of the Harvard University Press, 1966.
———, *Southern Politics in State and Nation.* New York, Alfred A. Knopf, 1949.
Kristol, Irving, and Weaver, Paul, eds., *The Americans: 1976.* Lexington, Mass., Lexington Books, 1976.
Lekachman, Robert, *Economists at Bay.* New York, McGraw-Hill, 1976.
———, *Inflation: The Permanent Problem of Boom and Bust.* New York, Vintage Books, 1973.
Lens, Sidney, *The Crisis of American Labor.* New York, Sagamore Press, 1959.
———, *The Labor Wars: From the Molly Maguires to the Sitdowns.* Garden City, N.Y., Doubleday & Company, 1973.
Lippmann, Walter, *Essays in the Public Purpose.* Boston, Little, Brown and Company, 1955.
———, *The Essential Lippmann.* Clinton Rossiter and James Lare, eds. New York, Random House, 1963.
Lloyd, Henry Demarest, *Wealth Against Commonwealth.* Thomas C. Cochran, ed. Englewood Cliffs, N.J., Prentice-Hall, 1963.
Malbin, Michael J., ed., *Parties, Interest Groups, and Campaign Finance Laws.* Washington, D.C., American Enterprise Institute for Public Policy Research, 1980.
Nevins, Allan, and Commager, Henry Steele, *A Short History of the United States,* 6th ed. New York, Alfred A. Knopf, 1976.
Novak, Michael, *The Rise of the Unmeltable Ethnics: Politics and Culture in the Seventies.* New York, The Macmillan Company, 1972.
Peabody, Robert L., *Leadership in Congress: Stability, Succession, and Change.* Boston, Little, Brown and Company, 1976.
Piven, Frances Fox, and Cloward, Richard A., *Poor People's Movements: Why They Succeed, How They Fail.* New York, Pantheon Books, 1977.
Prospect for America: The Rockefeller Panel Reports, Special Studies Project Reports 1–6, Rockefeller Brothers Fund. Garden City, N.Y., Doubleday & Company, 1961.
Reedy, George E., *The Twilight of the Presidency.* New York, World Publishing Company, 1970.
Reich, Charles, *The Greening of America: How the Youth Revolution Is Trying to Make America Livable.* New York, Random House, 1970.
Report of the National Advisory Commission on Civil Disorders. Washington, D.C., U.S. Government Printing Office, 1968.
Richardson, Elliot L., *The Creative Balance: Government, Politics, and the Individual in America's Third Century.* New York, Holt, Rinehart and Winston, 1976.

Riesman, David, *Abundance for What?, and Other Essays*. Garden City, N.Y., Doubleday & Company, 1964.

———, *Individualism Reconsidered, and Other Essays,* Glencoe, Ill., The Free Press, 1954.

Riesman, David, with Glazer, Nathan, *Faces in the Crowd: Individual Studies in Character and Politics*. New Haven, Yale University Press, 1952.

Riesman, David, with Glazer, Nathan, and Denney, Reuel, *The Lonely Crowd: A Study of the Changing American Character,* abr. ed. New Haven, Yale University Press, 1977.

Russell, Francis, *The President Makers, from Mark Hanna to Joseph P. Kennedy*. Boston, Little, Brown and Company, 1976.

Sale, Kirkpatrick, *SDS*. New York, Random House, 1973.

Sexton, Patricia Cayo, and Sexton, Brendan, *Blue Collars and Hard-Hats: The Working Class and the Future of American Politics*. New York, Random House, 1971.

Sundquist, James L., *Dynamics of the Party System: Alignment and Realignment of Political Parties in the United States*. Washington, D.C., The Brookings Institution, 1973.

———, *Politics and Policy: The Eisenhower, Kennedy and Johnson Years*. Washington, D.C., The Brookings Institution, 1968.

Taft, Philip, *The A.F. of L. in the Time of Gompers*. New York, Harper & Brothers, 1957.

Tolchin, Susan, and Tolchin, Martin, *Clout: Womanpower and Politics*. New York, Coward, McCann & Geoghegan, 1974.

Turner, Frederick Jackson, *The Frontier in American History*. New York, Henry Holt and Company, 1947.

Veblen, Thorstein, *The Portable Veblen,* Max Lerner, ed. New York, The Viking Press, 1948.

von Hayek, Friedrich, *The Road to Serfdom*. Chicago, University of Chicago Press, 1944.

Voters' Time: Report of the Twentieth Century Fund Commission on Campaign Costs in the Electronic Era. New York, The Twentieth Century Fund, 1969.

Wanniski, Jude, *The Way the World Works: How Economies Fail—and Succeed*. New York, Basic Books, 1978.

Weaver, Richard M., *Ideas Have Consequences*. Chicago, University of Chicago Press, 1948.

White, Theodore H., *In Search of History: A Personal Adventure*. New York, Harper & Row, 1978.

Will, George F., *The Pursuit of Happiness, and Other Sobering Thoughts*. New York, Harper & Row, 1978.

Wilson, William Julius, *The Declining Significance of Race: Blacks and Changing American Institutions*. Chicago, University of Chicago Press, 1978.

Wollstonecraft, Mary, *A Vindication of the Rights of Woman: With Strictures on Political and Moral Subjects*. Gainesville, Fla., Scholars' Facsimiles & Reprints, 1960.

II. Articles and Scholarly Papers

"The American Female," a special supplement of *Harper's* magazine, Vol. 225, Issue 1349, October 1962.

Axelrod, Robert, "Where the Votes Come From: An Analysis of Electoral Coalitions, 1952–1968," *The American Political Science Review,* Vol. 66, 1972.

Bolton, John R., "The Federal Election Commission: Government Astride the Political Process," *Regulation* magazine, July/August 1978.

Braungart, Richard A., "The Utopian and Ideological Styles of Student Political Activists," paper presented to the Second Annual Scientific Meeting of the International Society of Political Psychology, Washington, D.C., May 24, 1979.

Chapman, Stephen, "The Limits of Limits: The Failure of Election Reform," *The New Republic,* Vol. 181, No. 15, October 13, 1979.

"Domestic Consequences of United States Population Change," report prepared by the Select Committee on Population, U.S. House of Representatives, 95th Congress, Second Session, 1978.

"Doonesbury: Drawing and Quartering for Fun and Profit," *Time* magazine, February 9, 1976.

Drew, Elizabeth, "A Reporter at Large—Phase: In Search of a Definition," *The New Yorker,* Vol. 50, No. 28, August 27, 1979.

Duncan, Martha G., "Radical Activism and the Defense Against Despair," paper presented to the Second Annual Scientific Meeting of the International Society of Political Psychology, Washington, D.C., May 24, 1979.

Epstein, Edwin M., "The Business PAC Phenomenon: An Irony of Electoral Reform," *Regulation* magazine, May/June 1979.

Epstein, Noel, "May 17, 1954: 25 Years After *Brown,* A Rivalry for Injustice," *The Washington Post,* May 13, 1979.

Fallows, James, "The Passionless Presidency: The Trouble with Jimmy Carter's Administration," *The Atlantic Monthly,* Vol. 243, No. 5, May 1979.

———. "The Passionless Presidency II: More from Inside Jimmy Carter's White House," *The Atlantic Monthly,* Vol. 243, No. 6, June 1979.

"Federal Spending: The North's Loss Is the Sunbelt's Gain," *National Journal,* Vol. 8, No. 26, June 26, 1976.

Galbraith, John Kenneth, "The Great Wall Street Crash," *The New Republic,* Vol. 181, No. 15, October 13, 1979.

Greer, Ann Lennarson, and Greer, Scott, "Suburban Political Behavior: A Matter of Trust," *The Changing Face of the Suburbs,* Barry Schwartz, ed., Chicago, University of Chicago Press, 1976.

Heclo, Hugh, "Issue Networks and the Executive Establishment," *The New American Political System,* Anthony King, ed., Washington, D.C., American Enterprise Institute for Public Policy Research, 1979.

Kelber, Mim, "AFL-CIO—For Men Only?" *The Nation,* Vol. 229, No. 16, November 17, 1979.

Keniston, Kenneth, "Alienation and the Decline of Utopia," *The American Scholar,* Vol. 29, No. 2, Spring 1960.

Lamm, Richard, " 'Sell Colored' Challenged," *The Denver Post,* November 17, 1969.

McCarthy, Kevin F., and Morrison, Peter A., "The Changing Demographic and Economic Structure of Nonmetropolitan Areas in the 1970s," The Rand Paper Series, The Rand Corporation, Santa Monica, Calif., January 1978.

McPherson, Myra, "The VA's Max Cleland: A New Kind of Battle," *The Washington Post,* April 18, 1977.

"The Odds Against Logic," *Fortune* magazine, Vol. 100, No. 12, December 17, 1979.

Orren, Karen, "Standing to Sue: Interest Group Conflict in the Federal Courts," *The American Political Science Review,* Vol. 70, 1976.

Phillips, Kevin, "The Balkanization of America," *Harper's* magazine, Vol. 256, No. 1536, May 1978.

"The Revision of the Presidential Primary System," The Committee on Federal Legislation, *The Record* of The Association of the Bar of the City of New York, Vol. 33, No. 5/6, May/June 1978.

Reynolds, Reid T., Robey, Bryant, and Russell, Cheryl, "Demographics of the 1980s," *American Demographics* magazine, January 1980.

Roberts, Steven V., "Study Ties Oil Gifts to Voting in House," *The New York Times,* July 24, 1979.

Shapiro, Walter, "Lane Kirkland Punches In," *The Washington Post Magazine,* November 18, 1979.

Stanfield, Rochelle L., "Earning Their Stripes in the War on Poverty," *National Journal,* Vol. 11, No. 9, March 3, 1979.

Traugott, Michael W., and Katosh, John P., "Response Validity in Surveys of Voting Behavior," Center for Political Studies, The University of Michigan, 1979.

Vogel, David, "Clear as Kristol: Business's 'New Class' Struggle," *The Nation,* December 15, 1979.

Walsh, Kenneth T., "Politics: Early Warnings," *The Denver Post,* May 30, 1979.

Weber, Arnold R., "The Economic Scene: Labor Relations in Transition," *The New York Times,* December 21, 1979.

Weiner, Myron, "Political Demography: An Inquiry into the Political Consequences of Population Change," *Rapid Population Growth: Consequences and Policy Implications,* Roger Revelle, ed., Baltimore, Johns Hopkins Press, 1971.

Wertheimer, Fred, "Of Mountains: The PAC Movement in American Politics," paper presented to the Conference on Parties, Interest Groups, and Campaign Finance Laws, sponsored by the American Enterprise Institute for Public Policy Research, Washington, D.C., September 4 and 5, 1979.

Zimbalist, Andrew, "Worker Control over Technology," *The Nation,* Vol. 229, No. 16, November 17, 1979.

Zimmer, Basil G., "Suburbanization and Changing Political Structures," *The Changing Face of the Suburbs,* Barry Schwartz, ed., Chicago, University of Chicago Press, 1976.

IN ADDITION to the sources cited in the Bibliography, the research for this book was aided by innumerable reports and studies by federal agencies and congressional committees. Of particular help was the "Current Population Reports" series published by the Bureau of the Census in the Department of Commerce; we gratefully acknowledge the precision and scholarship of the Census Bureau staff in assisting the preparation of demographic data.

Index

For a complete list of books available from Penguin in the United States, write to Dept. DG, Penguin Books, 299 Murray Hill Parkway, East Rutherford, New Jersey 07073.

For a complete list of books available from Penguin in Canada, write to Penguin Books Canada Limited, 2801 John Street, Markham, Ontario L3R 1B4.